WANDSWORTH PUBLIC LIBRARIES
M.S.C.

D1629764

500 478 467 4X

WANDSWORTH LIBRARY SERVICE

AIR WAR
AT NIGHT

AIR WAR AT NIGHT

The
battle for
the night
sky since
1915

WANDSWORTH PUBLIC LIBRARIES

ROBERT JACKSON

Airlife
England

500478467

Copyright © 2000 Robert Jackson

First published in the UK in 2000
by Airlife Publishing Ltd

British Library Cataloguing-in-Publication Data
A catalogue reord for this book
is available from the British Library

ISBN 1 84037 100 5

The information in this book is true and complete to the best of our
knowledge. All recommendations are made without any guarantee on
the part of the Publisher, who also disclaims any liability incurred in
connection with the use of this data or specific details.

All rights reserved. No part of this book may be reproduced or transmitted in any form or by any means, electronic or mechanical including photocopying, recording or by any information storage and
retrieval system, without permission from the Publisher in writing.

Typeset by Servis Filmsetting Ltd, Manchester
Printed in China

Airlife Publishing Ltd
101 Longden Road, Shrewsbury, SY3 9EB, England
E-mail: airlife@airlifebooks.com
Website: www.airlifebooks.com

CONTENTS

CHAPTER ONE

THE FIRST BLITZ ON BRITAIN, 1915–18

A Maurice Farman of No 3 Squadron RFC made the first night flight by a military aircraft in Britain on 16 April 1913. (Philip Jarrett)

By the outbreak of World War I in August 1914, the threat of air attack on the British Isles was being taken very seriously by both the War Office and the Admiralty – especially the latter, which viewed Germany's Zeppelin airships as a considerable menace to the Royal Navy's vital dockyards. In theory it was the Royal Flying Corps, under the direction of the War Office, that bore the responsibility for the air defence of Great Britain, but the RFC had no aircraft or funds available for home defence.

The problem had not escaped the attention of the First Sea Lord, Winston Churchill, who in 1912 initiated the establishment of a chain of coastal aerodromes for use by aircraft working with ships at sea, or for air defence. In November 1913, after a great deal of wrangling, it was agreed that while the War Office retained overall responsibility for the air defence of Britain, the Admiralty, through the Naval Wing of the RFC (which was to reform as the Royal Naval Air Service on 1 July 1914) was to be responsible for the protection of naval bases.

It must be said that the Military Wing of the RFC, right up to the outbreak of war, had given little thought to the development of aircraft as an armed weapon of war, regarding it primarily as a reconnaissance tool. At the end of 1913, on the other hand, the Admiralty had issued a requirement for a 'home service fighting machine to repel enemy aircraft'. But it was the Military Wing that first demonstrated the feasibility of operating aircraft at night; on 16 April 1913 Lieutenant R. Cholmondeley of No 3 Squadron flew a Maurice Farman from Larkhill to Upavon and back by moonlight, and in June Lieutenant G.I. Carmichael took off and landed with the aid of petrol flares on the ground.

Experimental in nature though they still were, the German Navy's Zeppelins were beginning to prove their worth in North Sea reconnaissance operations by the end of 1914, and a plan now formed to extend their role to offensive operations over the British Isles. The plan had actually originated some three weeks after the war began, but it had been shelved because the handful of Navy airships available during the last months of 1914 were fully committed to patrol and reconnaissance duties.

On 25 December 1914 the German Army used its small fleet of airships to raid the French towns of Nancy, Dunkirk and Verdun. The Navy immediately requested the release of its own airships to attack selected targets on the east coast of England, but the request was turned down by the Navy Minister, *Grossadmiral* von Tirpitz, who believed that the bombing of these targets by single airships would have little or no material effect. He advised *Admiral* Hugo von Pohl, the Chief of Naval Staff, to defer such a move until both Army and Navy were in a position to mount a maximum-effort raid on London with all available airships.

Another serious obstacle to the Navy's plans at this time was the *Kaiser* himself, who was unwilling to authorise the bombing of targets in Britain, and particularly in London. It all added up to frustration for the planning staff of the Naval Airship Division. By the middle of December the division had enough airships to carry out both the primary task of reconnaissance in co-operation with the High Seas Fleet and long-range special missions over England, and every delay in obtaining authority to undertake the latter type of operation meant that favourable weather conditions were being allowed to slip by. There was also the danger that the Navy's new airships might be destroyed in enemy air attacks before they could be used to good effect, and this fear was expressed in a letter to von Pohl from *Konteradmiral* Philipp, the Chief of German Naval Aviation. There had already been a British air attack on the German Navy's airship facilities. On 21 November, three Avro 504s of the RNAS, flying from Belfort and piloted by Squadron Commander E.F. Briggs, Flight Lieutenant J.T. Babington and Lieutenant S.V. Sippe, had bombed the Zeppelin sheds at Friedrichshafen, where the airships were manufactured. A gas tank was set on fire and Zeppelin L7 (LZ32) slightly damaged. This was followed by a second raid on 24 December, when aircraft of the RNAS were launched by seaplane carriers in the German Bight to attack Zeppelin sheds at Nordholz, in northern Germany. On this occasion, no damage was caused.

More importantly, on this same day a Friedrichshafen FF29 seaplane of the Imperial German Navy's *Seeflieger Abteilung* 1 (Seaplane Detachment 1) dropped the first bomb on British soil, in the garden of an auctioneer living near Dover Castle. There were no casualties and little damage. On Christmas Day the same aircraft and crew dropped two bombs near Cliffe railway station, Kent. The FF29 was intercepted by a Vickers Gunbus of No 7 Squadron RFC and several bursts were fired at it, but it got away.

Pressure from Philipp and other senior naval commanders eventually resulted in von Pohl seeking an audience with the *Kaiser* on 7 January 1915, in which the *admiral* stressed the importance of attacking military objectives in England during the months of January and February, when weather conditions for long-range airship operations would be at their best.

Reluctantly, the *Kaiser* gave his consent to air attacks on the docks and military installations on the lower Thames and the east coast of England –

but not on London. After months of waiting, the Airship Division could at last go ahead with its plan, already worked out in minute detail by *Korvettenkapitän* Peter Strasser, commanding the Naval Airship Division. The plan, submitted to von Pohl on 10 January 1915 for his final approval, envisaged attacks on Tynemouth, the Humber, Great Yarmouth, Lowestoft, Harwich and the Thames Estuary by three airships, which would bomb their targets at dusk after a daylight flight over the North Sea and return to their bases under cover of darkness.

The first attack, made on the night of 19/20 January 1915, was abortive in that no military targets were hit, although two airships penetrated into Norfolk and dropped their bombs in the vicinity of Great Yarmouth and King's Lynn, causing some £8,000-worth of damage and killing four people, one a small boy. Further attempts, made by Army airships during the next two months, were also abortive.

The north experienced its first Zeppelin attack on the night of 14/15 April 1915. Earlier, the naval airship L9, commanded by *Kapitänleutnant* Heinrich Mathy, had set out on a reconnaissance flight to the west of Terschelling. She carried ten 110 lb high explosive (HE) and 40 incendiary bombs, and after flying all day without sighting any British ships Mathy obtained permission to carry out a raid on a British coastal target before returning to base. The objective selected by Mathy was Tynemouth, with its complex of shipyards, but landfall was made at Blyth, some miles to the north, and the L9's commander mistook the Wansbeck for the Tyne. Most of his bombs fell harmlessly in open country around the area's mining villages, although two people were injured at Wallsend when a near miss damaged their house. Convinced that he had inflicted considerable damage on the Tyne's shipyards, Mathy set course for home. A solitary Bristol TB8 took off from the Royal Naval Air Station at Whitley Bay, established six weeks earlier to counter Zeppelin attacks on the Tynemouth area, and patrolled at 5,000 feet over Newcastle for an hour, unassisted by any searchlights and without sighting the enemy. Its pilot, Sub-Lieutenant P. Legh, had never before flown at night. The TB8's gunner was a young Australian named Bert Hinkler, who later trained as a pilot and became famous for making the first solo flight from England to Australia in 1928.

At this time the air defence of Great Britain was the sole responsibility of the RNAS, mainly because the RNAS had more aircraft available than the RFC. Most of the naval aircraft assigned to air defence, however, were concentrated in the home counties and East Anglia, as were the relatively few anti-aircraft guns and searchlights, so that the

North's defences were minimal. The Whitley Bay station, for example, had three aircraft (two of which were unserviceable) at the time of the L9's incursion, and its weaponry comprised a few carbines with 209 incendiary rounds between them, twenty-four Hale rifle grenades without the rifles to fire them, and twenty Hale incendiary bombs with only one set of dropping gear.

On 16/17 May, for the first time, an airship was illuminated by a defending searchlight. She was *Hauptmann* Linnarz's LZ38, which dropped thirty-three bombs in the Dover area before making off. It was also the first time, thanks to the searchlights, that a Zeppelin was seen by defending pilots, but the three defence sorties by RNAS pilots from Dover and Westgate failed to come anywhere near her.

On the night of 31 May/1 June 1915 Linnarz led

Top and above: *The Avro 504 was one of the types used in attempts to intercept the early Zeppelin raids. It was also used by the RNAS to attack Zeppelin sheds.* (Philip Jarrett)

the first attack on London, LZ38 being joined by LZ39. Fifteen defence sorties were flown from Chingford, Eastchurch, Hendon, Rochford and Westgate, all by RNAS aircraft. Seven different aircraft types were involved; there was no co-ordination, and there were several landing accidents, one of them fatal.

On the night of 6 June Heinrich Mathy's L9 was once again active over the north, and this time the target was Hull. The Zeppelin dropped ten HE and fifty incendiary bombs, killing twenty-four people, injuring forty, and causing nearly £45,000-worth of damage. Naval aircraft took off from Killingholme and Yarmouth, but failed to make contact. Three Army Zeppelins which set out to raid London on this night failed to reach the English coast for various reasons, and one of them, LZ37, was destroyed over Belgium by Flight Sub-Lieutenant Reginald Warneford, flying a Morane Parasol, who dropped six 20 lb bombs on it after a chase lasting an hour. The encounter was accidental, as Warneford had been *en route* to attack the airship shed at Berchem Ste Agathe, but it proved that the Zeppelin was vulnerable to air attack provided the attacking aircraft had the advantage of height. In this case Warneford, who coaxed his Morane up to 11,000 feet, sighted the airship as it was passing through 7,000 feet, descending towards its base at Evère. A second airship, LZ38, was destroyed soon after docking at Evère when its shed was bombed by pilots of No 1 RNAS Squadron, based in France.

Following the loss of the two Army ships a tentative plan by the Navy to position its own airships at forward bases in Belgium was abandoned, and the next raid on Britain was made from Nordholz on the night of 15 June by the L10 commanded by *Kapitänleutnant* Hirsch. The L10 was an improved type of Zeppelin and was the forerunner of nine more airships of a similar class, all with a capacity of 1,126,000 cubic feet, which would be bought by the Navy before the end of 1915. The ships were 536 feet long and were powered by four 210 hp Maybach engines. They could cruise at 11,000 feet and fly as far as the west coast of England with a two-ton bomb load.

The L10's target on this June night was Tyneside. Hirsch crossed the coast near Blyth at a quarter to midnight, turned south, and for half an hour dropped 3,500 lb of bombs on Wallsend, Jarrow and South Shields, killing eighteen people, injuring seventy-two and causing damage amounting to nearly £42,000. No warning of the raid had been received, and much of the target area was brightly lit. Two sorties by BE2 aircraft were flown from Whitley Bay, but no contact was made. As a result of this raid, the Tyneside garrison commander advised Major-General H.M. Lawson, the GOC-in-C Northern Command, that the naval aircraft at Whitley Bay were inadequate for the defence task, and that an additional air station at Gosforth would be an advantage. The recommendation was approved, and a small RNAS detachment under Lieutenant Christopher Draper was operational there in July.

The next attack on the north, on the night of 9/10 August, was intended as a diversion for a major raid on London, which in the event was a dismal failure. The northern raider was once again the old L9, commanded this time by *Kapitänleutnant* Odo Loewe, who crossed the coast near Hornsea and bombed Goole in the belief that it was Hull. Air defence sorties were flown from Hornsea racecourse, Redcar – where there was a naval flying training establishment – and Whitley Bay, but although the L9 was sighted by pilots from Hornsea she was not engaged and escaped in thick mist.

On 7/8 September 1915 it was once again the Army's turn to raid London. The ships involved were the LZ74, LZ77 and the Schutte-Lanz SL2. The latter bombed Millwall, Deptford, Greenwich and Woolwich docks, causing a great deal of damage. Targets in England were attacked again on the following night, but only one ship managed to reach London; she was the L13, with Mathy in command, and her bombs started a huge fire among the textile warehouses to the north of St Paul's. In this one raid, Mathy caused one-sixth of the total damage inflicted on Britain during all the air raids of World War I; the total loss amounted to over half a million pounds.

Odo Loewe and the L9 returned to the north on the night of 8 September, crossing the coast near Whitby at 21.15 to raid the ironworks at Skinningrove. The attack was made with great accuracy but little damage was done, and the Zeppelin was well clear of the area before the first aircraft – a BE2 from Redcar – arrived on the scene. This was the last attack made on the north in 1915, and raids on southern England petered out a month later. For the remaining weeks of the year, the Navy's Zeppelins were either employed on co-operation work with the Fleet or were grounded by bad weather. When operations began again in January 1916, they were directed against targets spread along the whole length of England. The first raid of the year, on the last night of January, was a deep-penetration mission against Liverpool by nine Zeppelins. Twenty-two air defence sorties were flown without result, but one airship, the L19, came down in the North Sea through a combination of engine trouble and rifle fire from the Dutch Friesian Islands and was lost with all her crew, including her commander, Odo Loewe.

During 1915, it had become increasingly apparent that the RNAS was ill-equipped to deal with the Zeppelin threat, and it was clear that if matters were

Insert and above: *The BE2e/d variants proved quite successful in the anti-Zeppelin campaign if pilots had sufficient time to gain height and get above the airship to make their attack. Otherwise, they could be easily outclimbed.* (Philip Jarrett)

to improve the Royal Flying Corps, which had assisted the RNAS to a limited extent in the course of the year, would have to become much more involved, even to the extent of assuming the air defence commitment in full. The Admiralty and the War Office, however, found it hard to agree on anything, beyond the fundamental facts that Zeppelins were difficult to find in the dark and that night flying was fraught with peril, so while very brave young men in wholly inadequate aircraft were striving to confront the enemy, another war was being waged in Whitehall – a prolonged and unseemly wrangle over the responsibility for Britain's air defence.

In June 1915, the Director of Home Defence, General Launcelot Kiggell, had proposed that the Navy deal with enemy aircraft approaching the coast and that the Army take over once the enemy had come inland; this was firmed up by the Army Council in November, but it was not until 10 February 1916 that a formal agreement to this effect was endorsed by the War Committee. With effect from 12 noon on 16 February, 1916, the Commander-in-Chief Home Forces was to assume responsibility for the defence of London, and for

the rest of the country on the 22nd.

Meanwhile, by prior agreement with the RNAS, the RFC had positioned three BE2cs at Cramlington on 1 December 1915 for the defence of Tyneside, and on 18 March 1916 these formed the nucleus of the newly-formed No 36 Squadron, the first RFC squadron formed for the specific task of home defence. Flights were quickly established at Ashington, Hylton and Seaton Carew. Later in March, for the air defence of the southern part of the region, No 33 Squadron was transferred from Filton to Beverley in Yorkshire, with a detached flight at Bramham Moor, Tadcaster. In September 1916 No 76 Squadron formed at Ripon, with detached flights at Copmanthorpe, Helperby and Catterick, and in the following month No 77 Squadron was established at Edinburgh, with flights at Whiteburn, New Hagerston and Penston. By the end of the year, therefore, the north was defended by four front-line squadrons, all equipped with BE2 and, later, BE12 aircraft. Between them they had at their disposal no less than thirty-four landing grounds between Humber and Tyne and thirty-five between Tyne and Forth.

Despite these deployments, no raider was

BE2c 2473 Nightdress *of No 51 Squadron RFC, a Home Defence unit based at Thetford in Norfolk. The aircraft was written off on 29 July 1916. The squadron apparently had four named aircraft, the others being* Nighthawk, Nightclub *and* Nightmare. (Philip Jarrett)

The BE12 was widely used as a night fighter in WWI. This aircraft (6510), piloted by 2nd Lt (later AVM) W.A. McLaughry, was one of two flown from Dover on 12 August 1916. This later photograph shows the aircraft after a landing accident. Note the Le Prieur rocket rails. (Philip Jarrett)

destroyed by the northern air defences in the course of seven attacks that were made on targets from the Forth to the Humber between the beginning of March and the end of September 1916. Deployment of anti-aircraft weaponry to the north was still painfully slow, and it took a particularly costly raid on Hull on the night of 5 March 1916, after which a mob smashed up a vehicle belonging to the RFC, to bring about the hasty installation of two thirteen-pounder, two three-inch, one twelve-pounder and one six-pounder guns, while at the same time the defences around the Humber and along the east coast were generally strengthened.

Meanwhile, on 1 February 1916, the various air defence detachments in the London area had been brought together under No 19 Reserve Aeroplane Squadron, a newly-formed unit with its HQ at Hounslow. On 25 March the London defences were again reorganised and placed under the new No 18 Wing, and on 15 April No 19 RAS became No 39 (Home Defence) Squadron.

At the beginning of June 1916 eight RFC squadrons were dedicated to home defence. These were No 28 at Gosport and Newhaven; No 33 at Bramham Moor, Coal Aston, Beverley and Doncaster; No 36 at Cramlington, Turnhouse and Seaton Carew; No 39 at Hounslow, Hainault Farm, Sutton's Farm and North Weald; No 50 at Dover and Wye; No 51 at Thetford, Norwich and Narborough; No 52 at Hounslow, Goldhanger and Rochford; and No 54 at Castle Bromwich, Lilbourne, Papplewick and Waddington. Between them, they had an established aircraft strength of 134; their actual strength was sixty. At the same time, 271 anti-aircraft guns and 258 searchlights were available for the defence of key points, against a requirement of 487 and 490 respectively.

While the RFC strove to achieve some form of effective night defence organisation, a warning system was established and observer posts set up all over the country. These were connected with warning control centres and gradually began to prove their worth. Girls' names were used to identify individual Zeppelins, which were listed in alphabetical order as they crossed the coast. One of the first lines of defence against the incoming Zeppelins was the interception of their wireless traffic by direction-finding stations, and by the end of 1916 a network of huge sound locator mirrors, some built into cliffs, had also been set up.

By August 1916 the squadrons of the Home Defence Wing had adopted a system whereby aircraft operating from the landing grounds around the country were assigned individual patrol areas which overlapped, so that if a Zeppelin was sighted mutual support was readily available – at least in theory. Although aircrews had now amassed a considerable amount of experience in night operations, and were aware that night flying held no special complications, the Zeppelins remained notoriously hard to locate without searchlight assistance, anti-aircraft shellbursts or marker rockets, the latter fired by the coastal observers.

Then there were the allied problems of armament and interception techniques. Because the Zeppelin presented so vast a target, the favoured method of attack was from above, using small bombs, either the 20 lb Hale or the 60 lb incendiary designed at the Royal Laboratory, Woolwich, but there were alternative weapons. One was the Ranken Dart, devised by Engineer Lieutenant Francis Ranken, RN. Originally used by the RNAS, and also adopted by the RFC, the dart weighed about one pound and consisted of an iron-pointed metal tube containing high explosive and black powder. The tail unit embodied spring-loaded vanes which opened and locked into position to engage the Zeppelin's envelope after the head had penetrated inside, and at the same time activated a detonator rod. The dart, held fast to the envelope, would then burst into flames, igniting the gas from the airship's ruptured cells. The darts were carried in batches of twenty-four, which could be released all at once or in small groups.

Another anti-Zeppelin weapon was the Fiery Grapnel, which was carried in pairs attached to a BE2c. The idea was to approach the Zeppelin from right angles with the grapnel trailing behind, then to leap over the intended victim and allow the weapon to engage its envelope, whereupon an explosive charge would ignite leaking hydrogen.

The problem with these devices was that, because of the Zeppelin's superior rate of climb, it was usually difficult, if not impossible, for an attacking aircraft to get above it. The answer, clearly, was to be able to attack from any position, including below, using incendiary bullets.

Such bullets had existed for some years. One had been invented by a New Zealander, John Pomeroy, in 1908 and had been offered without success to the British government in 1914; it was only in 1916, after Pomeroy had written to David Lloyd George, that the Munitions Inventions Department agreed to sponsor development. In August that year, an order for half a million rounds was placed on behalf of the RFC.

The Admiralty had shown more interest in an explosive bullet designed by Flight Lieutenant F.A. Brock, and this was also ordered for both the RNAS and RFC, as was a phosphorus incendiary bullet designed by a Coventry engineer, J.F. Buckingham. This mixture of bullets was on issue to the home defence squadrons by the end of August 1916.

The result was immediate, and dramatic. On the night of 2 September, the Army's Schutte-Lanz airship SL11 (*Hauptmann* Wilhelm Schramm) was

The fiery end of Heinrich Mathy's L31, shot down in flames at Potter's Bar by Lt W.J. Tempest, RFC. The blazing mass has already broken in two. (Author)

Zeppelin L34 (Kaptlt Max Dietrich) falling in flames over Hartlepool Bay, 28/29 November 1916. (Author)

shot down in flames at Cuffley by Lieutenant William Leefe Robinson of No 39 Squadron. On 22 September L32 (*Oberleutnant-zur-See* Werner Peterson) fell in flames over Essex after being attacked by 2nd Lieutenant Frederick Sowrey, while Alois Bocker's L33 crash-landed near Little Wigborough, having suffered severe damage from anti-aircraft fire and the efforts of Lieutenant Alfred Brandon of 39 Squadron. Finally, on 1 October, one of a force of eleven Zeppelins that set out to raid England was shot down over Potter's Bar by 2nd Lieutenant W.J. Tempest. She was the L31, commanded by Heinrich Mathy.

All these successes had been in the south. But on the night of 28/29 November the northern air defences at last had their chance. Zeppelin L34, *Kapitänleutnant* Max Dietrich, was shot down off the coast by 2nd Lieutenant Ian Pyott of No 36 Squadron, flying a BE2c from Seaton Carew, soon after bombing targets in south-east Durham. All twenty crew perished. Another airship, the L21, was also destroyed that night by naval pilots from Great Yarmouth.

Although there were to be further Zeppelin attacks on the United Kingdom before the war's end, from May 1917 the emphasis switched to attacks on London and the south-east by heavier-than-air bombers, first by day and later by night. The principal bomber involved was the Gotha GIV,

which could carry a typical war load of six 110 lb bombs. Its maximum speed was about 85 mph, which even so was faster than some of the fighter aircraft sent up to intercept it, and its attack altitude of 16,000 feet made it a difficult target, unless defensive fighters had ample warning of its approach. The first attack on the British mainland, mounted by twenty-three Gothas in daylight on 25 May 1917, killed ninety-five civilians and injured 195 in Folkestone. More than seventy home defence aircraft were sent up to intercept, but the only ones to make contact were flown by two ferry pilots. Several Gothas were destroyed in subsequent raids, but these mostly fell to anti-aircraft fire or failed to regain their base because of adverse weather. The few home defence aircraft that did get close enough to intercept were usually beaten off by the Gotha's substantial defensive armament of three Spandau machine-guns.

In September 1917 the Gothas switched to night attacks, and they were now joined by an even more formidable bomber: the Zeppelin (*Staaken*) R Type, known as the *Riesenflugzeug* (giant aircraft). This monster was capable of carrying a 2,200 lb bomb at 14,000 feet at 80 mph under the power of its four 260 hp Mercedes engines; moreover, it was defended by five machine-guns, which made it a much tougher target than the Gotha. Only a small number of R Types were built, but they presented

Gotha GIVs of Kagohl 3 at Gontrode, Belgium. The GIV carried a typical war load of six 110 lb bombs. (Philip Jarrett)

The Zeppelin (Staaken) *R Type posed problems for the air defences. It was heavily armed and presented a difficult target for attacking fighters.* (Philip Jarrett)

an immense threat to British targets.

To meet this threat, the War Office implemented a new defence scheme whereby anti-aircraft guns and patrolling aircraft were allocated separate operating zones. In addition, balloons trailing steel cable 'curtains' floated in barriers up to 8,000 feet, theoretically forcing any attacking aircraft to fly above that height to a level where fighters would be patrolling. Sound locators – simple trumpet devices

at first, followed by more sophisticated fixed sound mirrors – were also playing their part by the end of 1917. The first sound mirror, a fifteen-foot reflector cut into the chalk cliff at Fan Bay, east of Dover, and focused on a point midway between Dunkirk and Calais, was operational by October 1917, and was able to detect aircraft sounds at up to fifteen miles.

The first German bombing raid of 1918 was

Gotha GIV bombers took part in most of the night attacks on London. (Philip Jarrett)

Gotha GIIIs parked in front of a Zeppelin shed, probably at Berchem Ste Agathe in Belgium. (Philip Jarrett)

mounted on the night of 28/29 January, when thirteen Gothas and two Giants were despatched to attack London. In the event seven Gothas and one Giant succeeded in doing so, killing sixty-seven civilians, injuring another 166, and causing damage of nearly £190,000. The raid was thwarted to some degree by fog, as far as the Gothas were concerned, while one of the Giants had engine trouble and was forced to turn back, having jettisoned its bombs into the sea off Ostende.

Crossing the English coast at intervals from 20.00 between Harwich and the North Foreland, three Gothas bombed London and the remaining four attacked Ramsgate, Margate, Sheerness and Sandwich. The Giant also reached London just after midnight, and one of its 660 lb bombs caused the worst single bombing incident of the war when it hit the Odhams Press building in Long Acre, killing thirty-eight people and injuring eighty-five.

One of the Gothas involved in the London attack dropped its bombs on Hampstead at 21.45 and was then tracked by searchlights as it flew over north-east London. The beams attracted the attention of two patrolling Sopwith Camel pilots of No 44 Squadron from Hainault – Captain George Hackwill and Lieutenant Charles Banks – who at once gave chase and independently picked up the glow from the Gotha's exhausts as it passed over Romford at 10,000 feet. Banks was flying a Camel with an unconventional armament; in addition to

its normal pair of Vickers guns it also carried a Lewis, mounted on the upper wing centre section and using the new RTS ammunition. Designed by Richard Threlfall and Son, this combined explosive and incendiary qualities.

It was Banks who attacked first, closing from the left to about thirty yards behind the Gotha and opening fire with all three guns. Hackwill meanwhile closed in from the right and also opened fire, effectively boxing in the German bomber and presenting an impossible situation to its gunner, whose field of fire was restricted. After ten minutes or so the Gotha caught fire and dived into the ground near Wickford, where it exploded. It would almost certainly have crashed anyway, even if it had not caught fire, for a subsequent examination of the crew's bodies revealed that the pilot had been shot through the neck. Hackwill and Banks were each awarded the Military Cross for their exploit. Other Gothas were also attacked that night, briefly and without result, by pilots of Nos 39, 50, 61 and 78 Squadrons RFC, and by a Sopwith 1½-Strutter of the RNAS from Dover.

An hour after the last Gotha had cleared the coast, the *Riesenflugzeug* was over Sudbury, having made landfall over Hollesley Bay, east of Ipswich, and was approaching London via a somewhat tortuous route. By this time, at least forty-four fighters were searching for it. It was sighted by two of them, from an unidentified squadron, not long after

The Gotha GV entered service in August 1917. Some 36 aircraft of this type were involved in night attacks on England. (Philip Jarrett)

crossing the coast, but they lost contact with it and it was next sighted by the crew of a No 39 Squadron Bristol fighter at about 23.00 near Harlow. The pilot of the Bristol, Lieutenant John Goodyear, positioned himself behind the Giant and fired a long burst from his Vickers, but was then hurled aside by the slipstream; this Giant, an R12, was fitted with six coupled engines driving three propellers, and the wash they created was enormous.

He tried again, and the same thing happened. On the third attempt, with the Bristol now running through heavy defensive fire, he attempted to position underneath the Giant so that his gunner, 1st Air Mechanic W.T. Merchant, could bring fire from his Lewis gun to bear. At that moment a burst of fire from one of the German gunners shattered the Bristol's petrol tank and wounded Merchant slightly in the arm. A few moments later the engine stopped and Goodyear glided down to make a faultless engine-off landing at North Weald, whose flarepath he had seen in the distance.

Shortly after it had released its bombs over London, the Giant was picked up east of Woolwich by a Sopwith Camel of No 44 Squadron flown by Lieutenant Bob Hall, a South African. Hall followed it as far as Foulness, cursing in helpless frustration all the way because he could not get his guns to work. The Giant got away.

The anti-aircraft barrage scored one success that night, but unfortunately its victim was a Camel of No 78 Squadron flown by Lieutenant Idris Davies, whose engine was stopped by a near shell burst at 11,000 feet over Woolwich. Davies tried to glide back to Sutton's Farm, but he hit telegraph wires near the Hornchurch signal box and was catapulted out of the cockpit. He fell between the railway lines, amazingly without injury, but the Camel was a complete loss. Forty minutes later Davies was sitting in another Camel, ready to take off if need be. Mostly, the anti-aircraft gunners co-operated very well with the RFC, and held their fire when friendly fighters were known to be overhead.

The following night witnessed the most remarkable night battle of the war, when three Giants out of four despatched, attacked southern England. The fourth, having developed engine trouble over the Channel, bombed fortifications near Gravelines before returning to its base, while the others crossed the English coast between Southend and the Naze. One of these, the R26, developed engine trouble soon after crossing the coast and began losing height, so its crew jettisoned the bomb load and limped back across the Channel on two engines, eventually landing at Ostende.

A second Giant, the R39, came inland via the Blackwater estuary just after 22.00, and ten minutes later it was sighted by Captain Arthur Dennis of No 37 Squadron, who was flying a BE12b. The latter, developed from the older BE2c, had enjoyed some success in the night fighting role, one of No 37 Squadron's aircraft having shot down Zeppelin L48 in June 1917. It was armed with a single Lewis gun, mounted on the port side of the cockpit and synchronised to fire through the propeller. Dennis

Sopwith Camel F1 B3834, oddly named Wonga Bonga *and based with the RNAS at Manston, was twice in action against Gothas. It shared in the destruction of an enemy bomber on 22 August 1917, flown by Flt Lt A.F. Brandon.* (Philip Jarrett)

opened fire from close range, braving fire from two of the Giant's machine-guns, and scored hits on the bomber's fuselage before drawing off to change his ammunition drum. On the second approach, however, he was buffeted by the Giant's slipstream, and on recovery found that he had lost contact with the target.

The R39 approached London from the

Crews of No 141 (Home Defence) Squadron at Biggin Hill, Kent, with their Bristol F2b Fighters in 1918. (Philip Jarrett)

Bristol F2b C4814 'D' of No 11 Squadron (Philip Jarrett)

north-west at approximately 11,000 feet and was next sighted by Bob Hall of No 44 Squadron, who pursued it until it became lost in the haze near Roehampton. Once again, Hall's guns gave trouble and he had no opportunity to open fire. Meanwhile, the Giant had dropped its bombs on residential areas between Acton and Richmond Park, the crew having apparently mistaken Hammersmith Bridge for Tower Bridge, which was several miles to the east. South of the Thames, the R39 was attacked briefly and with no visible result by Captain F.L. Luxmoore of No 78 Squadron, flying a Sopwith Camel. He fired fifty rounds on his first pass, but as he made a second firing run one of his bullets struck the Camel's propeller and the brilliant tracer element flew back into his face, temporarily blinding him. By the time his night vision was restored, the bomber had vanished.

Shortly after this the R39, now down to 9,500 feet and travelling very fast, was located by Captain G.H. Hackwill of No 44 Squadron, who was also flying a Camel. Hackwill gave chase and fired 600 rounds from long range before shortage of fuel compelled him to break off. The Giant was last seen as it crossed the coast near Hythe by 2nd Lieutenants F.V. Bryant and V.H. Newton, the crew of an Armstrong Whitworth FK8 of No 50 Squadron. They too gave chase, but lost the bomber in haze.

The third Giant, the R25, crossed the coast near Foulness at 10.50 pm and was almost immediately attacked by 2nd Lieutenant F.R. Kitton of No 37 Squadron, flying a BE2e. Diving his aircraft at a shuddering 100 mph, he got under the Giant's tail and fired a complete drum of ammunition at it, observing several hits, but lost the bomber while he was busy rearming. The R25 was next attacked by Bob Hall of No 44 Squadron at 23.15 over Benfleet, but his guns kept on jamming as he pursued it. He was joined by 2nd Lieutenant H.A. Edwardes, also of No 44 Squadron, who fired three long bursts before his guns also jammed.

By this time the R25 was taking violent evasive action. The battle had now attracted three more Camels, all from No 44 Squadron; the first on the scene was 2nd Lieutenant T.M. O'Neill, who fired 300 rounds before his guns jammed too. Next came the squadron commander, Major Murlis Green, who was flying a Camel equipped with two Lewis guns using RTS ammunition. He had already made one run, only to break away when he almost flew into O'Neill's fire. Now he closed in again to be greeted by the full attention of the Giant's rear gunner. Undeterred, he fired three-quarters of a drum at the bomber before suffering a stoppage which he was unable to clear. As his second Lewis also refused to function, he had no choice but to return to base to have the trouble put right.

Bristol F2bs of No 141 Squadron at Biggin Hill, late 1918. (Philip Jarrett)

Major G.W. Murlis Green, DSO, MC, OC No 44 Squadron, taking off from Hainault Farm, Essex, in a Sopwith Camel modified for night fighting. Note the machine-guns mounted above the upper wing – a special night fighting modification. (Philip Jarrett)

The R25 was now in trouble. The Camels' fire had put one of its engines out of action and some of its instruments had also been smashed. Although unable to maintain height with a full bomb load, and with their speed down to about 60 mph, the crew decided to press on to London. The Giant's bombs fell in open ground near Wanstead. Up to this point the R25 had been harried by Bob Hall, who was able to fire only five rounds before each stoppage; he now lost his target, but encountered the R39 a few miles to the west.

The R25 scraped home to Ostende, having survived successive attacks by five fighters. They had collectively fired over 800 rounds at her, and after landing she was found to have taken no fewer than eighty-eight hits. Had the fighters not suffered continual gun stoppages, there seems little doubt that they would have brought down the bomber.

23

This photograph of Sopwith Camel F1 of No 44 Squadron clearly shows the night fighting modifications. The pilot is thought to be Capt G.H. Hackwill. (Philip Jarrett)

Sopwith Camel, unit unidentified, in night fighting colours. Note the fuselage artwork. (Philip Jarrett)

Several armament installations, this one included, were tried out on the Sopwith 1½-Strutter. Something of a 'do-it-yourself' night fighter, the modified aircraft were known as Sopwith 'Comics' by their crews. (Philip Jarrett)

However, there were other factors in their failure to do so; analysing the action later, the Camel pilots of No 44 Squadron realised that the Giant's sheer size had led them to believe that they had been firing from a much closer range than was actually the case. Instead of closing to within 50 yards, as they had thought at the time, they must have been anything up to 250 yards away.

The last German aircraft raid on Britain in World War I took place on the night of 20/21 May 1918. Twenty-eight Gothas and three Giants set out to attack London, and were met by a vastly more effective night fighter force than had been the case four months earlier, at the time of the previous night raids. Seventy-four Camels and SE5s went up to intercept the bombers, shooting down three Gothas, while the anti-aircraft defences claimed two more and a sixth crashed in Essex after engine failure. It was the biggest loss suffered by the German bombers in a single night's operations over England, and it was to be more than two decades before they came again.

The cessation of attacks on England by heavier-than-air machines meant that fighters could be released for service in the night fighting role on the Western Front, and on 12 June 1918 No 151 Squadron formed for this purpose at Hainault Farm, combining one flight each from Nos 44, 78 and 112 Squadrons. The first flight of Camels crossed the Channel on 16 June; by the 26th the whole squadron was installed at Famechon, moving to Fontaine-sur-Maye on 2 July. Its first success was achieved by Captain A.B. Yuille, who sighted and attacked a Gotha in the early hours of 25 July. The

Gotha crash-landed behind the British lines with both engines out of action and its observer wounded. In the months that followed, No 151 Squadron was to carry out many night interceptions, as well as mounting night intruder operations against the German bomber airfields, and by the end of the war its pilots had claimed the destruction of twenty-six enemy aircraft. It was to remain a night fighter unit for most of its career, and the last aircraft it used in this role in the late 1950s was the potent Gloster Javelin – a far cry from the Camels with which it pioneered its night fighting techniques.

On 8 August, 1918 – a date later described by the German commander, Field Marshal Ludendorff in his memoirs as 'the black day of the German Army' – the First French Army under *Général* Debeney and General Rawlinson's Fourth British Army attacked on a fifteen-mile front east of Amiens. By 15.00 the Allied forces had made advances of up to seven miles and taken 7,000 prisoners; the offensive was supported by 430 tanks, the whole of the British Tank Corps less one brigade.

During the week preceding the offensive, the Allied air forces made numerous attacks on enemy airfields, notably those occupied by the *Schlachtstaffeln*, the German ground attack squadrons. In the early hours of 5 August, two Camels of No 151 Squadron, flown by Captain S. Cockerell and Captain W.H. Haynes, carried out intruder patrols over Estrées and Guizancourt aerodromes; Cockerell arrived over Estrées just as enemy aircraft were landing and dropped a bomb, which burst about fifty yards from it, and then

Top and above: *The Airco DH4, seen in these two photographs, made an excellent night fighter. It has been called the 'Mosquito' of WWI.*

(Philip Jarrett)

turned and fired 200 rounds at it from close range. At that moment all the lights went out and Cockerell was unable to see any result, so he dropped two more bombs in the hope of hitting something before returning to base. Shortly afterwards Haynes also appeared over Estrées, having found nothing worthwhile at the other airfield, and attacked one of three Gothas which he saw approaching. The Gotha took evasive action and he lost it. He dropped his bombs on a searchlight battery and then also headed for home, his guns having jammed.

On the next night, two Camels of No 151 Squadron again visited Estrées and Guizancourt. The first to arrive was Major C.J.Q. Brand, who dropped two bombs on the hangars at Guizancourt and then attacked a large two-seater which was coming in to land. He attacked it again on the ground, but broke off when all the lights went out. He remained in the vicinity of the airfield for the next half hour, dropping two bombs in the path of an aircraft which was about to touch down, then strafed the hangars and searchlights. Shortly after-

wards he attacked another enemy aircraft, but was himself attacked from the rear by a German scout and returned to base. In the 1939–45 war, this officer – then Air Vice-Marshal Sir Quintin Brand, DSO, MC, DFC – was to command No 10 Group, RAF Fighter Command, in the Battle of Britain. The other Camel of No 151 Squadron that night was flown by Captain Cockerell, who dropped four bombs on the hangars at Guizancourt and then shot up four searchlights until they went out. Soon afterwards he attacked a Gotha, which crash-landed some distance from the airfield.

It was on this night – 6/7 August, 1918 – that the German Naval Airship Division mounted its last raid on the British isles. Four airships were involved; they were the L53, L56, L65 and L70, and the latter was shot down in flames by a DH4 from Great Yarmouth NAS, crewed by Major Egbert Cadbury and Captain Robert Leckie. It fell into the sea near King's Lynn, Norfolk. The great irony was that among the twenty-two dead was the man who had been the original architect of the night offensive against Britain, Peter Strasser.

CHAPTER TWO

THE COMPLACENT YEARS, 1919–39

By the time the Armistice was concluded in November 1918, Britain's night air defences had reached a remarkable degree of sophistication. There were sixteen home defence squadrons under the command of No 6 Brigade, RAF, together with nine night training squadrons, with a total strength of 355 aircraft. Of these, 145 were Sopwith Camels and fifty-five Bristol Fighters; the remainder comprised eighty-two Avro 504s, sixty FE2bs/ds and thirteen BE12s.

By this time, air fighting tactics were well thought out, as was illustrated in a paper written by Murlis Green (who retired as a Group Captain, and whose name became hyphenated somewhere *en route*) in the early 1920s for the RAF Staff College.

> 'On a dark night with no moon the exhaust flames of a stationary engine machine will usually be seen before the outline of the machine itself, but on a clear moonlight night the outline of the machine is generally first seen.
>
> 'After patrolling for an hour or so in the dark without seeing anything there is a tendency, when a hostile machine is at last seen, to drive straight at it firing both guns. This method seldom leads to success as the flash of the machine-guns, even when shielded, usually impairs the pilot's sight to such an extent that after the first few rounds have been fired he loses the target.
>
> 'The method found most successful up to now is as follows. Once you have seen your objective you must not take your eyes off him until he is destroyed or you wish to break off the fight. Turn your machine quickly into the same direction as he is going and get behind and slightly below him. If you have a 45 degree mounting use it. If your guns fire in line of flight close up until almost colliding, throttle back and open fire.
>
> 'There are two reasons why it is important not to open fire until extremely close range has been reached. Firstly, it is difficult to distinguish friend from foe at night, as of course crosses cannot be distinguished from circles, so that one has to rely entirely on silhouettes. Secondly, range is very deceptive at night.'

Murlis Green was a firm advocate of upward-firing guns mounted at an angle of 45 degrees, and postulated a twin-engined night fighter armed with .5 in machine-guns in this configuration; but it was to be twenty years before the concept was adopted operationally, and then by the Germans, who used it with devastating effect against the RAF's night bombers.

From the summer of 1917, the RFC had used wireless telegraphy (W/T) in the fight against the German raiders. BE12s of Nos 37 and 50 Squadrons, operating in pairs and equipped with continuous-wave transmitters, patrolled north and south of the Thames and reported, by means of coded signals in Morse, the movements of incoming enemy aircraft to ground stations at Wormwood Scrubs and the Hotel Cecil in the Strand, London.

But the most significant development was radio telephony (R/T). Experimental work in this field was centralised at Biggin Hill early in 1917, and after successful trials the Bristol Fighters of No 141 Squadron were fitted with air-ground R/T sets in January 1918. Shortly afterwards, the principal airfields in the London Air Defence Area (LADA) were equipped with short-range transmitters so that they could communicate directly with their own squadron aircraft; in these early days, although all aircraft carried receivers, only those of the flight commanders were equipped to transmit. All the LADA squadrons were equipped with R/T by the end of August 1918, squadrons and their bases both being allocated callsigns. The collective callsign for all No 6 Brigade aircraft was Menagerie, and the other allocated callsigns were as follows:

Squadron	Base	Aircraft
37	Yukon	Husky
39	Bona	Buffalo
44	Niger	Hippo
50	Bark	Dingo
61	Rockies	Grizzly
78	Cub	Lion
112	Darling	Duckbill
141	Dollars	Rhino
143	Pouch	Kangaroo

Patrol areas were given geographical designations,

such as Brazil, Canada and Mexico, while other code words were used to precede orders transmitted from the ground. For example, Gulls meant the two highest aircraft on patrol, Penguins meant all other aircraft, and Rum signified recall. An aircraft forced to abandon its patrol transmitted the code-word Blanket. Height alterations were expressed in thousands of feet: 'Step up one' meant climb 1,000 feet, while 'Step down two' was the order to descend 2,000 feet.

The introduction of R/T led to vast improvements in the LADA control and reporting system. A central operations room was set up at Spring Gardens, near Admiralty Arch in London, and was declared operational on 12 September 1918. It was equipped with a large plotting table covered with a squared map of the London area and overlooked by a dais from which LADA's commander and subordinate officers could overlook the proceedings. The ten plotters received information through telephone head-sets from twenty-six sub-control centres, which in turn received their information from gun and searchlight sights, sound locators and observation posts, and transferred it to the map, using a disc to indicate single enemy aircraft and a rectangle to indicate a formation, with arrows denoting courses. During a major raid, coloured indicators were used to differentiate between enemy formations. Defending fighters were represented by aircraft-shaped counters. The commander of the London Air Defence Area, Major-General E.B. Ashmore, could break into the plotters' telephone lines if he needed further information, while Brigadier-General T.C.R. Higgins, GOC No 6 Brigade, had direct lines to his fighter wings.

In its definitive form, the new control and reporting system was installed too late to have a decisive impact on the air defence of Great Britain, for by September 1918 enemy air raids had ceased. But it was the foundation of a greatly enhanced and refined system which, with the priceless gift of radar, was to be the salvation of the nation in 1940, and which was ultimately to provide fighters with the eyes that would enable them to locate and destroy enemy bombers at night.

The four years of World War I marked an incredible leap forward in the embryonic science of military aviation – especially in Britain, which had progressed from aircraft that could barely fly across the Channel in 1914 to a strategic bomber (the Handley Page V/1500) that was preparing to bomb Berlin from East Anglia in 1918. Yet, almost before the guns had ceased firing, the British Admiralty and the War Office joined forces in a determined bid to abolish the Royal Air Force – the service in which technical advance was most apparent – as a separate organisation.

One man – the Chief of the Air Staff, Air Chief Marshal Sir Hugh Trenchard – was equally as determined that the RAF should retain its separate identity, but drastic cuts in post-war defence expenditure made his task a formidable one. By the end of 1921 the strength of the RAF was at a very low ebb; apart from training establishments, there were only five squadrons based in the United Kingdom, and only one of these (No 25) was a fighter squadron. Yet this was a mere three years after the government had published statistics showing that in four years of war, Zeppelins and German bombers between them had killed or injured over 4,000 British civilians, mostly during night raids.

The parlous state of Britain's air defences was highlighted by an article in *The Times* in March 1922, which alerted the British public to the fact that the French Air Force, far from dismantling its assets wholesale, possessed a front-line combat force of 300 bombers and 300 fighters. The shock was profound, especially as relations between Britain and her former ally were poor at this time; the Air Staff, carrying out an assessment of the probable damage such a bomber force might do, and basing it on the results of the Gotha raids, calculated that the French had the capability to kill 1,700 people and injure 3,300 in London in the first twenty-four hours of an air attack, followed by 1,275 killed and 2,475 injured in the second twenty-four hours, and 850 killed and 1,650 injured in every subsequent twenty-four hours. In other words, the French bombers would theoretically be able to kill and injure, in only three days, twice the number of casualties inflicted on British civilians during the whole of the war.

Within a month a defence sub-committee recommended that the strength of the RAF be greatly increased, and the Cabinet gave its approval to the formation of twenty new squadrons for home defence. In 1923 this was further increased to a recommended fifty-two squadrons, totalling 600 aircraft. It was not before time; in the spring of 1923 there was still only one fighter squadron, No 56, in the whole of the United Kingdom (the other, No 43, was on detachment to Turkey). Yet no thought was given to the formation of specialist night fighter squadrons, even though the French, armed with the excellent Breguet XIV, had shown considerable expertise in night bombing operations during the war.

Re-equipment proceeded at a relatively slow pace, the fighter squadrons standardising on the Sopwith Snipe, the RAF's most modern fighter when the war ended. A decade later, the biplane fighters with which the RAF's home defence squadrons were armed were not much further advanced, and although a new generation of monoplane fighters was on the horizon the prototypes, in

The magnificent Breguet XIV, seen here in civilian markings post-war, pioneered French night bombing techniques in WWI. (Author)

The Sopwith Snipe was the RAF's most modern fighter in the years immediately after WWI. This rare photograph shows Snipes in South Russia, 1919. (Author)

RAF pilots occasionally took to the night skies in biplane fighters such as the Bristol Bulldog . . .

. . . But day flying was hazardous enough, as this photograph of an upturned Armstrong Whitworth Siskin shows. (Both Author)

1934, had yet to fly.

On the technical front, however, decisions were being taken that would have far-reaching importance, particularly in the context of night fighter development. In 1934 A.P. Rowe of the Directorate of Scientific Research in the Air Ministry, seriously alarmed by the state of Britain's air defences, informed his Director, H.E. Wimperis, that unless science were applied to air fighting Britain would certainly lose any war fought within the next ten years. Wimperis was impressed by the argument, and proposed to the Secretary of State, Lord Londonderry, that a scientific committee should be formed within the Air Ministry to survey air defence. He further suggested that the chairman of this committee should be H.T. Tizard, a former

31

Royal Flying Corps pilot who was now Chairman of the Aeronautical Research Committee.

In 1935 one of the first matters to come before Tizard's committee was the so-called 'death ray', much beloved by science fiction writers, which had been proposed by various 'inventors' since the 1914-18 war. Tizard might have dismissed the concept out of hand; instead, he consulted on its possibilities with R.A. Watson-Watt, Superintendent of the Radio Department of the National Physical Laboratory. Watson-Watt and his staff buried the 'death ray' notion once and for all, but Watson-Watt recalled something odd. In 1932, the Post Office had reported that aircraft sometimes interfered with radio signals and re-radiated them. What if, Watson-Watt thought, a ground station transmitted a radio pulse which would be reflected back by an aircraft and picked up by the ground station?

One of Watson-Watt's staff, A.F. Wilkins, made further calculations, and as a result Watson-Watt submitted an historic document to the Air Ministry on 12 February, 1935. Its title was *Detection and Location of Aircraft by Radio Methods*. It was to change the course of air warfare.

While Watson-Watt and his team proceeded with their early experiments into what would even-tually become known as radar, the Air Staff had been turning its attention to the concept of a two-seat fighter suitable for both day and night operations, and in April 1935 Specification F9/35 was issued. Most of the major British aircraft constructors – Armstrong Whitworth, Boulton Paul, Bristol, Fairey, Hawker and Supermarine – submitted tenders, and in the end the choice was narrowed down to two proposals, those put forward by Hawker and Boulton Paul. (A contract was also drawn up around the Fairey submission, but this never went beyond the design stage).

Construction of the Hawker proposal, the Hotspur – basically a Hawker Henley with the addition of a power-operated gun turret – was delayed by Hawker's preoccupation with Hurricane production, and the sole prototype did not fly until 14 June 1938. In the meantime, in March 1937, Boulton Paul had received a contract for eighty-seven production examples of its design, the P82, to Specification F5/37, and the name Defiant was adopted. The full programme of flight trials was completed at the Aeroplane and Armament Experimental Establishment (A&AEE) at Martlesham Heath in February 1938, the prototype flying without its four-gun turret.

The turret, known as the Boulton Paul A Mk IID,

The Boulton Paul Defiant was a disaster as a day fighter, but adapted very well to the night fighting role. This example, N1751, served with No 256 Squadron in the winter of 1940–41. (Philip Jarrett)

The AI-equipped Bristol Blenheim 1F gave the RAF a limited night fighting capability. This example is seen bearing the code markings of the night fighter OTU, No 54. (Philip Jarrett)

was installed in the second prototype Defiant (K8620) which flew with a Rolls-Royce Merlin II engine on 18 May 1938. The first production Defiant I flew on 30 July that year. Fifty Defiants of the first production batch had been completed by the end of 1939, and the first Defiant squadron, No 264, began to rearm with the new type at Martlesham Heath on 8 December.

But the Defiant, at this stage, was not regarded as anything other than a day fighter; its part in the air war at night was to come much later, as we shall see.

In 1938, the Air Staff had identified a requirement for a long-range escort fighter, and this led to the conversion of a number of Blenheim Mk I bombers to the fighter role under the designation Mk IF. To convert the aircraft to a fighter proved relatively simple, by adding a self-contained battery of four forward-firing Browning machine-guns in a shallow pack fitting flush under the bomb bay. The first squadron to rearm with the Blenheim IF, in

September 1938, was No 600 at Hendon, and four others (Nos 23, 25, 29 and 604) had re-equipped by the end of the year. By the outbreak of war in September 1939 Nos 64 and 601 Squadrons had also rearmed with the type.

By the spring of 1940 it was becoming obvious that the Blenheim IF, allied with the still experimental airborne interception (AI) radar, was the only aircraft on the RAF's inventory capable of filling the night fighter gap, and on 18 April 1940 the Fighter Interception Unit was formed at Tangmere under the command of Wing Commander Peter Chamberlain, six Blenheims being allocated for operational trials with the AI Mk III.

Ten days earlier, the Germans had invaded Norway, and on 10 May 1940 their armies struck in France and the Low Countries. All the resources of Fighter Command would soon be put to the test.

CHAPTER THREE

NIGHT FIGHTERS IN THE BATTLE OF FRANCE

France's ANF les Mureaux 113 and 115 general purpose aircraft were used to develop night fighting tactics in the years before WWII. (ECP Armées)

When war broke out on 3 September, 1939, the only belligerent nation to have a dedicated night fighter unit on its order of battle was France. The French Air Ministry had been conscious of the need for air defence at night since 1934, and at the beginning of 1939 the night defence role was assigned to two *Groupes de Chasse de Nuit*, GCN 3/1 at Etampes and GCN 2/4 at Reims. Both were equipped with Mureaux 113 two-seat general purpose aircraft, GCN

GCN 2/4, the French Air Force pre-war night fighter unit, also operated a few Dewoitine D500s (seen here) and D501s. (ECP Armées)

2/4 also having an *escadrille* (flight) of Dewoitine D501 single-seat fighters. All these units had been assigned to other duties by the outbreak of war.

On 25 February 1939 another night fighter unit, the newly-formed GCN 1/13, took delivery of its first three twin-engined Potez 630 fighters at Reims. This aircraft was the result of a French Air Ministry specification, dated 31 October 1934, for a light multi-seat air defence fighter capable of night missions. Series production began at the beginning of 1939, and during the following year the 13e *Escadre de Chasse de Nuit*'s two groups, 1/13 and 2/13, progressively rearmed with a derivative, the Potez 631. This aircraft, powered by two Gnome-Rhône radial engines, had evolved from a 1934 specification for a three-seat strategic fighter; armed with two 20 mm cannon and two 7.5 mm machine-guns, it had an operational ceiling of 31,000 feet and a maximum speed of 275 mph at 14,800 feet.

From 22 September 1939, GCN 1/13 sent detachments to Melun-Villaroche for operational training, its pilots practising night interception techniques with the aid of searchlights on the ground. On 1 January 1940 both groups split up into four independent *escadrilles*, and on 10 May 1940 the order of battle was as follows:

Unit	Establishment (Aircraft)	Available	Base
ECN 1/13	12	8	Meaux-Villenoy
ENC 2/13	11	7	Melun-Villaroche
ECN 3/13	12	10	Le Plessis
ECN 4/13	12	7	Betz-Boulliancy
ECN 5/13	11	11	Loyettes

ECN 4/13, in fact, was seriously under strength, three of its crews having been sent to reinforce 2/13 and two more to reinforce 1/13. All flights stood alert from 10 to 16 May, but there were no night interceptions of enemy aircraft.

On 17 May 1940, ten days after the German assault in the west began, *Armée de l'Air* HQ – aware that the night fighter force possessed over forty serviceable aircraft that could usefully be employed elsewhere – decided to use them in the assault role. Accordingly, later that day eighteen Potez of ECN 1/13, 2/13 and 4/13 took off from their bases in the Paris area to attack enemy motorised columns near Fourmies.

It was a costly venture. Of the six Potez 631s of

The Potez 631 was of the same lineage as the Potez 63 reconnaissance aircraft, seen here, but had a redesigned 'solid' nose and a lengthened cockpit reminiscent of the Messerschmitt 110's – an aircraft for which it was often mistaken. (ECP Armées)

2/13, only two regained their base at Melun. Of the others, *Lieutenant* Guillier crash-landed near Montceaux; *Adjudant* Delmotte managed to land at Chantilly-les-Aigles, wounded and with his aircraft shot to ribbons, *Sous-Lieutenant* Reyter made a forced landing at Laon with his port engine out of action, and the *Groupe's* commander, *Capitaine* Petit de Mirbeck, was shot down in flames over the enemy lines. One of the four aircraft of 4/13 was hit and crash-landed at Cambrai with its pilot wounded; the gunner of a second was killed by a flak shell. The eight Potez of 1/13 returned to Meaux, but all were damaged.

The night fighter *escadrilles* scored their first victory on 18 May – during the daytime. At 14.00 three Potez of 1/13 flown by *Capitaine* Treilland, *Sergent-Chef* Post and *Adjudant* Guichard attacked a lone Heinkel 111 and forced it down north of Braine. That same afternoon, *Capitaine* Pierre Pouyade (who was later to rise to fame as commander of the *Regiment Normandie-Niemen*, the Free French air unit that fought on the Russian front), together with *Adjudants* Martin and Delage – all of 4/13 – intercepted a formation of ten He 111s and Me 110s over Creil. Two of the bombers were hit and damaged, but Delage was himself hit and had to make an emergency landing at Beauvais. On the way home, *Adjudant* Martin was successively attacked and hit by a He 111, a Me 110, French anti-aircraft fire and an errant Morane 406; he nevertheless managed to reach base safely.

On the morning of 19 May, six He 111s were intercepted by *Sous-Lieutenant* Merle, *Adjudant* Guichard and *Sergent-Chef* Post of 1/13. The French pilots made their attack through heavy friendly anti-aircraft fire, loosing off hundreds of rounds into a Heinkel that was lagging behind the rest. The bomber crash-landed near Braine with one engine in flames. In the early evening, *Adjudant-Chef* Chambrias, *Adjudant* Guichard and *Sergent-Chef* Post engaged six more Heinkels at high altitude. A Heinkel was set on fire and began to lose height steadily, streaming smoke, but at that point the French pilots were forced to break off the action through lack of fuel and the bomber was not seen to crash.

The Potez 631s of 2/13 also exchanged shots with a Dornier 17 in the evening of the 19th, but no result was observed. The following evening two aircraft of 2/13 were attacked by six Dewoitine 520s, which severely damaged one of the Potez before they realised their error. One could not blame the French fighter pilots; with its long cockpit canopy and twin fins the Potez 631 bore a strong resemblance to the Messerschmitt 110 when viewed from certain angles.

At 10.55 am on 21 May, *Sous-Lieutenant* Boursain and *Sergent-Chef* Post of 2/13 joined forces with a pair of Bloch 152s of GCN 2/1 and 2/9 in an attack on a Dornier 17. The four fighters each made two passes and shot the bomber down in flames in the forest of Halate, near Creil. That same day, the

Bloch MB152 fighters, seen here in Vichy markings, equipped France's local defence flights in the summer of 1940, operating in both the day and night role. They enjoyed some success in the former, but none at all in the latter. (ECP Armées)

problem of misidentification cropped up again with tragic consequences when two Potez of 4/13 were again attacked by D520s of GCN 2/3. The Dewoitines made five passes and the Potez were obliged to open fire to defend themselves. A D520 was hit and crashed in the forest of Chantilly, killing the pilot, *Sous-Lieutenant* d'Harcourt. Two days later, a Potez of 1/13 was attacked by Bloch 152s and crash-landed, seriously injuring the pilot. On 24 May, in an attempt to avoid further tragedies of this kind, several Potez 631s were sent on a tour of the fighter bases in the area so that the single-seater pilots could have a good look at them; they were also furnished with larger roundels and a white band was painted along their fuselage sides.

On 25 May the *Luftwaffe* made a series of heavy attacks on the airfields occupied by the night fighter *escadrilles*. At Le Plessis, a Potez 631 of 3/13 was destroyed on the ground and five others damaged. ECN 1/13, whose base at Meaux was badly hit, was transferred to Trilbardou and later to Moissy-Cramayel.

On 27 May, a Potez of 4/13 flown by *Adjudant* Guichard was attacked by seven Me 109s over the front line. Severely wounded, Guichard made a forced landing in enemy-held territory and the 109s continued to strafe the wreck of his aircraft on the ground. Guichard lingered on in hospital for more than a month before succumbing to his injuries on 18 June. On 28 May, 4/13 became the first night fighter unit to receive a modified version of the Potez 631 with heavier armament consisting of four additional machine-guns mounted under the wings. These modifications had been under way since

April, but they took six weeks to complete and in fact only a few machines were to be delivered before the final collapse.

The first day of June saw the operational debut of ECN 5/13, which was assigned to the defence of the Lyon–Saint Etienne–Le Creusot sector. Three of the unit's Potez 631s attacked nine He 111s over Vienne and damaged one of them, but the three Potez were also damaged and one crew member wounded. The next day 5/13 took part in two more battles; at 08.00 hours two Potez 631s attacked nine Heinkels over Lyon, but they were forced to break off when they themselves were attacked by four Me 110s. At 16.00, the same two French pilots – *Capitaine* Perdrizet and *Sergent* Farriol – attacked a formation of thirty-five He 111s at 25,000 feet over Vienne. Farriol chased a straggling Heinkel for over sixty miles, firing off all his ammunition at it, and the enemy bomber limped away, trailing a stream of smoke.

Also on 2 June, ECN 4/13 had yet another brush with friendly forces when *Capitaine* Pouyade and *Adjudant* Martin were fired on by a French anti-air-craft battery while on patrol over Villers-Cotterets. Pouyade, his aircraft in flames, made a wheels-up landing and escaped from the wreck with slight burns. His observer, however, was severely burned and his gunner wounded. *Adjudant* Martin, who had now been shot at by Frenchmen on three sep-arate occasions and who had collected no fewer than fifteen shell holes in his Potez, stormed into his CO's office on his return and demanded a trans-fer from the *Armée de l'Air*. His request was turned down.

In another incident that day, *Sergent-Chef* Post of 1/13 was also wounded by friendly shellfire while carrying out an air observation sortie over Lassigny. There seemed to be no end to the peril; on 3 June *Sous-Lieutenant* Merle of 1/13 was attacked in rapid succession by French anti-aircraft fire, seven Me 109s and a Bloch 152; he escaped by the skin of his teeth and pronounced the 109s to be the least dangerous adversaries he had met that day! Two Potez which took off from Melun later in the day to intercept a formation of Heinkels were also given a hot reception by their own base's AA defences on their return, fortunately without damage.

Sous-Lieutenant Biger of ECN 1/13 was lost on 3 June; he was patrolling over Lassigny with *Sous-Lieutenant* Boursain when they were surprised by five Me 109s. Biger went down in flames and Boursain managed to get away. Another Potez, flown by *Lieutenant* Guillier of 2/13, attacked a Dornier 17 and set it on fire, but it disappeared in the haze to the north of the forest of Compiègne.

During the week that followed the night fighter bases were hit repeatedly by the *Luftwaffe* and several Potez 631s were destroyed on the ground. The last air combat took place on 10 June, when *Adjudant* Ravet claimed an Me 109 probably destroyed over Rozay. After that there followed several days of confused withdrawal to the south; by 23 June ECN 1/13, 2/13, 3/13 and 4/13 had pulled back to Nîmes-Garons, while 5/13 was at Marignane.

At 13.00 that day, the four *escadrilles* were ordered to take off and attack armoured columns in the Moirans area. However, a heavy rainfall had turned the grass area into a quagmire and only seven out of fifteen aircraft managed to take off. Six of these attacked the target, and all returned to base.

It was the end. In six weeks of operations the night fighter *escadrilles* had destroyed nine enemy aircraft and claimed thirteen more probably destroyed. Ten Potez 631s had been destroyed through enemy action and three more by friendly aircraft and AA fire, together with three seriously damaged. Not once during those six weeks, although some night sorties had been flown, had the Potez crews had the opportunity to carry out a night interception. Nevertheless, GCN 1/13 deserves its place in history as the first unit of its kind to serve operationally with any air force.

CHAPTER FOUR

THE NIGHT DEFENCE OF BRITAIN, 1940–42

The defeat of France in June 1940 was followed by a growing number of incursions into British airspace by enemy aircraft at night. Many of these raids were intercepted by both day fighters and Blenheim night fighters, the latter having already registered some successes as intruders during the Battle of France. At 00.50 on 19 June, for example, an He 111H-4 of 2/KG54 was shot down into the sea off the Norfolk coast by Flight Lieutenant R.M.B Duke-Woolley in a Blenheim of No 23 Squadron, the German crew being captured; on the same night two Heinkels of 4/KG4 were also destroyed, both at 01.15. The first was shot down off Felixstowe by Flight Lieutenant A.G. Malan in a Spitfire of No 74 Squadron, and the second was shot down jointly by a Spitfire of No 19 Squadron and a Blenheim of No 23 Squadron at Fleam Dyke, Cambridgeshire. Unfortunately, the Spitfire pilot,

Flying Officer Petra, was forced to bale out during the combat after his aircraft was hit, while the Blenheim pilot, Squadron Leader O'Brien, baled out after losing control. Both his crew members were killed.

The third victory of the night was achieved at 02.15 by Flying Officer G.E. Ball of No 19 Squadron, who shot down a Heinkel 111H of 6/KG4 into the sea off Margate.

Three more Heinkels were destroyed in the early hours of 26 June. The first, an He 111P-2 of 3/KG4, was shot down into the sea off Hull by Pilot Officers R.A. Smith and R. Marples at 00.17, while two He 111H-3s of 3/KG26 were shot down by pilots of Nos 602 and 603 Squadrons off the Scottish coast.

Interceptions of this kind were aided by the clear, translucent nature of the summer nights, with their

Fighter Command's main adversary in the night skies of Britain was the Heinkel He 111, seen here under fighter attack during the main daylight phase of the Battle of Britain. (Author)

Barrage balloons were always a menace to the German night bombers. This He 111, brought down on British soil, is fitted with a cumbersome balloon 'fender'. (Author)

Blenheim Mk IF, showing AI aerial installation on port wing. (Philip Jarrett)

attendant good visibility. In the following months the *Luftwaffe's* main effort switched to attacks on coastal shipping. There were still opportunities for the day fighter pilots to make night interceptions, however; at 00.55 on 26 July, for example, an He 111H-4 of 1/KG4 on a mine-laying sortie over the

Bristol Channel was shot down by Pilot Officer Cock of No 87 Squadron, flying a Hurricane.

The development of airborne radar in Britain had meanwhile been proceeding well in the summer of 1940, by which time the RAF had five squadrons assigned to night fighting; these were equipped

First line of defence: a Chain Home (CH) radar station on the English coast. (Author)

with Bristol Blenheims and two of them, Nos 29 and 604, were just starting to carry out trials with rudimentary AI Mk III radar. The real pioneering work, however, was undertaken by the Fighter Interception Unit (FIU) at RAF Tangmere, and on the night of 22/23 July 1940 the long-awaited breakthrough came when a radar-equipped Blenheim of this unit intercepted and destroyed a Dornier Do 17 bomber. Flying Officer G. Ashfield, Pilot Officer G.E. Morris and Sergeant R.H. Leyland were patrolling at 10,000 feet when the Chain Home (CH) radar station at Poling established contact with a group of enemy raiders crossing the coast at about 6,000 feet. Information on the enemy's progress was passed to Tangmere Sector Operations Room where the FIU's CO, Wing Commander Peter Chamberlain, was acting as controller. Following Chamberlain's instructions, Ashfield closed on one of the enemy aircraft, the last phase of the interception being controlled by Morris's AI, and at a range of 400 yards identified it as a Do 17 and opened fire. The bomber, of 2/KG3, went down into the sea off the Sussex coast. All four crew members, although wounded, were picked up.

This was the first recorded success of a radar-assisted fighter, and although to some extent it was a lucky interception it showed that the concept was feasible, and the conversion of Blenheims to the night fighter role continued. However, a few squadrons of Blenheims, converted to carry airborne radar, did not provide a solution to the night defence problem; they were too slow, the equipment was very unreliable, and its operators lacked experience. A solution was on the horizon in the shape of the fast, heavily armed Bristol Beaufighter, which was just entering service; but this aircraft was beset by more than the usual crop of teething troubles. In November and December 1940, Beaufighters and radar-equipped Blenheims flew over 600 sorties, made seventy-one radar contacts, and succeeded in destroying only four enemy aircraft.

In an attempt to fill the gap Fighter Command was compelled to adopt what might best be described as desperation measures to counter the enemy night raiders, especially when the *Luftwaffe* began to step up its night offensive against Britain after the failure of its massed daylight attacks in August and September. In the latter month, Air Chief Marshal Sir Hugh Dowding, the AOC-in-C Fighter Command, was ordered by the Air Council to allocate three squadrons of Hawker Hurricanes to night defence, this decision having been taken following the creation of a high-level Night Air Defence Committee earlier in the month. Added to these were three squadrons of Boulton Paul Defiants, which, armed solely with a four-gun power-operated turret, had suffered appalling losses in the day fighter role during the Battle of Britain. During the closing weeks of 1940, these six squadrons of single-engined fighters flew 491 sorties on forty-six nights and destroyed eleven enemy bombers. Operating on a hit-or-miss basis,

41

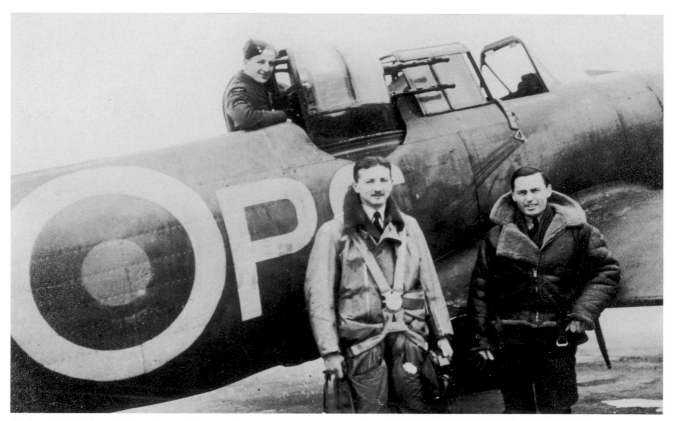

Boulton Paul Defiant Mk I and crew of No 264 Squadron. (Philip Jarrett)

pilots would seek out enemy bombers trapped in the glare of searchlights and would then go into the attack, risking being shot down by friendly anti-aircraft fire.

One such pilot was Flight Lieutenant Richard Stevens, a Hurricane pilot with No 151 Squadron at RAF Manston. A former civil pilot who had flown the cross-Channel mail route at night and in

Cannon-armed Hurricane IIcs of No 87 Squadron. No 87 was one of the 'specialist' Hurricane-equipped night fighter/intruder squadrons. Its main base was Charmy Down, in Somerset. (Philip Jarrett)

Above and right: *AI Mk IV scanner installation in the nose of a Beaufighter.* (Author)

all weathers, Stevens was thirty years old and a very experienced man by the time he joined No 151 Squadron at the tail-end of the Battle of Britain, in October 1940. At this time the Germans had switched most of their effort to night attacks, and night after night Stevens watched in frustration as the German bombers droned overhead towards the red glare of burning London. He constantly sought permission to try his hand at intercepting the raiders, and at last, one night in December, it was granted.

His early night patrols were disappointing. For several nights running, although the Manston controller assured him that the sky was stiff with enemy bombers, Stevens saw nothing. Then, on the night of 15 January 1941, the shellbursts of the London anti-aircraft defences led him to a Do 17 of 4/KG3, which he chased up to 30,000 feet and then almost down to ground level as the German pilot tried to shake him off. But Stevens hung on, and after two or three short bursts the bomber went down and exploded on the ground.

It was No 151 Squadron's first night victory, and there were more to come. On a second patrol that night, Stevens caught an He 111 of 2/KG53 at 17,000 feet, heading for London, and shot it down into the Thames estuary. Three of the four crew members baled out and were captured. The night's work earned Stevens a Distinguished Flying Cross.

Somehow, it seemed as though Stevens' brace of

kills had been a good omen. After that, the RAF's night fighter squadrons appeared to enjoy more success. Men like Flight Lieutenant John Cunningham of No 604 Squadron, now flying fast, heavily-armed Bristol Beaufighters, began to carve out reputations for themselves as bomber destroyers. Cunningham, known by the nickname of 'Cat's Eyes' bestowed on him by the popular press, and which he thoroughly detested, was to destroy no fewer than eight enemy bombers at night in April 1941, having been led expertly to his targets by his AI operator, Sergeant Jimmy Rawnsley. He was to end the war with a score of twenty enemy aircraft destroyed, two probably destroyed and seven damaged, most of them at night. (The 'Cat's Eyes' nickname, of course, was designed to divert attention from the AI radar, which was still highly secret and about which the public as yet knew nothing.)

It was eyesight alone, however, with a little help from searchlights and shellbursts, that brought Richard Stevens to his victims. Shortly after the award of his DFC, he developed ear trouble and was grounded for a while, but he celebrated his return to action on 8 April 1941 by shooting down two He 111s in one night. Two nights later he got another Heinkel and a Ju 88, and a few days later he received a Bar to his DFC. He destroyed yet another Heinkel on the 19th, and on 7 May he accounted for two more. Three nights after that, his claim was one Heinkel destroyed and one probably destroyed. He shot down a further Heinkel on 13 June, damaged one on the 22nd, and on 3 July sent a Ju 88 down in flames. There seemed to be no end to his success; at this time he was the RAF's top-scoring night fighter pilot, enjoying a considerable lead over pilots who flew the radar-equipped Beaufighters.

Stevens experienced a lot of frustration during the summer months of 1941. In June the Germans invaded the Soviet Union, and by the end of July they had withdrawn many of their bomber units from the Western Front. Raids at night over Britain became fewer, and although Stevens continued to fly his lone patrols, for weeks he never saw an enemy bomber. Then, one evening in October, he spotted a Ju 88 slipping inland over the coast of East Anglia and attacked it. The Junkers jettisoned its bombs and turned away, diving low over the water, but Stevens caught it with a burst of fire and sent it into the sea. It was his fourteenth victory.

Soon afterwards, Stevens was posted to another Hurricane unit, No 253 Squadron, as a flight commander, and he immediately set about devising a plan to take the war to the enemy by flying night intruder operations over the German airfields in Holland and Belgium. Later in the war, offensive operations of this kind would become routine, but in December 1941 Stevens was virtually pioneering a new technique. He flew his first night intruder operation on the night of 12/13 December, the day when it was announced that he had been awarded the Distinguished Service Order. He loitered in the vicinity of the bomber airfield at Gilze-Rijen, in Holland, but saw no aircraft and returned home in disappointment.

Three nights later he took off again, heading for the same destination, and never returned. The signal that his squadron commander sent to Group HQ was simple and concise. 'One Hurricane IIc (long-range), 253 Squadron, took off Manston 19.40 on 15 December 1941, to go to Gilze. It has failed to return and is beyond maximum endurance.' It later transpired that he had been shot down either by flak or return fire. He is buried in Bergen-op-Zoom war cemetery in the Netherlands.

The majority of the home-based Hurricane IIc squadrons took part in night intruder operations at one time or another during 1942, and some became specialists in the role. Number 1 Squadron, for example, which was based at RAF Tangmere, destroyed twenty-two enemy aircraft over occupied Europe between 1 April and 1 July that year before moving to Northumberland to convert to Typhoon fighter-bombers, and no fewer than fifteen of these victories were gained by one pilot, Flight Lieutenant Karel Kuttelwascher.

A highly competent and experienced pilot, Kuttelwascher – known by the simpler abbreviation of 'Kut' to his squadron colleagues – had flown with the Czech Air Force for four years before his country was overrun by the Germans, after which he had made his way to Britain via France. He scored his first three kills – all Me 109s – while flying convoy protection and bomber escort missions over the Channel in the spring and early summer of 1941, but it was when No 1 Squadron went over to night intruder operations in April 1942 that Kut really got into his stride. In April 1942 he destroyed three Ju 88s, three Do 217s and an He 111, and on the night of 4/5 May he shot down three He 111s over St André. He destroyed a Do 217 off Dunkirk on 2/3 June, and on the following night he visited St André again to destroy an He 111 and a Do 217, as well as damaging another Dornier.

St André was once again the target on 21/22 June, when Kut shot down a Ju 88 and damaged another. A Do 217 went down before his guns near Trevières on 28/29 June, and his last two victims, also Do 217s, were brought down near Dinard on the night of 1/2 July, when he also damaged a third Dornier. That brought Kut's score to eighteen destroyed, with one probable (an Me 109, his first combat in the RAF, on 2 February 1941) and five damaged. In addition, he may have claimed up to six victories while flying Morane 406 fighters in the Battle of France. After the war, he became a captain with British European Airways, flying Vikings and Elizabethans. He died of a heart attack on 17 August 1959, at the untimely age of 42.

Number 1 Squadron's other leading scorer in the summer of 1942 was the squadron commander, Squadron Leader James MacLachlan, but with five enemy bombers destroyed and three damaged, MacLachlan ws a long way behind his Czech colleague. A remarkable character, 'Mac' had scored six victories in the Battle of Britain and two more

Beaufighter Mk I showing the aerials of the AI Mk IV radar on nose and wings. Note the under-fuselage crew access hatches, which formed windbreaks to facilitate escape, and the 'cheese-grater' flame damping exhaust pipes. (Philip Jarrett)

over Malta, but had himself been shot down and badly wounded in February 1941, losing his left arm above the elbow. He took command of No 1 Squadron in November 1941, having been fitted with an artificial arm in the meantime.

Since the advent of the Bristol Beaufighter, night fighter developments in the RAF had been making steady progress. Delays in the production of AI Mk IV radar equipment had prevented the full complement of five Beaufighter units (Nos 25, 29, 219, 600 and 604 Squadrons) from becoming operational until the spring of 1941, but despite early teething troubles those that were operational had enjoyed some success. The first AI-assisted Beaufighter kill had been claimed on the night of 19/20 November

1940, when Flight Lieutenant John Cunningham and Sgt Phillipson of No 604 Squadron were credited with the destruction of a Ju 88, and by the time all five Beaufighter squadrons reached operational status their efficiency was greatly enhanced by the commissioning of six GCI (Ground Controlled Interception) radar stations on the south and east coasts of England. These could provide fairly wide coverage, and controllers could bring the fighter to within three miles of the target aircraft, at which point the AI Mk IV radar took over. The first GCI-controlled interception was made by John Cunningham on 12 January 1941, but was unsuccessful because the Beaufighter's guns jammed. Then, on 10 May 1941 – the last major

The Merlin-engined Beaufighter Mk II equipped seven RAF night fighter squadrons. (Philip Jarrett)

Boulton Paul Defiant Mk II AA370 with AI aerials. A trials aircraft for much of its career, AA370 went to Karachi in January 1944 and was struck off charge in SEAC in November that year. (Philip Jarrett)

Luftwaffe attack on London – GCI-controlled Beaufighters destroyed fourteen German bombers, the highest loss sustained by the *Luftwaffe* on any one night since the 'Blitz' began.

Thirteen more Beaufighter squadrons were assigned to the night defence of Great Britain in 1941–42, and many of the RAF's night fighter aces scored their early kills while flying the heavy twin-engined fighter. During the closing months of 1941 the *Luftwaffe*'s preoccupation with the eastern front meant that night raids on Britain were sporadic, but in the spring of 1942 the air offensive was renewed with the onset of the so-called 'Baedecker Raids', directed against Britain's historic cities.

Meanwhile, Fighter Command's Defiant night fighter squadrons were being progressively equipped with AI radar. A few Defiants were initially fitted with the AI Mk IV, but from August 1941 the improved Mk VI became available, and Defiants fitted with this set were redesignated Mk IAs. The installation on the Defiant had transmitter and receiver aerials on the wings and the side of the fuselage, the cathode-ray tube display being installed in the pilot's cockpit because there was not enough room in the gun turret. The first unit to be so equipped was No 264 Squadron, followed by No 96 Squadron by the end of 1941 and later by Nos 125, 256 and 410 Squadrons. Production of the Defiant I had now ceased, with a total of 712 aircraft, and the Defiant II had replaced it on the production line. The Defiant NF Mk II was used by Nos 141, 151 and 153 Squadrons, the last aircraft being delivered in February 1942.

Intruders

One principal headache for the RAF's night defence in 1940–41 was German intruder operations over the United Kingdom. In mid-May 1940, in the wake of the German *Blitzkrieg* in France and the Low Countries, Royal Air Force Bomber Command had begun operations for the first time against oil and communications targets in Germany, having hitherto confined itself to fringe attacks directed mainly against naval facilities. Such raids, mounted in growing strength, were intolerable to the Nazi leadership and in particular to *Reichsmarschall* Hermann Goering, the *Luftwaffe* C-in-C, who had earlier boasted that if enemy bombs ever fell on the *Reich* territory people might call him Meier – a predominantly Jewish name.

It is untrue, as has sometimes been suggested, that the *Luftwaffe*'s pre-war planners had given no thought to the night defence of Germany. Even before the war, an Me 109 squadron at Greifswald was assigned to night fighting practice with the aid of searchlights, and a specialist night fighter unit, 10/JG 26, also equipped with Me 109s, was on the order of battle in September 1939, although it was very much experimental and was not used operationally.

The unsuitability of the Me 109 for night fighter operations quickly became apparent, and following the start of the RAF's strategic offensive the first effective night fighter units were formed, equipped in the main with Me 110s. In addition to these, a specialist long-range night fighter unit, 1/NJG2,

Beaufighter Mk IIF of No 225 Squadron. This unit served in the UK and the Middle East. (Philip Jarrett)

was also established with three squadrons of Ju 88s and one of Do 17s. Tasked with long-range night fighter operations, this was the *Luftwaffe*'s first night intruder *Gruppe*, and early in August 1940 it deployed forward to Gilze-Rijn in Holland, from where it began operations against the British Isles in September under the command of *Hauptmann* Karl-Heinrich Heyse.

The *Gruppe*'s operational area over Britain was divided into three sectors. Sector One covered an area bounded by the Thames estuary, north London, the east Midlands and the Wash, taking in the whole of East Anglia; Sector Two ran inland from the Wash to Birmingham, then swung north to Sheffield and north-east to the Humber, covering Lincolnshire and south Yorkshire; while Sector Three ran from the Humber to Sheffield, Sheffield to Leeds, Leeds to Blackpool and finally from Blackpool to a point on the Northumbrian coast north of Newcastle-upon-Tyne. This was the only sector to extend as far as the west coast and was the largest in area – although by no means the most important, as the other two encompassed the two areas where Bomber Command had its densest concentration of airfields.

After some preliminary sorties over Lincolnshire

Beaufighter Mk I seen in 1940 with the first 'thimble' nose radome developed for the AI Mk VII centimetric radar. (Philip Jarrett)

R227, one of two Beaufighter Mk IIs experimentally fitted with a four-gun turret just behind the cockpit. (Philip Jarrett)

in late August 1940, the intruders claimed their first confirmed victory on 21 September, when *Hauptmann* Karl Hulshoff destroyed a Whitley of No 58 Squadron, the aircraft crashing near Thornaby with the loss of all four crew. Three nights later, *Feldwebel* Hans Hahn shot down a No 102 Squadron Whitley near Linton-on-Ouse. In the early hours of 28 September Lindholme was attacked by *Leutnant* Heinz Volker, who damaged a Hampden of No 49 Squadron as it was landing and shot down a second just off the coast.

During this initial period of operations the intruders lost four aircraft, although only one is thought to have been destroyed by the air defences – in this instance by anti-aircraft fire. During October and November the sortie rate was low, but in December several sorties were flown against the Lincolnshire airfields, in the course of which a Do 17 was destroyed and another damaged by Hurricanes of No 12 Group flying night patrols. During one of these sorties, the *Gruppe* commander, *Major* Karl-Heinrich Heyse, was shot down and killed by the Manby airfield defences.

In December 1940 No 4 Operational Training Unit – later renamed No 54 OTU – was established at Church Fenton to train night fighter crews. It may be that *Luftwaffe* Intelligence got wind of the OTU's activities, because on the night of 15 January 1941 the station was attacked by an intruding Ju 88 of NJG2, which badly damaged two Defiants and a Blenheim. Earlier in the month, another intruder had also attacked and badly damaged a No 10 Squadron Whitley near Catterick.

On 10/11 February 1941 the intruders threw their weight against the Lincolnshire airfields of No 5 Group, destroying seven aircraft returning from raids on Germany and Holland. Despite

encounters with RAF night fighters, all the intruders – nine aircraft – returned to base.

Since November 1940, No 600 Squadron, which had brought its Blenheim night fighters north to Catterick in the previous month, had been in the process of conversion to Beaufighters; it was declared operational in March 1941, when it moved to Drem for a fortnight before departing for Colerne in Wiltshire. Another Beaufighter squadron, No 68, also formed at Catterick early in the year, but in April it was assigned to the defence of the Midlands.

Also in the north, one Defiant squadron, No 141, was based at Ayr from the end of April 1941, and – with detachments at Acklington – found itself in the middle of the May 'Blitz' on Clydeside and Tyneside, its crews claiming eight victories. Although still not radar-equipped, the Defiant was proving itself unexpectedly suited to the night fighter role; experience had taught crews that if the pilot could manoeuvre his aircraft to a position beneath an enemy bomber, the gunner, elevating his guns at an angle, could usually inflict punishing damage on it. As mentioned elsewhere, it was a technique developed further by the *Luftwaffe*'s night fighter force later in the war, when aircraft fitted with upwards-firing guns inflicted severe losses on the RAF's heavy bombers.

The inauguration of Ground Controlled Interception (GCI) stations such as that at Patrington, on the Humber estuary, and the conversion of five of Fighter Command's six Blenheim squadrons to Beaufighters in March 1941, brought about a dramatic change in the Command's fortunes just in time to counter the *Luftwaffe*'s 'Blitz' on London, Merseyside, Tyneside, Clydeside and other targets. The Hurricane and Defiant squadrons allocated to night defence also added to

Beaufighter Mk VI in night fighter finish and with a flat tailplane; later production Mk VIs had dihedral on the tailplane. The Mk VI was the first Beaufighter variant to equip RAF squadrons in India. (Philip Jarrett)

this change as a result of their increased experience, and because they too derived assistance from GCI. The much more precise information provided by the GCI stations made the task of interception far easier, and matters improved still further with the introduction of AI Mk VII, which had a seven-mile range and a low-level capability. For the first time, the Mk VII, together with information passed on by the Chain Home Low radar stations – the low-level part of the general warning system – gave night fighter crews the ability to intercept low-flying minelayers and reconnaissance aircraft which had been operating off the north and east coasts almost with impunity.

The figures themselves reveal the general improvement in the overall air defence system by the summer of 1941. In February the enemy lost only four aircraft to fighters and eight to anti-aircraft, but during March night fighters shot down twenty-two enemy bombers and the AA guns seventeen. In April the score rose to forty-eight for the fighters and thirty-nine for the guns, and in the first two weeks of May the loss rate assumed serious proportions, ninety-six bombers being shot down by fighters and thirty-two by AA guns. In addition, ten others were lost due to unknown causes.

Following a final spate of intense attacks on London, the Midlands and Merseyside, the *Luftwaffe*'s spring 'Blitz' on Britain gradually petered out at the end of May 1941 as the Germans transferred the bulk of their bomber force to the east in readiness for Operation *Barbarossa*, the invasion of Russia, or to the Balkans. Although bombing attacks on the north continued on a sporadic basis during 1941, these tended to follow intruder-type tactics, only small numbers of aircraft being involved.

As for the dedicated intruder squadrons, these continued to concentrate on the bomber bases of Lincolnshire and East Anglia in the spring of 1941, and forays into northern airspace were few. Nevertheless, they did occur, and on the night 16/17 April a Ju 88 flown by *Feldwebel* Wilhelm Breetz, one of NJG2's most experienced pilots, fell victim to the Tyne anti-aircraft defences. Another experienced intruder pilot, *Leutnant* Heinz Volker, had better luck in the early hours of 26 April, destroying a Blenheim and a Defiant at Church Fenton and damaging two more aircraft in a combined bombing and strafing attack. Volker also claimed two more aircraft destroyed that night in attacks on the Lincolnshire airfields.

Intruder attacks continued during June and were again directed against Lincolnshire and East Anglia, but on the night 13/14th the intruders suffered a severe setback when three Ju 88s failed to return, all falling victim to the Beaufighters of No 25 Squadron from Wittering. This was not, however, by any means the beginning of the end for the intruders; Beaufighters accounted for only three more before the middle of October, although others fell to anti-aircraft fire and, in one case, to a

Although the Dornier 17 was the type used in early German intruder operations over the British Isles, it was later replaced by the Junkers Ju 88, pictured here. (Author)

Douglas Havoc night fighter of No 85 Squadron.

What spelled the end of intruder operations over England was a personal instruction from Adolf Hitler on 13 October 1941, ordering them to cease. The reason was purely one of propaganda. With the RAF's night-bombing effort steadily increasing, Hitler wanted the German people to see the 'terror bombers' destroyed over *Reich* territory; far-away victories over England did nothing to improve their morale. For *General* Kammhuber, commanding Germany's night defences, it was a bitter blow; what was potentially his most potent weapon had been struck from his hand, and no argument would sway the *Führer*.

What, then, had the intruder force – which never numbered more than twenty or thirty serviceable aircraft – achieved in just over a year of operations?

It had certainly destroyed more than fifty aircraft over England, together with an estimated thirty more over the North Sea. About forty others sustained damage as a consequence of intruder attacks. The cost to the Germans was twenty-seven aircraft, plus seven more destroyed in accidents.

Had the *Luftwaffe* been permitted to step up its intruder operations over the United Kingdom in the winter of 1941–42, as RAF Bomber Command prepared to launch a renewed offensive against Germany with its four-engined heavy bombers, it might have dealt a series of damaging blows to the Command, both materially and in terms of morale. It would return to intruder operations later in the war, but by then the intruders would have to contend with air defences vastly superior to those they had encountered previously.

CHAPTER FIVE

THE NIGHT DEFENCE OF GERMANY, 1940–42

At the beginning of World War II, although Germany had an air defence system in place, the emphasis was largely on anti-aircraft artillery, and a lot of misplaced faith was pinned on the ability of the *Fliegerabwehrkanone* (flak) units to defend the air space of the *Reich*. This was mainly a consequence of German experiences in the Spanish Civil War, where flak had proved very effective against low-flying aircraft; the fact that air power in Spain, apart from a few much-publicised attacks on cities, had been used almost exclusively in the tactical role, and that anti-aircraft weaponry would not be anything like as effective against high-flying targets, was ignored.

Fighters, according to the prevailing doctrine, were there for an altogether different purpose, which was to conduct offensive operations in enemy air space. The task of the bomber and fighter units of an air fleet (*Luftflotte*) was to co-operate closely with one another in support of ground campaigns. Each air fleet had to operate in concert with an army group; it was, in effect, a small self-contained air force operating within a defined area, and its commander-in-chief was responsible for both offensive and defensive operations within that area. This meant that when an army group was on the offensive in enemy territory, the C-in-C of the air fleet supporting it still remained responsible for the air defence of his original assigned region in Germany.

The Germans were very slow to recognise the need for a centralised system of air defence, probably made complacent by the speed of their early conquests, but with British night bombers attacking targets on the territory of the *Reich* during and after the Battle of France there was a clear requirement for a night air defence system based on fighters as well as flak, and in July 1940 the *Luftwaffe* established the 1st Night Fighter Division in Brussels under *General* Josef Kammhuber.

On 26 June 1940, just after the end of the fighting in France, the commander of 1/*Zerstörergeschwader* 1 (1/ZG1) was summoned to a high-level conference in The Hague. His name was *Hauptmann* Wolfgang Falck, and he had recently completed a lengthy report on attempts by his unit, which was

The Messerschmitt 110 became the Luftwaffe's *standard night fighter type in 1940, but initially crews were handicapped by a lack of AI radar.* (Author)

armed with Me 110s, to intercept British bombers passing over its base at Aalborg, in Denmark. Falck had trained his best crews in instrument flying and had held a battle flight on readiness every night, hoping to catch the elusive bombers with the help of a *Freya* radar station off the north German coast (an experimental unit that had been operating on the island of Wangerooge since the autumn of 1939).

The crews had met with no success, but they were the only fighter aircrew in the *Luftwaffe* with substantial experience of night flying, and the upshot of the meeting was that Falck was appointed to command the first night fighter *Geschwader*, NJG1, to be formed out of a *Gruppe* of ZG1 and one of JG2 (4/JG2, which had just converted from Me 109s to Me 110s.) These were now re-designated 1/NJG1, under *Hauptmann* Radusch, and 3/NJG1, under Major Blumensaat. In addition, a second *Gruppe*, 1/NJG2, was also formed under *Hauptmann* Karl-Heinrich Heyse, primarily for intruder operations over Britain; its activities have already been discussed.

It was apparent that NJG1's night fighters, lacking any aid to interception other than the eyesight of their crews, would have to co-operate closely with searchlights and sound locators. A belt of these was already in place on an oblique line west of Munster; Kammhuber now ordered it to be extended to north and south until it stretched for

some twenty-five miles along the approach to the Ruhr. Individual fighters were each allocated a sector within this belt, orbiting a radio beacon, their crews hoping to pick up a bomber once the searchlights were illuminated.

It was hardly surprising that the night fighters registered few successes with these tactics, and it was not until October 1940, with the introduction of the first *Wurzburg* fighter-direction radars, that matters began to improve. The system was somewhat cumbersome, involving a *Freya* station to provide early warning, and two *Wurzburgs*, one to track the incoming bomber and the other to direct the night fighter. The biggest snag with the whole system was that only one fighter could be controlled at any one time within each sector, and the fighter could not be handed over from one sector to another. The fighter controller could bring the interceptor to within a mile or so of its target, but it was in that last mile – with the fighter pilot depending on his eyesight alone – that the problems really began. Often, despite the fact that they knew they were within a few hundred yards of the bomber, the night fighters failed to intercept. When they did so, it was with a large element of luck. On the night 16/17 October 1940, for example, *Oberleutnant* Ludwig Becker, commanding 6/NJG2, and his radio operator, *Feldwebel* Staub, made the first successful ground-controlled interception of an enemy aircraft, assisted by

The German night fighters' principal opponent early in 1941 was the Vickers Wellington. The aircraft seen here belong to No 9 Squadron, whose motto was – and still is – Per Noctem Volamus (We Fly By Night). (Author)

Diagram showing the German early warning radar coverage in 1942, according to a British intelligence assessment. It turned out to be quite accurate. (Author)

information from a *Freya* set passed to them by the fighter controller, *Oberleutnant* Werner Schulze. They destroyed their target, a Wellington, but it was by pure chance that they spotted the bomber's exhaust flames in the night sky.

The night fighters' chances of success decreased in the spring of 1941, for the weight of Bomber Command's offensive was concentrated on the French Channel ports over a period of several weeks. When the main offensive again switched to German industrial targets in May the night fighter crews once more had their chance to score, and on the night 2/3 June 1941 an Me 110 crew, *Feldwebels* Kalinowski and Zwickl, became the first to destroy an enemy bomber – a Short Stirling – over the German capital, Berlin.

On 27/28 June, when seventy-three Wellingtons and thirty-five Whitleys were despatched to attack Bremen, returning crews reported, for the first time, that they had been subjected to intense night fighter attacks. Encountering bad weather, many crews attacked Hamburg in error, and five Whitleys were shot down by night fighters over the city – four of them by *Oberleutnant* Eckardt of 2/NJG1, the biggest success so far by a German night fighter pilot. Night fighters accounted for a further three bombers over Hamburg two nights later.

By mid-July 1941 the German night fighter force had 134 twin-engined fighters deployed in the west, and trained crews were reaching the *Staffeln* in growing numbers. On 1 August the 1st Night-Fighter Division was given Air Corps (*Fliegerkorps*) status, and Kammhuber set up a new HQ at Zeist, near Utrecht. The air defence system underwent a substantial reorganisation with the creation of the so-called 'Kammhuber Line'. This comprised a searchlight and flak belt, about twenty-two miles deep, and an overlapping network of circular air defence zones (known as *Himmelbett*, or 'four poster bed' zones) extending along the North Sea coast from Denmark to Belgium. From north-east to south-west the zones were code-named *Pelikan*, *Hummer* (Lobster), *Kuckuck* (Cuckoo), *Wal* (Whale), *Languste* (Spiny Lobster), *Jaguar*, *Delphin* (Dolphin), *Schlei* (Tench), *Löwe* (Lion), *Tiger*, *Eisbär* (Polar Bear), *Salzhering* (Salt Herring), *Hering*, *Zander* (Pike), *Seeadler* (Sea Eagle), *Rotkehlchen* (Redbreast), *Biber* (Beaver), *Gorilla*, *Schmetterling* (Butterfly), *Hamster*, *Bremse* (Horsefly) and *Wespe* (Wasp). A further searchlight and flak belt and nine more *Himmelbett* zones protected Berlin, while joint night fighter and flak zones were set up to defend the industrial areas of the Ruhr.

The system was as tightly controlled as Kammhuber could make it, but the fact remained that each ground controller could still only direct a single fighter, whose pilot then had to rely on his vision to make contact with the target; but this deficiency was about to be put right. As early as July 1939 the German communications firm, Telefunken, had shown that it was possible for an intercepting aircraft to be fitted with AI equipment, and had carried out a practical demonstration with a rudimentary set mounted in a Ju 52. The *Luftwaffe* Technical Office, however, had shown no interest in the device, and so Telefunken had developed it into a radar altimeter.

The AI concept was resurrected in the summer of 1940 and development went ahead, but there were a lot of snags to be overcome. One of them was that an internally-mounted antenna produced too weak a signal, so Telefunken had no choice but to opt for an externally-mounted aerial array – a far from satisfactory arrangement, not least because of the drag it produced.

In July 1941 a prototype set, named *Lichtenstein*,

Lichtenstein *AI radar installed in a Messerschmitt 110.* (Philip Jarrett)

was installed in a Me 110 based at Leeuwarden, Holland. On 9 August this aircraft, crewed by *Oberleutnant* Ludwig Becker and *Feldwebel* Josef Staub, intercepted a Wellington bomber with the aid of *Lichtenstein* and shot it down. Despite this success, Kammhuber had to maintain constant pressure to have his night fighters fitted with AI radar, and it was not until early in 1942 that *Lichtenstein*-equipped aircraft began to reach the night fighter wings (*Nachtjagdgeschwader*) in any numbers. Once they did, the effectiveness of the German night fighter force increased immeasurably, and some pilots began to achieve quite remarkable scores. One of them was *Hauptmann* Werner Streib, commanding 1/NJG1 at Venlo, who – accompanied by his observer, *Gefreiter* Lingen – had destroyed his first bomber, a Whitley, on the night 20/21 July 1940 while flying an Me 110. In August 1941 Streib destroyed three more bombers, and on the night 1/2 October he intercepted and destroyed three Wellingtons inside forty minutes.

Streib went on to gain sixty-six victories, and for a long time he was Germany's top-scoring night fighter pilot; but close behind him came *Leutnant* Helmut Lent, a veteran Me 110 pilot who had fought over Poland, Norway and in the defence of Germany against the early (and disastrous) daylight raids on the north German ports by RAF Bomber Command. On 1 November 1941, Lent formed a new night fighter *Gruppe*, 2/NJG2; his *Staffel* commanders were *Hauptmann* Rudolf Schönert, *Hauptmann* Prince Lippe-Weissenfeld, and *Hauptmann* Ludwig Becker. All of them went on to

achieve exceptional night fighting scores. Helmut Lent destroyed 102 aircraft at night and eight by day before his death in a flying accident on 7 October 1944; Lippe-Weissenfeld got fifty-one before his death in action on 12 March, 1944; and Becker had forty-six kills when he too was shot down, in February 1943. (See Appendix Two.)

Unfortunately for Germany's cities, Kammhuber's efforts to expand and streamline the night air defence system, and the growing prowess of his pilots, received scant attention in the corridors of the *Luftwaffe* High Command, preoccupied as it was with the German offensives in Russia. But there were some nasty shocks to come, beginning with a devastating incendiary attack by 191 RAF bombers on Lübeck on the night 28/29 March 1942 in which 200 acres of the Old Town were wiped out and sixty-two per cent of the town's buildings destroyed or damaged.

The raid represented Bomber Command's first major success against a German target, and it was followed in April by two major attacks on the Baltic port of Rostock and the adjacent Heinkel aircraft factory. Much damage was caused, and in reporting the raids the expression *Terrorangriff* (terror attack) was used for the first time by German radio announcers. The attacks still did not provoke major consternation, even though the German Propaganda Minister, Goebbels, noted in his diary that 'Community life in Rostock was practically at an end,' but there was much worse to come.

On the night 30/31 May, 1942, Bomber Command despatched 1,047 aircraft to Cologne. A

Dornier Do 217J-2 night fighter equipped with FuG202 Lichtenstein *B/C radar. The night fighter version of the Do 217 was used in small numbers in 1942–3.* (Philip Jarrett)

Cologne Cathedral stands forlornly amid the ruins of the ancient Rhineland city. (Author)

total of 868 aircraft bombed the main target area, dropping 1,455 tons of bombs, two-thirds of which were incendiaries. The city suffered very severe damage and the death toll was 469, the highest in any Bomber Command raid so far. Over 600 acres of Cologne's built-up area were destroyed, and about 250 factories were destroyed or badly damaged. The toll of property included 18,432 houses, apartments, workshops and public buildings destroyed and 40,586 damaged. Fifty per cent of the city's power supply was put out of action, and the gas and water supplies were seriously disrupted. The railway repair shops, employing 2,500 people, were totally destroyed and 12,000 fires were started, some of which burned for days. Bomber Command sustained a record loss of forty-one aircraft, of which twenty-nine were Wellingtons. Thirty-six were accounted for by fighters.

The massive onslaught demonstrated the limitations of the German air defence system, and Kammhuber strove to improve it still further. The coverage of the *Himmelbett* zones was extended; new night fighter *Gruppen* were formed, and new methods were introduced which permitted ground controllers to direct two fighters within a single zone. But the supply of night fighters was slow; the number deployed in September 1942 was 345, only ninety-five more than the figure for September 1941.

Despite mounting further raids involving 1,000 bombers in 1942, Bomber Command was unable to repeat the success of the Cologne attack. Had it done so, it is probable that Germany's leaders would have placed high priority on the massive reinforcement of the night fighter arm in 1942, with disastrous consequences for the RAF's night offensive in late 1942 and early 1943.

As it was, it would take a fearsome onslaught on Hamburg in July 1943 to bring about that result; and although subsequent events would bring the *Nachtjagdgeschwader* to a high point of effectiveness, it would not spare Germany's cities the ordeal that was yet to come.

CHAPTER SIX

NIGHT DEFENCE OF THE UK, JANUARY 1942-JUNE 1944

At the end of 1941 nine squadrons of Beaufighters were assigned to the night defence of Britain, one having formed during the summer and three having converted from Defiants. The squadrons were Nos 25 at Wittering (Northamptonshire), 29 at West Malling (Kent), 68 at High Ercall (Shropshire), 141 at Drem (East Lothian), 219 at Tangmere (Sussex), 255 at Coltishall (Norfolk), 307 at Exeter (Devon), 60 at Predannack (Cornwall) and 604 at Middle Wallop (Hampshire).

Six Defiant night fighter squadrons were also still on the Order of Battle. They were Nos 96 at Wrexham (Denbighshire), 125 at Fairwood Common (Glamorgan), 151 at Coltishall, 153 at Ballyhalbert (Co Down), 256 at Coltishall, and 264 at West Malling.

Added to these was No 85 Squadron at Hunsdon in Hertfordshire, equipped with Douglas Havocs. These aircraft were converted Douglas DB-7 bombers, part of a batch originally intended for France. The aircraft had been selected for the night fighter role because it had a good performance, a tricycle undercarriage – which made night landings and take-offs simpler – and its roomy interior readily lent itself to the fitting of AI radar.

Modification of the DB-7 (or Boston, as it was known in the RAF) was undertaken at Burtonwood, and two versions emerged. Both were known as the Havoc Mk I, but one featured a 'solid' nose containing eight .303 in machine-guns and was equipped with AI Mk IV radar; the other retained the transparent nose of the DB-7 and was in effect a night intruder, with four extra machine-guns in

The Douglas Havoc II in its basic night fighting form, with AI Mk IV radar and a twelve-gun nose. The gun ports are patched over in this photograph. Only No 85 Squadron operated this version. (Philip Jarrett)

Havoc Mk I of No 93 Squadron. This unit carried out experiments with various night fighting techniques, including the dropping of mines on enemy bombers. No 93 Squadron was the first to receive the Havoc. (Philip Jarrett)

the nose and no AI for obvious security reasons. This version was issued to No 23 Squadron at Ford, Hampshire, in March 1941; a few were also used by No 25 Squadron at Wittering between July and September 1941.

The first squadron to use the Havoc was No 93, which in December 1941 was in the process of disbanding at RAF Middle Wallop. No 93 Squadron had spent most of its career engaged in a series of rather bizarre experiments involving the dropping of aerial mines on enemy bombers; these had first been carried out in 1940, using Handley Page

A Havoc II (Turbinlite) of No 1459 Flight, showing the AI Mk IV radar aerials around the nose installation of the searchlight itself. Much time was wasted in experimenting with this quite useless arrangement. (Philip Jarrett)

Cockpit of the Mosquito NF Mk II, showing the observer's AI radar tube on the right-hand side. Positioning the radar operator alongside the pilot and not, as in the Blenheim and Beaufighter, at a remote location in the fuselage significantly improved crew teamwork. (Philip Jarrett)

Harrows. Havocs so modified were designated Havoc Mk I (LAM), the abbreviation standing for Long Aerial Mine. These operations, known as *Mutton*, were a predictable waste of time and effort, as was the Havoc I (Turbinlite). Trials with this had begun in May 1941 with the specially-formed No 1422 Flight. They involved the installation of a 2,700 million candlepower Helmore/GEC searchlight in the Havoc's nose, together with the AI Mk V. No armament was carried, the idea being that the Havoc would detect an enemy bomber, close in on it, and then illuminate it with the searchlight so that an accompanying Hurricane or Defiant could shoot it down. Ten Turbinlite flights were formed in 1941 following protracted development caused by many technical and operational difficulties, and remained operational throughout 1942, being given squadron identities (Nos 530–539) before they were eventually disbanded in January 1943. Between them they only succeeded in destroying one aircraft, and that was a Stirling of No 218 Squadron. Luckily, its crew escaped.

The real answer to the prayers of the RAF night fighter squadrons was the de Havilland Mosquito. The first Mosquito fighter squadron, No 157,

formed at Debden in Essex on 13 December 1941, its first aircraft, a dual-control Mk II, arriving at Debden's satellite airfield, Castle Camps, on 26 January 1942. Seventeen Mk IIs were delivered to Maintenance Units for the fitting of AI Mk V, and by mid-April No 157 Squadron had nineteen NF Mk IIs on its inventory, three of them without radar. By this time No 151 Squadron at Wittering had also begun to rearm with the NF Mk II, with sixteen aircraft on strength at the end of April.

As the two squadrons built up their night flying hours, practised interceptions and night gun-firing (which revealed the need for flash eliminators on the nose-mounted .303 in Browning guns, which, when fired, blinded the pilot to everything outside the cockpit) the crews became increasingly happy with their new aircraft. Its armament of four 20 mm Hispano cannon and four Brownings was formidable, and – unlike the arrangement in the Beaufighter – the radar observer sat facing forwards in the cockpit, on the pilot's right and slightly behind him.

Crews were less than happy, however, with the AI Mk V. As one No 157 Squadron radar operator, Squadron Leader Lewis Brandon, DSO, DFC, put

These early production Mosquito NF Mk IIs were delivered to the RAF in February-March 1944. (Philip Jarrett)

it in *Night Flyer*, published by William Kimber in 1961:

'Fighter Command had committed a blunder almost as bad as the Turbinlite fiasco. They had decided to install in our beautiful Mozzies, in fact in all the first batch of Mozzies to reach squadrons, a wretched new mark of AI. This was the Mark 5 AI, which had all the faults of the early Mark 4 plus many of its own. It was a retrograde step even when compared with Mark 4, but when compared with Mark 7 it was like going back to a divining-rod. There were times in the next few months when I thought that if I took a hazel twig, persuaded a Dachshund to lift a leg against it and then took the twig into the Mozzie with me, it would lead me to a German more readily than would Mark 5 AI.

'It had been wished on to Fighter Command by the experts of the Fighter Interception Unit. While it might have been all very well for these highly skilled pilots, it was not very practical for the average squadron pilot. It had the same aerial system as Mark 4 and the main difference was that it had an extra tube, placed so that the pilot could see it and could carry out the final stages of the interception himself. All the navigator needed to do was to read out the range. At night the pilot had his hands full enough without giving him an extra tube to look at. Then, too, when he should have been searching the sky for a visual, he would have to look at this indicator tube. Apart from these

points, the equipment suffered from very serious limitations that were not discovered until we had been struggling with it for several months ... Unfortunately a large number of sets had been made and it took some time to get them replaced.'

It was unfortunate that the Mosquito crews had to cope with inadequate equipment, for on the night 23/24 April the *Luftwaffe* launched the first of its so-called 'Baedecker' raids against British targets of cultural and historic value in reprisal for the Bomber Command attack on Lübeck on 28/29 March. The first raid, on Exeter by forty-five aircraft – mostly Do 217s of KG2 – proved abortive and was followed by two on Bath on 25 and 26 April. The city suffered heavily, and in three more successive raids Norwich was attacked twice and York once, the latter city suffering heavy damage from incendiary bombs. The most successful attack was on 3/4 May, when 131 tons of bombs were dropped on Exeter, severely damaging the city centre. During the remainder of the month Cowes, Norwich, Hull, Poole, Canterbury and Grimsby were all raided, but then the emphasis switched to more important strategic targets such as Birmingham, Southampton and Middlesbrough.

Although the two Mosquito night fighter squadrons made several contacts with enemy

(Trans) The speedy Dornier 217 was the Mosquito night-fighters' main target during the 'Baedecker' raids of early 1942. (Author)

aircraft during the first month of the German offensive, the Beaufighter squadrons remained in the forefront of the action, and it was not until 29 May that the first successful interception was made by a Mosquito, during a raid on Grimsby. At 04.30 Flight Lieutenant Pennington of No 151 Squadron was vectored on to an He 111 and opened fire on it over the North Sea. The Heinkel, with one engine on fire, spiralled down into the haze and

Pennington lost it, claiming it as a probable. His own aircraft was damaged by return fire and he flew back to base on one engine. In another incident, Pilot Officer Wain damaged a Do 217E, and on 30 May Squadron Leader Ashfield of No 157 Squadron damaged a Do 217 off Dover.

On 3 May No 264 Squadron began to rearm with Mosquitoes at Colerne, Wiltshire, the squadron flying its first night combat patrol on the 13th.

A standard Mosquito Mk II night fighter, DD750. This aircraft was delivered to the RAF in September 1942 and subsequently served with Nos 151, 264, 157, 410 and 239 Squadrons before being damaged beyond repair on operations on 28 June 1944. (Philip Jarrett)

It was not until the end of June that the Mosquito night fighters scored their first confirmed victories. On the night 24/25 June, aircraft of No 151 Squadron accounted for two Do 217E4s, shooting down a Dornier of 2/KG40 into the North Sea and another into the Wash. The squadron claimed two more enemy aircraft, an He 111 and a Do 217, before the end of the month, but there is no confirmation of these claims in records of enemy losses.

It was a frustrating time for No 157 Squadron; despite numerous patrols, its crews failed to score a confirmed victory until 22/23 August, when Wing Commander Gordon Slade and Pilot Officer Truscott shot down a Do 217 of 2/KG2 at Worlington, Suffolk. The Beaufighter crews were still claiming the lion's share of success, but that would soon change as more Mosquito squadrons formed. Number 85 Squadron began rearming with Mosquitoes in August, followed by Nos 25 and 410 Squadrons in October. Number 25 Squadron became the first Mosquito night fighter squadron in northern England, moving to Church Fenton and displacing No 54 OTU, which went to Charterhall on the Scottish Borders. Number 410 Squadron, at Acklington in Northumberland, became responsible for the night defence of Tyneside.

The advent of the Mosquito was timely, for KG2's fast Dorniers, which were capable of 300 mph at low altitude, were causing problems for the defences. And it was not only historic towns that were hit; Middlesbrough, for example, after a break of five months, was attacked four times between the middle of April and the end of July 1942. It is also worth recording that, outside the great conurbations of London and Merseyside, the hardest-hit city in Britain was Hull. By the war's end, only 6,000 out of 93,000 buildings in Hull had escaped bomb damage, most of it incurred during three major attacks in March and May 1941. Because of its geographical location, Hull was an easy target. It was heavily attacked twice during Operation *Steinbock*, the so-called 'Little Blitz' of January to May 1944, conducted by all available German bombers on the Western Front. During these two attacks, carried out by Ju 88s, Do 217s and He 177s, No 25 Squadron (Coltishall), 264 Squadron (Church Fenton) and 307 Polish Squadron (Drem) claimed eleven enemy aircraft between them. As a matter of note, the 'Little Blitz' cost the *Luftwaffe* 329

Mosquito victim: a Junkers Ju 88A-4 of 8/KG6 brought down by Flt Lt R.C. Pargeter and Flt Lt R.L. Fell of No 29 Squadron at Withyham, Sussex, on the night of 24/25 February 1944. Two crew members baled out and were taken prisoner. (Philip Jarrett)

aircraft, of which 129 were destroyed by Mosquitoes equipped with AI Mk VIII radar.

In 1943–4 the *Luftwaffe* once again mounted frequent intruder operations, using mainly Me 410 and Ju 188 aircraft. We can see a measure of what they might have achieved, had these aircraft been committed in greater numbers, in one attack on American air bases in East Norfolk on 2 April 1944, when intruders destroyed thirteen B-24 Liberators and, in the panic, two more were shot down by their own airfield defences. The Germans lost a single Me 410.

By the beginning of 1944, further improvements in the British air defences had made it hard for the *Luftwaffe* to penetrate UK air space at medium and low level. Increased numbers of anti-aircraft guns of all calibres, rocket batteries capable of firing salvoes of 128 missiles, and radar-directed searchlights able to illuminate targets up to 35,000 feet all contributed to frustrating the attackers, and the fast enemy bombers now began to penetrate at up to 30,000 feet before diving on their objectives and making a high-speed exit. These new tactics caused problems for the night fighters, since following an enemy aircraft in a dive meant that radar contact was often lost because of ground returns. The answer was to extend the night fighter patrol lines well out to sea; many intruders were trapped and destroyed in this way.

Had the *Luftwaffe* been in a position to launch a renewed night offensive against the north in the early summer of 1944, it would not have been left entirely to the RAF to counter the threat. By this time, radar-equipped Fairey Fireflies of No 784 Squadron, Fleet Air Arm, were operating from Drem as part of the integrated air defence system. It is interesting to note that the Navy's Fireflies did in fact operate against night intruders – but that was in Korea, in 1951, when several aircraft were deployed to Kimpo to form a defence flight against Po-2 biplanes making night attacks on United Nations forces. No claims were made.

At Scorton, in North Yorkshire, the 422nd and 425th Squadrons of the US IXth Army Air Force, which had been training there for some weeks, were declared combat-ready early in June 1944.

Northrop P-61 Black Widows of the US IXth AAF were based at Scorton, Yorkshire, in 1944 before departing for the Continent. (Philip Jarrett)

Serrate *installation in a Mosquito.* (Author)

Equipped originally with Beaufighters, these squadrons now had a full complement of Northrop P-61 Black Widow night fighters, and were also integrated with the air defence system before departing for the Continent in July.

Mention must be made of deception techniques, which contributed in no small measure to thwarting the enemy night offensive. By the end of 1941, airfields in the north and elsewhere were backed up by decoys known as 'Q' sites, with dummy flarepath and perimeter lighting laid out to resemble the pattern of the real aerodrome. According to some estimates, these decoy sites received seven times the number of bombs as those that fell on the real airfields. Most were closed down in the summer of 1944, when the bombing threat had receded.

Radio deception equipment was also installed; this included masking beacons, devised by the Radio Branch of the Post Office Engineering Department and designed to interfere with the *Luftwaffe*'s radio navigational aids. Three such beacons, known as Meacons, were situated in the North, at Marske near Redcar, Reston near Eyemouth and Mintlaw near Peterhead. They

achieved considerable success. On the night 6/7 July 1941, for example, thanks to the jamming of the Noordwijk beacon, three Ju 88s of *Kustenfliegergruppe* 106 operating between Holy Island and Whitby, became disorientated and all three flew into high ground near Bridlington.

By the beginning of 1943 the RAF's night fighter squadrons were turning increasingly from defence to offence. The Mosquito's long range and heavy armament of four 20 mm cannon made it highly suitable for the night-intruder role, as well as for local night air defence. The intruder Mosquitoes (and Beaufighters), although stripped of their AI for operations over enemy territory, were fitted with a device named *Serrate* which, developed by the Telecommunications Research Establishment as a result of information on enemy night fighting radars brought back by special countermeasures aircraft, enabled the British fighters to home in to the enemy's airborne radar transmissions. It had a range of about fifty miles, and was first used operationally in June 1943 by No 141 Squadron, which scored twenty-three kills in three months with its help.

Number 141 Squadron's commander was Wing Commander J.R.D. 'Bob' Braham, whose combat report describes a night action off the Dutch island of Ameland on 17/18 August 1943. Braham was flying a Beaufighter Mk VI, and his navigator was Flight Lieutenant H. Jacobs.

'We took off from Coltishall at 2200 hours on intruder patrol to Stade. We flew to a point north of Schiermonnikoog and then turned NE at 2254. We continued on course for about five minutes when we sighted one Me 110 flying east and jinking. We turned and followed him towards the coast, closing in on the aircraft until we were at 300 yards range, 20 degrees starboard astern and a little below. Fire was opened with a two-second burst from all guns and strikes were seen all over the enemy aircraft. Smoke came from the port engine and the Me 110 dived to port. We gave him another two-second burst from 250 yards and he caught fire and dived into the sea, burning on the water. Immediately afterwards we saw a second Me 110 (which had been chasing us) a little above and turning gently to starboard on an easterly course. We gave a one-second burst of cannon and machine gun at 50 yards in a gentle turn. The enemy aircraft appeared to blow up and we had to pull up and turn to port to avoid ramming it. At that point we saw one man bale out and his parachute open, and the enemy aircraft dived vertically into the sea in flames ... we landed at Wittering at 0145.'

Bob Braham, a pre-war regular RAF officer, had been involved in the development of night fighting techniques since the beginning of the war, and he destroyed his first victim – a Do 17 – while flying a Blenheim of No 29 Squadron on 24 August 1940. By July 1941 he had four kills to his credit, all at night, and he increased this score to six by the end of the year. During this period, his observer was Sergeant Gregory, who was later commissioned. After a rest from operations (during which, incidentally, they destroyed a Do 217 in a Beaufighter 'borrowed' while on a visit to their old squadron) they rejoined No 29 Squadron in July 1942, and in just a few weeks they destroyed three enemy bombers and damaged three more.

In October 1942 the Braham-Gregory team shot down a Ju 88 and a Do 217. In the following month, Braham was promoted and given command of No 141 Squadron, beginning night-intruder operations in June 1943. On his first such mission, on 14

A Mosquito Mk VI about to depart on an intruder sortie over Occupied Europe, 1944. (Author)

June, he shot down a Me 110, and by the end of September he had brought his score to twenty enemy aircraft destroyed, nineteen of them at night. He was now level with John Cunningham, but his second operational tour was at an end and it was not until February 1944 that he was again permitted to fly operationally, and then only on a limited basis, as Wing Commander (Night Operations) at HQ No 2 Group.

In the meantime, No 141 Squadron, together with Nos 169 and 239, had been transferred from Fighter Command to No 100 (Countermeasures) Group, the task of the three squadrons being bomber support. The Mosquito crews of Nos 169 and 239 Squadrons had no experience of *Serrate* operations; moreover, the Mosquito Mk II aircraft with which they were initially armed were worn out, and their operations had to be severely curtailed so that they could be re-engined with new Rolls-Royce Merlin 22s on a rotational basis. During their first three months of operations the three squadrons combined claimed only thirty-one enemy aircraft destroyed or damaged, and six of these were shot down by Bob Braham. In March 1944 No 100 Group's fighter force was joined by No 515 Squadron, operating Beaufighters and later Mosquito VIs. This unit, however, was not equipped with *Serrate*.

During this period, changing his tactics, Braham made six low-level daylight intruder sorties into occupied Europe in March and April 1944, and on five of these trips he destroyed seven enemy aircraft. On the first sortie on 5 March (he was now flying a Mosquito, borrowed from No 305 Squadron at Lasham) he shot down an He 177, the biggest aircraft he had so far destroyed. His run of luck came to an end on 25 June 1944, when, flying a No 21 Squadron Mosquito, he was hit by flak and had to make a forced landing on a sandbar near Ringkøbing, Denmark. He spent the rest of the war in prison camp, as did his Australian navigator, Flight Lieutenant Don Walsh. Braham's score at the time of his capture was twenty-nine confirmed kills, making him the leading RAF night fighter pilot. He was also the first RAF pilot ever to be awarded three DSOs and three DFCs.

During the early weeks of 1944 the AOC-in-C Bomber Command, Air Chief Marshal Sir Arthur Harris, had been making determined efforts to persuade the Air Staff to release more night fighter squadrons to No 100 Group as a matter of priority. In April he wrote a strong letter to the Vice Chief of the Air Staff in which he recommended the transfer of at least ten fighter squadrons to the Group; in the event, a conference convened at the Air Ministry on the 20th of that month decided to authorise the transfer of only two, Nos 85 and 157, both armed with Mosquitoes.

This meagre increase did little to improve the effectiveness of No 100 Group's night fighter force. One of the problems was that Mosquitoes equipped with the latest AI Mk VII/VIII radar were forbidden to operate over enemy territory, and the earlier Mk IV that equipped most of the 100 Group night fighters was subjected to increasing interference from enemy countermeasures. To make matters worse, the usefulness of *Serrate* was over. The German *Lichtenstein* AI radar on which it was designed to home had been replaced by the more advanced SN-2, which worked outside *Serrate*'s frequency cover. The end result was frustration for the night fighter crews. In June 1944, for example, only one enemy aircraft was destroyed in the course of 140 sorties. The situation improved somewhat towards the end of 1944, when Mosquitoes equipped with the latest AI radar were cleared to operate over enemy territory, and the old *Serrate* Mk I was replaced by a new version, the Mk IV. Some aircraft were also equipped with a new device known as *Perfectos*, which emitted a pulse that triggered the IFF (Identification Friend/Foe) sets of German night fighters and enabled the Mosquitoes to home on to the answering signal.

Nevertheless, No 100 Group's fighter force never really succeeded in getting to grips with the enemy night fighters. Quite apart from equipment problems, the Mosquito crews were faced with the formidable task of operating deep inside enemy territory as complete free-lancers, with no help from other quarters. Furthermore, enemy fighters had to be intercepted before they entered the bomber stream, because once they were inside it, it was extremely difficult to make radar contact with them owing to the profusion of other echoes. The tactics employed by the Mosquitoes usually began with a bombing and cannon attack on enemy night fighter airfields a few minutes before the bomber stream entered the area of German GCI radar coverage. Other Mosquitoes would work on the flanks of the stream, about forty miles from it and at a higher altitude, in the hope of intercepting enemy fighters before they reached the bombers. As the bombers were on their way home, more Mosquito fighter bombers loitered in the vicinity of the German airfields, waiting to catch the night fighters as they came in to land.

Few of the RAF's night fighter crews received publicity; in fact, many night fighter pilots achieved notable successes and remained almost entirely unknown outside the Service, at least until after the war. One of them was Flight Lieutenant George Esmond Jamieson, a young New Zealand pilot who, on the night 29/30 July 1944, set up an Allied record by destroying four enemy aircraft in one night. He was flying a Mosquito of No 488 RNZAF Squadron on patrol over Normandy, and

The pressurised Mosquito NF Mk XV carried nose radar and a ventral gun pack. It was designed for high-altitude operations, was powered by two-stage Merlin 61 engines, and was used only by No 85 Squadron. (Philip Jarrett)

Above and following spread: *The last night fighter Mosquito used in WWII was the NF30, which entered service with No 219 Squadron in June 1944.* (Philip Jarrett)

his navigator was Flying Officer Norman Crookes. Jamieson's combat report tells part of the story.

'I was patrolling the Coutance-St Lo area when I saw an unidentified aircraft approaching head-on at 5,000 feet height. Against the dawn I saw that it was a Junkers 88 and as I turned hard to port I followed him as he skimmed through the cloud tops. I closed to 300 yards and there was a series of explosions from the ground caused by the Junkers dropping his bombs as he tried to get away. I gave two short bursts as we came to the next clear patch, and after a fire in the port engine and fuselage the Ju 88 went down through the clouds vertically, hitting the ground near Caen.'

As Jamieson looked down at the debris of the Ju 88, Norman Crookes detected another aircraft on his radar and steered the pilot towards it. As he closed in, the unexpected happened: yet another Junkers suddenly burst out of the cloud, dead ahead of the Mosquito. The German pilot saw the danger and went into a diving turn, trying to regain the shelter of the clouds, but he was too late. Jamieson opened fire from a range of 350 yards, and flames were soon streaming back from the Junkers' starboard engine. The aircraft fell through the cloud layer, burning fiercely, and plunged into the ground.

'Almost immediately I obtained a brief visual on an aircraft crossing from port to starboard some 5,000 feet away and identified as a Ju 88. My navigator confirmed this and took over on his "box of tricks", keeping me behind the enemy aircraft, which was now taking violent evasive action and at the same time jamming our equipment. When we were down to almost treetop height I regained the visual at only 250 yards, opening fire immediately and causing the Junkers to pull up almost vertically, turning to port with sparks and debris falling away. The Ju eventually stalled and dived into a four-acre field where it exploded. This was near Lisieux and as the time was now 0515 hours I climbed back to 5,000 feet and requested control to vector me back to any activity, as I had already observed further anti-aircraft fire through the clouds ahead.'

The anti-aircraft fire, Jamieson soon established, was directed at a Do 217, whose pilot spotted the Mosquito as it closed in and began a series of violent evasive manoeuvres. Just as the Dornier was about to plunge into cloud, Jamieson opened fire and saw his shells bursting on the enemy's fuselage. The Dornier went down in flames, the rear gunner continuing to fire back almost until the bomber hit the ground.

Jamieson returned to New Zealand shortly after his exploit. His score was eleven enemy aircraft destroyed, one probably destroyed and two damaged, all of them at night or in weather conditions so bad that day fighters were unable to operate. Eight of the enemy bombers were shot down while trying to attack Allied forces in Normandy, and the four kills of 29 July were all achieved within twenty minutes.

One Mosquito night fighter/intruder team that enjoyed considerable success was Flight Lieutenant James Benson and Squadron Leader Lewis Brandon (navigator) of No 157 Squadron. Together, they scored seven confirmed kills, with a number of claims for aircraft probably destroyed and damaged, and also destroyed six V-1 flying bombs in the summer of 1944. On the night 11/12 September 1944, while flying bomber support operations with No 100 Group, they were flying over the island of Seeland, off the south-east coast of Denmark, when Brandon picked up a transmission from an enemy night fighter radar. A few moments later, he made contact with the suspect aircraft and steered Benson towards it. In the clear moonlight, the enemy was identified as a Ju 188; it was flying in broad circles, apparently orbiting a German radio beacon.

Benson slid in astern of the Ju 188 and fired a burst into it, seeing his 20 mm shells strike home on the night fighter's starboard wing root. The Ju 188 lost speed rapidly, its starboard engine catching fire, and Benson had to pull up sharply to avoid a collision. The Ju 188 was last seen plunging earthwards, streaming flames. At that moment, Brandon picked up another contact. It was a second Ju 188, and it had probably been engaged in a night fighting exercise with the first. Benson closed in rapidly and gave the Junkers a two-second burst; bright flames streamed back from the enemy's ruptured fuel tanks and it dropped away towards the Danish coast, shedding great chunks of wreckage. The Mosquito sped through the cloud of smoke and debris that the Junkers left in its wake; when Benson and Brandon returned to base they found their aircraft smothered in oil and scarred by pieces of flying metal.

Meanwhile, as the RAF's night intruders were fighting an increasingly successful battle in enemy skies, the home-based night fighter squadrons were fighting a defensive battle against the first of Hitler's 'revenge weapons' – the V-1 flying bomb.

CHAPTER SEVEN

'CONSIDER YOURSELVES EXPENDABLE'

The first V-1 flying bombs fell on British soil on 12 June 1944, and eleven squadrons of the Air Defence of Great Britain (as RAF Fighter Command was now known, albeit for a mercifully short period) were assigned to deal with the threat. Number 11 Group instituted so-called *Diver* patrols, which involved fighters patrolling along three clearly-defined lines: the first between Beachy Head and Dover, the second over the coast between Newhaven and Dover, and the third between Haywards Heath and Ashford. At the same time, nearly 400 anti-aircraft guns and 480 barrage balloons were deployed on the V-1s' approach route to London.

For the fighter pilots engaged in air defence against the V-1, the main problem was one of accurate response and accurate control. Their small margin of speed over the flying bombs, coupled with the short time available to make an interception, demanded that they should be quickly and accurately directed on to the V-1's course before the missile reached the gun and balloon belts. There was consequently a major problem of warning and control to be solved, because the network of radar stations, Observer Corps posts, telecommunications and Fighter Command operations rooms, which had evolved so successfully earlier in the war to counter attacks by piloted aircraft, became suddenly outmoded in the face of this new threat. The same was true of the defence system as a whole; it was not just a matter of improving the efficiency of the guns, searchlights, balloons and fighters as separate weapons, but of co-ordinating their activities. This co-ordination was vital, in particular, between guns and fighters.

As the Operations Room at No 11 Group HQ was fully occupied in controlling fighter activities over the Normandy beachhead in June 1944, all *Diver* defences were controlled by the Operations Room of the Biggin Hill sector. This was linked with the operations rooms of Anti-Aircraft Command in the *Diver* area, and all information from the radar stations and the Observer Corps was fed into it. However, the control that was exercised by Biggin Hill was general rather than specific; and much different from the procedure that had normally been employed in the defence against piloted aircraft where the direction of intercepting fighters was the responsibility of the Sector Operations Room. Instead, executive control of the patrolling fighters was vested in the same agencies that detected and plotted the flying bombs; the radar stations and the Observer Corps centres at Horsham and Maidstone were used as fighter direction stations. Similarly, Anti-Aircraft Command found it impracticable to control the firing of individual batteries from gun operations rooms, and so batteries were allowed to fire independently, except when the gun operations rooms ordered fire to cease – in order to safeguard friendly aircraft, for example.

The system worked in that it reduced the time between detection and interception, but it had to be supplemented by a set of standing orders designed to avoid mutual interference between guns, fighters and balloons. Weather, too, was a prime consideration. As early as 16 June Air Marshal Sir Roderic Hill, commanding the Air Defence of Great Britain (himself an accomplished pilot who flew sixty-two anti-*Diver* patrols, flying each type of defensive fighter in turn), decided that fighters would patrol over the Channel and the strip of land between the coast and the southern limit of the gun belt. They were permitted to pass over the gun belt only when in pursuit of a flying bomb, in which case the guns were not to open fire.

On 19 June it was decided that on days of very good visibility only the fighters would operate, and on bad days only the guns. On moderate days both guns and fighters would operate, each in their own areas. These principles were expanded on 26 June under the curious code-names of *Flabby*, *Spouse* and *Fickle*. In the case of *Flabby*, there was to be a total prohibition of gunfire when the weather was suitable for fighters; *Spouse*, which came into force when the weather was unsuitable for fighters, allowed complete freedom to the guns; and *Fickle*, in average weather conditions, permitted the guns to fire in the *Diver* belt up to 8,000 feet. Fighters were prohibited from entering the belt except when making a visual interception; outside the *Diver* belt fighters were given complete freedom of action, and light anti-aircraft guns were allowed to fire by day against visual targets if no fighters were present.

However, although these rules went some way towards tackling the problem, they did not solve it. Fighter pilots frequently reported that they had been engaged by the guns, and the gunners no less frequently reported that their shooting had been hindered by the presence of fighters.

By the end of June two new methods of controlling the ADGB fighters had been evolved, one for controlling the fighters over the Channel and the other for the direction of fighters patrolling over land. The first of these – the close control method – involved the direction of individual fighters by controllers located at radar stations on the coast. Approaching flying bombs were plotted in the control room of the radar station from which the controller, who was in R/T communication with the patrolling fighter, would issue detailed instructions on the bomb's course so as to bring the pilot into a position to intercept. The factor limiting the extent to which this method could be used was the number of control points available; by the middle of July only four radar stations – two at Fairlight near Hastings, one at Swingate and one at Beachy Head – were engaged in close control.

The main practical difficulty was that existing types of radar station could not, for technical reasons, provide sufficient early warning of an approaching bomb. The best of the stations rarely detected the bombs at ranges of more than fifty miles, which meant that the fighter had, even in theory, no more than six minutes in which to intercept before the bomb reached the coast.

In practice it was less; first because there was a substantial time lag between the initial detection of a bomb and the transmission of interception data from the fighter controller to the pilot, and secondly because patrols could not be carried out at the limit of the radar detection range because of the risk of being surprised by enemy fighters. In the Straits of Dover the ADGB fighters had three minutes at the outside in which to intercept a V-1 before the missile reached the Kent coast.

Despite the shortcomings, ADGB persevered with the close control method, because successful interceptions resulted in the bombs falling harmlessly into the sea. Over land, where there were no low-looking radar facilities, the running commentary method was used. The controllers using this technique were located at three radar stations – Beachy Head, Hythe and Sandwich – and two Observer Corps centres, Horsham and Maidstone. In the running commentary method, the position and course of the flying bombs was passed on the same R/T frequency to all patrolling fighters,

72 | *Hawker Tempest Mk V of No 501 Squadron, which fought at night against the V-1 flying bombs.* (James Grottick)

Personnel of No 501 Squadron, autumn 1944, together with some attached Mosquito aircrew. Left to right, perched on aircraft: Flt Lt Panton; two unknowns, both RCAF: Flt Lt Monty Burton; Flt Lt Bob Stockburn; Flg Off Bill Polley and Flg Off Bennett. Two unknown Canadians are on the tailplane. Standing, left to right: W/O Woyjinsky (Polish); an Army liaison officer; Flt Lt Robb; Flt Lt Hansen; Squadron Ldr Parker-Rees; Flt Lt 'Ollie' Willis; three unknowns; Flt Lt Jimmy Grottick; and the IO, name unknown. (James Grottick)

whose pilots then worked out their own course to intercept the target. This method was also used for fighters patrolling seaward, but it worked best over land where shellbursts, rockets from ROC (Royal Observer Corps) posts, searchlight beams and landmarks all helped the pilots to make speedy interceptions. The chief drawback was that more than one fighter often went after the same flying bomb, a waste of effort which meant that some V-1s slipped through unmolested.

The Mosquito night fighter squadrons opened their score against the V-1s on the night 15/16 June 1944, when a Mosquito Mk VI of No 605 Squadron from Manston (Flight Lieutenant J.G. Musgrave and Flight Sergeant Sanewell) exploded one over the Channel. Musgrave reported that:

'. . . it was like chasing a ball of fire across the sky. It flashed by our starboard side a few thousand feet away at the same height as we were flying. I quickly turned to port and gave chase. It was going pretty fast, but I caught up with it and opened fire from astern. At first, there was no effect so I closed in another hundred yards and gave it another burst. Then I went closer still and pressed the button again. This time, there was a terrific flash and explosion and the whole thing fell down in a vertical dive into the sea. The whole show was over in about three minutes.'

Four Mosquito squadrons – Nos 96, 219, 409 and 418 – were assigned exclusively to anti-*Diver* night patrols, and were joined later in June by Nos 85, 157 and 456, the first two temporarily reassigned from their intruder work. Other squadrons operated against the V-1s on a part-time basis, as priority was given to patrolling the Normandy beachhead. Between them, the seven full-time anti-*Diver* Mosquito squadrons claimed 471 flying bombs, while the part-timers claimed 152 to give a combined total of 623, or about one-third of the RAF's total claim against the V-1s.

Detachments of the USAAF's 422nd and 425th Squadrons also operated against the V-1s, their Black Widows being temporarily based at Hurn, but the crews were as yet inexperienced and they had little success, destroying nine flying bombs between them.

Although the ADGB's Mosquito squadrons bore the brunt of night operations against the V-1s, one other squadron played an extraordinary part in the defence against the flying bombs. This was No 501 (County of Gloucester) Squadron, armed with Tempest Mk Vs. The story is told by one of the squadron's pilots, Flight Lieutenant A.J. 'Jimmy' Grottick, who took part in these activities from first to last.

'On 2 August 1944 No 501 Squadron moved to Manston. The unit was now fully equipped with Tempests, and the move was preparatory to crossing over to the Continent to join the Second Tactical Air Force. It was at this point that the axe fell. Several of us were seen – mainly those who had more night-flying hours in their log books than the others – and given an option.

'Either we could be reappointed to another operational unit, or we could go off for a rest period, probably as instructors on an operational training unit. Together with others given the option, I elected to remain operational.

'We were transferred from 501 Squadron on to what was known as a Fighter Interception Unit, also at Manston. So great had the V-1 menace become that it was decided to set up a special night fighter unit under the command of Squadron Leader Joe Berry. This, flying Tempests, would attempt to provide an effective response to V-1s coming in at night. At first, the FIU was just twelve pilots strong, but within about a week the loss rate had become so great – mainly through accidents – that the strength had been almost halved.

'At the end of August 1944 the name Fighter Interception Unit was dropped, and the unit assumed the identity of No 501 Squadron. The day fighter pilots of the original 501 Squadron were allocated to 2nd TAF units, and so the County of Gloucester Squadron began an entirely new phase, operating solely at night in pursuit of its task. We were left in no doubt about the importance of the job we had to do. Squadron Leader Berry was called to HQ 11 Group and was given specific high-level instructions, which he passed on to us. He had been informed that Winston Churchill had taken a special interest in the new Tempest night-fighter set-up, and that the Prime Minister had issued the following directive:

"So great is the threat, especially at night, of the new V-1 menace, and the possibilities in terms of morale so dire, that No 501 Squadron must consider itself expendable. The Squadron will continue to fly, though there may be little chance of interception, however bad the weather."

'So, night after night, through September and onwards, patrols of 501 Squadron would take off in weather so bad that it sometimes grounded other squadrons during daylight hours. This, together with the fact that our own anti-aircraft gunners now had the benefit of radar gunlaying apparatus and proximity fuses, made our night operations decidedly hairy. Squadron Leader Joe Berry was one of our early casualties; he had been in the anti flying-bomb

business a long time, and by the time of his death his score stood officially at 61 destroyed, plus another which he shared with two more pilots. Berry was lost about the middle of September, at the same time as Flight Lieutenant Snowy Bond, a New Zealand pilot, and another New Zealander whose name I forget. Both had been members of the old 501 Squadron in the pre-Tempest days. [*Author: according to records, Squadron Leader Berry was shot down by flak over Veendam, Holland, on 2 October 1944*].

'The Squadron was taken over by Squadron Leader Parker-Rees, who came to us from No 96 Squadron and who was an experienced Mosquito night fighter pilot. At this time No 501 Squadron had seventeen pilots on strength, drawn from a wide area of operational experience.

'Midway through September 1944 No 501 Squadron was moved from Manston to Bradwell Bay, sixteen miles north-east of Southend in Essex, and continued its regular anti-*Diver* patrols from this new location. By the time of the move to Bradwell Bay our defences had become rather more organised; strong anti-aircraft forces had been mustered in the south-east corner of the country, and with their new equipment were beginning to take a substantial toll of the V-1s. We were all "zoned", and No 501 Squadron was responsible for an area over the Thames estuary between Southend and London. Fortunately, our patrol height was somewhat higher than the altitude setting of the anti-aircraft shells. It was also considerably higher than the normal height at which the V-1s flew. As I recall, they flew at between 500 and 1,000 feet. As you may well understand, this was not a comfortable height from which to deliver attacks on anything at night, especially something streaming a long, fiery tail and liable to explode in your face.

'We were equipped with a ground proximity warning device which was supposed to illuminate a red lamp in the cockpit at 500 feet above ground level. I don't think it ever worked.

'From this point on it was the anti-aircraft defences that got the majority of the V-1 intruders. Our task was to try to intercept those that got through the anti-aircraft net. The period of night fighting extended from August 1944 to the end of March 1945, and towards the end of this period No 501 Squadron was moved from Bradwell Bay to Hunsdon, in Hertfordshire, just north of London. During the whole of this period I managed to down two V-1s. I had attempted numerous interceptions throughout the winter, but I had always been beaten to the kill by the AA guns. My first V-1 kill was on the night of 29 October, the V-1 falling somewhere in the vicinity of Chelmsford. My aircraft was Tempest SD-V.

'My second V-1 was shot down on the night of 26 March 1945, when I was operating out of Hunsdon. It was an interesting kill, both for myself and for 501 Squadron. The V-1 crashed and exploded near North Weald, and as far as I can ascertain this was the last success scored against an enemy intruder over Britain. The V-1 offensive ended on 29 March, when a V-1 came down at Datchworth, near Hatfield, but this was not intercepted. At the end of March 1945 No 501 Squadron's role as a night fighter squadron came to an end.

'One point about the Tempest and the flying bomb. As I mentioned earlier, the V-1 was programmed to come across at low level, usually at between 500 feet and 1,000 feet and at high speed, but this was variable. According to official sources, the V-1's average penetration speed was 400 mph, but the second one I caught must have been doing close on 500. From 5,000 feet plus, my Tempest picked up some 580 mph IAS before I was able to catch up with it and destroy it.'

Officially, No 501 Squadron was credited with the destruction of more than 100 V-1s during that dark and freezing winter, but Flight Lieutenant Grottick believes this figure to be exaggerated. 'It was the anti-aircraft that got most of the flying bombs penetrating at night. All that was left for us to do was to try to catch the remnant that got through this first line of defence.'

Nevertheless, there is no disputing the courage and skill of the pilots, who launched themselves into the darkness night after night, in single-engined aircraft that were ill-equipped for the job they had to do, with the knowledge that they were officially expendable.

The Mosquito squadrons also began to take losses in the later phases of the campaign against the V-1. In September 1944, with their bases in the Pas de Calais overrun by the Allied advance, the enemy began flying bomb attacks on London and other UK targets, such as Portsmouth and Southampton, with V-1s air-launched from He 111s of KG53. Later in September air launches were made against east coast targets from positions off the Dutch coast. Catching the Heinkel launchers was very difficult, for they flew slowly at low level, and several Mosquitoes were lost to return fire, or because they stalled at low speed while trying to intercept. In an attempt to improve interception rates, a radar picket ship, the frigate HMS *Caicos*, and a specially-equipped radar Wellington of the Fighter Interception Unit were used to direct the Mosquitoes, which patrolled over the sea at about 4,000 feet between Britain and Holland. These operations continued until 14 January 1945, by which time KG53 had lost seventy-seven aircraft, forty-one of them on operations.

CHAPTER EIGHT

NORTH AFRICA, MALTA AND ITALY

Hurricane Mk IIc of No 94 Squadron at Gamil, May 1942. Note the plate just forward of the cockpit, fitted to protect the pilot's night vision from the glare of the exhaust. (Philip Jarrett)

Germany's entry into the North African theatre in April 1941 brought with it the threat of day and night bombing raids on the Suez Canal Zone, and in May No 94 Squadron, which had just exchanged its Gloster Gladiators for Hurricanes at Ismailia, was assigned to air defence duties, in which role it operated until relieved by No 213 Squadron in December. Both squadrons were equipped with Hurricane Is, which were not fitted with tropical filters and were deemed usuitable for desert operations. The Hurricanes' role as night fighters in the Middle East was short-lived, however, for in December 1941 No 89 Squadron arrived at Abu Sueir with Beaufighter Mk Is, and in May 1941 No 46 Squadron began reforming as a night fighter unit at Idku, initially using some of 89 Squadron's aircraft. These two squadrons remained responsible for the night defence of the Canal

Zone, and for protection of coastal shipping, throughout 1942, providing occasional detachments to Malta and, in 1943, carrying out intruder patrols over the Greek islands and Sicily.

Number 89 Squadron left for Ceylon in October 1943, while No 46 Squadron continued to provide air defence detachments around the eastern Mediterranean. In December 1942, meanwhile, another RAF Beaufighter night fighter squadron, No 153, had arrived in North Africa; based at Maison Blanche in Algeria, its task was to protect the North African ports following the Allied invasion of November 1942 (Operation *Torch*). In March 1943 No 108 Squadron, which had been operating in the night-bombing role from various locations in North Africa, reformed as a night fighter unit at Shandur with Beaufighter VIs, flying night patrols over Egypt and Libya before moving

The Mosquito Mk XIX, with Merlin 25 engines, equipped Nos 600 and 255 Squadrons in Italy from September 1944. (Philip Jarrett)

to Malta in June. Early in 1943 four USAAF night fighter units also arrived in North Africa; these were the 414th, 415th, 416th and 417th FS, whose crews had trained with RAF units in the UK. All four were armed with the Beaufighter VIF; they subsequently moved to Sicily and Italy, and were the only night fighter units operating with the United States Twelfth Air Force.

In December 1942 No 23 Squadron's Mosquitoes arrived at Luqa, Malta, from the UK, having flown there via Gibraltar, and at once began intruder operations over Sicily, with enemy airfields the principal targets. The squadron also carried out night operations against retreating enemy columns in the Tripoli area, and in February 1943 it extended its area of operations to southern Italy. By May 1943 it had destroyed fifteen enemy aircraft, with three probables and eleven damaged, and had also carried out 200 successful attacks on trains. The squadron flew 233 sorties in May, of which 175 were intruder patrols, claiming six enemy aircraft destroyed and sixty-five locomotives attacked, but at the cost of seven Mosquitoes lost. By July, now equipped with Mosquito Mk VI fighter-bombers fitted with drop tanks, the squadron was ranging as far afield as Rome and Foggia, but enemy aircraft

were encountered only occasionally; one exception was an Me 210, shot down by Flight Sergeant P. Rudd in the Taranto area on 26 July.

As mentioned earlier, No 108 Squadron brought its Beaufighter VIs to Luqa in June 1943, and in the following month it was joined by a detachment of six Mosquito Mk XIIs belonging to No 256 Squadron. Both squadrons operated intensively in support of the Allied invasion of Sicily, No 256 claiming sixteen enemy aircraft in a single week, its victims including Ju 88s, He 111s and Cant 1007s. The remainder of the squadron, armed with Mosquito Mk XIIIs, arrived in November. Its commitment was to defend Malta by day and night, with four and three crews repectively on standby during each period. Number 108 Squadron, in the meantime, soldiered on with its ageing Beaufighters, and the arrival of its first Mosquitoes in February 1944 was greeted with euphoria. It was short-lived; the new Mosquitoes were flown by crews drawn from 256 Squadron, and No 108 continued to fly Beaufighters until 5 April, when it flew its first Mosquito patrol. From then until July the squadron flew intruder patrols from Hal Far, using a mixture of Beaufighters and Mosquitoes; the Beaufighters then went to Libya for intruder operations over

Greece and the Aegean, while the Mosquitoes were assigned to No 256 Squadron. The squadron personnel, to say the least, were not happy.

Number 23 Squadron, meanwhile, had moved up to Sicily in October 1943, detachments going to Sigonella and Gerbini Main. In November a detachment moved to Pomigliano, on the Italian peninsula, which was heavily attacked by fifteen FW 190s on the 30th, luckily without causing any aircraft losses. Further detachments went to Alghero, Sardinia, in December 1943, so that the Mosquitoes could now range in an arc from Toulon to Rome. By the end of January 1944 No 23 Squadron had destroyed thirty-three enemy aircraft in air combat and thirty-nine on the ground, as well as attacking 331 locomotives. The squadron flew its last intruder sorties on 2 May, returning to the UK soon afterwards for bomber support operations with No 100 Group.

During 1944 No 256 Squadron, still based on Luqa in Malta, regularly deployed its Mosquitoes forward to Catania in Sicily, from where it flew night patrols over Allied convoys. In March a detachment moved up to Pomigliano to cover the Anzio beachhead, and in April there was a deployment to Algiers, from where patrols were flown over resupply convoys entering the Mediterranean. During these activities the squadron claimed three Ju 88s destroyed and one damaged. Returning to Italy, No 256 Squadron installed itself at Foggia in September 1944 to begin intruder patrols over Greece and the Balkans, and on 4 October two Ju 52s and an He 111 were shot down near Salonika.

The same month saw the arrival of the first Mosquito NF30s in the Middle East, and in December two Beaufighter squadrons, Nos 600 and 255, began rearming with Mk XIXs at Cesenatico and Foggia. Number 255 Squadron's main task was to provide night support for No 232 (Boston) Wing, which had been suffering losses, but there was no contact with enemy aircraft until the night 22/23 March, when a Ju 188 was destroyed.

With the war in Europe over, many Mosquito NFXIXs were transferred from Italy to India, where they replaced the Beaufighter VIs of Nos 89 and 176 Squadrons at Baigachi. Neither squadron saw action with their new aircraft before the end of hostilities.

CHAPTER NINE

THE NIGHT DEFENCE OF GERMANY, 1943–45

By the spring of 1943, General Josef Kammhuber had five *Geschwader* and 400 twin-engined fighters under his command on bases stretching from Holland to the Mediterranean. However, he was the first to realise that 400 night fighters were not enough to counter the great armadas of four-engined bombers that were beginning to make deeper inroads into Germany night after night, and he consequently proposed a major extension of the *Himmelbett* air defence system, with eighteen night fighter *Geschwader* covering the whole of Germany. The aircraft would be fitted with improved AI equipment and the ground radar network would also be modernised.

Kammhuber pushed relentlessly for the expansion of his night fighter force, and it was his undoing. Nothing could convince Hitler that the *Luftwaffe*'s night fighters were not already destroying enough enemy bombers to cripple the RAF's night offensive. Kammhuber rapidly began to fall from favour, and his cause was not helped when, during a series of heavy attacks on Hamburg in July 1943, Bomber Command rendered the *Himmelbett* radar system virtually impotent by the use of 'Window', bundles of tinfoil strips cut to the wavelength of the enemy warning radar and dropped from attacking aircraft to confuse the defences.

The paralysing of the *Himmelbett* system led to the evolution of new tactics, stemming from a

A Halifax bomber silhouetted against the fires of a German city – the view a Wilde Sau *pilot would see.* (Author)

proposal made by a Colonel von Lossberg of the General Staff. He recommended that night fighters be released from the confines of the *Himmelbett* zones, where their movements were too restricted and susceptible to radar jamming, and instead mix freely with the bomber stream, the pilots making visual attacks. The idea was approved, and it was decided as a first step to increase the strength of *Jagdgeschwader* 300, formed a month earlier under the command of Major Hajo Hermann, himself a fighter ace. This was the pioneer *Wilde Sau* (Wild Boar) unit; equipped with single-engined fighters, its task was to patrol directly over German targets, the pilots endeavouring to pick out enemy bombers in the glare of searchlights and fires.

The idea was quickly adopted by other night fighter units, including NJG1, and it achieved considerable success – although at great risk to the attacking fighters, which had to contend with German flak as well as defensive fire from the RAF bombers. The following combat report, one of the few to survive the wholesale destruction of *Luftwaffe* records that took place in the final days of the war, was made by *Leutnant* Musset of 5/NJG1. His observer was *Gefreiter* Hafner.

'At 2347 hours on 17.8.43 I took off from Berlin on a *Wilde Sau* operation. From the Berlin area I observed enemy activity to the north. I promptly flew in that direction and positioned myself at a height of 4,300 metres over the enemy's target, Peenemünde [*Germany's secret rocket weapons research establishment, hit by 597 heavy bombers that night – author*]. Against the glow of the burning target I saw from above numerous enemy aircraft flying over it in close formations of seven or eight.

'I went down and placed myself at 3,400 metres behind one enemy formation. At 0142 I attacked one of the enemy with two bursts of fire from directly astern, registering good strikes on the port inboard engine, which at once caught fire. E/A (enemy aircraft) tipped over to its left and went down. Enemy counter-fire from rear gunner was ineffective. Owing to an immediate second engagement I could only follow E/A's descent on fire as far as a layer of mist.

'I make four claims, as follows:

1. Attack at 0145 on a four-engined E/A at 2,600 metres from astern and range 30–40 metres. E/A at once burned brightly in both wings and fuselage. I observed it until it crashed in flames at 0147.
2. At 0150 I was in position to attack another E/A from slightly above, starboard astern and range 60–70 metres. Strikes were seen in starboard wing, and E/A blew up. I observed burning fragments hit the ground at 0152.
3. At 0157 I attacked another four-engined E/A at 1,830 metres from 100 metres astern. Burning brightly in both wings and fuselage it went into a vertical dive. After its crash I saw the wreckage burning at 0158. Heavy counter-

fire from rear gunner scored hits in both wings of our own aircraft.
4. At 0159 I was ready to attack again. E/A took strong evasive action by weaving. While it was in a left-hand turn, however, I got in a burst from port astern and range 40–50 metres, which set the port wing on fire. E/A plunged to the ground burning brightly, and I observed the crash at 0201. Enemy counter-fire from rear gunner was ineffective.

'A few minutes later I attacked another E/A which took violent evasive action by weaving. On the first attack my cannon went out of action owing to burst barrels. I then made three further attacks with MG and observed good strikes on the starboard wing without, however, setting it on fire. Owing to heavy counter-fire from enemy rear gunner I suffered hits in my own port engine. At the same time I came under heavy fire from aircraft on the starboard beam, which wounded radio operator in the left shoulder and set my Me 110's port engine on fire. Thereupon I broke off the action, cut my engine and flew westwards away from the target area. No radio contact with the ground could be established, and ES signals were also unavailing. As I was constantly losing height, at 1,800 metres I gave the order to bale out.

'As I did so I struck the tail unit with both legs, thereby breaking my right thigh and left shin-bone. After normal landings by parachute my observer and I were taken to the reserve military hospital at Güstrow.

'At 0250 the Me 110 crashed on the northern perimeter of Güstrow.'

Four heavy bombers, each with a crew of seven, destroyed in fifteen minutes, together with one probably destroyed and one damaged! And such engagements were by no means uncommon in the night battle over Germany. That night, forty RAF bombers failed to return from Peenemünde. The loss would undoubtedly have been higher, had it not been for a diversionary effort by a small force of Mosquitoes, which dropped flares over Berlin and duped the defences into believing that this was the objective. The result was that 148 *Wilde Sau* fighters patrolled over the capital for the best part of an hour without sighting a single enemy aircraft.

While *Wilde Sau* operations continued, Telefunken had been hard at work developing a new AI radar that would not be susceptible to *Window* jamming. In October 1943 the night fighter units began to receive the new *Lichtenstein* SN2 AI radar, which was free from both electronic and *Window* jamming. It had a maximum range of four miles and a minimum range of 450 yards, and it was not long before some night fighter crews began to register a formidable number of successes with its help. In the autumn of 1943 two more homing devices were also developed for use by night fighters, the *Naxos* Z and the *Flensburg*. The former enabled the fighters to

This and next page: Lichtenstein-equipped Ju 88. The drag caused by the 'toasting fork' aerial array knocked several knots off the aircraft's speed. (Philip Jarrett)

home on transmissions from the RAF's H2S blind bombing radar, and the latter was designed to lock on to radiations from the 'Monica' tail warning radar carried by the bombers.

In the summer of 1943 the German night fighters also began to receive a new type of armament, which was to prove extremely effective. Devised by an NCO armourer named Paul Mahle and known as *Schräge Musik* (Slanting Music), it involved the mounting of two 20 mm cannon, their muzzles pointing upwards at a fixed angle, on a wooden platform in the upper fuselage of a night fighter. This arrangement enabled the fighter to take advantage of a bomber's blind spot and attack it from directly below with the aid of a reflector sight mounted in the cockpit roof.

Schräge Musik was used for the first time on 17/18 August 1943, when two crews of 2/NJG5 destroyed six RAF bombers in the space of half an hour. The German airmen reported that the Halifaxes and Lancasters were extremely vulnerable to this form of attack. The large area of their wings was impossible to miss, and since the wings contained the fuel tanks a relatively short burst was usually enough to set a bomber on fire. Between the night of the Peenemünde raid and 2 October, the crews of 2/NJG5 scored eighteen victories with the aid of *Schräge Musik* for no loss to themselves.

It was a terrible irony that the original specification for the Lancaster and Halifax had included a ventral gun turret; it had been dispensed with at an early design stage to permit the carriage of a greater bomb load. As a result of losses caused by fighter attacks from below, some bombers – notably in No 6 (RCAF) Group – were locally modified to incorporate a lower fuselage hatch through which a 0.50 in machine-gun could be operated by a crew member.

Despite the problems of equipment and organisation that handicapped the German night fighter force, its success rate reached an unprecedented peak in the spring of 1944. In the course of three big air battles over darkened Germany, Bomber Command suffered crippling losses. On 19/20 February, seventy-eight out of a force of 823 heavy bombers despatched to attack Leipzig failed to

This Lichtenstein-*equipped Ju 88G-1 of 7/NJG2 landed in error at Woodbridge on 13 July 1944. It was extensively tested by the RAF.* (Philip Jarrett)

return; seventy-two more were destroyed during an assault on Berlin on 24/25 March; and then, five nights later, came the most catastrophic loss of all, and the greatest triumph for the night fighters.

At nightfall on 30 March 1944, 795 heavy bombers set out from their English bases to attack the important industrial centre and railway junction of Nuremberg. The night was cloudless and calm, and across a great arc of Europe stretching across Holland, Belgium, northern France and north-west Germany the *Luftwaffe* night fighter crews were at cockpit readiness. At 22.00 reports began to come in of small-scale attacks by Mosquitoes on several airfields in Holland and of minelaying operations over the North Sea, but the GOC I Fighter Corps, *Generalmajor* Josef Schmid, realised that these were simply diversions and kept his fighters on the ground. Then, at 22.30, the German coastal radar stations detected a major raid building up on the other side of the English Channel, and a few minutes later the bomber stream was reported to be heading south-eastwards towards Belgium. At 22.30 Schmid finally ordered his fighters into the air.

This time, instead of carrying out the normal procedure and making several changes of course to confuse the defences, the bomber stream continued due east for 150 miles after making landfall on the enemy coast, and the night fighters had no difficulty in locating their targets. The route to Nuremberg was marked by a series of fiery beacons as one heavy bomber after another fell burning from the sky. From all over Germany the night fighter *Gruppen* converged on the bomber stream, and several pilots scored multiple kills in the battle that developed. The greatest success was achieved by *Oberleutnant* Martin Becker of 1/NJG6, who destroyed six

Halifaxes in thirty minutes, between 00.20 and 00.50 hours. Nor was that all; after landing to refuel and rearm, Becker took off again in his Me 110 and shot down a seventh Halifax as it was on its homeward flight.

Other pilots who achieved notable successes that night were *Oberleutnant* Helmut Schulte of 2/NJG5, who destroyed four heavy bombers; *Leutnant* Wilhelm Seuss of 4/NJG5, who also shot down four; and *Oberleutnant* Martin Drewes of 2/NJG1, who destroyed three.

For RAF Bomber Command, the cost of the Nuremberg raid was stupendous: ninety-five bombers failed to return and seventy-one were damaged. The loss – 11.8 per cent of the attacking force – was the highest ever sustained by the Command. It was the greatest victory achieved by the German night fighter force during the war, but it was also its last. One by one, the leading German night fighter crews were swallowed up in the cauldron of the air war as 1944 wore on; the *Luftwaffe*'s night fighter resources dwindled steadily through attrition in combat and through Allied bombing. For example, 465 Me 110s, earmarked for night fighting, were destroyed by Allied bombing in February 1944 alone.

In the first half of 1943, *General* Kammhuber had pressed strongly for the production of new twin-engined types designed specifically for night fighting. At the forefront of these was the He 219 *Uhu* (Owl), the prototype of which had flown in November 1942 after months of delay caused by a lack of interest on the part of the German Air Ministry. By April 1943 300 examples had been ordered; Kammhuber wanted 2,000, but in the event only 294 were built before the end of the war. Formidably armed with six 20 mm cannon and

The Focke-Wulf Ta 154 (V3 pictured here) might have been a valuable addition to the German night fighter force, but it suffered serious structural bonding problems. (Philip Jarrett)

equipped with the latest AI radar, the He 219 would certainly have torn great gaps in Bomber Command's ranks had it been available in quantity. It also had a performance comparable to that of the Mosquito, which other German night fighters did not, and therefore could have fought the RAF's intruders on equal terms.

Admittedly, the He 219 suffered from a series of technical troubles in its early development career, but what it might have achieved in action was ably demonstrated on 11/12 June 1943 by *Major* Werner Streib of 1/NJG1. Flying a pre-production He 219 on operational trials from Venlo, he infiltrated an RAF bomber stream heading for Berlin and shot down five Lancasters in half an hour. The only sour note for Streib sounded when the flaps of the He 219 refused to function and the aircraft overran the runway on landing, breaking into three pieces. Streib and his observer escaped without injury.

Squadron Leader Lewis Brandon and Flight Lieutenant James Benson encountered one of these formidable aircraft on 5/6 January 1945, over northern Germany. They had been following a contact which, disappointingly, turned out to be a Lancaster bomber when Brandon suddenly picked up another trace on his radar screen. Whatever the strange aircraft was, it proved very hard to catch, climbing fast towards Hannover. Benson finally caught it at a range of half a mile over the burning city and identified it as an He 219, easily recognisable because of its twin fins and array of radar aerials.

Benson crept up behind the enemy aircraft and

opened fire at 200 yards, hitting the Heinkel's engines. Large pieces broke off and it went down in a steep dive, with the Mosquito following. At 6,000 feet the enemy night fighter entered a steep climb up to 12,000 feet, where it heeled over and dived almost vertically into the ground. The Mosquito crew saw it blow up. Later, it was learned that the He 219 was fitted with ejection seats, the first aircraft in the world to use them. From the aircraft's erratic behaviour after its initial dive, it seemed likely that the crew of this particular He 219 had ejected from their stricken machine.

Another promising night fighter design that fell by the wayside was the Focke-Wulf Ta 154 Moskito. The Ta 154 was of mixed metal and wood construction, and featured a tricycle undercarriage, with large-diameter tyres to facilitate take-offs from unprepared strips. Powered by two Junkers Jumo 211F engines, the Ta 154 carried a crew of two (pilot and radio/radar operator). Armament comprised two forward-firing 30 mm and two 20 mm cannon, with a single 30 mm cannon mounted obliquely in the rear fuselage. The prototype Ta 154V-1 flew in July 1943 and the type was ordered into production in November, but there were continual delays and in June 1944 the first two production Ta 154A-1s were accidentally destroyed – one when it fell apart because faulty glue had been used in its assembly and the other when its flaps broke away on a landing approach – and as a result the production order was cancelled. Seven more production Ta 154A-1s were completed, however, and these were used operationally for a while by

Above and below: *Messerschmitt Me 262B-1a/U1 night fighter with SN-2* Lichtenstein *AI. This is a captured example, bearing a British serial number. Note the under-fuselage drop tanks. The figure standing beside the aircraft in the second photograph gives a good impression of the Me 262's size.* (Philip Jarrett)

1/NJG3 at Stade and by NJGr10. There is no record of their combat achievements, if indeed there were any.

The Me 110 and the Ju 88 consequently formed the backbone of the German night fighter force. The Ju 88 was the real mainstay; 4,200 were produced as night fighters or converted to the night fighter role. But apart from the He 219, the Germans never fielded a purpose-built night fighter.

A few weeks before the end of hostilities the Germans belatedly realised the potential of the jet-propelled Me 262 as a night fighter, and a single night fighter *Staffel*, 10/NJG11, equipped with the jets in March 1945. On the night 30/31 March, the unit's commander, *Leutnant* Welter, destroyed four

Opposite and this page: *The battle against the German night fighters was never-ending, and the Telecommunications Research Establishment at Malvern was at the heart of it. These photographs show a variety of tail warning equipment under test on B-17 Fortress and Wellington aircraft.* (RRE)

Mosquitoes on the approaches to Berlin – the biggest individual claim against these fast, twin-engined light bombers. The next morning, Halifaxes of No 6 (RCAF) Group, operating over Hamburg by daylight without fighter cover, were attacked by thirty Me 262s of 10/NJG11 and eight of the bombers were shot down.

Many factors combined to bring about the defeat of the German night fighters, not least of which was a continual shortage of suitable aircraft. There was also the priority given to anti-aircraft guns and ammunition at the expense of fighter production, even though fighters were two or three times more effective in terms of kills than anti-aircraft artillery. It is a quite astonishing fact that the amount of aluminium used in manufacturing flak shell fuses throughout the war would have enabled the German aircraft industry to produce 40,000 more fighters, in addition to the 54,000 actually built.

But perhaps the biggest single factor was radio countermeasures (RCM), a field in which the British enjoyed an undisputed lead in their ongoing night offensive against Germany. Thanks to the 'Y' Service, *Ultra* and the various agencies that monitored German signals traffic, the threat presented by the German controlled night fighter system to the RAF's night bombing offensive was well known by the beginning of 1942, and much had been deduced about its operational methods. More knowledge was added in February 1942, when one of the system's key components, a *Wurzburg* precision GCI radar, was captured in a commando raid on Bruneval, near Le Havre, and by May 1942 an almost complete and very accurate picture of enemy GCI fighter control had been built up. At the same time, the loss rate suffered on bombing operations was steadily increasing, and there was no doubt that this was due to the large-scale introduction of radar-assisted control of both AA guns and fighters.

The value of radar countermeasures was not in doubt. The development of airborne jamming equipment had been started in late 1941 and was still in progress. One highly effective countermeasure – *Window* – had already been developed, but its use was not yet authorised on the grounds that Britain was still too vulnerable to air attack for the RAF to initiate a jamming war.

By the autumn of 1942, however, losses had become so severe that a continued embargo on radar countermeasures could no longer be justified, and on 6 October a meeting was held at HQ Bomber Command to consider their adoption. The first recommendation was that the bombers' IFF (Identification Friend/Foe) sets be modified to operate on the frequency (120–130 mc/s) of the *Freya* radars so that some jamming could be effected. It was realised that this countermeasure,

called *Shiver*, would not achieve much success, so the use of a second radar countermeasure was authorised. This was *Mandrel*, a radar jammer developed at the Wembley laboratories of the General Electric Company. It operated in the 120–130 mc/s band, and two aircraft per squadron were to be fitted with it. Its object was to reduce the range at which the *Freya* sets could identify and plot incoming bombers from 100 to about twenty-five miles. Two *Mandrel* ground stations, at Dover and Hastings, would also be brought into use to supplement the airborne equipment.

Steps were also taken to disrupt the vital radio communications link between the night fighters and their ground controllers. This was done by modulating the bombers' transmitters with noise produced by a microphone situated inside the aircraft. Each wireless operator was briefed to search a bank of 150 kc/s between 3 and 6 mc/s and to transmit on the frequency of any German R/T which he heard. This countermeasure, called *Tinsel*, and *Mandrel* were both introduced operationally in December 1942, and a squadron of Boulton Paul Defiants (No 515 Squadron) was also equipped with *Mandrel* and given the task of patrolling fifty miles off the enemy coast.

The effect of *Mandrel* was found to be less than had been hoped, mainly because the enemy extended the frequency range of the *Freya* from 120–130 mc/s to 120–150 mc/s in an effort to minimise the effect of jamming. He also developed a device called *Freya-Halbe*, which enabled night fighters to home on to the jamming aircraft, with the result that losses among the *Mandrel*-equipped bombers were high. It was never possible to raise the *Mandrel* barrage to the desired intensity, and although one estimate suggested that a force of 600 *Mandrel*-equipped aircraft would produce the required result, it was never possible, because of a shortage of equipment, to have more than 200 aircraft fitted with the device at any one time.

A greater success was achieved by *Tinsel*, and in April 1943 the 'Y' Service reported that the Germans were making increasing use of VHF radio communications, which operated between 38 and 42 mc/s and was therefore immune to this countermeasure. Another jamming device, *Ground Cigar*, was set up at Sizewell in Suffolk to deal with the new fighter frequency, but it suffered from a lack of range, with a coverage of only 140 miles from the ground station, and it also disrupted the 'Y' Service's VHF traffic. An airborne version was the obvious answer, and development of one – *Airborne Cigar*, more commonly called ABC – was set in motion.

All the frequencies on which the various German ground–air components of the German air defence system operated, could be monitored and identified

Jostle *noise jamming equipment installed in a Short Stirling.* (RRE)

from the United Kingdom, but the short-range airborne interception radars used by the German night fighters presented a different problem. The first German AI radar, the *Lichtenstein* BC, became operational early in 1942; it operated in the 490 mc/s band and had a maximum range of about two miles.

In July 1942, the 'Y' Service picked up indications that the German night fighters operating over Holland were using an airborne detection device referred to as *Emil*, but its exact nature could not be ascertained. In an attempt to gather more information, a special duties unit, No 1474 Flight, was formed, and its Wellingtons, equipped with radio detection gear, began operations over north-west Europe. Seventeen sorties were flown without result; then, on 3/4 December 1942, the radio operator of an eighteenth Wellington picked up weak signals at 04.30, possibly from German AI radar, on 487 mc/s. The signal strength increased rapidly, and the crew knew that an enemy fighter was locked on to them.

A few moments later the Wellington was heavily attacked by a Ju 88. The captain of the British aircraft, Pilot Officer Paulton, took evasive action and his rear gunner returned the fire. The specialist radio operator, Pilot Officer Jordan, was badly wounded by the night fighter's first burst of fire; he nevertheless went on transmitting information about the enemy radar signals back to base for some minutes before he collapsed. The Ju 88 finally broke off the attack when Paulton took the Wellington down in a long dive from 14,000 to 500 feet. The bomber was severely damaged; both its throttles were jammed, its gun turrets were out of action and most of its instruments had been smashed by shell splinters. As the aircraft limped homewards the second specialist wireless operator, Flight Sergeant Bigoray, continued to transmit data, although he was wounded in both legs. The Wellington ditched 200 yards off the British coast and the crew was rescued. For their part in the mission, Pilot Officer Jordan received the DSO, the pilot was awarded the DFC and Flight Sergeant Bigoray the DFM.

The electronic surveillance missions flown by No

Window, *seen here being manufactured, was – and still is – a very effective anti-radar weapon.* (Author)

1474 Flight were the first ever of their kind, and led to the development of a jamming device called *Ground Grocer*. This covered only a small area of Holland and Belgium and was of limited value. Of much greater importance was the development by the Telecommunications Research Establishment of *Serrate*, described earlier. However, there was no escaping the fact that in the autumn of 1943 Bomber Command's loss rate had once again risen to eighty per cent of the level it had reached prior to the introduction of *Window*, and furthermore British Intelligence was aware that the German night fighter units had begun to equip with the new FUG 220 *Lichtenstein* SN-2 AI radar, developed by Telefunken and resistant to both *Window* and the jamming equipment then in use. In the autumn of 1943 two more homing devices were also developed for use by night fighters, the FUG 350 *Naxos* Z and the FUG 227 *Flensburg*.

In the early months of 1944 the Allies knew very little about this new equipment, and went to great lengths to gather reliable intelligence data on it. Many perilous sorties were flown by No 192 Squadron – the former 1474 Flight – operating out of Gransden Lodge in Cambridgeshire with a mixture of Wellingtons, Halifaxes and Mosquitoes, but with no result. The Mosquitoes alone flew fifty-five sorties in the first three months of the year, five to the Berlin area.

The Germans had unrestricted use of *Lichtenstein* SN-2 for a full six months, during which Bomber Command suffered appalling losses. The only clues to the nature of the new equipment were some signals which had been picked up in the 160 mc/s range and which might have emanated from an AI radar, and a gun-camera photograph, taken by an American fighter, which showed a Ju 88 on the ground featuring a novel type of aerial array. The dimensions of the array, as deduced from the poor-quality photograph, suggested a frequency of around 100 mc/s, which was thought to be too low to produce reliable results. On the assumption – incorrect, as it turned out – that 160 mc/s was likely to be the frequency of the new enemy AI radar, a new type of *Window* called Type Y was produced.

It was never used operationally, for on 12/13 July 1944 a Junkers Ju 88G night fighter made a serious navigational error and landed at Woodbridge in Suffolk. The aircraft was equipped with both SN-2 AI radar and the *Flensburg* homing device, which were quickly subjected to a thorough evaluation by the Telecommunications Research Establishment. The examination showed that the SN-2 worked on a frequency of around 90 mc/s, and luckily a countermeasure was already available in the form of *Window* Type MB, which had been devised for use in connection with the D-Day landings and which covered all frequencies between 70 and 200 mc/s. Good stocks were still in hand, and on 23/24 July it was dropped on a normal operation. Almost immediately, bomber losses began to decline.

Several problems were experienced in the creation of No 100 Group's RCM force. The first lay in the choice of a suitable aircraft, which had to be big enough to carry the necessary equipment and able to fly fast and high enough to stand a chance of avoiding night fighters. The aircraft selected eventually was the Boeing B-17 Flying Fortress, which was considered to meet all the requirements. Fourteen B-17Fs were obtained, and necessary modifications were carried out early in 1944 by the Scottish Aviation Company at Prestwick. These included the replacement of the Fortress's chin turret by an H2S blister, the provision of mufflers to screen the exhaust flames and the fitting of the jamming devices in the bomb bay. The aircraft began operations with No 214 Squadron in June 1944. In addition, B-17s of the 803rd Squadron, United States Strategic Air Forces, were also equipped for the jamming role, and this unit was placed under the operational control of No 100 Group.

The RCM devices carried by these aircraft were called *Jostle* and *Piperack*. The first, a high-powered communications jammer, emitted a high-pitched wail and could effectively jam any frequency used by the German fighter controllers; the second, developed from an American RCM kit called *Dina*, designed to reinforce *Mandrel*, covered the 90–110 mc/s frequency used by the German AI radars. A third squadron, No 223, which was equipped with Liberators and which began operations in September 1944, was also equipped with these devices. *Mandrel* operations, which did not require fast, high-flying aircraft since they were usually conducted clear of enemy territory, were flown by the Stirlings of No 199 Squadron and the Halifaxes of No 171, joined at the end of 1944 by the Halifaxes of No 642 Squadron. Meanwhile, No 192 Squadron continued to monitor enemy radio and radar transmissions, and in late 1944 it wasted a lot of effort in searching for the radio signals that were mistakenly thought to guide V-2 rockets.

In their finalised form, the tactics used by No 100 Group's RCM force were as follows. *Mandrel*-equipped aircraft, employed mainly to provide a screen for the main bomber force, would operate in pairs with fourteen miles between them, forming a line positioned some eighty miles from enemy territory. With their *Mandrels* switched on, the orbiting aircraft formed an effective electronic curtain through which the enemy search radars were unable to penetrate. Aircraft equipped with *Jostle* and *Piperack*, on the other hand, flew 4,000 feet above the bomber stream at intervals of ten miles, providing an electronic umbrella to disrupt the German AI radar and voice communications.

The Germans tried desperately to remain a step ahead of Allied countermeasures developments. Early in 1944 they began work on two new types of AI radar, the FUG 218 *Neptun* VR and the FUG 228 *Lichtenstein* SN-3. The former worked in the 163-187 mc/s band, the latter in the 100–112 mc/s band, and the frequencies of both could be altered in the air to make jamming more difficult. Production of the SN-3 had already started when the Allies found an effective means of jamming the German *Freya* ground radar, which worked on the same waveband, so further work on the SN-3 AI set was stopped and production concentrated on *Neptun*. This was first used operationally in February 1945, but the Allies quickly discovered that it was vulnerable to *Window* of the right length and within three weeks effective countermeasures had been devised against it.

CHAPTER TEN

THE FAR EAST AND THE PACIFIC

The night fighter squadrons of RAF Fighter Command had been battling the *Luftwaffe* for more than a year when the Japanese launched their invasion of South-East Asia; and yet, despite all the warnings and all the lessons of experience, when Japanese bombers began intensive night raids on Singapore and Rangoon, there was not a single dedicated night fighter squadron to oppose them. Only one RAF squadron in Malaya, No 27, was equipped with Blenheim IF fighters, and these were assigned to the day fighting role. In the event the matter quickly became academic, for the Blenheims were soon destroyed by air attacks on their airfields, and it was left to the handful of RAF, RAAF and RNZAF single-engined squadrons – all equipped with the totally inadequate Brewster Buffalo – to fight on by day and night until they were eventually overwhelmed.

In Burma the scenario was similar, but here the Japanese Air Force encountered tougher opposition and better equipment. Here, one RAF Buffalo squadron (No 67) fought alongside the experienced pilots of the American Volunteer Group, who, flying Curtiss P-40s, had already been fighting the Japanese in China for some time. Between them, they inflicted substantial losses on the Japanese bomber formations that attacked the Burmese capital, Rangoon, by daylight in December 1941; and when two squadrons of Hurricanes arrived to replace the Buffaloes in January 1942 the enemy switched almost entirely to night attacks.

An early warning system of sorts was devised, relying on a network of ground observers to give warning of the Japanese bombers' approach by telephone. Ten minutes' warning was usually just enough to enable the defending fighters to gain a height advantage over the bombers as they approached their target. After that, the fighter pilots relied on their eyesight, moonlight and searchlights (of which there were very few) to locate the enemy.

War correspondent O.D. Gallagher, an accurate eye-witness to events in Burma (as far as censorship would allow), described a night battle early in 1942, in his book *Retreat in the Far East*, published by Harrap, London, 1942:

'At last two night fighter pilots arrived from Britain. We were in front of the club [the Mingaladon Golf Club – author] on the big lawn, with some twenty Blenheim pilots, observers and gunners. We heard the distant sirens of Rangoon ... We heard the night-fighter take off (the pilot was Squadron Leader Stone, DFC) and begin its sinister, unseen prowling of the sky. The moonlight was brilliant, although there were some high, patchy, still clouds. Indeed, they seemed to add to the brilliance of the moonlight by reflecting it.

'The Japanese night formation arrived with a trembling drone that filled the air. They were at a great height but we spotted them. They circled the airfield once or twice with their customary arrogance, their usual contempt for the feeble defences. Tonight it was a pleasure to see them keep tight formation, supremely ignorant of the single, higher-pitched sound that manoeuvred around them. They could not, of course, hear the Hurricane with its old night fighter pilot in the cockpit. They certainly could not see it, any more than we could. It was perfectly blacked out – not a twinkle of light from its shielded exhausts ...

'A line of red tracer bullets pierced the sky and shot up vertically. Another – the tracers chased each other upwards until they burned out. Seconds later we heard the rat-tat-tat of Stone's guns ... Tracers shot from another point, obviously fired by the gunner of a Japanese bomber. But at that same moment a new line of red tracers poured downward from an invisible source above them. It was Stone, who had drawn their attention to a spot below the formation, then climbed all out above them and caught them unawares ...

'One of the bombers burst into fire and crashed to the ground. An immense flash as it hit, and later a heavy crump ... In the light of the following day they found the bodies and remains of five Japanese around the wreck. That was the first night fighter success from Mingaladon airfield ...'

Whatever limited success the improvised night fighters in Burma may have enjoyed, it was short-lived. The Allied forces were soon in full retreat towards the Indian border, and the air squadrons, decimated by attacks on their airfields, ceased to exist as a fighting force.

The successful campaign by the Japanese in Burma brought their army to within striking distance of the Plain of Bengal and its teeming capital city of Calcutta. But the enemy needed to regroup and strengthen his forces, and the expected invasion of India failed to materialise in 1942. It was not until December that a threat began to develop and, as a preliminary, the Japanese began to send small numbers of bombers over Calcutta in an attempt to panic the civilian population. Initially, Nos 17 and 79 Squadrons were responsible for the air defence of Calcutta; but as most of the air attacks came in at night, they achieved little result. Matters began to improve in January 1943, when No 176 Squadron formed at Dum Dum from a flight of No 89 Squadron, newly arrived from the Middle East with eight Beaufighter Is. These went into action immediately, and in less than a week they destroyed five Japanese bombers at night – three of them falling to one pilot, Flight Sergeant Pring, on 15/16 January 1943. The Japanese bombers, one observer recalled, were 'uncamouflaged and gleaming like silver fish in the moonlight.'

In May 1943 No 176 Squadron formed a second flight, armed with Hurricane IICs. These were fitted with AI Mk IV, the installation closely following that in the Defiant, and they remained operational until January 1944, when they were replaced by Beaufighter VIs. Meanwhile, a detachment of Beaufighters had been sent to Ceylon in September 1943 to counter Japanese reconnaissance aircraft. In August 1944, after a period operating from advanced bases in Burma, the squadron moved to southern India, returning to the Burma front in June 1945 and converting to Mosquitoes.

At the time of the Japanese attack in December 1941, the United States Army Air Corps, as it then was, had no specialised night fighter. In fact, scant thought had been given to night fighting at all until the late summer of 1940, when Lieutenant-General Delos C. Emmons, Commanding General of GHQ Air Corps, visited Britain and saw at first hand the threat posed by night bombers. As a result of his recommendations, the USAAC drew up preliminary specifications for a night fighter and passed them to the Northrop Company, which at that time was working on a night fighter design on behalf of the British Purchasing Commission in the USA. The design that was taking shape involved a radar-equipped aircraft with a crew of two, heavy armament and long endurance, so that incoming bombers could be intercepted long before they reached their targets.

Before negotiations could begin with the British on construction of a prototype, the USAAC stepped in and virtually commandeered the project, although British involvement was maintained for the time being; the RAF relinquished its interest when the Beaufighter began to prove its worth in the night defence role. In January 1941 Northrop received a contract for the construction of two prototypes under the designation XP-61. The aircraft would later be called the Black Widow.

In December 1941, however, the first flight of the XP-61 was still several months away, and the USAAF (which it had become in June that year) identified a pressing need for an interim night fighter. The most logical and speedy solution seemed to be to convert the Douglas A-20 bomber to the night fighting role, as the RAF had done with the Boston/Havoc, and sixty such conversions were authorised under the designation P-70. British AI Mk IV radar was installed in the nose, the antenna being mounted in the nose and wings. A ventral armament pack of four 20 mm cannon, with sixty rounds per gun, was fitted in place of the bomb bay. Deliveries of the first sixty aircraft began in April 1942 and were completed in September, most being allocated for training purposes to the 481st Night Fighter Operational Training Group at Orlando, Florida.

As crews became proficient in handling their aircraft and equipment, they were assigned to squadrons and sent overseas. The first P-70 unit to be sent to the Pacific Theatre was the 6th Night Fighter Squadron (NFS), which arrived in Hawaii in September 1942 and left a detachment there before proceeding to Guadalcanal in March 1943. The 421st NFS was sent to New Guinea. Both proved quite incapable of catching the Japanese bombers they were supposed to intercept, prompting Admiral Halsey, concerned about shipping losses caused by night attacks, to request a new night fighter, possibly the Mosquito. The request was denied, and instead five brand-new P-61As were rushed out to the 421st NFS; P-38 Lightnings were also locally modified to two-seat configuration and fitted with an SCR-540 radar mounted in a drop tank, but they were not used operationally. Instead, unmodified P-38Gs and P-38Js were used as night fighters by the 418th and 421st NFS in New Guinea and the 419th NFS on Guadalcanal, and a few successful interceptions were made. Two single-seat P-38Js fitted with APS-4 radar in Australia were used with some success by the 547th NFS, which operated in the Philippines from late 1944.

However, it was not until the Black Widow began to reach the Pacific Theatre in numbers that the USAAF had a really effective night fighter. The 421st NFS was the first to rearm with the new type, operating from Mokmer in New Guinea, and on 7 July 1944 one of its aircraft scored the first P-61 victory in the Southwest Pacific by shooting down a Mitsubishi Ki46 *Dinah* over Japen island.

The 421st, which was joined in the theatre at later dates by the 418th and 547th NFS, moved to Tacloban, Leyte, on 25 October 1944, and on 29

Above and below: *The Northrop P-61 Black Widow proved deadly in night actions over the Pacific.* (Philip Jarrett)

November the Black Widows were ordered to make a night attack on a Japanese convoy in Leyte Gulf. The convoy, consisting of two escort destroyers and a number of smaller vessels, was heading towards Ormoc to land reinforcement troops and supplies. The convoy was duly harassed throughout the night, preventing the landing of its troops, and one of the destroyers was sunk by United States surface forces at daybreak.

In the Central Pacific, the United States Seventh Air Force had three Black Widow squadrons, the 6th, 548th and 549th. In June 1944 seven P-61s of the 6th NFS moved to Aslito airstrip on Saipan, and on 27 June one of its aircraft claimed a Nakajima B5N *Kate* as probably destroyed. There was no doubt about the outcome on 6 July, when two P-61s sent two Mitsubishi G4M *Betty* bombers down in flames. Two more G4Ms were destroyed on 25/26 December by Lieutenant Dale Haberman (pilot) and Lieutenant Raymond Mooney (RO). The combat report tells the story:

> 'Scrambled from Condor Base then to Coral Base and vectored to the north of the island at altitude of 15,000 ft. Coral Base ordered figure 8 orbits since they had no Bogies in the vicinity but much Snow (fuzzy radar image) was in the area. Contact made with airborne radar at five miles. Control notified ... reported Bogies in vicinity but could give no information. Went into starboard orbit but airborne radar kept picking up Bogie which seemed to be in orbit. Chased Bogie to the north and let down to 9,000 ft when visual contact was made. Opened fire at 1,500 ft and closed to 700 ft. Bogie made violent turns and hits observed to go into wings and fuselage. Bogie was in a slight dive indicating 300 mph. Bogie last seen to roll to port in semblance of Split-S and nose straight down with fires observed coming from the right wing and engine. Visual lost as Bogie was at 6,000 ft still going straight down, apparently out of control.
>
> 'At the same time the Radar Observer called for a starboard turn as a second Bogie was out about two miles. Closed fast on second Bogie letting down to 4,500 ft where visual was made at about 2,500 ft. Closed in to 700 ft and opened fire with hits observed to spray the entire ship. Bogie exploded with its debris hitting P-61 with damage to left cowling. Bogie went down in flames and was seen to hit the water ...'

Two more Black Widow squadrons, the 548th and 549th, arrived in the Pacific on 7 and 24 March 1945 respectively, being assigned to the Seventh Air Force on Iwo Jima. The 548th NFS soon moved up to Ie Shima to provide forward air defence and also to carry out night intruder operations over Kyushu, scoring five kills during these operations; the 549th NFS remained on Iwo Jima, sending detachments to Saipan and Guam as required.

There were two Black Widow squadrons in the China–Burma–India (CBI) Theatre. The first was the 426th NFS, which was activated on 1 January 1944 at Hammer Field, California, and arrived at Chengtu, China, under Fourteenth Air Force command on 5 November 1944. It operated from a number of bases thereafter, mostly in the night ground-attack role, as there was virtually no air opposition. The other was the 427th NFS, which

was activated on 1 February 1944 and deployed to Myitkyina, Burma, in December by way of Italy and India. During the next few months, under the command of the Tenth and later the Fourteenth Air Force, the 427th NFS flew seventy-three defensive patrols without encountering a single enemy aircraft and so its aircraft were modified to carry bombs and rockets for intruder operations against Japanese troop concentrations and supply dumps. A detachment at Kunming, China, carried out similar work.

The hardest-worked P-61 squadron in the Pacific, however, remained the 418th, which saw considerable action against enemy intruders from successive bases in New Guinea, the Schouten Islands, Leyte, Mindoro and Okinawa. A combat report by Lieutenant Bertram C. Tompkins, dated 27 January 1945, describes one of its actions. The squadron was then based on Mindoro.

> 'Approximately 1½ hours after becoming airborne the GCI controller vectored me onto a Bogey approaching from the north-west. Flying Officer Wertin made radar contact with Bogey at 0010 at a distance of six miles and altitude of 10,000 ft on heading of 280 degrees. He directed me to 2,000 ft directly behind and below Bogey and I obtained a visual and identified it as a *Tony* (Kawasaki Ki-61). I closed to 150 ft and fired one short burst. The *Tony* exploded and fell burning into the water approximately twenty miles west of base. No evasive action was used by enemy aircraft.
>
> 'Immediately GCI vectored me onto second Bogey, which was twenty miles south-east of me. Flying Officer Wertin made radar contact at six miles and directed me to 3,000 ft directly behind and slightly below the Bogey, where I got a visual. I closed to 300 ft and fired one burst, and enemy aircraft exploded and fell to the water burning. Kill was made approximately five miles west of Mindoro coast. Enemy Aircraft was identified as a *Tony*. Violent evasive action was used.'

Early night fighting in the USN, like its land-based counterpart, was also an improvised business. It had its beginnings in November 1943, when six heavy and five light carriers of the USN's Task Force 50 opened the campaign to capture the Gilbert Islands with a two-day series of strikes on Japanese airfields and installations in support of American landings on Tarawa and Makin Atolls. The Task Force Commander, Rear-Admiral Pownall, was concerned about Japanese night attacks on his ships, and invited ideas on how they might be protected.

Lieutenant-Commander Edward H. (Butch) O'Hare, commanding Air Group 6 on the carrier USS *Enterprise*, and some of his fellow pilots came up with a possible answer. The *Enterprise* had one of the new radar-equipped Grumman TBF-1C

Close-up of the AN/APS-6 radar pod on the starboard wing of a Grumman F6F-3N Hellcat. (Philip Jarrett)

Avengers, and the plan was to form an interception team with this aircraft and two Hellcat fighters. The Hellcats, each of which would be flown by a pilot with night experience, would form up on the Avenger; the formation would be vectored to the vicinity of an enemy contact by the carrier's Fighter Director and the Avenger's radar would then take over, bringing the fighters to within visual range of the target.

The first sortie, on 24/25 November, did not result in any intercepts, but on 26/27 the trio got in amongst a formation of G4M bombers and caused havoc. The Avenger was the aircraft that scored, its pilot and gunner accounting for two of the *Betty*s; the Wildcats also attacked separate targets, with the result that the enemy raid was severely disrupted. 'Butch' O'Hare went missing during this engagement and was never seen again.

From this point onwards *Enterprise* began to specialise in night operations, both offensive and defensive. On 17/18 February 1944, during a heavy assault by US carrier aircraft on the island of Truk, twelve radar-equipped TBF-1Cs of VT-10 from *Enterprise* carried out the first night bombing attack in the history of US carrier aviation, making a low-level raid on the harbour and scoring several direct hits on shipping.

For this campaign, night fighter detachments of

VF(N)-76 and VF(N)-101, armed with F6F-3 Hellcats and F4U-2 Corsairs equipped with AI radar, were assigned to five carriers, and although they were not widely used they were occasionally vectored against enemy night raiders. The first success by a radar-equipped Corsair had in fact been registered on 31 October 1943, when Lieutenant H.D. O'Neil of VF(N)-75 operating from Munda, New Georgia, destroyed a *Betty* during a night attack off Vella Lavella, ground-based fighter direction being provided by Major T.E. Hicks and T/Sgt Gleason of VMF(N)-513.

Eighteen F6F-3E Hellcat night fighters were built, an AN/APS-4 AI radar being fitted into a radome on the starboard wing. The -3N, 150 of which were built, used the improved AN/APS-6 radar. The most numerous of the Hellcat night fighter variants was the F6F-5N, which also had the AN/APS-6; 1,435 were produced in total. Two Royal Navy squadrons, Nos 891 and 892, were equipped with F6F-5Ns under the designation Hellcat IIs.

Like the F6F-3N Hellcat, the Vought F4U-2 Corsair was developed, or rather modified, in response to the need to keep Japanese night intruders at bay. Twelve F4U-2s were converted from F4U-1s drawn from stock and assigned to two units, VF(N)-101 on the USS *Essex* and VF(N)-75

A Grumman Hellcat NFII of the Fleet Air Arm, pictured in March 1945. (Philip Jarrett)

The F4U Corsair night fighter was used by US Marine Corps squadrons in the Pacific, and later in Korea. (Philip Jarrett)

at Munda. Other night fighter versions of the Corsair to serve in the Pacific were the F4U-4E with the AN/APS-4 radar, and the -4N with the AN/APS-6.

On 14 August 1945, the day before the Japanese surrender, a United States Marine Corps night fighter squadron arrived at the Pacific battlefront. This was VMF(N)-533, armed with the potent twin-engined Grumman F7F-2N Tigercat. An aircraft in which the USN had shown little interest, the Tigercat was deployed too late to see action in World War II; its chance would come later, in Korea.

CHAPTER ELEVEN

NIGHT DEFENCE OF JAPAN, 1944–45

On the night of 9/10 March, 1945, B-29s (Superfortresses) of the USAAF's 21st Bomber Command, operating from bases in the Marianas, launched their first major incendiary attack on Japan. The target was Tokyo. At 23.00 a small force of B-29 pathfinder aircraft dropped clusters of 70 lb M47 napalm bombs on an aiming point at the centre of a rectangle measuring three miles by four. During the next three hours the pathfinders were followed by 279 more B-29s, routed individually to the target and stripped of weapons and armour plating to enable them to carry an enhanced load of 500 lb M69 oil-bomb clusters. Each cluster consisted of sixty 6 lb jellied-oil bombs, released from the main canister at 2,000 feet by a time fuse.

The raid and its catastrophic results were witnessed by Major David H. James, a British intelligence officer in the PoW camp at Omori, just over seven miles south of the Imperial Palace in Tokyo. In his book *The Rise and Fall of the Japanese Empire* he subsequently wrote:

> 'The alert came at 11pm and soon after the alert the air-raid warnings were being sounded all over Tokyo. About midnight there was the drone of aircraft as the first wave came in from the north-east. They were travelling in two streams – from north-east to south-west and from north-west to south-east.
>
> 'Ground defence came into action as the first fires appeared at Oji-ku ... almost at the same time as the leading planes crossed overhead. Planes were flying very low. A strong wind was fanning the fires as wave after wave came over and dropped "baskets" of fresh incendiaries over the industrial districts north and east of the Imperial Palace and the factory area to the south-west, bordering Tokyo Bay. Wind direction was north to south. Wave followed wave; they destroyed and then went on into the darkness beyond the flames, their bodies glistening as the beams of searchlights followed them until they were lost to sight in cloud.'

The B-29 bomb aimers in the last waves found their task made difficult by the dense clouds of smoke that billowed over the capital and by the tremendous upcurrents of hot air bursting from the inferno below. There was considerable anti-aircraft fire; nine B-29s were destroyed over the city, and five others were so badly damaged that they had to ditch in the sea; all their crews were picked up safely. Forty-two other bombers sustained varying degrees of flak damage. Seventy-six fighters were sighted and forty attacks were reported, but none of these inflicted any damage.

The 1,667 tons of incendiaries dropped by the B-29s caused a glow in the sky that could be seen 150 miles away. The following morning, photographs brought back by high-flying B-29 reconnaissance aircraft revealed that 15.8 square miles of Tokyo had been razed to the ground, and that twenty-two major industrial targets had been destroyed. Firestorms had swept through a quarter of the city's built-up areas, destroying 267,000 buildings and rendering 1,008,000 people homeless. The official Japanese casualty figures gave the number of dead as 83,793, with 102,000 injured; in fact the total was probably higher. After the war, an official told Allied investigators:

> 'People were unable to escape. They were found later piled upon the bridges, roads and in the canals, 80,000 dead and twice that many injured. We were instructed to report on actual conditions. Most of us were unable to do this because of horrifying conditions beyond imagination.'

From his vantage point at Omori, Major James observed the horrific consequences of the raid after daybreak.

> 'All day an acrid smell filled our nostrils ... when the tide lapped our fences it cast up hundreds of charred bodies. We stared through the knot-holes at the men, women and children sprawled in the mud or jammed against the logs from the demolished timber-yards – men, women and children, the remains of human beings left there to rot alongside others who floated in after other raids on the capital.'

The Tokyo raid served to underline the painful inadequacy of the Japanese defences. The early warning system was hopelessly outdated by western standards, and although Tokyo's fire service was the

Above and below: *The Kawasaki Ki-45* Toryu *was a formidable night fighter, having upward-firing cannon mounted in the fuselage, but like all Japanese night fighters it had no AI radar.* (Philip Jarrett)

best in Japan it was completely unable to cope with the outbreak of so many large fires over so wide an area. The result was that the inferno got out of hand within half an hour of the start of the raid. The anti-aircraft batteries were not radar-directed; had it been otherwise, they might have inflicted far more damage on the attackers.

The lack of AI radar also handicapped the Japanese night fighter force. The only operational night fighter available to the Japanese Army was the Kawasaki Ki-45 Toryu, known to the Allies by the codename *Nick*. With its armament of two 20 mm cannon and one 7.92 mm machine-gun it was a for-midable enough interceptor, but it was not equipped with AI radar, and although it claimed successes against the B-29 night raiders the burden of night home defence came to be borne increas-ingly by single-engined day fighter types, using tactics similar to the German *Wilde Sau*.

The ordeal of Japan's cities continued. On 12/13 March it was the turn of Nagoya, the centre of Japan's aircraft industry. Shortly after midnight industrial areas of the city were marked by napalm-carrying B-29 Pathfinders, and during the next three-and-a-half hours 285 bombers unloaded 1,790 tons of incendiaries on and around the aiming points. Nagoya, however, was spared the catastro-phe that had engulfed Tokyo. The city's fire brigade had had the foresight to space firebreaks at key points, the water supply was plentiful, and above all there was only a light wind to fan the flames. On this occasion too the bombers released their M69 clusters at intervals of 100 feet instead of 50 feet as had been the case in the Tokyo raid, with the result that the incendiaries had been too widely spaced to build up dangerous firestorms. Nevertheless, although only two square miles of the city were dev-astated, eighteen major industrial plants were destroyed or badly damaged. All the B-29s returned to base; twenty suffered damage, two of them in fighter attacks.

Two nights later the Superfortresses visited Osaka, the second largest city in Japan. Two hundred and seventy-four B-29s made a radar-directed attack on this target through eight-tenths cloud, razing over eight square miles with 1,732 tons of fire bombs. The enemy death toll was 3,988, with a further 9,000 people injured; while 119 fac-tories and 135,000 houses were wiped out. The B-29 crews reported forty attacks by enemy fight-ers; two bombers failed to return and thirteen more were damaged.

On 17 March, 21st Bomber Command's effort was switched to Kobe, a vital enemy port. Once again the attack was radar directed. To achieve a better bombing concentration the aiming points were grouped in a confined area and the duration of the raid was reduced. This time, as supplies of M47

napalm and M69 oil bombs were running low in the Marianas, the B-29s carried M17A1s, magnesium thermite incendiary clusters containing 110 four-pound bombs. The Kobe raid was the largest to date, with 307 Superfortresses taking part. In the space of just over two hours they dropped 2,355 tons of incendiaries on the target, totally destroying an area of 2.9 square miles. The Kawasaki shipyards were heavily damaged, while 500 industrial instal-lations were destroyed and 162 damaged. The con-flagration destroyed 66,000 houses, making a quarter of a million people homeless; 2,669 were killed and 11,289 injured. Although enemy fighters made ninety-three reported attacks on the raiding force, no B-29s were lost.

On 7 April 1945 21st Bomber Command, now escorted by long-range P-51 Mustang fighters, turned its major effort to a daylight offensive against Japan's principal aero-engine plants. Night attacks continued, however, and on 13/14 April the Americans launched another incendiary attack on Tokyo in which 327 B-29s dropped 2,139 tons of incendiaries, wiping out 11.4 square miles of the city. Vast explosions rocked the city as the fires touched off the contents of munitions factories and arsenals. Two nights later 303 more B-29s bombed Tokyo Baty, Kawasaki and Yokohama, destroying over a quarter of a million buildings.

By mid-May 1945 four B-29 wings (the 58th, 73rd, 313th and 314th) were committed to the air offensive against Japan, and on 14 May all four took part in a daylight attack on Nagoya. The same target was attacked again on 16/17 May, when 475 B-29s dropped 3,609 tons of incendiaries on the docks area. Each aircraft in the main force carried eight tons of M50 magnesium bombs. The destruc-tion amounted to 3.8 square miles and included one of Mitsubishi's aircraft factories. It was the last time that devastated Nagoya was subjected to an aerial attack.

On 23 May, 21st Bomber Command launched its biggest attack so far. Late in the afternoon 562 Superfortresses took off from their bases in the Marianas, arriving over Tokyo shortly after mid-night. Attacking through intense flak between 8,000 and 15,000 feet, they unloaded over 3,600 tons of napalm and oil bombs through nine-tenths cloud, smoke and the glare of searchlights, razing 5.3 square miles of the city. Four B-29s were shot down and sixty-nine damaged, all of them by anti-aircraft fire.

Two nights later Tokyo was subjected to its most fearful holocaust yet. A total of 502 aircraft dropped 3,262 tons of incendiaries on the enemy capital; vast firestorms raged through its shattered streets, destroying an area of 16.8 square miles. The Americans, however, did not have things all their own way. The flak was the heaviest ever encountered by 21st Bomber Command, and the Japanese fighters were up in force; twenty-six B-29s failed to return and 100 more were damaged, many of them severely.

On 17/18 June, following a series of daylight precision attacks on targets in Japan's major cities, the weight of the strategic offensive was switched to Japan's smaller industrial towns. Between that night and the end of the war 21st Bomber Command flew 8,014 sorties against these targets, dropping 54,184 tons of incendiaries. Fifty-seven towns were attacked, thirty-five of them on nine nights in July, when the bombers destroyed a total area of 35.4 square miles.

The massive air attacks continued, even after the dropping of the two atomic bombs on Hiroshima and Nagasaki on 6 and 9 August. On 14 August 449 Superfortresses, escorted by 186 Mustangs and Thunderbolts, struck at the last remaining targets – the naval arsenal at Hikari, the Osaka Army Arsenal, the Marifu marshalling yards near Hiroshima and the Nippon Oil Co. plant at Atika. That night the B-29s carried out a heavy incendiary raid on Kumagaya and Isezaki, north-west of Tokyo.

Even before this raid took place the Japanese had decided to accept the Allies' unconditional surrender terms. The last hours were described by Japanese fighter ace Saburo Sakai, in his book *Samurai*.

'Japan was about to *surrender*.

'"Sakai." I looked up. "Saburo, it ... it is just about the end now." Kawachi spoke. "We have very little time left. Let us make one more flight together, one last flight." He kicked the ground idly with his foot. "We just can't quit like this," he protested. "We have to draw blood once more."

'I nodded. He was right. We told the maintenance men to move our two Zeros out to the runway, to prepare them for flight. We knew that the Superfortresses would bomb tonight. The weather forecast appeared promising, and there were so many bombers overhead every evening that B-29s could be intercepted almost anywhere. For a long time they had flown over Oppama without opposition, using the field for a landmark. They would not expect fighters.

'Kawachi and I kept our plans strictly to ourselves, not even telling the other pilots ... The afternoon passed and we remained seated, almost invisible in the darkness. Shortly after midnight the tower radio spluttered. "Alert. Alert. A B-29 formation is now approaching the Yokosuka-Tokyo area."

'We jumped to our feet and ran across the field to our planes. The air base lay in blackness, not a light showing. There was just enough light from the stars to enable us to make our way. When we reached the Zeros, we discovered that we were not the only pilots determined to go up for a

last mission. At least eight other fighters were lined up at the edge of the runway, fuelled and armed.

'The moment we were airborne, I swung in close to Kawachi's fighter and took up a position off his wing. Eight other Zeros were in the air with us, forming into two flights behind our planes. We climbed steadily, then circled at 10,000 feet over Tokyo Bay.

'Kawachi's fighter banked abruptly and pulled away to the east. I flew with him, the two flights close behind. For a few moments I failed to see any other planes in the air. Then Kawachi's cannon started firing, and I made out the big bomber flying northward. I had him now, clear in my sights. I pulled up almost alongside Kawachi's plane and opened fire. We each had four cannon now, and we would need every weapon against the tremendous airplane. I had never seen anything so huge! As I swung around after completing my firing pass, I saw the eight other fighters storming the Superfortress. They appeared like tiny gnats milling round a tremendous bull. How could we hope to shoot down an airplane of such incredible size?

'I came in again, climbing and sending my fire into the B-29's underside. The counterfire was terrible. Tracers spilled into the air from the multiple turrets of the B-29, and I felt the Zero shudder several times as the enemy gunners found their mark. We ignored the bomber's guns and kept pressing home the attack. The Superfortress turned and headed south. Apparently we had damaged the big plane, and now he was running for home. I clung to Kawachi and slammed the engine on overboost. The other eight fighters were already lost far behind us, and it was doubtful that we could keep up with the bomber. It possessed remarkable speed and was, in fact, faster than the Zero I had flown at Lae.

'Kawachi, however, had no intention of losing the big plane in the dark. He cut inside the B-29's wide turn and led me down in a shallow diving attack. This time we had a clear shot, and both Kawachi and I kept the triggers down, watching the tracers and shells ripping into the glass along the bomber's nose. We had him! Suddenly, the Superfortress's speed fell off and the pilot dropped the airplane down for a long dive. We came around in a tight turn, firing steadily in short bursts, pouring the cannon shells into the crippled plane.

'The great bomber descended quickly. I saw no fire or smoke. There was no visible damage, but the airplane continued to lose altitude steadily, dropping towards the ocean. We kept after the fleeing plane. O Shima island suddenly loomed up out of the darkness. We were fifty miles south of Yokosuka.

'We pulled up out of our dives, and climbed to 1,500 feet. A volcano on the island reared 1,000 feet above the water, and we dared not risk a collision in the blackness. I could make out the bomber faintly as it dropped. Presently it ditched with a splash of white foam in the ocean, several miles off O Shima's southern coastline. In less than a minute the B-29 disappeared beneath the water.

'Back at the airfield, we learned that at least three cities had been gutted during the night. The fires were still

Above and below: *The Yokosuka P1Y1 Ginga was a superb aircraft as a fast bomber, but an attempt to convert it into a night fighter proved disappointing.* (Philip Jarrett)

burning fiercely, unchecked, sweeping before the wind.

'The war was to end less than twelve hours later ...'

In summary, it is clear that the dwindling Japanese fighter force never had any real hope of halting the onslaught by the B-29 night bombers. But it might have inflicted considerably more damage on them, had it not been for a wrong decision made in the closing months of 1944.

The subject of the decision was the Yokosuka P1Y1 Ginga (Milky Way) fast twin-engined bomber. Known by the Allied code-name *Frances*, it was perhaps the nearest Japanese equivalent of the de Havilland Mosquito and the Ju 88. During its flight test programme, this aircraft, which had a top speed of 340 mph, attracted the attention of Japanese Navy pilots, who were attempting to create a night fighter force to counter expected bombing attacks. The Kawanishi company was instructed to produce a night fighter variant under the designation P1Y2-S; this was armed with a pair of 20 mm cannon, mounted obliquely in the upper fuselage, and retained the bomb bay of the Ginga for intruder operations. First flown in June 1944, the P1Y2-S went into production as the Navy Night Fighter Kyokko (Aurora), but its performance at altitude proved disappointing and the ninety-six examples built had their 20 mm cannon removed and reverted to the bomber role.

The Japanese had no means of knowing that most of the devastating B-29 attacks would be made from medium and low level, where the Kyokko might have shown its true potential.

CHAPTER TWELVE

POST-WAR DEVELOPMENTS, 1945–50

The United States

In the late summer of 1943, North American Aviation Inc began design work on an aircraft to meet a USAAF requirement for a twin-engined, long-range escort fighter for service in the Pacific Theatre. Part of the specification was that the aircraft should have two pilots to ease the strain of long over-water flights.

North American's simple solution was to join two P-51H Mustang fuselages by means of a new wing centre section, so creating a two-seat, twin-engined aircraft with greatly enhanced long-range performance. The USAAF liked the concept and ordered 500 examples of the production variant, designated P-82B, but with the sudden ending of the war this was cut back to just twenty examples for service

with the Air Defense Command. Eighteen were completed as P-82Bs, but the tenth and eleventh production aircraft were completed as P-82C and P-82D Twin Mustang night fighters for evaluation as replacements for the Northrop P-61 Black Widow in this role. The P-82C (44-65169) was fitted with an SCR720 AI radar in a large central pod, while the P-82D (44-65170) carried the APS-4. The radar operator sat in the right-hand cockpit at his AI console, the radar aerials being installed under the outer wing sections.

Trials with the two aircraft showed that the night fighter variant of the Twin Mustang would be more than adequate as a P-61 replacement, and in March 1946 orders were placed for an additional 250 aircraft. In the event, however, the first 100 were completed as escort and ground-attack

The North American F-82 Twin Mustang filled a crucial post-war night and all-weather fighter gap for the USAF. (Author)

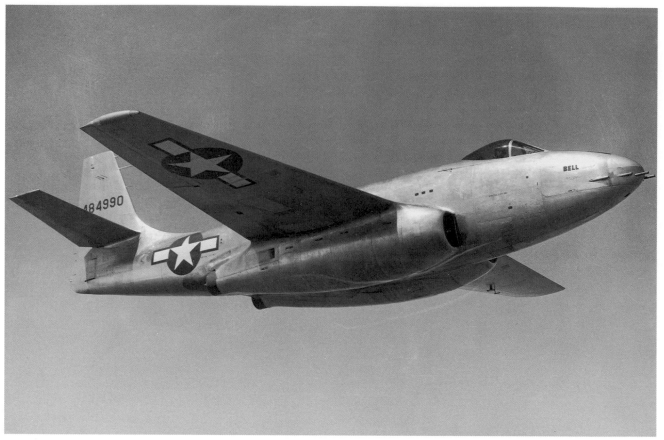

The Bell XP-83 was proposed to meet a specification for a jet-propelled night fighter for the USAF, but it was outclassed by later designs. (Author)

fighters for the newly-established Strategic Air Command, which came into existence on 21 March 1946. Only ninety-one were completed as F-82F night fighters (the 'P' prefix now having been dropped by the USAF) with APS-4 radar, and fifty-nine as F-82Gs with the SCR-270. These aircraft, which were also fitted with APN-1 radar altimeters and APS-13 tail warning radars, equipped the 51st Fighter Interceptor Group (16th, 25th and 26th Squadrons), the 52nd All-Weather Fighter Group (2nd and 5th Squadrons), the 325th All-Weather Fighter Group (317th, 318th and 319th Squadrons), and the 84th Reserve Fighter Group (496th, 497th and 498th Squadrons).

In the Far East, Twin Mustangs were also assigned to the 4th Fighter Squadron (All-Weather) at Naha on Okinawa, the 68th Fighter Squadron (All-Weather) at Itazuke on Kyushu, and the 339th Fighter Squadron (All-Weather) at Yokota, near Tokyo. As we shall see in the next chapter, the Twin Mustangs were to play a vital part in the early, critical phase of the Korean War.

The Twin Mustang, however, was in reality an interim aircraft, pending the development of a suitable jet-propelled night fighter. The USAF issued a specification for such an aircraft in May 1946; among possible early candidates was the Bell XP-83, which began life as a heavy single-seat long-range fighter and flew for the first time on 25 February 1945, powered by two General Electric J33-GE-5 turbojets. Two prototypes were built and extensively tested, their performance figures including a maximum speed of 525 mph at 45,000 feet, together with a range of 1,730 miles at 30,000 feet. The proposed armament for the XP-83 was six 0.5 in machine-guns, with either four 20 mm or four 37 mm cannon as alternatives. The XP-83's airframe had the potential for conversion to a two-seat configuration and the inclusion of AI radar, but there would have been a substantial weight penalty and the existing engines were not powerful enough. This, together with the fact that the XP-83 was outclassed by later designs, led to development being abandoned.

Meanwhile, three American aircraft companies, Curtiss, Northrop and Lockheed, were busy working up designs to meet the USAF requirement, which called for a two-seat radar-equipped aircraft armed with either cannon or machine-guns and possessing a top speed of at least 600 mph and a ceiling of 40,000 feet.

The design submitted by the Airplane Division of the Curtiss-Wright Corporation, the XP-87, was the first multi-seat jet combat aircraft specifically designed for the radar intercept role at night. Developed from an earlier wartime project, the XA-43 attack aircraft, it was powered by four Westinghouse XJ34-WE-7 turbojets, installed in

This page and following page: *The Northrop F-89 Scorpion was the mainstay of USAF Air Defense Command during most of the 1950s.* (Philip Jarrett)

pairs in two nacelles, and was armed with four 20 mm cannon. Provision was also made to install 0.5 in machine guns in a dorsal turret, but this was never fitted. The XP-87 prototype (49-59600) flew for the first time on 5 March 1948, and work began on a second aircraft, the XP-87A, which was intended to have two General Electric J47-GE-15 engines. The first aircraft was known as the Nighthawk, the second as the Blackhawk. However, the second machine never flew, and an order for eighty-eight J47-powered production aircraft was cancelled to release funds for the development of two more promising designs that were eventually to give the USAF a truly potent night/all-weather capability, the Lockheed F-94C Starfire and the Northrop F-89 Scorpion. The XP-87 passed into aviation history as the last combat aircraft produced by Curtiss-Wright.

The first of two Northrop XF-89 prototypes flew on 16 August 1948, and after USAF evaluation Northrop received an order for an initial batch of forty-eight production aircraft. The first of these flew late in 1950 and deliveries to the United States Air Force Air Defense Command began soon afterwards, the first Scorpion squadrons being assigned to Arctic defence zones such as Alaska, Iceland and Greenland. The first production model of the Scorpion, the F-89A, was powered by two Allison J35-A-21 turbojets with reheat and carried a nose armament of six 20 mm cannon. The F-89B and F-89C were progressive developments with uprated

Allison engines, while the F-89D had its cannon deleted and carried an armament of 104 folding-fin aircraft rockets (FFAR) in wingtip pods. Additional fuel tanks under the wings gave an eleven per cent range increase over the F-89C and the aircraft was fitted with an automatic fire control system. The F-89H, which followed the F-89D into production, was armed with six Hughes GAR-1 Falcon missiles and forty-two FFAR, and could also carry the MB-1 Genie nuclear AAM. The Falcons were housed in the wingtip pods and were extended prior to firing. The F-89H's armament was fired automatically, a sighting radar and fire control computer forming a fully integrated attack system.

The other night/all-weather design conceived in the 1940s, the Lockheed F-94 Starfire, was developed from the T-33A trainer, two production T-33 airframes being converted as YF-94s. The first of these flew on 16 April 1949, and four months later the USAF placed contracts for seventeen F-94A-1-LO and ninety-two F-94A-5-LO fighters, together with one YF-94B – the latter having centrally-mounted wingtip tanks instead of underslung tanks.

The F-94A, which incorporated seventy-five per cent of the components used in the T-33 and F-80 Shooting Star, had 940 lb of radar equipment in the nose and an armament of four 0.50 in Colt-Browning machine-guns. The aircraft was powered by an Allison J33-A-33 centrifugal-type turbojet with reheat. F-94As were fitted with 195 imp gal Fletcher wingtip tanks. The F-94A went into

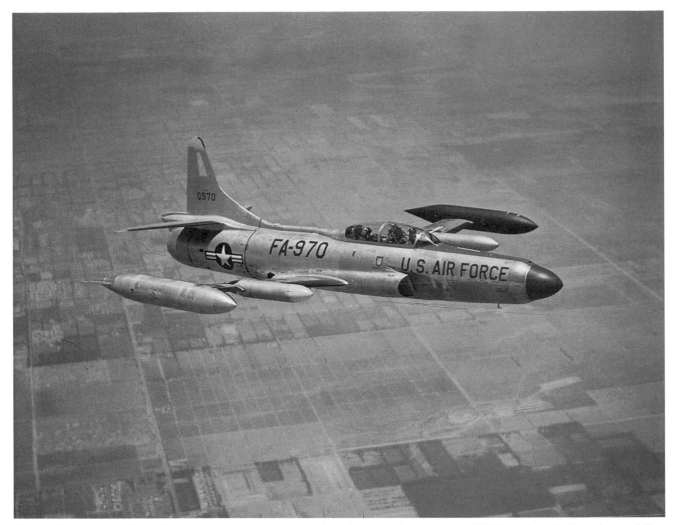

The Lockheed F-94 Starfire, with its powerful missile armament, brought a new dimension to the USAF's night and all-weather capability. (Philip Jarrett)

production in 1949; 200 were built, the first entering service in June 1950 with the 319th All-Weather Fighter Squadron.

The YF-94B was converted from the nineteenth F-94A in 1950, and 357 F-94Bs were built. Apart from the revised wingtip tanks, they differed from the F-94A mainly in having a modified hydraulics system and avionics, including a Sperry Zero-Reader flight recorder. The next variant, the F-94C, differed so extensively from its predecessors that it was originally known as the YF-97A. This designation remained in force from the aircraft's maiden flight on 16 January 1950 until 12 September that year, when the designation YF-94C was officially adopted.

The F-94C was fitted with an afterburning Pratt & Whitney J48-P-5, and other changes included an increase in wing dihedral and a reduction in thickness/chord ratio from thirteen to ten per cent, the introduction of a swept tailplane, and the replacement of the gun armament by twenty-four unguided FFAR in a ring of tubes around the nose-cone. Later, provision was made for a further twenty-four rockets in wing pods. The F-94C carried 1,200 lb of electronics, and two 1,000 lb

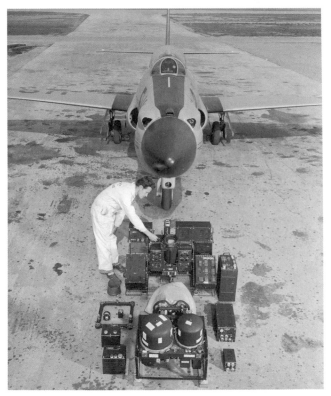

The 'black boxes' that brought the F-94 to its target; the system had as many different parts as 200 TV sets. (Philip Jarrett)

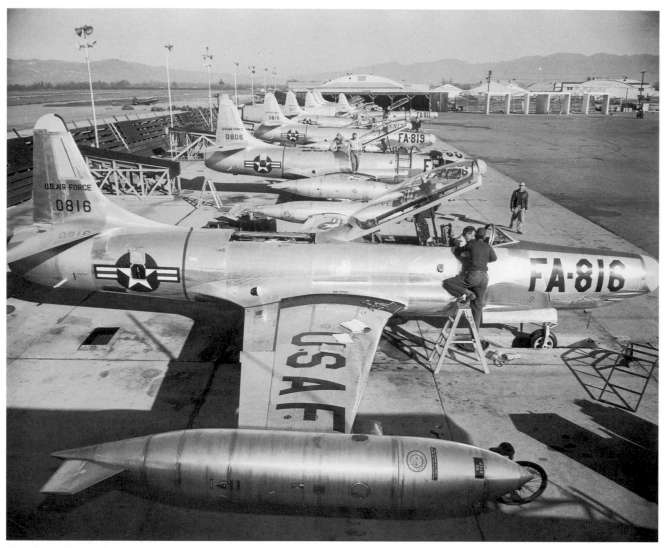

F-94C Starfires being made ready for delivery to the US Air Defense Command. (Philip Jarrett)

thrust RATOG (rocket assisted take-off gear) packs could be fitted under the fuselage. Total production of the F-94C came to 387 aircraft before the series was completed in 1954.

Great Britain

In January 1946 six squadrons – Nos 23, 25, 29, 85, 141 and 264 – were responsible for the night defence of Britain. All of them were armed, or in the process of rearming, with the de Havilland Mosquito NF36. With the advent of jet aircraft, it was apparent that the Mosquito needed to be urgently replaced, and in December 1946 the Air Staff issued Operational Requirement OR227, calling for a jet-propelled, twin-engined, two-seat night and all-weather fighter. (Another requirement, OR228, covered a replacement for the Gloster Meteor in the day fighter role; it would eventually be met by the Hawker Hunter).

In January 1947 OR227 crystallised into Specification F44/66, modified to F4/48 a year or

so later, but none of the early proposals submitted satisfied the requirement, so the Gloster Aircraft Company was asked to investigate the possibility of developing a night/all-weather version of the Meteor to bridge the gap. Gloster had already carried out radar installation trials on Meteor F3 and F4 aircraft in conjunction with the Telecommunications Research Establishment, and the Company now looked to the two-seat Meteor T7 airframe as a suitable vehicle for adaptation to night fighter configuration.

Specification F24/48 was issued and written around the Gloster aircraft, and the fourth production Meteor T7 was converted as an aerodynamic prototype, flying in October 1949. The first true prototype of the Meteor NF11, as the night fighter variant was designated, flew on 31 May 1950. The aircraft featured the T7's tandem cockpit, the F8's tail unit and long-span wings similar to those of the PR10 high-altitude photo-reconnaissance version, and was fitted with a lengthened di-electric nose containing the scanner for the AI Mk X radar. This equipment, of American origin (it was the SCR720

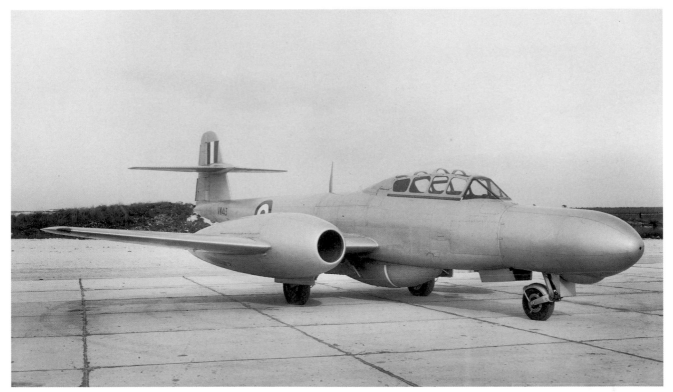

The Meteor NF11 prototype was based on the T7 trainer airframe, with the addition of a Mk 8 tail unit. (Philip Jarrett)

This plan view of the Meteor NF11 clearly shows the 20 mm cannon mounted in the outer wing panels. (Philip Jarrett)

The de Havilland Sea Hornet NF Mk 21 prototype, PX230. The aircraft was used by No 809 Squadron until 1954, when it was replaced by the Sea Venom. (Philip Jarrett)

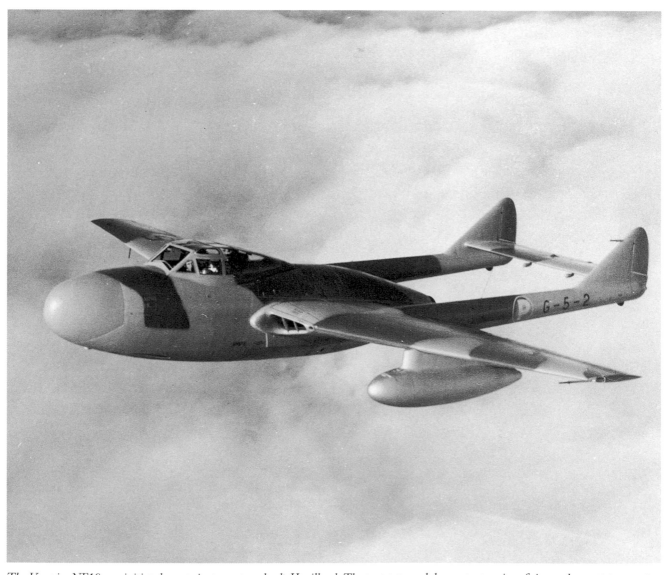

The Vampire NF10 was initiated as a private venture by de Havilland. The prototype and demonstrator aircraft is seen here. (Philip Jarrett)

set carried by the Black Widow) was the same as that fitted in the Mosquito NF36; it had proved very effective in the closing stages of World War II, but by 1950 its performance was rapidly degrading. Its use was dictated by the failure of the British Mk IXc, developed by TRE at Malvern; far better AI equipment was being produced by the American company, Westinghouse, but although it would be ordered later for use in later marks of Meteor no attempt to purchase it was made at this stage.

As Gloster was fully occupied in building the Meteor F8 day fighter, and in working on the prototype of the aircraft that would eventually meet F4/48 – the GA5, later to be called the Javelin – it was decided to transfer responsibility for NF11 production to Armstrong Whitworth. The first production Meteor NF11 (WD585) was delivered to No 29 Squadron at Tangmere in August 1951; the operational career of the NF11 and the follow-on Meteor night fighter marks will be examined in chapter fourteen.

De Havilland produced two night fighter types in the late 1940s. The first was the Sea Hornet NF21, developed in 1946 to meet an urgent need for a high-performance night fighter for the Royal Navy. After lengthy trials this variant entered service with No 809 Squadron at Culdrose in January 1949, the unit embarking on HMS *Vengeance* in May 1951. The Sea Hornet NF21 was used by 809 Squadron until 1954, when it was replaced by the Sea Venom.

The other de Havilland night fighter type was the Vampire NF10, which served with both the RAF and the Italian Air Force. The NF10 entered service with Nos 23, 25 and 151 Squadrons, which

used it for a short period before it was replaced by other types.

The Soviet Union

During World War II, the Soviet Air Force had no aircraft designed specifically for night fighting. During the aerial battles that took place over Moscow and Leningrad in 1941, and later over Stalingrad, some converted Pe-2 dive bombers were used in the night fighter role, as was a heavily-armed interceptor variant, the Pe-3, but the Russians had no AI equipment and had to depend on visual interception techniques.

It was not until 1948 that the Russians, with the help of German technology, succeeded in developing a viable AI radar known as *Izumrud* (Emerald), which was intended to equip a new generation of night and all-weather fighter aircraft. Pavel Sukhoi, whose Su-9 twin-jet fighter prototype had flown in 1946, now came up with the Su-15, also known as the *Samolyot* (aircraft) P. Powered by two RD-45 (Rolls-Royce Nene) turbojets, the aircraft had a mid-mounted wing with a leading-edge sweep of thirty-seven degrees, the twin engines being mounted one above the other in a deep centre fuselage, and exhausting below the fuselage aft of the wing trailing edge. The AI scanner was housed in a small radome situated above the nose air intake, and armament was two 37 mm cannon, one mounted on either side of the nose. With a loaded weight of 23,000 lb the Su-15 was a very heavy aircraft; nevertheless, its designers estimated that it would have a maximum speed of 641 mph, a service

The twin-engined Suckhoi Su-15, also known as the Samolyot-P, was fitted with Izumrud *(Emerald) AI radar. The sole prototype was destroyed during flight testing.* (Author)

Mikoyan's I-320(R) all-weather fighter was based on the MiG-15. Its flight characteristics were poor and it was abandoned. (via Author)

ceiling of 46,000 feet, and the ability to reach 32,800 feet in six and a half minutes.

These figures were never proven, because the Su-15 disintegrated following severe vibration on an early high-speed run, the pilot ejecting, and no further prototypes were built.

The other main contenders in the race to produce a Russian night fighter were Mikoyan, Lavochkin and and Yakovlev. Mikoyan's design, the single-seat I-320(R), was powered by two Klimov VK-1 turbojets and first flew in 1949; it was based on the MiG-15, but the engine installation resulted in a bulky, ungainly aircraft with poor handling characteristics and even worse visibility for the pilot, whose forward view was badly obscured by the long nose and radome. Lavochkin's design, the La-200A, was a better proposition from several points of view, but suffered from the same engine arrangement as the I-320(R). In both cases, the VK-1 engines were fed via a common nose air intake, but in the La-200A they were installed in tandem, the first exhausting under the fuselage and the second under the tail, and this necessitated some complex ducting that resulted in an inordinately large fuselage. A central air intake cone housed the La-200A's *Izumrud* radar and the fighter

The La-200B was designed to the same requirement as the Yak-25, to which it proved inferior. With its massive radome, it was one of the ugliest fighter aircraft ever built. (via Author)

was a two-seater, the pilot and radar observer seated side by side. The La-200A had a fuselage-mounted undercarriage and carried an armament of three 37 mm cannon, which contributed to the high all-up weight of 22,873 lb. Like the I-320(R), the La-200A flew in 1949, and during trials reached a maximum speed of 660 mph at 16,400 feet; the service ceiling was 59,700 feet. Neither aircraft underwent extensive operational trials, because in 1950 a developed, lighter version of the *Izumrud* AI radar was successfully installed in a two-seat MiG-15 variant known as the SP-5; both MiG-15s and MiG-17s were subsequently equipped with AI.

These variants, however, did not meet the urgent requirement for an all-weather fighter fitted with long-range AI radar, and a specification for such an aircraft was issued in November 1951. Lavochkin set about modifying the La-200A to carry a new radar scanner in a lengthened fuselage nose, and the result was the La-200B, one of the ugliest fighter aircraft ever flown. The massive radome ruled out a single air intake, so the engines were fed by three ducts, one on either side of the nose and one underneath it. Bulky auxiliary fuel tanks were fitted under the wings, and to compensate for the extra weight – the aircraft now weighed 24,750 lb loaded – the undercarriage was strengthened.

The La-200B was not the solution to the Soviet Air Force's night and all-weather interception problems. That still lay over the horizon, and it would be provided by Alexander S. Yakovlev – the designer who, above all others, had given the Russians fighter superiority over the Eastern Front.

CHAPTER THIRTEEN

NIGHT BATTLE OVER KOREA

When Communist North Korean forces launched their surprise attack on the Republic of Korea (ROK) on 25 June 1950, one of the first priorities was to evacuate US and other foreign nationals from the South Korean capital, Seoul. A number of freighters were already standing by in Inchon harbour, ready to take the evacuees to safety in Japan, and in the early hours of 26 June, with North Korean tanks only a few miles from Seoul, General Douglas MacArthur, the Supreme Commander Allied Powers in the Pacific Theatre, ordered General Earle T. Partridge, the United States Fifth Air Force Commander, to provide air cover over the evacuation area.

The only aircraft really suitable for the patrol task, because of the distances involved from the Japanese airfields, were the long-range F-82s of the 68th Fighter All-Weather Squadron at Itazuke on Kyushu, but there were only twelve of them, too few to carry out effective standing patrols. In an effort to resolve the problem, General Partridge ordered the 339th All-Weather Squadron to redeploy its F-82s from Yokota to Itazuke, and also requested the Twentieth Air Force to despatch eight F-82s of the 4th Squadron to Itazuke from their base on Okinawa.

The evacuation got under way at first light on 26 June, the majority of the refugees embarking on a Norwegian vessel. Overhead, the F-82s circled watchfully in flights of four, a few hundred feet below the cloud base. The evacuation proceeded without interference during the morning, but at 13.30 there was a sudden alarm when a North Korean La-7 fighter dropped down out of the clouds and attacked a flight of F-82s. The American fighter pilots took evasive action, and after this single pass the enemy fighter climbed steeply back into the clouds and disappeared. This action was taken to present a direct threat to the evacuation, and during the remainder of the day the F-82s ventured inland to cover evacuation convoys *en route* from Seoul to Inchon. After dark the fighters

Crews of the 339th FS (all-weather) in the process of converting from Northrop P-61 Black Widows to North American F-82 Twin Mustangs at Johnson AB, Japan, in 1949, some months before the outbreak of the Korean War. (Martin Bambrick)

North American F-82G Twin Mustang on patrol over Korea, 1950. (Robert F. Dorr)

continued to accompany the merchantman as it headed out into the Yellow Sea, only breaking contact when the ship was met by an escort of American destroyers. On the 27th, the maritime patrol task off the Korean coast was assumed by Navy Patrol Squadron VP-47, based at Iwakuni and equipped with Martin PBM-5 Mariners.

The airlift of evacuees from Seoul and Kimpo also got under way on 27 June, the day on which United States President Harry Truman ordered sea and air forces in the Far East to give support and cover to the ROK forces, in effect authorising an armed conflict if necessary. Finding transport aircraft to carry out the airlift had presented something of a problem; the C-54s of the 374th Wing were widely dispersed on routine duties, and only two were immediately available. The situation was saved by the arrival of eleven C-47s, hastily assembled from various FEAF (Far East Air Force) transport units. The first transports took off from Itazuke before dawn, escorted by F-82s. At daybreak, while the transports landed at Kimpo and Suwon under the protection of the Twin Mustangs, two flights of F-80 Shooting Stars of the 8th Fighter Bomber Wing arrived over the Han river and began a high-level patrol, covering the approaches to the South Korean capital.

The patrolling fighters encountered no enemy opposition until midday, when five Yak-7s appeared over Seoul and initiated an attack on Kimpo. They were intercepted by five F-82s of the 68th and 339th Squadrons, and in a five-minute air battle three Yaks were shot down, the first by Lieutenant William G. Hudson of the 68th Squadron, to whom fell the distinction of destroying the first communist aircraft over Korea. The other American pilots who scored were Major James W. Little and Lieutenant Charles B. Moran.

The Twin Mustang featured prominently in the 'shopping list' of reinforcement aircraft sent to Washington at the end of June 1950, but the USAF was unable to meet the requirement for additional aircraft. There were only 168 F-82s in service, and apart from the fact that most were needed for the all-weather defence of the continental United States (a role they would continue to fulfil until the deployment of the Northrop F-89 Scorpion from 1950) there was a critical shortage of spares, which frustrated any move to make good the attrition suffered by the Fifth AF's F-82s in Korea.

During the bitter winter of 1950–51, a winter that saw the massive involvement of Chinese troops in Korea, night intruder operations were carried out by Douglas B-26 Invaders of the 3rd Bombardment Wing, while the night air defence task was assumed by two squadrons of the Marine Air Wing. One of these, VMF(N)-513, was armed with F4U-5N Corsairs; the other, VMF(N)-542, with F7F-3N Tigercats. In March 1951 VMF(N)-542 returned to El Toro, California, to rearm with the Douglas F3D-1 Skyknight jet night fighter; its Tigercats were assigned to VMF(N)-513, together with a pair of F-82 Twin Mustangs. The unit retained its Corsairs, which operated by day in the

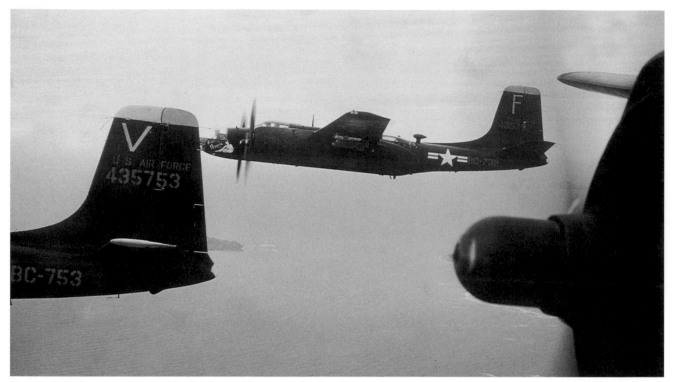

Douglas B-26 Invaders of the 3rd Bombardment Wing carried out night intruder operations. (Robert F. Dorr)

The Grumman F7F Tigercat night fighter served with VMF(N)-542 and -513 in Korea. (Author)

ground-attack role.

During World War II, the Russians had made extensive use of light aircraft, notably Polikarpov Po-2 biplanes, to carry out night attacks on German positions and installations on the Eastern Front. Within a year of the outbreak of hostilities in Korea, once the front line had stabilised, the North Korean Air Force adopted similar tactics.

The first of these nuisance raids took place in the early hours of 14 June 1951, when two Polikarpov Po-2s took off from Sariwon airstrip. One attacked Suwon, dropping two bombs that narrowly missed the runway, and the other released its bombs on an Eighth Army motor transport park at Inchon, causing splinter damage to several vehicles. On the next night a third raider – identified as an MBR-2 amphibian – made a low-level strafing run over Kimpo airfield, fortunately without hitting anything.

The next attack, on 16/17 June, produced spectacular results. On this occasion, two Po-2s led by Lieutenant La Woon Yung arrived over Suwon, the crews finding to their surprise that the airfield was brightly lit. La Woon Yung had no difficulty in picking out the F-86 Sabres of the 4th Fighter Interceptor Wing in their dispersals and dropped his pair of bombs on a flight of 335th Squadron aircraft, destroying one Sabre and damaging eight others, four of them seriously. The other pilot dropped his bombs on the parked vehicles of the 802nd Engineer Aviation Battalion, severely damaging several of them.

The nightly visits by the Po-2 raiders, nicknamed 'Bed Check Charlies', continued to be a thorn in the Allies' flesh throughout the summer of 1951, and steps were taken to combat them. The biplanes, cruising at 80 knots and at low level down the valleys on the approach to their targets, proved incredibly difficult to detect by radar, and when night fighters were sent up to intercept them the Po-2 pilots made full use of their low speed and high manoeuvrability to evade them. However, two

F4U-5N Corsair night fighters of Composite Squadron VC-3 on a carrier in Yokosuka Bay, Japan, during the Korean War (Robert F. Dorr)

Po-2s were intercepted and destroyed during June 1951; the first on the night of the 23rd by Captain Dick Heyman, flying a B-26 of the 8th Squadron, and the second on the 30th over the Han river by Captain E.B. Long of Marine Squadron VMF(N)-513, flying an F7F Tigercat. His radar intercept officer (RIO), Warrant Officer R.C. Buckingham, steered him to the black-painted target, which he shot down on his third pass after reducing speed to the absolute safe minimum. It was the Tigercat's first combat victory.

Shortly after midnight on 12 July, a Corsair night fighter of VMF(N)-513 surprised a Po-2 raider and shot it down in flames over Seoul. This success was followed, on 23 September, by another scored by an F7F Tigercat. A Po-2 had attacked Kimpo in the early hours and was intercepted by Major Eugene A. Van Gundy and his RIO, Master Sergeant T.H. Ullom. Van Gundy closed in to 500 feet and destroyed the enemy aircraft with 20 mm cannon fire.

Fears of large-scale enemy air attacks on Allied air bases in Korea proved unfounded, but the nuisance raids by Po-2s continued to keep the night defences on the alert. Four T-6 Texans armed with .30 calibre machine-guns were kept on readiness at Kimpo during the hours of darkness, but they never

had any luck; neither did the 68th Fighter Interceptor Squadron's (FIS) Lockheed F-94B Starfires, which replaced the unit's North American F-82 Twin Mustangs in December 1951. Two F-94s were deployed to Suwon, where they were joined in March 1952 by the 319th FIS, whose F-94s were deployed to Korea from McChord AFB, Tacoma, Washington. One F-94 did manage to shoot down a Po-2 by throttling right back and lowering landing gear and flaps to reduce its speed, but it stalled immediately afterwards and spun into the ground, killing its crew. Another F-94 was lost when it collided with a Po-2.

Royal Navy Fairey Fireflies also joined the battle against the night intruders towards the end of the war in Korea. An observer with No 810 Squadron, R.K. Simmons, on HMS *Ocean* recalls that:

'On 7 July 1953 I was detached with the CO, Lieutenant Cdr A.W. Bloomer, RN, to the 319th FIS at K-13 (Suwon) to determine whether the Firefly V could be used as an interceptor to counter the threat posed by Po-2s which were operating from road strips just short of the front line. These aircraft were flying at night just below the level of the air defence radar, with ladies in the back throwing out 40 lb bombs by hand. We were patrolling at night with wheels and flaps down at 95 knots, just above the stall.

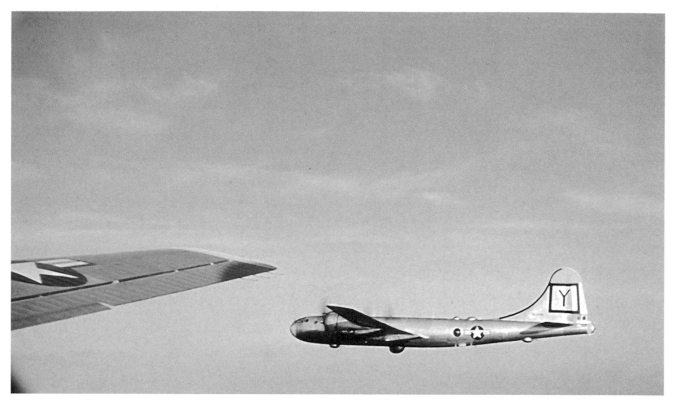

Boeing B-29s of FEAF Bomber Command on a daylight mission to North Korea. Communist MiG-15 night fighters came near to sweeping the B-29s from Korea's night skies. (Robert F. Dorr)

'It was soon found impracticable to operate the Firefly from a jet base, so we were transferred to K-6 (Pyongtaek-ni) with Marine Air Group 12. We had no luck with Po-2s; indeed, the only bogey we had managed to outpace us, and was believed to be a Yak-9.

'It is interesting to note that the 319th FIS was supposed to have a complement of twenty-four aircraft. In fact they were reduced to eighteen aircraft after a number of landing accidents. During the time I was with them they managed a maximum serviceability rate of six aircraft, and frequently could put only two aircraft into the sky. The squadron had a complement of 117 aircrew (i.e. about fifty-eight crews) who were lucky to get a flight once every ten days. With so little flying practice it was no wonder that many aircraft were damaged in landing accidents when weather was marginal.'

Late on in the war the Po-2s were joined by other training types, notably Yak-18s. Their heckling missions reached a climax of success on 16/17 June 1953, when they destroyed five million gallons of fuel in a dump at Inchon. Between 30 June and 16 July Lieutenant Guy P. Bordelon, a pilot with an F4U-5N detachment of VC-3 deployed to K-6 from the USS *Princeton* for anti-intruder operations, destroyed three Yak-18s and two other aircraft (either Lavochkin La-9s or La-11s) in the Seoul area. He was the USN's only ace of the Korean War.

Almost from the beginning of hostilities in Korea, targets in enemy territory were attacked by B-29 Superfortresses of the United States Far East

Air Force Bomber Command, assisted by Strategic Air Command (SAC) units deployed from the United States. Despite the fact that these attacks were carried out in daylight, often against strong opposition from MiG-15 fighters and flak, the Command lost only six B-29s in action between the beginning of the conflict and October 1951, but when that month ended five more had been destroyed by flak or fighters and eight others seriously damaged. In one week, fifty-five aircrew had been posted dead or missing and twelve others had been wounded. The aircrew losses were particularly serious, because by now the B-29 units in the Korean theatre were having to rely heavily on Air Force Reserve personnel who had flown B-29s during World War II in order to avoid an unacceptable drain on SAC's aircrew resources.

The outcome was inevitable; the B-29 force was restricted to night operations. By the end of November 1951 most of the Superfortresses had been fitted with Shoran short-range air navigation and bombing equipment, and although early Shoran night raids met with only limited success, the B-29s soon began to inflict heavy damage on the North Korean airfields. The enemy set up heavy flak batteries along the arcs followed by the bombers on their radar bombing runs, but although several B-29s were damaged none was lost. As yet, the communists possessed no effective night fighter force; the few night interceptions reported by the B-29 crews were carried out on a hit-or-miss basis by MiG-15s, relying on searchlights to

Top and above: *B-29s of Far East Air Forces Bomber Command attacking targets in North Korea.* (Author)

illuminate their targets. The only B-29 lost in November was on a leaflet dropping mission along the Yalu; it was hit by flak but succeeded in reaching the coast, where its crew parachuted to safety.

During these latter weeks it was clear that the communists were making extensive use of radar in carrying out their fighter interceptions. On several occasions, Allied fighter bombers were attacked by MiGs which dropped down through a cloud layer, obviously vectored to their targets by radar controllers. Early warning radars had been in place since December 1950, and had been identified by 91st Strategic Reconnaissance Wing RB-29 reconnaissance aircraft as being American-manufactured SCR-270 sets, supplied to the Soviet Union under lend-lease during World War II. They had an effective range of about 150 miles, but were able to detect an aircraft flying higher than 40,000 feet at a greater range. Another American-built radar, the SCR-584, formed a second component of the system, automatically tracking an intruding aircraft detected by the SCR-270 and directing anti-aircraft fire on to it.

The ground controlled interception (GCI) radar identified in 1952, however, was of Russian design and was code-named *Token*, and it was better than anything that had been deployed previously. The communists lost no time in using it to develop countermeasures against the B-29 night strikes; hitherto, such countermeasures had taken the form of searchlight and anti-aircraft batteries directed by the SCR-584 stations, but by the end of May 1952 the deployment of *Token* made it possible for the enemy to form at least one specialist night fighter unit, using Tupolev Tu-2 light bombers equipped with AI radar. These aircraft assumed the role of master night fighters; having located the bomber stream they would fly immediately above it and control the final interception phase, the other fighters having been guided to the scene by *Token*. The B-29s would then be constantly tracked by searchlight batteries, with the aid of which the night fighters would launch their attacks.

These tactics produced results. On 10 June 1952, four B-29s of the 19th BW were suddenly illuminated by twenty-four searchlights after being shadowed for some minutes by an unidentified aircraft. A few moments later they were attacked by twelve MiG-15s. One B-29 exploded over the target, a railway bridge at Kwaksan, and another went down somewhere over North Korea. A third was so badly damaged that it barely made an emergency landing at Kimpo. The fourth aircraft used countermeasures to break the searchlights' radar lock and got away unharmed.

Because of the growing danger from enemy defences, FEAF Bomber Command's operations were now restricted to nights when there was substantial cloud cover in the target areas. This was predicted when thirty B-29s set out to bomb the power plant at Suiho on 12/13 September 1952, but when the bombers reached the objective they found the skies clear. Six more B-29s orbited to the east of Suiho, jamming the enemy radars with electronic countermeasures, but the enemy put up a very concentrated box barrage and several of the attacking bombers were damaged. A few bombers were illuminated by searchlights, and one 307th Wing aircraft was shot down by night fighters. The other B-29s destroyed the target with 2,000 lb bombs.

A further threat to Bomber Command's night operations over north-west Korea developed in December 1952, when FEAF Intelligence received strong indications that two Russian night fighter squadrons had been deployed to the Antung airfield complex and were already in operation. Between 18 November 1952 and 31 January 1953 the communist air defences achieved notable successes at night, destroying five B-29s and damaging three more so badly that they had to be withdrawn from service. In the words of the official history:

'On the night of 18/19 November 1952 the Reds revealed new tactics when they shot down a 98th Wing B-29 coming off its supply-centre target at Sonchon. Riding above the B-29, a Red spotter dropped flares every time the bomber changed direction. The flares allowed searchlights to lock on the bomber, and four Red fighter passes riddled the bomber, forcing its crew to abandon ship over Cho-do. On the night of 30/31 December, when a full moon was at its zenith and contrails were streaming at bombing altitudes, Red searchlights coned three 19th Group B-29s which were attacking an ore-processing plant near the Yalu at Choak-tong. A conventional airplane called signals from above the bombers, and Red fighters shot down one B-29 and damaged two others so badly that their crews were forced down at Suwon. Bomber Command blamed the moonlight and the contrails for the losses, but in the dark of the moon on the night of 10/11 January 1953 a 307th Wing B-29 was coned by searchlights, hit by flak, and shot down by fighters over Anju's marshalling yards. The position of this bomber was apparently betrayed by light contrails.

'On the night of 12 January Red fighters intercepted and shot down a lone 91st Reconnaissance Squadron RB-29 which was distributing leaflets along the Yalu. On 28/29 January enemy fighters apparently silhouetted a 19th Group B-29 against a full moon over Kimpodong and needed no other illumination to shoot it down. Moonlight again betrayed 307th Wing B-29s when they bombed the Unjong-ni supply area on the night of 30/31 January. Some ten Red fighters prosecuted attacks which so badly damaged a B-29 that it barely made an emergency landing in South Korea. The total number of Red interceptions was not great. Bomber Command reported only twenty non-firing and twenty-three firing passes made

The Douglas F3D Skynight flew effective bomber support night missions over Korea from November 1952. (Author)

against its aircraft in January 1953. But the Red night interceptions were becoming extremely effective.

'Darkness was no longer affording the old B-29s the protection they needed to attack targets in North Korea ...'

Nevertheless, Bomber Command was to lose no more B-29s to enemy action after January 1953. This was due to a number of countermeasures as well as to natural causes, such as the raising of the contrail-forming level with the onset of spring. Attacks were arranged on an irregular basis; attack altitudes were varied as much as Shoran direction allowed; the bomber stream was compressed so that attacking aircraft passed through the target area in the minimum time; contrail-forming altitudes were avoided, and heavily defended targets were attacked as far as possible in the dark of the moon.

Another solution to the enemy night fighter problem was to provide bomber support, using night intruders to penetrate deep into enemy territory. Since June 1952 Marine Fighter Squadron VMF(N)-513 had been making four F7F Tigercats available for bomber support each night,

the fighters preceding the bomber stream by about five minutes in the run-up to the target area. They proved ineffective against the enemy's MiG-15s, and it was not until VMF(N)-513 re-equipped with twelve Douglas F3D-2N Skynights early in November 1952 that matters began to improve.

On 3/4 November, during the Skynight's second bomber support mission, Major William T. Stratton Jr, was brought to within visual range of a target by his radar operator, Master Sergeant Hans Hoglind. Stratton put three bursts of cannon fire into it and it went down in flames. The enemy aircraft was identified as a Yak-15 (Russia's first jet fighter), which is unlikely; it was more probably a piston-engined Yak-9 or a Yak-3, from which the Yak-15 was developed. Five nights later another Skynight crew destroyed an enemy aircraft, believed to have been a MiG-15, near Sonchon.

Later in November, General Hoyt S. Vandenberg, the USAF Chief of Staff, personally authorised the removal of the restrictions that had hitherto prevented the 319th Fighter Interceptor Squadron's F-94 Starfires from operating over enemy territory for fear that their modern fire

123

A Lockheed F-94 Starfire of the 319th FIS. Its crew, Capt Ben Fithian and Lt Sam Lyons (RO) were credited with the first Starfire kill over Korea. (Author)

control system might fall into enemy hands. From then on, flights of four to six F-94s flew barrier patrols about thirty miles ahead of the bomber stream while the Skynights took up position 2,000 to 3,000 feet above the bombers. These new tactics quickly produced results, the Skynights scoring two kills in moonlight conditions, one each on the nights of 28 and 31 January 1953. On the night of 30 January Captain Ben Fithian and Lieutenant Sam R. Lyons scored the F-94's first kill in Korea, shooting down an La-9. Between them, the Skynights and Starfires destroyed fifteen enemy aircraft in the first half of 1953. It was a relatively small contribution in terms of enemy aircraft destroyed, but it helped the war-weary B-29s to survive those last months of conflict in Korea.

Another factor that helped the B-29s to survive was electronic countermeasures, the development of which was accelerated by FEAF after June 1952.

Data on enemy radars and electronic systems, collected by the 'ferret' RB-29s of the 91st SRS, was collated, evaluated and disseminated by a special section of the 548th Reconnaissance Technical Squadron. Despite the use of old equipment and partly-trained operators, Bomber Command's ECM programme produced results. Between 1 January and 27 July 1953, in the course of 534 B-29 sorties, 114 aircraft were illuminated by searchlights, and in at least eighty-seven cases the searchlight lock was broken by the use of ECM. Had ECM not been available, Bomber Command's losses would almost certainly have been triple what they were. And there was another inescapable fact. If the communists had possessed an effective night/all-weather air defence system – or even if they had used the existing one properly – the night sky over North Korea might have been completely denied to United Nations bombers.

CHAPTER FOURTEEN

COLD WAR

The Yakovlev Yak-25 Flashlight *was the mainstay of the Soviet Air Force's night/all-weather interceptor force during the 1950s.*
(Philip Jarrett)

The failure of the communist air defences to stem the B-29 night offensive against targets in North Korea did not pass unnoticed in the Soviet Union. Neither did the fact that American reconnaissance aircraft like the RB-29, RB-36 and RB-50 were making frequent night incursions into Soviet airspace, radar-mapping Russian airfields and other facilities. These two facts combined to accelerate the development of a viable Soviet night and all-weather jet fighter, and there were only two real contenders. The first, as we have seen, was the unwieldy Lavochkin La-200B; the second was the Yakovlev Yak-25, and it was this aircraft that was selected for production, although not without a good deal of political

lobbying by the Yakovlev design team. The problem was that Semyon Lavochkin had the backing of Lavrenti Beria, the all-powerful Soviet Chief of Secret Police; but Yakovlev went directly to Josef Stalin, and managed to win him over.

In every respect, the Yak-25 was a better aircraft than the La-200B. A mid-wing monoplane with forty-five degrees of sweep, it was a tandem two-seater and featured a bicycle undercarriage with outriggers under the wings. It was fitted with an improved version of the *Izumrud* AI radar under a large plastic radome and was armed with two 30 mm cannon mounted under the fuselage. The Yak-25 prototypes had two 6,000 lb static thrust (s.t.) Mikulin AM-5 engines, but production aircraft had the more powerful AM-5F, the F denoting *Forsazh*, or reheat. Several prototypes were flying by the summer of 1952 and the aircraft entered service with a Soviet Air Force development unit in 1955, becoming fully operational in the following year. The Yak-25 was allotted the NATO code-name *Flashlight*.

The Yak-25 was to be the mainstay of the Soviet Air Force's night/all-weather fighter force throughout the 1950s, and in that role it was complemented by the shorter-range MiG-19 Farmer, a night fighter variant of Russia's first truly supersonic jet-fighter having been produced. By the late 1950s, however, an extra requirement had been built into specifications for a new generation of Soviet night and all-weather fighters: extended combat radius. No longer was it necessary for American strategic bombers to penetrate into Soviet airspace; they were now armed with stand-off missiles that could be launched from points well outside Soviet territory, and the priority of the IA-PVO, the Soviet Air Force's Air Defence Command, was to destroy SAC's B-52 bombers before they came within launch range.

Soviet Intelligence circles were doubtless well aware, at an early stage, that the USAF was developing such weapons. In the mid-1950s, the Bell Aircraft Corporation had extensively tested an air-launched strategic missile, the XB-63 Rascal, which was designed to be carried by a modified version of the B-47 Stratojet known as the DB-47. The missile, which was capable of 1.6 M and had a stand-off range of about seventy-five miles, made some forty test flights from DB-36 and DB-47 carrier aircraft between 1953 and 1957, and by the end of the series was achieving a 1,500-foot circular error probable (CEP), which was acceptable with a nuclear warhead. SAC's entire Rascal programme was to have been concentrated in one squadron of the 321st Bomb Wing at McCoy AFB, Florida, and this unit carried out operational trials with the weapon in 1958, having received some modified DB-47s.

On 29 November 1958, however, the Rascal programme was cancelled by HQ USAF in deference to a far more promising air-launched missile system, the North American GAM-77 Hound Dog. This forty-three-foot missile had small canard fore-planes, a rear-mounted delta wing fitted with ailerons, a small fin and rudder, a very slim fuselage and a 7,500 lb s.t. Pratt & Whitney J52-6 turbojet in an underslung rear pod. The missile was designed to carry a one-megaton warhead over a range of between 500 and 700 miles, depending on the mission profile, and could operate between tree-top level and 55,000 feet at speeds of up to 2.1 M. The weapon was fitted with a North American Autonetics Division inertial system, which was linked to the aircraft's navigation systems and continually updated by a Kollsman astro-tracker in the launch pylon.

The first powered test vehicle was launched from a converted B-52D over the Gulf Test Range on 23 April 1959, and on 23 December that year the first missile was handed over to the 4135th Strategic Wing (SW) at Eglin AFB, Florida. This unit, armed with B-52Gs – the Stratofortress variant designed to carry two Hound Dogs slung under its wings – was responsible for supporting Category III Hound Dog trials in co-ordination with Air Research and Development Command's Air Proving Ground Center, leading to SAC acceptance of the weapon system. The first SAC Hound Dog launch was made by a B-52G of the 4135th SW on 29 February 1960.

All B-52Gs and, later, B-52Hs armed with the Hound Dog carried one pylon-mounted round under each wing. The Hound Dogs' turbojets were lit up during take-off, effectively making the B-52 a ten-engined aircraft, and were subsequently shut down, the missile's tanks being topped up from the parent aircraft. After launch, the missile could follow a high or low flight profile, with dog-legs and diversions as necessary. Later, anti-radar and terrain contour matching (TERCOM) modifications were introduced. At the missile's peak in 1962 there were 592 Hound Dogs on SAC's inventory, and it is a measure of the system's effectiveness that it remained in operational service until 1976.

The urgent IA-PVO requirement for an aircraft capable of intercepting Strategic Air Command B-52s before they reached their missile launch points led directly to the development of the Tu-28 long-range, missile-armed all-weather interceptor, first seen by western observers at the Tushino air display of 1961. With a length of eighty-five feet and a wing span of sixty-five feet, the Tu-28, which was given the code-name *Fiddler*, was the largest interceptor to see service anywhere, and Western experts noted with interest, after they had gathered more intelligence on the aircraft, that its designation carried the suffix 'P' for *Perekhvachnik* (interceptor). The interesting point was that this suffix was only applied to the designations of Soviet aircraft which had been adapted to the fighter role, indicating that the Tu-28 had originally been designed as a low-level strike aircraft, possibly in the anti-shipping role. The Tu-28 was estimated to have a combat radius of around 1,500 miles with maximum fuel, and it was armed with four AA-5 Ash air-to-air missiles on underwing pylons.

The long-range Tu-28 was complemented by a series of medium-range fighters, products of the Sukhoi design bureau, which effectively formed a second barrier of defence. These were the Su-9/11 *Fishpot* and the larger twin-engined Su-15 *Flagon*.

The latter achieved brief notoriety in September 1983, when one destroyed a Korean Airlines Boeing 747 at night off Sakhalin Island, probably because Soviet air defence controllers had confused the airliner with an RC-135 reconnaissance aircraft that was in the vicinity.

Canada, forming the first line of defence against the threat of bombers attacking the North American continent across the great wastes of the Arctic, was quick to identify the need for a long-range night and all-weather interceptor during the early post-war years. In response to this requirement, Avro Canada designed the CF-100, at that time the largest fighter aircraft in the world. The prototype CF-100 Mk 1 flew on 19 January 1950, powered by two Rolls-Royce Avon RA3 turbojets; production aircraft were fitted with the Avro Orenda.

In September 1950 an order was placed with Avro Canada for 124 CF-100 Mk 3s for the RCAF. These were powered by two Orenda Mk 8s and armed with eight 0.5 in Colt-Browning machine-guns. In fact only seventy were built, the first entering service with No 445 Squadron. The next production version was the Mk 4A, powered by two

Orenda 9s and equipped with a Hughes AGP-40 fire control radar. This variant could be armed with forty-eight 'Mighty Mouse' high velocity aircraft rockets (HVAR), eight 0.5 in machine-guns or four 30 mm cannon in a ventral pack, plus fifty-eight HVAR rockets in wingtip pods. The first

Top and above: *The Convair F-102 all-weather interceptor's design was based on the XF-92 research aircraft, pictured here.* (Author)

production Mk 4A flew on 24 October 1953 and the aircraft entered service with No 445 Squadron in the following year. In all, 510 Mk 4As and 4Bs (the latter with Orenda 11 engines) were built, and by the end of 1957 nine RCAF squadrons were operating the type, providing round-the-clock air defence coverage of Canada's far north. Four CF-100 squadrons also served in Germany as part of Canada's NATO commitment, and fifty-three examples of the last production version, the Mk 5, were delivered to Belgium.

The CF-100 was to have been replaced in RCAF service by the very advanced Avro Canada CF-105 Arrow delta-wing interceptor, which flew for the first time on 25 March 1958, powered by two Pratt & Whitney J75 turbojets. Four more aircraft were built, designated CF-105 Mk 1, and four more – designated Mk 2, with 22,000 lb thrust Orenda PS-13 engines – were almost complete when the project was cancelled in February 1959. The Arrow was to have been armed with eight Sparrow AAMs.

In 1950, the USAF formulated a requirement for a night and all-weather interceptor incorporating the latest fire control system. This was eventually to emerge as the Convair F-102, whose design was based on experience gained during flight testing of the XF-92 delta-wing research aircraft. Two prototype YF-102s were built, the first flying on 24 October 1953. This aircraft was damaged beyond repair only a week later, but testing resumed with the second machine in January 1954. Eight more YF-102s were built for evaluation, and it soon became apparent that the aircraft's performance fell short of expectations. After substantial airframe redesign the machine re-emerged in December 1954 as the YF-102A, and the type was ordered into full production. The first F-102A was handed over to Air Defense Command in June 1955, but it was another year before the type was issued to squadrons.

In the interim, Air Defense Command had acquired an aircraft that went a long way to solving the problem of accurate interception at night and in bad weather. This was the North American F-86D, an aircraft bold in concept. Not only did the design envisage the replacement of the traditional interceptor armament of cannon or machine-guns by air-to-air missiles; it also envisaged that a single pilot would control the whole weapons system. Admittedly, the original F-86D design, begun in May 1948, had involved a two-seater aircraft, with a second crew member assisting the pilot in making radar-controlled interceptions and being responsible for navigation, but the performance limitations imposed by the installation of a second crew position – coupled with other attendant problems such as restricted fuselage fuel tank space – led to this concept being reconsidered. In the end, it was the availability of improved automated AI radar, reducing the operator's workload, that tipped the scales in favour of the single-seater.

Engineering design work on the single-seat F-86D was begun on 28 March 1949. The USAF showed an immediate interest in the project, and on 7 April work was started on the production version, the NA-165, and North American started building a mock-up in June.

The first of two YF-86D prototypes went to Muroc on 28 November 1949 and flew for the first time on 22 December. Much of the early test flying involved the evaluation of the electronic control system fitted to the afterburning General Electric J47-GE-17. At an early stage in the aircraft's design, it had been realised that pilots would find difficulty in monitoring the engine behaviour, especially during an AI radar intercept requiring the use of afterburner, so to overcome this problem North American and General Electric joined forces to develop a complex engine control system for installation in production F-86Ds. This involved the use of a single throttle lever control which, by means of an electronic fuel selector, determined the amount of fuel being supplied to the engine and afterburner to maintain maximum efficiency, even when the throttle was slammed open and shut rapidly.

Both YF-86Ds were flown without the fire control system, which was still under development by the Hughes Aircraft Corporation. The prototype system, the 50-kilowatt E-3, was approved by the Air Materiel Command on 17 February 1950 and was delivered to North American on 26 May; after some changes, it was installed in the second YF-86D and tested in September. The test programme was delayed when the YF-86D was damaged at Edwards Air Force Base (as Muroc was now known) as the result of an undercarriage malfunction, resuming on 17 October 1950.

The E-3 fire control system was installed in the first thirty-seven production F-86Ds pending delivery of the more complex 250-kW E-4, but even at this stage delays began to beset the programme. It was not until July 1951 that the first production E-3 system was delivered to NAA, and since aircraft could not be accepted for service without the system, it was October 1952 – three years after the original letter contract – that the USAF took delivery of the last of its thirty-seven F-86D-1s.

The situation with the E-4 system was just as bad, if not worse. The first set was delivered in December 1951, three months behind schedule, and was found to have a power output of only 180 kW instead of the planned 250. The first batch all suffered serious malfunctions, mostly because of extremely poor quality control at the manufacturer's works. Components were wired incorrectly or were of the wrong type, and foreign objects such as screwdrivers were found in the systems' innards. The upshot was that some systems had to be returned to the sub-contractors for repair, and for eleven modifications demanded by the USAF. At one time, in the winter of 1952–3, there were more than 320 F-86Ds awaiting the installation of the E-4 system and other electronic components.

Meanwhile, aerodynamic flight testing had revealed a number of problems created by changes of design from the original F-86A. The wing of the F-86D was generally similar to that of the F-86A, except that it was strengthened; the fuselage was dimensionally larger, the vertical tail surfaces were increased in area and a slab-type tailplane adopted for improved longitudinal control. The most noticeable external change was the design of the nose, which now featured a lowered nose intake topped by a 30 in fibreglass radome housing the antenna of the Hughes AN/APG search radar.

The F-86D's innovative weapons system also produced some teething troubles, all of which contributed to the slippage of the production programme. Early problems with the F-86D's armament, which comprised twenty-four 2.75 in folding fin aircraft rockets (FFAR) mounted in a retractable ventral pack, lay in its electronic linkage with the fire control system.

The weapons system was designed to work as follows. On a typical air defence mission beginning with a cold start, the F-86D would be off the ground in about four minutes, which included warming up time, and would then take eleven minutes to climb to 45,000 feet at full power. The pilot would then initiate the search phase, the AN/APG-36 (AN/APG-37 in later models) radar antenna sweeping an area 68.5 degrees left and right of the centreline in a three-and-a-half second cycle and also, if required, 33.5 degrees up and 13.5 degrees down. When a target was acquired at a range of up to thirty miles the radar locked on to it and the AN/APA-84 computer then worked out a lead collision course, which the pilot followed by keeping the 'blip' on his radar scope inside a one-inch circle.

When the automatic tracking system indicated twenty seconds to go, the system instructed the pilot to turn on to a 90-degree collision course, at which point he elected to launch six, twelve or all twenty-four rockets and pressed the trigger switch. The computer controlled the actual firing, extending the rocket pack in half a second and initiating the firing sequence when the target was about 500 yards away. It took only one-fifth of a second to fire the full salvo of rockets, each weighing eighteen pounds, the missiles fanning out like a charge of shotgun pellets to make sure of a hit. The rocket pack retracted in just over three seconds, and a symbol on the radar scope, which illuminated at a range of 250 yards, warned the pilot to break off.

Launching a full rocket salvo presented few problems; these tended to arise when the pilot selected a ripple-firing sequence, a procedure that saw frequent malfunctions. The system was updated and refined, but by the time the snags were ironed out the programme had slipped by two years, and it was

During the 1950s and early '60s, France made a valuable contribution to NATO's night and all-weather air defences with the Sud-Aviation Vautour IIN, pictured here. The type equipped the 6e and 30e Escadres de Chasse. (Philip Jarrett)

Meteor NF11s taking part in the Royal Review of the Royal Air Force at RAF Odiham in 1953 (Philip Jarrett)

A fine echelon formation by the Meteor NF12s of No 25 Squadron. The NF12 was a progressive development of the NF11, having a 17 in longer nose housing a US-built APS-21 AI radar. (Philip Jarrett)

not until April 1953 that the F-86D began to enter service with active Air Defense Command units. Thereafter, deliveries proceeded rapidly, and by the end of 1953 600 F-86Ds were in service with Air Defense Command. Eighteen months later, 1,026 – seventy-three per cent – of the Command's 1,405 interceptors were F-86Ds serving with the USAF overseas; some were assigned to the Fifth AF in Korea late in 1953, but the 'Sabre-Dog' was a much heavier fighter than the standard F-86 and it did not take kindly to operations from the still fairly primitive South Korean airfields. It was withdrawn after only a brief period of service in the peninsula. However, F-86Ds did equip the 199th Fighter Interceptor Squadron of the 154th Fighter Group, Hawaiian Air National Guard, until they were replaced by Convair F-102A Delta Daggers in the early 1960s.

F-86Ds also served in the United Kingdom, equipping the 406th Fighter Wing (512th, 513th and 514th Fighter Interceptor Squadrons) at RAF Manston from November 1953. They provided a much-needed boost to the UK night and all-weather air defences, which were reliant on six squadrons of Meteor NF11s and two of Vampire NF10s. Two Meteor NF11 squadrons, Nos 68 and 87, were based in Germany, at Laarbruch and Wahn respectively, and in addition to their main

The last and most elegant Meteor of all, the NF14 equipped ten RAF squadrons. The aircraft pictured here in 1955 bear the markings of No 264 Squadron. (Philip Jarrett)

role of high-level defence they also trained for low-level defence and for night intruder operations, the latter involving night attacks on airfields, troop and armour concentrations. In the low-level air defence role their opponents were usually the A-26 Invaders of the USAF's 38th Bomb Group (Tactical) at Laon. The Meteor night fighter crews found these aircraft difficult targets, as many of the A-26s had served in the night intruder role in Korea and carried specialised night optics which enabled them to detect the attacking fighters at considerable ranges.

In November 1952 a new night fighter appeared on RAF Fighter Command's inventory. This was the de Havilland Venom NF2, the prototype of

which, like its Vampire NF10 precursor, had been produced as a private venture at the company's own expense. The first and only squadron to equip with the new aircraft, which was fitted with the AI Mk X, was No 23 at Coltishall, for after a number of crashes in 1954 the unit's aircraft were grounded for structural modifications, and the squadron did not become fully operational until the summer of that year.

Further modifications were carried out, and in the spring of 1955 the first of the modified aircraft, designated Venom NF2a, entered service with No 253 Squadron at Waterbeach. Venom NF2as were also issued to Nos 33 and 219 Squadrons, and the three squadrons formed an important element in

The de Havilland Venom NF3 equipped five RAF night fighter squadrons, in some cases replacing the Meteor NF11. (Philip Jarrett)

The de Havilland DH110 was in direct competition with the Gloster Javelin for a new RAF night/all-weather jet fighter. (Author)

Fighter Command's expanding night/all-weather fighter force. Ninety aircraft were built, the NF2a being followed into service by the NF3, which had the improved AI Mk 21 radar; this mark equipped Nos 23, 89, 125, 141 and 151 Squadrons.

The shortcomings of the RAF's night fighter force, meanwhile, had been demonstrated time and again by its inability, during air exercises, to get to grips with high-flying Canberra jet bombers. The Venom, which had an excellent high altitude performance, could intercept Canberras at up to 43,000 feet, but the Meteor NF11 had little chance. Indeed, on many occasions NF11 crews suffered the ignominy of having a Canberra turning the tables on them at high altitude and claiming them as its victim.

Both of the aircraft that Fighter Command was eagerly awaiting to replace its Meteor and Venom night fighters, the Gloster Javelin – designed as the GA5 to Specification F4/48 – and its direct competitor, the de Havilland DH110, had suffered serious misfortunes during their development careers. De Havilland's swept-wing, twin-boom DH110 flew for the first time on 26 September 1951, powered by two Rolls-Royce Avons, and six months into the test programme, on 9 April 1952, this aircraft (WG236) became the first twin-engined two-seater to exceed Mach 1.0 in a dive. The second DH110 prototype, WG240, flew on 25 July 1952. Painted a rather sinister all-black, WG240 was demonstrated by test pilot John Derry at that year's Farnborough air show on every day except 6 September, when it went unserviceable. Derry switched to the other DH110, WG236, and went into his usual display routine. He was pulling a high G turn about a mile outside the airfield perimeter when the aircraft broke up without warning as a

result of the structural failure of the starboard outer wing section. The results were catastrophic; Derry and his observer were killed and debris plunged into the crowd, causing many fatalities and injuries.

The second prototype DH110 was grounded as a result of this tragic accident, and in 1953 the RAF decided to fill its night/all-weather requirement with the Gloster Javelin. Yet in many respects, the DH110 was the better design; it was certainly more manoeuvrable, its handling qualities comparing closely with those of many smaller single-seat fighters, and it was very stable in a high G turn right down to the stall, which the Javelin was not. Nevertheless, de Havilland resumed testing with the second DH110 after further structural modifications, with a naval requirement in mind, and in September 1953 it undertook carrier trials aboard HMS *Albion*. A production order for a developed naval version followed, and this eventually entered Fleet Air Arm service as the Sea Vixen F(AW)1 – an aircraft which, for the first time, gave the Royal Navy a true round-the-clock all-weather fighter capability.

Construction of the prototype Gloster GA5, the world's first twin-jet delta and an extremely radical design for its day, began in April 1949, and the aircraft (WD804) flew for the first time on 26 November 1951, powered by two 7,000 lb thrust Armstrong-Siddeley Sapphires. The maiden flight was attended by a serious snag in the shape of rudder buffeting, and further flight testing was delayed while modifications were carried out. Then, on 29 June 1952, the protoype lost both elevators and was destroyed in a crash landing at Boscombe Down. (The test pilot, Squadron Leader W.A. Waterton, was subsequently awarded the George Medal for his action in retrieving the vital

Line-up of Gloster Javelins of No 46 Squadron, the first to receive the type. (Philip Jarrett)

flight recorder from the blazing wreckage).

Testing continued with the second prototype, WD808, which flew on 21 August 1952, but this aircraft was also destroyed on 11 June 1953 as the result of a super-stall condition. Three more prototypes had been ordered in the meantime: the third aircraft (WT827) flew on 7 March 1953 and carried an armament of four 30 mm cannon, while the fourth featured a modified wing shape and the fifth, which flew on 20 July 1954, was up to full production standard, with British AI Mk 17 radar.

As the Javelin FAW1, the new fighter was ordered into 'super-priority' production for the RAF. The first production aircraft flew on 22 July 1954 and deliveries began to No 46 Squadron at RAF Odiham in February 1956. Javelin FAW1s were also issued to No 87 Squadron, which formed part of 2nd TAF in Germany. In October 1955 a new variant, the Javelin FAW2, made its appearance; this was basically similar to the FAW1 apart from its radar, which was the American-designed AI22 (APQ43) and avionics, and replaced the earlier production model in No 56 Squadron.

Next on the production line was the FAW4, the prototype of which was the 41st FAW1 with an all-moving tailplane. This variant entered service with No 141 Squadron early in 1957, and except for the tailplane was essentially similar to the FAW1. Later that year, No 151 Squadron received the first examples of the Javelin FAW5, which had a modified wing structure and increased internal fuel capacity, and in 1958 the Javelin FAW6 – which was basically an FAW5 with the same radar as the FAW2 –

entered service with No 89 Squadron.

In November 1956 the Javelin's already formidable combat potential was given an extra boost with the appearance of the FAW7, which was fitted with Sapphire ASSa7R turbojets developing 12,300 lb thrust with reheat in place of the 8,300 lb thrust Sapphire ASSa6 engines used in earlier marks. The Javelin FAW7, which incorporated further structural modifications and increased wing fuel tankage, had an armament of two 30 mm ADEN cannon and four Firestreak AAMs. It entered service with No 33 Squadron at RAF Leeming in July 1958. The FAW8, which flew on 9 May 1958, was externally similar to the FAW7; it incorporated the US Mk 22 radar, a simplified afterburning system, a Sperry autopilot, drooped wing leading edges and dampers on the yaw and pitch axes. The FAW8 was the last production model of the Javelin, the final aircraft being completed in June 1960, but a number of Javelin FAW7s were brought up to FAW8 standard (although with British AI radar) and designated FAW9.

The Javelin, which at various stages in its service career equipped sixteen RAF squadrons at home and overseas, was a vital component in NATO's European night and all-weather air defence system. It helped to pioneer a number of night fighting techniques, one of which was a mixed night fighter force of Javelins and Hunters, the former leading the latter to the target in a way not unreminiscent of the Havoc-Hurricane-Defiant combination of 1941–2. The technique was tested by Nos 33 and 92 Squadrons at RAF Middleton St George in the late

Javelin FAW9s of No 29 Squadron, armed with Firestreak AAMs. (Philip Jarrett)

1950s and was quite successful unless large numbers of aircraft were operating, when it was less so.

In the early 1960s the Javelin was progressively replaced in the air defence role by the English Electric Lightning, while the USAF's night and all-weather interceptor force's F-102s and F-106s were supplanted by the McDonnell F-4 Phantom, an aircraft that would also see RAF service in the interceptor role. The day of the dedicated night/all-weather fighter was fast approaching its end: the interceptor capable of operating round the clock, in all weathers, armed with air-to-air missiles capable of killing targets at extreme radar range – far beyond the limits of the human eye – was on the horizon.

But there was still a night battle to be fought, with methods not far removed from those of Korea and the closing stages of World War II; but the battleground was far removed from the unpredictable skies of Europe.

CHAPTER FIFTEEN

LAST BATTLES

When USAF and USN fighter-bombers began attacking targets in North Vietnam in August 1964, any doubts the crews may have harboured about the capability of the small North Vietnamese Air Force (NVAF) were soon dispelled. The NVAF's most numerous type, the MiG-17, proved to be a serious threat to the much heavier, bomb-laden F-4s and F-105s, while the MiG-21 could match the latest American types in every respect except quality of weapons and avionics.

Neither the MiG-17 nor the MiG-21 were specialised night fighters, but they often operated in that capacity, particularly when the American night bombing campaign against the North intensified during 1972. One USN pilot, Captain R.E. Tucker, recalled that:

'During 1972, when Navy A-6s were making a number of single aircraft low-level night strikes all over the area between Haiphong and Hanoi, MiGs were known to launch, making the A-6 drivers nervous (although I personally felt that the MiGs had no night/IFR capability against an A-6 at 300 feet). As a result, we started positioning a single F-4 on MIGCAP along the coastline at night. We figured a single F-4 didn't have to worry about a mid-air with his wingman and had plenty of potential at night against a single MiG. If a MiG launched and headed towards an A-6, the F-4 would vector for the MiG. Invariably MiGs would run for home when the F-4 got to within 25–30 miles of them. Some pilots weren't too overjoyed about the night MIGCAP missions, but I personally felt it was a golden opportunity and my MiG kill proved it. I figured that the MiG had a negligible opportunity to do anyone bodily harm at night with his limited weapons system and Atoll/guns load, whereas the F-4 had a good solid head-on or tail shot against any MiG he could find and get close enough to shoot at.'

Tucker, then a Lieutenant-Commander, was flying an F-4 Phantom of VF-103, operating from the USS *Saratoga*, when he destroyed a MiG-21 on 10/11 August 1972. The Phantom was armed with two AIM-7E Sparrows and two AIM-9D Sidewinders.

Tucker was refuelling from a KA-6D tanker when he heard the fighter controller vector another Phantom on to a MiG. He immediately broke contact and joined the other F-4 in the search, the controller advising him that the enemy aircraft was at 8,000 feet, 140 degrees at twelve miles range. Tucker descended to 8,000 feet and his RIO, Lieutenant (JG) Bruce Edens, got a radar contact at once. Lighting his afterburners, Tucker accelerated to 650 knots and closed to within five miles of the MiG, at which point Edens advised the pilot that he had lost radar contact. Realising that the MiG pilot had probably descended, Tucker went down to 3,500 feet; Edens announced that he had regained contact and that the MiG was seven or eight miles ahead.

Tucker jettisoned his centreline fuel tanks and accelerated to 750 knots, overtaking the MiG from directly astern. At a range of about two miles he launched two Sparrows, the second one leaving the under-fuselage rack just as the first warhead detonated. Tucker reported:

'There was a large fireball, and the second missile impacted in the same spot. I came right slightly to avoid any debris. The target on our radar appeared to stop in mid-air and within a second or two the radar broke lock. The MiG-21 pilot did not survive. If he ejected after the first missile, the second missile must have done him in. We couldn't see any debris in the dark ... The kill was confirmed about three days later.'

In May and June 1972, B-52 bombers ventured into heavily defended North Vietnamese airspace for the first time to make limited night attacks on airfields and oil storage facilities, and also to lay mines in the waters of Haiphong and other strategic ports. These minelaying operations, carried out by modified B-52Ds, were also flown under cover of darkness, and no losses were sustained.

On 20 October 1972, when it seemed as though peace talks in Paris were at last leading to an agreement that would end the war, air operations over North Vietnam were once more halted. They were resumed when the peace talks again broke down amid indications that the North Vietnamese were preparing to renew their offensive in the

Top and above: *B-52D bombers operating from Guam and Thailand carried out an intensive campaign against North Vietnam in December 1952, and suffered heavy losses – but to surface-to-air missiles, not night fighters.* (Philip Jarrett)

south. There followed an eleven-day bombing campaign against the north which developed into the heaviest bombing offensive of the war, with round-the-clock attacks on targets which had mostly been on the restricted list until then. They included rail yards, power plants, communications facilities, petrol, oil and lubrication (POL) stores and ammunition supply dumps, as well as the principal North Vietnamese Air Force fighter bases and SAM sites. The target list numbered thirty-four strategic objectives, over sixty per cent of which were situated within a twenty-five-mile radius of Hanoi.

The original plan called for the B-52s to attack at night, in three waves, with F-111s and A-6s continuing the offensive in daylight. The B-52 bomber streams were to be preceded by F-111

interdictors, attacking fighter bases at low level, and F-4 Phantoms dropping *Window* – still a very effective countermeasure, thirty years after it was first used in the Battle of Hamburg.

The B-52s were to approach their target areas from the north-west, using strong high-altitude winds to give them a much increased ground speed, and after bomb release they were to swing away from the target in tight turns in order to clear SAM defences as quickly as possible. Attacks would be made by cells of three aircraft, generally bombing from 33,000 feet. The three aircraft were to fly in close formation to pool their ECM resources, which included the GE ALQ-87 and ITT ALQ-117 jammers and the Lundy ALE-24 chaff dispensing system. In fact, the B-52D was better equipped with ECM than SAC's main force B-52Gs, some of which were brought in to augment the bombing force during *Linebacker* II.

The operation began on 18/19 December 1972, when 129 B-52s took off from their respective bases in Thailand and on Guam. Thirty minutes before the first cells arrived over their targets, F-111s carried out strikes on enemy airfields and F-4s sowed two chaff corridors to screen the attacks on the target areas of Kinh No and Yen Vien, north of Hanoi. Unfortunately, the strong north-west wind had dispersed the chaff before the B-52s arrived.

The first B-52 wave to attack the Yen Vien rail yards flew over a cluster of SAM sites as it began its final run-in to the target, and Charcoal 1 – the leading aircraft in the 'Charcoal' cell – sustained a near miss from an SA-2 just as its bomb doors were opening. Crippled and out of control, with its pilot, co-pilot and gunner either dead or incapacitated, the bomber began its long plunge to earth. The navigator, radar navigator and electronic warfare officer ejected and were taken prisoners. A second B-52, attacking with 'Peach' cell in the second wave four hours later, was luckier; it was also crippled by an SA-2, this time just after completing its bombing run, but managed to reach friendly territory with wing and engine fires before its crew were forced to abandon it.

The third wave of eighteen B-52s, attacking five hours later, encountered fierce opposition over the target (the Hanoi railway repair shops). More than sixty SAM launches were observed, but the bombers' ECM worked well and there were no losses, although one aircraft was damaged by a near miss. Another wave of twenty-one aircraft, attacking from the west, also encountered heavy opposition from eleven SAM sites in the Hanoi area and lost the leading aircraft in the last cell to bomb, Rose 1. On this first night of *Linebacker* II, therefore, in which the enemy had launched more than 200 SAMs and expended massive quantities of AAA ammunition, the SA-2s had destroyed three B-52s and damaged three more. The situation might have been much worse, because the MiGs were up in strength, but the Phantom MIGCAP kept them at arm's length and they achieved no successes.

The B-52s suffered no casualties on 19/20 December, when 120 bombers attacked several targets in the Hanoi area. However, the North Vietnamese had by now realised that the bombers were approaching their target areas along the same tracks each night, and they evolved new tactics that included sending up MiGs to shadow the incoming bomber stream and verify its altitude, so that the defences could fuse their missile warheads and AAA shells accordingly.

During the third night of operations, on 20/21 December, SA-2s knocked down two B-52s as they completed their bombing runs, and both of them crashed in Hanoi. A third B-52, badly damaged, struggled back to Thailand, only to crash on landing, killing four of its crew. Two more B-52s in the last wave that night were destroyed by SAMs; a third was crippled and crashed in Laos. In the nine-hour operation the enemy had fired 220 SAMs and claimed six B-52s, four of which were B-52Gs.

On the fourth night, 21/22 December, the tactics employed by the bomber stream were modified. The time between attacking waves was greatly reduced, attacking altitudes were varied and the cells were randomly spaced. In addition, individual crews were given freedom of action in evasive manoeuvring; most favoured a shallow post-attack turn followed by a dive to low altitude and a high-speed run clear of the Vietnamese defences over the Gulf of Tonkin. All sorties on this night were flown from U-Tapao, the Guam-based B-52s being released for *Arc Light* missions (carpet-bombing attacks on suspected NVA troop movements in the south) and there were no losses.

The B-52 force was stood down for thirty-six hours over the Christmas period, but on 26/27 December 120 B-52s, flying in tightly compressed waves and accompanied by 113 defence suppression and ECM aircraft, attacked ten targets in Hanoi, Haiphong and Thai Nguyen, the more vulnerable B-52Gs being assigned to the latter objectives. Two streams attacked Hanoi from the north-west, flying in from Laos and out over the Gulf of Tonkin, while two more attacked on a reciprocal track. All the bombers passed through the target areas within fifteen minutes and only one B-52 fell to the SAM defences, although a second, severely damaged, crashed short of the runway while attempting to land at U-Tapao in Thailand.

The last three nights of *Linebacker* II, in which sixty B-52s were committed on each night, cost SAC five more bombers, all victims of SAMs. By this time the North Vietnamese defences had been virtually neutralised, and the enemy had expended most of their stock of about 1,000 SA-2s. On 30 December, North Vietnam announced that it was ready to resume peace negotiations.

In all, 729 B-52 sorties had been flown during *Linebacker* II, and more than 15,000 tons of bombs dropped out of a total of 20,370 tons. Fifteen B-52s had been lost to the SAM defences, and nine damaged. Thirty-four targets had been hit, and some 1,500 civilians killed. Of the ninety-two crew members aboard the shot-down bombers, twenty-six were recovered by rescue teams, twenty-nine were listed as missing, and thirty-three baled out over North Vietnam to be taken prisoner and later repatriated.

Compared with the threat from North Vietnam's SA-2 *Guideline* surface-to-air missiles, the threat from night fighters and AAA had been small during the eleven nights of *Linebacker* II. On the first night of the operation, a MiG-21 was shot down in a radar-directed gun engagement by Staff Sergeant Samuel O. Turner, the tail gunner in a B-52D; and a second MiG was destroyed by B-52 gunners before the brief campaign was over.

These were the last occasions in the history of air warfare when attacking night fighters were destroyed by a bomber's defensive gunfire.

CHAPTER SIXTEEN

FROM NIGHT FIGHTER TO STRATEGIC FIGHTER

For the former Soviet Air Defence Forces – which had to cope with the threat of air attack from virtually any direction – the deployment of strategic interceptors in considerable numbers around the country's vast periphery was of paramount importance during the years of the Cold War. The first of them, as we have seen, was the Tupolev Tu-28.

The United States Air Force, on the other hand, faced a threat of attack by manned bombers flying over the Arctic, and was consequently able to place its strategic fighter defences well forward, in Alaska, Greenland and Iceland. For many years, the front line was held by the Convair F-102A Delta Dagger and its development, the F-106 Delta Dart, armed with the Douglas AIR-2 Genie or Super Genie nuclear-tipped AAM. These older aircraft were later replaced by the F-4 Phantom and, ultimately, the F-15 Eagle.

Although the Soviet-manned strategic bomber threat was never particularly great at the height of the Cold War – the Soviet leadership having opted instead for the development of advanced strategic missiles – it was revived in the latter years with the deployment of a version of the Tu-95 Bear armed with cruise missiles and of the Tu-160 Blackjack supersonic variable-geometry bomber, the broad equivalent of America's B-1.

America's principal NATO partner, Britain, also faced an air threat from one main axis, but the British air defences had to expect a much shorter warning time. It was therefore imperative to deploy an aircraft with a rapid reaction time, and in this respect the BAC Lightning was excellent. With the aircraft off the ground interception was a fairly straightforward matter, even though the main medium between pilot and controller was voice communication. (It had always been intended that the Lightning be equipped with a datalink for the passage of data from a ground-based computer to the aircraft's auto-attack system, but this was never fitted.) In a rear-sector attack with the Lightning's Firestreak AAM missiles the target would have been well within visual range during the final stage, provided it was daytime, so there was little danger of engaging a friendly aircraft.

The replacement of the Lightning by the McDonnell Douglas Phantom FG1/FGR2 brought about some dramatic changes in the RAF's Rules of Engagement, because the Phantom carried an impressive array of weapons, including some with a genuine 'beyond visual range' capability, and this raised many issues of identification, classification and tactics which had to be solved by tighter controls and realistic training if the risk of a costly error was to be eliminated. The AIM-7 Sparrow was capable of engaging targets at ranges well in excess of twelve miles, and at that distance the foolproof identification of a target without some form of visual enhancement was virtually impossible. The Phantom entered full RAF service in the air defence role without any aid to visual identification, although US variants had carried an electro-optical device for this purpose for some time. The British variant was eventually fitted with air-to-air IFF, radar warning sensors and a telescope system.

Principally, the RAF's air defence system had to guard against attacks by a new generation of fast Soviet aircraft armed with long-range missiles, which generated a requirement for an interceptor capable of spending lengthy periods on patrol on the axis of the potential air threat, a long way from its home bases. At the beginning of the 1970s the Lightning was reaching the end of its useful life and its systems left a lot to be desired, while the Phantom, although expected to fulfil the air defence role adequately, would need to be phased out in favour of a more advanced weapons system in the late 1980s.

In 1971, therefore, the Ministry of Defence issued Air Staff Target 395, which called for a minimum-change, minimum-cost but effective interceptor to replace the British Aerospace Lightning and the F-4 Phantom in the air defence of the United Kingdom. Primary armament was to be the British Aerospace Dynamics XJ521 Sky Flash medium-range air-to-air missile, and the primary sensor a Marconi Avionics pulse-Doppler radar. The result was the Air Defence Variant (ADV) of the Panavia Tornado interdictor/strike (IDS), an aircraft that provides a good illustration of a modern round-the-clock interceptor and its

Top and above: *The English Electric (BAC) Lightning gave RAF Fighter Command a round-the-clock defensive capability, replacing the Hunter and Javelin in their respective day and night roles.* (Philip Jarrett)

The Phantom was the first RAF aircraft to be armed with missiles that could hit targets beyond visual range. (RAF)

associated systems.

The original Tornado ADV study envisaged four Sky Flash missiles under the wings, long-range tanks under the fuselage and a modified nose to accommodate the AI radar. Early aerodynamic trials, however, showed that with pylon-mounted missiles the ADV's performance fell short of requirements, giving little or no advantage over the Phantom it was intended to replace, even allowing for further engine developments. The answer was to carry the AAMs semi-submerged under the fuselage, providing a low-drag configuration. To accommodate the front pair of missiles some lengthening of the forward fuselage was necessary, but this produced an added bonus in that it increased internal fuel capacity by ten per cent. A further armament change involved the deletion of one of the ADV's two planned Mauser 27 mm cannon, providing more space for the installation of avionics. The overall structural changes involved stretching the fuselage by 53 in; the wing root glove was also given increased sweep, moving the centre of pressure forward to compensate for the resultant change of centre of gravity and to reduce wave drag.

Because of the minimum-change requirement, the only changes permitted to the Tornado IDS weapon system were those that would produce an effective air defence aircraft at minimum cost. First of all, this involved the removal of all equipment not required for the air defence role, including the Texas Instruments terrain-following/ground mapping radar. The next stage was to identify equipment that only required modification to perform the air defence role. This included the Command Stability Augmentation System (CSAS), which required inputs to reduce stick pitch forces and increase roll rates for air combat. The result was a system common to both Tornado ADV and IDS, with the air defence equipment added. This comprised the Marconi Avionics AI radar, with integrated Cossor IFF interrogator, Singer-Kearfott secure datalink, Marconi Space and Defence Systems radar homing and warning receiver, Smiths Industries/Computing Devices missile management system, and a new electronic head-down display in the front cockpit. All this required a considerable re-write of the main computer software and resulted in more changes than had originally been envisaged. Each step was approved separately by the MoD, which considered a number of alternatives – including the F-14 and F-15 – before finally approving the whole ADV project in 1976.

The aircraft that eventually emerged was a long-range interceptor, with long on-CAP (Combat Air Patrol) time, capable of engaging multiple targets in rapid succession, in all weathers and in complex ECM conditions. It was designed to operate with the United Kingdom Air Defence Ground Environment (UKADGE), airborne early warning (AEW) aircraft, tankers and air defence ships, all linked in due course to a secure ECM-resistance data and voice command and control net. The problem of navigation at extreme range from fixed navigational systems was overcome by a highly accurate twin inertial platform, the Ferranti

141

Top and above: *The prototype Panavia Tornado Air Defence Variant (ADV) taking off from BAe Warton, Lancashire . . . and in a powerful climb out with reheat on.* (BAe)

FIN1010, which provided the computer with accurate position data for steering to a large number of fixed or moving positions. This could be done automatically by use of the autopilot, allowing the crew to concentrate on the tactical information provided by the AI radar and datalink.

The intercept radar selected for the Tornado ADV was the Marconi (later GEC Marconi) Avionics AI24 Foxhunter, development of which began in 1974. The essential requirement was that detection ranges should in no way be limited to target altitude. Look-down capability against low-level targets was the most demanding case, particularly when the interceptor itself was at low altitude. Severe and sophisticated electronic countermeasures also had to be overcome.

By the time the first Tornado ADV was ready to fly, late in 1979, the external stores fit had also undergone changes. The four Sky Flash AAMs were now joined by four AIM-9L Sidewinders on underwing stations, and the capacity of each drop tank increased from 1,500 litres to 2,250 litres to extend unrefuelled range and time on CAP.

Three Tornado ADV prototypes were built. All were powered by the Turbo-Union RB199 Mk 103 turbofan, which was also to power the initial production batch of Tornado F-2s for the RAF. These aircraft also featured manually-controlled wing sweep, which would be automatic on later production aircraft. The first development Tornado ADV, A01, was a single-stick aircraft assigned to handling, performance and general systems evaluation. Early in 1982, to demonstrate that the ADV could fulfil its CAP requirements in all respects, this aircraft flew a CAP of two hours twenty minutes over the North Sea, involving a flight of 325 nm to the CAP area and a similar return flight. The aircraft was climbed out of Warton, Lancashire, and cruised at high altitude over the North Sea, then descended to medium altitude to take up a CAP racetrack pattern. On arriving back at base the aircraft loitered in the local area for fifteen minutes at low level before landing with more than five per cent internal fuel remaining after a total flight time of four hours thirteen minutes.

It was a very promising indication of the ADV's capability. So were the armament trials, carried out by A02 in the same year. Sky Flash firings were carried out from 0.9 M into the supersonic envelope, while Mauser gun firing trials covered the subsonic flight envelope above 200 kt from zero G to the angle of attack limit, and up to 30,000 feet. By the end of 1982, A03 had done most of the necessary radar and weapon system integration flight trials and pre-production radar flight trials were scheduled to start in the near future, although it was now apparent that deliveries of the operational AI24 were going to be alarmingly late.

Despite problems with the AI radar there was nothing wrong with the aircraft and its other systems, and orders for the RAF now stood at 165, to be delivered in three batches. Pilots of 'A' Squadron of the Aeroplane and Armament Experimental Establishment (A&AEE) at Boscombe Down, who evaluated it, were very enthusiastic about all aspects except the radar, which failed to meet its specification in no fewer than fifty-two areas.

The problems with the Foxhunter were still far from resolved when the first Tornado F-2s were delivered to No 229 Operational Conversion Unit (OCU) at RAF Coningsby, in Lincolnshire, in November 1984. The first eighteen aircraft were all powered by Mk 103 engines; aircraft after that had the more powerful Mk 104, which combined a 360 mm reheat extension with a Lucas Aerospace digital electronic engine control unit (DECU). These later aircraft, designated Tornado F-3 – the definitive production version of the design – also featured the full armament of four Sky Flash and four AIM-9Ls, auto wing sweep, and automanoeuvre devices with the slats and flaps deploying as a function of angle of attack and wing sweep.

It was not until 1986 that the first modified AI24 Foxhunter radars were delivered for installation in the OCU aircraft, the necessary modifications having cost an additional £250 million. The first squadron, No 29, formed at RAF Coningsby in May 1987 and was declared operational at the end of November. The aircraft eventually armed seven squadrons in addition to No 229 OCU (which became No 56 Reserve Squadron on 1 July 1992).

The Tornado F-3 opened up a whole range of tactical possibilities for No 11 Group RAF, the air defence group responsible for its operations. Its excellent take-off and landing characteristics mean that the aircraft can, if necessary, deploy to small airfields or even sections of motorway, together with its Auxiliary Power Unit and datalink. All the crew needs to do is remain on cockpit alert, monitoring tactical developments on the multi-function displays via the datalink, and wait for the order to scramble. Long before combat is joined, pilot and navigator will have an accurate appraisal of the tactical situation.

Normal air defence operations with the Tornado F-3 involve what is known as a 'heavy combat fit', which means four Sky Flash, four Sidewinders and no external tanks. CAP fit with the two tanks is reserved specifically for long-range sorties. A good example of what the F-3 can achieve without the long-range tank was given on 10 September 1988, when two aircraft of No 5 Squadron were scrambled from RAF Coningsby to intercept a pair of Tupolev Tu-95 Bear-D maritime radar reconnaissance aircraft over the Norwegian Sea. A VC-10 tanker was scrambled from RAF Leuchars to rendezvous with the Tornados, which carried out the intercept successfully.

The Tornado F-3 is, first and foremost, a missile platform. The aircraft's AI24 radar uses a technique known as frequency modulated interrupted continuous wave (FMICW), with which is integrated a Cossor IFF-3500 interrogator and a radar signal processor to suppress ground clutter (which, in fact, was one of the major problems associated with its protracted development). The radar's high pulse repetition frequency (PRF) enables it to detect targets at an initial range of about 100 nm, while FMICW allows the range of the target to be determined from the frequency change between transmission and reception.

As they are detected, the targets are stored in the Central Digital Computer, which is the same as that in the Tornado IDS variant. Since the radar continues to scan normally, the targets are unaware that they are the subject of detailed analysis. The system rejects unwanted signals, leaving only real targets which then pass through the radar data processor prior to display to the aircraft's crew. While the radar keeps up a 'running commentary' on ranges, velocities and tracks of established targets, it continues to scan and report new plots. With the computer fully updated, the crew plan their approach to engage the maximum number of targets. Displays are duplicated in the front cockpit for the pilot, who steers to the engagement on his head-up display. The symbology for Sky Flash, Sidewinder or gun attacks is very clear, and an important feature is the target indicator which aids the pilot in an early visual sighting.

For a long-range interception, the Sky Flash semi-active radar homing AAM would be used. This weapon was developed from the AIM-7E Sparrow and features several areas of improvement, including early discrimination between grouped targets, positive target detection and tracking against ground radar clutter, ECM resistance, more accurate guidance resulting in reduced miss distance, better proximity fusing and improved reliability. The original version required continuous-wave illumination by the launch aircraft's radar all the way to the target, but the latest version is fitted with an MSDS monopulse radar homing head. It can engage targets at high altitude or down to 250 feet in the face of heavy ECM and at stand-off ranges of more than 25 nm.

The Sky Flash launch sequence lasts less than a tenth of a second, the missile being driven down from its fuselage recess by two gas-operated, long-stroke rams (developed by Frazer-Nash) through the flow fields around the aircraft. Additionally, the rams stabilise the missile in roll and yaw during ejection, and are then retracted to avoid adding post-launch drag. The system enables the F-3 to launch its missiles across the entire flight envelope. The Tornado F-3 is also compatible with the AIM-120 Advanced Medium Range AAM (AMRAAM).

For engagements at closer range the AIM-9L infrared homing AAM Sidewinder would be used. To respond quickly to a close-in threat, the pilot can take control of the weapons systems by selecting the air-to-air override mode. This mode, optimised for visual combat, is controlled by two multi-function buttons mounted on the throttle. Pressing the buttons in sequence selects the close combat radar mode and associated HUDs (Head-Up Display), as well as the required weapons, without the pilot having to take his hands off the throttle or stick. A hand controller, located aft of the throttles, may be used to slew the radar scanner or missile homing heads if the automatic HUD scan pattern is insufficient to acquire the target. Once the target is in scan, lock-on is automatic. The AIM-132 Advanced Short Range AAM (ASRAAM) is also integrated on the F-3.

Although not a fighter in the strictest sense of the word, the Tornado F-3 gives an excellent account of itself in combat with other contemporary aircraft, including the F-16 Fighting Falcon. With its wings swept at forty-five degrees the Tornado can hold its own in a turning fight with most combat aircraft of its generation. The aircraft's Spin Prevention and Incidence Limiting System (SPILS) provides care-free handling, and stick forces are about thirty per cent lighter than those of the Tornado GR1. Another useful feature is that the pilot can bang the throttles open and shut without penalty. The F-3 is capable of 2.2 M at high level, and more than 800 kt at low level; in both cases, fuel consumption is surprisingly low. A 'clean' Tornado F-3 can fly for one hour at 420 kt, low level, and still have enough fuel for half an hour's flying time.

No modern fighter, whether designed for air superiority over the battlefield or long-range interception, can function successfully without being fully integrated with airborne and ground-based electronic surveillance systems. Today's ground-based systems combine a centralised command structure with a decentralised sensor network that is secure, survivable and capable of functioning even after sustaining substantial damage. They are based on advanced portable ground radars, enabling sensors to be deployed almost anywhere, and telecommunications technology providing a network of lines and exchanges that would continue to route both voice and data transmissions along any path so long as some sort of physical connection remains.

The Improved United Kingdom Air Defence Ground Environment is typical of such a system. IUKADGE involves three different types of new-generation radar, operating in two wavebands. There are two General Electric GE592 and four

GEC/Marconi Martello 23 cm radars, operating in the L-band, and six Plessey/ITT 10 cm radars operating in the S-band. All are three-dimensional radars capable of measuring target range, bearing and height. Each radar is deployed in a convoy of about fifteen vehicles to a pre-surveyed but unmarked site indistinguishable from the surrounding countryside. The radar head is located remotely from its associated reporting post, and is protected by decoys intended to confuse anti-radar missiles. The overlapping L- and S-band coverage also reduces the risk of enemy jamming. As an extra insurance, an electronic counter-countermeasures officer forms part of the reporting post (RP) trailer crew, his function to assist the radar in overcoming any jamming problems.

Associated with four of the twelve RPs are hardened Command and Reporting Posts (CRPs) with local tracking and fighter control capability; these provide backup facilities for the Command and Reporting Centres (CRCs), which under normal circumstances are responsible for tracking and interceptor control and which are the nerve centres of the UK air defence system.

The process of building up a picture of a possible air threat begins with the first receipt of radar plots (target positions) and strobes (the bearings of enemy jammers). This information is fed into the air defence system via a narrow-band datalink. At the CRC, the plots are combined with those of other radars for multi-radar target tracking; these active tracks are then combined with passive tracks derived from jamming strobes. Tracks from airborne early warning (AEW) and interceptor aircraft are also introduced, together with those from other CRCs, and track-to-track correlation is carried out to produce the local picture. Then the recognition process begins, an automatic interface with the principal air traffic control centre ensuring instant access to all currently filed civil flight plans.

With the threat revealed, the fighter controllers can now marshal and direct their forces. Sea tracks are introduced into the system to produce the final recognised air-sea picture; this mutual exchange of information between elements ensures that all centres share the same constantly updated picture of the UK Air Defence Region (UKADR), so that even if an element is lost, the big picture will remain intact. In addition, the CRCs interface with the NATO Air Defence Ground Environment (NADGE) and France's STRIDA II air defence

systems for target data exchange.

Another key element in the air defence system is the airborne early warning aircraft, and in this respect the NATO requirement is filled by the Boeing E-3 Sentry. The Boeing E-3, originally known as the EC-137, stemmed from a NATO requirement for an early warning aircraft equipped with radar systems capable of extending the low-altitude radar view of Warsaw Pact territory by as much as 150 miles, thereby filling the existing gaps in low-altitude coverage left by ground-based radars, and providing a major advance in early warning protection. Although the perceived threat from the east has receded over the horizon, if not vanished entirely, the core of the E-3's role today remains the detection of an air threat. Its primary function in the 1991 Gulf War was to detect the movement of Iraqi aircraft and to direct Allied fighters to the point where a successful interception could be made. It has been used extensively for surveillance of Bosnia (Operation *Deny Flight*), providing intelligence of aircraft, helicopter and missile battery movements that might present a threat to UN peacekeeping forces, and in directing NATO air attacks on targets in Serbia and Kosovo (Operation *Combined Force*).

At the heart of the E-3's systems is its Westinghouse surveillance radar, which can track targets more than 300 nm away while the E-3 orbits at 30,000 feet. The thirty-foot diameter radome turns at six revolutions per minute when the equipment is active, and has various operating modes depending on the task in hand. The standard E-3A's radar was later modified to track ships, and other modifications included the fitting of a faster central computer with expanded memory, together with improved communications equipment. This included the Joint Tactical Information Distribution System (JTIDS), which ensures an unbroken transmission of data if main communications links are disrupted and gives fighter and attack crews an unprecedented picture of the air battle. Fighters equipped with the system include the F-15 and Tornado F-3. The E-3 Sentry fulfils the Airborne Warning and Command System (AWACS) role with the USAF, the RAF and NATO, and with the French Air Force.

It is technology far removed from the primitive AI that led a Blenheim of the Fighter Interception Unit to the first radar-aided destruction of an enemy bomber, on that July night in 1940.

RAF NIGHT FIGHTER VICTORIES, JULY 1940–MAY 1941

Date	Enemy a/c	Unit	Attacking a/c	Unit	Remarks
23/24 July 1940	Do 17Z	2/KG3	Blenheim	FIU	Off Sussex
25/26 July 1940	He 111H-4	1/KG4	Hurricane	87 Sqn	Nr Honiton, Devon
11/12 August 1940	He 111H-3	2/KG27	Unknown		Nr Wimborne, Dorset
16/17 August 1940	Ju 88	4/NJG1	Blenheim	29 Sqn	Off Spurn Head
24/25 August 1940	He 111P	9/KG55	Unknown		Off Hastings
29/30 August 1940	Do 17Z	2/KG2	Unknown		Crashed in France
	He 111H	3/KG27	Spitfire	92 Sqn	Nr Hale, Cheshire
5/6 September 1940	He 111H-3	1/KG1	Blenheim	25 Sqn	Rendlesham, Suffolk
	He 111H-3	2/KG26	Unknown		Crashed in Holland
14/15 September 1940	He 111H-4	3/KG4	Blenheim	25 Sqn	Nr Sheering, Essex
17/18 September 1940	Ju 88A-1	1/KG54	Defiant	141 Sqn	Maidstone
15/16 October 1940	He 111H-4	2/KGr126	Defiant	264 Sqn	Hutton, Essex
15/16 November 1940	Do 17Z	9/KG76	Unknown		Harlow, Essex
19/20 November 1940	Ju 88A-5	3/KG54	Beaufighter	604 Sqn	Chichester
22/23 December 1940	He 111P-4	3/KG55	Defiant	141 Sqn	Etchingham, E. Sussex
15/16 January 1941	Do 17Z-2	4/KG3	Hurricane	151 Sqn	Nr Brentwood, Essex
	He 111H-5	2/KG53	Hurricane	151 Sqn	Off Canvey Island
4/5 February 1941	Do 17Z-3	7/KG2	Defiant	151 Sqn	Weldon, Northants
15/16 February 1941	He 111P-2	7/KG27	Beaufighter	604 Sqn	Haberton, Devon
17/18 February 1941	Do 17Z-3	3/KGr606	Beaufighter	219 Sqn	Windsor Great Park
25/26 February 1941	Do 17Z-2	4/KG2	Hurricane	85 Sqn	Lavenham, Suffolk
4/5 March 1941	He 111H-5	1/KG28	Beaufighter	604 Sqn	Beer Head, Devon
12/13 March 1941	He 111H-4	4/KG27	Defiant	264 Sqn	Off Hastings
	He 111P-4	5/KG55	Defiant	264 Sqn	Ockley, Surrey
	He 111P-4	6/KG55	Hurricane	96 Sqn	Widnes, Lancs
	Ju 88A-5	6/KG76	Beaufighter	604 Sqn	Kingston Deverill, Wilts
	Ju 88A-5	9/KG76	Defiant	307 Sqn	Wychbold, Worcs
13/14 March 1941	Do 17Z-2	Stab/KG2	Beaufighter	29 Sqn	Off Skegness
	He 111H-5	7/KG26	Beaufighter	219 Sqn	Shipley, Sussex
	He 111P-2	7/KG55	Beaufighter	219 Sqn	Bramdean, Hants
	He 111H-3	1/KGr100	Blenheim	600 Sqn	Dunure, Ayrshire
	Ju 88A-5	3/Ku106	Spitfire	72 Sqn	Off Amble, Northumberland
	Ju 88C-4	4/NJG2	Beaufighter	29 Sqn	Dovendale, Lincs
14/15 March 1941	He 111H-3	2/KG1	Beaufighter	29 Sqn	Off Skegness
	He 111P-4	6/KG55	Beaufighter	604 Sqn	Falfield, Glos
	Ju 88A-5	1/KGr806	Beaufighter	Unknown	Off Beachy Head
3/4 April 1941	Ju 88A-5	7/KG1	Beaufighter	604 Sqn	Off Isle of Wight
4/5 April 1941	He 111H-5	3/KG26	Beaufighter	604 Sqn	Weston-super-Mare
7/8 April 1941	He 111H-5	9/KG26	Hurricane	87 Sqn	Branscombe, Devon
	Ju 88A-5	5/KG54	Defiant	256 Sqn	Southport, Lancs
	He 111P-4	1/KG55	Beaufighter	219 Sqn	Off Worthing
8/9 April 1941	He 111H-5	9/KG26	Defiant	264 Sqn	Hitchin, Herts
	He 111H-5	2/KG27	Hurricane	151 Sqn	Warwicks
	He 111P-4	3/KG55	Hurricane	151 Sqn	Desford, Leics
	He 111P-4	8/KG55	Defiant	151 Sqn	Windsor
9/10 April 1941	He 111P-2	5/KG55	Defiant	264 Sqn	Busbridge, Surrey
	Ju 88A-5	3/KG77	Defiant	151 Sqn	Bramcote, Warwicks
	He 111H-3	2/KGr100	Beaufighter	604 Sq	Cranborne, Dorset
	Ju 88C-4	4/NJG2	Beaufighter	25 Sqn	Oakham, Rutland
	He 111H-2	2/KG1	Unknown		English Channel
	He 111P	4/KG27	Defiant	264 Sqn	Smethwick, Staffs

RAF NIGHT FIGHTER VICTORIES, JULY 1940 – MAY 1941

Date	Enemy a/c	Unit	Attacking a/c	Unit	Remarks
10/11 April 1941	Ju 88A-5	2/KG1	Hurricane	151 Sqn	Murcott, Oxford
	He 111H-5	3/KG26	Defiant	264 Sqn	Seaford, Sussex
	He 111H-5	8/KG26	Defiant	256 Sqn	Radway, Warwicks
	Ju 88A-5	1/KG54	Beaufighter	604 Sqn	Off Swanage, Dorset
	He 111P-2	9/KG55	Hurricane	151 Sqn	Kettering, Northants
	He 111H-3	3/KGr100	Beaufighter	604 Sqn	Isle of Wight
11/12 April 1941	He 111P-2	9/KG27	Defiant	307 Sqn	Lydlinch, Dorset
15/16 April 1941	Ju 88A-5	2/KG54	Beaufighter	604 Sqn	Holcombe Burnell, Devon
	He 111P-4	2/KG55	Beaufighter	604 Sqn	Off Portland Bill
	He 111P-2	8/KG55	Beaufighter	604 Sqn	Southampton
16/17 April 1941	Ju 88A-5	4/KG1	Beaufighter	219 Sqn	Cranleigh, Surrey
	He 111H-5	2/KG28	Beaufighter	219 Sqn	Wormley, Surrey
	Ju 88A-5	3/KG76	Beaufighter	219 Sqn	Wimbledon
17/18 April 1941	Ju 88C-4	4/NJG2	Unknown		Nr Peterborough
19/20 April 1941	He 111H-5	7/KG4	Hurricane	151 Sqn	Stockbury, Kent
1/2 May 1941	He 111P	4/KG27	Beaufighter	219 Sqn	Off Shoreham
2/3 May 1941	Ju 88A-6	8/KG77	Beaufighter	604 Sqn	Lyndhurst, Hants
3/4 May 1941	He 111H-5	3/KG26	Beaufighter	604 Sqn	Crowcombe, Somerset
	He 111H-5	8/KG26	Beaufighter	219 Sqn	Sidlesham, Chichester
	He 111P-2	9/KG26	Beaufighter	604 Sqn	Corton Denham, Somerset
	He 111H-4	3/KG53	Defiant	151 Sqn	Sharrington, Norfolk
	Ju 88A-6	2/KG54	Defiant	307 Sqn	Lostock Gralam, Cheshire
	Ju 88A-5	1/Ku806	Beaufighter	600 Sqn	Stoke St Michael, Somerset
4/5 May 1941	Ju 88A-5	8/KG1	Beaufighter	25 Sqn	Eastgate, Lincs
	Ju 88A-5	6/KG54	Beaufighter	604 Sqn	East Burton, Dorset
	Ju 88A-5	2/Ku106	Unknown		Idle, Bradford
5/6 May 1941	He 111H-5	1/KG54	Defiant	141 Sqn	Whorlton Park, Newcastle-on-Tyne
	Ju 88A-5	4/KG54	Beaufighter	604 Sqn	Chawleigh, Devon
6/7 May 1941	He 111H-5	7/KG27	Beaufighter	600 Sqn	Oborne, Dorset
	Ju 88A-5	5/KG30	Defiant	141 Sqn	Holy Island, N'land
	Ju 88A-5	2/Ku106	Defiant	141 Sqn	Lennoxtown, Stirling
7/8 May 1941	He 111H-5	1/KG54	Hurricane	151 Sqn	Withernsea, Yorks
	He 111P	2/KG27	Beaufighter	600 Sqn	Weston-Super-Mare
	He 111P	2/KG27	Beaufighter	600 Sqn	Isle of Wight
	He 111H-5	7/KG27	Beaufighter	604 Sqn	Weston Zoyland, Somerset
	He 111H-3	1/KG53	Defiant	255 Sqn	Scrooby, Notts
	He 111P-4	1/KG55	Defiant	265 Sqn	Stockport, Cheshire
	He 111P-4	3/KG55	Beaufighter	604 Sqn	Off Portland
	He 111P-4	3/KG55	Defiant	256 Sqn	Bagillt, Flintshire
	He 111P-4	6/KG55	Defiant	256 Sqn	Wrexham
	Ju 88A-5	3/KG76	Unknown		Gradbach, Staffs
	He 111H-2	3/KGr100	Defiant	256 Sqn	Malpas, Cheshire
	Do 17Z-10	2/NJG2	Beaufighter	25 Sqn	Carrington, Lincs
8/9 May 1941	He 111H-5	2/KG27	Beaufighter	29 Sqn	Wimbledon
	He 111H-5	4/KG53	Defiant	255 Sqn	Patrington, Hull
	He 111H-5	6/KG 53	Defiant	255 Sqn	Long Riston, Yorks
9/10 May 1941	Ju 88A-5	9/KG1	Beaufighter	219 Sqn	Off Selsey
10/11 May 1941	He 111P-2	7/KG2	Beaufighter	29 Sqn	Off Seaford, Sussex
	He 111P-2	8/KG27	Beaufighter	219 Sqn	Cranleigh, Surrey
	He 111H-5	1/KG28	Unknown		Chelmsford, Essex
	He 111H-5	3/KG53	Defiant	Unknown	Upchurch, Kent
	He 111P	9/KG55	Unknown		Withyham, E. Sussex
15/16 May 1941	Ju 88A-5	7/KG1	Beaufighter	600 Sqn	Plymtree, Devon
	He 111P-2	7/KG55	Beaufighter	219 Sqn	Sompting, Sussex

Although night attacks on the British Isles continued, the *Luftwaffe*'s bomber force was now preoccupied with operations over the Soviet Union, which was attacked on 22 June 1941. Attacks on Britain now tended to be small-scale affairs, and would never again reach the intensity of the night raids inflicted on the British people during the spring 'Blitz' of 1941.

THE TOP-SCORING *LUFTWAFFE* NIGHT FIGHTER PILOTS

Thirty German night fighter pilots scored forty or more victories in the night battle over the *Reich*. Between them, they destroyed 1,800 aircraft, the equivalent of 120 RAF Bomber Squadrons.

The Leading German Night Fighter Aces

Name	Unit(s)	Score	Remarks
Schnaufer, *Maj* Heinz-Wolfgang	NJGs 1, 4	121	
Lent, *Oberst* Helmut	NJGs 1, 2, 3	102	+8 by day k.7.10.44
Sayn-Wittgenstein, *Maj* Prince	NJGs 3,2	83	k.21.1.44
Streib, *Oberst* Werner	NJG 1	66	
Meurer, *Hauptmn* Manfred	NJGs 1,5,	65	k.21.1.44
Radusch, *Oberst* Gunther	NJGs 1,3,5,2	64	
Rokker, *Hauptmn* Heinz	NJG 2	64	
Schonert, *Maj* Rudolf	NJGs 1,2,5,100	64	
Zorner, *Maj* Paul	NJGs 2,3,5,100	59	
Raht, *Hauptmn* Gerhard	NJG 2	58	
Herget, *Maj* Wilhelm	NJGs 4,3,71	57	+14 by day
Becker, *Hauptmn* Martin	NJGs 3,4,6	57	
Francsi, *Oberlt* Gustave	NJG 100	56	
Kraft, *Hauptmn* Josef	NJGs 4,5,1,6	56	
Struning, *Hauptmn* Heinz	NJGs 2,1	56	k.24.12.44
Frank, *Hauptmn* Hans-Dieter	NJG 1	55	k.27.9.43
Vinke, *Feldwbl* Heinz	NJG 1	54	k.26.2.44
Geiger, *Hauptmn* August	NJG 1	53	k.27.9.43
Lutje, *Oberstlt* Herbert	NJGs 1,6	53	
Drewes, *Maj* Martin	NJG 1	52	
Hoffmann, *Maj* Werner	NJGs 3,5	52	
Lippe-Weissenfeld, *Maj* Prince	NJGs 2,1,5	51	k.12.3.44
Welter, *Oberlt* Kurt	JG 300, NJG 11	50+	
Greiner, *Hauptmn* Hermann	NJG 1	50	
Kollack, *Stabsfeldwbl* Reinhard	NJGs 1,4	49	
Becker, *Hauptmn* Ludwig	NJGs 2, 1	46	k.26.2.43
Frank, *Leutnant* Rudolf	NJG 3	45	k.26.4.44
Gildner, *Oberlt* Paul	NJG 1	44	k.24.2.43
Knacke, *Hauptmn* Reinhold	NJG 1	44	k.3.2.43
Jabs, *Oberstlt* Hans-Joachim	NJG 1	28	+22 by day

BIBLIOGRAPHY

Aders, G. *History of the German Night Fighter Force*. Jane's, 1979.

Ashmore, Maj-Gen E.B. *Air Defence*. Longmans, 1929.

Bekker, Cajus. *The Luftwaffe War Diaries*. Macdonald, 1966.

Brandon, Sqn Ldr L. *Night Flyer*. William Kimber, 1969.

Brew, A. *The Defiant File*. Air-Britain, 1996.

Chisholm, R. *Cover of Darkness*. Chatto & Windus, 1953.

Cole, C. and Cheesman, F. *The Air Defence of Britain 1914–18*. Putnam 1984.

Darlington, R. *Night Hawk*. William Kimber, 1985.

Delve, K. *Nightfighter. The Battle for the Night Skies*. Arms & Armour Press, 1995.

Gentil, R. *Trained to Intrude*. Bachman & Turner, 1974.

Gunston, Bill. *Night Fighters. A Development and Combat History*. PSL 1976.

Held, W. and Nauroth, H. *The Night Fighters. German Fighters in World War II: a Photographic History of the German Nachtjäger 1940-1945*. Schiffer Publications (USA) 1995.

Held, W. and Nauroth, H. *The Defence of the Reich. Hitler's Nightfighter Planes and Pilots*. Arco (USA) 1982.

Hermann, H. *On Eagles' Wings*. Guild Publishing 1991.

Hinchcliffe, P. *The Other Battle. Luftwaffe Night Aces versus Bomber Command*. Airlife 1996.

Howard-Williams, J. *Night Intruder*. David & Charles 1976.

Hunt, L. *Defence Until Dawn. The Story of No 488 (NZ) Squadron*. Crecy Books 1993.

Jackson, R. *Air War over Korea*. Airlife 1998.

Jackson, R. *Air War over Flanders, 1914–18*. Airlife, 1999.

Jackson, R. *The High Cold War*. PSL, 1998.

Johnen, W. *Duel Under the Stars. A German Night Fighter Pilot in the Second World War*. Crecy Books 1994.

Lindsay, R. *Service History of the Gloster Javelin Mks 7 to 9R*. Privately published and undated.

Middlebrook, M. and Everitt, C. *The Bomber Command War Diaries*. Viking 1985.

Nauroth, H. and Held, W. *Messerschmitt Bf110 Zerstörer*. Motorbuch, 1978.

Philpott, B. *Meteor*. PSL 1986.

Price, A. *Battle over the Reich*. Ian Allan 1973.

Rawnsley, C.F. and Wright, R. *Night Fighter*. Collins, 1957.

Robinson, A. *Nightfighter. A Concise History of Nightfighting Since 1914*. Ian Allan 1988.

Spooner, T. *Night Fighter Ace*. Sutton Publishing 1997. (Story of Wg Cdr Bob Braham.)

INDEX

AIRFIELDS/AIRSTRIPS

KU-153-503

DUBLIN
A GRAND TOUR

JACQUELINE O'BRIEN

DUB

A GRAND

WEIDENFELD

Reading 901595
Batt 151
C 90

0297 832 247 0 973 81

Reading Borough Council

34126004036680

WITH DESMOND GUINNESS

LIN

TOUR

BERKSHIRE COUNTY LIBRARY

AND NICOLSON

C O N

TENTS

For Vincent and David O'Brien

TEXT © JACQUELINE O'BRIEN AND DESMOND GUINNESS 1994
PHOTOGRAPHS AND ARCHITECTS, ARTISTS AND CRAFTSMEN © JACQUELINE O'BRIEN 1994

FIRST PUBLISHED IN 1994 BY
GEORGE WEIDENFELD AND NICOLSON LTD
ORION HOUSE, 5 UPPER ST MARTIN'S LANE,
LONDON WC2H 9EA

ALL RIGHTS RESERVED. NO PART OF THIS PUBLICATION MAY BE REPRODUCED,
STORED IN A RETRIEVAL SYSTEM, OR TRANSMITTED, IN ANY FORM OR BY ANY MEANS,
ELECTRONIC, MECHANICAL OR OTHERWISE, WITHOUT THE PRIOR
PERMISSION IN WRITING OF THE COPYRIGHT OWNERS.

BRITISH LIBRARY CATALOGUING-IN-PUBLICATION DATA
A CATALOGUE RECORD FOR THIS BOOK IS AVAILABLE FROM THE BRITISH LIBRARY.
ISBN 0-297-83224-7

EDITED BY COLIN GRANT
DESIGNED BY HARRY GREEN
MAP BY TAS LTD

PHOTOTYPESET BY KEYSPOOLS LTD, NEWTON LE WILLOWS, LANCS.
COLOUR SEPARATION BY NEWSELE LITHO LTD
PRINTED IN ITALY BY PRINTERS SRL, TRENTO
BOUND BY L.E.G.O., VICENZA

PAGE I
PLASTERWORK DECORATION ABOVE THE STAIRCASE AT 20 LOWER DOMINICK STREET.
PAGE 3
WAX IMPRESSIONS OF THE THIRTEENTH-CENTURY DUBLIN CITY SEAL,
REPRESENTING THE CITY AT WAR AND PEACE.
PAGE 4
LEFT THE NAVE OF CHRIST CHURCH CATHEDRAL.
RIGHT THE FRONT DOOR OF 67 MERRION SQUARE.
PAGE 5
TOP THE DRAWING ROOM OF 18 NORTH GREAT GEORGE'S STREET.
BOTTOM THE BANKING HALL OF THE ALLIED IRISH BANK, 5 COLLEGE STREET.
ENDPAPERS
FRONT GREAT COURT YARD, NOW KNOWN AS UPPER CASTLE YARD, DUBLIN CASTLE,
FROM MALTON'S 'VIEWS OF DUBLIN', 1799.
BACK ST STEPHEN'S GREEN, FROM MALTON'S 'VIEWS OF DUBLIN', 1799.

READING CENTRAL LIBRARY
REFERENCE DEPARTMENT
CLASS 720.9418
ADDED 9-11-94   PRICE £30-00
DISPOSED OF/FILED

ACKNOWLEDGEMENTS

I would like to thank my co-author, Desmond Guinness, for his wonderful help in writing this book. His extensive knowledge of Dublin, his love of its Georgian architecture, coupled with his great concern for Ireland's heritage and his enthusiasm for preservation have been a source of inspiration. It has been an unforgettable experience to explore the buildings of Dublin and we have both learnt a great deal during our researches. I also want to put on record my gratitude to Penny Guinness at Leixlip, who was always so welcoming and hospitable. During our long writing sessions, she most patiently endured the inconvenience of an untidy library, spread with books and endless drafts from the computer, as well as the temporary loss of her husband.

David O'Brien was an invaluable source of information and support throughout and also compiled the index – for him a special debt of gratitude. Dr Edward McParland and Frederick O'Dwyer read the manuscript and made many valuable suggestions for which I am most grateful; they were both very generous in sharing their vast accumulation of knowledge. I am indebted to David Griffin of the Irish Architectural Archive, and to his most obliging staff, for help with the manuscript and the list of architects, artists and craftsmen, and for advice on locations to photograph. Much information was obtained and obscure points clarified from the excellent sources of the Archive.

My sincerest thanks to all those, both public bodies and individuals, who allowed their premises to be photographed, for the enthusiasm and warmth with which they welcomed me and for tolerating the inconvenience of lights, cables and rearranged furniture. Photography is never easy and always disruptive but their co-operation helped and encouraged me enormously. I was deeply touched to find how many wanted to help with the book and welcomed the opportunity of making their particular building known to the world.

John Derby has assisted in nearly all the photography and has shared with me the joys and frustrations alike. I have valued so much his single-minded focus on the job in hand and his calmness under pressure and would like to record my gratitude for all

he has done to help make the photographs successful. I would also like to thank John Slater for giving invaluable help and encouragement particularly in the use of large format photography. For the guides in the public buildings who often re-routed their groups while a final shot was being taken, a special word of thanks and also to the caretakers who opened early and stayed on late, to the readers who 'froze' in the libraries and to those who vacated the front benches in the churches. I warmly thank the motorists who carefully skirted the twelve-foot tripod and step-ladder in the street as well as those who helped me sweep the pavements or held my parking place.

Colin Grant, our ever-patient editor, and the designer, Harry Green, deserve the highest praise. They were always open to suggestions that would improve the book. Street signs, parking meters, lamp-posts, modern lights and office equipment often meant that they rejected good pictures but thanks to their demands the pristine appearance of Dublin here shows how it might have looked without the trappings of the twentieth century.

This book would not have been possible without the scholarly publications of an ever-increasing band of art and architectural historians, of whom the most important is Maurice Craig; his *Dublin 1660–1860* is still unsurpassed after forty years. For the Architects, Artists and Craftsmen I relied heavily on the outstanding works of Howard Colvin, Rupert Gunnis, Rolf Loeber and Walter Strickland, as well as on the *Macmillan Encyclopedia of Architects* (ed. A. Placzek) and on the RIBA's *Directory of British Architects*, all listed in the bibliography.

Desmond and I would like to express our warmest thanks to the following among the many who helped with this book: The President, Mrs Mary Robinson, and Nicholas Robinson; An Taoiseach, Albert Reynolds; Dublin City Manager, Frank Feely; John Abernethy; Jonathan Armstrong; Lindsay Armstrong; Dr Barra Boydell; David Boylan; Joe Brennan; Tony Brown; David Byers; Canon Carmody; Dr Christine Casey; Michael and Aileen Casey; Dr Anthony Clare; Mary Clark; Geoffrey Codd; Michael Colgan; Dr Desmond Connell, Archbishop of Dublin; Sybil Connolly; Rev. John Crawford; Dr Darling; Barbara

Dawson; Philip Doyle; Tom Doyle; John Dunne; T. Austin Dunphy; Liam Egan; Canon Empey; Sergeant Eamon Fennessy; Allen Figgis; Sandra Fisher; Pascal Fuller; Lieut.-Col. Furlong; Máire Geoghegan-Quinn, Minister for Justice; Claire Gogarty; Rev. Thomas Gould; Vona Groarke; Patrick Guinness; John Gyves; Dr Peter Harbison; Frank Hardy; Dan Harrington; Capt. Colette Harrison; Arlene Hogan; Eugene Hogan; Raymond Keaveney; Paul Kelly; Dr Noel Kissane; Ralph Lalor; Brian Lord; Muriel McCarthy; Susan Magnier; Harry Meyer; Michael Mills; Dr Thomas and Lynn Mitchell; Ken Monaghan; Sister Brigid Mulholland; Jimmy Murphy; Senator David Norris; Catherine O'Brien; Michael O'Doherty; Comdt. Eamon O'Donoghue; Eleanor O'Neill; Siobhan O'Rafferty; John O'Sullivan; Dean Patterson; Peter Pearson; Fred Penco; Gawain Rainey; Rev. Father Shiel; Desiree Shortt; Professor Roger Stalley; Jean Stanley; Dean and Mrs Stewart; Dr Patrick Wallace; Alex Ward; Catherine Ward; Dean Woodworth; and Comdt. Peter Young.

We would like also like to express our gratitude to the following who gave us permission to include them in this book: Allied Irish Banks, An Taisce, Bank of Ireland, Dáil Eireann, Daughters of Charity of St Vincent de Paul, Department of Education, Department of Foreign Affairs, Department of Justice, Department of the Taoiseach, Dublin Corporation, Eastern Health Board, Grand Lodge of Freemasons of Ireland, Hugh Lane Municipal Gallery of Modern Art, Incorporated Law Society, King's Inns, Knights of St Columbanus, Lord Mayor of Dublin, Marsh's Library, National Gallery, National Irish Bank, National Library, National Museum, National Youth Federation, National University of Ireland, Natural History Museum, Office of the Ombudsman, Office of Public Works, Representative Church Body, Rotunda Hospital, Royal College of Physicians, Royal College of Surgeons, Royal Irish Academy, Society of Jesus, Stephen's Green Club, Trinity College, University College Dublin.

Finally my heartfelt thanks to my own family for their patience and understanding.

Broadstone
Station

St. Mary's
Chapel
of Ease

Belvedere
House

Connolly
Station

Hugh
Lane Gallery

Abbey Presbyterian
(Findlater's Church)

St.Saviour's

Rotunda
Hospital

Gate
Theatre

St. Mary's
Pro-
Cathedral

King's
Inns

No. 20

Tyrone
House

Custom
House

Blue Coat
School

KING STREET NORTH

GPO

Collins
Barracks

St. Mary's
Abbey

St. Mary's

O'Connell Bridge

St. Michan's

St. Paul's

Four
Courts

AIB
Bank

Garda Station

Bank of
Ireland

St. Michael & St. John's

AIB Bank

Trinity College

College Park

St. Augustine &
St. John's

Christ
Church
Cathedral

St. Audoen's

City Hall

The Castle

National Irish
Bank

Provost's
House

St. Andrew's

St. Catherine's

Tailors
Hall

St.
Werburgh's

Royal Irish Academy of Music

Iveagh Market

Powerscourt
House

Merrion Hall

St. Nicholas
of Myra

Freemason's
Hall

St. Ann's

Leinster
House

Rutland
Fountain

Merrion
Square

N

St. Patrick's
Cathedral

Marsh's
Library

Royal
College
of Surgeons

Mansion
House

St. Patrick's
Deanery

St. Stephen's
Green

Merrion
Square
South

St. Stephen's

University
Church

No. 52

Ely House

Newman
House

Iveagh
House

0   500 metres

0   500 yards

Ashtown

Cabra

Dunsoghly Castle
4 miles

Marino
Casino

Marino

Clontarf

Navan Road

Royal Canal

Drumcondra Rd

Phoenix
Column

Áras an
Uachtaráin

Phoenix
Park

Cabra Road

Royal
Hibernian
Military
School
Chapel

Cottage
Orné

D U B L I N

Wellington
Testimonial

Royal
Military
Infirmary

CAR FERRY TERMINAL

R. Liffey

Garden of
Remembrance

Heuston
Station

Dr. Steevens'
Hospital

Pearse St.

Kilmainham
Gaol

Royal
Hospital

St. Patrick's
Hospital

Sir Patrick Dun's
Hospital

Sandy-
mount

Inchicore

Drimnagh

Grand Canal

National
Concert
Hall

Harcourt
St. Station

Naas Road

Crumlin Road

Parnell Road

Portobello House

Leeson Street

Merrion Road

Strand Road

Drimnagh
Castle

Rathmines

1 Newcomen Bank
2 Royal Irish Academy
3 Stephen's Green Club
4 Shelbourne Hotel
5 Government Buildings
6 Natural History Museum
7 National Museum
8 National Library
9 National Gallery
10 Royal College of
   Physicians
11 St. Francis Xavier's
12 Mountjoy Square

INTRODUCTION

Dublin has many natural advantages, lying as it does between picturesque mountains and the vast natural harbour to which the city owes its very existence. Described by Jonathan Swift as a river which 'never roars but always murmurs', the Liffey also greatly enhances the beauty of the city through which it flows before reaching the sea. The main purpose of this book is to show the architecture of the heart of Dublin, the area that is bounded by the two canals, Royal to the north and Grand to the south, and by the Phoenix Park to the west. Such a remarkable wealth of material is crowded together within these confines that many wonderful places have had to be left out. The buildings are arranged in chronological order, although it was sometimes difficult to assign a specific position under one date to a building or group of buildings which had undergone substantial alterations or additions since it was first built. The buildings of Trinity College, for example, span a wide range of historical periods but, since they form a single campus, it seemed preferable to keep them together rather than split them up into the relevant chapters.

With the coming of the railway those who could afford it moved out of the city and some of the best streets and squares in Dublin degenerated into tenements and slums; however, a movement to restore these to their former beauty is now gathering momentum. In the 1950s a massive programme of clearance and re-housing was initiated and new suburbs were created, as much of the city, particularly on the north side, had degenerated sadly. Some of the better parts of Dublin were torn down during the office boom of the 1960s, but the more that were lost the more concern began to be felt. The brave stand taken by protesting students, who occupied threatened houses at the corner of St Stephen's Green and Hume Street in 1969, was an important milestone, followed in 1976 by the battle for Wood Quay. The loss of this thousand-year-old Viking site between Dublin Castle and the river did more than anything to galvanize public opinion in the cause of preservation. When the lawyer for Dublin Corporation described these unique remnants of the city's past as 'medieval junk', Father F.X. Martin, Professor of Medieval History at University College Dublin, was inspired to lead a protest march which attracted 20,000 angry people. Although this battle was lost and the site

was built over with new offices for the Corporation, the effect on public opinion was salutary. Many of the worthwhile and successful restoration schemes that have developed owe their existence to this important turning-point as well as to the dedicated work of the Dublin Civic Group. It would be hard to find a Dubliner today who is able to remain indifferent to the destruction of the architectural heritage of his city.

The recent exemplary restoration of the Custom House by the Office of Public Works is a shining example of the state's pride in, and concern for, the architectural masterpieces in its care. The refurbishment of the Royal Hospital, Kilmainham, has given back to Dublin a superb building of great value that had all but crumbled to dust. Private funds have restored Newman House on St Stephen's Green so that two great adjoining town houses are in the process of being furnished in period and opened to the public. The fact that, in a capital city endowed with such fine houses, not one has been opened to the public before is surprising but true. An authority has recently been established to revitalize the run-down Temple Bar area between Dame Street and the river where several streets of early eighteenth-century houses, shops and warehouses form a district of particular character and charm. This endeavour has come about at the eleventh hour and Dubliners have great hopes for the scheme.

The future of the city churches is a serious problem. With dwindling congregations many have been deconsecrated and it is not always easy to find an alternative use. St Catherine's, Thomas Street, which was closed for worship in 1967, was restored by a voluntary body but has since suffered badly at the hands of vandals; it now awaits a purchaser. By contrast, the 'Black Church', until recently semi-derelict and apparently without a future, has been turned into offices in a most imaginative way.

This *Grand Tour* ends in 1920, just as the last wave of Classicism petered out, giving way to the international modern style of architecture which makes one capital so like another. Much of the historic city has miraculously survived. The future of Dublin, with its literary, academic, artistic, theatrical, musical and sporting worlds, is probably better now than it has been for a very long time. It can take its place with pride among the great cities of Europe.

EARLY DUBLIN

When the dawn of history broke in Ireland it found a land covered in forest and scrub, interspersed by large areas of lake and marsh. The first of many waves of settlers is thought to have arrived about ten thousand years ago and to have come from the north European plain. The next groups of people started to appear in about 4,000 BC probably from Britain, France and the Iberian peninsula. They introduced agriculture and a settled way of life and they integrated with the earlier nomadic hunter and fisher population. Over the following thousand years or more – the Neolithic period, as it is known – they built great stone ancestor-shrines in the form of megalithic tombs, perhaps to mark their hegemony over the surrounding lands. Although nothing remains from the Neolithic period in the city of Dublin itself, within a ten-mile radius there are dolmens as well as passage, portal and wedge tombs.

The early Bronze Age period, 2000–1200 BC, is marked by the introduction of metal-working and the exploitation of Ireland's rich copper deposits as well as the gold found in the Wicklow hills; beautiful lunulae and sun discs fashioned from sheets of gold show sophisticated craftsmanship. The gold work of the later Bronze period, 1200–600 BC, was even more highly skilled and intricate, using bands and bars of the metal as well as sheets. The National Museum in Dublin contains superb examples of the artefacts of this time.

The next great wave of arrivals was the Celts, who stamped the personality of the country with a permanent die; they spoke a language ancestral to the Gaelic which is Ireland's national language today. Scholars are generally agreed that the Celts were established in Ireland by 600 BC or even earlier. They sprang from eastern Europe and spread in every direction, migrating to France, Britain, Germany, Spain, Italy and Greece; their dominance of Europe was extinguished by the Romans and, as they were illiterate, it is through the Romans that most knowledge about them has come down. The Celts were accomplished artists in bronze as well as other metals and have left a legacy of many astonishing artefacts. In their barbaric magnificence these can stand comparison with the contemporary arts of ancient Greece which

inspired them, just as two thousand years later they were to inspire the artists and craftsmen of Georgian Ireland. The Romans considered the Irish climate so bad that they christened the island Hibernia, 'winter', and left the country strictly alone. If Ireland has retained some of its Celtic character and culture to the present, it is in part because there was no Roman conquest.

The existence of Dublin as a trading port was known beyond the bounds of the Roman world, as the Greek cartographer, Ptolemy, marks it as Eblana on a map drawn by him in the second century AD. His information would have been based on reports brought back by mariners he considered reliable. Native sources – admittedly written down many centuries later – also feature Dublin at about the same period, when Conn of the Hundred Battles defeated Mogha of Munster and carved up Ireland into his half and Mogha's half, with a line drawn from Dublin to Galway.

Christianity was almost certainly established in the south-east of Ireland by the fourth century AD, but St Patrick's mission, which started when he landed at Skerries in north County Dublin some time in the following century, proved to be more effective and far-reaching. Legend avers that the national apostle passed through Dublin where he performed a miracle, striking his staff on the ground to reveal a well of pure spring water in which he baptised converts. Later generations continued to revere this as a holy well, and the church which was subsequently built beside it was dedicated to the saint and is now the site of St Patrick's Cathedral. Within a century of St Patrick's arrival, the country experienced a phenomenal growth in the monasteries which were to foster learning, literature, arts and crafts. Ireland acted like a beacon, illuminating afresh a European continent that was badly in need of rejuvenation after the heavy devastation of the wandering Germanic hordes. Irish teaching spread across Europe as missionaries from Ireland founded monasteries and churches, bringing learning and the faith as far afield as Italy and Russia. In this period Ireland came to be known as the 'Isle of Saints and Scholars'.

At the end of the eighth century AD the Vikings, or Norsemen, descended on Ireland, attacking with the speed and unpredictability of lightning, plundering the treasures of the defenceless monasteries and murdering the populace. The country at this time was divided into small kingdoms which were frequently at war with one another; had they only been united, they might have had some chance of repelling the Viking attacks which continued over the next fifty years. Eventually, from 841 onwards, due to the pressure of increased population and internal strife in Scandinavia, the Vikings came to settle along the coast of Ireland in Limerick, Cork, Waterford, Wexford and Wicklow as well as Dublin. In each place they established trade depots for the transport and storage of merchandise which they had acquired by commerce or by the sword along the shores of Atlantic Europe and beyond. It is to the Vikings that Ireland owes the establishment of its ports and harbours.

One of the first and most thriving Norse settlements was founded along the banks of the Liffey. This was probably not on the site of the present city of Dublin but upstream at Islandbridge, where a cemetery with Viking weapons and jewellery has been discovered in the area now occupied by the Garden of Remembrance. Perhaps the Vikings felt they were too vulnerable to attack from the native Irish, and by the early tenth century they had moved downstream nearer to the last ford across the river. This crossing was known as *Átha Cliath*, the origin of *Baile Átha Cliath*, the name by which Dublin is known today in the Irish language meaning 'town of the ford of the hurdles'. A black pool at the confluence of the Liffey with a small river called the Poddle gave the future city its English name; in Irish 'black pool' is translated *Dubh Linn* and in Norse, *Dyfflin*.

The Vikings built themselves a wooden fortress on the ridge above the black pool, in which their ships could ride safely at anchor, and they established a *longphort*, a base for raiding and trading. The new settlers were probably of mixed Scandinavian stock, as indicated by the names the native Irish gave them: *Fionn-Ghaill*, the fair foreigners, the bulk of whom probably came from south-western Norway, and the *Dubh-Ghaill*, the dark strangers, who are thought to have come from Denmark. These Vikings were quick to make, but equally quick to break, alliances with other Viking groups elsewhere – as for instance with Northumbria which, at one stage, was allied with Dublin under a single ruler, King Olaf.

Knowledge of the Vikings in Ireland has come from archaeological excavations at Wood Quay, Fishamble Street and High Street undertaken by the National Museum, which has an excellent range of material from this period. The early settlement was surrounded by a ditch and earthern bank; the only surviving examples of Viking engineering visible in Ireland today are parts of the stone wall which replaced it after the Battle of Clontarf in 1014. This wall is up to 10 feet high and 5 feet thick with a number of offsets for support. The houses in the settlement were small and single-storey, usually consisting of one room with partitions for privacy. The walls were made of rows of upright posts interwoven with layers of hazel, ash or elm wattle daubed with mud. The roofs were thatched with no chimney; the houses were badly ventilated, hot in summer and freezing in winter. The floor was covered with rushes or wattle mats and the furniture simple: stools, tables and benches. The life of the houses was short and as soon as they became uninhabitable they were demolished. On one site in Christ

Church Place the remains of six houses have been found, one on top of another, with little passage of time between each rebuilding. The domestic architecture of the Vikings bears little or no comparison with their superb shipbuilding skills.

Since the Dublin Vikings were surrounded by the Irish it was inevitable that they would soon accept their customs and religion, learn the native language and intermarry. The Norse King Sitric who ruled from 989 to 1036 married the daughter of Brian Boru, King of Munster and High King of Ireland. By the eleventh century Irish and Viking would appear to have lived in comparative peace with one another, side by side in Dyfflin. This period of calm came to a violent end after Brian Boru married King Sitric's Irish mother. Finding her a dishonest schemer, Brian Boru discarded her, whereupon she incited the people of Leinster against him; a great battle ensued at Clontarf in 1014. Viking warriors, who had come from as far afield as Northumbria and Orkney to support the King of Leinster, Mael Mórdha, were routed, but the victorious Brian Boru and his son lost their lives.

The result was an end to Viking expansion in Ireland. The Battle of Clontarf may not have had such a devastating effect upon the embryonic city as earlier historians were apt to imagine. Rather than a catastrophic clash between Viking and Irish, it may have been more in the nature of a feud between Mael Mórdha and Brian Boru who wanted to create a united Ireland. The foundation in the 1030s of Dublin's first cathedral, Christ Church, by Sitric, is symptomatic of the lack of enmity; the first bishop was an Irishman named Dunan. King Sitric had ruled the city for twenty-five years before Clontarf and continued his long reign for another twenty-two years after it, so he must have kept aloof from that conflict.

The next momentous event came a century and a half later when Dermot McMorrough, King of Leinster, who had abducted the wife of the O'Rourke of Breffni, incited the anger of the other Irish kings who united against him. He was deposed by the last High King of Ireland, Rory O'Connor, and sailed for England to seek the assistance of King Henry II. Richard de Clare, Earl of Pembroke, commonly known as Strongbow, was despatched to go to his assistance. Having succeeded in taking the Viking town of Waterford, Strongbow married Dermot McMorrough's daughter, Aoife, on the battlefield. An immense Victorian painting of this event, by Daniel Maclise, hangs in the National Gallery of Ireland (see illustration on pp.224–5). Strongbow marched on Dublin, coming across the Wicklow mountains and avoiding the defenders who were posted at the passes. While Archbishop Laurence O'Toole was discussing surrender terms with him, a small party of knights breached the walls and slaughtered many of the inhabitants. Giraldus Cambrensis, a medieval chronicler, described how the miracle-working Cross of the Holy Trinity in Christ Church Cathedral, could not be carried away by the fleeing natives: 'the whole population of the city failed to move it from its place either by force or contrivance.' This crucifix attracted gifts from rich donors including Strongbow himself, who provided funds to supply it with perpetual light. The Vikings abandoned the town to its fate, ran for their ships and sailed away; they returned a year later with a large fleet but were defeated as were the Irish who launched an attack on Anglo-Norman Dublin shortly afterwards.

Henry II reached Dublin at Christmas in 1171, when he attended Mass on Christmas Day in Christ Church, the cathedral built by the Vikings. He entertained the Irish chieftains in a 'palace' hastily built of wattle, and issued a charter presenting the city of Dublin to the men of Bristol. This ensured that the town would belong to his loyal subjects in Bristol rather than the Anglo-Norman lords who in fact had conquered it. In a second charter of 1174 he declared Dublin to be free from all duties throughout his Kingdom of England, Scotland, Wales and France.

The Normans soon set about reclaiming the swampy land on the southern bank of the Liffey to provide anchorage for their ships. They deepened the channel and began to erect permanent buildings clustered around the old stockade of the Vikings. Henry's son John ordered the erection of Dublin Castle in 1204 on this site, and henceforth it was centre of the government and the seat of the treasury as well as housing the law courts and parliament. Guilds were established under a charter from Prince John in 1192, which gave them power to exercise control over their own trades and professions and to devise conditions of work, including apprenticeships. The guilds subsequently developed into powerful bodies. Dublin expanded under Norman rule and trade prospered; the two cathedrals, Christ Church and St Patrick's, were under construction by the early thirteenth century. The city was controlled by elected bailiffs from 1215 and a mayor was first appointed in 1229.

For the townspeople conditions of life were still hard. In 1244 during the reign of Henry III the first domestic water supply was provided: a cistern and water course which consisted of a stream running through the middle of the streets. Those who could afford it drank beer or ale because of the scarcity of pure water. Pigs roamed the narrow dirty streets scavenging for food. Houses had changed little since Viking days and the risk of fire was ever-present. There was no food for wintering cattle, so the beasts were slaughtered in the autumn and the meat salted down to last the winter; nonetheless it often decayed. Fish was plentiful and was sold in Fishamble Street; Church teaching prescribed fasting for two days in the week and for Lent.

In 1315 after a string of victories Edward Bruce, brother of Robert Bruce, King of Scotland, was crowned King of Ireland by the Irish at Dundalk. His army advanced on Dublin, where the inhabitants burnt part of the city, destroyed the one bridge across the Liffey and took down the belfry of the church of St Mary del Dam using the stones to strengthen the city walls. A serious loss was Bruce's destruction of the Hospital of St John, which had stood at Newgate outside the walls. Bruce's attack failed but this episode resulted in a change of attitude by the Normans, who increasingly settled themselves within an area which came to be known as the Pale. This was a ring of fortified castles built by them to protect the rich flat land north and west of Dublin, which changed its boundaries according to the ebb and flow of their fortunes; they regarded the Irish 'beyond the Pale' with enmity and suspicion.

Dunsoghly Castle, a Pale castle near Dublin, was built by Sir

LEFT Sections of Dublin's medieval city walls still survive next to two adjacent churches of different denominations dedicated to St Audoen: Catholic on the left, in High Street, and Protestant (the tower) on the right, in Cornmarket.

RIGHT Dunsoghly Castle, Dunsoghly, was built c.1470 by Sir Thomas Plunkett. A typical Pale castle, it is situated eight miles north of Dublin and surrounded by a moat in the form of an exceptionally deep ditch.

ABOVE A limestone plaque over the chapel door at Dunsoghly is carved with the instruments of the Passion, the initials 'I P M D D S' and the date '1573'.

LEFT Some of the original oak roof timbers have survived at Dunsoghly Castle, providing a model for the restoration of the roofs at Bunratty Castle, Co. Clare, in the 1950s and more recently at Drimnagh Castle, Co. Dublin.

Thomas Plunkett in about 1470; it is a four-storeyed tower house with a small square tower at each corner and is typical of the fortified residences that were built by both Norman invaders and native chieftains all over Ireland. One of the towers contains the spiral stone staircase and the other three once had a little square room at each storey. Uniquely in Ireland, Dunsoghly Castle retains some of the original fifteenth-century roof timbers, and when Bunratty Castle, Co. Clare, was restored in 1954, this roof was used as the model.

After the Norman invasion the Norsemen had gravitated towards the north side of the city, which became known as Oxmantown. Here they organized their own defences and had their own marketplace and their own church, St Michan's. Most of the land north of the Liffey was owned by St Mary's Abbey, the most powerful of the ten monasteries that surrounded Dublin. Founded by the Benedictines in 1139, it came under Cistercian rule eight years later. At the peak of its power its holdings of land, much of which by then was coastal land to the south, amounted to 17,000 acres. Although little is left of the abbey today, in the fourteenth century it was the finest assemblage of buildings in

Dublin and was frequently used by the King's Council as a meeting place throughout the medieval era. It was here in 1534 that Silken Thomas, the son of the Lord Deputy, Garret FitzGerald, flung down the Sword of State at a meeting of the King's Council and renounced his allegiance to the Crown, thereby initiating his short-lived rebellion. Soon after this, during the Dissolution of the Monasteries in the late 1530s, Henry VIII closed St Mary's and confiscated the land and riches that it had accumulated.

The great Abbey of St Thomas the Martyr was founded by Henry II between Thomas Street and the Coombe, out of remorse for the murder of Thomas à Becket in Canterbury Cathedral. Henry VIII seized the lands of Thomas Court, which he granted to Sir William Brabazon, ancestor of the Earls of Meath, who was appointed Vice-Treasurer of Ireland in 1534. The loss of the monasteries sounded the death knell of the old medieval order. They had cared for the sick, dispensed charity and provided education through the centuries. By means of their gradual amassing of wealth they had brought about a stability which endured beyond any change of administration. Little attempt was made to provide hospitals and schools to replace those of the monasteries.

Until the reign of Henry VIII, while the English Crown controlled Dublin and the Pale, it had little authority over the rest of the country. Henry VIII assumed the title of King of Ireland in 1541, after the Dissolution of the Monasteries. The successive Tudor monarchs ruthlessly brought the rest of Ireland under the control of the English government, and where they failed to stamp out Irish resistance, they carried out a brutal policy of plantation, replacing Irish landowners with loyal English and Scottish colonists. By the end of the seventeenth century ownership of land by the Irish had fallen from 90 to 15 per cent.

In 1610 John Speed published his map of Dublin, showing the medieval walled town with its new streets spilling outside the gates. Trinity College, founded only twenty years before, stands well away to the east. By the seventeenth century Dublin had its first Custom House and the port was beginning to develop in earnest. A sanitation system was established, together with a fire brigade, and there was even a city band. The guilds were becoming more powerful and controlled the election of the city council.

The restoration of Charles II in 1660 was celebrated with fireworks, pageants and banquets, and it marked the beginning of a period of progress for Dublin. New ideas, inspired by continental architecture, were to reach Ireland thanks to the Viceroy, the Earl of Ormonde, who had been in exile with King Charles in Paris.

ABOVE The last remaining panelled door (c.1600) of the old Archbishop's Palace of St Sepulchre (now the Kevin Street Garda Barracks) beside St Patrick's Cathedral. The original palace was built by Archbishop Comyn in 1192.

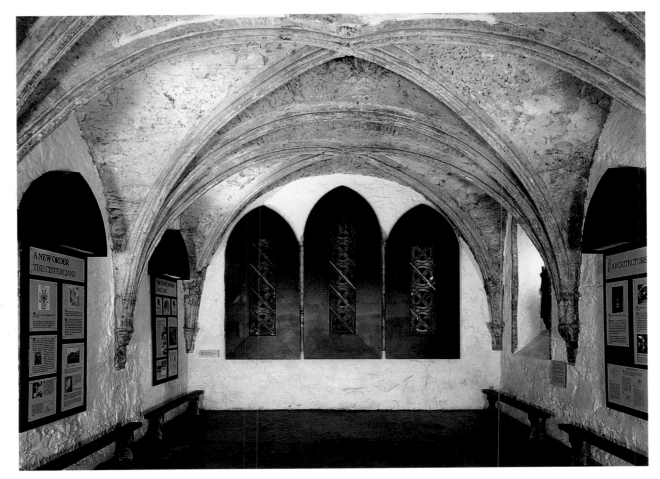

LEFT The vaulted chapter house of 1180 at St Mary's Abbey, off Capel Street, is all that remains of the greatest medieval abbey in Dublin.

CHRIST CHURCH CATHEDRAL
Christ Church Place

Christ Church Cathedral, dedicated to the Holy Trinity, stands on a ridge above the River Liffey overlooking the site of the former Viking settlement. It was at the centre of the walled medieval city and was a place of worship, refuge and even commerce. Today, the cathedral with its stepped battlements, lancet windows, flying buttresses and many conical towers contrasts with the surrounding modern architecture and provides an oasis of tranquillity in the endless stream of Dublin traffic.

The original church, thought to have been a wooden construction, was built in 1038 by Dunan, the first bishop of Dublin, with funds provided by Sitric, the Norse, or Viking, king. It was during Sitric's reign that Christianity came to be accepted by the Norse community in Dublin and the king gave extensive land holdings to endow the church. The revenues which paid for its erection and upkeep continued for over eight hundred years until the disestablishment of the Church of Ireland in 1871.

In 1162 Bishop Laurence O'Toole was appointed Archbishop of Dublin, and in 1163 the cathedral chapter became monastic, joining the Arroasian order based on the Abbey of Arras in northern France and affiliated to the Augustinians. Until the Dissolution of the Monasteries in the late 1530s Christ Church remained a priory. In 1541 its constitution was altered by Henry VIII, but the personnel remained the same, the last prior, Robert Paynswick, becoming the first dean.

In 1170 Dublin was captured by the Normans, led by Richard de Clare, Earl of Pembroke, known as Strongbow. In the following year Henry II came to Dublin and attended Mass on Christmas Day in the church then standing here. The Normans were great church builders and it was probably as an act of reconciliation with the Irish chieftains that they offered to replace the old structure with an impressive stone cathedral. Archbishop O'Toole, who was uncle to Strongbow's wife,

Aoife, is said to have been involved with the planning and the commencement of the building in 1172, but both he and Strongbow died at an early stage of the construction. They are nevertheless both remembered as the originators of the building. Strongbow, who died in 1176, was buried in the cathedral and is commemorated by a monument in the south aisle. Laurence died in 1178 at Eu in Normandy, where he is buried. Following his canonization in 1225, his heart was brought back 'with solemn rejoicing' in a heart-shaped metal casket which now hangs in one of the eastern chapels. This relic survived when much else was destroyed in the Reformation era, and recently a Peace Candle has been placed opposite the heart in what is now designated the Peace Chapel. Here pilgrims pause to pray for the peace and reconciliation which the saint, in his day, had striven to achieve.

ABOVE The monument known as Strongbow's Tomb, commemorating Richard de Clare, Earl of Pembroke, is in fact the effigy of a Norman knight named FitzOsbert. It replaced the original monument which was destroyed in 1562 when the roof fell in. The small figure at the side may lie on a chest containing entrails or a fragment of the original monument.

LEFT Christ Church Cathedral and the Synod Hall (left) are joined by a bridge over the road.

RIGHT The great nave has five bays of triple arches and dates from the thirteenth century. The floor has copies of the original medieval tiles.

The Norman builders of the cathedral at once encountered major difficulties because the soil was too soft to carry the weight of a great stone building, so they constructed massive stone columns with vaulted arches to create the foundation. Thus the groin-vaulted crypt extends under almost the entire cathedral as the foundation for the nave, aisles and the three chapels at the eastern end. No other crypt in England or Ireland extends under an entire upper church.

Following the death of Laurence O'Toole, an Englishman, John Comyn, was appointed archbishop in 1181. His mission was intended as largely political; he at once sought freedom from the asceticism of the Arroasian canons at Christ Church and attempted to distance himself from the jurisdiction of the city fathers. He built the fine Palace of St Sepulchre to live in outside the city walls and beside it erected a new collegiate church, St Patrick's, for the better education of the diocesan clergy. In the early thirteenth century Henri de Londres, who was not only archbishop (1213–38) but also viceroy, extended Comyn's church and raised it to cathedral status. Both these archbishops continued with the building of Christ Church, which was completed in the 1230s. The building of the nave commenced in about 1213 under the supervision of 'the Christ Church Master', a mason known to have come from Worcestershire. He created elaborate capitals for the columns, with a variety of foliage themes, some with crowned heads and grimacing faces.

Professor Roger Stalley suggests that Christ Church was modelled on the cathedrals of Glastonbury and Wells. Maurice Craig describes it as a 'totally English building erected in Ireland'. Some of the very white decorative stone is believed to have been imported from quarries at Dundry, near Bristol. The north and south transepts from this period survive, with intricate carving surrounding paired arches, which are slightly pointed and decorated with chevron mouldings; the exterior door with its row of double chevrons, now at the south entrance, is likewise a fine example of twelfth-century workmanship.

One of the most dramatic historical events which has taken place in Christ Church Cathedral during its nine-hundred-year history was the crowning in 1487 of Lambert Simnel as King Edward VI of England and France. The Great Earl of Kildare, Garrett Mór FitzGerald, supported those who maintained that the boy was Edward of Warwick, the Yorkist heir to the throne. Henry VII claimed that he was the twelve-year-old son of an Oxford tradesman and that the real earl was at the time incarcerated in the Tower of London. The crown used in the elaborate coronation ceremony was taken from a statue of Our Lady in the nearby church of St Mary del Dam, which incidentally gave its name to the modern Dame Street. The Pretender King and his followers invaded England, but were defeated at the Battle of Stoke (1487). Simnel became a servant of Henry VII and was made to work as a kitchen scullion.

Tragically, at the time of the Reformation, Archbishop Browne made a bonfire of all 'superstitious reliques', including the celebrated *Baculum Iosa*, the miraculous golden crozier of St Patrick, though one rare survival from the period is a wooden statue of Our Lady, originally in St Mary's Abbey and now in the Carmelite Church, Whitefriar Street.

King James II attended Mass in Latin at Christ Church in 1689, the year before his defeat at the Battle of the Boyne. The tabernacle and candlesticks on display in the crypt are said to be those used on this historic occasion. After the battle, William of Orange presented a magnificent set of silver-gilt communion vessels, alms dishes and candlesticks to the cathedral as a gesture of thanksgiving. These are still used on ceremonial occasions. George IV worshipped here when

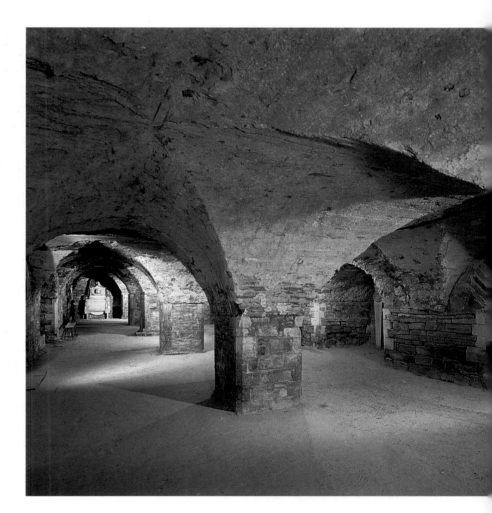

he visited in 1821, and Edward VII, as Prince of Wales and Earl of Dublin, also attended a service here.

By the middle of the fourteenth century the cathedral had taken on its present aspect and it is not known why, during the Archbishopric of John de St Paul, it was decided to extend the choir 40 feet to the east. It was here that the English Prayer Book was used for the first time on Easter Sunday 1551 and that the Bible was read in the vernacular from the sixteenth-century eagle lectern.

Until 1814, when the Chapel Royal was built in Dublin Castle, Christ Church was the church of the government. To this day it contains the State Pew (1667) where successive Presidents of the Republic have sat quite happily behind the arms of the House of Stuart. This is balanced by the Civic Pew, which bears the arms of the city of Dublin and brass fittings to hold the mace and sword when the lord mayor and civic dignitaries attend service. The ceremonial sword was presented to the city by Henry IV.

For a time in the sixteenth and seventeenth centuries the extensive crypt of the cathedral was directly accessible through doors on the

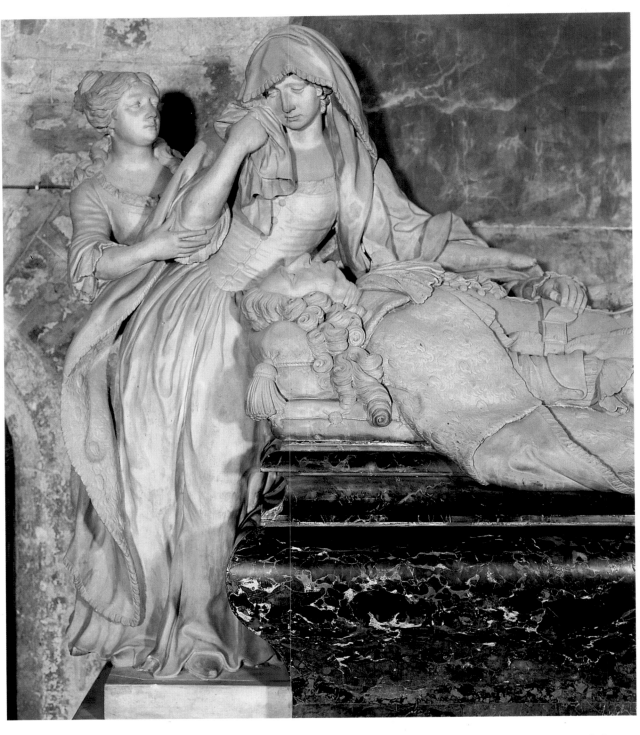

RIGHT Part of a memorial in the south transept by Sir Henry Cheere to the nineteenth Earl of Kildare (died 1744).

ABOVE Grotesque medieval carving on twin capitals in the north ambulatory, which dates from the thirteenth century.

LEFT The twelfth-century crypt extends the entire length of the building. It once contained three chapels and during the seventeenth century it was let to shops selling tobacco and to 'tippling houses'.

north side and was leased out as a maze of small shops. These included a tavern and in 1633 Primate Bramhall complained to Archbishop Laud that 'the vaults ... are made into tippling rooms for beer, wine and tobacco ...' The church authorities had some difficulty in removing the tenants and Lord Deputy Strafford eventually issued an order banishing them. In a corner of the crypt are two life-sized statues of Charles I and Charles II, carved by William de Keyser. These adorned the facade of the Tholsel, or city hall, which stood opposite the cathedral. They were transferred to the crypt when the Tholsel was demolished at the end of the eighteenth century. The dean of Christ Church had authority to lock up in the stocks those who offended within the 'Liberty' (area of jurisdiction) of the cathedral. These stocks, made in 1670, are preserved in the crypt. Burials continued here until 1866, but the stone coffins collapsed into an unseemly heap and nearly all the bones were re-interred during the 1870s restoration.

By the mid-nineteenth century the fabric of Christ Church was in a semi-ruinous condition, and in 1871 the chapter accepted an offer from a generous Dublin distiller, Henry Roe, who undertook to finance its

renovation. The famous English architect, George Edmund Street, was employed and made a very extensive restoration, preserving as much as possible of the old, but rebuilding the east end in conformity with the original plans and replacing a blank south wall, which had been erected when the original collapsed in 1562. Street also designed for Roe the adjacent Synod Hall, which incorporates the seventeenth-century tower of the old St Michael's Church, and is linked to the cathedral by a ceremonial neo-Gothic bridge. The Synod Hall now contains a historical exhibition of medieval Dublin.

Music has long played an important role in the worship here. In 1993 the choir celebrated the 500th anniversary of its foundation by Prior David de Wynchestyr. The splendid Jones organ installed in 1984 is one of the finest in Ireland and is known worldwide through its use for the Dublin International Organ Festival.

Christ Church is now the cathedral of the Protestant Diocese of Dublin and Glendalough and the Metropolitan Cathedral of the Province, being second in Ireland only to Armagh. The Christian faith has been professed within this wonderful cathedral for over 900 years.

ST AUDOEN'S CHURCH
Cornmarket

St Audoen's is the only surviving medieval church in Dublin as well as being the city's oldest parish church in continuous use. It was built within the city walls, probably by the men of Bristol who had been granted the city of Dublin by Henry II in 1172. It replaced an earlier church on the site said to have been dedicated to St Columba. St Audoen, who died in AD 684, was Bishop of Rouen and is the patron saint of that city. In northern France there are many churches dedicated to him, besides a chapel in Canterbury Cathedral and, significantly, a church in Bristol.

The nave dates from 1190 and is the only part of the church that is still roofed. As the population of Dublin grew, a chancel was added to the east in 1300, with a sanctuary beyond. Beside the nave and parallel to it is the Guild Chapel of St Anne, added in 1431. In 1455 the Portlester Chapel was added to the south side of the chancel and named after Sir Roland FitzEustace, Lord Portlester, Chancellor and Treasurer of Ireland. Recumbent effigies of Sir Roland and his wife Margaret can be seen at the base of the tower, although they were buried at Castlemartin, Kilcullen, Co. Kildare, in a recently restored chapel.

The tower dates from the seventeenth century although it looks older with its rubble plaster and crenellations, but it lacks the batter (sloping base) found in Irish medieval buildings and, besides, the round-headed windows and the classical doorway point to a later period. The tower originally had a small spire which was taken down on the orders of Charles Cobbe, Archbishop of Dublin from 1743 to 1765. This prompted Jonathan Swift to write:

> Christ's Cross from god's house,
> Cursed Cobbe has pulled down
> And put in its place
> What he worships – the Crown.

The tower contains three of the oldest bells in Dublin, cast in 1423; these were not rung between 1898 and 1983 on account of the condition of the tower, but now their gentle peal rings out again on Sunday mornings.

In the porch beside the tower stands the Lucky Stone, probably an early Christian grave stone, secured against the wall by iron clamps

ABOVE The baptismal font was discovered during the restoration of 1848 built into the wall of the porch. It dates from the original Norman foundation in 1190.

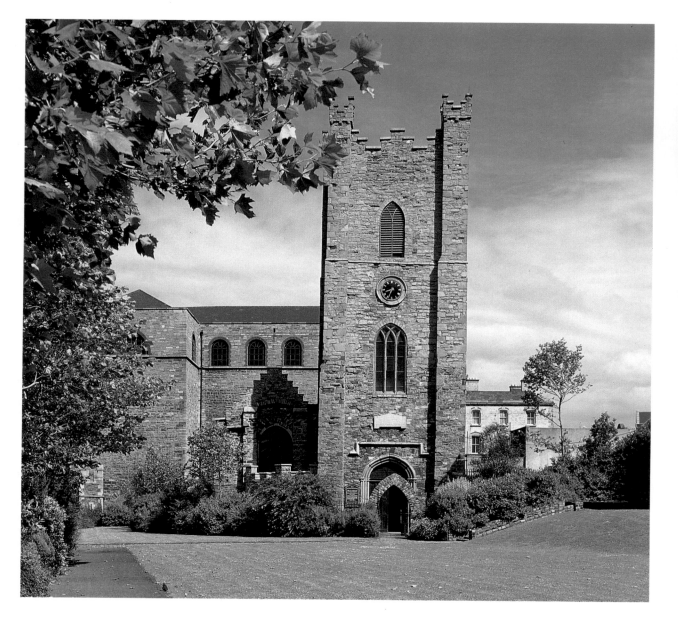

LEFT The seventeenth-century tower of the Protestant church of St Audoen's, Cornmarket, which has been continuously used for worship for longer than any other parish church in Dublin.

because of its tendency to wander. Over the years this stone has frequently vanished only to reappear as mysteriously as it left. According to local superstition among the merchants and traders, a daily visit to touch the stone ensured good business.

St Audoen's was the church of the Lord Mayor and Corporation of Dublin, and the city coat of arms in the top light of the east window is among the few remaining fragments of early stained glass. It was one of a group of churches serving the Dublin craftsmen's guilds. There was a school attached to the church where the pupils were taught by guild priests and many of the guildhalls were in the immediate vicinity. The Tanners' Guild had their hall in the tower of St Audoen's Arch from the fourteenth to the middle of the eighteenth century and the Bakers' Guild occupied 'the College' adjoining the church in 1618.

The hearth rolls of the 1660s show St Audoen's parish as a fashionable area, occupied by the cream of Dublin society. However, in the eighteenth century the area started to decline as the Georgian city expanded to the north and the east. By 1773 the building was too large for the needs of the parish, and the chancel and Portlester Chapel were unroofed as were the south aisle of the nave and the chapel of St Anne in 1820. In 1826 the tower was remodelled by Henry Aaron Baker and in 1848 a complete restoration was financed by the Ecclesiastical Commissioners for Ireland. During the 1860s Sir Thomas Drew led an architectural and archaeological survey of the church; the drawings he made are in Marsh's Library.

The importance of St Audoen's is attested to by the successive efforts over the years to ensure its survival. The Office of Public Works is at present engaged in routine restoration work, pointing the stonework in the ruined part which is now in their care. Preliminary plans have been drawn up for roofing the Guild Chapel of St Anne and the intention is to mount a permanent exhibition within these hallowed walls devoted to life in medieval Dublin. Funds from the EC have been allocated to help defray the cost. With the building of apartments in the vicinity the congregation is on the increase again. Besides those attending services here, tourists and school groups will be able to absorb the atmosphere of St Audoen's while learning about the history of medieval Dublin.

ABOVE The Lucky Stone, reputed to bring good fortune if touched, is attached to the wall by iron clamps to counteract its tendency to wander.

RIGHT Only this part of the nave, which dates from 1190, is still roofed. The seventeenth-century stucco monuments on a wooden frame are two of the very few to have survived in Ireland. During a recent restoration twelve coats of paint were removed showing that the larger of the two monuments had been defaced, probably during the time of Cromwell.

ST PATRICK'S CATHEDRAL
St Patrick's Close

S t Patrick, Ireland's patron saint, is said to have baptised converts in the fifth century at a holy well beside the present St Patrick's Cathedral during the course of a journey from Wicklow to Armagh. The site of this well was discovered during excavation work in 1901 revealing the ninth-century stone slab which once covered it; this can now be seen within the cathedral. An early wooden church dedicated to St Patrick, one of the four main Celtic churches in pre-Viking Dublin, was built near this holy place.

Seven years before the coming of the Normans Laurence O'Toole, Archbishop of Dublin, brought Arroasian canons into Christ Church Cathedral. John Comyn was appointed by Henry II to succeed O'Toole as archbishop in 1181. Comyn, a layman, was an able diplomat and administrator as well as a trusted friend of the king. He had no wish to join the Arroasians established at Christ Church, nor did he want his palace within the jurisdiction of the city fathers. He deliberately chose a site outside the city walls, took down the old wooden church of St Patrick's that stood there and built a new one 'in hewn stone, in the form of a cross, right goodly to be seen with fair embowed works, fine pavements and an arched roof overhead with stonework'. His new church was dedicated on St Patrick's Day 1192. He built the Palace of St Sepulchre beside it where he installed 'a secular College of clerics of approved life and learning'. St Sepulchre's remained the seat of successive Archbishops of Dublin until 1806.

Comyn's successor, Henri de Londres, raised the status of St

RIGHT The great Gothic nave with its vaulted roof is over 50 feet high. The Lady Chapel is beyond the High Altar. The cathedral was saved from total collapse by the generosity of Sir Benjamin Lee Guinness, who restored it in 1865.

BELOW St Patrick's Cathedral from St Patrick's Park, with Archbishop Minot's tower of 1370 on the right; the tower is 150 feet high and diminishes in width at each of the string courses. The Lady Chapel is on the left.

LEFT The baptistry is the oldest remaining part of the original cathedral and may have formed the entrance to Archbishop Comyn's church at the end of the twelfth century.

BELOW The tomb of Archbishop Fulk de Saundford, who was responsible for adding the Lady Chapel and died in 1271.

BOTTOM Brass memorial on the wall of the south choir commemorating Dean Robert Sutton, who was dean of the cathedral from 1527 to 1528. For fear of the plague he never set foot in St Patrick's during his deanship.

Patrick's to a cathedral in 1213, and it was reconstructed between 1220 and 1254 to reflect its new standing. It became the largest church in Ireland, with essentially the same layout as it has to-day. Dublin has had two Protestant cathedrals in the same diocese ever since, a unique situation as they are less than a half mile apart. Rivalry between them was finally resolved in 1872 when St Patrick's became a national cathedral for all the dioceses of Ireland and Christ Church was made the diocesan cathedral of Dublin and Glendalough.

St Patrick's was built in the early English Gothic style by English masons. The Lady Chapel was added in about 1270 by Archbishop Fulk de Saundford whose recumbent effigy, dressed in his prelate's robes, can be seen in the north choir aisle. In 1315 the spire of the cathedral was blown down and in the same year the fabric was damaged by fire when, on the approach of Edward Bruce, brother of Robert, the citizens set the suburbs of Dublin alight. In 1370 after yet another fire, this one attributed to the carelessness of 'John the Sexton', Archbishop Minot rebuilt the great north-west tower; it remains the most impressive medieval monument in Dublin today. The present granite spire was added in 1749, built to a most sensitive design by George Semple, thanks to a legacy from Bishop Stearne, a former dean.

The first university in Ireland was founded at St Patrick's in 1320 by Archbishop de Bicknor with the approval of Pope John XXII. Owing to lack of funds the university was not a success and it was finally closed in 1539 by decree of Henry VIII.

In 1492 the ancient feud between the FitzGeralds (war-cry 'Crom-a-Boo') and the Butlers (war-cry 'Butler-a-Boo') came to a dramatic head when Lord Ormonde of the Butler family and his men took refuge in the chapter house of the cathedral, with the Earl of Kildare in hot

LEFT The choir, with the
banners, swords and helmets of
the Knights of St Patrick, an
order founded in 1783, above
their stalls.

pursuit. A hole had to be cut through the wooden door to enable the
opponents to shake hands and seal a truce, giving rise, it is said, to the
expression 'to chance your arm'. The old wooden door with the hole
cut through it can still be seen at the west end of the building. The
mayor and council of Dublin were suspected of being pro-FitzGerald
and the whole episode was considered sacrilegious. To atone for it, all
of them had to take part in the annual Corpus Christi procession
wearing nothing but a shirt and each carrying a lighted candle.

In 1537, at the time of the Reformation, Thomas Cromwell, in the
name of Henry VIII, ordered the destruction of all the statues of saints
and images in the cathedral. These were to be replaced with framed
excerpts of religious texts. Not long afterwards the king appropriated
all the revenues of St Patrick's. In 1550, during the reign of Edward VI,
the cathedral was reduced to the status of a parish church and it was
decreed that a part of the building should be used as a courthouse. Five
years later under the Catholic Queen Mary its former position as a
cathedral was restored and Mass was once again celebrated here. In
1558, with the accession to the throne of Elizabeth I, St Patrick's
remained as a cathedral, but returned to the reformed faith.

During the Commonwealth period Oliver Cromwell is said to have
used St Patrick's as a stable for his horses and a place for holding courts
martial. In 1661 after the Restoration, Anglican services were again
held here, but by now the fabric was in urgent need of repair. The
building was re-roofed ten years later, using 40 tons of oak generously
provided by the son of the Earl of Strafford, from his estate at
Coolattin, Co. Wicklow. In 1680 the new stone vault above the choir
was painted blue and adorned with gold stars.

From the fourteenth century onwards the north transept was used
for worship by the parishioners of St Nicholas Without. The Liberties
(areas under cathedral jurisdiction) beside St Patrick's were settled in
the seventeenth century largely by French Huguenots engaged in the
weaving trade. From 1666 they held services in French in the Lady
Chapel where a commemorative tablet records the fact. For a time
therefore there were three different congregations at worship in
different parts of the cathedral.

The most famous name associated with the cathedral is Jonathan
Swift, Dean of St Patrick's from 1713 to 1745, when he died after a long
illness. He was the outstanding intellectual figure of the eighteenth century and one of the greatest satirists in the English language. Born in
Dublin at Hoey's Court beside St Werburgh's in 1667, he studied at Trinity
and left Ireland after the troubles of 1689, not returning until 1713. As
Dean of St Patrick's he presided over his Liberty with its right to a
gaol, a court and shelter for fugitives. The area around the cathedral
was a maze of tiny crowded streets, a centre for the weaving industry,
which was hit hard by regulations imposed by England at the end of
the century. Swift was indignant, intolerant, short-tempered and

LEFT The Lady Chapel, which was beautifully restored in the 1840s by Dean Pakenham. This part of the cathedral had been used by the Huguenots for worship, a fact commemorated by a plaque on the wall.

RIGHT The Boyle Monument was carved in 1630 by Edmund Tingham during the lifetime of the Great Earl of Cork and represents the earl and his family. The central niche contains the figure of Robert Boyle, later to became the famous scientist. The earl is buried in an equally florid tomb in Youghal, Co. Waterford.

crusty but full of compassion for the poor. A brass plate in the south-west of the nave bears his epitaph, which translates, 'He lies where furious rage can rend his heart no more.'

The Most Illustrious Order of St Patrick was founded by the Viceroy, the Marquess of Buckingham, in 1783, modelled on the Order of the Bath in England. St Patrick's Cathedral was the chapel of the order, and the banners, swords, and helmets of the knights can be seen above their stalls in the choir. No new knights have been elected since 1936 so the order is now extinct.

The Lady Chapel was very well restored in the 1840s by Dean Pakenham in spite of the fact that it virtually had to be rebuilt from the ground up; the architect was R.C. Carpenter. In 1845 Carpenter had drawn up plans for the restoration of the entire cathedral but after the Lady Chapel was rebuilt additional funds were not available. The architect died in 1859. In 1860 Sir Benjamin Lee Guinness MP, sometime Lord Mayor of Dublin and sole owner of the brewery, undertook the rescue and restoration of the cathedral at his own expense. The work was to take four years and cost £160,000. Sir Benjamin used Carpenter's drawings as a basis for the restoration although he made considerable alterations to them. He received some professional advice before starting construction but carried out the work without architectural supervision. Although this restoration has been criticized for being a virtual rebuilding, it saved the cathedral from total collapse and it saw the removal of the partitions that had divided the building into three so that the cathedral became whole again. Sir Benjamin's statue by John Henry Foley was erected in 1875 and stands outside the cathedral. The restoration of the choir, not tackled by Sir Benjamin, was undertaken by his son Lord Iveagh in 1899–1904 with Sir Thomas Drew as architect.

By far the most impressive monument here is that inscribed 'To Richard Boyle, Earle of Corke', designed by Alban Leverett, Athlone Pursuivant-at-Arms, and carved during the earl's lifetime in 1630 by Edmund Tingham. On its completion Tingham received a bounty from the earl of £32 and £28 worth of iron. The many-tiered monument originally stood behind the high altar but the Earl of Strafford and Archbishop Laud caused it to be dismantled stone by stone and re-erected on the south side of the sanctuary in 1634. In 1863 it was moved again to its present position on the south wall of the nave. Robert Boyle, the young son of the Earl, occupies the central niche; he went on to become a famous scientist and formulated Boyle's Law, which deals with the relationship between the temperature and pressure of a gas. When the present earl received an appeal for the restoration of the monument, he replied that he would be happy to make a contribution if and when it was returned to its rightful position.

The Choir School was founded in 1432 and the cathedral choir took part in the first performance of Handel's *Messiah* in 1742, conducted by the composer, joining forces with the choir of Christ Church Cathedral. The splendid musical tradition is still fully maintained with Matins and Evensong being sung daily.

In common with any large medieval building, the cost of upkeep of St Patrick's is exorbitant. The increasing income from the thousands of tourists who visit it every year has, to a degree, compensated for the dwindling revenues but the problem of finance remains acute. No visitor to Dublin should fail to visit St Patrick's Cathedral. On a sunny day, when the light outside contrasts with the darkness of the interior and shafts of sun illuminate the banners that hang above the choir, the experience on passing through its tall wooden doors is not easily forgotten.

DRIMNAGH CASTLE
Long Mile Road

Drimnagh Castle was built in the thirteenth century for the Barnewall family, a powerful Norman clan who owned vast tracts of land including Ballyfermot and Terenure. It was lived in until 1954, the last occupants being the Hatch family who ran a dairy farm here.

The castle, which stands in the grounds of a Christian Brothers School, was in a dangerous structural condition by 1986 and was due for demolition. The principal of the school, Brother Hegarty, was approached by Peter Pearson, a dedicated conservationist, with a plan to rescue the building. A committee was formed comprising members of An Taisce, the National Trust for Ireland, and interested local people, and in 1986 the restoration work began. Dublin Corporation, to its eternal credit, has provided nearly £50,000 towards the cost.

The castle has a moat fed by an underground stream called the Bluebell; it is said to be the only castle in Ireland completely surrounded by its original moat. Until 1780 there was a wooden drawbridge where the present stone bridge now stands: this leads through the gatehouse tower into the castle precincts. The sixteenth-century tower is three storeys high and once afforded clear views of the western approaches to the city from the Phoenix Park to the Dublin mountains. A minstrels' gallery takes up three sides of the Great Hall where the Barnewalls and their retainers once sat at meat; the recently made copies of medieval floor tiles are based on the heraldic motifs of the Barnewall family.

Two stonemasons and a carpenter from France on an exchange training programme, together with Irish trainees, made the roof and carried out repairs to the stonework. Craftsmen from Germany and Italy have also been involved with the project. They use only traditional methods of craftsmanship and are being trained in skills which might otherwise be lost. The saving of Drimnagh Castle has provided Dublin with another attraction open to the public.

RIGHT Built in the thirteenth century, Drimnagh Castle has stepped battlements and is the only castle in Ireland surrounded by a functional moat.

LEFT The Great Hall has an oak-beamed roof copied from Dunsoghly Castle, Co. Dublin. It is surrounded on three sides by a wooden minstrels' gallery. The castle has recently been restored using traditional methods of craftsmanship.

THE EMERGENCE
OF CLASSICISM

Charles Brooking's map of Dublin (see pp.242–3) was published in 1728. It showed the great development that had taken place in the city during the previous fifty years. As well as a plan of the city streets the map has a panorama and the whole is bordered by vignettes illustrating elevations of all the major public buildings existing at that date; nearly all of these had been erected since the Restoration. The map makes a most useful record of the architecture of the period. Naturally Brooking includes the Royal Hospital, Kilmainham, and Dr Steevens' Hospital nearby, as well as the Great Library in Trinity and the Mansion House. An equestrian statue of King George I is shown standing on an island in the Liffey with access to Essex Bridge where there are two sentry boxes. Iron railings surround the statue as well as spikes at water level for the king's greater protection. The roofscape in the background is jagged like the teeth of a saw. By 1728 there were five bridges over the Liffey, of which Essex Bridge was the most easterly as well as being the earliest in date.

The restoration of the monarchy in 1660 had found Dublin in a sad plight. The Dissolution of the Monasteries by Henry VIII in the previous century had done away with the long-established medieval structures, and then, just a hundred years later, came the murderous Cromwellian regime. The death of Charles II in 1685 heralded another period of unrest when his brother and heir, the Catholic James II, attempted to rally the Catholic population under his banner. Forced to give up the throne of England to his son-in-law William of Orange, he had fled to France in 1688. King James hoped to regain his English throne by first establishing a foothold in Ireland where he knew the Catholics were seething with bitterness; they wanted the return of their confiscated land, the freedom to practice their religion and the right to govern their country. King James came to Dublin in 1689 where he summoned the so-called 'Patriot Parliament', the first assembly in Ireland that represented the Irish people and the last until Dáil Eireann (the Irish parliament) met for the first time in 1919.

When James' aspirations were dashed at the Battle of the Boyne in 1690 by King William, he fled into exile in France. His disastrous

campaign had unfortunate results for Ireland, as it led to the imposition of the iniquitous Penal Laws to ensure that Catholics could never again regain power. The Protestant Ascendancy was confirmed in government and in the ownership of land, the principal source of wealth. Under these conditions Dublin became the second largest city in the English-speaking world, a position that it retained for a hundred years. The city enjoyed these years of expansion during a period of exceptional taste in architecture and the decorative arts.

This great period of Dublin's history can be said to have originated in 1662 with the return, as viceroy, of James Butler (1610–88), Earl and later Duke of Ormonde. Ormonde had originally held this position under Charles I, but left when Parliament defeated the king in 1647. He returned briefly to Ireland in 1648 to rally support for King Charles II but after Oliver Cromwell's conquest of the country for the Parliamentarians he fled to Charles II's court in exile in Paris. For the next ten years he was one of Charles' closest advisers. While in Paris he was influenced by the grandeur and culture of the court there. It was at Ormonde's instigation that Dublin gained its first great Classical building, the Royal Hospital, Kilmainham, which occupies a commanding site, a gift from the king, on high ground to the west of the city. Designed by Sir William Robinson (c.1643–1712), it expressed Ormonde's confidence in great things to come; it was the precursor of Dublin's 'golden age' of architecture.

A viceregal residence called Phoenix House had been put up in what was later to become the Phoenix Park, and from 1616, for the next forty years, this was the principal residence of the viceroys. The Great Earl of Cork recorded in his diary in 1616, 'I and mine were this day feasted at the Phenix by the Lord of Ranelagh.' Among the chief governors of Ireland before the Restoration were Strafford, Ormonde, Fleetwood and Henry Cromwell, the son of Oliver, all strong administrators. At various times they inhabited Phoenix House, situated on the high ground where the magazine fort now stands and commanding a splendid view of the Dublin hills and the Liffey valley. Henry Cromwell added one wing to the building and Lord Orrery, an amateur architect, later added another to balance it. Ormonde lived there for

The Royal Hospital, Kilmainham, Ireland's first great classical building, was designed in 1680 by the Surveyor-General, Sir William Robinson. for the accommodation of old soldiers.

just four years; in 1734 the house was demolished to make way for a powder magazine satirized by Swift in his famous lampoon:

> Behold a proof of Irish sense
> Here Irish wit is seen
> When nothing's left that's worth defence
> They build a magazine!

The creation of the Phoenix Park was one of Ormonde's most lasting achievements. 'It is of importance to keep up the splendour of the government,' he wrote to his son, Lord Arran. The nucleus of the park was land originally confiscated from the monasteries of St Mary's Abbey and the Knights Hospitallers. Ormonde's intention was to create a royal deer park, not just a demesne surrounding the viceregal

residence. The king was enthusiastic and wrote sanctioning the purchase of further land; by 1669 a total of 2,000 acres had been acquired on both sides of the river. Ormonde undertook to surround the park with a wall. Deer were imported from England, and Marcus Trevor, Viscount Dungannon, was appointed ranger. When the king donated land at Kilmainham for the building of the hospital it was decided to confine the park to the northern bank of the river, and its boundaries have changed little since then. As a result Dublin now has one of the finest parks in Europe not far from the centre of the city.

Sir Humphrey Jervis (died 1708), a prosperous merchant and ship owner, was a notable figure in the beautification of the city, although he was not without self-interest. He purchased twenty acres of land, which had been part of St Mary's Abbey, on the northern bank of the

LEFT Collins Barracks, Benburb Street, formerly Royal Barracks, was built in 1700 by Thomas Burgh and at the time was the largest purpose-built barracks in the British Isles.

RIGHT St Ann's Church, Dawson Street, built in 1720, whose design has been attributed to Isaac Wills. In 1723 Lord Newtown left an income for the purchase of loaves of bread for the poor, which are still placed on the shelving beside the altar.

BELOW St Mary's Church, Mary Street, built to the designs of Sir William Robinson from 1701, is the earliest galleried church in Dublin. The Renatus Harris organ has a handsome carved wood case stained dark brown. The church was closed in 1986.

river. He succeeded in persuading the viceroy at the time, the Earl of Essex, that a new bridge should be built and, to tempt him, suggested that it should be named Essex Bridge and embellished with his coat of arms. Furthermore, a fine street leading north from it across Jervis's land would be called Capel Street, the Essex family name being Capell. Essex had been appointed viceroy during a brief period when Ormonde was out of favour. Happily for Dublin, Essex fell in with the scheme, and when Ormonde returned to power in 1677 he also supported it but insisted that the new buildings along the quay face the river as they do in Paris, instead of backing onto it as had been planned and as they do in Florence and Rome. As Maurice Craig has written:

> This suggestion of Ormonde's was of immense importance to the future development of Dublin, because it was this prototype which inspired the whole system of quays in their final beauty. Otherwise Dublin might well have been like so many other towns, through which the river slinks shamefacedly between tall buildings which give it no chance to be seen.

At Ormonde's insistence Jervis built a stone quay which he named Ormonde Quay after the viceroy, and Arran Quay, built about the same time, was named after Ormonde's son. Jervis also built a market behind Ormonde Quay with a central rotunda; the area is now called Ormonde Square. The Liffey bank was later built up making a new quay to the east, which was planted with trees and is known as Bachelor's Walk.

The development of the city proceeded on the south side as Dublin burst out of the old medieval walls. St Stephen's Green was the first grandiose planning scheme initiated by Dublin Corporation. In 1664 the perimeter of a 27-acre area of open common was drained and laid out in building lots to form a square; it was called after St Stephen, patron saint of the leper hospital which had stood nearby, and it was approached by a winding lane which is now Grafton Street, the most fashionable shopping street in Ireland. Members of the corporation and others drew for the ninety lots marked out. Each allottee received a 'fee farm grant' of his plot and had to pay a small ground rent of one penny per square foot for lots on the north, east and west sides, and a half-penny for those on the south side – the 'fines for each lease to be applied to walling-in and paving the Green for the ornament and pleasure of the city'. It was decreed that trees should be planted and that the houses were to be of brick, stone and timber covered with tiles or slates; no thatched roofs were permitted after the Great Fire of London in 1666.

A good deal of buying and selling ensued so that those ready and able to build found themselves in possession of a lot. There was no attempt at imposing architectural uniformity as is found in the later Dublin squares. Beside the double avenue of trees, a broad gravel walk, 35 feet in width, was laid out around the four sides of the Green, a distance of approximately one mile. 'Why don't you walk in the Green of St Stephen? . . . the walks there are finer gravelled than the Mall,' Swift writes to Stella and Mrs Dingley in 1710. It had not taken long to create a fashionable place of assembly and promenade, but the interior was still reserved as a pasturage for cattle and horses. The earliest printed map illustrating the Green, drawn by Hermann Moll in 1714, shows it already built up on two sides, the north and west. The early brick houses had gable ends facing the Green, some of which have survived, although squared off later to conform with the horizontal parapet that became *de rigueur* in Dublin from 1750. By the time of Brooking's map in 1728 only one-third of the south side remained open.

The sash window and the use of brick are supposed to have been introduced to Ireland around the time of William III's arrival and presumably also the Dutch gables which faced the Green. Glazing bars were thick and heavy, and the window frames were almost flush with the wall so there were practically no reveals as are found in the later eighteenth century. In most of the houses the rooms were small and sparsely furnished; there were corner fireplaces without a shelf and with plain mantels which formed an extension of the oak or pine wall-panelling.

King William III ordered the construction of Dublin (Royal from 1803, now Collins) Barracks, the largest in his dominions, in 1700, ten years after the Battle of the Boyne. It was a new idea to house the military in purpose-built barracks instead of cramming them into forts or billeting them in private households. The barracks were to be 'plain and useful without any unnecessary ornament'. The squares are surrounded by arcades in the manner typical of the architect Thomas Burgh (1670–1730), with three storeys and central pediments to relieve the monotony; there is beautiful vaulting behind the arcades. There were quarters for 5000 men by 1704, and after restructuring in the 1750s 3000 men and 1000 horses could be accommodated. After the founding of the Irish Free State in 1922 the barracks was renamed after General Michael Collins, the first Commander-in-Chief of the Irish Army. The Irish army still occupies Collins Barracks but a new use for this imposing building is now being sought.

In 1701 a magnificent statue of King William III on horseback was erected on College Green in front of Chichester House where at that time parliament sat. The statue was made in London by the foremost sculptor of the day, Grinling Gibbons, and unveiled with great ceremony during the king's lifetime. The statue suffered every kind of indignity before it was finally blown up in 1929; bits of it were sawn off and it was regularly daubed with paint, often by the boisterous students from Trinity nearby. Since the blowing up of Viscount Gough on horseback in the Phoenix Park, Dublin has become the only capital city in Europe without an equestrian statue.

The Surveyor-General, Sir William Robinson, is believed to have designed Dublin's first galleried church, St Mary's, Mary Street, setting a pattern that was to last for over a hundred years. Isaac Wills, who, it can be assumed, was the master-carpenter of the same name working for Thomas Burgh at Dr Steevens' Hospital, is thought to have designed St Ann's, another large galleried church, on Dawson Street in 1720. The church has Victorian stained glass including a window dedicated to the poetess, Felicia Hemans, remembered for her immortal lines about the boy who stood on the burning deck. This window was financed by public subscription. Charles Dickens was sent an appeal but declined to contribute; 'I would rather read Mrs Hemans by her own light than through the colours of any painted window,' was his response.

It may be thought that, by comparison with the great period that followed, the architecture of the late seventeenth and early eighteenth centuries was severe. Considering that the two major architects, Robinson and Burgh, were soldiers, more at home in the building of military installations, Dublin fared well. This period led up to the advent of the Palladian style in all its beauty and to the work of architects who could no longer be considered anything but professional.

THE ROYAL HOSPITAL
Kilmainham

In 1662, after the Restoration, Charles II appointed as Viceroy of Ireland his old friend and ally in exile, James Butler, who was then twelfth Earl of Ormonde and was created first Duke of Ormonde twenty years later. On 29 April 1680 Ormonde laid the foundation stone of Dublin's first great Classical building, the Royal Hospital at Kilmainham, which antedates Wren's Chelsea Hospital in London by two years. The founding charter stated 'that such of the . . . Army, as hath faithfully served . . . in the Strength and vigor of their Youth, may in the Weakness, and Disasters, that their Old Age, Wounds or other Misfortunes may bring them into, find a comfortable Retreat and a competent Maintenance therein'. The Royal Hospital was built to house 300 old soldiers and was used for this purpose from 1684 until its closure in 1929. The military commander-in-chief in Ireland served also as the master of the hospital. He and his family had accommodation at the north-west corner of the courtyard.

The inspiration for the Royal Hospital came from Louis XIV's Hotel des Invalides in Paris, built in 1671–6. There were many old soldiers in Ireland who were homeless and had become a nuisance, hanging about the forts and garrison towns. The fact that troops would now be properly cared for when they were retired or wounded would increase morale among the serving men; the cost of the building ($£23,559$ 16s 11¼d by 1687) was to be met by a levy on military pay.

The elevated site chosen, on the southern side of the Liffey, was situated a mile west of the city in what was then the Phoenix Park, with splendid views across the river. The architect was Sir William Robinson, a Yorkshireman, appointed Surveyor-General of Ireland in 1671, which post he retained until 1700. A military engineer as well as an architect, he worked simultaneously on the great star-shaped Charles Fort guarding the harbour of Kinsale, Co. Cork. The Royal Hospital was built in the form of a quadrangle with the dining hall, chapel and master's accommodation taking up the north range of the building; arcades on the other three sides were used for exercise in wet weather. Four of the entrances are surmounted by beautiful tympana carved in pine, with a rich profusion of classical heads and military trophies, all in a surprisingly good state of preservation.

ABOVE One of four overdoors elaborately carved with military trophies, cannon and sacks of gun-powder.

RIGHT The chapel, which has a superb Carolean ceiling and woodwork by the Huguenot craftsman, James Tabary, was dedicated to Charles I, King and Martyr, in 1687.

LEFT The north front of the Royal Hospital, which looks across formal gardens to the River Liffey and the Phoenix Park, bears the arms of the first Duke of Ormonde.

The principal front faces north across formal gardens towards the river, the central axis closing on an enchanting little building with twin towers, originally a garden banqueting house, the design of which has been attributed to Sir Edward Lovett Pearce. The central feature of this north front consists of a pedimented portico of four giant Corinthian pilasters, which spring out of the ground without the customary plinth, or 'socle'. The entrance door, beneath the Ormonde arms carved in Portland stone, is surmounted by a segmental pediment,

previously occupied this site, but it is unlikely that more than fragments of the medieval tracery were used. James Tabary, a Huguenot woodcarver, assisted by his relatives John and Louis Tabary, executed the altar-table and all the carving at the east end of the chapel. The quality and movement of Tabary's floral carving is unmatched by any contemporary carving in Ireland. The rest of the panelling in the chapel is of dark brown Baltic oak with a natural wax finish, providing an anchor for the profuse decoration of the coved

LEFT Detail of carved woodwork in the chapel by James Tabary.

RIGHT The dining hall and tower from the recently gravelled courtyard. The entire complex, which had become dangerous, was rescued and beautifully restored from 1980 onwards for the Office of Public Works. Park of it houses the Museum of Modern Art, with its fine collection of paintings and sculpture.

whose dentils converge inwards instead of being vertical. The artisans at work on the Royal Hospital, Ireland's first major Classical building, were evidently not yet completely at home with the Classical vocabulary. The tower above is not unlike the spire of a seventeenth-century church. This was completed in 1701 to Robinson's design by his successor as surveyor-general, Thomas Burgh.

The chapel was dedicated in 1687 to Charles I, 'King and Martyr' in his role as an Anglican saint; during the brief reign of his son, James II, Catholic Mass was celebrated here. Musical accompaniment at services used to be supplied by a military band as there has never been an organ. It has always been said that the great arched east window of the chapel originally came from the Priory of the Knights Hospitallers, which

ceiling. Among the foliage there are cherubic winged heads as well as fruit, flowers, shells, pumpkins, grapes, carrots and cabbages. The elaborate stuccowork of the ceiling was originally mounted on green oak twigs, with the idea that the plaster would not crack as it dried out, but with the passage of time the twigs decayed and the ceiling had to be taken down in 1902. Various proposals were put forward for a new ceiling and fortunately it was decided that a papier-mâché replica of the original, far lighter in weight, was the best solution. Although Carolean ceilings of this type are no rarity in England or Scotland, they are virtually unknown in Ireland and the survival of this example, even as a replica, is fortunate.

In 1849 Queen Victoria presented stained glass for the east window,

the sill of which had to be lowered to accommodate it. The handsome carved reredos was removed at this time but is now back in place once more. The coats of arms of successive masters displayed in the side windows of the chapel are the work of Michael O'Connor, an Irish artist living in London, who died in 1867. Between the dining hall and the chapel, both of which take up the full height of the building, there is a set of blue wrought-iron gates with the arms of Queen Anne, for which a Mr Greenway was paid £50 in 1706.

The entrance to the great dining hall, which measures 100 feet by 50 feet, is at the centre of the north side of the quadrangle. The panelling in the hall, now white, was formally stained dark brown and was covered with military trophies, swords and armour. Twenty-two early eighteenth-century full-length portraits, including Charles II, William and Mary, Queen Anne, Archbishop Marsh and the Duke of Ormonde, are fortunately still *in situ*. Several have recently been restored. At the centre of the compartmented ceiling there was once a gigantic clock, a constant reminder to the pensioners of the inevitable passage of time. A gallery used to run along the south wall, so that the master could attend chapel services, seated beneath his carved canopy, without descending to the level of the old soldiers. This gallery was

'supported by brackets of carved oak, representing different figures, as large as life'. An elaborate, carved timber tympanum above the door leading to the chapel is original and may be the work of James Tabary; music is the theme. The entablature once supported the royal arms but these were removed to the Royal Hospital, Chelsea, in 1928 leaving an unfortunate empty space. Now that the building has been restored, the arms should be returned to their rightful place, or at least a copy installed.

In 1820 some alterations to the master's quarters were made by Francis Johnston; he has been criticized for extending the dining room into the arcade, thereby upsetting the symmetry of the quadrangle. Johnston also designed the Gothic gateway at the end of the formal avenue of lime trees on the axis to the west of the Royal Hospital. This originally stood beside the River Liffey at Bloody Bridge, but when the Great Southern and Western Railway came into being in 1844 and Kingsbridge Station was built here, the traffic congestion necessitated its removal. The architect had put his personal coat of arms above the arch, concealed by a piece of wood painted to match the stone, his idea being that his arms would be revealed to future generations after the wood became rotten. However, his innocent ruse was uncovered when

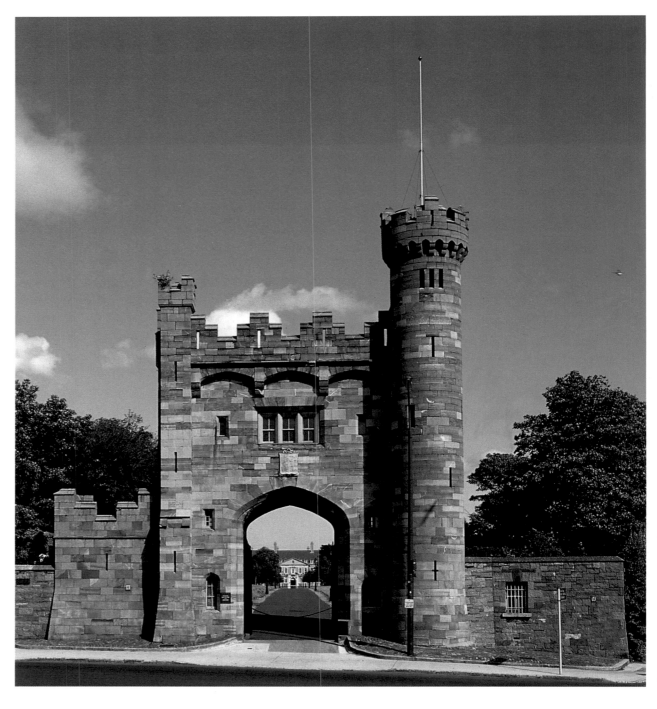

LEFT The dining hall, used for banquets and concerts, has twenty-two full-length portraits, including William III, Queen Anne, James, Duke of Ormonde, and Archbishop Narcissus Marsh; the latest dates from 1737.

RIGHT The Gothic gateway was designed by Francis Johnston and originally erected at Bloody Bridge. It was moved to its present site in 1844 on the coming of the railway to Kingsbridge.

the gateway was taken down; the coat of arms at present on the structure is that of the Royal Hospital.

In 1922 the commander-in-chief formally handed over the building to General Mulcahy who accepted it on behalf of the Irish Free State. Seven years later the remaining pensioners were transferred to Chelsea and the last service was held in the chapel, which was then closed for worship. The building was offered to University College, Dublin, but the college authorities considered it unsuitable and the Garda Síochána (Irish police force) took possession. By 1949 the roof and general structural condition had deteriorated and the Gardaí departed; the National Museum of Ireland then used it as a store. In 1980, thanks to the inspiration of the Taoiseach, Jack Lynch, major restoration work that was to cost £20 million was commenced for the Office of Public Works by Costello, Murray and Beaumont, architects.

It was decided to restore the building as closely as possible to the way it had stood after Francis Johnston had completed his alterations in 1820. The architect in charge, John Costello, has been much commended for his scholarship and sensitivity in carrying out the works here. The Irish Museum of Modern Art has occupied part of the Royal Hospital since 1991 and is beginning to build up a collection of modern pictures and sculpture; already Sir Sidney Nolan and Senator Gordon Lambert have made significant contributions to it. Unfortunately some modern alterations have been made which are out of place in a seventeenth-century building, in particular a hung glass staircase, relegating two of the finest seventeenth-century staircases in Ireland to the status of fire exits.

The dining hall, chapel and other reception rooms of every shape and size are in constant demand for plays, concerts, balls and banquets as well as commercial promotions of various kinds. The martial drums may be silent now but the old building echoes instead to the strains of the dance band and chamber orchestra. Its rescue at the eleventh hour has restored the Royal Hospital to the life of Dublin, returning to the city one of its most precious possessions.

The Duke of Ormonde who was recalled to England in 1685 by James II attended a farewell banquet here as an old man and in replying to the toast he filled his glass to the brim and addressed the pensioners as follows: 'See, gentlemen, they say that I am old and doting, but my hand is steady nor does my heart fail.' He deserves our applause for the Royal Hospital, a magnificent adornment of the capital, just as much as he earned the cheers of the soldiery on that occasion.

ST MICHAN'S CHURCH
Church Street

St Michan's Church was first built in the year 1095 in the Viking settlement of Oxmantown north of the Liffey; for the ensuing six centuries it was the only city parish church on that side of the river. St Michan is thought to have been a Dublin Norseman, although the *Martyrology of Christ Church* describes him simply as an Irish saint and confessor; the church was served by the monks of Christ Church. After the Norman conquest many of the descendants of the Vikings settled in this area; it is not known whether they left the south side voluntarily or if they were forced to move. A medieval recumbent effigy in the church is thought to represent Bishop Samuel O'hAingli (died 1121), who founded the original church. He made St Michan's his seat instead of Christ Church and the chronicles report that in 1100 he was 'parading around Dublin like an Archbishop' even though his see did not become an archdiocese until 1152; he was reprimanded for this behaviour by Anselm, Archbishop of Canterbury.

The present church dates from the rebuilding of 1685 and the design has been attributed to Sir William Robinson. This rebuilding was probably at the instigation of Sir Humphrey Jervis, as St Michan's was the parish church of his fashionable new rectilinear suburb on the north side. In 1697, as the population on the north side had increased rapidly, the parishes of St Paul's and St Mary's were carved out of the west and east sides of St Michan's boundaries; Jervis also planned a church for

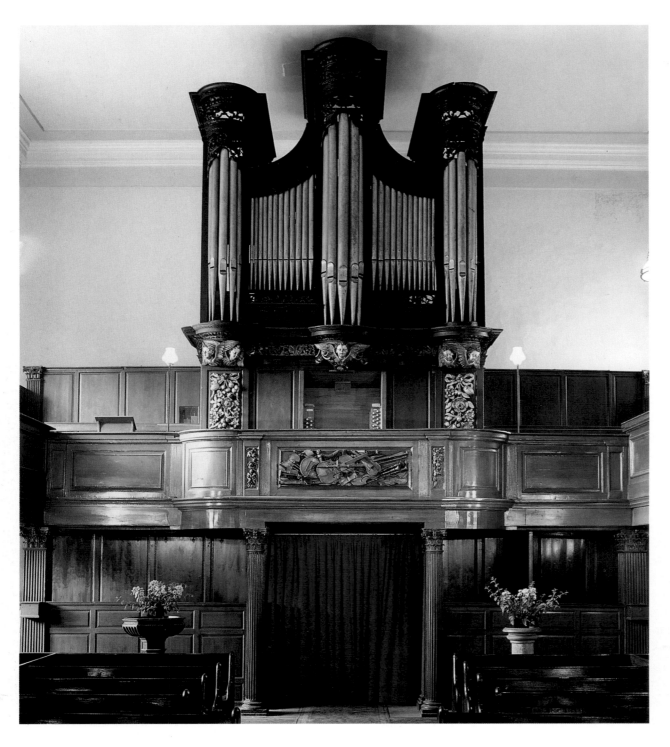

LEFT The organ at St Michan's was built by John Baptiste Cuvillié in 1725. A wood panel carved with musical instruments adorns the front of the organ gallery.

RIGHT Founded in 1095, St Michan's was for centuries the only church on the north side of the Liffey. The present building dates from 1685 and may have been designed by Sir William Robinson.

The corpses in the vault are in a remarkable state of preservation thanks to the magnesium salts in the limestone which absorb the moisture.

the site of St Mary's. The tall grey tower of St Michan's with its distinctive crenellations has long been a well-known landmark in north Dublin; it is built of rough-hewn Dublin calp (a local limestone) and rubble. At its base there is a seventeenth-century stone doorcase with a scrolled pediment. The interior of the church, which is in the Greek-Revival style, only dates from 1828 when it was also re-roofed.

Barra Boydell, in his authoritative account of the organ at St Michan's, has pointed out that at the time of Cromwell an ordinance of 1644 resulted in 'the speedy demolishing of all organs, images and all manner of superstitious monuments in all cathedrals and collegiate or parish churches and chapels'. The parishioners of St Michan's in 1724 were however of the firm opinion that church music was 'not only . . . lawful in itself but also highly serviceable to excite and actuate the devotion of good men, by composing and fixing the mind, moving the passions and assisting the voice, whereby they are better disposed to receive the influence of the Holy Spirit'. The parish worked hard to raise the cost of a new organ, gathering a total of £467 7s 10d from contributions, the sale of seats and burials.

The organ in the gallery was built in 1725 and there is a tradition that it was played by Handel when he was in Dublin in 1741–2 for the first performance of *Messiah*. A carved wooden panel of seventeen musical instruments, faded now to a golden honey colour, decorates the gallery of the church and the corners of the organ case are carved with winged angel heads, ribbons, fruit and flowers. This carving has for long been attributed to the builder of the instrument, John Baptiste Cuvillié.

Presumably of French origin, he came to Ireland as assistant to Renatus Harris, the famous English organ-builder who worked in Dublin both at St Patrick's and Christ Church. The singing of psalm tunes was the only type of choir-singing at this time, and at St Michan's one of the organist's duties was to train the children.

St Michan's is famous for the mummified corpses in the vaults which have been preserved because the magnesium salts in the limestone absorb the moisture from the air. Dr Leask has pointed out that this part of the building is seventeenth century and not medieval, so the claims that one of the caskets contains a 'crusader' can be dismissed. It might seem preferable and more correct to shut up the coffins and leave the occupants in peace but the 'mummies' are a popular attraction and, as funds are urgently needed for the maintenance of the church, they serve a useful purpose.

Preserved in St Michan's is the only Stool of Repentance remaining in Dublin, and among the church plate there is a silver-gilt chalice dated 1516. Also in the church is the font where Edmund Burke, the orator, was baptised in 1729 and there is an early nineteenth-century moveable pulpit. The unfortunate Sheares brothers, who gave their lives heroically in the 1798 rebellion, are buried in the vaults. Dr Charles Lucas, physician, patriot and founder of the *Freeman's Journal*, whose statue by Edward Smyth is in the City Hall, died in 1771 and lies buried here. The east window was shattered during the shelling of the Four Courts in 1922 and has been replaced with a window based on designs from the Book of Kells.

MARSH'S LIBRARY
St Patrick's Close

One of the earliest and least known of Dublin's public institutions can also lay claim to being the most charming and intimate of all. From a Victorian iron gateway steep steps ascend through a rockery to the old door in the narrow front of red brick. Archbishop Narcissus Marsh (1638–1713) provided Dublin with its first public library in 1701. Marsh's Library, as it is known, was erected in the grounds of his Palace of St Sepulchre to the designs of Sir William Robinson, the architect of the Royal Hospital, Kilmainham. Although the library was originally built of brick with a steeply pitched roof, the side facing St Patrick's Cathedral was faced in stone at the time of Sir Benjamin Lee Guinness's restoration of the cathedral in the 1860s. The curved road that separates the library from the deanery was made at this date.

The ground floor contains an apartment for the librarian opening on to a small private garden; the original staircase with its barley-sugar balusters leads to the library on the upper floor. On first entering, the visitor is struck by an other-worldly atmosphere of scholarship and repose, heightened by shafts of sunlight falling on the old bindings. The dark oak panelling is punctuated by brilliant white decorative carving and a magical smell of old leather pervades the whole. The two galleries that contain the books converge at right angles on the office enabling the librarian to supervise the whole collection from one spot. Each of the dark oak library stalls is surmounted by a bishop's mitre, with decorative plaques numbered to indicate the method of finding a book. In the past, books were put on chains that ran along wooden rods attached to the shelves, and three elaborately carved cages were provided for scholars who were locked in with especially rare and valuable volumes.

The nucleus of Marsh's Library consists of 10,000 books the archbishop purchased for £2,500 in 1705 from the heirs of Edward Stillingfleet (1635–1699), Bishop of Worcester. Archbishop Marsh bequeathed his own books to the library as did the first librarian, Dr Elias Bouhéreau, a Huguenot. John Stearne (1660–1745), Bishop of Clogher, also left his books, which included Cicero's *Letters to his Friends*, printed in Milan in 1472. The collection of 25,000 books of the sixteenth, seventeenth and eighteenth centuries covers a wide range of subjects including law, medicine, science, travel and mathematics; there are bibles in many languages. The library also contains a large

RIGHT Marsh's Library, which was given to Dublin by Archbishop Narcissus Marsh in 1701, is the earliest public library in Ireland. The entrance front, with its steeply pitched roof, is approached through a Victorian Gothic gateway.

LEFT The books are housed on the upper floor, which overlooks a small private garden.

collection of early manuscript material including an account of the lives of the Irish saints dating from about 1400.

Jonathan Swift was a governor of the library from the time of his appointment as Dean of St Patrick's in 1713 until his death in 1745; his dislike of the archbishop, whom he blamed for impeding his promotion, was well known. Swift wrote of Marsh:

> He is the first of the Human race, that with great advantages of learning, piety and station ever escaped being a great man . . . He is so wise to value his own health more than other men's noses so that the most honourable place at his table is much the worst especially in summer . . . No man will be either glad or sorry at his death, except his successor.

Among mementos of Swift on display here are his death mask, his writing cabinet and the plain wooden table on which he is thought to have written *Drapier's Letters* and *Gulliver's Travels*.

When he established his library Archbishop Marsh laid down rules and regulations which state: 'We order and appoint that all graduates and gentlemen shall have free access to the said library on the days and hours before determined; provided they behave themselves well, give place and pay due respect to their betters.' There is a monument to Marsh in the cathedral by Grinling Gibbons and he is buried in the graveyard. According to a legend the ghost of the archbishop haunts the library, searching for a letter left in a book by his niece, who apparently wrote to him apologizing for a misdemeanour.

An Act passed in 1707 laid down that the governors of the library should consist of the Archbishop of Dublin (chairman), the Archbishop of Armagh, the Deans of St Patrick's and Christ Church, and the Provost of Trinity; the Chief Justice has recently been added to the list. Mrs Muriel McCarthy, the librarian, has written a history of the library entitled *All Graduates and Gentlemen* and has recently established a conservation bindery thanks to the generosity of Mr Jean-Paul Delmas and Mrs Gladys Delmas. The Ireland Fund has paid for restoration to the fabric of the building as well as essential treatment work on the books themselves. It has also provided some display cases which have enabled the librarian to mount regular exhibitions based on the material in her care.

RIGHT Although only 'graduates and gentlemen' were allowed to use the library, they were locked up with rare volumes in these decorative 'cages'.

TAILORS HALL
Back Lane

Among Dublin's public buildings Tailors Hall must have had the most varied collection of tenants during its chequered past. The hall faces south across a little paved garden on Back Lane opposite Mother Redcap's pub and, as it houses An Taisce, the National Trust for Ireland, it is now at the forefront of the conservation movement in Ireland.

The establishment of Dublin guilds began soon after the arrival of the Normans, and in Prince John's charter to the city in 1192 provision is made for artisans to associate for their mutual protection and to establish standards of work. The guilds laid down conditions of employment and rules for apprenticeships. Over the centuries the number of guilds in Dublin varied between sixteen and twenty-five. They became powerful as they took over control of the municipal government, each guild having the right to fill a number of seats on the city council. In 1840 with the passing of the Irish Municipal Reform Act members of Dublin Corporation were to be elected by the general public; this led to the collapse of the guild structure.

The Guild of Tailors, dedicated to St John the Baptist, was inaugurated in 1418 and by 1583 it was established in a wooden guildhall, possibly in Back Lane. In 1703 the cornerstone of the present building was laid and it was completed in 1707. The architect was probably Richard Mills, who was assistant to the Masters of the City Works and is known to have overseen the building, for which he was paid the sum of £23. Until the Music Hall in Fishamble Street was built in 1741, Tailors Hall was considered to be the fashionable place to hold meetings, dances and every kind of social function.

Tailors Hall is of red brick, as would be expected at this date, and is one of the few buildings in Dublin surviving from the reign of Queen Anne, besides being the only surviving guildhall in the city. The entrance is approached from Back Lane through a handsome limestone archway with a broken segmental pediment. The hall itself is lit by four tall round-headed windows, and there is an oval minstrels' gallery at one end surmounted by an ogee canopy which acts as a sounding board. A large wooden panel at the other end carries the names of the masters of the guild from 1419 to 1841 in gold lettering. The white marble mantel is inscribed 'the gift of Christopher Neary, master; Alexander Bell and Hugh Craigg, wardens, 1784'. The stairs, in a projection at the back of the building, have a low balustrade supported on barley-sugar balusters.

In common with the other Dublin guildhalls, Tailors Hall was always available for hire and an astonishing variety of tenants, ranging from dancing classes to temperance organizations, have met here over the years. From 1755 to 1818 the Grand Lodge of Freemasons used the hall for meetings. The hall's great moment of glory, when an important part of Irish history was enacted within these walls, came in 1792. On 2nd December of that year it was leased by Wolfe Tone, himself a Protestant, who was secretary of the Catholic Committee. Representatives of the Catholic community from all over Ireland met here under

RIGHT The guildhall of the tailors dates from 1703. It was rescued in 1966 by a voluntary committee and now serves as the headquarters of An Taisce, the National Trust for Ireland.

LEFT The main hall has a minstrels' gallery, a marble mantel and, at the other end, a large wooden panel inscribed with the names of the officers of the guild. The tailors used the hall for their banquets.

the chairmanship of Archbishop Troy, beneath the very walls of Dublin Castle, to debate and petition for Catholic emancipation. This Catholic Convention came to be known as the Back Lane Parliament. On 3 January 1793 five members of this committee presented their petition to George III in London.

An humble application to our gracious sovereign, submitting to him our loyalty and atttachment – our obedience to the laws – a true statement of our situation – and of the laws which operate against us; and humbly beseeching – that we may be restored to the ELECTIVE FRANCHISE, and an equal participation in the benefits of TRIAL BY JURY.

The very fact that the delegation was received by the king was regarded as a moral victory for the Catholics although little came of it and the Catholic Convention concluded its business, which lasted only a few days. The hall continued to be the meeting place of the Dublin Society of United Irishmen, who assembled here every second Friday until their meetings were suppressed in 1794.

In 1960 the building was declared unsafe by Dublin Corporation, and the last tenant, the Legion of Mary, was obliged to leave. It was then shuttered and shored up and left to the mercy of vandals and the elements. The gutters soon became choked and the hall mantel was stolen but fortunately recovered in Co. Cork. In 1966 a voluntary committee, the Tailors Hall Fund, was set up which took a lease of the building for one shilling a year in order to save it. Tailors Hall is now leased to An Taisce as their National Headquarters and is available, as in the past, for meetings of every kind.

THE MANSION HOUSE
Dawson Street

The Mansion House today is a cheerful building, covered with frilly Victorian ironwork and laden with colourful flowers and window boxes which add to its charm. There has been a civic government in Dublin since 1172, just after the coming of the Normans, and in 1229 the office of mayor was instituted by Henry III to administer the affairs of the city. The first lord mayor was Sir Daniel Bellingham in 1665, and in 1841 Daniel O'Connell became the first Catholic lord mayor to be elected since the reign of James II. Dublin preceded London by twenty years in the provision of an official residence for its lord mayor.

The Mansion House began as a private house, built by Joshua Dawson for himself in 1710. Dawson had purchased the land here five years previously and in 1707 laid out the street that bears his name, then described as the finest street in Dublin. The house was a two-storey, seven-bay, red-brick dwelling with stone quoins and curved sweeps, set well back from the street; a broken pediment over the front door contained a bust. The parapet was surmounted by four stone urns and ornamented with figures in panels, presumably made of stone or plaster, as can be seen in a vignette of the house on Brooking's map of Dublin, 1728.

In 1715 Dawson sold the property to Dublin Corporation and it has served as the Mansion House ever since. The price was £3,500, a yearly rent of 40 shillings and a loaf of double refined sugar weighing 6lbs at Christmas, the price to include the building of an extra room. The corporation decided that this room should be on a more elaborate scale than stipulated in the contract and paid the difference. This has always been known as the Oak Room although the panelling and top-lighting of the Oak Room today appear to be twentieth century. Dawson was also prepared to part with the following household goods: 'all the brass locks and marble chimney pieces, as also the tapestry hangings, silk window curtains and window seats and chimney glass in the great bed chamber; the gilt leather hangings, four pairs of scarlet calamanco window curtains and chimney glass in the walnut parlour; the Indian calicoe window curtains . . . in the Dantzick oak parlour.'

The facade was radically altered in the nineteenth century. The brick was plastered over, and elaborate Victorian surrounds were added to

LEFT Built in 1710 as a private residence, the Mansion House was purchased by Dublin Corporation in 1715 as an official residence for the lord mayor.

ABOVE The Oak Room has dark panelling that appears to be Edwardian and is surrounded by coats of arms of successive lord mayors. The portraits are, on the left, Richard Manders (lord mayor in 1802) by Hugh Douglas Hamilton and, at the end, Charles Stewart Parnell (lord mayor in 1892) by Thomas Alfred Jones.

the windows, designed by Hugh Byrne, city architect, in about 1851. The cast-iron porch with its glass roof was added by D.J. Freeman in 1896 and ten years later a handsome cornice and pediment, containing the arms of the city, gave the Mansion House the appearance that it has today.

The great Round Room behind the house, nearly 100 feet in diameter, was designed by John Semple, father of the architect of the Black Church. The domed ceiling was 'painted to represent a beautiful sky', and the room was built in six weeks so as to be ready for entertaining George IV on his visit to Dublin in 1821. This was the first visit of a reigning monarch to Ireland since that of the victorious William of Orange in 1690 and elaborate preparations were made for

LEFT The drawing room has a fine collection of portraits, including those of George, Lord Townshend, painted by T. Hickey (1771) on the left and John, Earl of Westmorland, by Romney (1790) on the right.

BELOW The dining room with the table laid for an official luncheon in honour of a Russian delegation, with the flags of Russia, Ireland and Dublin. The carpet, with a Celtic design, was made in the Dun Emer workshops. The portrait on the right, painted by Solomon Williams, is of George, Marquess of Buckingham, viceroy from 1782 to 1787, wearing a ceremonial chain. The other portrait is of Charles II.

his reception, particularly in Dublin. Over two centuries later it was in the Round Room that the first Republican Dáil met in January 1919 and adopted the Declaration of Independence.

The Lord Mayor of Dublin is elected on an annual basis and is chairman of Dublin Corporation. He works hard during the term of office receiving foreign dignitaries, attending countless functions and receptions, sometimes five or six during the course of a day. The Round Room and the Supper Room are used throughout the year for exhibitions, fairs, sales, concerts, dances and charitable events of all kinds. As an example of the wide variety of activities that take place here, the Irish winner of the 1953 Grand National, Early Mist, was paraded through the streets of Dublin and then received outside the Mansion House by the lord mayor. Forty years later, in 1993, three elephants from Fossett's Circus were brought into the forecourt of the Mansion House to launch an appeal for arthritis.

ST WERBURGH'S CHURCH
Werburgh Street

St Werburgh's Church, standing in the heart of the medieval city beside Dublin Castle, is reputed to be one of the oldest foundations in Dublin. St Werburgh (died about AD 700) was the Abbess of Ely and the daughter of Wulfhere, King of Mercia. In 876, to prevent her tomb being plundered by the Vikings her body was removed from Ely to the Benedictine Abbey of Chester, now the cathedral. Chester, like Bristol, had close links with Dublin and from the twelfth century a succession of churches on this site in Dublin have been named after St Werburgh.

In 1716 a church with a tall Baroque facade culminating in an octagonal domed cupola, was designed by Thomas Burgh, the surveyor-general, who signed payments for its building from that date onwards. Rolf Loeber believes that the elevation was inspired by da Volterra's church of Santa Chiara in Rome. The main body of Burgh's church was destroyed by fire in 1754 leaving only the tower and the lower section of the Baroque facade intact; this corresponds exactly with the elevation illustrated on Brooking's map of Dublin, 1728. Kenneth Severens, in the *Irish Georgian Society Bulletin 1992/3*, suggested that Alessandro Galilei, the architect of Castletown, Co. Kildare, may

have had a hand in the design of the facade, which does seem too Italianate for Burgh.

The present interior dates from 1759 and is the finest of any Classical church in Dublin, with its dark profusion of panelling and carving. The original pews and gallery are still in place, stained a wonderful shade of brown in contrast to the light that streams in through the large plain windows above; being in an unfashionable district, St Werburgh's escaped the intrusion of Victorian stained glass. Michael Maguire was responsible for the excellent plasterwork in the chancel; the original floor, paved in large black and white squares, has fortunately survived. Richard Stewart carved the intricate Gothic pulpit designed by Francis Johnston and originally made for the Chapel Royal.

As Severens has written, Michael Wills, John Ensor, Joseph Jarratt, George Semple and others were invited to provide estimates for repairing the church after the fire in 1754. Joseph Jarratt and Francis Goodwin appear to have been responsible for the rebuilding. A spire was added to the tower in about 1768, which can be seen both in Pool and Cash's elevation, 1780, and later in Malton's *View of Upper Castle*

RIGHT The truncated facade is all that remains of St Werburgh's Church built in 1716. The church school on the right has been adapted to form a private residence for the Dean of Christ Church.

RIGHT The present interior dates from 1759. The Gothic pulpit, originally made for the Chapel Royal in Dublin Castle, was carved by Richard Stewart.

LEFT Due to the church's proximity to the castle, the viceroy and his entourage worshipped here until the Chapel Royal was built, hence the royal arms on the front of the viceregal pew in the gallery.

Yard. After the uprisings of 1798 and Emmet's rebellion of 1803 the authorities became nervous at having such a vantage point overlooking Dublin Castle. They produced seven architects to pronounce the spire unsafe, and it was taken down despite Francis Johnston's offer to make it secure; in 1836 the tower on which it had stood was also dismantled.

The eighteenth-century organ is one of the few antique instruments in Dublin that has never been rebuilt. It has the usual golden pipes and a royal crown, flanked by two bishop's mitres; a balustraded gallery for the choir extends to either side. St Werburgh's was the viceroy's church until the Chapel Royal was completed in 1814 within the walls of Dublin Castle; the viceregal pew in the organ gallery was adorned with the royal arms in 1767.

Jonathan Swift was born in Hoey's Court around the corner and was christened in the church that stood here in 1667. In 1766 the wardens of St Werburgh's passed a resolution forbidding 'any seat in the church to be lined with any kind of cloth, silk or stuff, so as to prevent, as much as possible, any lodgement of vermin'. The bell in the aisle bears the name of James Napper Tandy, the popular patriot. By day he was church warden at St John's, a neighbouring church but by night he was one of the leaders of the rebellion of 1798.

The most famous person buried here is Lord Edward FitzGerald who died in Newgate prison of wounds inflicted by Major Sirr, his captor, on the eve of the 1798 rebellion. His coffin, which bore no name, had the initials 'E F' scratched onto it by an old man who recognized Lord Edward's aunt, Lady Louisa Conolly, as the lone mourner at his burial. By a strange coincidence Major Sirr himself lies buried only a few feet away.

The Select Vestry of St Werburgh's was the local government authority of the area and it kept the fire engines that belonged to this district in the spacious front porch of the church, where they can still be seen. One is the size of a wagon and the other resembles a wheelbarrow; known as 'water-engines', they both have solid wooden wheels and may date from as early as 1706. The school-house next door to the church has recently been converted into a residence for the Dean of Christ Church; this was cleverly adapted for him by John Redmill.

DR STEEVENS' HOSPITAL
Steevens' Lane

Dr Steevens' Hospital was designed by the Surveyor-General, Thomas Burgh, and building was begun in 1721. The architect died in 1730, before it was finished, and the building was completed by his successor, Sir Edward Lovett Pearce, in 1733, the year in which the hospital at last opened. When it closed in 1987 it was the oldest public hospital in Dublin. It was founded by Dr Richard Steevens (1653–1710) whose father, a clergyman from Wiltshire, had come to Ireland at the time of Cromwell. Dr Steevens became a Fellow and was twice President of the Collge of Physicians. He bequeathed his fortune to his twin sister Grizel, upon whose death it was to be used to 'build . . . within the city of Dublin . . . an Hospital for maintaining and curing from time to time such sick and wounded persons whose Distempers and Wounds are curable.'

Madam Steevens, as Grizel was known, determined to proceed with the building during her lifetime, retaining £100 per annum for herself. Under the terms of her brother's will she had the right to live in the

he was presumably the same Isaac Wills who designed St Ann's Church, Dawson Street, in 1720. The hospital was equipped to house forty patients and cost Madam Steevens £15,000; forty beds were purchased for a total of £50 and 40 pewter chamber pots at 8d each. By the end of the first year, 164 out of 248 admissions were 'dismissed cured'.

A portrait by Michael Mitchell of Madam Steevens shows her wearing a white veil; in her right hand she holds a drawing of the front of the hospital showing a more elaborate plan than was built; the design must have been simplified for the sake of economy. The fact that she always wore a veil gave rise to the popular myth that her nose was shaped like the snout of a pig, resulting from a curse that was hurled at her mother by a beggar. To refute this legend it is said she used to sit for hours by an open window on Steevens' Lane, her veil cast aside. She died in 1746 at the age of ninety-three and is buried in the grounds, close to the site of the old chapel.

LEFT The first public hospital in Dublin, Dr Steevens' Hospital opened in 1733, thanks to a bequest from Dr Richard Steevens and the generosity of his sister, 'Madam' Grizel Steevens. The architect was Thomas Burgh, who died three years before it opened.

RIGHT The arcaded courtyard is characteristic of the architect, who designed the cupola and tower although he did not live to see them completed. The clock is one of the oldest in Dublin.

hospital and she took an active part in the running of it. In 1717 she appointed fourteen trustees among whom were Archbishop King, who acted as treasurer, and Burgh, the architect, who waived his fee. Thomas Proby, surgeon-general of the army and a friend of Dr Steevens, not only gave expert advice but also provided the stone for building the hospital free of charge, from a quarry he owned north of the Liffey. In 1721 Dean Swift joined the board of trustees, and when his companion, Stella, died in 1728, she left £1,000, the bulk of her estate, to endow the hospital with a chaplaincy.

The trustees purchased 3½ acres situated just on the Dublin side of the Royal Hospital, Kilmainham, some distance away from the city for reasons of health. Isaac Wills worked under Burgh as master-carpenter;

The hospital, with its steeply pitched roof and dormer windows, is essentially a late seventeenth-century design and it marked the end of Burgh's long and successful career. It was built around an arcaded courtyard used for exercise by the patients, inspired by that of the neighbouring Royal Hospital. Arcades feature in most of Burgh's buildings, such as the great library in Trinity College, the old Custom House and the Royal (now Collins) Barracks. An obelisk bearing a lamp was erected at the centre of the courtyard in about 1790. A delightful clock tower with a copper weathervane, made by Hugh Wilson, carpenter, dates from 1735; the clock was bought in that year and is among the oldest in Dublin. A bell in the tower was rung with a rope from the porter's lodge when consultants entered the hospital.

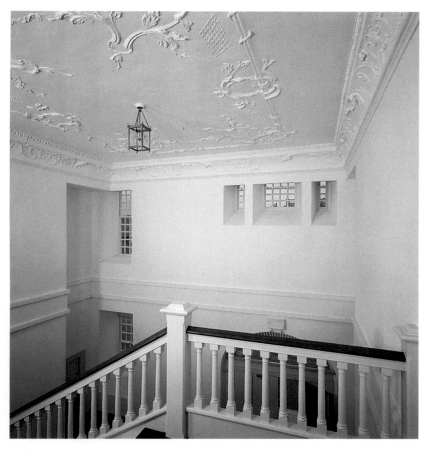

LEFT The Rococo ceiling was rescued from Johnstown Kennedy House, Co. Dublin, and installed by the Eastern Health Board, which purchased the hospital after it was closed in 1987 and has undertaken a magnificent programme of renovation.

The finest interior is the Worth Library, which has early eighteenth-century panelling and fluted Corinthian columns; the design is attributed to Pearce and was executed by Hugh Wilson. It is one of the most intact interiors of this period in Dublin, lined with bookcases and formerly hung with old portraits. The collection included a full-length portrait of Dr Edward Worth (1678–1733) by an unknown Irish artist; Worth bequeathed his important library of some 4,500 volumes to the hospital. Not all of these are, in fact, medical and many have beautiful bindings by the finest Irish and continental bookbinders of the seventeenth and eighteenth centuries. Dr Worth was the son of John Worth, Dean of St Patrick's; he studied medicine at Trinity and abroad and was a trustee and governor of the hospital but died before it opened. The books and pictures from the library have been in the care of Trinity College since the hospital was closed in 1987, and it is hoped that they will soon return.

The hospital was purchased in 1988 by the Eastern Health Board as its administrative headquarters; they commissioned a total restoration and refurbishment, which was carried out by Arthur Gibney and Partners, architects. This received a European Architectural Heritage Award from the EC Commission. The building was re-opened in 1992, but the main entrance on Steevens' Lane, with the plaque in Latin commemorating Dr Richard Steevens and his sister Grizel, could no longer be used because the lane was so narrow and full of traffic. The carved limestone pedimented doorway and steps were sensitively reproduced on the north front, providing a new main entrance identical to the original. The entrance hall created here now has a wonderful Rococo ceiling, rescued from Johnstown Kennedy House, Co. Dublin. The windows were given small panes, and the red-brick Victorian nurses' home and outpatients' department, which had hidden the northern facade, were demolished, opening up a huge forecourt with cobbles and formal tree planting. It is almost as if Dublin has suddenly been presented with an old building it never had before, giving a majestic send-off to those on the road to Galway or taking the train to the south.

RIGHT The panelled library, designed by Sir Edward Lovett Pearce in 1733, awaits the return of the important collection of books, the bequest of Dr Edward Worth, for which it was built. Portraits of Dr Worth and 'Madam' Grizel Steevens, which used to hang here, will also, it is hoped, return.

EARLY GEORGIAN
DUBLIN

Peace had come to Ireland after the bitter struggles of the seventeenth century, and with peace came one hundred years of prosperity for the Anglo-Irish Ascendancy who governed the country. The Irish Catholics had been deprived of their land by confiscation, and while they smouldered in resentment the Protestant landlords grew rich from their rents. This ruling class consisted of a wide spectrum; there were the old Irish families who had changed their religion, for example the O'Briens of Dromoland, and there were Norman families such as the Plunketts of Dunsany and the Talbots of Malahide, who were forced to abandon the old faith in order to retain their lands. These were joined by families like the Brabazons, who had governed the country for Henry VIII, and the descendants of the Great Earl of Cork, who made his fortune in the reign of Elizabeth I. The Maudes and the Cuffes were among many Cromwellian settlers who achieved prominence in the century following their arrival.

In spite of their diverse backgrounds, the great landowning families were united in one ambition: they were determined to provide themselves with a city of which they could be proud. In the words of Thomas Pakenham, 'They had a style and a sense of pride, a pride of community, colonial nationalism of a sort, bigoted and narrow as it was, that set them apart from a mere English garrison taking its orders from London.' The more enlightened among them, who felt confident of being able to govern Ireland satisfactorily with the minimum of interference from England, had a spokesman in Swift, who said:

> Were not the People of Ireland born as Free as those of England? Is not their Parliament as fair and as Representative of the People as that of England? Are they Subjects of the same King? Does not the same Sun shine on them? And have they not the same God for their Protector? Am I a Free-Man in England and do I become a Slave in six hours by crossing the Channel?

It was in this heady climate that the decision was taken to build a magnificent Parliament House, even more splendid than Westminster. There was no streak of Puritan modesty in the blood of the Anglo-Irish, but then modesty does not make for good architecture. The foundation stone of the new building was laid in 1729 and when it was completed it must have outshone its neighbours and made them seem old-fashioned. The primitive Dutch-Palladian facade of the west front of Trinity College with its curved gables and the little town houses clustered around it suddenly found a new star in their midst. From now on Dublin architecture assumed a professionalism hitherto unknown; the age of Pearce and Castle had arrived, many of whose architectural splendours have fortunately survived to the present.

The architect of Dublin's great Parliament House was Sir Edward Lovett Pearce, who died in 1733 at the early age of thirty-four. His death was a serious loss to Ireland. No comparable genius has ever, before or since, been at the official helm of Ireland's architecture, and as surveyor-general there is no knowing how his capabilities would have grown. It was indeed fortunate that such an important commission as the Parliament House should have gone to such an unknown figure at such an early age. At its ceremonial inception Henry Nelson is quoted by Maurice Craig in *Architectural Drawings at Elton Hall* as having written:

> Next let my gratitude and due respect
> Be humbly paid to the great architect
> Let every tongue in softest note rehearse,
> Time after time, the worth of Capt. Pearce;
> All hail to thee! who only is the man
> That by your art has formed this noble plan.

Richard Castle (*c.* 1690–1751) came to Ireland in 1728 and is believed to have worked for Pearce as a draftsman in his office. Pearce wrote in that year:

> I know nobody in this Town whom I could employ capable of drawing from designs of this nature but one Person, and he, indeed, has done them infinite justice, his name is Castle, he is at present employed in building a House for Sir Gustavus Hume near Enniskillen but I hope will find more and constant employment. I thought I could not do a better service than mentioning this to Gentlemen who may have occasion for such a person.

The Bank of Ireland, or Old Parliament House (centre), and Trinity College (foreground). The front block of the college encloses Parliament Square, so-called because the funds for building it were voted by the Irish parliament, then across the street. The Provost's House is on the left (foreground).

Pearce could not have known, when writing this recommendation, that he was to die so soon or that Castle, thought to have come from Germany via England, would enjoy such a successful career and remain in Ireland for the rest of his life.

Already in 1731 Castle was building two of Ireland's most important country seats, Westport House, Co. Mayo, and Powerscourt, Co. Wicklow. Just as Palladio found himself at work in the Veneto when a great spate of villa building was about to commence, Castle's arrival in Ireland in 1728 was equally propitious. Apart from his extensive country-house practice he also built canals and at least one church, at Newtownbreda near Belfast, as well as fulfilling both public and private commissions in Dublin. He wrote a treatise on the canal system in Newry which was never published, but in the landscape view on the title page he tactfully incorporates an Irish round tower. He calls himself Richard Castle both on this treatise and in his will, but he is frequently known by variants of this name. Leinster House, Tyrone House and 85 St Stephen's Green are his most important private commissions in Dublin and, happily, all three are intact – more than can be said for his work at Trinity College which was beset with problems and failure. His buildings were massive, solid and correct but by the end of the century they were considered heavy and old-fashioned. If Pearce was the one who introduced the Palladian style, it was Castle who caused it to be accepted. Of all his houses, Russborough, Co. Wicklow, is justly the most famous and the best loved. His buildings have had an enormous influence on Irish architecture.

With the attractions of the viceregal court and parliament sitting in Dublin, it became desirable for the aristocracy to have a town house. From 1730 the characteristic Dublin streetscape began to develop with wide and generous streets and squares. Larger houses were now built that could be used for entertaining on a grand scale. These formed terraces of brick with a simple granite parapet and were devoid of ornament on the facade, giving little or no idea of the splendours within. Only the entrance doorways with their handsome fittings, the distinctive fanlights and the ironwork of the railings and balconies varied in design and showed the individuality of the owner. The eighteenth-century door furniture would have been of iron, and brass fittings were introduced in the nineteenth century. Even the granite-paved footpaths are worthy of note, punctuated as they are now by remarkably decorative coal-hole covers.

The modest Dutch-gabled brick houses that were built at the beginning of the eighteenth century were now out of date. After 1730 the interior walls were plastered instead of panelled in wood, and the great school of Dublin stuccodores developed and flourished at this time. Although it is generally assumed that decorative plasterwork was the work of foreigners, in fact the only craftsmen on record who came

from overseas to work in this medium were the Swiss stuccodores, Paul (1695–1770) and Philip (1702–79) Lafranchini and Bartholomew Cramillion (*fl.* 1755–72), whose work showed a German influence. Like their Irish imitators they worked freehand, adding plaster, layer upon layer as it dried out, to build up the birds and cherubs in their design. Their influence on the native exponents of the craft was very important. The Rococo flights of fancy indulged in by the Dublin stuccodores relieve the severity of the architecture and bring the houses to life with the spirit of the eighteenth century. It is sad to consider the amount of furniture, paintings, books, glass and silver that must have once adorned these houses and has now disappeared, but at least much of the plasterwork remains.

In 1731 the Dublin Society was formed by a group of cultured and enlightened citizens to promote improvements to the quality of life and

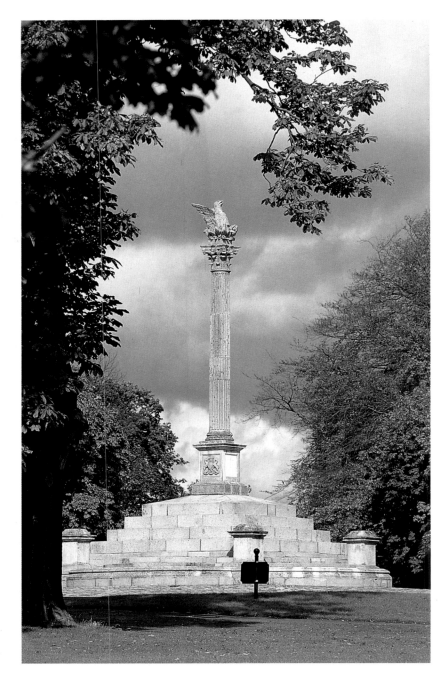

ABOVE LEFT The staircase at 6 South Leinster Street, with its spacious proportions and rich stuccowork, is one of the finest in Dublin of the mid-eighteenth century.

ABOVE St Stephen's Green (centre) with Iveagh Gardens in the foreground. Building lots surrounding the Green were laid out by Dublin Corporation in 1664. The Green was given its present aspect in 1877 by Sir Arthur Guinness, first and last Lord Ardilaun, who bought out the key-holders, landscaped the grounds and opened them to the general public. His statue by Thomas Farrell faces the College of Surgeons.

ABOVE Phoenix Column, Phoenix Park, was erected by the Viceroy, the Earl of Chesterfield, in 1745 and stands outside the main entrance to Áras An Uachtaráin, formerly the Viceregal Lodge.

LEFT The Dublin Writer's Museum, 18 Parnell Square, devoted to the great writers of Ireland, is accommodated in a grand old house on the square, once the property of the Jameson family. The drawing room has delicate Adamesque platerwork and a deep Edwardian lincrusta frieze.

RIGHT St Catherine's Church, Thomas Street, has the most distinguished facade of any eighteenth-century church in Dublin. The architect was always thought to have been John Smyth but recent evidence has connected the name of Joseph Jarratt with its design.

FAR RIGHT Dating from 1769, St Catherine's Church was de-consecrated in 1966 and restored by the Bell Tower Trust, a voluntary organization. It was given to a local group but vandals have done their worst and St Catherine's is again in need of rescue and repair.

culture in Ireland. Its interests were wide, encompassing science, agriculture and literature as well as the fine and decorative arts. For the latter, the principal centre of training was the excellent school of figure drawing, painting and sculpture set up from 1746 by Robert West (died 1770) and James Mannin (died 1779). In *c.* 1760 the Irish architect, Thomas Ivory (*c.* 1732–86), himself a superb draftsman, established a School of Architectural Drawing, which instructed the pupils in plans, elevations, sections and perspective views, and in the vocabulary of the classical orders: Tuscan, Doric, Ionic, Corinthian and Composite. To learn the practicalities of building, the students were apprenticed to an architect. This arrangement whereby first-class tuition was available free of charge, in conjunction with the apprenticeship system, brought Dublin in line with the major capitals of Europe.

In 1749 to celebrate the peace of Aix-La-Chapelle, an elaborate fireworks display was held in St Stephen's Green master-minded by the Surveyor-General, Arthur Jones Neville. In the centre was a twelve-sided temple of peace 64 feet high and 32 feet wide, illuminated from within, the sides adorned with statues. Over the temple, in which 1,100 yards of Persian silk were used, was a gilt dome with a statue of peace. St Stephen's Green was almost built up by 1750, but there was no uniformity as the plots were of different sizes, a deliberate arrangement designed to appeal to different pockets. Although the perimeter was a fashionable place to promenade, the ground in the middle of the square was still swampy and in 1752 the lord mayor directed that no-one should break through the hedges to shoot snipe or else they would be punished. With the development of the Green and the building of Leinster House, Grafton Street became a fashionable residential area. It was named after Charles Fitzroy, the second Duke of Grafton, who was the illegitimate son of Charles II and the Duchess of Cleveland. Molesworth Street and Dawson Street, where the Mansion House was in use by the lord mayor from 1715, were soon developed.

An Act that had far reaching consequences for Dublin was passed in

1757, 'for making a wide and convenient Way, Street, or Passage, from Essex-bridge to the Castle of Dublin'. The Wide Streets Commissioners were appointed, who, except for the lord mayor, were all members of parliament. They stayed together as a highly influential body to carry out further improvements in the planning of Dublin over the next fifty years. As Dr McParland has said, 'Modern Dublin between the canals is largely as planned by them.' They were men of political power, taste and vision and were prepared to look beyond London to the continent for their inspiration. As patrons and builders in their own right the commissioners were only too ready to discuss the problems of the city with the eminent architects they employed.

During the first half of the eighteenth century the rivalry between the Gardiners with their development schemes on the north side of the city and the Fitzwilliams on the south began in earnest and lasted for a hundred years. Luke Gardiner purchased land which had belonged to St Mary's Abbey on the north side of the city and laid out Henrietta Street, which, although for many years sadly neglected, remains the grandest street in Dublin. He also laid out Sackville (later O'Connell)

Street, named after the Viceroy, Lionel Cranfield Sackville, Duke of Dorset. The land in this development included Drogheda Street and extended from Great Britain Street (now Parnell Street) to Abbey Street. Gardiner demolished the buildings on the west side and created a fine street 150 feet wide with brick houses and a mall in the centre enclosed by low ornamental stone walls; the houses on the eastern side were larger and intended for professional people and parliamentarians. The finest house on Sackville Street was built by Alderman Richard Dawson, a wealthy banker, on a lease from Luke Gardiner dated 30 May 1751. It was then purchased by Charles, sixth Earl of Drogheda, for £5,000 and became known as Drogheda House. The mall soon became a fashionable promenade. Parnell Square (formerly Rutland Square) is one of Gardiner's most distinguished and successful compositions, and if only the centre of the green had been left unencumbered by later buildings, it would still be one of the great sights of Dublin. On the south side of the river Lord Fitzwilliam began

to develop the huge expanse of Merrion Square in the 1760s. He must have benefited considerably from the proximity of Kildare (later Leinster) House, by far the most important private mansion in Dublin.

The intense building activity that took place in Dublin from 1730 brought about a rapid increase in the population. A veritable army of doctors, lawyers, agents, civil servants and clerks was essential to make life run smoothly. People came up from the country to work as labourers, artisans, tradespeople and domestic servants in the new houses. Access to the guilds of master craftsmen was, however, difficult, as there were strict rules governing admission and apprenticeship in order to protect the membership. In the seventeenth century Catholics were not admitted to the guilds; later they tended to engage in the food, drink and leather-based trades. The guilds of craft workers had control of industries such as weaving, printing, felt making, silverwork and joinery (furniture making) from medieval times. In the Weavers' Guild, one of the most important, were to be found Quakers, Presbyterians and Huguenots, all making cloth in the Liberties.

The city seethed with life, despite the squalor and poverty in some parts, and there was pride in the splendour of the new buildings that were going up, particularly when they compared favourably with those in London of the same date.

THE BANK OF IRELAND/OLD PARLIAMENT HOUSE
College Green

The first great Palladian building in Dublin is still unrivalled in terms of nobility and splendour, and forms a distinguished partner for the majestic west front of Trinity College opposite. The monumental facade of the Old Parliament House, with its giant colonnaded forecourt, faces south across College Green in the heart of the city. It stands on the site of a building erected by the Lord Deputy, Sir George Carew, at the end of the sixteenth century as a hospital for 'poor, sick and maimed soldiers', a purpose it apparently never served. The Law Courts sat here for a few terms before the palatial house passed into the ownership of the Lord Deputy, Sir Arthur Chichester, and came to be known as Chichester House. It had ten or twelve windows on the facade and there were two storeys with an attic. After the Restoration in 1660 it served as the Parliament House with the Commons on the ground floor and the Lords above. But as Dr C.P. Curran has observed, the members of parliament 'allowed the fabric of their building to fall about their ears while busy with writing the blackest pages of the Statute Book'.

A committee was appointed in 1727 to consider the building of a new Parliament House; on that committee sat Colonel Thomas Burgh, MP for Naas and Surveyor-General, who was asked to prepare plans. It is not thought, however, that he had any hand in the design of the new building because he was passed over and the commission was given to his successor, Captain Edward Lovett Pearce. Although it is not known exactly why Pearce came to take the place of Burgh, it was fortuitous for Dublin, which gained a masterpiece far beyond the capability of the older man.

The foundation stone was laid on 3 February 1729 with Speaker Conolly of Castletown in attendance. Pearce, by now the Member of Parliament for Ratoath, was of course present at this ceremony but

ABOVE The top-lit corridor by Pearce, which extended around three sides of the Commons chamber, has survived subsequent alterations.

RIGHT The former House of Lords has a tapestry of Dublin manufacture, depicting William of Orange at the Battle of the Boyne. The chandelier was made for the room.

LEFT The Bank of Ireland, College Green, formerly the Parliament House, was designed by Sir Edward Lovett Pearce in 1729 to house the Irish parliament.

Burgh did not attend. At the time Pearce, Ireland's architectural genius, was not yet thirty years of age, but unfortunately he was destined only to live for four more years. He was born in about 1699, the son of General Edward Pearce. The general was first cousin to Sir John Vanbrugh, the great English architect, among whose masterpieces is Blenheim Palace, designed for the Duke of Marlborough. Pearce may have been apprenticed to his cousin Vanbrugh. He travelled in France and Italy in 1723–4 and his profusely annotated copy of Palladio's *I Quattro Libri* (1570) is in the library of the Royal Institute of British Architects. He designed Bellamont Forest, Co. Cavan, for his cousin Charles Coote and the Cashel Palace, Co. Tipperary, for Archbishop Bolton. The front hall of Castletown,

Co. Kildare, Speaker Conolly's great country seat, and 9 and 10 Henrietta Street are also his creations.

The main front of the Parliament House consists of an open portico of giant Ionic columns raised on a continuous flight of steps and forming three sides of a square. All the emphasis of the building was concentrated on the entrance axis which led straight through the Court of Requests and Lobby into the House of Commons, whereas the House of Lords was in a subordinate position to one side. It has been suggested that this arrangement was at the behest of that great commoner, Speaker Conolly, who could never be tempted to desert the Commons for the Lords.

The octagonal Commons chamber was surrounded on three sides by

LEFT Detail of the plasterwork in the former House of Lords, which can be visited during banking hours by courtesy of the bank.

RIGHT The Corinthian portico on Westmoreland Street, designed by James Gandon, was added in 1785 to provide the House of Lords with an entrance of its own.

a remarkable corridor, which has survived subsequent alterations; it consists of a sequence of arches and domes lit by shafts of light from above that play on the bold architectural features. The chamber itself was surmounted by an octagonal coffered dome, supported on tall Ionic columns which rested in turn on arcades at floor level. John Wesley described the wainscotting as being of Irish oak that 'shamed all mahogany'. According to Sir Jonah Barrington MP, lawyer, writer and wit:

> A gallery behind the colonnade accommodated seven hundred spectators and commanded an ininterrupted view of the Chamber. Orators addressed the gallery which unlike Westminster was never cleared on a division. In every important debate it was filled, not by reporters, but by the superior orders of society, the first rows being generally occupied by ladies of fashion and rank who diffused a brilliance over and exerted a gallant decorum in that assembly which the British House certainly does not appear very sedulously to imitate.

The canopied Speaker's chair, bearing the royal arms, was placed beneath a tall Venetian window and there were *œil-de-bœuf* windows in the dome. The 300 members of the Commons were ranged on four tiers of mahogany benches upholstered in green; some of these have

survived and can be seen at St Patrick's Hospital as well as at the Royal Irish Academy.

The House of Lords was designed to accommodate 120 peers and is one of the most remarkable interiors in Dublin. It has a coffered, barrel-vaulted ceiling and is lit by two Diocletian windows; there is a curved apse at one end and a vaulted space at the other. Dr McParland has noted the similarity between the section of this room and that of the Temple of Venus in Rome as published by Palladio. Two immense tapestries, framed by giant Corinthian pilasters, were commissioned in 1728 from Robert Baillie of Dublin and woven by 'Jan van Beaver ye famous tapestry weaver'. One of them represents the Battle of the Boyne and the other the Siege of Derry; they were designed by a Dutchman named Johann van der Hagen, an itinerant topographical artist. The original wooden mantel, which is still *in situ*, was carved in 1748 or 1749 probably by John Houghton and 'to the designs of Inigo Jones', according to the Commons Journal. The upholstery in the House of Lords was red, as Dr Curran describes in his masterly history of the building, 'An upholder's estimate of 1749 details expenditure on red cloth for cushions, wool packs, stools, chair and table-carpet with red silk lace and red cloth for five forms and the table and a large Turkey carpet to fit under the throne.' The mace from the Irish House

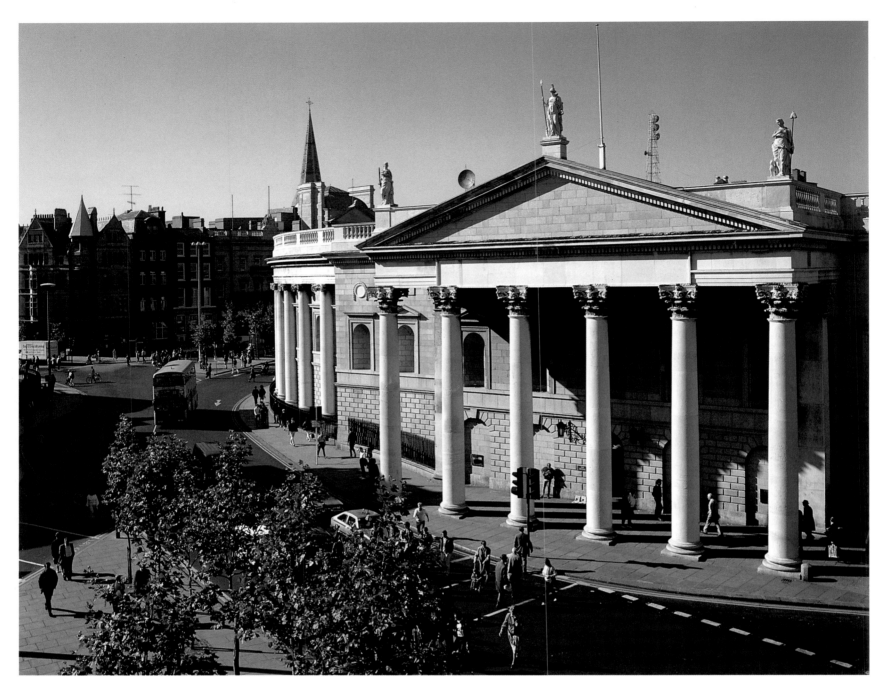

of Commons, made by John Swift of London in 1765, is on display here; the House of Lords mace forms part of the silver collection at the National Museum. The glass chandelier, probably made in Dublin rather than Waterford, was installed in 1788 but sold when gas lighting was introduced in the 1840s. It was later repurchased by the Bank of Ireland.

Pearce was knighted by the viceroy in 1732 in the partly finished Parliament House and made a Freeman of the City of Dublin as a reward for creating its most noble adornment. His early death in 1733 robbed him of the pleasure of seeing his masterpiece completed. This task fell to Arthur Dobbs, MP, who, although a political economist rather than an architect, succeeded Pearce as surveyor-general. The cost of the building up to Pearce's death was £35,000, and when completed the final amount was £95,000. Pearce himself charged nothing for 'his own great expenses, skill and pains' but the Commons twice voted him £1,000.

In 1785 James Gandon designed a great portico to provide the House of Lords with its own entrance; this was added to the east of the building, facing Westmoreland Street, and was adorned with statues of Wisdom, Justice and Liberty by Edward Smyth. The new portico was built in the Corinthian style in deference to the great Ionic south front.

When asked why he was introducing a different style, the architect replied that he was 'working to the Order of the House of Lords' – in fact the Corinthian columns with their taller proportions took up the fall in levels. Gandon linked his new portico to the south front by a curved screen wall pierced with niches.

In 1787 the Commons, needing more space, expanded to the west, and Robert Parke was commissioned to design an Ionic portico on Foster Place. He joined this by means of an open curved colonnade to the main south front. The building thus became lop-sided and the design was much criticized. In 1792 the House of Commons was destroyed by fire and rebuilt, 'meanly' according to Craig, by Vincent Waldré, architect to the Board of Works. He gave it a round dome of brick even lower than the original, which had itself been too low to be appreciated from College Green – the only criticism ever levelled at Pearce's building. Waldré, also an artist, painted the ceiling in St Patrick's Hall, Dublin Castle.

Parliament sat here for the last time on 2 August 1800, and the Act of Union, whereby Ireland was to be ruled from Westminster, became law on 1 January 1801. The Parliament House was then used for art exhibitions and became a military barracks during the rebellion of Robert Emmet in 1803. In that year it was purchased by the Bank of

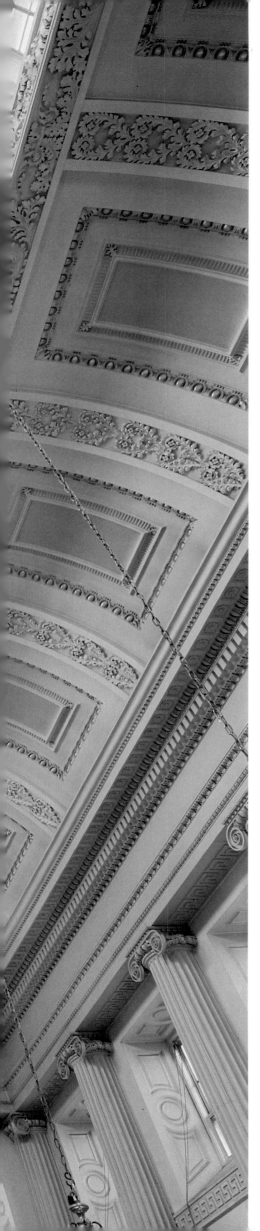

LEFT Ceiling of the cash office, which was designed by Francis Johnston in 1804. After the Act of Union in 1801 the Irish parliament was disbanded and in 1803 the great Parliament House was purchased by the Bank of Ireland, who remodelled the interior.

RIGHT AND BELOW Until recently the directors lunched beneath a Rococo ceiling which was rescued from the La Touche Bank in Castle Street in 1945 through the good offices of Dr C.P.Curran. In the centre Venus and Cupid rest on a cloud (right) and there are swans in the four corners (below).

Ireland for £40,000; fortunately the architect chosen for the consequent alterations was Francis Johnston. The foundation stone for the new works was laid by the Viceroy, the Earl of Hardwicke, in 1804. A magnificent cash office took the place of the Court of Requests and the Commons Lobby, and Johnston blocked up the windows overlooking College Green, as it was felt the bank was safer without them. The interior walls of the cash office are of Bath stone with fluted, Ionic, engaged columns of Portland stone. It has for long been said that a covenant required the bank to alter the chambers to prevent their ever being used for public debates, but the story is without foundation. In any case, Johnston made no alterations to the House of Lords. It was he, in his capacity as architect to the Board of Works, who stumbled on the tapestries in 'the depository of decayed furniture in the Castle' and put them back where they belonged. He improved the exterior by making the curved screen walls match: he filled up Parke's open colonnade, engaging the columns, and repeated this treatment on Gandon's plain curtain wall – an admirable solution. In 1811 Johnston closed off the end of Foster Place with a monumental guard room, which was entered by a triumphal arch and surmounted by military trophies carved in Portland stone by Thomas Kirk.

In 1945 a delicate Rococo ceiling, which had been rescued from the La Touche Bank in Castle Street, was installed in the directors' dining room. This dates from the late 1750s and Joseph McDonnell has attributed it to Bartholomew Cramillion. It represents Venus and Cupid resting on a cloud with four swans in the corners, the design taken from an engraving by Hendrik Goltzius (1596).

The Bank of Ireland has recently undertaken a major programme of restoration work here, replacing the perished stonework and cleaning the exterior which is now a warm golden colour. The facade has been ingeniously lit from behind the columns and the bank looks particularly splendid at night when the flood-lighting gives the building an ethereal quality.

HENRIETTA STREET

Henrietta Street, which took its name from Henrietta, Duchess of Grafton, wife of the viceroy, was the most fashionable enclave in Dublin in the early eighteenth century. It was a street of noble houses on the north side of the city, laid out in about 1721 by Luke Gardiner who purchased land in this area. This had been part of the estates of St Mary's Abbey since time immemorial and was surrendered to Henry VIII in 1539 on the Dissolution of the Monasteries. Gardiner was to become the great developer in the north of the city in rivalry to Lord Fitzwilliam on the south side.

Henrietta Street can be seen in Rocque's map of Dublin, 1756, and comparison with the plots in the neighbouring streets shows that those in Henrietta Street were more than twice as large. On his large-scale map Rocque also shows the layout of the formal French or Dutch gardens that separated the stables from the houses. This street marked the beginning of a new era of domestic opulence in the city; it set a fresh example and exacting standards by virtue of the superb proportions of the rooms, the grandeur of the staircases and the quality of the carving in marble and wood. It attracted a distinguished group of aristocratic families and was given the name 'Primate's Hill' because successive powerful and influential Archbishops of Armagh resided here.

Gardiner built No. 10 for himself in about 1731; it was later called Mountjoy House and subsequently Blessington House, as his family assumed these titles. Together with No. 9 next door, it was designed by Sir Edward Lovett Pearce, architect of the Parliament House. No. 10, which adjoins the archway at the top of the street, has a seven-bay facade and some of the original interior is still intact; the upstairs drawing room now serves as a chapel for the Daughters of Charity. The

famous writer, Lady Blessington, who was born Marguerite Power in Fethard, Co. Tipperary, was introduced to her husband's Irish friends in this house. Unfortunately for Dublin, it was not here but in London that she established her remarkable literary salon.

Pearce built No. 9 for his cousin, Thomas Carter MP, Master of the Rolls. The front door surround with its unusual blocking is nearly identical to that designed by Pearce for the Cashel Palace, Co. Tipperary. The front is rusticated up to the first floor with brick above. The interior is the finest to survive on the street and is Pearce's masterpiece in its genre. Both elevation and plan were inspired by a house designed in 1721 by the 'Architect' Earl of Burlington for the Earl of Mountrath at 30 Old Burlington Street, London. Although lacking in the flights of stucco fancy that adorn the Dublin houses of twenty years later, the ceilings at Nos. 9 and 10 are coved, coffered and compartmented, the strength of the plasterwork decoration providing the perfect foil to the bold and simple lines of the Palladian architecture. These houses belong to the Daughters of Charity and are used as workshops by St Vincent's Trust. Pearce also designed Nos. 11 and 12 opposite.

The King's Inns Library, designed by Frederick Darley in 1826, stands at the top of Henrietta Street on the site of the palatial residence of Primate Stone, Archbishop of Armagh. Richard Cumberland described the street in his *Memoirs*: 'Nothing I have seen in England could rival the Polish magnificence of Primate Stone, or the Parisian luxury of Mr Clements.' Nathaniel Clements, architect, contractor, builder and developer, built Nos. 3 to 7 and lived in No. 7 from 1733 until his death in 1777. He is best known for building Phoenix Lodge, later to become the Viceregal Lodge in the Phoenix Park and now the residence of the President of Ireland.

A street directory of 1792 lists one archbishop, two bishops, four peers, and four MPs among the inhabitants of Henrietta Street. The Union of 1801 had an even more deleterious effect on the north side of Dublin than on the south and much of the northern side degenerated into tenements. That Henrietta Street has survived is indeed fortunate and its survival is a testimony to the competence of the original builders and the strength of the proportions then in fashion, rather than the quality of the maintenance over the years. The slum landlords were in the habit of removing the grand staircases, thereby being able to cram two more poor families into the generous space they occupied, leaving only the narrow service stairs which ran from basement to attic.

Michael Casey purchased No. 13 in 1975, with the help of an interest-free loan of £13,000 from the Irish Georgian Society. At the time there were thirty-six unfortunate souls living in this one house, in wretched conditions; the occupants were rehoused by Dublin Corporation and

LEFT No.9 Henrietta Street was designed by Sir Edward Lovett Pearce in 1731 for his cousin, Thomas Carter MP, Master of the Rolls.

RIGHT The entrance hall and staircase of 9 Henrietta Street are the best of their date in Dublin and are united to form one space.

ABOVE Compartmented ceiling over the staircase of 9 Henrietta Street, in the bold and elegant proportions that preceded the Rococo style.

RIGHT No.13 Henrietta Street was purchased by Michael Casey in 1975 and at the time it was inhabited by thirty-six people (since rehoused) living cheek by jowl in dreadful conditions. He has been restoring it gradually ever since.

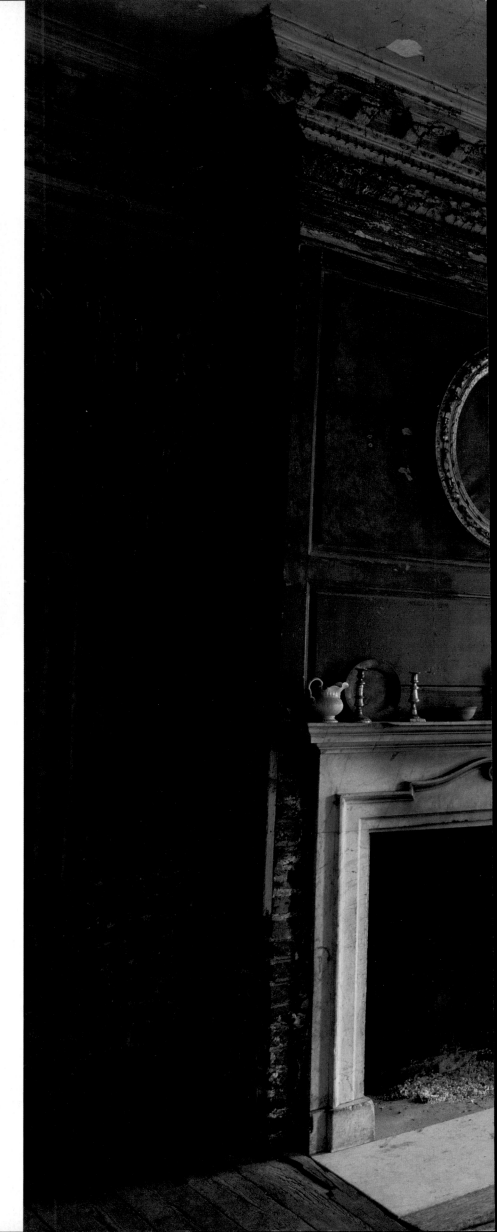

the Caseys set about restoring the house to its former glory. An early eighteenth-century staircase has been given by the Irish Georgian Society, as the original one had been removed. Restoration work proceeds as funds allow, and the Caseys regard it as a lifetime vocation.

The upper end of the street was closed off by James Gandon's King's Inns, much to the displeasure of most of the residents, who lost their view of the open fields beyond. The King's Inns is placed at an angle across the top of the street to accommodate the right of way which existed before it was built. The archway, not envisioned by Gandon, was designed by Francis Johnston and erected in 1820; the royal arms were carved by John Smyth.

Henrietta Street is a prince among streets, and its fortunes, which were for many years on the decline, look brighter now. Dublin Corporation is aware of its importance and is laying cobbled setts, which will greatly enhance its appearance as well as providing an added incentive for film makers in search of a period street location.

IVEAGH HOUSE
80 St Stephen's Green

The great Portland stone facade of Iveagh House dominates the south side of St Stephen's Green. Now the Department of Foreign Affairs, it was the most opulent private Dublin town house of its time and is still used for elegant entertaining today. Two houses, Nos. 80 and 81, were united in 1862 by Sir Benjamin Lee Guinness MP (1798–1868), sometime Lord Mayor of Dublin and sole owner of the Dublin brewery that bears his name. His son Edward became the first Earl of Iveagh, and his grandson Rupert, the second earl, gave the house to the Irish government on the eve of the Second World War, thereby avoiding, as his wife used modestly to say, the immediate problem of procuring nine housemaids.

Robert Clayton, Bishop of Killala, was the original builder of No. 80 and a man of cultivation and taste. He was appointed Bishop of Cork and Ross in 1735, in which year Lord Orrery wrote

> We are not entirely void of Elegance at Corke. We have a bishop, who, as He has travel'd beyond the Alps, has brought home with him . . . the Arts and Sciences that are the ornament of Italy and the Admiration of the European world. He eats drinks, and sleeps in taste. He has pictures by Carlo Morat, Music by Corelli, Castles in the Air by Vitruvius, and on High-Days and Holidays We have the honour of catching Cold at a Venetian door

It is hardly surprising that in 1736 the bishop employed Richard Castle, the most distinguished Irish Palladian architect of the day, to design his new town house. Castle had established his reputation already in the building of Powerscourt, Co. Wicklow, and Westport House, Co. Mayo, and No. 80 was to be the first of several magnificent Dublin town houses designed by him.

The original house, No. 80, was free standing, three bays wide, and

RIGHT The wooden mantel in the front hall of Iveagh House is Victorian and was probably designed by J.F. Fuller, the architect, to support the magnificent mid-eighteenth-century carved overmantel, depicting a scene of sacrifice. In the left-hand niche there is a statue of *Mercury* by Thorwaldson and in the right *Modesty* by Corbellini; both statues were purchased at the 1865 Dublin Exhibition.

BELOW Dating from the 1860s, when 80 and 81 St Stephen's Green were joined together, the facade of Iveagh House was modelled on Aldborough House in Dublin. It now houses the Department of Foreign Affairs.

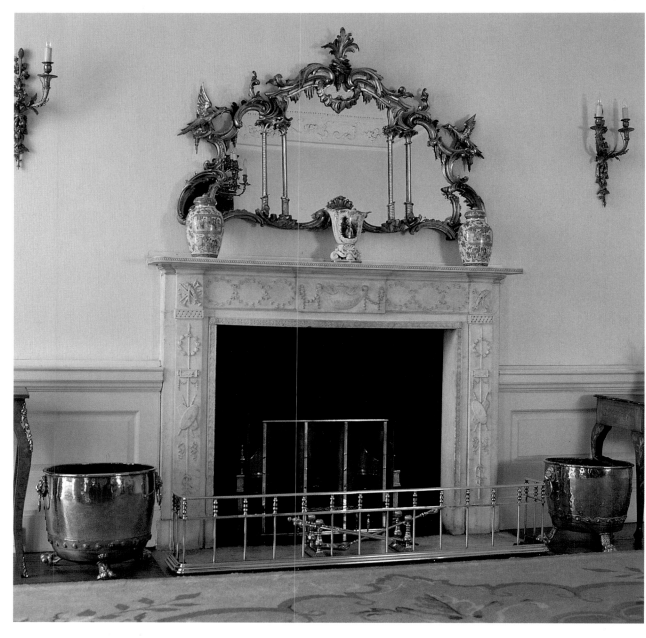

ABOVE White marble mantel in the music room which faces the garden. A pretty Rococo ceiling here, with musical instruments in the plasterwork, is part of the eighteenth-century interior of No. 80 that has survived.

LEFT The office of the Minister of Foreign Affairs, with the flags of Ireland and the European Community. The ceiling is a convincing Victorian copy of the dining-room ceiling of the Provost's House, Trinity College.

built of red brick with the basement and ground floor of cut stone. A four-columned entrance portico spread across the full width of the facade, an unusual feature which did not prove a success as the lead covering on its flat roof was a temptation for thieves. On the *piano nobile* the saloon with its coved and compartmented ceiling took up the entire width of the house. This has survived subsequent alterations and is still in use as the dining room. It opens into the music room facing the garden with its delicate Rococo ceiling incorporating musical instruments and scores. In 1766 No. 80 was purchased by the Earl of Mountcashell and became known as Mountcashell House. His son sold the house in 1809 to the famous barrister John Philpot Curran MP, wit and patriot, whose daughter Sarah had been engaged to the ill-fated Robert Emmet.

In 1856 Sir Benjamin Lee Guinness purchased No. 80 and six years later he also acquired No. 81. Acting as his own architect, he created a new Portland stone facade in the Georgian style based on Aldborough

LEFT The ballroom was added in 1896 by the first Earl of Iveagh and designed by William Young of Glasgow. The walls are lined in alabaster with marble and onyx.

RIGHT An opulent double staircase was designed by James F. Fuller in c.1880, incorporating eighteenth-century wrought-ironwork. The walls were later lined in alabaster to match the ballroom by Young.

House in Dublin, with his family arms and the motto *Spes Mea in Deo* in the pediment. The two houses were united, but the eighteenth-century interior of No. 81 seems to have been lost in the remodelling of the house. The drawing room of No. 81 is now the Office of the Minister of Foreign Affairs. It was given a compartmented ceiling, which was modelled on the dining room in the Provost's House and looked so deceptively like an eighteenth-century ceiling that it was photographed in 1909 for *The Georgian Society Records*. The richly worked cast-iron railing at pavement level in the form of a foliage scroll must have been made by the firm that produced the similar railing of the Shelbourne Hotel across the Green.

Sir Benjamin died in 1868 and left the house to the youngest of his three sons, Edward Guinness, later first Earl of Iveagh, who renamed it Iveagh House. He employed the architect James F. Fuller (1835–1924), who from 1880 to 1884 linked Nos. 78 and 79 to Iveagh House. No. 79 was rebuilt with a link-building and a first floor corridor to No. 80. It is thought that Richard Castle's staircase was removed at this time and the present grand double staircase installed, incorporating the wrought-iron balustrade of Castle's house and leading to the main reception rooms. The walls were later lined in alabaster to match those of the ballroom. Edward Guinness's third son, Walter, later first Lord Moyne, was born here in 1880. In 1896 Lord Iveagh commissioned William Young (1843–1900) from Glasgow to add a large ballroom at the back of the house, much used today for official banquets. The walls are lined in alabaster inlaid with marble and onyx, and the domed ceiling has lincrusta ornamentation; there is a minstrels' gallery at each end. The set of three Donegal carpets was designed by Raymond McGrath, chief architect to the Office of Public Works, in 1952. The second Earl of Iveagh's gift of the house to the nation was formally accepted by the Taoiseach, Eamon de Valera, in 1939.

ABOVE Detail of the decoration on the ballroom ceiling dome.

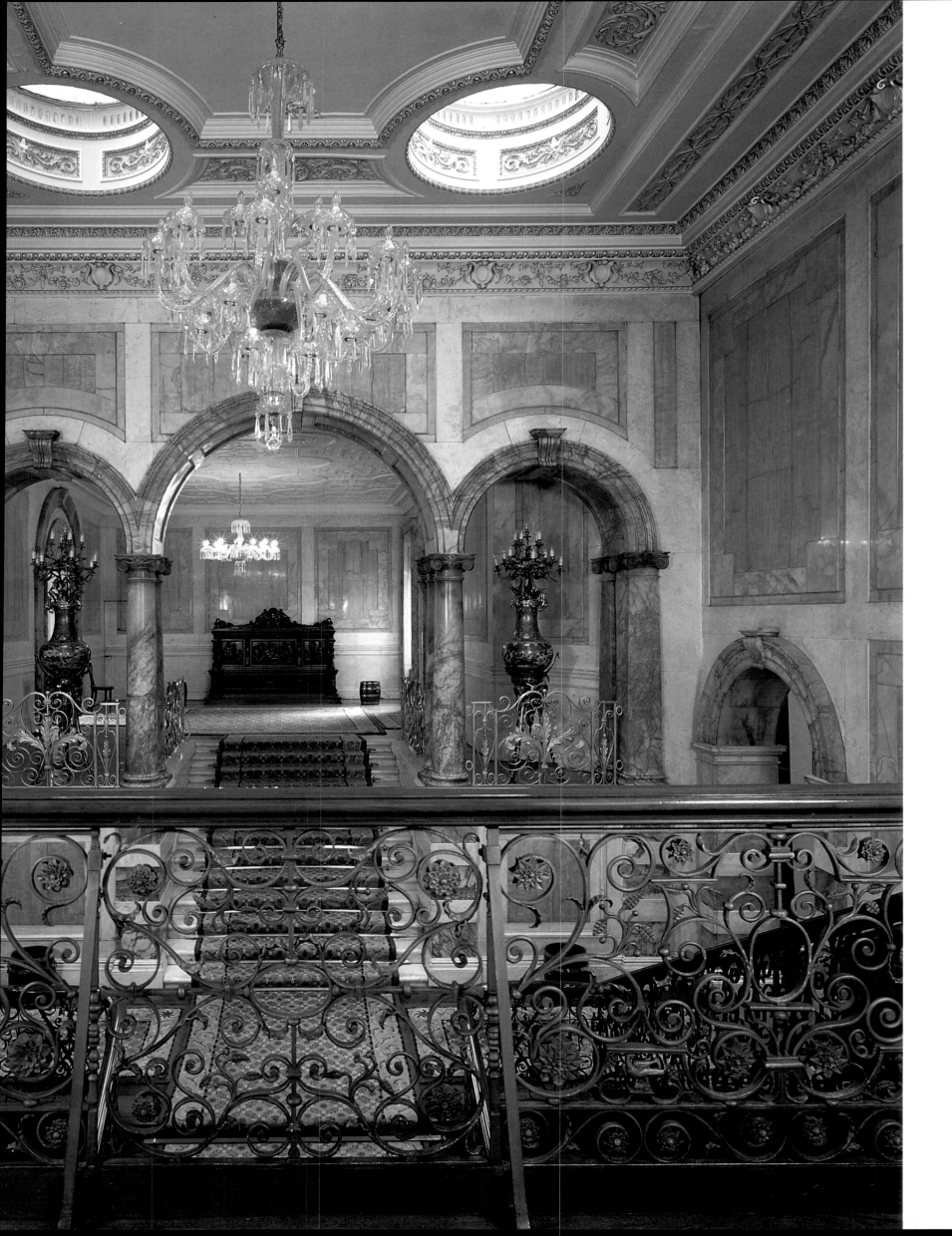

NEWMAN HOUSE
85/86 St Stephen's Green

The two great stone town houses that now constitute Newman House were joined together in the mid-nineteenth century by the newly created Catholic University of Ireland and are named after the university's first rector, John Henry Newman (1801–90), who was later made a cardinal. Although nearly thirty years apart in date and therefore as different in style as they are in scale, these houses both have superb interiors with some of the finest plasterwork in the city. They have recently been opened to the public on a regular basis. Happily they are also still used on occasion for entertaining, the purpose for which they were built and the reason the interiors were so elaborately adorned in the eighteenth century.

No. 85 dates from 1738 and its design is attributed to Richard Castle. It was built for Captain Hugh Montgomery of Colonel Hayes' Regiment of Foot. Montgomery possessed extensive lands in the vicinity of Drogheda and leased the site on the Green from Abel Ram. Montgomery died three years after the house was begun. It became known as Clanwilliam House after the Earl and Countess of Clanwilliam, who were given it by the countess's mother in 1785. Although dwarfed now by its taller neighbours, when built it was free-standing; it was one of the first houses on the Green to be faced in stone.

The front hall, with its black-and-white floor and black Kilkenny marble mantelpiece, leads to the Apollo Room, which is decorated with the sun god and his muses, the daughters of Zeus and Mnemosyne, superbly executed in stucco by the Lafranchini brothers. Joseph McDonnell has discovered the source for the Apollo plaque to be the de Rossi engraving of the Apollo Belvedere from P.A. Maffei, *Raccolta di Statue Antiche e Moderna*, published in Rome in 1704. The nine muses are modelled on engravings, in the same publication, of

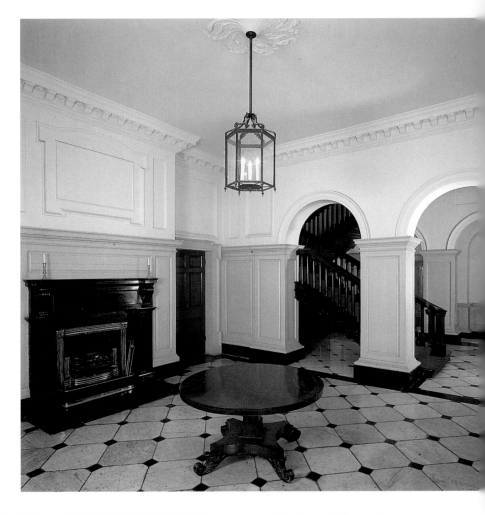

ABOVE The front hall at 85 St Stephen's Green has a black Kilkenny marble mantel and an arcaded back wall to admit light to the magnificent carved mahogany staircase.

LEFT Nos 85 and 86 St Stephen's Green, with the entrance to University Church on the right. The two houses were joined together in 1865 by the Catholic University of Ireland.

RIGHT The Apollo Room at 85 St Stephen's Green, which was built in 1738 by the German-born architect Richard Castle. The god stands above the mantelpiece surrounded by the nine muses; the plasterwork is by Paul and Philip Lafranchini.

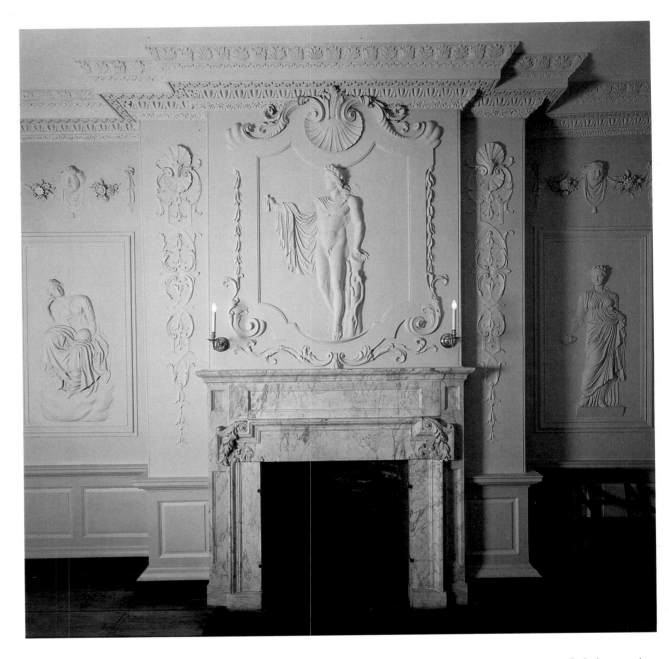

statues which were formerly the property of Queen Christina of Sweden. They represent Thalia, muse of comedy; Melpomene, muse of tragedy; Terpsichore, muse of dancing; Erato, muse of lyric poetry; Clio, muse of history; Euterpe, muse of music; Polyhymnia, muse of sacred song; Calliope, muse of epic poetry; and Urania, muse of astronomy. The two overdoor panels of putti at play with hares come from an engraving of a ceiling fresco by Pietro da Cortona. When No. 85 was joined to No. 86 in 1865 a passage was pushed through this wonderful room and the back wall was removed. Fortunately the plaster deities were re-erected nearby so that it has been possible to restore the room to its former glory.

The mahogany staircase is beautifully carved and can be compared to those at Tyrone House and Russborough; both houses were also designed by Richard Castle at about the same time and presumably the same craftsmen were at work. The wrought-ironwork here is of the highest quality and incorporates the star-shaped La Touche crest;

George La Touche lived at No. 85 from 1818 to 1823. It is interesting to contrast the Grecian waves which follow the line of the landing here, almost modern in their simplicity, with their flowing Rococo counterpart in the neighbouring house. The Venetian window, which lit the stairs, was given mirror glass in 1876 when the university built the red-brick Aula Maxima next door; it has recently been re-glazed and the sashes restored to the correct early Georgian dimensions.

The great glory of No. 85 is the saloon which takes up the entire width of the house facing over the Green. The year after they worked here the Lafranchini executed a larger version of the ceiling at Carton, Co. Kildare, representing 'The Courtship of the Gods'. The ceiling at No. 85 is described by Dr C.P. Curran: 'Its scheme is allegorical – an allegory shall we say of good government and prudent economy exercised over earth, air, and water – and it is conducted through pairs of figures [framed] in a series of six ovals broken into quatrefoils.' In between the ovals twelve playful putti in various attitudes cling to garlands. This room was used as a chapel from 1865, so it was decided to clothe the naked figure of Juno or Air with a bodice of rough plaster. This bodice is still in place, although two of her female companions have been deprived of theirs. The plaster frieze below the cornice was missing and may never have been executed although the base for it has always been there. A copy of the frieze in the saloon of Tyrone House was installed here as part of the recent restoration. On the short walls are representations of Justice and Prudence, keeping a close watch on the four elements. The composition is grand and full of movement; the saloon of Clanwilliam House is the supreme example of Dublin Baroque. It has recently been painted beige to copy the original stone colour. Castle's original chimneypiece, long removed, has been copied from the drawing in *The Georgian Society Records* (vol. 1), and the replica has been recently installed. A tall plain room opposite, with three elongated Gothic windows which look out over the garden, was extended to its present dimensions, probably during the ownership of the Clanwilliams.

ABOVE Three of the muses in the Apollo Room: Erato (left), the muse of lyric poetry; Clio (centre), the muse of history; and Euterpe (right), the muse of music.

RIGHT The saloon at No.85, with allegorical figures in the plaster ceiling executed by Paul and Philip Lafranchini. They made a larger variant of this ceiling at Carton, Co. Kildare, in 1739.

Richard Chapell Whaley, MP for Co. Wicklow, purchased No. 85 in 1755. While living here he began to build a much larger house next door but never moved in to it as he died before it was completed. James Malton in his *Views of Dublin*, 1799, describes No. 86 among the edifices of St Stephen's Green: 'The structure which claims principal attention, is the Mansion of JOHN WHALEY Esq; . . . it is of stone, with dressings about the windows; over a handsome Doric door is an excellent figure of a couchant Lion, cast by the celebrated VAN NOST.'

An inscription on the stone kitchen fireplace at No. 86 reads '16 April 1765 R.C.W', recording the date that building commenced. The architect was probably Robert West who was also responsible for the plasterwork, particularly splendid on the staircase. Although not as dramatic at West's famous staircase at his own house, 20 Lower Dominick Street, the staircase decoration at No. 86 comes a close second. The coving contains evil-looking birds, some in full flight, some feeding their young or perched on stucco branches, all very much alive with their angry beaks and twisted necks. The staircase walls are decorated in panels, with musical instruments hanging from rings or suspended from the beards of grotesque masks.

The mahogany doors with their pedimented timber surrounds have carving of superb quality, so fine indeed are they that one of them has found its way to the National Museum. In the absence of the original contents copies have been made of furniture of the right date and the appropriate scale. The Victorian character of the Bishops' Room has been preserved in fond memory of the long tenure of Cardinal Newman and his successors.

Richard Whaley was a notorious priest-hunter and he was nick-named 'Burn-Chapel' on account of his bigoted religious opinions. It is ironic therefore that his house should have become the seat of the fledgling Catholic university. He is remembered for writing a rhyming cheque in favour of his wife:

> Mr. La Touche,
> Open your pouch,
> And give unto my darling
> Five hundred pounds sterling:
> For which this will be your bailey,
> Signed, Richard Chapell Whaley.

His younger son was the famous eccentric Thomas 'Buck' Whaley MP (1766–1800), a notorious rake who once for a bet leapt from the back of the lead lion above the front door over the pavement and onto the box of a carriage. He ran through the fortune he had inherited at a great rate. In 1788 at a dinner in Leinster House he wagered that he would travel to the Holy Land and back within a year. He succeeded in this adventure and claimed his winnings of £20,000, boasting that he had played handball at the Wailing Wall of Jerusalem.

The origins of the Catholic University of Ireland date from 1845

RIGHT The staircase at 86 St Stephen's Green, which was built in 1765 by the Irish architect and stuccodore Robert West for Richard Chapell Whaley MP, father of the notorious 'Buck' Whaley.

LEFT Detail of the plasterwork in the coving of the saloon, showing the figure of Justice.

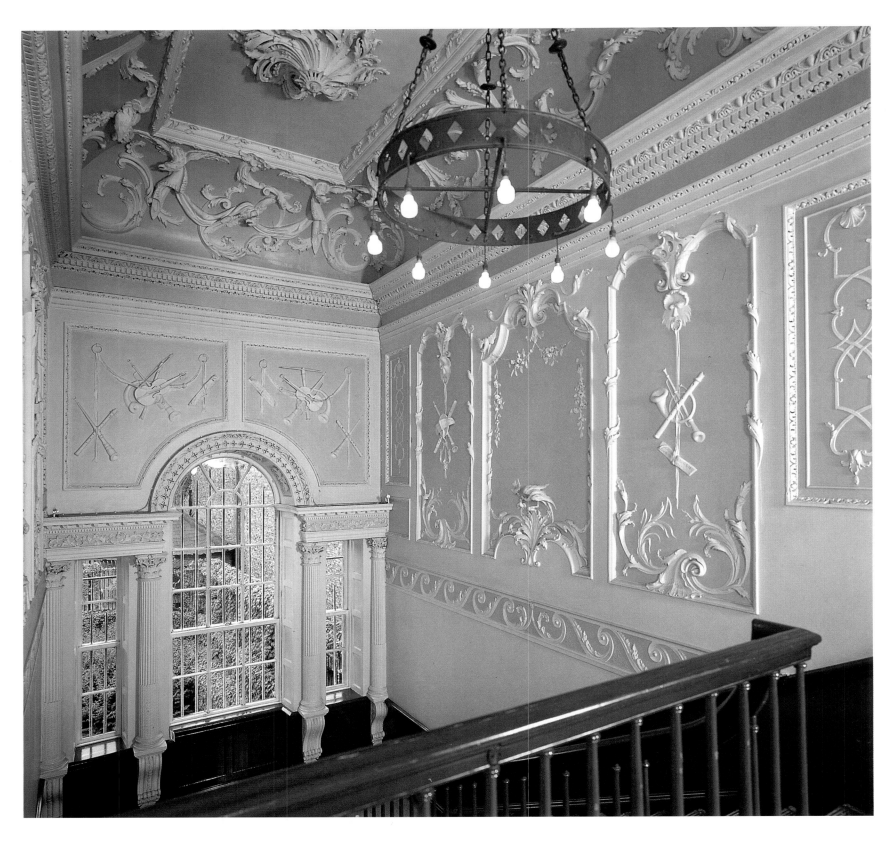

when the Prime Minister, Sir Robert Peel, promoted a bill to establish the Queen's Univeristy of Ireland, with colleges in Cork, Galway and Belfast. The first National Synod of Catholic Bishops to be convened since the seventeenth century was held in 1850 in Thurles, Co. Tipperary, and the Catholic hierarchy took the decision there to set up a university in Dublin to cater for the education of Catholics. Dr John Henry Newman was invited to becme its first rector and remained for four years. No. 86 was bought in 1853 and No. 85 in 1865 when the university was extended. The poet Gerard Manley Hopkins came to the university in 1884 as Professor of Classics and remained until his death. From 1883 to 1908 the university was governed by the Society of Jesus. In 1908 the National University of Ireland was founded, incorporating the newly named University College, Dublin, under its

umbrella. The university moved to a new campus south of the city at Belfield, Stillorgan, in 1968.

Newman House has been under restoration for the university over the past four years, supervised by David Sheehan, of Sheehan and Barry, architects. The facade of No. 85 is shortly to be restored with the help of the Getty Foundation, California, and the National Heritage Council, Dublin. The initiation of this immense project was made possible through the generosity of Gallaher (Dublin) Ltd, tobacco manufacturers, and the co-operation of Bord Fáilte and Dublin Tourism. According to Dr Christine Casey, a former curator, this has involved 'the revival of traditional crafts, the painstaking cleaning, conservation and repair of plasterwork and joinery, and the sheer excitement of discovering a building's inner secrets . . . .'

TYRONE HOUSE
Marlborough Street

Tyrone House was built in 1740 for Sir Marcus Beresford, later Earl of Tyrone, grandfather of the first Marquess of Waterford. The architect was Richard Castle and it is Castle's second most important Dublin house after Leinster House, which it antedates by five years. Drastic alterations have been inflicted on the facade, which now gives little indication of the splendours within. The location of Tyrone House encouraged some important families to establish themselves on Marlborough Street, including the Earl of Annesley, whose wife was the daughter of Lord Tyrone; his house was later demolished to make way for the Pro-Cathedral. Other neighbours included Lord Avonmore and Lord Drogheda with Lord Aldborough not too far distant.

The seven-bay house of Irish granite has three storeys and once stood surrounded by a garden and park extending to five acres, hidden from view by a high wall. Beside it was the Bowling Green, a fashionable resort; in 1761 a duel took place there in which Lord Delvin, heir to the Earl of Westmeath, was killed. Soon afterwards the green was closed, partly as a result of competition from the Rotunda Gardens nearby.

Fortunately the original design for the facade is illustrated by Pool and Cash in their *Views of the City of Dublin*, 1780; the house had a tripartite pedimented front door with a Venetian window above and an oculus at the centre of the top floor. None of these features survive and, to make matters worse, an ungainly porch has been added. The heavy

cornice which can be seen below the top floor windows is unusual in a Dublin house but was employed elsewhere by the architect, for example at Russborough, Co. Wicklow. Although the main facade of Tyrone House is disappointing, the garden front, with its beautifully cut granite blocks, is distinguished but unfortunately seldom seen.

The front hall has a black Kilkenny marble mantel; Castle was fond of putting a black mantel in the entrance halls of his houses: Russborough still has one, and the incredibly elaborate black mantel he designed for Westport House, Co. Mayo, has recently gone to Mme Schlumberger in Paris. Throughout the house there is lavish use of mahogany in doors and panelled dados in a very similar way to Russborough. The mahogany staircase is one of the finest in Dublin and appears to be the work of the same craftsman who made the stairs at Russborough as well as those at 85 St Stephen's Green. Pool and Cash can be forgiven for describing Tyrone House as being 'in the old heavy stile' but they are forced to admit that the 'workmanship . . . is remarkably good'.

As at Russborough and 85 St Stephen's Green, the plasterwork here is by the Lafranchini brothers. The female heads with haloes on the wall of the staircase can be compared to similar, haloed heads in the saloon at Carton, Co. Kildare, a house designed by Richard Castle in 1739. The noted authority on Irish plasterwork, Dr C.P. Curran, believed these to be Victorian, perhaps because of their likeness to the queen, but their similarity to the haloed heads on the staircase at

LEFT Before the porch was added to Tyrone House, there was a pedimented front door with a Venetian window above. The house was designed in 1740 by Richard Castle for Sir Marcus Beresford, later Earl of Tyrone, and is now used as offices for the Department of Education.

RIGHT The Minister for
Education has his office in this
upstairs reception room with a
handsome coved ceiling by Paul
and Philip Lafranchini. They
also worked at Curraghmore, the
Earl of Tyrone's country seat.

ABOVE The carved mahogany
staircase resembles those at 85 St
Stephen's Green, now part of
Newman House, and at
Russborough, Co. Wicklow,
both designed by the same
architect, Richard Castle, at
about the same date.

Tyrone House suggests that the Carton heads may be eighteenth-century work by the Lafranchini brothers.

The saloon at Tyrone House is a few feet higher than the other reception rooms; as a result a windowless servant's room on the floor above was reached by steps up the coving. The Lafranchini plasterwork of the saloon is one of their finest creations and the frieze was closely studied when it came to replacing that in the saloon of 85 St Stephen's Green. In a small room on the *piano nobile* the panelling has curious curl graining, made by cutting the mahogany at the junction of two large branches, giving the effect of walnut.

During the rebellion of 1798 it was said that Beresford's corps of yeomanry were instructed not only in riding but in torture, and a notice board was placed outside Tyrone House which read, 'Mangling done here by John Beresford & Co.'. The son of the builder of the house, the Rt Hon. John Beresford, was responsible for the building of the Custom House and was one of the most prominent members of the Wide Streets Commissioners. Although unpopular he was a man of great taste, with the power and influence to put his ideas into practice.

In 1835 Tyrone House was bought by the government and a free-standing replica of it was built to the north with, in between, the Central Model Schools, famous for their past pupil, George Bernard Shaw. The whole complex now belongs to the Department of Education and the minister is privileged to work in one of the most beautiful rooms in Dublin.

LEINSTER HOUSE
Kildare Street

Leinster House was built in 1745 for James FitzGerald, the twentieth Earl of Kildare, for whom the Dukedom of Leinster was created in 1766. Kildare House, later renamed Leinster House, remains unequalled in Dublin to this day in terms of its scale and grandeur. Lord Kildare, who was only twenty-three at the time the building began, employed the same architect, Richard Castle, as his father had used for his country house at Carton, Co. Kildare, six years earlier. Until he inherited in 1744, the family town house was in Suffolk Street, at the foot of Grafton Street and close to Trinity College. Lord Kildare paid Lord Molesworth £1,000 for land in the Molesworth

the one chosen, had pilasters and pedimented doors leading to the stables. The grandest of all was for a colonnaded forecourt modelled on that at Burlington House on Piccadilly.

The front hall, paved in black and white squares, takes up two storeys, and the original chimneypiece of Portland stone is still *in situ*. The room is crowned with a coffered ceiling and is lit by the three central windows on the *piano nobile*. Opposite these windows there are square apertures which light the upstairs corridor. The layout of the house, with its axial corridor, derives from Castletown, Co. Kildare and inspired James Hoban, the Irish architect, when he built the White

LEFT Richard Castle built Leinster House in 1745 for James FitzGerald, the twentieth Earl of Kildare, created first Duke of Leinster in 1766. It now houses Dáil Eireann, the Irish parliament.

Fields, considered both remote and unfashionable at the time, but the earl silenced his critics with the famous words, 'Wherever I go, fashion will follow me.'

In 1747 he married Lady Emily Lennox, daughter of the second Duke of Richmond, who was scarcely fifteen at the time. She was so beautiful as to drive Sir Joshua Reynolds to despair when painting her: 'There is a sweetness of expression in the original which I have not been able to give in the portrait, and therefore cannot think it finished,' he said. Her husband was a great popular hero and, whenever possible, he took a stand against the official English policy of the viceroy. Crowds thronged to see him wherever he went. As the Earl of Malmesbury recalled, he sometimes dressed 'in a long, light blue silk coat, embroidered all over with gold and silver, and turned up with white satin which among a company of distinguished people had made him seem the most distinguished'.

The great forecourt on Kildare Street was entered through a rusticated triumphal arch. Castle produced several alternative designs for his young client to choose from; one showed a Palladian archway, another had the walls of the forecourt pierced with niches and a third,

House in Washington in 1792. His winning design was a three-storeyed building closely modelled on Leinster House, but George Washington asked that the plan be reduced to two storeys. Hoban could not remove the top floor because of the applied portico so he took away the ground floor; the design of the White House today is derived from the top two floors of Leinster House.

James Malton describes in 1792 'a beautiful Lawn, with a handsome Shrubbery, on each side, screening the adjacent Houses from view: enjoying, in the tumult of a noisy Metropolis, all the retirement of the Country'. The unadorned garden front of the house, faced with Golden Hill granite, gives into the garden hall on axis to the front door. This room is used for the reception of visiting dignitaries and contains a statue of Daniel O'Connell by Andrew O'Connor. The two-tiered mantel and grate were measured for *The Georgian Society Records* (vol. IV), which described them as 'as handsome specimens of this style as could be found in any mansion in the United Kingdom'. It notes the doors were dark brown with gilded panels and shouldered architraves of egg and dart moulding. There is a delicate Rococo ceiling.

David Griffin of the Irish Architectural Archive has discovered that

RIGHT The front hall takes up
two storeys. The square
openings below the coving
admit light to the upstairs
corridor.

BELOW The garden hall, which
opens out onto Leinster Lawn, is
used for the reception of foreign
dignitaries.

the library on the ground floor at the northern end, which can be dated
to about 1759, was designed by Isaac Ware to replace the three small
rooms of Castle's plan. The twin mantels are based on a drawing by
William Kent published by Ware in his *Designs of Inigo Jones and Others*
(1727). The ceiling is derived from a drawing in Serlio's *The Book of
Architecture* (1611, London edition) and the Ionic pedimented doorcase
is illustrated in Ware's *A Complete Body of Architecture* (1756). Some of
the columns surrounding the room were removed by the Dublin
Society in the early nineteenth century and incorporated in the gallery
of the Drawing School, now part of the National College of Art and
Design.

James Wyatt (1746–1813) remodelled the picture gallery, a vast
apartment taking up the entire depth of the house, for William Robert,
the second duke. Pool and Cash wrote in 1780 of the duke's 'elegant
taste in some considerable alterations lately made at the north end of
the house'. The barrel-vaulted ceiling is one of the finest in Dublin in
the Neoclassical style, with winged sphinxes in pairs contained in demi-
lune panels. Dr C.P. Curran identified the hand of Michael Stapleton at
work here thanks to similarities in the central section with the drawing

room at Clonmell House. Stapleton, the leading exponent in Dublin of
the Adam and Wyatt schools of decoration, would have been an
obvious choice to carry out Wyatt's design. This noble room once
contained works by Rembrandt, Claude, Giordano, Rubens, Van
Dyck and many other old masters.

The patriotic hero, Lord Edward FitzGerald, brother of the second
duke, gave his life in the cause of Irish freedom on the eve of the
rebellion of 1798, which proved to be one of the prime factors that led
to the Act of Union of 1801. This dissolved the Irish parliament, and as
a result Dublin's social life became gradually more provincial. In 1815,
having no need to keep up a town house, Frederick Augustus, the third
duke, sold Leinster House to the Dublin Society for £10,000 and a
yearly rent of £600.

The Dublin Society was founded in 1731 for improving 'Husbandry, Manufacturing and other useful Arts and Sciences'. It became the
Royal Dublin Society at the time of the visit of George IV in 1821. The
society engaged in all kinds of activities: a significant library was built
up which became the nucleus of the National Library, prizes were
offered to encourage the manufacture of silk, linen, glass and paper,

RIGHT The picture gallery was remodelled for the second Duke of Leinster to the designs of James Wyatt and was completed by 1780. It is used today as the Senate Chamber.

LEFT The library on the ground floor was designed in 1759 by Isaac Ware to replace three small rooms on Castle's plan.

and premiums were awarded for drawing and sculpture. Schools were established to promote education for craftsmen in these fields in conjunction with the apprenticeship system; horse shows were held in the forecourt of Leinster House and the society was responsible for the establishment of the Veterinary College. In 1795 the society purchased land in the vicinity of Glasnevin from the family of Thomas Ticknall and established the Botanic Gardens 'to increase and foster a taste for practical and scientific botany'. This cultural and industrial activity led to the building of four major institutions at the four corners of Leinster House during the second half of the nineteenth century; these were the Natural History Museum, the National Gallery, the National Library and the National Museum. Unfortunately the elegant forecourt was unnecessarily demolished in the name of culture; the forecourt of Burlington House in London, now occupied by the Royal Academy, suffered the same fate in the same cause.

In 1924 the Royal Dublin Society sold Leinster House to the government for £68,000 and moved to Ballsbridge where they had owned land since 1880. The picture gallery became the Seanad (Senate), and the lecture theatre, built in 1897 by the Royal Dublin Society, now houses the Dáil.

A prophetic Latin inscription on the foundation stone, laid by the earl in 1745, translates: 'Learn, whenever, in some unhappy day, you light on the ruins of so great a mansion, of what worth he was who built it and how frail all things are, when such memorials of such men cannot outlive misfortune.' The earl's descendants no longer own 67,227 acres of land in Co. Kildare, as they did in 1871, but their great town house has survived intact and continues to play a significant role in modern Ireland.

ST PATRICK'S HOSPITAL
St James's Street

In the shadow of Guinness's Brewery, partially hidden behind a high wall, stands the hospital generally known as Swift's Hospital, which still takes care of the mentally ill after 250 years of radical progress in this field of medicine. When Jonathan Swift, Dean of St Patrick's, died in 1745 almost insane, he left money for founding a hospital for 'idiots and lunaticks'. In his poem of 1731 entitled 'Verses on the Death of Dr Swift' he wrote:

> He gave the little wealth he had,
> To build a house for fools and mad:
> And showed by one satiric touch,
> No nation wanted it so much . . .

Swift sat on the board of governors of Dr Steevens' Hospital with Sir William Fownes, a former Lord Mayor of Dublin with whom he discussed his scheme for an asylum. Fownes advised him to build it on the outskirts of the city because 'the cries and exclamations of the outrageous would reach a great way and ought not to disturb the neighbours'. Swift was familiar with the appalling conditions at Bethlem (nicknamed Bedlam) in London and determined that Dublin should be provided with an institution where patients would not be chained up and treated as criminals. Under the terms of his will he appointed ten clerical and legal friends as trustees and directed that the hospital should be built near Dr Steevens' Hospital, whose governors donated the land. It was only the second hospital in the British Isles built to house the insane.

St Patrick's was begun in 1749 and was designed by George Semple (*fl.* 1748–80). The author of a treatise on bridge-building called *The Art*

ABOVE The staircase, with a bench from the former Irish House of Commons.

LEFT St Patrick's Hospital was built in 1749 by George Semple out of proceeds from the estate of Jonathan Swift left to provide care for the mentally ill.

RIGHT The boardroom contains a portrait of Swift, with paintings of his companions Stella and Vanessa on either side.

of *Building in Water*, Semple was later involved in a scheme for the rebuilding of Essex Bridge. The main granite front of the hospital, consisting of seven bays with a pediment, is rusticated on the ground floor and scored horizontally on the floor above, where the windows have Gibbsian surrounds. Twin projections at the back housed the patients, one for men and the other for women, with sixteen cells on each floor and wide corridors. Flanking wings were added to the facade by Thomas Cooley in 1778; he also extended the projections at the back so that a total of 108 patients could be accommodated.

Semple sought advice from a Mr Jennings, 'a person well recommended for his skill in the care of lunaticks'. The architect's annotated 'Book of Plans' containing details of the cells, is preserved here. The cell doors were made of 'very stout whole deal'; there were iron doors at the entrances to the wards, each of which had 'a chair firmly fixed near the wall in order to secure raging lunaticks during their extreme illness'. Each cell had a window $2\frac{1}{2}$ feet square, unglazed, with two bars and shutters, set 7 feet above the floor. All were 'to be built convex in shape so that the patients may have nothing to take hold of, when they

offer to climb up to the windows.' It may well be imagined that cold was a dreadful problem.

The hospital opened in 1757, when it took in the first ten 'pauper lunatics'; it was always short of funds but received help from lotteries, charity sermons and donations as well as from the government. Many extensions were made and 150 patients were accommodated here by 1817. Surgeon Richard Leeper, who was superintendant from 1899 to 1941, renovated and added to the old building; he made a collection of Swiftiana including copies of Swift's books and personal memorabilia. In the 1940s with the advent of greater understanding of mental illness and its treatment, conditions for the patients improved greatly.

In the 1970s Charles Haughey (later Taoiseach) and Lady Goulding chaired a committee which raised nearly half a million pounds and financed the erection of a scientific and clinical research unit in St Patrick's; today there are beds for over 300 patients. The hospital is the main centre for psychiatric care in Ireland besides being an important teaching hospital. The wisdom, foresight and generosity of its founder have been amply justified.

DUBLIN CASTLE
Castle Street

In 1170, the year after they first landed in Ireland, the Anglo-Normans under Strongbow captured Dublin. The building of Dublin Castle was ordered in 1204 by King John, who desired 'a castle . . . for the custody of our treasure . . . for the use of justice in the city & if needs be, for the city's defence with good dykes and strong walls'. The castle has been the seat and symbol of alien power in Ireland from then until 1922 when it was handed over to the Irish Free State. Henri de Londres, Archbishop of Dublin from 1213, is generally credited with having taken charge of the construction. An elevated position was chosen dominating the city, and a walled enclosure was erected with circular towers at the four corners. The entrance was through a portcullis flanked by twin towers at the centre of the northern side, facing the Liffey; the cupola of Castle Hall is in the approximate position of one of these towers. The River Poddle gave protection to the east and south and was later channelled to form a moat; it now flows underground.

In 1245, during the reign of Henry III a Great Hall was built within the walls of the castle; this must have been the most lavish building yet seen in Ireland. There were marble columns and a rose window; a raised dais at one end was enhanced by a mural depicting the king and queen surrounded by their court.

The history of the castle was at times violent. Thomas FitzGerald, known as 'Silken Thomas' because of his fine apparel, was a grandson of the Great Earl of Kildare. In 1534 he was acting deputy in place of his father who had been called to London. Hearing a rumour, later proved false, that his father had been executed in London, he threw down the Sword of State and renounced his allegiance to Henry VIII before the Council of State in St Mary's Abbey. He then laid siege to the castle but was defeated, and in 1537 he was hanged, drawn and quartered at Tyburn along with five of his uncles. His female relatives were held hostage in the castle after his abortive rebellion. In 1584 Archbishop O'Hurley of Cashel was chained up here in a 'dark, dismal and fetid' cell before being hanged for his Catholic faith.

At various times the courts and parliament sat in the Great Hall until it burnt down in 1671. The castle served at times as the viceroy's residence, besides housing the government offices, the exchequer and the mint and providing a secure home for the state papers. It was also an arsenal, a barracks and a prison.

Thomas Wentworth, Earl of Strafford, became Lord Deputy in 1633 and on landing in Dublin he found that his apartments in the castle were in a ruinous condition. He also had to take down one of the towers, reporting to Secretary Coke 'the others are so crazy that we are still in fear part of it may drop on our heads'. After the Restoration in 1660 plans were made for the improvement of Dublin Castle by Captain John Paine, Director-General and Overseer of the King's Fortifications, with the assistance of John Mills, Master Carpenter of Ireland. Many of the improvements they effected would have been destroyed in another fire of 1684. The Duke of Ormonde's son, the Earl of Arran, who prevented this fire from reaching the powder magazine, was not unduly distressed, writing that the king had 'lost nothing other than the worst castle in the worst situation in Christendom' and that now 'his majesty may have a noble palace built, and I believe there are a hundred projectors at work already about

RIGHT The statue of Justice, by John Van Nost, makes a pair with that of Fortitude. They surmount the stone arches with broken curved pediments on either side of Castle Hall. These arches being on a larger scale than the building they flank add to the unreality of the composition.

FAR RIGHT Castle Hall, Dublin Castle, was built in the 1750s. The army band used to play in the upstairs portico during military parades in Upper Castle Yard.

framing proposals'. Hardly a trace now survives of the medieval castle which occupied more or less the site of today's Upper Castle Yard. Practically the only visible remains of the original fortress are the lower walls of the Record Tower beside the chapel, the base of the Bermingham Tower, the curtain wall beneath St Patrick's Hall and the newly uncovered foundations of the Powder Tower to the north.

Sir William Robinson, the surveyor-general under Ormonde, was the architect of the Royal Hospital, Kilmainham. In 1685 he designed a similar arcaded building at the south-east corner of the Upper Yard. His plans set the style for the further development that was to follow at the hand of Thomas Burgh, who succeeded Robinson in 1700, and Joseph Jarratt, who was deputy to the Surveyor-General in the 1750s. Burgh built the east range, or lower cross block, of the Upper Castle Yard in 1711 and the west range which matches it in 1714. He was also responsible for the Treasury offices in the Lower Castle Yard in 1712, although he objected to the site. Under the Surveyor-General, Colonel Thomas Eyre, Joseph Jarratt extended the State Apartments in 1758–9, designing the stone-faced facade on the south front of Upper Castle Yard facing the garden. This block suffered fire damage in 1941,

Jarratt's arched corridor survived but had to be subsequently rebuilt. This was originally top-lit and is one of the most impressive architectural features of the whole ensemble. J.B. Maguire has connected Jarratt's drawings with Eyre's account book, now in the Irish Architectural Archive, to show that the earlier attribution to Pearce of this work was mistaken.

Castle Hall, variously known in the past as the Genealogical Office, the Office of Arms and the Bedford Tower, is one of the most magical mid-eighteenth century buildings in Dublin and dates from the 1750s. A military band used to perform in the upstairs portico when there was a parade in the yard below. The giant gateways on either side support lead statues of Fortitude above the western gate and Justice above its twin, both by John Van Nost. The rain used to tilt Justice's scales as one side was protected by her arm, inciting sardonic comments from the populace regarding British justice, until holes were drilled in the pans to drain them. It was also remarked that she stands with her back to the city. The crown jewels of Ireland were stolen from this building on the eve of a state visit by Edward VII and Queen Alexandra in 1907 and no trace of them has ever been found.

The State Apartments occupy the entire southern range of the Upper Yard and are used for such ceremonies as the inauguration of the president as well as official entertainment, just as in viceregal days. Mary Delany (1700–1788) attended a ball in Dublin Castle in 1731 and described it as follows:

> Monday at eight o'clock went to the Castle. The room where the ball was to be was ordered by Capt. Pierce [Edward Lovett Pearce], finely adorned with paintings and obelisks, and made as light as a summer's day. I never saw more company in one place; abundance of finery, and indeed many very pretty women. There were two rooms for dancing. The whole apartment of the Castle was open, which consists of several very good rooms; in one there was a supper ordered after the manner of that at the masquerade, where everybody went at what hour they liked best, and vast profusion of meat and drink, which you may be sure has gained the *hearts* of all guzzlers!

The whereabouts of the ballroom described by Mrs Delany is uncertain but it was probably the principal reception room, known as the Old Hall. This was at ground level, entered through a rusticated ceremonial

LEFT St Patrick's Hall has a magnificent ceiling depicting scenes from Irish history. It was painted by Vincent Waldré in c.1700.

RIGHT The Throne Room, originally Battle Axe Hall, was remodelled to form a Presence Chamber in the late 1780s.

The State Drawing Room, which suffered a disastrous fire in 1941, was restored in 1968 by McGrath with Oscar Richardson and J.B. Maguire as project architects, who have given it an opulent Victorian look. Beyond the drawing room is the Apollo Room, a reproduction of the back drawing room of Tracton House, 40 St Stephen's Green, which was demolished in 1912. The original, Baroque, figured ceiling has been re-erected here with appropriate panelling. The figure of the sun god, his hand resting on the signs of the zodiac and seated on a cloud with his lyre, is surrounded by trophies of the Arts, Hunting, Music and Love. It is rare to find a plaster ceiling either signed or dated but the Tracton House ceiling is an exception, being inscribed with the date 1746 on the Arts trophy in one of the corners. If only a signature could have accompanied the date!

Parts of two Rococo ceilings from Mespil House dating from about 1751, which have been attributed to Bartholomew Cramillion, have been re-erected in two of the small reception rooms. One represents Medicine with the Arts and Sciences and the other, Minerva introducing the Arts to Hibernia. The Hibernia ceiling is in a room

archway with the royal arms, which can be seen on Charles Brooking's map of 1728.

The Old Hall was replaced by its much larger successor, St Patrick's Hall, in 1746–7. Originally known simply as the Ballroom, it acquired its present name in 1783 when the Order of St Patrick was inaugurated by the Viceroy, the Marquess of Buckingham, as an Irish equivalent of the Order of the Bath. The ceiling was painted by Vincent Waldré who was brought to Ireland in 1787 by Buckingham, for whom he had worked at Stowe. Divided into three sections, it is by far the most important painted ceiling in Ireland. The panels represent St Patrick converting the Irish to Christianity at the western end, George III supported by Justice and Liberty in the centre and Henry II receiving the submission of the Irish chieftains in 1171. A small painted version of the ceiling by Waldré serves as a table top at the Royal Dublin Society. The walls of the room are hung with the insignia and banners of the Knights of St Patrick, and at either end there are galleries, one for spectators and the other for musicians, with the star of St Patrick above them.

The Throne Room or Presence Chamber was originally built as Battle Axe Hall and remodelled as a presence chamber in the late 1780s. It is rich with red velvet and white and gold decorative mouldings. The throne, traditionally believed to have been the gift of William of Orange, is in fact early nineteenth century. The twin mantels and the doors can be attributed to Francis Johnston but much of the rest of the room, including the crown-shaped mirrors, dates from the 1830s. The painted roundels have been attributed to the Venetian artist, Giambattista Bellucci. The carpet is one of several designed for the castle by Raymond McGrath, chief architect of the Office of Public Works.

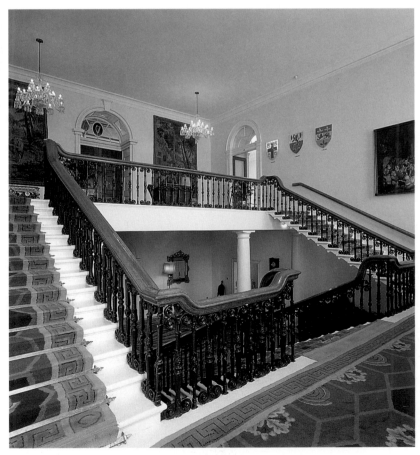

ABOVE The double staircase in the State Apartments leading up to the Throne Room and St Patrick's Hall.

LEFT The State Drawing Room was severely damaged by fire in 1941 and was given an opulent Victorian interior in the restoration. The room contains a pair of late eighteenth-century marble mantels.

RIGHT The Picture Gallery, formed out of three rooms overlooking Upper Castle Yard, has a collection of viceregal portraits.

fitted out with furniture and pictures presented in memory of Beatrice, Countess of Granard, and her husband the eighth earl.

The Picture Gallery, which is almost 100 feet long, was originally a Supper Room and was later divided into three rooms, which were used for entertaining. The ceiling appears to date from about 1820, when the room was returned to its original layout. The gallery houses a collection of portraits of former viceroys, with their coronets surmounting the gilt frames. This gallery leads into the top-lit Wedgwood Room, formerly a billiard room, which in turn leads into the Bermingham Tower or Supper Room – a vast circular room with attenuated Gothic windows and plasterwork, created in 1775. In December 1921 the treaty was signed by which the twenty-six counties became the Irish Free State. Peter Somerville-Large in his book *Dublin* describes the scene: 'Nine hundred and fifty years after the Normans arrived the English were leaving. Tommies abandoned their numerous

barracks to the Free Staters and marched for the Mail Boat as bands played "Come back to Erin . . ." At the castle some untidy young men led by Michael Collins tumbled out of two taxis to take over "the Devil's Half Acre".' Sean O'Casey, the author and playwright, describes how the last Viceroy, Lord Fitzalan 'handed over the place known as Dublin Castle and seemed to be doing it all in a dream . . . "Here's the key to the throne room, and this one's the key of St. Patrick's Hall, my good man." '

Except when there is a state ceremony of some kind or when it is Ireland's turn to host the European Parliament, the most spectacular parts of Dublin Castle are open to all. The faded brick facades, the calm gentle atmosphere and intimate scale of the Upper Yard provide a cloak which hides the turbulent history once enacted here. Dublin Castle resembles a seat of learning more than the administrative hub of the alien power that ruled Ireland for centuries.

TRINITY COLLEGE
College Green

COLLEGE BUILDINGS

LEFT Trinity College campus from the north-west.

RIGHT Library Square with the Rubrics (to the left) and the great library on the right, partly hidden by one of the famous Oregon maples. Dating from 1700, the Rubrics is the oldest building in college, although the Dutch gables were added in 1890.

Trinity College ranks with Oxford and Cambridge as one of the great universities of the world, known for its scholarship, tradition and the beauty of its campus. In 1590 a group of learned citizens petitioned the city council for the establishment of a university. The council recommended the proposal to Lord Deputy Fitzwilliam and were prepared to hand over the Augustinian Priory of All Hallows, which had been suppressed in 1538, as a site for this purpose. Henry Ussher, Archdeacon of Dublin and graduate of both Oxford and Cambridge, presented the city's petition to Queen Elizabeth I with the support of the lord deputy and Archbishop Loftus, who afterwards became the first provost. In 1592 the queen founded 'the College of the Holy and Undivided Trinity near Dublin whereby knowledge and civility might be increased by the instruction of our people there, whereof many have usually heretofore used to travaill into ffrance, Italy, and Spaine to gett learning in such foreign universities, whereby they have been infected with poperie and other ill qualities, and soe become evil subjects'. The royal endowment was minimal, however, and in its first years the college was financed by public subscription. King James I later provided a significant

endowment from estates in Ulster, which increased its income threefold. In 1593 the first students were enrolled, and by 1613 their number had risen to sixty-five.

The earliest surviving drawing of the college dates from about 1600; it is the property of the Marquess of Salisbury and shows a single red-brick quadrangle with hall and chapel taking up one side, and the old spire of All Hallows, a landmark for navigators sailing into Dublin. A drawing of the college by Thomas Dineley in 1681 shows that after nearly a century it had trebled in size. During the provostship of Narcissus Marsh, 1678–83, the benefactor who gave Dublin its first public library, the chapel was rebuilt and beautified. Dr McParland has discovered references to 'an east window with Gothic tracery, elaborate armorial carving within, "carved work at ye Alter", and a coved ceiling with four "Panells of Enricht Stucco work"'. This interior seems to have been akin to the chapel of the Royal Hospital, Kilmainham, designed in 1680 by Sir William Robinson, who was also to be the architect of Marsh's Library.

In 1689 Archbishop King described the depredations inflicted on Trinity by the Catholic James II and his army when they marched into

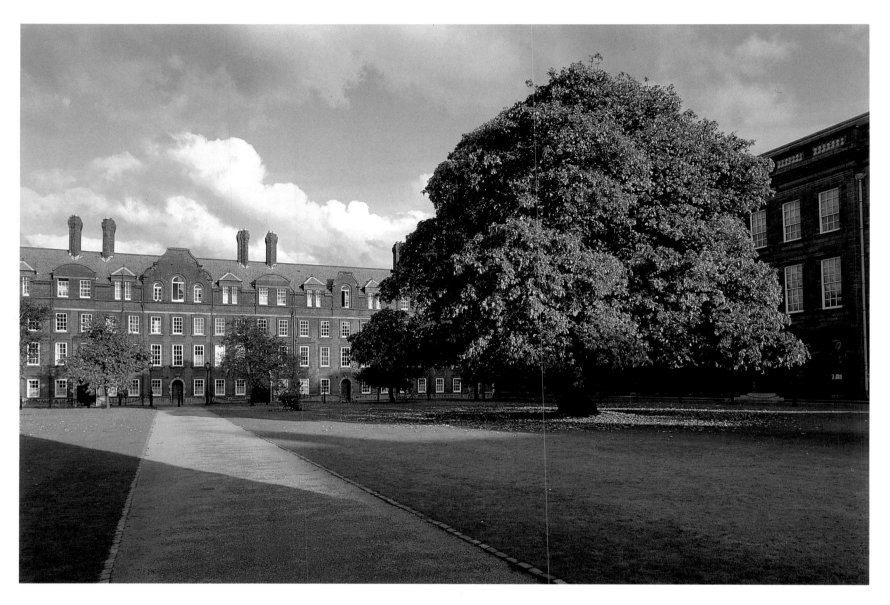

Dublin. 'King James and his party ... turned out the Vice-Provost, Fellows, and Scholars; seized upon the Furniture, Books, and publick Library, together with the Chappel, Communion-Plate, and all things belonging to the College ... In the House they placed a Popish Garison, turn'd the Chappel into a Magazine, and many of the Chambers into Prisons for Protestants.'

Nothing remains of any building at Trinity from before 1700. The college of today began to take shape when a royal grant of £3,000 and a bequest of £1,200 from Provost George Browne made it possible for the building of Library Square to commence. The first side to be erected was the Rubrics and, although the gables date from 1890, this red-brick range is the earliest building in college. The year 1712 saw the laying of the foundation stone of the great library, which was sited at right angles to the Rubrics and built to the design of Thomas Burgh, the surveyor-general. This magnificent building which took up an entire side of Library Square, stood on open arcades to protect the books from damp; these have since been glazed in. The library was built of pinkish St Bee's sandstone while the arcades were in a darker limestone; these contrasting colours added greatly to the beauty of the

whole. Unfortunately, the sandstone must have weathered badly, as in the nineteenth century the library was refaced in a dead grey granite.

The Long Room of the library was formerly approached at the west end by the magnificent staircase designed by Richard Castle; this however is no longer in general use and the great room is now approached by modern concrete stairs. The Long Room is one of the glories of Ireland and it was here that the famous illustrated Celtic manuscripts, the Books of Kells, Durrow and Armagh, used to be displayed; they are now housed in the Treasury. The lower part of the room remains as Burgh designed it, with beautiful dark woodwork providing the perfect backdrop to the two rows of white marble busts by Scheemakers, Roubiliac, Vierpyl and others. The room originally had a flat compartmented plaster ceiling painted white, with light and spacious galleries on either side. In 1860 more space was needed for books and the galleries were filled with bookshelves, repeating the rhythm of those below. The original flat ceiling was sacrificed and the vertical axis of the bookcases now culminates in a great dark timber ceiling in the shape of a barrel vault; transverse ribs which spring from the top of the bookcases add emphasis to the perspective of the

ABOVE The Dining Hall, designed by Richard Castle in 1741. The marble statue is of George Salmon, provost from 1888 to 1904.

LEFT The Long Room of the library designed by Thomas Burgh in 1712, with its great Victorian barrel-vaulted ceiling, is one of the most spectacular sights in Dublin and regularly open to the public. It contains marble busts by Vierpyl, Roubiliac and Scheemakers.

receding arches. These alterations were designed by Deane and Woodward and, in the words of Dr McParland, 'what had been superb they made sublime'.

Among the outstanding rare books in the library there is a First Folio Shakespeare and there are Egyptian papyri, Greek and Latin manuscripts, besides extensive collections of Irish maps, bookbindings and documents of the sixteenth and seventeenth centuries. Another of the library's treasures is an ancient harp which was once thought to have belonged to Brian Boru. Trinity has had a copyright library since 1801 and enjoys the right to receive a free copy of every book published in Great Britain and Ireland.

In 1734 Richard Castle designed a little Doric temple as a printing house, thanks to the generosity of John Stearne, Bishop of Clogher, who endowed it. *The Georgian Society Records of Eighteenth Century Domestic Architecture and Decoration in Dublin* (vols I–V) were printed here from 1909 to 1913. Castle also designed the Dining Hall in the 1740s but experienced severe difficulties with the construction, and

LEFT Above the door inside the Dining Hall is a portrait of Frederick, Prince of Wales, by Thomas Hudson in an elaborate carved frame by Paul Petit. The orginal mantelpiece was moved up to the Common Room and the present one was carved by George Darley at a cost of £55 15s 8d.

RIGHT The west front was built in 1752 to the design of Theodore Jacobsen, an amateur architect. The central block was recently cleaned for the university's 400th anniversary.

Hugh Darley, at that time engaged on the west front, was given the task of rebuilding it in 1760. The Dining Hall is faced in granite with a frontispiece that breaks forward and four Ionic pilasters supporting a pediment. It is approached by a generous flight of steps much used by the students for relaxation in fine weather. A large entrance hall, with the Common Room above, leads to the Dining Hall – a vast coved room surrounded by panelling with full length portraits above, as at the Royal Hospital, Kilmainham. The painting by Thomas Hudson (1701–79) of Frederick, Prince of Wales, Chancellor of the University, hangs over the door. The elaborate gilded frame, surmounted by the Prince of Wales' feathers, is particularly worthy of note and was made by Paul Petit, a Frenchman working in London. The black marble chimneypiece, designed by Castle for the Dining Hall and carved by David Sheehan, is now in the Common Room.

In 1740 Richard Castle added a handsome classical entrance, surmounted by a domed bell-tower, to the Gothic chapel. This belfry appears on old engravings of Dublin, towering above the west front. After some years it was pronounced unsafe so that the great college bell could no longer be rung; in the 1780s the tower was demolished, together with the chapel. Castle whose brand of Palladianism was of the solid, enduring variety, seems to have fared ill when it came to building for the college. He prepared a scheme for a new west front but it is hardly surprising, given his record here, that this was not carried out. The present front was in fact built the very year after he died.

The main west front of Trinity leads into Parliament Square, so named because the college obtained grants totalling £40,000 from the Irish parliament to build it. Work began in 1752 but the identity of the architect had for long remained a mystery; it has now been established by Dr McParland that Theodore Jacobsen, an amateur English architect, was responsible. He originally intended that a dome should crown the main entrance with cupolas above the terminal buildings to either side; the northern cupola was actually erected by 1756 but only lasted three years. It was taken down on the advice of an unidentified but 'well-travelled friend', who wrote that such features should be abandoned as they 'are nowhere to be met with in Italy in such buildings'. The octagonal foundations for the intended central dome can be seen in the main entrance lobby. The Regent House, a double-storeyed room above the front archway, with mortar boards in the

Rococo plaster ceiling, owes its existence to the abandonment of this scheme. Statues of Edmund Burke and Oliver Goldsmith by John Henry Foley stand on either side of the main entrance; these were erected by public subscription in 1864 and 1868. Edmund Burke (1729–97), the famous philosopher and statesman, entered Trinity at the age of fifteen and proved a precocious scholar. Oliver Goldsmith (1730–74), poet and dramatist, who is remembered for his poem *The Deserted Village* and his play *She Stoops to Conquer* among many other works, also studied here.

The Theatre, or Examination Hall, which terminates the southern side of Parliament Square, was built to the designs of Sir William Chambers in 1777 and completed in the mid-1780s. Chambers never came to Ireland and it was left to the college architect, Christopher Myers, to execute his plans. Chambers wrote: 'If there be any merit in the general intention I may claim some share of it; but the whole detail on which the perfection of these works must greatly depend, is none of mine and whatever merit that has is Mr Myers' who I understand is the operator.' It is not known precisely what Chambers meant by this – he did not know Myers' capabilities. Had the building not succeeded, he could have escaped any blame; as it turned out, he could claim a share in the applause. The Examination Hall is a temple-fronted building which faces its twin of ten years later, College Chapel, also designed by Chambers, across the end of Parliament Square. The accomplished Dublin stuccodore, Michael Stapleton, gave both buildings superb Adamesque interiors, noting in his bill that the Examination Hall had 'Antique Composed Capitals ... Copied from Design in "Stewards Grecian Antiquities"'. The impressive marble monument in the Examination Hall was carved in Rome by Christopher Hewetson, an Irish sculptor, in memory of Provost Richard Baldwin, who left the college a fortune in the will he is depicted as holding in his left hand. The case of the organ in the gallery is seventeenth century, and the chandelier of gilded wood was originally made for the Parliament House. One of the great beauties of the Chapel, which was consecrated in 1798, is the curved organ gallery in dark wood, exquisitely carved and resting on six fluted Ionic columns; there is unusual free-hand plasterwork behind the organ. The original panelled stalls are still *in situ* facing inwards in the collegiate manner.

After the spire of All Hallows was demolished, some time elapsed before its exalted place was taken by Richard Castle's magnificent, but short-lived Bell Tower. This in turn eventually gave way to the Campanile, which stands in the heart of the college just as it occupies the hearts of those who have belonged here. This symbol of Trinity was designed by Sir Charles Lanyon in 1852 to house the two college bells. The Campanile was the gift of Lord John Beresford, Archbishop of Armagh and Chancellor of the University.

In 1853 the firm of Deane and Woodward, with ideas from John McCurdy, produced designs for the Museum Building which is the finest example of Victorian architecture on the campus. It is heavily influenced by Ruskin's *The Stones of Venice* and the round plaques which serve as punctuation between the windows were inspired by the Palazzo Dario (above) and the Palazzo Ducale (below). The great beauty of the interior is the top-lit staircase made of stone, with two domed ceilings in multicoloured glazed tiles or brick. The capitals are the work of the O'Shea brothers from Cork and have lively carving of flowers, leaves and animals, bringing exotic and even Byzantine references to a northern clime.

Although Queen Elizabeth I founded Trinity as a Protestant institution it opened its doors to Catholic and Dissenter alike. But in 1637 parliament imposed strenuous conditions on Catholics wishing to go to the college. Except for a short period in the 1680s when James II was on the throne, this situation prevailed until 1793 when the Relief Act was passed, removing restrictions on Catholics attending Trinity. However they were later discouraged from attending the college by their own religious leaders – an attitude that fortunately is in the past. The university chapel is now ecumenical and Trinity is attended by students of many nationalities and religions.

RIGHT The pews in College Chapel face inwards in collegiate style. Like the Examination Hall opposite, it was designed by Sir William Chambers and he seems to have allowed the architect who executed the interior much discretion. Both have good plasterwork by the Dublin stuccodore Michael Stapleton.

RIGHT The landing ceiling with the oval opening in the floor of the pilastered lobby above, which leads into the saloon, and the skylight beyond.

Andrews was adept at cultivating those in authority and would have needed all his powers of persuasion to secure for himself and his successors such a magnificent house as this.

The design of the Provost's House had for many years been attributed to John Smyth, the architect of St Thomas's Church (now destroyed), which was a version of Palladio's Church of the Redentore in Venice. Smyth was evidently a deep-dyed Palladian, and because the college bursar in June 1759 made a payment of £22 15s 'To Smith Architect for a plan for the Provost's House', everything pointed to him as the designer. Dr McParland, the recognized authority on the buildings of Trinity, has however found evidence of a much larger payment of £108 6s 8d (then the exact equivalent of £100 sterling) by the college to an unnamed architect whom, he suspects, may have been Henry Keene, the English architect working at the time on the west front of Trinity. Perhaps Smyth was responsible only for the Palladian

exterior of the Provost's House, leaving the refined interior to Keene.

The front hall is very masculine in feeling, and quite unlike the hall of any other Dublin house. The walls are boldly rusticated in ashlar blocks made of wood painted to resemble stone and left uncluttered so that the niches, arches, vaulting and the shadows thrown by them can be best expressed. The octagonal-plan staircase is one of the finest in Dublin, and the walls are blocked out in ashlar like the hall up to the level of the landing above. The ironwork, which is such an outstanding feature of the house, is first admired on the grille above the entrance gates, can next be seen protecting the tall arched window on the landing, and then on the staircase itself. A portrait of Primate Boulter by Francis Bindon hangs on the stairs in an amazingly ornate wooden frame, stained black. This was carved by John Houghton with a profusion of acorns, oak leaves, wheat ears, swags, coins, books, grapes and tassels, all silhouetted against the white background of the walls.

LEFT The saloon, with a full-length portrait of John, Duke of Bedford, by Gainsborough on the left and a portrait of Queen Elizabeth I, who founded the college in 1592, over the mantel.

RIGHT The painting over the mantel in the dining room, *Coriolanus Receiving the Embassy* by P. Lastman (1625), is one of a collection of pictures given to the house by the Rev. Samuel Madden.

LEFT The saloon, with a full-length portrait of John, Duke of Bedford, by Gainsborough on the left and a portrait of Queen Elizabeth I, who founded the college in 1592, over the mantel.

A lively Vitruvian scroll, or 'running dog', continues the level of the upper landing around the staircase octagon. The pilastered lobby at the head of the stairs is lit from a domed skylight on the storey above, the light filtering down through an oval opening surrounded by a beautiful wrought-iron balustrade. This, like the rest of the ironwork in the house, was made by Timothy Turner. The saloon, which takes up all five windows of the *piano nobile*, is the climax to any visit here, and a room quite without equal in Dublin. It is entered through a handsome pedimented doorcase with fluted Corinthian columns, which is flanked by a pair of carved wood mantels with caryatids. The ingenious manner in which the two ends are separated from the main body of the room by a pair of Corinthian columns makes the saloon at once more intimate and less awesome.

John, Duke of Bedford, viceroy from 1757 to 1761, was Andrews' friend and became Chancellor of Trinity in 1765; he presented a full-length portrait of himself by Gainsborough, which hangs at one end of the saloon with a stucco satyr peeping over the frame. On either side of the duke is a pair of lion-head brackets in gilded wood, thought to have been made by Richard Cranfield in 1771. The two paintings over the mantels are of Queen Elizabeth I, the foundress of Trinity, and James Ussher, an early provost. There is lively Rococo humour in the wall decoration and the frieze; the main ceiling is very fine, subtly coved and compartmented. The magnificent plasterwork in the house was executed by Patrick and John Wall and is in the transitional style which came after the freedom of the Rococo period and was soon to be eclipsed by the 'dead hand of Adam'.

As would be expected in a house of this quality the dining room, which faces over the garden at the back, is very ornate with beautiful plasterwork on the walls and ceiling. In 1765 the Rev. Samuel Madden bequeathed twenty oil paintings to the college, on condition that they were hung in the Provost's House – a magnificent gift, and one of these, *Coriolanus Receiving the Embassy* by Peter Lastman, is over the mantel. The building has remained unaltered with the exception of a library and ante-room added to the ground floor in the 1770s.

THE ROTUNDA HOSPITAL
Parnell Street

The dreams of most men die with the dawn. Two hundred and fifty years ago Dr Bartholomew Mosse had a dream that he could relieve the suffering of the Dublin poor at childbirth, and it not only came true but lives on yet. Bartholomew Mosse (1712–59) was the fifth son of the Rector of Maryborough, now Portlaoise, Co. Laois. He qualified as a surgeon in Dublin at the age of twenty-one and five years later accompanied a troop of soldiers to Minorca during the Wars of the Spanish Succession. On the way home he visited the famous Hotel Dieu in Paris which was noted for its expertise in midwifery. He made this his speciality when he returned to Dublin, obtaining the Licentiate of Midwifery from the Royal College of Physicians in 1742. At the time conditions at childbirth, especially among the poor, were appalling and the death rate was high for both mother and child. T. Percy Kirkpatrick in *The Book of the Rotunda Hospital* (1913) writes: 'their lodgings were generally in cold garrets open to every wind, or in damp cellars subject to floods from excessive rains, destitute of attendance, medicines, and often of proper food.'

In 1745 Dr Mosse opened a lying-in hospital in a former theatre in George's Lane; this was the earliest maternity hospital in these islands, preceding by three years the first in London. He engaged in every kind of fund-raising activity to support his charity, with the help of an influential board of management. For example on 11 February 1747 the first performance in Ireland of Handel's oratorio, *Judas Maccabaeus*, was held at the Music Hall in Fishamble Street 'For the Benefit of the Hospital for Poor Distressed LYING IN WOMEN in George's-Lane'.

In 1748 Dr Mosse leased 'four acres and one rood plantation measure on the north side of Great Britain Street [now Parnell Street] for three lives, renewable forever at a fine of a peppercorn on the fall of each life'. To raise money for the new building he laid out gardens which were inspired by Vauxhall Gardens in London; these were opened to the public in the following year and admission was one shilling. The venture proved a great success and the Pleasure Gardens soon became a fashionable promenade; they were equipped with an orchestral hall where concerts, banquets and other entertainments were held and they soon became a northside rival to Beaux Walk on St Stephen's Green.

In 1750 Dr Mosse engaged his friend Richard Castle to build a maternity hospital at the lower end of these gardens, designing the layout of the delivery rooms himself; they are still in use after 250 years, the layout unchanged. Castle, who apparently provided the design free of charge, died in February 1751, and the building was supervised by his pupil and assistant, John Ensor. The elevation closely resembles Leinster House designed by Castle five years previously. The present cupola was substituted by Ensor for Richard Castle's design which was shown on an early lottery ticket sold in aid of the hospital. The cupola once carried a gilded ball and a weather vane in the shape of a cradle. Both the front and the back of the building were framed by curved colonnades and niches, similar in design to those at Russborough, Co. Wicklow, also designed by Richard Castle. The front hall, which contains a bust of Dr Mosse by Van Nost, has four free-standing Doric columns, and the black and white paving extends into the corridor beyond. The master's quarters were originally situated here and

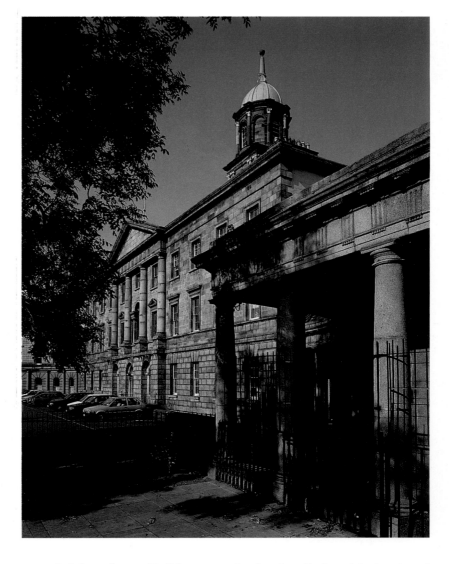

occupied three floors; Dr Mosse was the first in a distinguished series of masters. A royal charter was granted by George II in 1756 and in the following year the Viceroy, the Duke of Bedford, opened the new hospital on 8 December, now the Feast of the Immaculate Conception.

Directly above the hall is the chapel, once Church of Ireland (Protestant) but now used by all denominations. Dr Mosse, who was not one to squander hard-earned contributions, spent a large sum on its decoration, hoping to attract a prosperous congregation with charitable instincts – a good tear-jerking sermon could raise a considerable sum in those days, provided the right people came to listen. Bartholomew Cramillion was paid 300 guineas in 1755 for the amazing stucco ceiling; the three principal groups of plaster figures in the coving represent Faith, Hope and Charity, surrounded by an abundance of cherubs and angels interspersed with vines. It is the most extravagant figured plasterwork to be found in Dublin and must surely have inspired the local exponents of the art to ever greater flights of fancy. In 1756 Robert West, the Irish stuccodore, received nearly £1,000 for 'cornishes and plaistering' and for 'plaster and stucco' in the rest of the hospital and it is tempting to suppose that he watched Cramillion at work. Painted coats of arms of distinguished patrons of the hospital, including Mosse himself, surround the chapel. The

ABOVE Detail of the chapel
ceiling above the organ,
showing part of a decorative
scroll with the quote: 'Sons shall
grow up as the young plants and
our daughters as the polished
corners of the temple.'

RIGHT Bartholomew Cramillion
was responsible for the
astonishing stucco ornament in
the chapel, which is now
ecumenical.

LEFT Designed by Richard Castle
and built in 1751, the Rotunda
Hospital was the earliest
maternity hospital in the British
Isles.

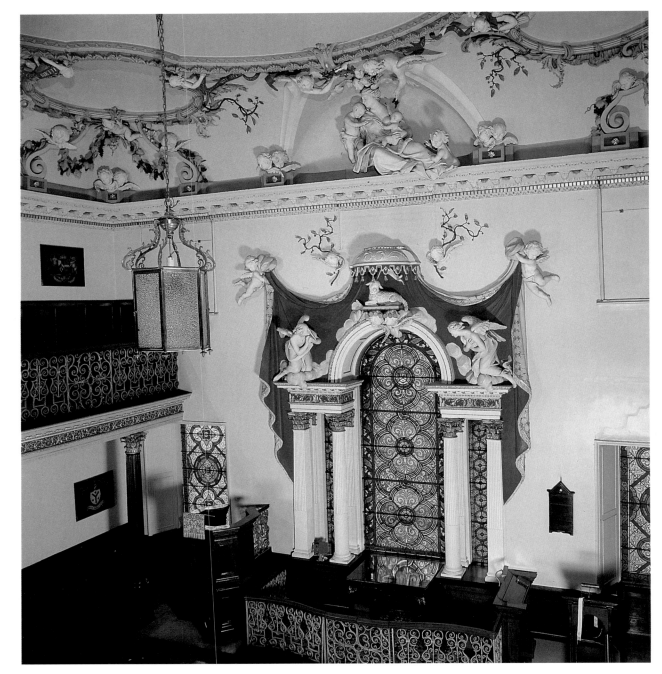

Victorian stained glass not only makes the chapel dark but also detracts
from the beauty of the entrance front of the building.

Dr Mosse chose the motto *Solamen Miseris*, or 'Succour for the
Needy', for the hospital. He, who had devoted his life to the
underprivileged, himself died a poor man in 1759 at the early age of
forty-seven, and his widow was forced to seek help from the governors
of the hospital in her financial distress. Before his death plans were
under way for a theatre, an assembly room and rooms for dining and
card-playing to bring in additional revenue. In 1764 Ensor added a
circular assembly room to the east, which is the origin of the name
Rotunda. Although quite splendid inside, the brick extension looked
out of place; in 1786 James Gandon raised the drum, gave it a
Coadestone frieze by Edward Smyth and plastered the brick to
resemble stone. He also designed a handsome entrance block at the
same time with niches, swags and stone urns on the parapet, which
provided the Rotunda with a foyer. Malton in his *Views of Dublin*
shows this addition duplicated on the other side of the entrance front.
The Rotunda was at the hub of Dublin life and was used for gatherings
of every kind. The Volunteer Convention, which sought to establish a
parliament independent from England, took place here in 1783,
presided over by the Earl of Charlemont; John Field, the Irish

composer who devised the Nocturne, held recitals, and Charles
Dickens gave his 'Readings' in the great round auditorium. The
Ambassador Cinema was the last tenant and the building is now empty.

In 1784–86 Richard Johnston, brother of the more famous Francis,
designed an assembly room (now the Gate Theatre), with an additional
function room below called the Pillar Room, in the grounds of the
hospital. Frederick Trench, a governor of the hospital and an amateur
architect, devised the layout of these rooms, which still bring an
income to the Rotunda Hospital. The Gate Theatre was opened in 1928
by Hilton Edwards and Micheál MacLiammóir for 'the production of
modern and progressive plays unfettered by theatrical convention'.
They were later joined by the Earl of Longford; their touring company
travelled the length of Ireland and even went as far afield as Cairo.
Orson Welles made his acting debut at the Gate, which has recently
enjoyed a successful revival.

Dr Mosse's hospital is the oldest purpose-built maternity hospital in
continuous service in these islands and has been responsible for saving
the lives of innumerable mothers and babies. The Rotunda is in the
forefront of obstetrical services in the world today, universally
recognised as a teaching hospital, equipped as it is with the latest
technological advancements.

ÁRAS an UACHTARÁIN
Phoenix Park

Áras an Uachtaráin, which means 'the house of the President' in Gaelic, is the official residence of the President of Ireland. The Áras stands in its own grounds, which form an island within the broad expanse of the Phoenix Park.

In 1751 the Rt Hon. Nathaniel Clements MP (1705–77) had been appointed Ranger and Master of the Game in the Phoenix Park. He was granted 92 acres here for the duration of his life and the lives of his three sons. While he was responsible for the park he proved a strict administrator, as the *Freeman's Journal* recounts: 'Under the rule of Mr Clements every impropriety was rigorously expelled from that beautified spot. Ill-looking strollers of either sex could never get admittance at the gate except on public occasions. Cars and noddies [the cheapest form of shay] were refused passage.'

On his estate Clements built himself a delightful red-brick country retreat called Phoenix Lodge which still stands at the heart of the Áras. It was a plain house with handsome stone urns on the parapets and stone balls on the curved sweeps which led to single-storey wings. The main block was five bays wide and above the front door there was a demi-lune, or Diocletian, window. On the garden front the wings had steep pediments with urns. The gates to the yard had carved phoenixes on the piers and there were, and still are, wrought-iron obelisks carrying lanterns on either side of the front steps.

Clements, who was an amateur architect and a friend of both Pearce and Castle, obtained plans from John Wood of Bath. Frederick O'Dwyer has noted that, although the dimensions of the house correspond to these, the layout of the rooms is different; it was sometimes the practice for amateur architects to commission designs from one or more professionals and alter them to suit their own taste. It was reported at the time: 'Last week a great variety of curious small Figures and Statues were landed at the Custom House, to ornament the fine gardens of Nathaniel Clements Esq. in Phoenix Park.'

Clements was a friend and associate of Luke Gardiner MP in politics and business: they both had town houses in Henrietta Street, Clements

at No. 7 and Gardiner at No. 10, and were jointly involved in the development of Georgian Dublin on the north side of the city. It is not surprising to learn that Gardiner also built a house in the Phoenix Park, now the headquarters of the Ordnance Survey.

In 1782 Robert Clements, later first Earl of Leitrim, sold Phoenix Lodge to the government to provide a summer retreat for the viceroy and it was re-named the Viceregal Lodge. The modest country house was subsequently enlarged several times as space was needed to accommodate visiting royalty and for official entertaining. In 1802 the garden front was extended at both ends under the supervision of Robert Woodgate. A carpenter by trade, Woodgate had been employed as an assistant to Sir John Soane before taking up the post of architect to the Irish Board of Works in 1802. In 1808 Woodgate's successor, Francis Johnston, added the front porch and in 1815 he designed the vast Ionic portico on the garden front which can be seen from the road. In 1849 Jacob Owen further extended the garden front to the east adding a ballroom for Queen Victoria's visit; five years later he balanced this addition on the western end of the facade. The queen returned for the Great Exhibition in Dublin in 1853 and for this occasion the park was lit by gas lamps, which are still in use.

In spite of all these additions, Clements' house of 1751 is still intact at the core of the present building. The front hall resembles the hall at Westport House, Co. Mayo, designed by Richard Castle in 1731, which also has a barrel-vaulted ceiling terminating in a demi-lune above the front door. The hall leads straight into the drawing room which has a compartmented ceiling made more ornate by the gilding of the plasterwork. The original pair of white marble mantels with key pattern ornament are still *in situ* as are the mahogany doors whose panels are edged in gilded egg and dart moulding. The Savonnerie carpet made at the Donegal carpet factory is based on a French Empire design. Two smaller rooms on either side of the drawing room – the library and the small dining room, which is used for meetings of the Council of State – are part of the original house.

LEFT Áras an Uachtaráin in the Phoenix Park, showing the entrance front with the central block, curved sweeps and wings of the original house built by Nathaniel Clements MP in 1751.

RIGHT The main drawing room at the centre of the original house has a compartmented gilded ceiling and a pair of white marble mantels. It opens out into the formal garden.

The plaster ceiling in the library was rescued from Mespil House in Dublin, which was built in the same year as the Phoenix Lodge and has since been demolished. It represents Jupiter with his thunderbolts, seated on a cloud and surrounded by the four elements with the four seasons in the corners. In the lightness of its flowing lines it embodies the true spirit of Rococo. The small dining room has a ceiling original to the house, which depicts scenes from Aesop's Fables. The long sides illustrate the story of the Fox and the Stork, and the short sides, the Fox and the Crow at one end and the Fox and the Grapes at the other; two groups of putti on clouds represent the seasons. Joseph McDonnell ascribes both these ceilings to Bartholomew Cramillion, the stucco-dore who is known to have decorated the chapel at the Rotunda Hospital.

The ballroom, built in 1802, is now known as the State Reception Room; it is where foreign envoys present their credentials to the president. Both here and in the corridor beyond there are plaster casts of plaques on the walls and ceiling at Riverstown House, Co. Cork, the work of Paul and Philip Lafranchini in 1745. The installation at Áras an Uachtaráin of mid-eighteenth-century plasterwork from Mespil House, which was demolished, and Riverstown House, whose future at the time was precarious, was the brilliant idea of Dr C.P. Curran, a personal friend of President Sean T. O'Kelly (1882–1966), and it is now hoped to establish a collection of eighteenth-century Irish furniture to complement the fine architecture of the house. Since her inauguration the president, Mary Robinson, and her husband Nicholas have welcomed to the Áras many people, both from Ireland and abroad, enabling them to enjoy the beauty of the house and grounds.

RIGHT The ceiling decoration in the small dining room is original to the house and is based on Aesop's fables. Illustrated here is the tale of the Fox and the Stork.

NO. 20 LOWER DOMINICK STREET

One of the most dramatic interiors of any Dublin house is concealed behind the uniform brick facade of 20 Lower Dominick Street. It was built in 1755 by Robert West (died 1790), architect and stuccodore. It was one of the first houses on this once fashionable street and is now one of the few to survive. Although the street is dominated today by the Dominicans who built their church of St Saviour here, its name comes from the Dominick family who owned the land on which it was laid out. Sir Christopher Dominick's daughter, Elizabeth, who inherited the property, married Lord St George of Headford, Co. Galway. Their daughter Emilia became the wife of the second Duke of Leinster in 1775, and the old estate office of the Dukes of Leinster continued to be run from their house, 13 Dominick Street, until 1957 when it was demolished as part of the clearance of the area by Dublin Corporation.

West leased three plots on Dominick Street from Elizabeth St George and, although he built No. 20 for himself, it was immediately leased to the Rt Hon. John Beresford, later First Commissioner of the Revenue. In 1758 West sold the house to the Hon. Robert Marshall, a Justice of the Court of Common Pleas, for £3,200. It passed through various hands until in 1856 it became a Protestant school where the sister of the playwright Sean O'Casey, Isabella, was a teacher and Sean himself lived here with his mother after 1887. In 1927 the Dominicans set up an orphanage in the house and today it is the headquarters of the National Youth Federation.

ABOVE Detail of the staircase decoration. West's ubiquitous birds may have been inspired by the seagulls that accompanied the sailing ships into Dublin harbour, as his workshop stood beside the River Liffey.

LEFT No. 20 Lower Dominick Street is now the home of the National Youth Federation. Robert West, the Irish architect and stuccodore, built this house for himself in 1755 but never lived here.

RIGHT Staircase decoration. With five bays, No. 20 was the largest house in the street and West gave it a spectacular staircase, including stucco birds projecting 16 inches from the surface of the wall.

The chief beauty of the house is the plaster decoration, the work of Robert West. He was employed as stuccodore in the Rotunda Hospital where Bartholomew Cramillion was completing the spectacular ceiling of the chapel and would have been influenced by Cramillion's masterpiece. West's particular hallmark was the bird, and as his workshop and builders' yard stood beside the River Liffey, he is thought to have been inspired by the seagulls flying overhead as they came up the river in the wake of the sailing ships. At No. 20 the birds, which are mounted on wire beneath the plasterwork and perched on asymmetrically placed Rococo stands, project 16 inches clear from the wall surface, incredibly lifelike and graceful. The main drawing room at the top of the stairs has the best ceiling. In the centre two putti are at play, a bird perched on one of their hoops, and eight other children, in various attitudes, are interspersed among musical instruments, flowers and Rococo arabesques. Joseph McDonnell has traced the origin of the putti to François Boucher. West is considered the greatest of the Irish stuccodores and No. 20 is his most flamboyant creation. Long may it survive.

THE STEPHEN'S GREEN CLUB
9 St Stephen's Green

No. 9 St Stephen's Green is remarkable in that it retains its full plot as laid out for it by Dublin Corporation in 1664, and the present house is probably only the second to stand here. Like so many Dublin houses its fortunes have alternated over the years with periods of splendour and periods of neglect, but for the last 150 years it has been cherished by the Stephen's Green Club, a centre of professional life in Dublin.

The building which is marked on Rocque's map of 1756 probably dates from that year, when an existing house of 1730 was renovated for the Rev. Cutts Harman, Dean of Waterford, possibly by Joseph Jarratt. Harman lived here from 1757 until his death in 1784 and gave the house its outstanding interior, making it a delight for enthusiasts of figured plasterwork in Ireland.

The dean bequeathed No. 9 to his nephew, Laurence Parsons, created first Earl of Rosse in 1806. The second earl sold the house in 1812 to the Huguenot banker, Peter La Touche of Bellevue, who died aged 95 in 1828; in 1831 it belonged to 'R. La Touche of Harristown'. It was seemingly during that family's ownership that the house was used as garrison lodgings. Sir Walter Scott came to Dublin in 1825 to visit his son, Captain Walter Scott of the 15th Hussars, and was surprised to find him sharing such a splendid house on St Stephen's Green with a fellow officer. Lockhart, the great author's son-in-law, quotes him in his *Life of Scott*: 'We reached Dublin in time for dinner, and found young Walter and his bride established in one of those large and noble houses in St Stephen's Green (the most extensive square in Europe), the founders of which little dreamt that they should ever be let at an easy rate as garrison lodgings.' In 1840 the Stephen's Green Club, formerly the Union Club, occupied the house and has been here ever since.

As is so often found in Dublin houses, the most lavish plaster decoration at No. 9 was on the staircase, too lavish for a living room where stucco on the walls would have made it impossible to hang

LEFT The stuccowork on the staircase of the Stephen's Green Club is by Paul and Philip Lafranchini and includes a panel on the landing of Juno's metamorphosis of Antigone into a stork.

RIGHT The reading room also has plasterwork by the Lafranchini brothers, whose decoration of the house has given it one of the most outstanding interiors in Dublin.

BELOW Detail of the reading room ceiling, representing the winged figure of Fortitude resting on clouds and surrounded by attendant putti symbolising different attributes.

paintings. At a reception a great deal of time would have been spent on the main staircase, as the drawing rooms were upstairs and the dining room had to be on the ground floor to be near the kitchen, which was in the basement. The walls and ceiling of the staircase at No. 9 were decorated by the Lafranchini brothers in 1756. Three years later they executed a larger version for 'Squire' Tom Conolly at Castletown, Co. Kildare, which is arguably the most beautiful staircase in Ireland. The panels with their elaborate Baroque frames surmounted by plumed heads were left empty of plasterwork in the country house, whereas at No. 9 they contain figures representing classical themes, creating a slightly overcrowded look. The metamorphosis by Juno of Antigone, the sister of Priam, into a stork can be seen at the head of the stairs. The Lafranchini brothers filled up the space between the frames in the same way as at Castletown, only in the town house there are medallions of Roman emperors instead of stucco family portraits.

The reading room upstairs has a Rococo ceiling full of life and symbolism, dominated by the Amazon-like figure of Fortitude with her sword, shield, attendant lion and cannon; an odd choice indeed for

an ecclesiastic. Joseph McDonnell has discovered that this figure is based on an engraving by M. Dorigny after a painting by Simon Vouet. The same authority has pointed out how influential the plasterwork surrounding this figure was on the evolution of Dublin Rococo, for example, at 86 St Stephen's Green across the square.

In the small drawing room, now part of the same room, there is a great winged figure of Fame resting on clouds and surrounded by her attendant putti. One of these is a child-king receiving suppliants and another represents Wisdom, with mirror and serpent. Mercury, bearing his caduceus, has two attendants, one pouring coins and the other emptying a cornucopia of fruit upon a starry sphere representing Earth. In the fourth corner Liberty is being crowned with a cap at the freeing of a slave.

It is enjoyable to contrast the sober-suited club men with the classical deities, cherubs and clouds that float above their heads. The Stephen's Green Club is faced with heavy expenditure on upkeep and its members are to be congratulated for maintaining their commitment to this great house.

MERRION SQUARE

Of all the Georgian squares in Dublin, it is Merrion Square that stands supreme for the purity of its architecture, the excellent state of its preservation and the subtle variety of its fanlights and doorways. The sheer length of the vistas of warm red brick, with the contrasting green of the park and the ever-changing Irish sky, combine to produce a streetscape that is uniquely Dublin. The great squares of Edinburgh and Bath were conceived as finite architectural entities, replete with pediments and pilasters, whereas the squares of Dublin depend for their effect on the cliff-like massing of the street as a whole. If Merrion Square happened to be longer or shorter by three or four houses, it would make little difference to the general appearance of the scheme. The facades are plain and reticent, enlivened by the white of the window reveals and differing from one another in the doorways and fanlights. A few houses have had elaborate wrought-iron balconies added in the nineteenth century. The subtle variations in roof and parapet lines and the diversity of window heights also enliven the square. The Wide Streets Commissioners, a planning body who from 1757 laid down rules that have resulted in the uniformity of the Dublin streetscape, did not apply them rigorously to the Fitzwilliam Estate, of which Merrion Square was a part, and there were certainly no rules to be obeyed when it came to the adornment of the interiors.

These terraced houses were usually built in groups of two or three, as may be readily seen by a glance across the square at the roof line opposite; sometimes the builder of three houses would live in one and rent out the others. When built, these houses had four storeys over a basement, with a garden leading to a mews and stabling at the back. The basement kitchen and servants quarters were lit from the lower ground area; wood and coal were stored beneath the pavement. A narrow front hall or vestibule led to the dining room on the ground floor. The main staircase, which often had an arched window on the landing, generally only went as far as the *piano nobile*, where the main drawing room faced the street and took up the entire width of the house. This gave into the smaller drawing room, sometimes with a rounded or bowed end, that faced the garden. These rooms were frequently thrown together in the Regency period to create one large L-shaped apartment. A secondary staircase led up to the bedrooms and nurseries at the top of the house.

Merrion Square was laid out from 1762 on land belonging to the sixth Viscount Fitzwilliam of Merrion, whose name is perpetuated in the nearby streets. The great house of the Earls of Kildare faced the square across its lawn from the west and this, together with the proximity of the Parliament House, helped to entice prospective purchasers to come and live here. Lord Fitzwilliam employed the architect John Ensor, who had been Richard Castle's assistant and had inherited his practice, to lay out the square. Ensor had been working for Luke Gardiner in the development of Rutland (now Parnell) Square, and in spite of being enticed to the south side by Fitzwilliam, he later returned to the Gardiner Estate.

The north side of Merrion Square was the first to be built and started with No. 1; most of the thirty-four houses on this side are faced in rusticated granite up to first-floor level. They have more individuality than their neighbours on the eastern and southern sides, having been built at an earlier date and by eight different builders and speculators.

The east side of the square was laid out in 1780 by Samuel Sproule, architect to the Wide Streets Commissioners. It forms one end of the longest Georgian streetscape in Dublin, which also incorporates Upper and Lower Fitzwilliam Street, Fitzwilliam Square and Fitzwilliam Place. Sixteen houses in Lower Fitzwilliam Street were demolished in 1965 by the Electricity Supply Board and replaced by a building which is out of context, but the rest of the vista survives. The sixteenth Earl of Pembroke, who owned the ground rents of these houses and was anxious to save them, was forced to sell the freehold in 1964. He gave half the compensation of £2,000 he received to the Irish Georgian Society, which had campaigned strenuously for the preservation of the facades.

The south side was completed in the 1790s and here the houses are taller and more uniform. It leads to Mount Street Crescent where the little 'pepper canister' church, on its island site, provides the focal point of one of Dublin's best-loved vistas. The land on which Merrion Square was built was low-lying and marshy, and in January 1792 part of the south wall of the Liffey collapsed. The *Dublin Chronicle* reported: 'His Grace the Duke of Leinster went on a sea-party, and after shooting the breach in the south wall sailed over the low ground in the south lots and landed safely at Merrion Square.'

Most of the west side of Merrion Square is bounded by Leinster Lawn, the garden of Leinster House, and was never developed. The lawn is flanked by the Natural History Museum and the National Gallery. Facing the National Gallery is the Rutland Fountain, built in 1791 to the designs of Francis Sandys to commemorate Charles Manners, fourth Duke of Rutland, the popular young viceroy who died in Ireland at the age of thirty-three. This lovely drinking fountain had fallen into disrepair and was restored in 1975 at the instigation of Dr James White, Director of the National Gallery, in memory of Sybil Le Brocquy, a passionate devotee of literature and the arts and mother of the artist, Louis Le Brocquy.

Until the Act of Union the square flourished, and many prominent citizens, members of parliament, peers and baronets lived here. After 1800 the aristocracy gradually gave place to the professional classes. George Herbert, eleventh Earl of Pembroke, inherited the Fitzwilliam Estate through the female line in 1816 and continued to develop it; the property was well run and proper maintenance ensured its survival. From then on the street names are associated with his family and with Wilton, his great house near Salisbury. Whereas the Gardiner Estate on the north side was split up and sold, the Pembroke Estate remained intact and is a good example of the advantages to an area that can result from private ownership. The south side of the Liffey had for long been

LEFT The north side of Merrion Square, with No. 1 on the corner, which was the residence of Sir William Wilde, surgeon and antiquarian, and the father of Oscar; Lady Wilde, the poetess 'Speranza', held her literary evenings here.

RIGHT The Rutland Fountain was designed by Francis Sandys as a drinking fountain in 1791 and restored in 1975 for Architectural Heritage Year in memory of Sybil Le Brocquy.

fashionable, and during the nineteenth century the more prosperous Dubliners gravitated even further south towards Ballsbridge and Donnybrook, greatly to the advantage of the Pembroke Estate.

In 1751 a few houses had been built to the north and south of Kildare House (later Leinster House) and are shown on Rocque's map of 1756 as being on Merrion Street, which now forms part of Merrion Square. No. 90 was purchased in 1986 by the National Gallery of Ireland which has embellished it with superb mirrors and furniture; some of these originally came from Russborough, Co. Wicklow, as part of the Milltown Bequest. Among the paintings here are portraits of Patrick Sarsfield, the Earl of Lucan and Jonathan Swift as well as works by Angelica Kauffman, Robert Hunter, Smith of Chichester and George Barret. No. 90 is one of the few Dublin houses today where the contents are superior to the architecture; it has been restored 'to suggest the home of a collector of the period' and a formal garden has been created at the back. The house is used for meetings by the Friends of the National Gallery and is available for holding receptions.

No. 1 Merrion Square was the home of Sir William Wilde, the surgeon and antiquarian, whose poetess wife 'Speranza' held her literary evenings here; their son Oscar had been born in 1854 at 21

ABOVE The Georgian streetscape of Merrion Square West, including Nos. 88–90, the first three houses from the left, which belong to the National Gallery.

RIGHT Formerly the home of Dr Arthur Chance, 90 Merrion Square was purchased in 1986 by the National Gallery of Ireland and is now used by the Friends of the Gallery. It is one of the few notable Georgian houses in Dublin where the contents are superior to the architecture.

LEFT The front hall of 90 Merrion Square, with a superbly carved mirror that once hung at Russborough, Co. Wicklow, and came to the National Gallery of Ireland as part of the Milltown bequest.

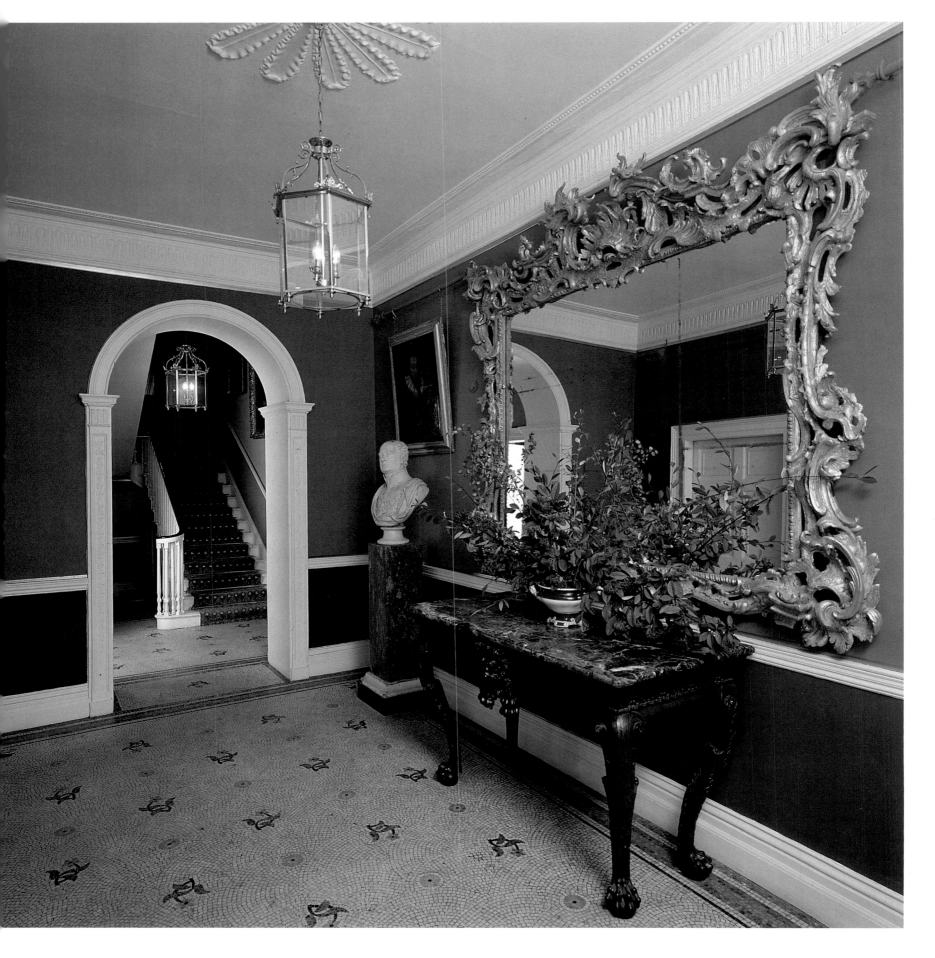

Westland Row, just around the corner. No. 39 Merrion Square belonged to the British Embassy; it was set on fire by an angry mob in 1972, as a result of an incident in Londonderry known to history as 'Bloody Sunday'. The house has since been restored by T. Austin Dunphy for the Electricity Supply Board and the plaster ceilings replaced. Sir Jonah Barrington (1760–1834) lived at No. 42; he was an MP, lawyer and the author of *Personal Sketches of his Own Times*, the raffish and amusing memoirs of a great original.

No. 49 belongs to National University of Ireland, whose constituents are the University Colleges of Dublin, Cork and Galway. The house dates from the 1790s but was renovated in 1814. Four years later it was leased by Robert Way Harty of Prospect Hall, Dublin; he was created a baronet in 1831, in which year, shortly before his death, he became Lord Mayor of Dublin. He commissioned a series of mural paintings for Mount Prospect and another for No. 49, which is illustrated here, the work of an unknown artist. As Marguerite Lillis has discovered, they represent Italian scenes taken from engravings of Paintings by Claude Lorrain, Salvatore Rosa, Rubens and others. These murals combine to create a romantic interior of nobility and style for the L-shaped room, which is used for meetings of the Senate of the National University.

Daniel O'Connell, the 'Liberator', lived at No. 58. No. 70, which now houses the Irish Arts Council, once belonged to Sheridan Le

ABOVE The front door of 71 Merrion Square, with a peacock-tail fanlight.

RIGHT The Senate Room of the National University of Ireland at 49 Merrion Square was painted with pastoral landscapes in *c*.1820. Lake Albano after G.F. Grimaldi is depicted above the mantel on the left and a landscape after Claude Lorrain above the mantel to the right.

ABOVE The dining room at No. 71. Princess Margaret of Hesse, the daughter of Lord Geddes, was born in this room.

LEFT The private drawing room at No. 71, which is both the residence of Miss Sybil Connolly, the Irish couturière, and the showroom for her clothes.

Fanu, one of the founding fathers of the Gothic novel. The Irish Architectural Archive, which has built up an invaluable collection of architectural drawings and photographs as well as a reference library devoted to Irish architecture, is established at No. 73. The poet, W.B. Yeats, lived at No. 82 from 1922 to 1928, and the poet, painter and journalist, George 'AE' Russell, whose bust is in the park, worked at No. 84.

No. 71 was built in 1782 for Judge Henn, one of the Henns of Paradise House in Co. Clare. Princess Margaret of Hesse and the Rhine was born here earlier this century, the daughter of Lord Geddes, Professor of Anatomy at the Royal College of Surgeons. For the last thirty-seven years No. 71 has served as workshop, showroom and home for Sybil Connolly, the well-known Irish couturière, famous for the pleated linen with which the walls of her salon are covered. Besides her fashion house she has made a name for herself designing china, glass, linen and textiles as well as being an interior decorator of great skill.

The Catholic hierarchy purchased the park in the centre of Merrion Square in the 1920s with a view to building a cathedral here but the idea was abandoned; in 1974 it was taken over by Dublin Corporation who have created an extensive public garden, beautifully cared for by the Parks Department.

THE LATE
GEORGIAN PERIOD

The 1760s could be taken as a turning point in architectural styles. From then on the design of the buildings and their interiors became less robust and more refined, with the introduction of the Neoclassical or Adam style. Dublin was the centre of taste and fashion and led the way when it came to architectural styles, introducing them, as it were, to the rest of the country. In the provinces things were slow to change and the Palladian idiom with Rococo plasterwork continued to flourish. The Mayoralty House in Cork, for example, was built by the Savoyard architect, Davis Ducart, in 1770 and is embellished with Rococo plasterwork by Patrick Osborne of Waterford.

These were the years of the Grand Tour, when it was the ambition of architects and their patrons to visit Rome and, if possible, Greece to study the ancient buildings at first hand. Lord Charlemont spent several years in Rome, where he was acquainted with Giambattista Piranesi (1720–1778), whose etchings depicted Roman antiquities in a new light. His magnum opus *Antichità Romane* was dedicated to Lord Charlemont.

Neoclassicism began as a reaction to the excesses of the Baroque and Rococo styles; it was seen as a desire to revert to purity and to go back to the source, that is, to the ancient buildings of Greece and Rome in their 'noble Simplicity and calm Grandeur'. Geometrical restraint and the use of antique sources for ornament, together with a tendency towards severity, were the hallmarks of Neoclassical building and the orders were used with a structural purpose rather than being applied to gain a decorative effect. Plain clear-cut lines came to be valued.

Within, the plasterwork was more delicate and in less high relief, almost flat on the surface of the wall. Michael Stapleton (*fl.* 1770–1801), who was both architect and stuccodore, inherited Robert West's practice and became the leading exponent of the Adam style in Ireland. The best private house designed and decorated by him is Belvedere House, Great Denmark Street, and his work at Trinity College in the Chapel and the Examination Hall is equally fine. It is often regretted, however, that the use of moulds, introduced at this time, put an end to the freehand plasterwork in which Dublin is so rich, although Michael

Stapleton was unusual in that he continued to work freehand as well as in the Adam style.

The earliest Neoclassical building in Ireland is the Marino Casino at Clontarf, designed by Sir William Chambers (1723–1796) in 1758 for the Earl of Charlemont. The Casino was also one of the first buildings of its type in Europe and well ahead of trends in Dublin. A later example, designed by the Irish architect Thomas Ivory (*c.* 1732–86), is the Newcomen Bank on Castle Street, with its cut-stone swags and medallions, which, as Maurice Craig has written, 'is the only building in Dublin which looks as though it might have been designed by one of the Adams'.

The competition for the design of the Royal Exchange in 1768 caused great interest in the architectural profession on both sides of the Irish Sea. There was a strong feeling that no Irish architect was fully conversant with the Neoclassical style and the Dublin merchants wanted a building that was right up to date. Thomas Cooley (1740–84) from London emerged the winner and came to Ireland where he remained for the rest of his life. James Gandon, whose drawings for the competition are lost, came second; had he won, he would have come to Ireland ten years earlier than he did. In 1771 Cooley designed a chapel in the grounds of the Royal Hibernian Military School in the Phoenix Park, now St Mary's Hospital for the aged; he only lived for five years after the Royal Exchange was completed in 1779.

Powerscourt House, South William Street, was designed by Robert Mack (*fl.* 1765–1780) in 1771, a date that would appear much too late for its busy Baroque exterior. The interior of the house is in two different styles, Rococo plasterwork in the hall and staircase by James McCullagh and Adamesque plasterwork elsewhere by Michael Stapleton, who used the same plaques here as are found at 16 St Stephen's Green. The wood-carving, especially fine on the staircase, is by Ignatius McDonagh. This was one of the grandest private houses in

The drawing room of the Royal Irish Academy of Music, 36 Westland Row, has an elaborate Adamesque ceiling. The house was built for Nicholas Tench of Fassaroe, Co. Wicklow, in 1771.

ABOVE Aspects of the Royal Irish Academy of Music: a door (above) with a pressed pewter surround, which leads to the drawing room with its painted roundels, and a Gothic mantel (top) with a grate to match.

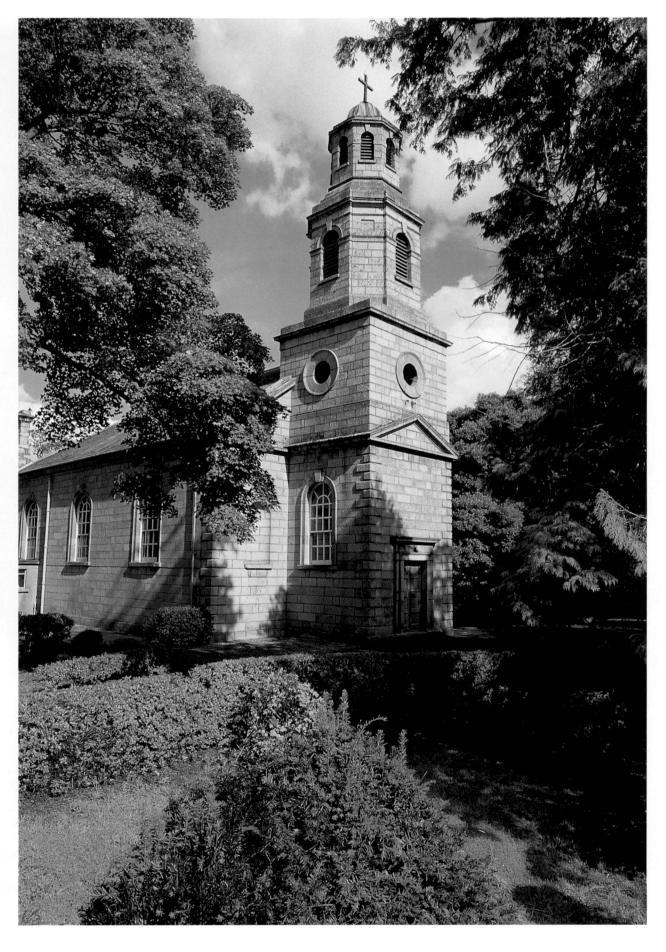

RIGHT Chapel built by Thomas Cooley in 1771 in the grounds of the former Hibernian Military School, now St Mary's Hospital, Phoenix Park.

RIGHT The architect of
Powerscourt House, South
William Street, was Robert
Mack, the Rococo plasterwork
was by James McCullagh, the
Adamesque interiors were by
Michael Stapleton and the wood
carving on the staircase was by
Ignatius McDonagh.

BELOW Powerscourt House
stands on a narrow street and is
the least known and most
extraordinary of Dublin's great
stone mansions. Its busy
Baroque facade and attendant
arches seem to belong to an
earlier date than 1771 when it was
built.

Dublin, built of granite from Lord Powerscourt's own quarry in the Wicklow Hills. The house has little curved sweeps on either side, attached to triumphal arches with bands of elaborate rustication. It is difficult to obtain a good view of the facade as Powerscourt House is tucked away in a narrow street beside the Civic Museum. This is the Museum of the City of Dublin, which makes an ideal starting point for exploring the capital. In 1981 Powerscourt House was converted into a large shopping centre and the courtyard was glazed over; the developer was Robin Power, whose treatment of the house has been sensitive.

The present Deanery of St Patrick's Cathedral dates from 1783; it was built on the site of the original house lived in by Swift, which had been destroyed by fire two years previously. In Swift's day the garden extended to a quarter of an acre but as he was such an enthusiastic gardener even this was not enough. He leased the Cabbage Garden, now the site of the Meath Hospital, where Cromwell had grazed his horses, and renamed it Naboth's Vineyard. Swift planted fruit trees here as well as flowers and shrubs, interspersed by serpentine paths. He was in close touch with Alexander Pope in England, who shared his dislike of the stiff formal garden fashionable at the time. Pope's three rules were: Contrasts, the Management of Surprises and the Conceal-ment of Bounds. Swift's friends, Dean Patrick Delany and his wife Mary, who lived at Delville, Glasnevin (now demolished), shared these views on gardening.

James Gandon (1742–1823) came to Ireland to build the Custom House at the behest of the Rt Hon. John Beresford, Chief Commis-sioner of the Irish Revenue. Gandon was the son of a French Protestant father and a Welsh mother. He was born in London and was apprenticed to Sir William Chambers at the age of fifteen. Chambers' theory was set out in his *Treatise*; he recommended forming 'if you can a style of your own in which [you] endeavour to avoid the faults and blend the perfections of all'. Gandon designed three major public buildings in Dublin – the Custom House, the Four Courts and the King's Inns – and added on a handsome new portico to the great Parliament House. In 1786 he built the Royal Military Infirmary in the Phoenix Park, now Army General Headquarters.

In 1777 the Wide Streets Commissioners, who had been established in 1757 to create a wide street from Dublin Castle to Essex Bridge and had subsequently stayed together as the city planning body, were given a grant to extend Sackville Street (now O'Connell Street) to the river, which involved demolishing a warren of lanes and houses. In 1785 it was decided to continue the street over the river with a new bridge. A grant of £15,000 was obtained and Carlisle (now O'Connell) Bridge was completed to Gandon's designs in 1795. His original design included colonnades over the footpaths which were never built because of the expense. He commissioned Edward Smyth to carve the keystone heads for the central arch but, when the bridge was widened in 1880 and renamed, these were replaced; the original heads can be seen on the front of a warehouse at 32 Sir John Rogerson's Quay.

ABOVE The Four Courts, overlooking the River Liffey, with Tailors Hall in the immediate foreground and across the road to the left the two neighbouring churches of St Audoen's (Protestant left, Catholic right).

FAR RIGHT BELOW Life-sized portrait of Dean Swift by Francis Bindon in St Patrick's Deanery, with St Patrick's Cathedral in the background of the painting.

RIGHT Detail of the blackened frame of the Swift portrait at St Patrick's Deanery, incorporating a serpent, a Hibernia and an open book. It was carved by John Houghton, who was paid £18 13s.

ABOVE The present Army General Headquarters, Phoenix Park, was built as the Royal Military Infirmary in 1786 to the designs of James Gandon.

Sackville Street became a wide avenue with shops that were part of the architectural plan. The Wide Streets Commissioners had thought in terms of a broad boulevard before London or Paris had done so. Westmoreland Street across the river was also developed to make a continuing thoroughfare to Trinity and the Parliament House. Thus the city began to move east and Sackville Street became its main north-south axis, replacing Capel Street and Essex Bridge.

Gandon was by far the most brilliant architect of his day at work in Ireland and his public buildings rank with the finest in Europe. Many years after his retirement he was told that George IV intended to honour him with a knighthood when the royal cortège passed through Lucan in 1821. The old man was wheeled down in his chair to wait beside the road but the king took another route and Gandon was pushed back up the hill without the honour being conferred. On grounds of old age he declined the position of the Presidency of the Royal Hibernian Academy, offered him by Francis Johnston on its foundation in 1823. Gandon died at his house in Lucan later that year at the age of eighty. He was buried in Drumcondra graveyard.

During this period tensions between the English and Irish parliaments came to a head. Poynings Law of 1494, followed by a law of George I in 1719, had bound Ireland to obey laws made by king and council at Westminster. England had thus assumed the power to

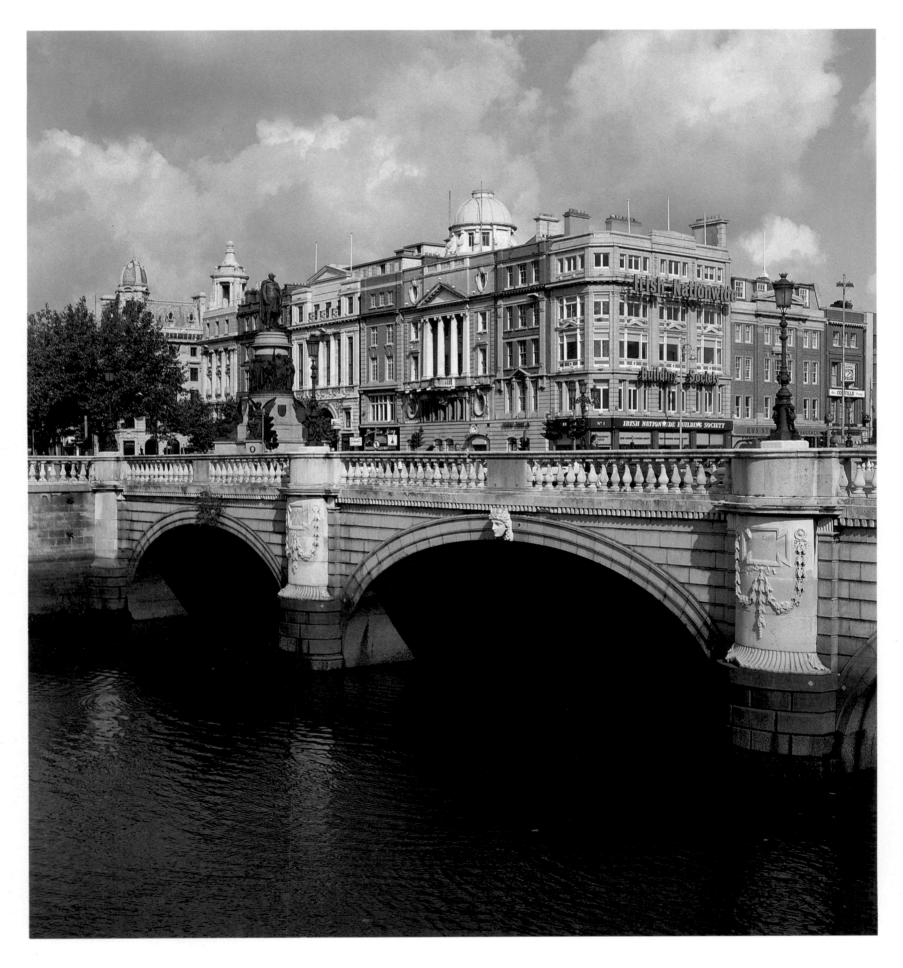

LEFT O'Connell Bridge and Monument. The monument was made by John Henry Foley (1818–74), who died before it was completed. On the base there is a figure of Erin depicted holding the Act of Catholic Emancipation in her left hand while pointing to Daniel O'Connell with her right.

RIGHT Aldborough House, North Circular Road, was the last great private house built in Dublin. It was completed just before the Act of Union and was hardly lived in by the Stratfords, Earls of Aldborough, who also built Stratford House in London.

override the Irish parliament and did not hesitate to impose any trade restrictions or embargoes which suited its own economic situation. It had prohibited imports of Irish cattle into England and had similarly attacked the wool trade. Watching the struggle of the colonies for independence, the Anglo-Irish Ascendancy became restive and sought freedom for their own parliament and the right to free trade. The situation was further exacerbated by bans and embargoes on trade with the colonies as a result of the American War of Independence. The 'Volunteer Movement' arose from this Anglo-Irish unrest and was formed from nobility and gentry led by the Earl of Charlemont; at its National Convention in 1783 its members numbered 80,000.

In 1782, due in some measure to Henry Grattan (1746–1820), an honest, courageous and powerful politician, the Irish parliament was granted legislative independence from Britain and control over its trade. Grattan's famous speech – 'Spirit of Swift! Spirit of Molyneux! Your genius has prevailed, Ireland is now a Nation' – invoked the great figures who had sought this freedom in the past. The nineteen years of this parliament were the peak of Anglo-Irish political achievement. The favourable economic conditions to which it gave rise were reflected in the amount of money which was available to spend on public buildings and for the establishment of the Grand and Royal Canals, the embankment of the Liffey and the laying down of roads.

The last decade of the eighteenth century culminated in the rebellion of 1798. The Ascendancy, which had become sympathetic to the Catholics, began to be afraid, especially after the French Revolution, which opposed the aristocracy and was jealous of its property and power; as a result the Volunteer Movement collapsed and anti-Catholic feeling grew. Although the Penal Laws had been relaxed, the five and a half million Catholics in Ireland had no satisfactory representation in parliament and could hold no public office. The 'United Irishmen' was an organization formed in Belfast, which aimed to overthrow the government, declare an independent republic and redress the grievances of the Catholic population. The headquarters were moved to Dublin and Wolfe Tone, a Protestant, emerged as the leader. The rebellion of 1798 was a peasants' revolt and, as the rebels were armed

only with pikes, they stood no chance against the soldiery; the slaughter was appalling, costing an estimated 30,000 lives. In 1796 a hoped-for French invasion had been aborted when gales in Bantry Bay forced the ships carrying 20,000 men to return to France. French troops did land at Killala, Co. Mayo, in 1798, but after marching half-way across Ireland they were defeated.

The 1798 rebellion resulted in the Act of Union with Britain long dreaded by those who opposed it. Henry Grattan, who had done so much to stir up feelings of patriotism among his fellow members of the House of Commons, practically had to be carried to his seat so that he could attend on the fatal day when the Act was debated. This was to abolish the Dublin parliament and establish direct rule from Westminster; the Act was passed with the help of considerable bribes. In spite of his physical condition Grattan spoke memorably:

> The constitution may be *for a time* so lost; the character of the country cannot be so lost; the Ministers of the Crown will, or may perhaps at length, find that it is not so easy to put down forever an ancient and respectable nation, by abilities, however great, and by power and by corruption, however irresistible . . . Identification is a solid and imperial maxim, necessary for the preservation of freedom – necessary for that of empire; but without union of hearts identification is extinction, is dishonour, is conquest.
>
> Yet I do not give up the country; I see her in a swoon, but she is not dead. Though in her tomb she lies helpless and motionless, still there is on her lips a spirit of life, and on her cheek a glow of beauty.

The Union left a situation worse than before. The effect on Dublin was sad; it became 'an echoing shell, full of grand but redundant buildings' in the words of the historian, R.F. Foster. The viceregal court carried on but without its glitter, and the members of parliament with their bribes went back to their estates to 'improve' their country seats with ill-gotten Gothic battlements. They were badly missed by the Dublin tradespeople. It was estimated that the members of the Lords and the Commons between them may have spent half a million pounds a year in the capital. The last great Dublin town house,

LEFT The front hall of Sir Patrick Dun's Hospital. The architect, Sir Richard Morrison gave the hospital a grand interior with good, if rather heavy, plasterwork, which is still intact.

RIGHT Portobello House, Portobello Road, was built as a hotel for passengers on the Grand Canal, which went as far as the River Shannon, linking Dublin and Limerick. It was designed in 1807 by Thomas Colbourne, the canal company's architect and engineer.

Aldborough House, was completed in the unhappy year of 1798 and hardly lived in by its builder, the Earl of Aldborough, who died three years later. The east wing once contained a theatre; another unusual feature was the circular drawing room which opened out into the garden on axis to the front door. This great mansion is now owned by Telecom Éireann and is used as offices and a depot.

Although the building of great private houses came to an end, the nineteenth century was noted for the erection of public buildings and institutions. One of the earliest of these, Sir Patrick Dun's Hospital, was designed in 1803 by Sir Richard Morrison (1767–1849), who had one of the largest country-house practices in Ireland, working in partnership with his son William Vitruvius in both Neoclassical and

ABOVE Sir Patrick Dun's Hospital, Grand Canal Street, Lower, was designed in 1803 by Sir Richard Morrison and was well restored in 1987 by the Institute of Clinical Pharmacology.

Gothic styles as well as Tudor and Jacobethan. The building was purchased in 1987 by the Institute of Clinical Pharmacology, which effected an extensive restoration programme, removing partitions, uncovering original ceilings and replacing the glazing bars. It is said to have been modelled on the Royal Military Infirmary designed by Gandon and has similar niches, blank arches and plaques on the facade. Sir Richard also designed the wooden triumphal arch erected beside the Rotunda for the visit of George IV in 1821, which appears in Turner de Lond's painting of the royal procession that hangs in the National Gallery of Ireland.

Francis Johnston (1760–1829), the leading architect in Ireland after Gandon, was equally at home in both Neoclassical and Gothic styles. He started his career as a pupil of Thomas Cooley in Armagh, and when his master died in 1784, Johnston completed the buildings begun by Cooley for the primate. He came to Dublin where he built up a huge practice and was made architect to the Board of Works in 1805. The exteriors of his Classical buildings are plain and without any ornament, rendering them severe in contrast to the sumptuous interiors, which although heavy and masculine are full of interest and ingenuity. His Gothic castles are masterly, the finest being Charleville Forest, Co. Offaly. He began his career in Dublin in 1802, designing the Classical St George's Church, Hardwicke Place, with its beautiful slender spire, and ended it with the Royal Hibernian Academy, Abbey Street, which he erected at his own expense. His best-known work in Dublin is the General Post Office in O'Connell Street, built in 1814, with statues by John Smyth of Fidelity, Hibernia and Mercury crowning the pediment. It is a historical building now because of its role in the Easter Rising of 1916, when the Proclamation of Independence was read from its steps. A memorial in the form of a statue of Cúchulainn by Oliver

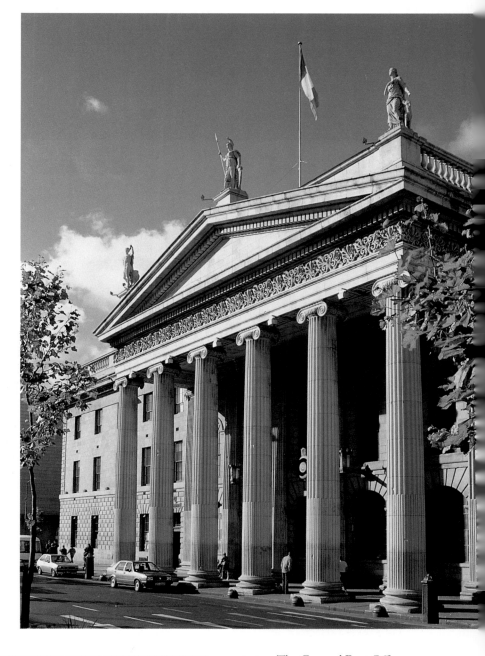

ABOVE The General Post Office, O'Connell Street, was built in 1814 to the designs of Francis Johnston. The building was seized during the Easter Rising in 1916 and became the rebel headquarters; the Proclamation of Irish Independence was read from the steps by Patrick Pearse. As a result of the fighting and shelling most of the street was destroyed.

LEFT The Gate Theatre, Cavendish Row, and the Pillar Room beneath were built as assembly rooms. Both were part of the Rotunda Hospital complex and helped earn revenue for the upkeep of the hospital.

RIGHT Inside the Gate Theatre, which together with the Pillar Room, was designed in 1784 by the architect Richard Johnston, brother of the more famous Francis.

ABOVE The Wellington Testimonial, Phoenix Park, was designed by Sir Robert Smirke in 1814 as a gesture of thanks to the Iron Duke and paid for by public subscription. After the Duke's death Joseph Robinson Kirk, Thomas Farrell and John Hogan each designed a panel in bronze for the base of the monument.

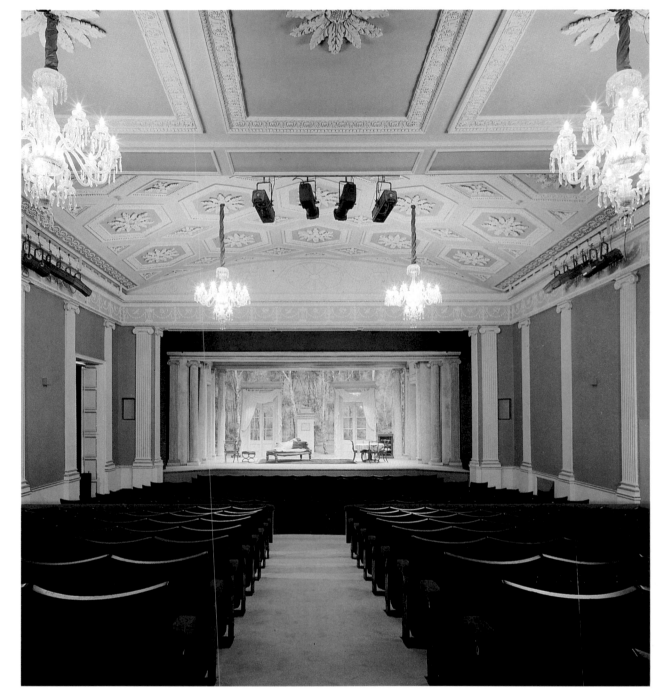

Sheppard stands in the public office, to commemorate all those who lost their lives here in the struggle for freedom.

The Chapel Royal in Dublin Castle is one of Johnston's few Dublin buildings in the Gothic style. Johnston lived in Eccles Street where, at the end of his garden, he built a timber replica of a Gothic church tower, in which he installed a peal of bells. He greatly enjoyed ringing them himself, to the dismay of his neighbours, and the story goes that he was eventually persuaded to present the bells to St George's Church, which he had designed nearby. The Assembly Room, which is now the Gate Theatre, was designed in 1784 by Richard Johnston, brother of Francis, and, together with the Pillar Room below, was used for balls and assemblies to raise funds for the Rotunda Hospital. The general

plan was devised by Frederick Trench, one of the Wide Streets Commissioners and a governor of the hospital.

In spite of the general decline in the fortunes of Dublin in the aftermath of the Union, the nineteenth century saw great activity in the building of churches. It is sometimes forgotten that half the population of Dublin was Protestant and churches were better attended then than they are today – overcrowding in churches and chapels was a problem for both denominations. It was hoped in vain that Catholic Emancipation would be granted with the Act of Union, but full representation in parliament was not won for the Catholics until 1829. A spate of church building then ensued – a valuable adornment to the city in terms of art and architecture as well as spirituality.

THE HUGH LANE MUNICIPAL GALLERY OF MODERN ART/CHARLEMONT HOUSE

Parnell Square

James Caulfeild, first Earl of Charlemont (1728–99), commissioned Sir William Chambers to build his great town house in 1762. He purchased a double site at the centre of the north side of what is now Parnell Square; this side came to be known as Palace Row on account of the magnificence of his house. It looked down across the Rotunda Gardens to Richard Castle's Lying-in Hospital, which resembled a country house with curved colonnades. Charlemont House is built of brick with a limestone facade and curved sweeps to either side. A pair of obelisks found in the basement by the curator,

cabinet for the display of medals and seals; the cabinet was designed by Chambers and is now on view at Somerset House in London, of which he was also the architect. The smaller, 'Venus' Library contained a marble statue of Venus by Joseph Wilton, who carved the attendant Egyptian lions or leopards at the Marino Casino. Charlemont commissioned James Gandon to build a library in 1789 which has now been demolished. It was Gandon's most important domestic work in Dublin after the apartments in the Custom House that he designed for the Rt Hon. John Beresford. The library had a half-domed apse at

LEFT Charlemont House (now the Hugh Lane Municipal Gallery of Modern Art) was designed in 1762 by Sir William Chambers for the first Earl of Charlemont. Much of the original interior survives.

RIGHT *The Breton Girl* by Roderic O'Conor hangs in the front hall above a mantel designed by Chambers, which has been in the house since it was built.

Patrick O'Connor, in the 1950s have been re-erected in their original position beside the front door, placed with the help of the engraving in Pool and Cash's *Views of the City of Dublin* (1780). Chambers, who also designed the Casino at Marino for Lord Charlemont, made the new house five bays wide and three storeys high, the landing on the top floor lit by a cupola. Some interesting original features remain in the interior, notably the stone fireplace designed by Chambers in the entrance hall, and the handsome staircase with its wrought-iron balusters, lit by *œil-de-bœuf* windows. This leads up to a series of rooms, which have also escaped alteration, with compartmented ceilings typical of the architect. One room contains an inlaid marble mantel by Pietro Bossi, an Italian who lived in Dublin and made this type of work his speciality.

Charlemont was a man of taste and refinement and a great collector. He owned paintings by Rembrandt, Titian and Hogarth as well as a great number of books. As his book collection grew he was obliged to add on new libraries at the back of the house. The large library, which Charlemont used as his study, contained a very grand architectural

either end and was lit by round windows high up in the side walls. A bust of the Marquess of Rockingham, after whom the room was named, stood above a mantel at one end, opposite a bust of General Wolfe.

Charlemont became one of the cultural leaders of Dublin. As a young man he had made a prolonged Grand Tour between 1746 and 1755. During this time he spent eight years in Rome where he met and befriended Chambers, Reynolds, Robert Adam and many other leading artistic figures of the day. In 1748–9 he made a pioneering trip to Turkey, Egypt and Greece where his draftsman made the first accurate measured drawings of the Parthenon. He was a close friend and ally of Henry Grattan and in 1779 became leader of the Volunteer Movement, which supported the Irish parliament in its fight for legislative independence. Edmund Burke, the orator, said of him: 'Lord Charlemont is a man of such polished manners, of a mind so truly adorned, and disposed to the adoption of whatever is excellent and praiseworthy, that to see and converse with him, would alone induce me, or might induce anyone who relished such qualities, to pay a visit

LEFT The staircase hall. Charlemont House was purchased by Dublin Corporation in 1929 to house the city's municipal art collection. Some of it was bequeathed by Sir Hugh Lane, a brilliant connoisseur and art collector, who was drowned when the Lusitania was torpedoed in 1915.

RIGHT The sculpture gallery, which includes a bust of Sir Hugh Lane (left) by Albert Power and the painting *Eva Gonzales* (centre) by Manet.

BELOW A superb Bossi mantelpiece with an engraved grate in an upstairs room used for special exhibitions.

to Dublin.' (Francis Hardy's *Memoirs of the Earl of Charlemont*.) Despite being so much involved in the cultural affairs of the city, Charlemont was unable to speak in public. As he said himself:

> I have gone down to the House determined to speak. Nay, I have often gone so far as to write my speech, and to get it by heart. But all in vain. When I attempted to rise, every effort of my mind was baffled by my bodily weakness. My recollection was lost, my courage was gone; and the aggregate of those very men, whom singly and individually I despised, was sufficient to terrify me from my purpose.

Lord Charlemont died in 1799, just before the passing of the Act of Union which he had opposed for so long and dreaded so much. His son, Francis William, who lived to be the last surviving member of the old Irish House of Commons, kept up Charlemont House until his death in 1863. His nephew, James, the third earl, sold the house to the government in 1876, and it was used as the General Register Office for the next fifty years.

In 1929 Charlemont House was purchased by Dublin Corporation for the display of the Municipal Art Collection which belongs to the city. The building was partly chosen because, as it stood on its own, it was thought to be safer from the risk of fire. A sculpture hall and nine galleries were erected at the back of the house. A room here was, for a time, purposely kept empty for the French masterpieces belonging to Sir Hugh Lane (1875–1915), who drowned when the Lusitania was torpedoed off the south coast of Cork. Lane, whose father was an Anglican minister in Cork for a time, was the nephew of Lady Gregory who introduced him to W.B. Yeats and other leaders of the Irish literary revival. He was inspired to found a gallery of modern art in

Dublin, believing that the absence of a talented school of modern Irish painting was due to the lack of good examples. Lane became a brilliantly successful art dealer and from 1914 to 1915 he was Director of the National Gallery of Ireland, to which he presented many great paintings.

Lane had left his collection of French Impressionist masterpieces to the National Gallery in London. In 1915, before departing on the fatal voyage, he added a codicil to his will leaving these paintings to Ireland; he signed the codicil but omitted to have it witnessed and therefore it was declared invalid. Legally the pictures belonged to England but morally to Ireland; the collection remained in London. After prolonged negotiations a satisfactory compromise was agreed between Dublin and London whereby the majority of the paintings in the bequest are on loan to the Hugh Lane Gallery.

The gallery was renamed the Hugh Lane Municipal Gallery of Modern Art on the one hundredth anniversary of Lane's birth, despite the fact that he had modestly asked that his name should not be used. Besides the Lane collection the gallery owns a collection of paintings of remarkable quality, including works by Corot, Monet, Bonnard, Degas, Rouault, and Boldini. The sculpture collection includes the Age of Bronze by Rodin and a bust of Lady Gregory by Epstein. Among the Irish artists represented are Yeats (father and son), Lavery, Orpen, Osborne and Mainie Jellett. Free lectures and concerts are held in the Sculpture Hall on Sundays, and an excellent restaurant has been started in the vaulted basement.

If Lord Charlemont could see the use to which his great house has been put, and the joy it gives to both to Dubliners and visitors, he would surely be very pleased.

THE CASINO AT MARINO
Clontarf

The Marino Casino is one of the most exquisite buildings in Europe, equally beautiful from whatever aspect it is viewed; its sculptural ornament is original in its detail and fastidious in its execution. The Casino was built for the first Earl of Charlemont from 1758 to the design of Sir William Chambers, who wrote that he had originally conceived it as a wing pavilion in his rejected plans for Harewood, Yorkshire. Marino House, Lord Charlemont's marine villa, was situated where he could take the air and entertain at a distance of only a mile from his Dublin town house. The Casino is all that is left of the house and the elaborate landscaped park, with a lake and a rustic cottage, which surrounded it.

The Marino Casino, or 'little house by the sea', as it translates from the Italian, is said to have cost £20,000 to build, a huge sum in those days. The workmen are supposed to have been cautioned that 'every broken stone is another townland gone'. It is an uncommonly perfect building, deceptive in that it appears to contain one room whereas in fact there are fifteen rooms on three floors. T. Austin Dunphy notes that from the exterior the building looks like one room for a giant, whereas the interior is designed with doll's house proportions, like a miniature palace. A canopy could be erected on the flat roof in fine weather so that Lord Charlemont could admire the view of Dublin harbour, with the gentle contours of the Wicklow hills as a distant backdrop.

The carving of the four attendant lions (John Hardy, the noted

RIGHT The saloon, with its wooden inlaid floor and coved ceiling, once had a mantelpiece and marble table, both inlaid with lapis lazuli; the table was supplied by Joseph Wilton.

ABOVE Three mahogany doors in the entrance hall.

LEFT The Marino Casino, Clontarf, is an elaborate garden pavilion which was designed by Sir William Chambers.

scholar, has described them as Egyptian leopards) that guard the building is attributed to Joseph Wilton, best known for having made the gilded state coach used at coronations in London, which was also designed by Chambers. Some of the twelve free-standing columns that surround the building are hollow, to take the rainwater from the roof while avoiding any unsightly drainpipes; the fluting on the urn above the lower ground area is pierced to allow the water to escape. Simon Vierpyl, who was in charge of the building work, was also responsible for most of the beautiful carved ornament, including the urns on the parapet, once functional chimneys.

The miniscule front hall has a fireplace on one side with a window opposite; a glass screen above the front door, which could be pulled down to make a window, turned the hall into an additional room from where the northern side of the park could be enjoyed. The compartmented ceiling has a plaster trophy with the lyre of Apollo in the centre, and the frieze is decorated with garlands of flowers, urns and musical instruments. The dado is in the form of Vitruvian waves, and the most unusual feature is the floor, inlaid with an intricate arrangement of rare woods. Three mahogany doors in the apse face the entrance, surmounted by a coffered semi-dome. The double door leads to the saloon where the head of Apollo, amidst his sun-burst, looks down from the centre of the coved and coffered ceiling. Chambers wrote to Charlemont in 1769 recommending 'that the Entablature, door(case) etc. of the room should be dead white touched with blue and that the cove parts of the ceiling . . . be of a more brilliant white'. The original chimneypiece, which had a lapis-lazuli plaque, was carved in Rome by Francis Harwood in about 1768. A table with a matching lapis-lazuli top was made by Wilton in London; both mantel and table disappeared during the nineteenth century.

Two small rooms open off the saloon: on the left is the library with a domed ceiling surrounded by the signs of the zodiac and on the right is the china closet, formerly a bedroom with the best inlaid floor to be

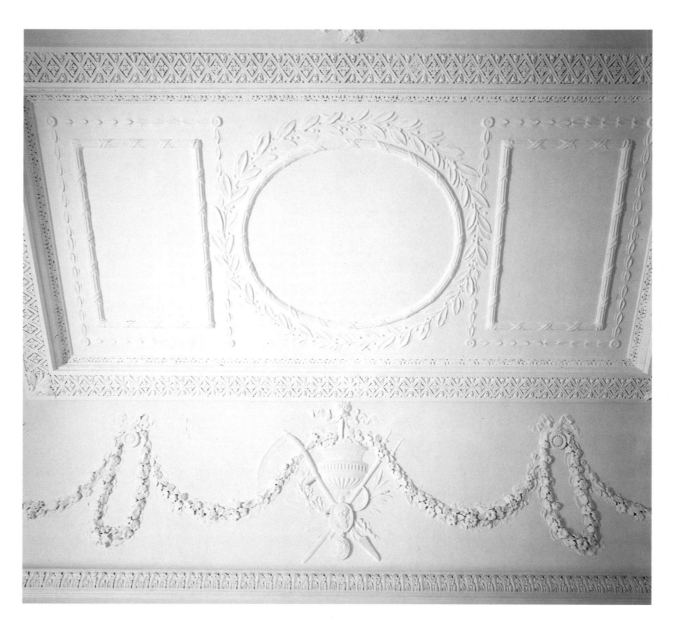

ABOVE The ceiling of the china closet, with a scythe and a pitch-fork in the coving.

LEFT The china closet, lit by a section of the one large window on this side of the building. The floor is the most intricate of all the inlaid wood floors at the Casino.

found here. Séan O'Reilly, author of the Casino guide, describes the decoration in the coving: '... hanging garlands frame rustic variants of antique trophies. Instead of the ancient Roman shield, spear and sword, we find ... the rake, spade and scythe.' A narrow flight of stairs, whose only decoration is a gigantic stucco shell, leads up to the bedrooms where the State Bedroom has a floor inlaid with the Greek key pattern, echoed in the entablature and on the mantel.

In 1930 the National Monument Act was passed to protect historic buildings. The only post-medieval building to be covered by the Act was the Casino; indeed, concern for this building was instrumental in getting the Act passed at all. A major work of restoration has recently been carried out for the Office of Public Works by T. Austin Dunphy, who was awarded the Architectural Restoration Medal for his achievement. He was assisted by John Redmill and John O'Connell. The Casino is now open to the public as the grounds were in the eighteenth century. In 1783 it was reported that 'the utmost liberality of admission is permitted here; the inhabitants of Dublin may at all times amuse themselves with an agreeable walk.'

THE CITY HALL/ROYAL EXCHANGE
Dame Street

Looking south from Grattan Bridge, the view uphill is crowned by one of the most accomplished and sophisticated buildings in Dublin, remarkable for the perfection of its exterior detail and the wonder of the domed hall within. The City Hall was built originally as the Royal Exchange, to provide the merchants of Dublin with a place to transact business. Bills of Exchange were bought and sold beneath the central rotunda and, until the Irish currency was abolished in 1826, money was exchanged here. The Tholsel, or old City Hall, on Christ Church Place, where the Guild of Merchants had met previously, was becoming semi-ruinous and was finally abandoned in 1791.

The Wide Streets Commissioners were set up in 1757 for the purpose of creating a wide and convenient way from Dublin Castle to

RIGHT The central stone rotunda, with statues of Daniel O'Connell in a Roman toga by John Hogan on the left and of Thomas Drummond, also by Hogan, on the right.

Essex Bridge, as Grattan Bridge was known until 1874. The resulting street, Parliament Street, was opened in 1762. The Commissioners stayed together as a body and eventually had complete control of city planning. As they were all powerful men with taste and an interest in architecture, Dublin owes them a great deal. Dr McParland has written: 'The story of how their interests and their powers were extended until the development of the whole city was under their control is one of the most important episodes in the history of Irish architecture in the late eighteenth and early nineteenth centuries.'

At the top of the newly created Parliament Street was the former site of Cork House, erected in 1600 for the Great Earl of Cork and later used by Cromwell's hated government as its headquarters. In the 1760s a scheme for building a Chapel Royal with a cupola here was abandoned, as was another plan for a square to be named Bedford Square after the viceroy. The merchants exerted pressure through their allies in parliament and Dublin Corporation and, in spite of the opposition of the Wide Streets Commissioners, they succeeded in purchasing the site in May 1768 for £4,000.

ABOVE Statue of Dr Charles Lucas MP, who died in 1771. Edward Smyth carved this when he was only in his early twenties.

ABOVE LEFT City Hall (formerly the Royal Exchange), Dame Street, was designed by Thomas Cooley in 1769, who came to Ireland to build it and remained to establish a successful practice.

LEFT The coffered ceiling in the dome. Dublin Corporation is considering a major restoration programme to restore the interior to its original appearance.

RIGHT The ceiling above one of a pair of staircases, with plasterwork by Charles Thorp.

FAR RIGHT The lord mayor's Great Chair in the council chamber, with decorative Irish wolfhounds carved by Arthur Jones in Irish oak in 1852.

A competition for the building of an exchange was advertised in both England and Ireland. Sixty-one entries were sent in from fifty-five architects, thirty-three from England, twenty from Ireland and two who remained anonymous; the designs were put on display at the Assembly Rooms in South William Street, now the Civic Museum. It was rightly feared that the imported article would be favoured over the native, and three of the Irish competitors gave initials only, while three used pseudonyms. The competition aroused enormous interest and the exhibition attracted a large attendance, including the Provost of Trinity and the viceroy. Among the detractors was one who wrote in the *Freeman's Journal*: 'Do not build – we cannot afford it – when the very life-blood of the nation is sucked, by a shoal of lazy leeches, that are almost bursting with over-gorged pernicious pensions.' A second exclaimed: 'What! build the Exchange amongst brothels and coal yards!'

The first prize of £100 was awarded to Thomas Cooley, a young English architect who beat James Gandon into second place while Thomas Sandby came third; all three were from London. Thomas Ivory, Joseph Jarratt and the partnership of Samuel Sproule and Christopher Myers were chosen from among the Irish entrants for consolation prizes.

Thomas Cooley (1740–84), who started his career as a carpenter, was

a pupil of Robert Mylne, the architect of Blackfriars Bridge in London. He came to Dublin to build the Royal Exchange and established a successful practice in Ireland, never returning to the country of his birth. Besides working for the Archbishop of Armagh, where Francis Johnston was apprenticed to him, and building a country seat for the Earl of Caledon in Co. Tyrone, he designed many buildings in Dublin. Dr McParland says of Cooley: 'He is not a major architect by international standards but in Ireland in the 1770s he played an important part in the early development of Neoclassicism.'

The foundation stone of the Royal Exchange was laid by the Viceroy, Lord Townshend, on 2 August 1769, on which occasion the bells rang out, the sailing vessels unfurled their flags and the trustees entertained the viceregal party at the old Tholsel. The government provided funds and the merchants organized lotteries to pay for the building, which took ten years to complete. Because trade was burgeoning at this time, they were determined to provide themselves with spacious and elegant surroundings of which they could be proud.

The Royal Exchange makes a handsome climax for the vista at the top of Parliament Street and was remarkable in its day for the refinement of the carved ornament executed by Simon Vierpyl. It was the earliest of Dublin's green-domed buildings and is the only one to survive intact from the time that it was built. The plasterwork is by

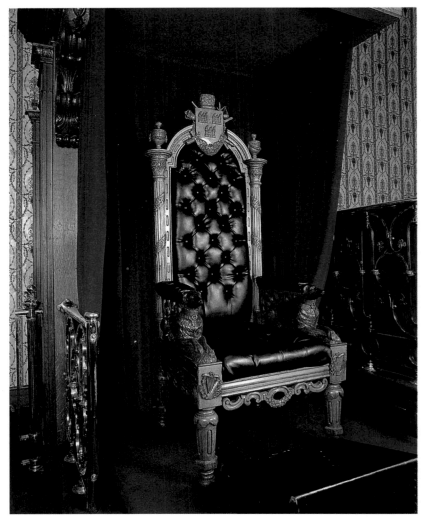

Charles Thorp, who was later to become Lord Mayor of Dublin. His work in the coffee-room, now the council chamber, was of high quality but it was largely destroyed by a fire in 1908. Lit by circular windows and supported by composite columns, the central rotunda forms a grand and formal, if somewhat chilly, stone interior. The twin staircases, flanking the entrance, are particularly fine.

The building has stood witness to many dramatic events. Volunteer rallies were held here during the 1780s when, as Sir John Gilbert describes, '... from the clang of arms the vibrating dome caught the generous flame, and re-echoed the enlivening sound of liberty.' During the 1798 rebellion it became a military depot and was used as a torture chamber; in 1800 Daniel O'Connell, the 'Liberator', made his first public speech here. In 1814 many people were killed and wounded when the balustrade in front collapsed beneath the weight of a crowd of spectators, assembled to witness a public whipping.

In 1852 Dublin Corporation, which had been meeting in the Assembly Rooms in South William Street since the Tholsel was abandoned in 1791, acquired the building and renamed it the City Hall. Indoors, the open colonnades on the ground floor were closed in with partitians and a staircase was inserted on the south side. The architect was Hugh Byrne. The lord mayor's Great Chair in the council chamber, which cost £25 10s, was made by Arthur Jones, and green morocco leather cushions were provided for the members' seats. The lord mayor and corporation have met in the Council Chamber here ever since, and the building also houses the offices of the city manager. At the time of writing elaborate plans are being considered for restoring the interior of the building to its original appearance.

Dublin Corporation has been fortunate in that its magnificent collection of civic regalia has survived intact and is preserved in the City Hall. The collection includes 102 royal charters, deeds, maces, swords, including the sword of Henry IV, the Great Mayoral Chain donated by William III and seals dating back to the twelfth century.

The rotunda makes an ideal home for the statuary belonging to the city. The statue of Dr Charles Lucas MP, who persuaded parliament to contribute £13,500 to the cost of the building, was carved by Edward Smyth when he was only in his early twenties. The plinth has a bas-relief of Liberty, with her rod and cap; Lucas was praised by Grattan as a 'pioneer of Irish liberty'. Other statues are of Thomas Drummond, Daniel O'Connell and Thomas Davis. Twelve wall paintings high up in the rotunda represent episodes in Irish history; these are the work of James Ward and were completed in 1919. The mosaic floor of the rotunda is ornamented with the arms of the city of Dublin and a Latin inscription which translated means: 'An obedient citizenry creates a happy city.'

NO. 52 ST STEPHEN'S GREEN

No. 52 St Stephen's Green was built in 1771 on ground let by Gustavus Hume to David La Touche of Marlay; No. 53 was built by Hume. David La Touche was of Huguenot origin and he, as well as his father and grandfather, married Huguenots in Ireland. His grandfather had started a thriving factory for the manufacture of poplin but turned to banking after successfully investing the money of other Huguenots. Dr C.P. Curran describes David La Touche as a man of taste who travelled in Italy bringing back treasures for his houses. He was the head of the banking house in Castle Street and was succeeded here by his son and namesake who died in 1817. La Touche was also Governor of the Bank of Ireland. His daughter Elizabeth was an outstanding beauty and used to act with Grattan in outdoor theatricals at their country house, Marlay. In 1870, after a succession of owners and tenants, No. 52 was purchased by the Representative Church Body. It is now owned by Canada Life and leased to the government for the ombudsman. It has a frontage of 60 feet and spacious rooms with lavish decoration.

The ceiling of the back drawing room of the *piano nobile* has been attributed with more certainty than is usual to Angelica Kauffman on the grounds that she was known to have been a friend of David La Touche. She spent six months in Ireland in 1771 when she also painted portraits of the Viceroy, Lord Townshend; the Earl of Ely, for whom she worked at Rathfarnham Castle; and Sir Philip Tisdall, the Attorney-General and Secretary of State for Ireland. The central plaque of the drawing room is after Guido Reni's *Aurora*.

The most unusual room in the house is the Music Room, now the office of the ombudsman, with wall paintings by Peter de Gree, a Flemish artist with whom La Touche had become acquainted in Antwerp. De Gree came to Dublin in 1785 at the joint invitation of La

RIGHT No. 52 St. Stephen's Green (now the Ombudsman's Office) was built in 1771 for David La Touche of the Huguenot banking family.

BELOW The ceiling of the back drawing room with Adamesque plasterwork and painted inserts, which have a good claim to be by Angelica Kauffman as she is known to have been a friend of David La Touche.

RIGHT The Music Room, showing the wall paintings by Peter de Gree, *c.*1785, including Apollo with his muses, painted in green and white on account of the green marble mantel.

Touche and William Burton Conyngham, bearing recommendations from Joshua Reynolds who evidently thought highly of the painter. Decorative grisaille panels by him can be seen at Lucan House, Abbey Leix and Luttrellstown Castle, but his work at No. 52 is unusual in being green and white, to match the verd-antique marble mantel.

Apollo and the Muses preside over this chimneypiece, while Orpheus and Euridyce adorn the north wall and a Nereid surmounts the door. De Gree also painted a series of grisaille panels – this time they were grey and white – for the dining room; they represent the Elements and are now hanging in George's Hall, Dublin Castle.

ELY HOUSE
8 Ely Place

The sober frontage of Ely House must surely hide one of the most unexpected interiors in Dublin. In 1771 Henry Loftus, Earl of Ely (1709–83), whose country seat was Rathfarnham Castle, Co. Dublin, erected the first house on Ely Place. He was descended from Adam Loftus, Archbishop of Dublin, Lord Chancellor, Lord Justice and the first Provost of Trinity College, who had built Rathfarnham Castle in 1585. The family title comes from the ancient Irish chieftain, Eli O'Carroll, and has no connection with Ely in England. In 1767 Lord Ely succeeded his nephew, whose mother was the daughter and heiress of Sir Gustavus Hume, a surgeon and speculative builder. Having inherited the title and estates late in life, the earl lost no time in building a grand town house. He leased from Hume a large plot of land, 140 feet wide, on which to build his new house facing down Hume Street to St Stephen's Green East.

Lord Ely's first wife, Frances Monroe, was the aunt of the reigning beauty in Dublin, Dorothea (Dolly) Monroe. During her brief sojourn in Ireland, Angelica Kauffman painted Lord and Lady Ely attended by a negro page bearing a cushion with their two coronets; Dolly, seated at the harpsichord, is included in the picture, now in the National Gallery of Ireland. Having no children of her own, Lady Ely was anxious to see her beautiful niece Dolly married to the Viceroy, Lord Townshend, a widower, who was a friend and a frequent visitor. He did pay court to Dolly and attended balls and masques in Ely House as well as driving to Rathfarnham Castle in his coach and six, with six running footmen. In the event, however, he married another. The earl

ABOVE The plaques on the staircase represent figures from the Labours of Hercules. A statue of the god himself, clad in his lion's pelt, stands guard at the foot of the staircase.

LEFT Ely house faces down Hume Street to St Stephen's Green in an unspoilt enclave of Georgian streets.

built a magnificent hunting lodge near the 'Hell Fire Club' above Rathfarnham; this he named Dollymount after his niece and he filled it with fine marble and statuary.

The plain terraced exterior of Ely House, made of Bridgewater brick imported from England, glows red in the setting sun, the shadows of the wrought-iron balconies etched diagonally across it. A pair of wrought-iron lamp standards flank the entrance. The outer hall, once used for the accommodation of sedan chairs, gives into a small waiting room, now an oratory, which once formed part of the front hall. The door to the inner hall and staircase could be unlocked by a clever arrangement of lever and bolt operated from the floor above by means of a wire through the ceiling, a device which is still in place.

The staircase is one of the most remarkable to be found in Dublin. In a house that was constantly alive with lavish entertainment, the guests must have presented a spectacular sight as they mounted the stairs in all their finery. No more theatrical backdrop for them could be imagined. The bizarre decoration comes from the story of the Labours of Hercules and includes a life-sized statue of the god wearing his lion's

pelt, with a club in one hand and apples from the Garden of the Hesperides clutched behind his back in the other. Birds and animals from the legend, carved in wood and painted to look like bronze, mount the stairs beyond him: first the Erymanthian boar, next a Stymphalian bird on the corner, then the Nemean lion carrying Hercules' club, followed by a second Stymphalian bird making another corner. The Cretan bull takes up the third flight, and the landing has the Arcadian stag, so fleet its brazen hooves scarce touched the ground, and Cerberus, the three-headed dog and guardian of the nether regions. Small lead medallions below the handrail also represent the labours and depict the Nemean lion, the Cretan bull and the Mares of Diomedes, which fed on human flesh. The whole concept was closely modelled on the staircase of a house in Brussels, built in 1731; this once served as the residence of the Governors of the Low Countries and now houses the Musée Moderne.

The style of the interior ornament is transitional and the freehand plasterwork in the staircase hall is in higher relief than might have been expected in 1771. Above the pedimented doorcase at the foot of the

ABOVE The elaborate silver doorhandles which are an unusual feature of the house were made by Messrs Boulton and Fothergill of Birmingham in 1772 and are based on a design by Robert Adam.

RIGHT The dining room with a plasterwork roundel called *The Young Bride* and a marble plaque on the mantel representing the sleeping Hercules having his club stolen by putti.

157

LEFT The mantel plaque in the back drawing room depicts Venus, goddess of love, with two turtle doves symbolizing love and marriage and a group of cherubs and cupids. Hymen, the god of marriage, carries a flaming torch.

RIGHT Plasterwork roundel from a painting called the *Aldobrandini Marriage*, showing a Greek bride parting from her mother (*c.* 350 BC).

stairs there is a large medallion of Hercules, festooned with the inevitable pelt; to the right there is a medallion of Mars and to the left one of Zeus, the father of them both. These are suspended, along with trophies of war, from a massive chain affixed to a double-ended spear stretching the entire length of the wall beneath the landing. The panelled doors are of West Indian mahogany with elaborate silver handles supplied by Messrs Boulton and Fothergill of Birmingham in 1772. The design for them was later published in Volume II of Robert and James Adam's *Works in Architecture* (1779).

The main dining room on the ground floor is decorated with a variety of allegorical stucco plaques linked together by supremely ornamental and delicate ribbon decoration, attributed to Michael Stapleton, the chief exponent of the Adam style in Ireland. Hercules appears again in the plaque on the Siena marble mantel; exhausted after his labours, he lies sleeping on the hide of the boar with the lion's skin around him, while putti make off with his club. The high standard of decoration in the dining room is also found, as would be expected, in the other reception rooms on the floor above.

Lord Ely, the builder of the house, died in 1783, but his much younger second wife survived him by nearly forty years. She fitted up a little theatre, joining together two rooms on the upper floor, which could hold an audience of sixty besides an orchestra and the stage. In the *Freeman's Journal* of April 1786 it is recorded that the tragedy of *The*

Distressed Mother and the farce of *All the World's a Stage* were performed here with Leslie Westenra, Mrs Monroe, and Miss St Leger among those taking part. Besides amateur theatricals, musical evenings were held, the chamber orchestra playing in one room and, by means of an ingenious concealed aperture, being audible in the next.

Lady Ely sold the house in 1809 and it passed through many hands over the next century. It was rented by the Rev. James Hamilton in 1812 and subsequently occupied by Sir William Leeson and then by Francis Synge of Glenmore Castle, Co. Wicklow. The next occupant was the Hon. Robert Leeson, who was followed by Ladies Kathleen and Jane Hely Hutchinson and then by William Sandford Pakenham. From 1890 to 1911 it was the residence of Sir William Thornley Stoker, and in 1910 the house was photographed and described for *The Georgian Society Records*, showing how suitably it was furnished in his day. The Vicereine, Lady Aberdeen, leased Ely House on behalf of the Women's National Health Association, which operated from here until 1922. In that year it was purchased by the Knights of St Columbanus, an Irish Association of Catholic laymen founded in 1915, who wish to fulfil their Catholic ethos in a practical way. They are affiliated with similar bodies worldwide and concern themselves with the betterment of their members in matters of faith as well as with such problems as unemployment and education. They have cared for this wonderful house for over seventy years.

THE BLUE COAT SCHOOL/BLACKHALL PLACE
Blackhall Place

The original King's Hospital, or Blue Coat School, was begun in 1669 on Queen Street, north of the Liffey. Charles II awarded it a royal charter; it was to be 'a mansion house and place of abode for the sustentation and relief of poor children, [and] aged and impotent people inhabiting or residing in the city of Dublin'. The prospectus of 1673 warned that it was 'not intended to be an Hive for Drones, but a Profitable Nursery . . . '. The correct title of the school was 'The Hospital and Free School of King Charles the Second, Dublin', although it was variously known as the Blewcoat Boys Hospital, the Blue Coat School and later as the King's Hospital. The uniform was a 'dark blue brass-buttoned, cutaway coat and dark blue knee breeches, yellow waistcoats and long yellow stockings and silver shoe buckles'; the blue coat was worn by the pupils until 1864. This

Master of the Dublin Society's School of Architectural Drawing, was the winner.

Ivory was born in about 1732 in Cork, where he was trained as a carpenter; he came to Dublin early in life and was employed in carving stocks for guns. He was a supreme draftsman and Dr McParland has described his drawings for the Blue Coat School as 'the loveliest architectural drawings produced in Ireland in the eighteenth century'. His winning plan was drastically curtailed, as the expected government funds did not materialize. In 1776 George III was presented with the magnificent set of Ivory's twelve drawings bound in morocco, but even this gesture was of no avail in procuring funds. George IV later presented the set to the British Museum.

Ivory's design looked backwards to the architecture of Pearce and

RIGHT The Blue Coat School, or King's Hospital, was designed by Thomas Ivory in 1772, but his central spire or tower was never completed on account of the cost. It is now occupied by the Incorporated Law Society and has been re-christened Blackhall Place, the name of the street on which it stands.

LEFT The Blue Coat School governors painted by John Trotter in 1779 with the architect, Thomas Ivory, in the centre, supposedly being given the news that the central tower was to be omitted for reasons of economy. Sir Thomas Blackhall, lord mayor in 1769 and the instigator of the building, is presumed to have been among those represented.

was followed by a blue suit with yellow cuffs and the traditional cap and buttons, which was the uniform until 1923.

The original school, on a site to the east of the present building, consisted of a low range with dormer windows surmounted by a clock tower, and a ceremonial entrance door with a scroll pediment bearing the arms of the city of Dublin and the royal arms above. Both houses of parliament met here while waiting for Pearce's new Parliament House, begun in 1729, to be ready. However, by 1769 the old school became derelict and was apparently 'about to fall'; in that year the governors, who included William Robert FitzGerald, later second Duke of Leinster, decided to rebuild. In anticipation of government funds they purchased a site from Dublin Corporation adjoining the Royal Barracks to the west. In May 1772 an architectural competition was initiated but no English-based architect entered. The competitors included Francis Sandys, Rowland Omer, Samuel Sproule and Thomas Cooley, who was by now established in Dublin, having won the competition for the Royal Exchange in 1769. Thomas Ivory, the first

Castle. His plan was for a central block linked with curved quadrants to wings in the Palladian manner. This arrangement was popular in country-house architecture, not only with great houses such as Castletown, Co. Kildare, but also with more modest 'agricultural complexes' like Kilcarty, Co. Meath, itself designed by Thomas Ivory. The northern wing contained the chapel which was balanced to the south by the school hall. These pavilions have some fine detailing in the stonework, carved by Simon Vierpyl, with swags, niches, oculi and wooden cupolas above. At the centre there was to have been an elegant spire, taller again than the main block, to tie the design together. Due to lack of funds this spire was never built and the base now supports a dumpy copper dome, designed by Robert Stirling in 1894 as a substitute. Ivory's original drawing for the spire shows a circular base but as built the base is octagonal; the proposed spire was illustrated at full height by both Pool and Cash in 1780 and Malton in 1799.

At the back, on land adjoining the barracks, Ivory proposed an arcaded courtyard with dormitories above and a great dining hall centered on the western range, but none of this was ever built. In 1775, at the request of the corporation, Ivory produced a 'Map of Oxmantown Green laid out into Streets' in a grid pattern, with his building as the focal point.

In the eighteenth century, institutional buildings tended towards extravagance on the exterior while economizing indoors; considering this, the Blue Coat School came off well. The axial corridor dividing the main block in two is sensitively articulated with niches, arches and cross-vaulting above a diagonally paved floor. Much space is given to

The plasterwork in the boardroom by Charles Thorp seems stylistically older than the date 1773 would suggest, but suitable for a building which itself looks backwards. The ceiling was damaged by fire in the 1930s and was restored by the Dublin firm of Sibthorpe and Son.

the ornamental staircase which leads to a magnificent boardroom with an elaborate, transitional ceiling by Charles Thorp, for which he was paid £72. The chapel, although it lacks the coffered ceiling and mural ornament in Ivory's design, has elegant round-headed windows and between them twin Corinthian pilasters supporting an elaborate cornice at the eastern end; the reredos (now removed) was carved by Richard Cranfield. A painting by John Trotter, which Strickland dates to 1779, shows the architect seated in the centre, talking to Simon Vierpyl in his white working jacket, with the rest of the board of governors grouped to either side. Ivory resigned from the project in 1780, disgusted at the curtailment of his plans.

In 1968 the school decided to move out of Dublin and purchased Brooklawn, an eighteenth-century house near Palmerstown, Co. Dublin, beside the Liffey, with land that was ideal for playing fields. Ivory's building was sold for £105,000 to the Incorporated Law Society of Ireland. It is now called Blackhall Place after the street in which it stands; this in turn is named after Sir Thomas Blackhall, chairman of the school building committee and lord mayor in 1769.

The Incorporated Law Society is the controlling body of solicitors in Ireland. It is responsible for regulating the practice of solicitors, representing the interests of the profession, and providing professional training for students as well as continuing legal education for those already in practice. The new owners instigated a thorough programme of renovation, which included the replacement of decayed stonework. A statue of Judge Stephen Trotter, who died in 1764, has found a new home in a niche in the front hall. This is attributed to Peter Scheemakers (1691–1781) and came from the Church of Ireland church in Duleek, Co. Meath. Fortunately the stained-glass window depicting the Resurrection, made by Evie Hone (1894–1955), one of Ireland's great modern stained-glass artists, is still in the east window of the chapel. No Dublin building has been more successfully adapted to a new use with more exemplary concern for its character.

THE NEWCOMEN BANK
Castle Street

The Newcomen Bank occupies a prime position, with the main front facing Dublin Castle and the east front being opposite City Hall. It was built for Sir William Gleadowe, who married into the Newcomen family of Carrigglas, Co. Longford, and assumed his wife's name. This provoked the print-makers into publishing a view of his handsome new bank with the following caption:

> Though many years I've lived in town
> As New-Come-In I'm only known.

Sir William was knighted in 1781 and sat in the Irish parliament where he represented Co. Longford. He was bribed to vote for the Union with the offer of a peerage for his wife Charlotte. His acquiescence was in marked contrast to his competitors, the La Touche family of bankers; four of them were MPs and all voted against the Union. Richard Lovell Edgeworth wrote the following lines at this time which turned out to be prophetic:

> With a name that is borrowed – a title that's bought
> Sir William would fain be a gentleman thought;
> His wit is but cunning, his courage but vapour
> His pride is but money – his money but paper!

Sir William's son, Viscount Newcomen, inherited the bank and the title bestowed on his mother, but the business failed in 1825 and he shot himself, aged forty-eight. As he died unmarried the title died with him and he left all his property to his eight illegitimate children.

The Newcomen Bank was designed in 1781 by Thomas Ivory

ABOVE Part of the wall and ceiling of the vast oval room, which was Sir William's office and originally faced in three directions. A small section of the ceiling paintwork has been cleaned, and it is hoped that the whole ceiling will be restored.

LEFT The Newcomen Bank was designed for Sir William Gleadowe Newcomen, MP and banker, by Thomas Ivory in 1781. In 1858 it was doubled in size, showing a salutary respect for Ivory's building; the old half on the left was joined to the addition by a large Victorian porch.

LEFT The dome over the main staircase.

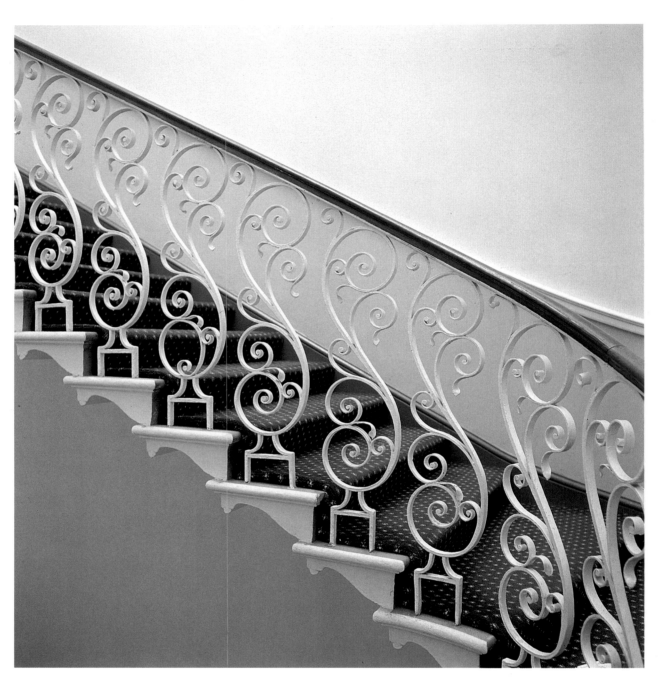

RIGHT The elegant ironwork on the stairs leading to the oval room.

(*c.* 1732–86), architect of the Blue Coat School and Master of the Dublin Society's School of Architectural Drawing. James Hoban, the architect of the White House in Washington, was among his pupils, and in 1792 Hoban offered to import help from Ireland to work on the building of the president's house, since he was 'universally acquainted with men in the Building line in Ireland, particularly with many able Stone Cutters in Dublin with whom I have been concerned in building, as the Royal Exchange, New (Newcomen) Bank, and Custom House . . .' An anonymous eulogy on Thomas Ivory, which has been ascribed to James Gandon, was published in *Anthologia Hibernica* after Ivory's death. It praises his professionalism and derides the amateurish architectural creations that are 'scattered about, to the disgrace of the taste of the country'.

Ivory favoured the Adam style and the east front of the bank is ornamented with a delicate Adamesque frieze, stone swags and niches, rather unusual for Dublin. The original tall, narrow building of three bays, faced in Portland stone, contained Sir William's superb oval upstairs office with a painted ceiling and windows facing north, south and east, approached by an elegant stone staircase with iron balusters, which winds on upwards to the top floor.

In 1831 the Hibernian Bank took over the premises and in 1858 the building was doubled in size, the east front being extended to the north and exactly duplicated. However, the stone swags of the original were imitated in composition stone which has weathered badly. The old and new facades are linked together by a handsome Victorian curved porch with four columns and a balustrade. The building was further extended in the 1880s and another oval room was created at the back. The building is now used as rates offices by Dublin Corporation.

NORTH GREAT GEORGE'S STREET

On Rocque's map of Dublin, 1756, North Great George's Street has not been named, nor are there as yet any buildings but the street is shown as a handsome avenue of trees approaching, through a pair of lodges, the site of the present Belvedere House. The owner of the land was Nicholas Archdall of Castle Archdall, Co. Fermanagh, who sold off sites in the mid-eighteenth century; building commenced in the 1770s. In 1773 eleven houses had been built on the south-west side and by 1798, except for three houses, the street was finished, with Belvedere House closing the vista at the top of the hill. Edward Archdall was involved in developments with the Gardiners in Gardiner Street, Mountjoy Square and Temple Street.

The street leads from Parnell Street up to Great Denmark Street and was once a distinguished element in the planning of the north city. Although the houses have plain exteriors there are examples here of the most elegant and varied interiors to be found in Dublin: beautiful

RIGHT The drawing room of 18 North Great George's Street, which was built *c.*1780.

BELOW The landing and entrance to the drawing room of No. 18, owned by Senator David Norris, who is at the forefront of the campaign to save the street.

ceilings, fireplaces, stairs, ironwork and gardens. Michael Stapleton, Charles Thorp and Francis Ryan were among those building and decorating here before the Act of Union in 1801. Among those who lived in the street in 1798 were the first Earl of Kenmare, the Dowager Viscountess Powerscourt and Mrs Catherine Clements, the daughter of the Rt Hon. John Beresford. After the Union the street attracted many in the legal profession – QCs, barristers and solicitors.

The Rev. J.P. Mahaffy (1839–1918) occupied No. 38 from 1865 and was living here when he founded the Georgian Society in 1908. Among the first to appreciate the beauty of Georgian Dublin, he determined to make a record of buildings and interiors doomed, as he put it, to 'decay

and disappearance'; in 1914 Mahaffy became Provost of Trinity. He had been the erstwhile tutor and friend of Oscar Wilde but he abandoned Wilde after he was sent to gaol saying: 'We no longer speak of Mr Wilde at Trinity.' He described James Joyce and George Moore as ne'er-do-wells and thanked God that they had 'cleared out of Dublin', though 'not before they had squirted stink upon all the decent people like a pair of skunks'. When informed that Provost Traill had been taken ill, Mahaffy, who hoped to succeed him, said: 'Nothing trivial, I hope?'

No. 41 belonged to an attorney, Sir Richard Orpen, who purchased the house before 1819. In the front drawing room there were faded wall

LEFT The dining room of 38 North Great George's Street. Built in 1785, No. 38 became known as Mahaffy House as it was for forty years the residence of Professor John Pentland Mahaffy, sometime Provost of Trinity College.

RIGHT The living room of Mahaffy House. When the current owner, Miss Desiree Shortt, rescued the house there were twenty-seven people living here in crowded conditions.

paintings of Italian coastal scenes, viewed between the pillars of a loggia, attributed to Gaspare Gabrielli (*fl.* 1805–30) and since painted over. There was also a Gothic private chapel in the house. Isaac Butt MP, leader of the Irish Party prior to Parnell, purchased the house following the death of Orpen in 1876. No. 41 was eventually added to five houses in the street already occupied by the Loreto Convent and is now part of the Montessori Education Centre.

saved No. 16 and bequeathed it to the Irish Georgian Society, which has sold the house to the architect, John O'Connell. Many of the houses were bought and restored with tenants still in them, but at No. 38 the owner, Desiree Shortt, waited until 1993 and the departure of a tenant who had been there for nearly twenty years before restoring the main drawing room. Miss Shortt has established a successful studio and school for restoring china here.

LEFT Ceiling of the main drawing room at 35 North Great George's Street (now the James Joyce Cultural Centre), which was built in 1784 for Valentine Browne, later the first Earl of Kenmare. Michael Stapleton and Charles Thorp worked on the interior.

RIGHT The dining room of No. 35 has unusual giant pilasters decorating the walls. The painted ovals depict the Dancing Academy of Professor Denis J. Maginni, as mentioned in Joyce's *Ulysses*.

In common with its neighbours on the north side of the city, North Great George's Street had largely degenerated into tenements by the First World War. In the 1960s, however, several houses were saved and restored by idealists who were attracted by their beauty and central location. Among the early pioneers in this movement was Harold Clarke who lived for twenty years at No. 19, a house containing arguably the finest Adamesque interior on the street. Brian Molloy

No. 22 was among a group of houses at the lower end of the street demolished by the corporation in the 1960s as unfit for human habitation. It was the home of William Swan, assistant Town Major at the time of the 1798 rebellion, who, together with a party led by Major Sirr, captured Lord Edward FitzGerald, later to die of his wounds in prison. Major Swan took Lord Edward's dagger in the fray, in which two men lost their lives. Sheridan Le Fanu's memoirs, *Seventy Years of*

Irish Life (1893), describe how his mother, Emma, had stolen the dagger 'on a patriotic impulse' from Major Swan's house in North Great George's Street and hidden it in her feather mattress.

In 1976 Senator David Norris, the prominent Joycean scholar, came to live at No. 18. He organized a conference to celebrate the centenary of Joyce's birth, which was attended by devotees of the writer from all over the world. The proceeds were used for the purchase of No. 35 to

from the EC a major restoration, recently completed, was carried out under the supervision of the architect, James O'Connor, and the watchful eye of the senator across the street.

Having attended Belvedere College, Joyce would have been all too familiar with the street. It was in No. 35 that a Mr Maginn opened his dancing academy where he advertised himself as 'Mr Denis J. Maginni, Professor of Dancing'; he is mentioned thus in *Ulysses*. Joyce is said to

serve as the James Joyce Cultural Centre. The house was built by Francis Ryan in 1784 for Valentine Browne, who was created Earl of Kenmare in 1801, and has a magnificent interior with plasterwork by Thorp and Stapleton. The giant pilasters in the dining room on the ground floor are a most unusual feature. The house was to have been demolished by the corporation, as the condition of the fabric had deteriorated so far as to become dangerous. With the help of funding

have claimed that if ever Dublin were destroyed it could be rebuilt from the pages of Ulysses. His love-hate sentiments for his native city are epitomized in his description of Dublin as 'the centre of European paralysis ... the brown brick houses of Dublin [represent] the incarnation of that spiritual paralysis'. Despite this accusation No. 35 will house a permanent display on Georgian Dublin as well as containing the James Joyce Archive.

BELVEDERE HOUSE
6 Great Denmark Street

Belvedere House is the Neoclassical masterpiece of Dublin's private houses. Drawings for the interior by Michael Stapleton, architect, builder and stuccodore, form part of the Stapleton collection in the National Library of Ireland; it is presumed that he also designed the house. This great free-standing mansion was completed in 1786 for George Rochfort, second Earl of Belvedere, and faces down North Great George's Street to the Dublin mountains beyond. Up to the first-floor level, the facade is of Portland stone, with red brick above and delicate stone balustrades beneath the five windows on the *piano nobile*. The fluted Portland stone frieze and the cornice at roof level are refinements seldom found in Dublin houses. The brickwork is new and when it was replaced the white reveals were omitted; the recent replacement of glazing bars in the windows has, however greatly improved the facade.

The interior is the ultimate expression of the Adam style in Dublin and shows Michael Stapleton at his best. The front hall, now a passage, originally had two windows on the street but it was later divided and a sitting room created out of the right-hand portion. Although some of the plasterwork was doubtlessly made with the help of moulds, much of it is freehand, notably the decoration beneath the main stairs. As is usual in a great Dublin house, this staircase leads up to the main drawing-room floor and goes no further; he who ascends it cannot fail to be dazzled by the riotous extravagance of the stucco ornament all around. The walls have plaster panels with elliptical plaques at the centre, surrounded, within the frame, by decorative arabesques. A double frieze with lions, urns and swags continues the line of the landing, a Neoclassical version of the Grecian wave. The arched window on the half-landing is flanked by pilasters, richly decorated in stucco with emblems from classical antiquity, and the wrought-iron balusters have medallions bearing the head of Apollo.

The principal rooms on the *piano nobile* are the Diana Room, the Apollo Room and the Venus Room. The ceiling of the Diana Room, now the library, shows the goddess in her chariot pulled by stags, surrounded by emblems of the chase. The antlered stags in the demi-lunes at either end are an allusion to the stags which appear in the Rochfort coat of arms. The Apollo Room, now the chapel, shows the sun god with his lyre in a sunburst and groups of putti playing musical instruments, including the cello, flute, tambourine, lute and drum. For reasons of modesty the undraped figure of Venus was removed from the ceiling of the Venus Room when the Jesuits took over the building but the demi-lunes remain, representing Astronomy, Painting and Sculpture; there are tablets ornamented with stylized birds from the Rochfort crest.

One of Lord Belvedere's country seats was a modest-sized house of 1740 called Belvedere. It was built by his father on the shores of Lough Ennell, Co. Westmeath, and boasts a delicate Rococo interior that is the finest of its kind in Ireland. The second earl married twice but had no children. On his death in 1814 his widow, Jane, married Abraham

ABOVE The design of Belvedere House is attributed to Michael Stapleton and it was completed in 1786 for George Rochfort, second Earl of Belvedere. The Jesuit College has occupied it since 1841.

RIGHT The staircase is Michael Stapleton's masterpiece. He was the greatest exponent of the Adam style in Dublin and enjoyed a huge practice.

Boyd KC. Their son, George Boyd-Rochfort, inherited Belvedere House in 1836 and sold it to the Society of Jesus five years later. There was considerable prejudice against the sale of great houses to the Catholic clergy at that time and Boyd-Rochfort was obliged to make use of the services of a middle-man to negotiate the deal; he chose Sylvester Young, the brother of one of the priests. Belvedere House is one of many distinguished buildings in Ireland that have been preserved by the timely intervention of the Catholic Church.

The Jesuit school moved here in 1841 from Hardwicke Street and took the name Belvedere College; it has cared for the building with pride ever since. James Joyce is the most illustrious past pupil 'but the visitor who enjoys the courtesy of the Fathers will do well to talk of other subjects', writes Maurice Craig. Tony O'Reilly, the great rugby player, chairman of Heinz and newspaper magnate, is a past pupil of Belvedere as was Harry Clarke, the stained-glass artist. Two others who attended Belvedere College were the patriots, Cathal Brugha and Kevin Barry, who lost their lives in the fight for Irish freedom.

THE CUSTOM HOUSE
Custom House Quay

The Custom House is built to be seen from all four sides and, although each is different, they are married together with consummate skill. The massive gleaming white facade of Portland stone with back and sides of Irish granite is one of the most spectacular sights in Dublin, at its best reflected in the waters of the Liffey at the brief moment when the high tide is on the turn.

The Rt Hon. John Beresford was appointed Chief Commissioner of the Irish Revenue in 1780, a department that was administered from offices in the Custom House because duty on imported goods was an important source of revenue. The old Custom House had stood on the southern bank of the Liffey where ships bearing cargo were obliged to dock. This was a handsome, if somewhat antiquated building, designed by Thomas Burgh in 1707. It was twelve bays wide with a clock in the pediment and stood on arcades well back from the quayside on the present Wellington Quay, beside Essex Bridge (renamed Grattan Bridge in 1874). At the time this was the last crossing over the Liffey before it flowed out to sea.

RIGHT James Gandon came to Dublin for the express purpose of building the new Custom House in 1781 and remained in Ireland for the rest of his life. Widely regarded as his masterpiece, the building has recently been restored to its pristine glory.

BELOW The north front at night, with the arms containing the harp of Ireland, carved by Edward Smyth, and his statue of Commerce on top of the dome. The building is designed to be admired from each of its four fronts.

Beresford was a man of vision, power and great taste; his brother-in-law, Luke Gardiner, was busy developing Dublin to the north-east and the success of Gardiner's schemes would be assured if a new bridge could be built over the Liffey to the east. (This was to be Carlisle Bridge, which was eventually built in 1792–5 by James Gandon and is now O'Connell Bridge.) Because the path of the cargo ships would be blocked by the bridge there was nothing for it but to have the old Custom House declared unsafe and build a new one downstream. The

vested interests in the heart of the city were however vehemently opposed to this move on account of the prosperity brought to their doorstep in terms of goods and warehousing in the vicinity of the busy quayside. The new scheme was equally unpopular with the dockers because their place of work would be moved further away from their place of abode.

In 1781 Beresford invited an almost untried architect named James Gandon, who was English of Huguenot stock, to undertake the

174

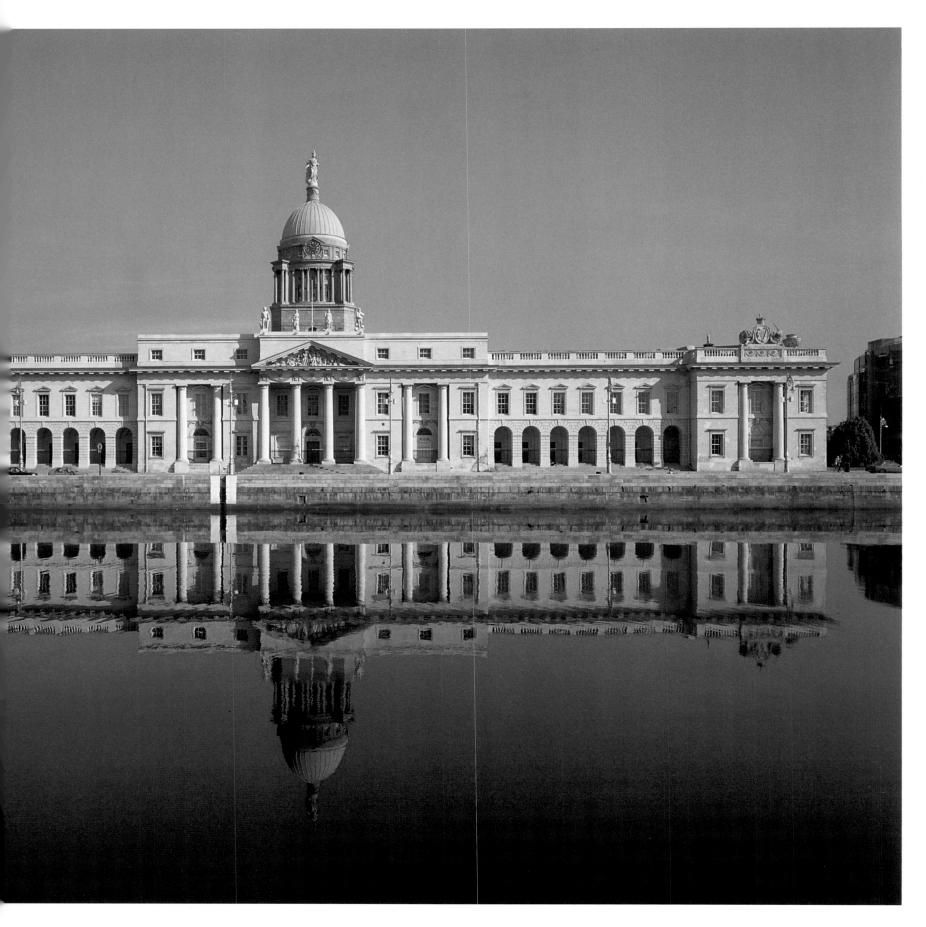

building of a new Custom House for Dublin, cautioning that 'this business must be kept a profound secret'. Apprenticed for seven years to Sir William Chambers, Gandon had entered a competition for the Royal Exchange building in Dublin in 1768, finishing in second place. He had been considering going to St Petersburg at the invitation of Catherine the Great when the summons came that had such happy results for Ireland.

The foundation stone was laid by Beresford in 1781 'without any

formality as we were apprehensive that a riot might be got up'. The site chosen was on the northern bank, nearly a mile downstream of the old Custom House; on Brooking's map of 1728 the land here is described as being 'walled in but as yet overflowed by ye tide'. Because the ground was marshy, trenches had to be dug and piles, made of enormous tree trunks bound together, were sunk to support the foundations. Gandon assembled the best team of local contractors he could obtain: John Semple for brickwork, Henry Darley for stone-

ABOVE Detail of the carving on the entrance front, the work of Edward Smyth, which incorporates heads of cattle, in place of the more conventional ox skulls, and swags of hide, symbolic of Ireland's export trade in cattle.

LEFT The main portico. The carving in the pediment was designed by Agostino Carlini and carved by Smyth; it represents Britannia and Hibernia embracing while Neptune drives away Famine and Despair, with statues of Mercury, Plenty, Industry and Neptune above.

cutting and Hugh Henry for carpentry. The building took ten anxious years to complete and on 8 November 1791 the newspapers reported that twenty vessels had discharged goods at the new Custom House quay and that for the first time 'the general business of the port of Dublin was transacted at the New Custom House'. The cost had amounted to £200,000.

Sculptural ornament of superb quality adorns this great building. The decorative urns on the parapet which once served as chimneys are direct descendants of those at the Marino Casino, which were designed by Gandon's master, Chambers. On the main fronts, as Dr McParland has written, 'snarling lions and haughty unicorns support the arms of the kingdom of Ireland in the most beautiful heraldic sculpture ever carved in stone in Ireland'. These are the work of Edward Smyth who also carved the fourteen riverine head keystones, representing the rivers of Ireland and the Atlantic ocean, with the River Liffey above the front door. The sculpture in the main pediment was designed by Agostino Carlini and carved by Smyth; it represents Britannia and Hibernia embracing, while Neptune drives away Famine and Despair. The frieze below is adorned with the heads of fat cattle, symbolic of the meat trade, interspersed with swags of tanned leather and medallions of Hibernia. The four statues above the pediment represent Mercury, Plenty, Industry with her beehive and Neptune. Mercury and Neptune are by Carlini, and Smyth carved the others to Carlini's designs as well as the statue of Commerce which crowns the dome. Thomas Banks, who like Carlini had worked for Chambers at Somerset House in London, designed the four statues at the centre of the north front which represent the continents of Europe, Asia, Africa and America; no trade was forthcoming at this date from the newly colonized continent of Australia.

In 1921 the Custom House was set on fire by the Dublin Brigade of the IRA and burned for five days; of the original interior only the North Hall survives. Beresford had apartments in the building, which were no doubt designed and fitted out to reflect his taste and position, but sadly no record of their appearance survives. There were, according to the Dublin Evening Post in 1789, fifty mahogany doors at six guineas each: when completed these apartments would 'vie with oriental magnificence – with the palaces of Kings and Princes'. Soon after the fire, when nothing was left except a smouldering shell, a vast rebuilding programme was initiated which saved the building and made it usable. Unfortunately the drum supporting the dome was replaced in the darker Ardbraccan stone instead of the original Portland.

Spurred on by a fall of masonry in the late 1970s, the huge task of restoring the fabric again was initiated by the Office of Public Works, under the supervision of David Slattery. This time there were no short cuts, and by its financial commitment the government showed it was proud to own such a monument as this. A team of sculptors replaced the damaged statuary and carved detailing on the building; the entire balustrade and cornice of Portland stone is new. The Custom House (which now houses the Department of the Environment) should not only be seen from a distance; examination at close quarters is also highly recommended, now that the immense project has been completed with such exceptional care and devotion.

THE FOUR COURTS
Inns Quay

Sited at a bend in the River Liffey, James Gandon's Four Courts is a majestic building, providing a dramatic focal point from the west, especially fine in the setting sun. The great copper dome that crowns it dominates the heart of the city. The law courts had been situated across the river beside Christ Church Cathedral from the beginning of the seventeenth century, occupying a building belonging to the cathedral known as the King's Courts. In 1776 Thomas Cooley, who had come to Dublin to build the Royal Exchange, began work on a new Public Records Office on Inns Quay which was also to house the King's Inns. In 1781 a commitment was made to build the law courts here also, in order to compensate those with vested interests in the old

heart of the city who were vehemently opposed to the building of a new Custom House to the east. This had been Gandon's first Irish commission and he travelled to Ireland to fulfil it.

Cooley died in 1784, and two years later Gandon started work on the Four Courts as they are seen today, incorporating Cooley's building in the western wing; it was designed to house both the law courts and the Public Records Office. The Viceroy, the Duke of Rutland, laid the foundation stone in 1786. In deference to complaints that his vast Corinthian portico projected too close to the river, Gandon brought it back to its present position. On either side of the central block he created two courtyards, which were linked by arcaded screen walls

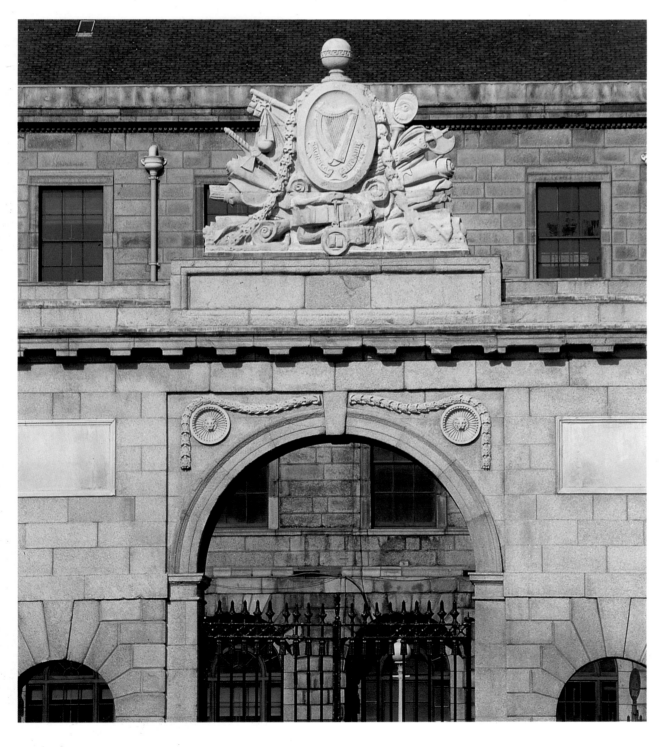

LEFT Emblems of Justice and Law, carved by Edward Smyth, surmount each of the two triumphal archways on either side of the main block of the Four Courts, designed by James Gandon in 1786.

RIGHT The central portico and drum. The statues of Wisdom, Justice, Moses, Mercy and Authority, carved by the Irish sculptor, Edward Smyth, decorate the length of the main front block of the Four Courts.

ABOVE The central rotunda. During the Civil War in 1922 this great edifice was destroyed and Gandon's interior was lost. Fortunately the building was restored and still serves its original purpose.

LEFT The Four Courts and the Custom House are Gandon's two spectacular adornments to the north bank of the Liffey. O'Donovan Rossa Bridge beyond was designed by J. Savage in 1813 and was formerly known as Richmond Bridge.

centred on triumphal arches. These carried emblems of Justice and Law, surmounted now by balls where formerly there had been crowns; in the centre an Irish harp bears the legend Saorstát Éireann. These arcades help to lighten the solid granite facade.

The four courts of law contained in the central block were the Courts of Exchequer, Common Pleas, King's Bench and Chancery; they converged on a magnificent central rotunda. When Gandon came to build the Custom House, he had already consulted the sculptors Thomas Banks and Agostino Carlini in London regarding statuary to adorn it. For the present undertaking he had no need to look further than the Irish sculptor, Edward Smyth, who had worked with him so successfully at the Custom House. Smyth provided the five statues on the central block representing Wisdom, Justice, Moses, Mercy and Authority.

Above the door of each court were four historical friezes showing William the Conqueror establishing courts of justice, King John signing the Magna Carta, Henry II granting Dublin its first charter and James I abolishing the Brehon law. These were designed by Gandon and executed by Edward Smyth, who also gave the hall eight colossal stucco figures: Justice holding her hand to her eyes, Wisdom, Mercy, Law, Eloquence, Liberty, Prudence and Punishment. These were linked together by a florid, scroll-like frieze above the windows separating the figures and surmounted by a domed and coffered ceiling.

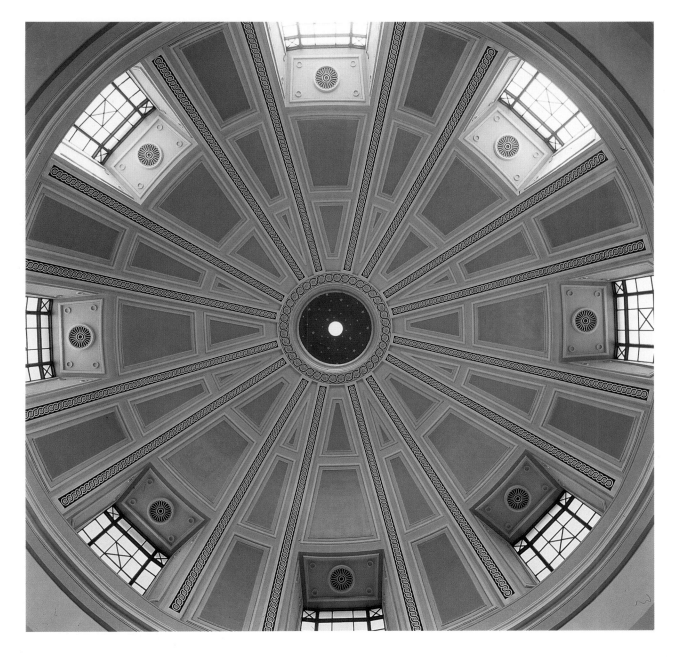

The domed ceiling of the drum, which floats above the city forming a distinctive landmark.

The great round room overhead, which floats above the city and has the best views in Dublin, was used for storing documents. Dr C.P. Curran, an authority on decorative plasterwork in Ireland, worked as a lawyer and official at the Four Courts and could remember seeing papers being lowered by rope through the circular aperture down to the hall below. His photographs of this interior, which was destroyed during the Civil War, are the only record of it besides the sectional drawings by Gandon himself. Curran has described the change in the traffic in the hall following the erection of the law library where the barristers now congregate: 'As that provision was gradually made the loungers in the hall gave way to statues and the two applewomen who, to our own day, had their stands for oranges, apples and ginger-bread under the clock . . .' In Gandon's drawing for the hall the eight niches, now empty, were filled with statuary.

The building was bombarded and burnt during the Civil War in 1922 by Free State troops, and battle scars can be seen on the columns of the portico. Not only was Gandon's beautiful interior lost but even worse the Public Records Office which occupied a separate building beside the west wing was destroyed at the same time; the fire lasted for days. The Public Records Office was full to overflowing with papers, specially brought in for safe-keeping during those times of trouble and change. To lose the records that had been accumulated over centuries was an appalling tragedy; these included parish records from all over the country, the deeds of Christ Church from its foundation and archives from country houses as well as maps and surveys of great historical importance. As with the Custom House, a magnificent programme of rescue and renovation was soon under way and by 1932 the building was functional once more, although the interior was drastically changed. The two wings which used to project beyond the line of the portico were shortened by twelve feet in the rebuilding to facilitate the flow of traffic along the quays; a major element in Gandon's magnificent design was thus lost.

KILMAINHAM GAOL
Inchicore Road

The history of Kilmainham Gaol reflects the long and bitter struggle for independence in Ireland and many of the country's heroes were imprisoned here during the 140 years following its construction in 1787. The prison was built at Gallows Hill, Kilmainham, to the design of John Traill, High Sheriff of Dublin and architect of the Marshalsea, the debtors' prison, and replaced the gaol at Old Kilmainham, which was begun in 1210 and built as part of the priory complex of the Knights of St John of Jerusalem. This had continued in use after the confiscation of the priory in 1542. John Howard, Sheriff of Bedford, visited the old gaol more than once and described its appalling condition in *The State of the Prisons*. As a result a Bill was put through Parliament by Sir Edward Newenham in 1786 to authorize the present building; four years later he was to find himself locked up in Kilmainham for failing in the payment of a debt.

A sinister doorway greeted the unfortunate prisoner as he entered: five entwined serpents cast in bronze and known as the Five Devils of Kilmainham are set in a rusticated stone lunette above the door, and above that is the gibbet where public hangings took place.

During and after the rebellion of 1798 the gaol was filled with political prisoners, who mingled with the ordinary criminals. In 1803, after his abortive insurrection, Robert Emmet and two hundred others were crammed in although there were only fifty-two cells in all. Emmet was taken from here to his execution outside St Catherine's Church. There are three fearful dungeons beneath the gaol containing punishment cells.

In 1857 the architect John McCurdy was awarded a prize for his plans for the redesigning and enlargement of the gaol. This was completed in 1863 and the building has changed little since. In 1866 the Fenians were imprisoned here. In 1881 Charles Stewart Parnell spent six months in the gaol after his election as President of the Land League. He signed the No Rent Manifesto and negotiated the Kilmainham Treaty with Gladstone from his cell.

In 1914 the gaol was turned into a military barracks to accommodate extra troops recruited for the First World War. Two years later it was a prison once more and all those sentenced to death for their part in the Easter Rising were executed in the stone-breaking yard here, apart from Roger Casement, hanged in London. Among the national heroes executed were Pearse, Ceannt, McDonagh, McDermott, Plunkett, Clarke and Connolly, who was shot seated on a chair, as he had been wounded in the fighting. One of the last great Irishmen to be held in the gaol was Eamon de Valera in 1923. This was his second internment at Kilmainham; he had escaped execution in 1916 as he was an American citizen.

In 1924 the doors of the prison clanged shut for the last time and the grim, old building was abandoned to the elements. A voluntary committee began collecting funds for its restoration in 1960 on account of the exceptional historical interest of the building. The committee was determined to preserve the gaol as a shrine dedicated to those who suffered in the long and bitter struggle for Irish freedom. The gaol is now open to the public and a museum has been established here.

ABOVE The entrance door of Kilmainham Gaol, with the five chained serpents, or demons, known as the Five Devils of Kilmainham in the arch above.

LEFT Many famous Irishmen were incarcerated here and it has now been restored and converted into a museum.

KING'S INNS

Henrietta Street

The King's Inns, which bestrides the top of Henrietta Street, serves as the Dublin headquarters of Ireland's barristers. Built of silver-grey granite, with Portland stone dressings, it is resplendent now after its recent cleaning. The King's Inns is the third monumental building given to Dublin by James Gandon, after the Custom House and the Four Courts, and is the least well known of the three. It is also the best preserved, having escaped destruction during the Civil War, and its dining hall is the most important original Gandon interior to have survived in Dublin. In Henrietta Street are the grandest houses on the north side of the city; this street had always been a cul-de-sac and the residents, having enjoyed an open view of grass and trees at the top of their street, were by no means pleased at the loss of this amenity when the King's Inns was built, with its back to them.

The earliest Inn of Court in Dublin was in existence at the end of the thirteenth century in St George's Lane; it occupied Collett's Inn where accommodation was provided for lawyers and judges. A tradition was established that has endured to the present day, whereby those studying for the bar sat down to dine with their elders and betters as a means of learning their profession, and some manners, at first hand. In 1541 Henry VIII proclaimed himself King of Ireland and in that year his Privy Council was petitioned by the Dublin lawyers who 'thought it mete to be in one house together at board and lodging in term time'. They went on to say that a common Inn would assist 'the bringing up of gentlemen's sons within this realm in the English tongue, habit and manners'. The king presented to the Irish judges and teachers of the

ABOVE The front hall with its vaulted ceiling leads to the great dining hall.

RIGHT The dining hall is the only major Gandon interior in Dublin to have survived intact. Obligatory dinners still form part of the training for a barrister.

LEFT The principal facade of the King's Inns faces a park. James Gandon designed the central portion of the building and the cupola in 1800, and it was subsequently enlarged by three bays on either side. The central figure, known locally as Henrietta, used to bear a gas-light aloft in the central rotunda of the Four Courts.

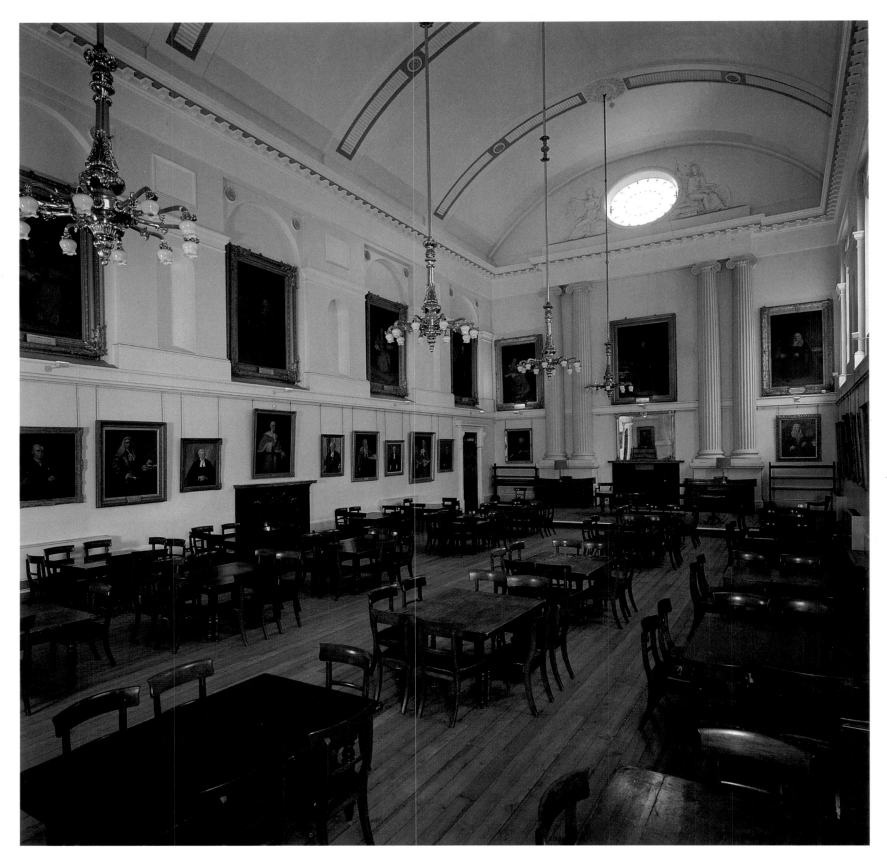

law the monastery of Friar Preachers, the Dominican Friary of St Saviour, which had recently been confiscated. It was situated on the north bank of the Liffey where the Four Courts now stands. As a mark of gratitude for this gesture the Inn of Court henceforth called itself The King's Inns and put up a building on Inns Quay which became part of history when it was used by James II in 1689 to hold his last parliament.

By 1750 this building was becoming derelict. As part of it housed the parliamentary and judicial records, vital when the ownership of land came into dispute, George II was petitioned for a grant of £5,000, which he approved. Thomas Cooley produced a design for housing the

King's Inns and the record office as well as courts. The foundation stone, probably only for the record office, was laid in 1776. Cooley died in 1784 and two years later James Gandon took over the commission, building the Four Courts to hold the Courts of Law and the Public Record Office on Inns Quay. The King's Inns were still without a home and were forced to lease accommodation; in 1792, for example, they rented as a dining hall the theatre in Fishamble Street where the first performance of Handel's *Messiah* had taken place some fifty years earlier.

In 1793–4 the treasurer of the King's Inns, William Caldbeck, leased two parcels of land at the top of Henrietta Street: the Plover Field from

Lord Mountjoy and the primate's garden from the Dean and Chapter of Christ Church. In 1794 Caldbeck, who was an amateur architect, submitted plans and elevations for a dining hall and library which were approved by the benchers. However, at the eleventh hour the project was deferred due to a dispute about the lease of the land. It was later felt that a professional architect should be engaged for a building of such importance, and in 1800 the benchers were considering plans for a library and dining hall submitted by Richard Morrison, Graham Myers and James Gandon, who was to be the successful candidate. John

top floor has three plaques and a number of medallions in place of windows. Edward Smyth also carved these three plaques: the one on the left shows mythological figures, the one in the centre is thought to represent either Queen Elizabeth I receiving gifts or the restoration of the King's Inns in 1607, while the one on the right has eleven figures including Time, History, Wisdom, Security and Law.

The entrance hall is vaulted and leads up a shallow flight of steps to the great dining hall, where the bold clear-cut lines impart a masculine severity suitable to its purpose. It is twice as long as it is broad and

LEFT The royal arms surmounting the triumphal archway in Henrietta Street are by John Smyth, son of Edward. Francis Johnston closed the top of Henrietta Street with this archway leading to the King's Inns in c.1820.

Fitzgibbon, Earl of Clare, the Lord Chancellor, laid the foundation stone on 1 August 1800.

Gandon's plan placed the hall and library at an angle to Henrietta Street. An eleven-foot wide right of way, dividing the two original plots, led from the top of the street at an angle to the west and this pathway was a determining factor in the layout of the present building. Gandon allowed the old right of way to run between them. Instead of facing down the noble row of houses, the main facade of the King's Inns looks west across lawns and trees. It was intended that a crescent containing chambers for the barristers would be built here but this scheme came to nothing. The hall and library were linked together by a triumphal arch surmounted by an upstairs corridor forming a bridge, with a cupola to cap it all and bind the design together.

A pair of grand entrance doorways, quite without parallel in Dublin, are flanked by giant Portland stone caryatids, carved by Edward Smyth. On the left the doorway that leads eventually to the great dining hall is supported by Ceres, goddess of Plenty, and a Bacchante, or female follower of Bacchus, the god of Wine, holding a goblet. The doorway to the right, originally intended to lead to the library, has male caryatids representing Law with book and quill, and Security with key and scroll. Gandon's dislike of windows is evident in the facade of this building. The central section is completely blind and the

was heated by three cast-iron chimneypieces; two of these are elaborately ornamented with a gilded Irish crown surmounting an open book, which displays twin Hibernias and the motto *Nolumus mutari*. The ceiling is barrel-vaulted and light comes from tall round-headed windows facing south, with panels in the opposite wall designed to take full-length portraits of legal figures. At either end two pairs of fluted Ionic columns support an imposing entablature; above the entrance are the figures of Temperance emptying a container of wine and Prudence holding a mirror and an arrow entwined with an eel. Presumably these figures were intended to serve as good examples for the students at table below. Above the benchers' dais are the figures of Justice reclining on a globe, holding her sword and scales, and Wisdom resting on three large books, one marked 'Solomon', with a paraclete displayed on the shield she is holding. These figures were moulded in stucco by Edward Smyth.

In 1808 Gandon, depressed by the endless delays that were caused by the shortage of money, resigned from the project leaving his partner, Henry Aaron Baker (1753–1836), in charge. The King's Inns proved to be Gandon's swan-song and the great man retired to Canonbrook, Lucan, at the age of sixty-five. His letter of resignation was full of disappointed pride. It was, however, left to Francis Johnston to complete the building and to convert the unfinished library into the

RIGHT The King's Inns library, designed by Frederick Darley in 1826, has specially made cast-iron tables and the ceiling boasts a vast plaster acanthus. The library contains an important collection of books and manuscripts, including two Folio Shakespeares.

ABOVE Cast-iron fireplace in the dining hall, one of a pair incorporating a gilded Irish crown in the decoration above an open book bearing the legend '*Nolumus Mutari*'.

Registry of Deeds, which purpose it serves to the present day. Johnston finished the cupola to Gandon's plans and in about 1820 designed an ingenious curved triumphal archway at the top of Henrietta Street surmounted by the royal arms, the work of Edward Smyth's son, John. In the 1840s the main facade was prolonged by three bays on either side, sensitively blending them with Gandon's work; this extension has been attributed to Jacob Owen, chief architect to the Board of Works, but there are grounds for believing that the north wing may have been designed by Frederick Darley, who was responsible for the main staircase.

The King's Inns has amassed a fine collection of portraits of their most notable members, including the work of painters such as John Lavery, William Orpen, James Sleator, Leo Whelan and John Butler Yeats. Facing the staircase hangs *High Treason* by Lavery, a large canvas depicting the court room scene of Sir Roger Casement's unsuccessful appeal held in London in 1917.

The female statue facing the west front is known by the boys of the neighbourhood as Henrietta; she was moved here from the Four Courts in 1880. Dr C.P. Curran, writing in his notebook about the Four Courts, says:

No one knows whence came this figure of Truth which was the first statue to grace our hall nor on what date it alighted on its stony ground.

Holding her torch aloft, I find her first mentioned in *The Citizen* (Dec. 1840) when she is already the butt of ribaldry. 'For the interior of the Courts', says the architectural writer, probably Mulvany, 'we daily tremble. The gas-woman whom we have recently been scandalized to see established in the centre of the Hall is below all comment of a critical kind.' Who subscribed for it, who made it, was it an effort of the Board of Works, was it set up in allegory or satire, was her torch in truth gas-lit? I do not know.

In 1822 the benchers decided to build a law library and what had been the primate's house at the top of Henrietta Street adjoining the King's Inns was demolished to make way for it. The Greek Revival library building was designed by Frederick Darley, and work on it commenced in 1826. Darley was one of a building, quarry-owning and brewing family; he designed both New Square and the exquisite Magnetic Observatory, a small Greek Revival building (now re-erected at UCD, Belfield), for Trinity College. The interior of the library is very handsome with remarkable cast-iron tables especially created for it. The room has a gallery supported on columns and a vast plaster acanthus centrepiece adorns the ceiling. The library contains over 110,000 volumes about half of which relate to the law. There are two Folio Shakespeares, several incunables and a collection of fifteenth- to nineteenth-century manuscripts in the Irish language.

THE CHAPEL ROYAL, DUBLIN CASTLE
Castle Street

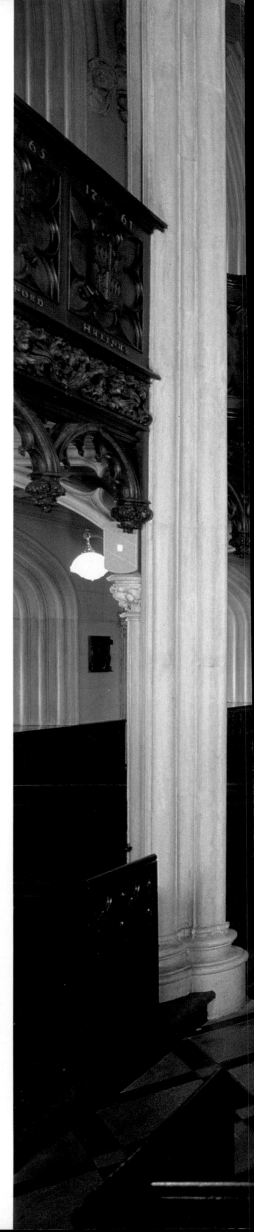

The Chapel Royal was the private chapel for the viceroy, his family and his court; services here were attended by much pomp and ceremony. The viceroy could approach his pew in the chapel gallery from the State Apartments, without going out of doors, by means of a battlemented Gothic corridor which skirts the south side of the Record Tower.

James Gandon prepared plans for a chapel for Dublin Castle in 1801, but withdrew from the project as he considered that the commission rightly belonged to the architect of the Board of Works. Francis Johnston was appointed to this position in 1805 and work began on the chapel to his designs in 1807. Johnston was an eclectic architect, equally at home whether working in the Neoclassical, Greek Revival or Gothic manner. The Chapel Royal is in the pointed Gothic style and the exterior is broken by a series of 'buttresses' which terminate in elegant finials; twin Gothic towers at the east end flank the door to a spacious basement. There are over a hundred carved heads, in Tullamore limestone, decorating the exterior of the building and representing religious, legendary and historical figures; these are the work of Edward Smyth and his son John. Heads of St Peter and Jonathan Swift are on either side of the entrance door which adjoins the medieval Record Tower. It leads into the main body of the chapel with its oak galleries, beautifully carved by Richard Stewart and displaying the coats of arms of the viceroys from 1172. Later arms can

RIGHT The vaulting in the Chapel Royal is made of plaster and painted to resemble stonework. The carved woodwork, by Richard Stewart, displays the arms of each successive viceroy from 1172, and the last panel available was filled with the arms of Lord Fitzalan in 1922.

BELOW Work began on a Gothic Revival chapel for the viceroy and his court within the walls of Dublin Castle in 1807. The architect was Francis Johnston.

The viceregal pew with the arms of Devonshire, Harrington, St Patrick, Carteret and Bolton, with their dates.

be seen on the chancel walls and in the stained-glass windows. It is remarkable that the last available space should have been filled with the arms of the last viceroy, Lord Fitzalan, in 1922. The panel at the front of the primate's pew is devoted to St Patrick, with his coat of arms and the date 432, flanked by the arms of the Earl of Harrington (1755) and Viscount Carteret (1724).

Michael Stapleton's son George was responsible for the fantastic plasterwork of the fan vaulting, made to imitate medieval stone tracery. Edward Smyth and his son John made the plaster heads and the full-length figures above the east window. Among the wide range of people represented here between the stained-glass windows and the plasterwork are Moses with the ten commandments, Christ, the Virgin Mary, the Evangelists, Pontius Pilate, St Peter, St Patrick, Brian Boru and Dean Swift.

The floor is elegantly paved in black and white stone, set on the diagonal. Some of the original pews designed by Johnston are now in the entrance hall of the State Apartments and the pulpit is in St Werburgh's. The four central panels of the east window contain early stained glass, depicting scenes from the Passion of Christ; these windows were purchased on the continent by the viceroy, Earl Whitworth, and presented to the Chapel Royal.

The first service was held on Christmas Day 1814, and the viceregal court worshipped here until 1922. In 1943 the Chapel Royal was reconsecrated as the Church of the Most Holy Trinity and is one of the few churches in Ireland to have changed from Protestant to Catholic. A major refurbishment programme was recently undertaken and the church is now used for ceremonial occasions as well as being open to the public in conjunction with the State Apartments.

THE ROYAL COLLEGE OF SURGEONS
St Stephen's Green

The dignified granite facade of the Royal College of Surgeons faces a fine statue of Robert Emmet, the heroic rebel and orator, beside the railings of St Stephen's Green. The college was founded in 1784 and under the terms of its royal charter it was given the power to control the practice of surgery and to provide surgical education; it was also freed from the guild partnership it had hitherto enjoyed with the barbers, described by William Dease as 'that preposterous union'. Dease was responsible for achieving this separation and is commemorated in a handsome seated statue in the front hall of the present building. Thanks to George Renny, a surgeon and Director-General of the Army Medical Department in Ireland, £6,000 was voted by the Exchequer for the purchase of the site at the corner of St Stephen's Green and York Street.

It was here that the surgeons built their first headquarters to the

and respondent pilasters, is similar in design to that of the Rotunda Hospital. It leads to a magnificent top-lit staircase, designed by Parke with flowing Adamesque plasterwork. The barrel-vaulted boardroom at the top of the stairs, also by Parke, has very fine plaster decoration. Among the portraits is one by William Cuming of George Renny holding a drawing of the original three-bay building.

During the Easter Rising in 1916, a contingent of the Citizen Army, led by Michael Mallin and Countess Constance Markievicz, attempted to hold St Stephen's Green, digging trenches in the park oblivious to the fact that it was overlooked on all sides. The Shelbourne Hotel was quickly occupied by troops and the rebels decided to retreat into the College of Surgeons. The countess rang the door bell, but receiving no answer blew in the lock with her revolver. Their contingent held out here to the end. As Diana Norman recounts in *Terrible Beauty, A Life of*

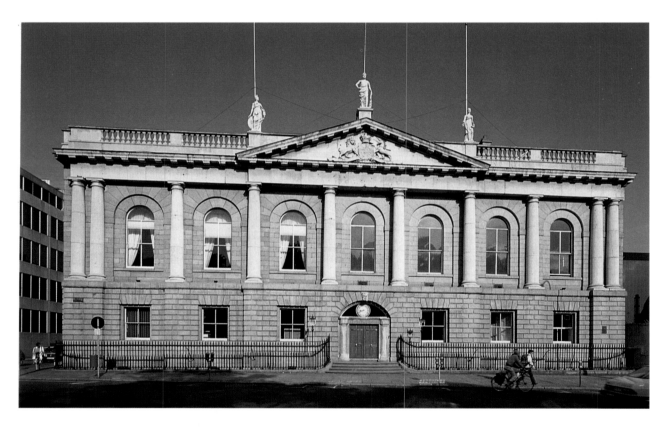

Edward Parke designed the original building for the Royal College of Surgeons in 1810. This occupied the southern, or left-hand, three bays of the facade and in 1825 William Murray added four more bays to the north.

designs of Edward Parke, and the building was opened in 1810. The architect was the brother of Robert Parke, responsible for the design of the western extension to the Parliament House in 1787. The original college occupied the southern three bays of the present facade with a five-bay return on York Street, later extended. The present front was designed in 1825 by William Murray, cousin of Francis Johnston. He extended the building northwards by four bays and recentred the pediment, which originally stood in front of three bays to the south of the facade. The pediment was given three statues by John Smyth: Asclepius, the god of Medicine, is in the centre, on the right is Athena, goddess of Wisdom and War and patroness of the Useful Arts, and on the left stands Hygiea, goddess of Health; the royal arms are set in the tympanum.

The entrance hall by Murray, with its four free-standing columns

Constance Markievicz, '. . . you can see the College of Surgeons roof from the Constitution Room at the top of the [Shelbourne] hotel. At noon every day of the Rising week, they say, "for humanitarian reasons", Con would hoist a flag which brought about a truce between the two forces, stopping the firing just long enough for a hotel employee to nip across into the park and feed the ducks.'

The countess surrendered the building to Captain de Courcy Wheeler, whose brother, Sir William, was a fellow of the college and shortly to become its president. Mallin was captured and executed but the countess's death sentence was commuted on account of her sex. After the General Amnesty of 1917 she was released and later became the first woman to be elected to Westminster. These were stirring times; it was not long before the martyrdom of the few led to Irish independence.

ABOVE The top-lit staircase was part of the original building designed by Edward Parke and has fine plasterwork in the Adam style.

LEFT The front hall resembles the hall of the Rotunda Hospital. The seated statue facing the entrance door is of William Dease, one of the founders of the college, and was commissioned from Sir Thomas Farrell by Dease's grandson in 1886.

Many colourful characters have passed through the college. The legendary anatomist, Tom Garry, whose portrait is in the Anatomy Room, boasted that 'the name of Tom Garry was a household word even in the depths of Africa where the name of the Lord was not yet known'. He claimed that only God and he possessed a genuine appreciation of anatomy, and of the two he had the greater knowledge. Another was Philip Crampton, who, at an advanced age, claimed that he had swum across Lough Bray, ridden into Dublin and amputated a limb before breakfast. Dominic Corrigan has his statue here, even though he was a physician, and Gustavus Hume, who besides being a surgeon was the property developer of Hume Street and Ely Place, is represented by a portrait in the Council Room.

The college is unique among Dublin institutions in that it has never suffered from sectarian discrimination and in 1885 it became the first such institution in the British Isles to admit women. In 1977 the building was greatly extended along York Street and the medical school established here accommodates 800 students, many from overseas; the college is also reponsible for postgraduate training of surgeons in a number of specialities connected with surgery. Recently it acquired the adjacent Mercer's Hospital where there is now a fine medical library and hostel accommodation for overseas students. The college looks back with pride on two hundred years of progress in the field of surgery and looks with confidence to the future.

ST MARY'S PRO-CATHEDRAL
Marlborough Street

Although the Pro-Cathedral is used for state occasions, it has always had a special place in the hearts of the Dublin people, to whom it is known affectionately as 'The Pro'. A constant stream of several thousand faithful passes through here every day to attend Mass, say a prayer or light a candle. In 1993 the church suffered a serious fire but, to ensure the daily throng were not disappointed, the administrator, the Very Rev. Thomas Gould, saw that the church did not close while repairs were carried out.

The Pro-Cathedral, dedicated to St Mary, exists today thanks to the unstinting effort of John Thomas Troy, appointed Catholic Archbishop of Dublin in 1786. He began collecting funds to build 'a dignified spacious church' in central Dublin but did not live to see its completion, and the first Mass in the unfinished church, known then as

RIGHT The nave is flanked by Greek columns which continue round the apse, where there is an immense stucco representation of the Ascension by John Smyth.

LEFT The foundation stone of the Pro-Cathedral was laid in 1815, but the identity of the architect is not known for certain. The main portico, which is derived from the Temple of Theseus in Athens, is surmounted by statues of the Virgin Mary, St Patrick and St Laurence O'Toole.

the Roman Catholic Metropolitan Chapel, was his own requiem. The Catholic community in Dublin is still, to this day, without a cathedral although the Protestant Church of Ireland maintains two: Christ Church and St Patrick's.

The first site under consideration for St Mary's early in the nineteenth century was where the General Post Office now stands on O'Connell Street. However, it was felt that such a public position might jeopardize the introduction of Catholic Emancipation; prejudice against Catholics was still rife after the 1798 rebellion, in which some parish priests had played a leading role. A less conspicuous site was chosen on Marlborough Street opposite Tyrone House; formerly the town house of the Earl of Annesley, it was purchased for £5,100 and a deposit was paid in 1803.

In 1814 advertisements announced a competition and invited designs for the new church; a Greek Revival entry signed only with the letter 'P', was chosen as the winner. The identity of the architect has never been established for certain, although John Sweetman, an active Catholic layman, has been credited with the design. Frederick O'Dwyer has detected the influence of Louis Hippolyte Le Bas, a French architect who had undertaken work for Napoleon. This could

LEFT Monument to Cardinal Paul Cullen, who became archbishop in 1852 and was one of the most important figures in the church of his day. The sculptor was Sir Thomas Farrell.

RIGHT The base of the Cullen monument depicts scenes from his life and ministry: working for the sick and poor, training priests and educating the young.

FAR RIGHT Our Lady's Altar, with flickering candles placed by the constant stream of faithful that come to pray. The pedimented altarpiece is beautifully carved and has a pair in the Sacred Heart altar on the opposite side of the church.

explain the secrecy surrounding his involvement so soon after the Napoleonic Wars between England and France. The church of Notre Dame de Lorette, which was completed in 1824, closely resembles the exterior of St Mary's and was designed by Le Bas. The interior of the Pro-Cathedral is similar to another Parisian church, Saint Philippe-du-Roule by Chalgrin. Sweetman was exiled in Paris after taking part in the 1798 rebellion and he could have sent over the plans from there. Whoever the architect may have been, he designed a powerful facade, too powerful in its massive proportions perhaps for the narrow street where it stands.

The foundation stone was laid by Archbishop Troy in 1815, and the following year a model of the building was made to a scale of one inch to one foot. This is certainly the largest architectural model ever made

in Ireland; it is possible for a person to walk inside. At present being restored, the model will be returned to the special room constructed for it at the top of the Pro-Cathedral. It was constantly referred to during the construction of the building and faithfully copied, except for the inappropriate addition of a dome.

The main portico is derived from the Temple of Theseus in Athens and the pediment is surmounted by statues of the Virgin Mary, St Patrick and St Laurence O'Toole; the fluted Doric columns without bases continue inside in a grand internal colonnade. A half-dome above the altar contains a stucco representation of the Ascension with highly stylized cloud effects, the work of John Smyth. The high altar was carved by the Irish sculptor, Peter Turnerelli (1774–1839), and among the monuments are two of Sir Thomas Farrell's finest works: a statue of

Archbishop Daniel Murray, who is depicted kneeling, and another of Archbishop Paul Cullen, which is embellished with scenes of his ministry around the base.

On the feast of St Laurence O'Toole in 1825 Archbishop Murray celebrated the inaugural High Mass to a packed congregation, which included Daniel O'Connell. The choir sang Mozart's *Mass in C Minor*. At the reception following, Richard Sheil, later an MP, said: 'At last an edifice worthy of the loftiness of our creed stands in the centre of the metropolis. Our religion has at last lifted up its proud and majestic head.' Catholic Emancipation came at long last in 1829.

In 1848 the Greek-Doric south portico was completed by closely following the great wooden model. It was executed by John B. Keane, who had designed the fine Church of St Francis Xavier in Gardiner Street, and is more original, with its twin pavilions, than the main front; the recessed portico had been designed to support four statues of saints. Stained-glass windows depicting Our Lady flanked by St Laurence O'Toole and St Kevin were installed behind the sanctuary in 1886.

Edward Martyn of Tulira Castle, Co. Galway, a leading figure in the Irish literary and artistic revival, endowed the Palestrina choir for male voices in 1902. In 1903 a young man from Athlone wrote to ask if he could join it; his name was John McCormack. He sang with the choir, directed by Dr Vincent O'Brien, for some years, won the gold medal at the Feis Ceoil and went on to become a world-famous tenor. The William Hill organ, which was rebuilt in 1971 by J.W. Walker, is much used for recitals as well as for daily services.

VICTORIAN AND EDWARDIAN DUBLIN

The early years of the nineteenth century saw a decline in the economic and political importance of Dublin which had held the position of second city in the United Kingdom throughout the eighteenth century. By the 1860s it only ranked fifth and was even surpassed by Belfast before the end of the century. The Act of Union of 1801 abolished the Irish parliament, and with its removal the aristocracy returned to their country seats taking with them the glamour and glitter of the social scene. No private houses of any importance were built in the city after 1800, as the more affluent still living in Dublin retreated to the new suburbs leaving the city centre as a place of work. The fate of the great eighteenth-century mansions was left to chance. Leinster House fared well, being purchased by the Dublin Society as its headquarters, but others were less fortunate; Aldborough House became a school and Powerscourt House a government stamp office. Moira House, with its wonderful interior, was acquired by the Association for the Suppression of Mendicancy in Dublin, later known as the Mendicity Institution which attempted to care for street beggars and provide a public wash-house. Many were used as government offices and business premises for professional people. Worse still was the fate of those houses that found no suitable alternative use; they became slum dwellings and a survey at the time showed that one third of the population lived in single-room tenements. The wide staircases of the Georgian houses were removed and the service stairs used instead so that extra rooms could be crammed in. The north side of the city suffered particularly badly from such exploitation and destruction.

During the Napoleonic Wars the blockade of the continental ports resulted in an unprecedented demand in England for Irish agricultural produce; when the wars came to an end, however, this market collapsed. As a result many unemployed farm workers drifted into the city to join the throngs left unemployed by the falling demand for builders, craftsmen, dressmakers and domestic servants. One of Dublin's most important and labour-intensive industries from the seventeenth century onwards had been the weaving of wool, linen and silk. After the Act of Union Ireland became part of a free trade area

with Britain; the removal of protective tariffs in the textile industry exposed it to competition with England where the industrial revolution had introduced methods of mass production. As a result the weaving industry in Dublin declined, contributing to the general depression in the city.

Although Dublin never became industrialized, it was the administrative capital of Ireland and as such required an expanding civil service. It was also the centre for banking, law and medicine, and the army maintained a large permanent garrison in the city. The building industry declined due to the lack of new large private houses, but the nineteenth century was notable for the building of institutions such as prisons and mental asylums as well as cultural buildings such as the museums and galleries. While traditional crafts declined, the brewing and distilling industries expanded rapidly; Guinness's, for example, became the largest brewing enterprise in the world. Transport developed into a major industry, as Dublin was the chief point of entry for the passenger boats from Britain as well as for imported goods such as coal, iron, clothing, hardware and consumer goods, and the point of departure for the export of live cattle, hides and other agricultural produce.

The railway age reached Ireland in the 1830s and by the middle of the century a nationwide network radiated from the city. Dublin gained some fine buildings in the great railway termini serving the lines that crossed the country. The railways provided employment and reduced transport costs benefiting the Irish economy. From the 1870s trams were introduced to Dublin and made the suburbs such as Rathmines and Clontarf more accessible.

Daniel O'Connell, a lawyer from Co. Kerry, was the great popular hero of the time; he fought for the right of Catholics to stand for parliament and hold high office. In spite of the opposition of the Duke of Wellington, the arch-Tory prime minister who was born in Dublin, O'Connell stood for a vacant parliamentary seat in Co. Clare in 1828 and was elected by an overwhelming majority; legislation for Catholic Emancipation was rushed through to avert a civil war, and in 1830 O'Connell was permitted to take his seat in Westminster thus

Cottage *orné* at the entrance to the Zoological Gardens in the Phoenix Park by Decimus Burton (1800–1881), an English architect who designed the Ionic screen at Hyde Park Corner. He worked on improvements at the Phoenix Park from 1834 to 1849, designing the park gates as well as the cottage *orné*.

becoming the first Irish Catholic to hold a legislative position since 1692.

After Emancipation in 1829 there was a great increase in Catholic church building. At first these churches followed the Classical tradition looking to Rome, but later the Gothic style became popular, principally due to the influence of A.W.N. Pugin and his son Edward. Of the Irish-born architects, Patrick Byrne was the principal exponent of the Classical style, and J. J. McCarthy designed many churches in the Gothic idiom. The established Protestant Church was quicker to embrace the new fashions, building Gothic churches from the 1820s. Later in the century other Victorian styles were used, as can be seen in the polychromatic Romanesque facade given to St Ann's by Thomas Newenham Deane in 1868. The restoration of the two Gothic cathedrals, St Patrick's and Christ Church, was carried out during the 1860s through the respective generosity of Sir Benjamin Lee Guinness and the Dublin distiller, Henry Roe.

With the availability of new building materials and the lower cost of transport, architectural styles changed and the reserved Georgian buildings gave way to the more ornate Victorian styles, which varied from Scottish Baronial to Lombardo-Romanesque. During the nineteenth century banks and insurance buildings were constructed to give an impression of solidity and worth; fine examples may be seen in College Green and Dame Street. Granite was difficult to work for detailed carving and was replaced by limestone and sandstone. Red brick became available from England and stone of various types and colours was combined with it.

The influence of John Ruskin was apparent in the fine work of the architectural firm of Deane and Woodward. Benjamin Woodward (1816–61), the designer of the partnership, was one of the most brilliant architects of the nineteenth century and was responsible for putting the firm into the forefront of the profession in the British Isles. Woodward trained as an engineer but a passionate interest in medieval architecture led him to change professions. He entered the practice of Sir Thomas Deane (1792–1871) in 1845 and was made a partner in 1851 together with Dean's son Thomas Newenham (1828–99). Deane and Woodward were the first and most successful architects to apply the principles of John Ruskin, as put forward in his books *The Stones of Venice* and *The Seven Lamps of Architecture*. Ruskin emphasized a return to early medieval styles, beauty imitated from nature, building for posterity, irregular massing, the use of the best materials and the freedom of craftsmen to express themselves. The firm's first important commission was the Museum Building at Trinity College (1853–57)

LEFT The Genealogical Office and Alliance Française, formerly the Kildare Street Club, Kildare Street was built by Deane and Woodward in 1858–61 with the collaboration of C.W. Harrison for the naturalistic sculptural ornament. After the club sold the building and moved to St Stephen's Green, the great Victorian staircase was demolished; its only crime had been that it took up too much space.

BELOW The game of billiards has ever been synonymous with club life, and at the base of the twin capitals on the ground floor of the former Kildare Street Club is the well-known scene of monkeys playing billiards.

and in 1853, with Ruskin's influence, they won the competition for the design of the Oxford Museum.

The emphasis on ornamentation and freedom of expression for craftsmen, as advocated by Ruskin and implemented by Deane and Woodward, resulted in the emergence of two outstanding firms of stone-carvers during this period, the O'Shea brothers from Cork, whose work can be seen on the museum buildings at Trinity and Oxford, and C.W. Harrison, originally from Yorkshire who was responsible for the carving on the former Kildare Street Club (1858–61), also by Deane and Woodward. Henry Acland in his book *The Oxford Museum* (1858) writes: 'The capitals are partly designed by the men themselves and especially by the family of O'Shea who bring wit and alacrity from the Emerald isle to their cheerful task.' Although stone-carving continued to play an important part in Victorian architectural ornamentation, by the 1880s stone was frequently replaced by yellow and red terracotta, easily moulded and less expensive. The South City Markets and McKee Barracks were built of red brick dressed with terracotta.

The great advances in technology in the nineteenth century made possible the use of cast iron, wrought iron and glass in construction. The Allied Irish Bank in Foster Place has a three-bay glazed roof and the passenger sheds of the railway stations were built of the new materials. Two Dublin-based engineers achieved fame as iron-workers: Richard Turner of the Hammersmith Works, who roofed the original Westland Row and Broadstone Railway Stations, and Robert Mallet of Ryder's Row, who constructed the roofing at Kingsbridge. Turner also made the glass palm houses at Glasnevin and Belfast Botanic Gardens and at Kew Gardens.

In the 1840s Ireland was devastated by famine, a national disaster of unprecedented proportions. The potato blight struck in 1845, and again from 1846 to 1848. As a result one million people died from starvation and another million were forced to emigrate; emigration became part of life for the masses; 300,000 people left the country in 1851 alone. Many starving families converged on Dublin, which was already crowded with beggars.

Queen Victoria first visited Ireland soon after the famine in 1849 and her visit was a great success; it was love at first sight. She took to the country with enthusiasm, promising to return, which she did, four years later, to visit the International Exhibition. According to Dublin legend, when the Book of Kells was placed before her in the library of Trinity College, she seized a pen to sign it before anyone realized what she was going to do. In fact she signed a sheet of parchment which was later bound in with the famous book. The queen returned late in life saying that her visit was out of gratitude for the bravery of the Irish regiments in the Boer War.

At the Great Exhibition of 1851 in London, Queen Victoria bought two copies of the exquisite Tara Brooch, which had been found on the beach near Drogheda in 1850 and is one of the most important examples of Celtic Irish metalwork. From about this time there was a new interest in native Irish design, which gave birth to the Celtic Revival. Irish motifs, often sentimental, such as harps, Hibernias, wolfhounds, shamrocks and round towers, intertwined with Celtic filigree patterns, came to be widely used in graphic designs. With the Anglo-Irish influence waning, Irish craftsmen were beginning to look to Celtic sources such as the Book of Kells and other medieval manuscripts for inspiration. This movement was reflected in ceramics, silver and textiles, and also in furniture where the wood was often disguised to resemble bog oak with Irish decoration.

The cultural centre of Dublin was Leinster House, the headquarters of the Dublin Society, which was made 'Royal' during the visit of George IV in 1821. The large lawn that separated it from Merrion Square, which was the site of the International Exhibition in 1853, soon afterwards had matching museum buildings, one on either side, the Natural History Museum and the National Gallery. The first of these, the Natural History Museum, was designed by Frederick Villiers Clarendon in 1856. This was built in the Italian palazzo style in order to blend in with Leinster House. The niches facing the lawn were to have had life-sized statues of famous naturalists carved in Caen stone but this scheme was abandoned. The narrow panels above are carved with serpents and crocodiles, and over the entrance can be seen the figure of Neptune with a dolphin on either side.

The museum houses the society's extensive collection of geological and zoological material, formerly in Leinster House itself. The geological collection includes fossils, minerals and rocks. The building was inaugurated in 1857 by none other than Dr David Livingstone, who spoke on his 'African Discoveries'. Three giant skeletons of Irish red deer, extinct since 8,000 BC, greet visitors as they enter, and most of the ground floor is devoted to native Irish birds and animals, which has earned it the schoolchildren's nickname of 'the dead zoo'. The great gallery upstairs is reserved for the museum's international collection of mammals and invertebrates. The manner of display is attractive, reminiscent of an eighteenth-century cabinet of curiosities. The National Gallery was built on the north side of Leinster Lawn to balance the Natural History Museum and was opened in 1864.

ABOVE The Natural History Museum, Upper Merrion Street, was designed by Frederick Villiers Clarendon in 1856 and built on Leinster Lawn. It was opened in the following year by none other than Dr David Livingstone, who spoke on his 'African Discoveries'.

LEFT Affectionately known to school children as 'the dead zoo', the Natural History Museum has a most attractive manner of display, reminiscent of an eighteenth-century cabinet of curiosities. The ground floor is principally devoted to Ireland; here the visitor is greeted by the skeletons of three giant Irish red deer.

One of the best known Victorian landmarks in Dublin is the Shelbourne Hotel, which stands on St Stephen's Green on the site of the old house of the Fitzmaurice's, Earls of Shelburne. Its doors first opened in 1824 and among its most famous visitors was William Makepeace Thackeray, who described his visit in 1842 in *The Irish Sketchbook*. The present building dates from 1867 and was designed by John McCurdy, the architect of the Royal Marine Hotel in Dun Laoghaire. His design is said to be based on the Langham Hotel in London. Elizabeth Bowen writes in *The Shelbourne*:

The departure in splendour, from the hotel, of guests bound for a ball or Drawing-room was one of the spectacles of Dublin, a drama played to an audience of old-timers, critical, but well-mannered . . . All eyes, expectant, were fixed on the Shelbourne's door – which, frequently opening, exposed to view the bright-lighted hall, ivory pillars, and crimson carpet . . . ladies' plumes nodded, satins gleamed, jewels shot out rays; the black-and-white of the gentlemen was immaculate.

ABOVE Iveagh Market, Francis Street, was built for the first Earl of Iveagh by Frederick Hicks in 1907 to provide the street traders of the area with a covered market. Lord Iveagh, who was the sole proprietor of the Guinness brewery for a time, was criticized by the Temperance movement for providing the poor with a convenient place to sell their rags, so that they could buy another pint of his stout.

ABOVE LEFT The Shelbourne Hotel, St Stephen's Green, is a famous Dublin landmark and is now part of the Forte worldwide chain of hotels. The constitution of the Irish Free State was drafted in 1922 in an upstairs room which is kept unaltered on account of its historical importance.

LEFT University College, Dublin, in Earlsfort Terrace was the second home of the Catholic University after Newman House and was built in 1912 by R.M. Butler. At the back an earlier hall, by Alfred Gresham Jones, has recently been converted into the National Concert Hall. UCD has now moved most of its faculties to Belfield on the outskirts of the city.

The Shelbourne today remains the fashionable meeting place for Dubliners, particularly at the time of the Royal Dublin Society's Horse Show traditionally held in early August. The constitution of the Irish Free State was drafted in a room on the first floor of the hotel in 1922 and because of its historical interest the room remains unaltered. The Victorian iron railings that surround the hotel can be compared to those at Iveagh House opposite. There is a statue to the memory of Wolfe Tone on the corner of St Stephen's Green opposite the hotel; the patriot is surrounded by granite piers, nicknamed 'Tone Henge'.

Just across the Green from the Shelbourne Hotel, a few yards up Earlsfort Terrace, stands the great facade of University College, Dublin, which housed the university until it moved to Belfield leaving only a few sections of faculties here. The design of this facade and that of Government Buildings on Merrion Street owe much to the river front of Gandon's Custom House. Edwardian architecture represented a return to grand and simple lines, which had been largely forgotten in the watered-down classicism of the second half of the nineteenth century. The architect for University College, Dublin, was Rudolph Maximilian Butler (1872–1943), who won an architectural competition in 1912. An earlier building, which originated as the Great Hall of the Dublin International Exhibition in 1865, designed by Alfred Gresham Jones, was incorporated in the new structure; since 1981 it has served as Dublin's Concert Hall.

Poverty had always been an appalling aspect of life in Dublin and some of the worst city slums were beside St Patrick's Cathedral, which was restored by Sir Benjamin Lee Guinness in the 1860s. Anxious to help alleviate the dreadful conditions among the poor, his third son, Edward, later the first Earl of Iveagh, set up a charitable trust to rehouse the slum dwellers and create a park on the north side of the cathedral, St. Patrick's Park. He built the red brick, Dutch-gabled flats at Bull Alley and a play-school for the children of the area. There were also public baths, a swimming pool and a hostel for men, which has recently been refurbished. He provided a market on Francis Street nearby, so that the street traders could sell their wares under cover. The Iveagh Market was designed in 1907 by Frederick Hicks. The Iveagh Trust still flourishes and now provides 692 flats in the area as well as 140 apartments for the elderly between Bull Alley and Rathmines.

Whereas the design of the Iveagh Market looks backwards to Palladio with its arcaded front and Classical pediment, only five years later the Office of Public Works built the Pearse Street Garda Station where the elevations alluded to contemporary British revivals. The police station was designed in 1912 by a team led by Andrew Robinson (1858–1929). Its long sparkling gabled frontage faces Trinity College; on either side of the entrances are carved heads wearing Dublin Metropolitan Police helmets and caps, to distinguish the entrance for officers from that of other ranks.

Andrew Robinson's other works include George's Hall, the new Supper Room at Dublin Castle added for the visit of George v and Queen Mary in 1911 and the west wing added on to the Viceregal Lodge at the same time. The royal visit was an unqualified success and Robinson was given the Royal Victorian Order. It made up for the previous visit by Edward VII in 1907 when the Irish crown jewels were stolen on the eve of the king's arrival. When Robinson, who came from

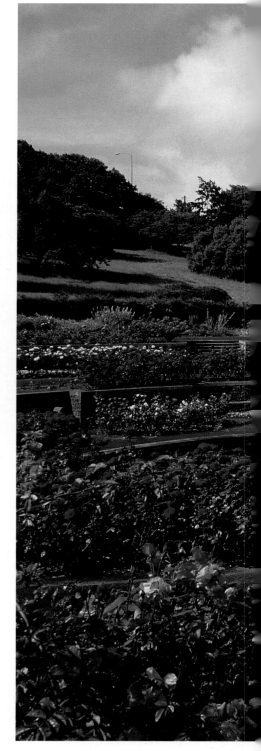

Co. Antrim, was pressed by a reporter for information about the theft, he replied blandly 'I did not take them.'

From the middle of the nineteenth century the demand for Irish independence gathered pace, bitterly opposed by the Protestant Unionists in Ulster. It was not however until 1914 that an Act was finally passed setting up a parliament in Dublin subservient to that in Westminster, with a provision allowing the opt-out of the Ulster counties. This legislation was suspended due to the outbreak of the Great War. In the event it was pre-empted by the Easter Rising of 1916 when the Irish Volunteers, led by Pearse, and the Citizen Army under James Connolly took possession of several key Dublin buildings, including the Four Courts, the Royal College of Surgeons and the General Post Office, where Pearse proclaimed an independent Irish Republic. O'Connell Street was the scene of fierce fighting and all buildings from the Post Office to O'Connell Bridge were destroyed by British artillery. After six days the rebels surrendered leaving over 450 people dead. The uprising had no hope of success and little support from the public, but the British government's draconian measures, executing the fifteen leaders by firing squad and imprisoning 3,500 Irish, swung public opinion behind the radical Republican groups.

The demand for independence was now relentless and in a general election in 1918 seventy-three out of a hundred and five members elected to Westminster were members of Sinn Féin, led by Eamon de Valera. Boycotting Westminster, they set up their own assembly, the first Dáil Éireann, or Parliament of Ireland, which met in the Round Room of the Mansion House on 21 January 1919 and declared the Free State of Ireland. The Anglo-Irish war of 1919–21, known as 'the Troubles', followed with violent clashes between the British troops, the Royal Irish Constabulary and the infamous Black and Tans on one side and the Irish Republican Army, using guerilla tactics, on the other. A treaty was negotiated with the British government in July 1921, under which Southern Ireland was to become the Irish Free State, a self-governing dominion within the British Empire. The state was to

ABOVE The long gabled frontage of Pearse Street Garda Barracks faces Trinity and was designed in 1912 for the Dublin Metropolitan Police by Andrew Robinson of the Office of Public Works.

RIGHT The Garden of Remembrance, Islandbridge, commemorates those who gave their lives in the Great War and was opened in 1937. It is now being completed to Lutyens' original design and will commemorate those who lost their lives in both World Wars as well as on peace-keeping missions.

have a governor-general and MPs would have to take an oath of allegiance to the Crown. The first governor was Tim Healy and the present Áras an Uachtaráin became known as 'Uncle Tim's Cabin'.

The treaty was signed in December 1921 and a provisional government took over from the British authorities. The following year a bitter Civil War broke out between the forces of the provisional government under Michael Collins, who had accepted the treaty, and the anti-treaty Republicans led by Eamon de Valera, who wanted a full Republic; peace was not restored until 1923, by which time the government had executed 77 people and imprisoned 12,000 more. The Irish Free State shed its remaining ties with Britain during the next twenty years and a Republic was declared in 1948.

The troubled years from 1916 saw the burning and destruction of the Custom House and the Four Courts, including the Public Records Office where centuries of Ireland's most precious records from medieval times were housed. The eastern side of O'Connell Street was bombed by government troops during the Civil War and the buildings razed to the ground; as a result very little remains in O'Connell Street of the eighteenth- or nineteenth-century buildings. The street was rebuilt in the 1920s in differing late-Classical styles with heights and materials regulated by the city architect.

In 1919 a memorial committee was established to commemorate the 35,000 Irishmen who lost their lives fighting in the Great War. £50,000 was collected and various schemes were proposed, including one for Merrion Square and another for O'Connell Street. Because of the Civil War the undertaking was delayed until 1931 when the Taoiseach, W.T. Cosgrave, agreed to the present site at Longmeadows on the south bank of the Liffey at Islandbridge. Sir Edwin Lutyens (1869–1944), the distinguished English architect, provided the design; his other Irish commissions include work at Lambay Island and Howth Castle, both in Co. Dublin, as well as the design of the gardens at Heywood, Co. Laois, now in the care of the Office of Public Works. The original

building work at Islandbridge was carried out by ex-servicemen using wheelbarrows to move the earth and block-and-tackle to erect the stonework; during excavations Viking graves containing skeletons and artefacts were discovered on the site.

Today a stone cross looks down on an elaborate symmetrical garden layout with four classical pavilions of granite linked by pergolas, symbolic of the four provinces of Ireland. There are round ponds and terraced flowerbeds, but due to a shortage of funds the ornamental bridge over the Liffey and other features were abandoned; the memorial was opened in 1937. In 1993 a bandstand was erected in the form of a domed temple with a Tuscan order, broadly based on the ideas of Lutyens. It is hoped that a footbridge will be constructed to provide a link between the Magazine Fort in the Phoenix Park with the Garden of Remembrance and then on to Kilmainham. In 1988 the monument was refurbished and rededicated to the 49,400 Irish servicemen who fell in both World Wars.

CHURCH ARCHITECTURE

FROM CLASSICAL TO GOTHIC

In the eighteenth century the plain, rectangular structures of the Protestant churches were generally Classical, even when attached to a Gothic tower. The two last great Dublin churches of the established Church in the Classical style were St George's, Hardwicke Place and St Stephen's, Mount Street Crescent. Francis Johnston lived in Eccles Street, beside which he built the church of St George, begun in 1802 and completed in 1814. It has the finest Wren-type spire in Dublin and stands on the crossroads of three formerly important Georgian streets. The church was deconsecrated in 1990 and its future is uncertain. St Stephen's, known as the 'pepper-pot' church because of the shape of its tower and cupola, was designed by John Bowden in 1821 in the Greek-Revival style and closes the vista of the southern side of Merrion Square in a most pleasing way. Although still used for services it is also the venue for classical concerts and other events.

The Gothic Revival came to Ireland in the 1760s mainly introduced through domestic architecture but ironically it did not become popular in the building of churches until the following century, even though the style was itself inspired by early Gothic church architecture. After 1780 Gothic windows were sometimes inserted into existing churches, while the plain glazing was often replaced with stained glass in the nineteenth century. The Gothic Chapel Royal, designed by Francis Johnston, was built in 1807 in Dublin Castle.

Some Protestant churches in the Gothic style were built in the new suburbs by the ecclesiastical Board of First Fruits, who employed John Bowden and John Semple. St Mary's Chapel of Ease was designed by John Semple (1830) in a unique style of Gothic architecture, and St Andrew's in Suffolk Street, another Gothic church, was constructed in 1860 by Lanyon, Lynn and Lanyon of Belfast, replacing an earlier church which was destroyed by fire. The restoration of the two Cathedrals during the nineteenth century by two generous individuals was of major importance; Sir Benjamin Lee Guinness rebuilt St Patrick's Cathedral at a cost of £160,000 from 1860 to 1864, and Henry Roe, a Dublin distiller, underwrote the cost of a major restoration of Christ Church Cathedral, which was re-opened for worship in 1878. The *Dublin Penny Journal* observed in 1832 that:

> The new protestant Churches are generally in what is called the Gothic or pointed style of architecture, but those of the Roman catholics are more usually in the Greek or Italian style – a choice which may be variously accounted for, either from the taste for such a style acquired by the ecclesiastics in their foreign travels, or by the wish to have their places of worship distinguished from those of the established Church.

The earliest Catholic churches, barely tolerated under the Penal Laws, were known as 'chapels'. To avoid attracting attention, they were very plain on the outside but many were luxuriously decorated inside with furnishings from the continent. The Franciscan Church on

LEFT Built on an island site, St Stephen's Church, Mount Street Crescent, faces down the entire length of Merrion Square South, creating one of Dublin's best known vistas. Known as the 'pepper-pot' church, it was designed by John Bowden in 1821 and completed after his death by Joseph Welland.

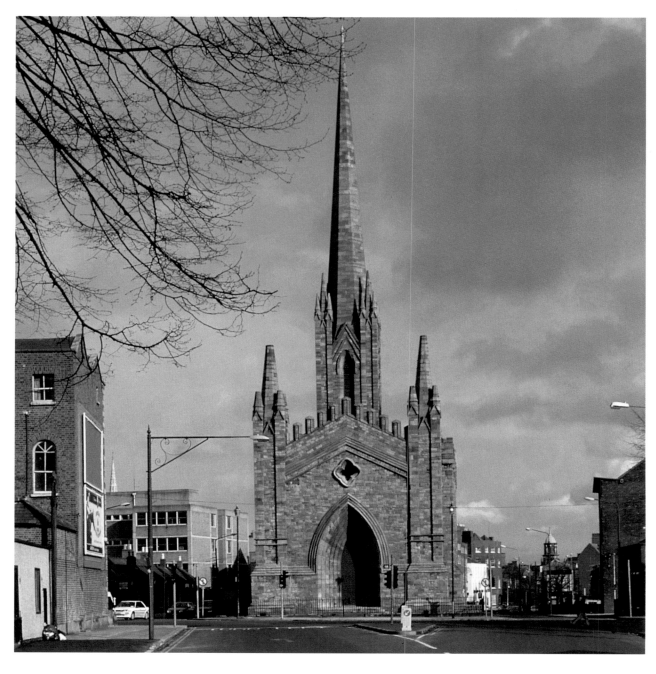

LEFT Popularly known as the Black Church, because the local black calp limestone of which it is constructed turns black when wet, St Mary's Chapel of Ease, St Mary's Place, is one of the most extraordinary buildings anywhere and was John Betjeman's favourite Dublin church. The church was designed by John Semple in 1830 and the Gothic finials were even more tapering when it was built, as can be seen from an old photograph in *Dublin Churches* by Peter Costello.

BELOW The interior of St Mary's Chapel of Ease is in the form of a single parabolic arch so that the walls begin to lean inwards from floor level. It was deconsecrated in 1962 and now belongs to M.G.M. Financial Services, which has retained the amazing architectural features intact.

Merchants Quay is still known as Adam and Eve's because the original Mass House was located at the rear of a tavern of this name. None of these 'chapels' survive in Dublin but the cathedral in Waterford, built from 1793 to 1796, is a 'chapel' from penal times and still known locally as the 'Big Chapel' or 'Great Chapel'

The gradual relaxation of the Penal Laws from the last decades of the eighteenth century gave the Catholics the confidence to worship more overtly. One of the earliest surviving Catholic churches in Dublin, although now deconsecrated, is St Michael and St John's. This is a very early example of a Gothic Catholic church, stylistically a grandchild of Walpole's Strawberry Hill – Gothick within and without. It was designed by John Taylor in 1815 and comes a quarter of a century ahead of the movement towards Gothic architecture in the Catholic Church. Those churches built in Dublin after the introduction of Catholic Emancipation in 1829 generally tended towards the Classical style associated with Rome. Patrick Byrne (1783–1864) was an able exponent, working expertly in this manner for many years: St Audoen's on High Street, St. Paul's on Arran Quay and the frontispiece of St Nicholas of Myra are examples of his work in the Classical style. John B. Keane built the Church of St Francis Xavier in 1829 for the Jesuits on Gardiner Street, with a handsome Ionic portico. St Andrew's, Westland Row, was designed by James Bolger and, at the

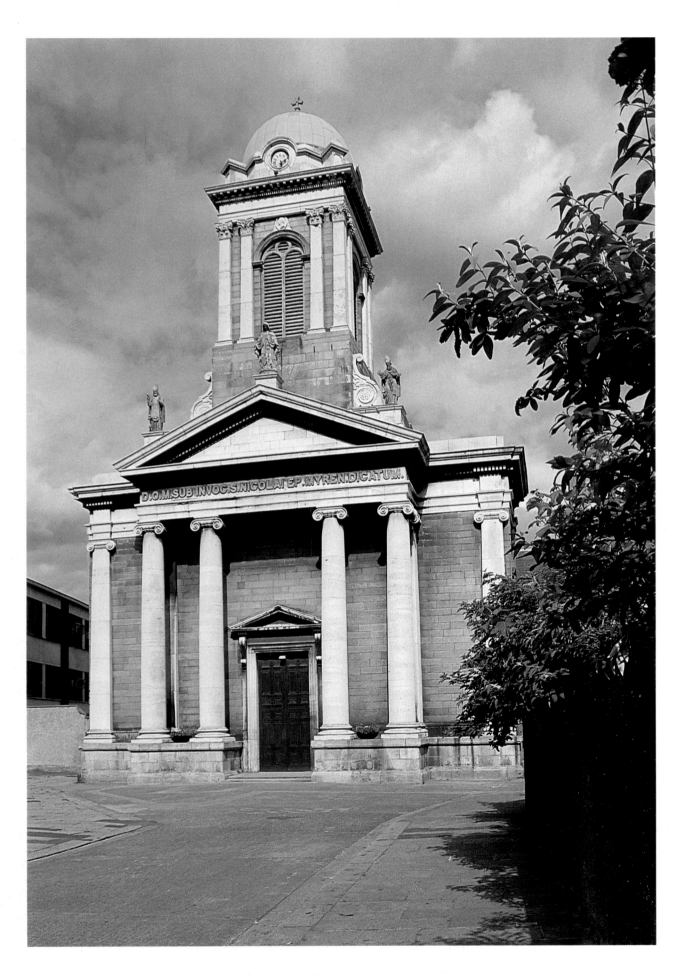

LEFT St Nicholas of Myra, Francis Street, was begun in 1829, the year of Catholic Emancipation, and designed by John Leeson. The portico and cupola however were added by Patrick Byrne in 1860. The three statues on the pediment are of the Virgin Mary, St Patrick and the patron saint of the church, better known as Santa Claus.

RIGHT The colourful interior of St Nicholas of Myra has a lovely *pietà* over the altar carved by John Hogan, who also sculpted the angels at each side. Hogan modelled the plaster reliefs of the Last Supper and the Marriage of the Virgin. Above the sanctuary are the Twelve Apostles, each painted with his appropriate symbol. The nuptial chapel has a stained-glass window by Harry Clarke depicting the Marriage of the Virgin.

time of its building in 1832, it was the largest Catholic church in Dublin. Its giant Greek-Revival portico is surmounted by a statue of St Andrew with his cross. Daniel O'Connell, who lived nearby in Merrion Square, was involved with the selection of the site and construction of the church. Mr Bloom in James Joyce's *Ulysses* arrives at St Andrew's late for Mass.

During the second half of the nineteenth century Catholic church building came under the influence of A.W.N. Pugin and his son, Edward Welby Pugin, who, with their Irish counterpart, J.J. McCarthy, were passionate devotees of the Gothic. McCarthy designed St Saviour's, Lower Dominick Street, in 1852, and E.W. Pugin with George Ashlin, his partner and brother-in-law, built the Church of St Augustine and St John, Thomas Street, in 1862. This has been described as the finest example of Gothic Revival in the city.

The Nonconformists, like the Catholics, began to get some freedom around the turn of the century. Most of their churches are simple preaching halls with elaborate facades like the Evangelical church, Merrion Hall, designed by Alfred Gresham Jones in 1862, and the

ABOVE St Andrew's Church, Westland Row, where Joyce's Mr Bloom attended Mass, was the largest Catholic church in the city when it was built in 1832. It was designed by James Bolger and the statue of St Andrew bearing his cross surmounts the Grecian pediment. The church is cleverly integrated into the street it stands in.

RIGHT The high altar of St Andrew's Church was imported from Rome and consists of four scagliola columns supporting a pediment. Daniel O'Connell, who lived in Merrion Square around the corner, was a parishioner and was involved with the choice of site and with the building of the church.

FAR RIGHT The elaborate Gothic interior of St Augustine and St John, Thomas Street, which has a many-spired Gothic altar. In 1862 Edward Welby Pugin and his partner George Ashlin were commissioned to design a large church on Thomas Street for the Augustinian Friars, who had been established in the area of St John's Lane since 1704. It took almost fifty years to complete although the church was opened for worship in 1874.

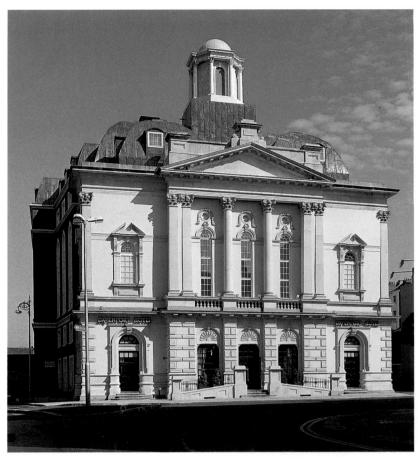

ABOVE Davenport Hotel, Lower Merrion Street, formerly Merrion Hall, was designed as a gospel hall in 1862 by Alfred Gresham Jones. The pulpit was at the centre and over 2,000 seats rose up steeply in galleries. The building was already out of date when it was put up at the height of Victorian evangelical fervour. It is now the Davenport Hotel and the facade has been preserved.

ABOVE The Abbey Presbyterian Church, Parnell Square, is known to Dubliners as Findlater's Church out of gratitude to Alexander Findlater, a local merchant, who paid for its construction. Designed by the Scottish architect Andrew Heiton, it stands on the site of Bective House, the eighteenth-century town house of the Earls of Bective.

Unitarian church in St Stephen's Green, which was designed by the Belfast architect, William H. Lynn, in 1863. An exception was the Abbey Presbyterian or Findlater's Church in Parnell Square, built in 1863 by Andrew Heiton and paid for through the generosity of the merchant Alexander Findlater, by whose name it is generally known. The spire on this beautiful Gothic building is a prominent landmark on the north side of the city.

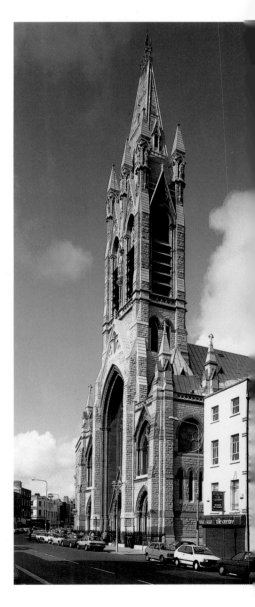

RIGHT The Church of St Augustine and St John, with statues of the Apostles by James Pearse, father of the patriot Patrick Pearse, the leader of the Easter Rising. Ruskin loved the church and described it as a 'poem in stone'.

UNIVERSITY CHURCH
ST STEPHEN'S GREEN

In 1853 the Catholic University opened in the magnificent stone house built in 1765 at 86 St Stephen's Green. The Catholic hierarchy invited Dr John Henry Newman, later to be made a cardinal, to become its first rector. He had converted to Catholicism in 1845, having been a vocal member of the controversial Oxford Movement. Newman considered that a university church was an essential ingredient of the new institution. It would symbolize 'the great principal of the university, the indissoluble union of philosophy with religion'. He purchased 87 St Stephen's Green, an unpretentious brick house which had the advantage of a long garden stretching back to the wall of Iveagh Gardens; this provided the site for his new church. He summoned his friend, John Hungerford Pollen (1820–1902), from England and appointed him Professor of Fine Arts in the new university. Like Newman, Pollen had been ordained an Anglican priest but was received into the Catholic Church in 1852. In his spare time while up at Oxford Pollen had designed and painted the ceiling of Merton College Chapel; he had travelled extensively making drawings of buildings he admired. Newman invited Pollen to decorate the interior of his new church and later wrote, 'My idea was to build a large barn and decorate it in the style of a basilica with Irish marbles and copies of standard pictures.' Building started in mid-1855 and the church was opened in May 1856, although not finally completed until November of that year.

Ignoring the Classical and Gothic styles of church architecture that were prevalent in the 1850s, Newman chose the Byzantine style for his church. The multi-coloured Irish marbles that line the walls create an effective and mysterious backdrop; there is green marble from Galway, red from Cork, brown from Laois and Armagh, and black from Kilkenny. Because of the relatively narrow site it was impossible to break the monotony of the walls with real arches but an arcaded effect was created by the use of painted columns, interspersed by lunettes decorated with saints and angels by Pollen. These columns have alabaster capitals carved in relief which carry the Stations of the Cross. Pollen did not employ highly skilled craftsmen for the carving, as he was afraid that they 'would have attempted smoothness, and what they call finish and so ruin the design'. Ordinary workmen were employed who had 'little to unlearn'.

The culmination of Pollen's decoration was the golden apse, which he painted himself, inspired by the Church of San Clemente in Rome. In the centre is the Virgin enthroned as the Seat of Wisdom and surrounded by ever-diminishing portraits of saints bearing palm branches. These circular paintings are framed by the dark coils of an immense vine which seems to grow out of the canopy that crowns the raised altar. An elevated choir faces across the sanctuary, a reminder of Newman's abiding love of liturgical music. The green-tinted bull's-eye windows are at the top of the walls, only just beneath the beamed roof which is painted in red, green and gold.

The building cost £6,000 instead of the £3,500 estimated; the extra cost was borne by Newman himself, who went into debt as a result. A bust of him by Sir Thomas Farrell, dated 1892, takes pride of place in the centre of the right hand wall.

LEFT The red-brick Byzantine entrance of University Church, St Stephen's Green, built by Cardinal Newman beside the Catholic University of which he was the first rector. It was designed by his friend John Hungerford Pollen, an amateur architect, and opened in 1856.

BELOW Newman's idea for University Church was 'to build a large barn and decorate it in the style of a basilica with Irish marbles'. Newman was pleased with his creation and said, 'The more I looked at the Apse, the more beautiful it seemed to me – and, to my taste, the church is the most beautiful one in the three Kingdoms.'

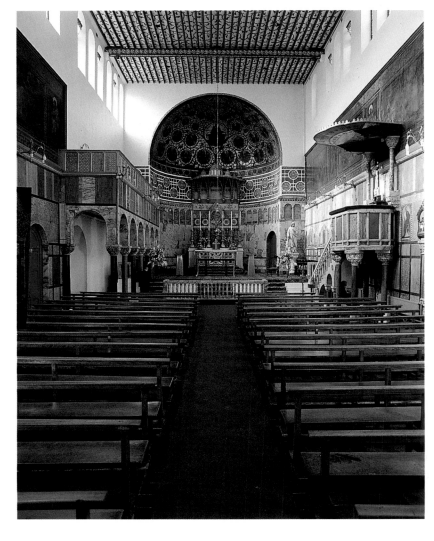

RAILWAY STATIONS

The novelist, Charles Lever (1806–72), has described the varied types of people that made use of the Dublin suburban train:

The 8.30 train is filled with attorneys; the ways of Providence are inscrutable; it arrives safely in Dublin. With the 9.00 train comes a fresh jovial looking sort of fellows with bushy whiskers and geraniums in buttonholes. They are traders. 9.30 the housekeeper train. 10.00 the barristers . . . fierce faces look out at the weather . . . 11 o'clock the men of wit and pleasure.

The railway age came to Ireland in 1834, only ten years later than in England, when George Stephenson had opened the first steam locomotive line between Stockport and Darlington. The romance of the Irish railways has been immortalized by Percy French in his famous song about the West Clare railway. He would surely have approved of the first-ever journey in an Irish railway train, drawn by horses from Westland Row to Kingstown (Dun Laoghaire) on 31 July 1834. By December a steam-powered engine was pulling the first regular passenger train, the Hibernia, on the same line. 'The little carriages, pulled by a high-stacked engine, were painted different colours, purple-lake, yellow-green and Prussian blue according to class,' as Peter Somerville-Large recounts in his book *Dublin*. The railway boom had come to Ireland and developed rapidly so that Dublin is now surrounded by railway stations, although not all of them are still running trains.

The earliest station of architectural importance is Connolly Station, formerly Amiens Street Station, the terminus of the Dublin and Drogheda Railway. This line was later extended to reach Belfast and became the Great Northern Line. The station, designed by William Deane Butler in 1844, is a handsome Italianate building with a two-storeyed central tower that closes the vista down Talbot Street. In 1879, at the northern side of the station, John Lanyon of Belfast designed a red-brick railway office with Dumfries sandstone dressings and a tower echoing Butler's design.

Amiens Street derives its name from Viscount Amiens, created Earl of Aldborough in 1777, the builder of Aldborough House, Dublin's last great private house, which stands nearby. The earl, apparently attempting to lengthen his pedigree, chose Amiens for a title as he claimed descent from Gualtara de Lupella, a native of Picardy, who came to England with William the Conqueror; Amiens is the capital of that province in France. In 1966 the station was renamed after James Connolly, who had been executed for his part in the Easter Rising fifty years before.

Heuston Station, originally Kingsbridge Station, was built in 1845 as a terminus for the Great Southern Railway and later served the Western Railway, linking Dublin with Cork and Limerick. An architectural competition for the design was won by Sancton Wood of London over the Irishman, John Skipton Mulvany. Wood had been a pupil of Sydney Smirke, sometime Professor of Architecture at the Royal Academy and brother of Sir Robert Smirke, who designed the British Museum. The station stands beside the Liffey and took its

ABOVE Heuston Station, St John's Road West, formerly Kingsbridge Station, was built by Sancton Wood, an English architect, after a competition. Inscribed on the parapet are the date of the building, also given as 'Vic VIII', or the eighth year of Queen Victoria's reign, as well as the stone coats of arms of Dublin, Cork and Limerick.

LEFT Connolly Station, Amiens Street, formerly Amiens Street Station, derives its former name from Viscount Amiens, created Earl of Aldborough in 1777, the builder of Aldborough House. The architect was William Deane Butler, who built the station in 1844.

former name, Kingsbridge, from the cast-iron bridge beside it. In 1966 both bridge and station were renamed after Captain Sean Heuston, a former employee of the railway company, who was executed in 1916 for his part in the Easter Rising. He had been in command of the Mendicity Institution on Usher's Quay, formerly Moira House. The station, now beautifully floodlit, looks like an Italianate country house, and the granite facade is busy with giant, engaged columns and carved ornament, including the arms of Dublin, Cork and Limerick; twin cupolas crown the pavilions to either side. The entrance facade on John's Road is, by contrast, severely Neoclassical.

Broadstone Station was commenced in 1841 although it was not finally completed until 1850; it is outstanding for the flawless simplicity of its neo-Egyptian lines. The architect was John Skipton Mulvany (c.1813–1870), an Irishman whose father wrote a life of James Gandon. Mulvany also designed the Royal Irish Yacht Club and the railway station in Dun Laoghaire. Broadstone Station was the terminus of the Midland Great Western Railway; the line to Mullingar was opened in 1849, later continuing on to Galway and Sligo. The station was formerly approached over a drawbridge that floated on the Royal Canal basin, but in 1879 this was filled in. The great colonnade, which once sheltered the jarveys (hackney coachmen) waiting for passengers, was added in 1861 to the design of George Wilkinson (c.1814–90). The roof of the passenger shed was made by the celebrated ironworker, Richard Turner, best known for his glass palm houses at Dublin and Belfast Botanic Gardens and at Kew Gardens. The station closed to rail traffic in 1937 and is now used as a bus depot.

Harcourt Street Station, which opened in 1859 is a noble building with simple lines, free of the ornamentation that might have been expected well into Victoria's reign. It was the terminus of the Dublin and South Eastern Railway, which ran a suburban line to Bray, Co. Wicklow, and was in operation for exactly one hundred years. Thirty-five years after its closure there is talk of re-opening the line to alleviate the city's traffic problems. The station was designed by George

Wilkinson, the railway architect, who was also reponsible for building workhouses and asylums. The grand entrance archway in the brick facade is flanked by a generous classical colonnade of granite. Oval *œil-de-bœuf* windows, just below the parapet, ornament the great walls of the passenger shed, which are constructed from Dublin calp (limestone) and terminate in a magnificent rounded end to the north. The building is now used as offices, and the vaulted basement, which originally housed bonded stores, has recently been restored to use by Findlater's wine merchants.

The building of stations presented a new challenge to Victorian architects, and they responded magnificently. They had to solve the problems of roofing and lighting enormous sheds and experimented with new materials such as wrought and cast iron which had become available in commercial quantities after the industrial revolution. Just as the railways had sounded the death knell to the canal system, so, in turn, the bus and car have taken business from them. Fortunately new uses have been found for the great stations that have closed.

ABOVE Broadstone Station, Phibsborough Road, now closed, was the terminus of the Midland Great Western Railway and was built in the Egyptian style by John Skipton Mulvany in 1841. It is greatly admired for the noble simplicity of its lines.

LEFT Harcourt Street Station, Harcourt Street, was the terminus of the Dublin and South Eastern Railway, which ran a suburban line to Bray, Co. Wicklow, from 1859 for exactly one hundred years. It was designed by George Wilkinson.

THE ROYAL IRISH ACADEMY

19 Dawson Street

The Meeting Room of the Royal Irish Academy was added on in 1854 by Frederick Villiers Clarendon.

Most visitors to Dublin admire the Irish gold objects in the National Museum without realizing that most of this amazing collection in fact belongs not to the museum but to a learned body established in the eighteenth century, which began acquiring early Irish art, artefacts and manuscripts from the time of its inception.

The Royal Irish Academy was founded in 1785 as a society for 'promoting the study of science, polite literature and antiquities'. The Earl of Charlemont, one of Dublin's most learned and cultivated figures, became its first president, and initially meetings were held in his house. The academy's first premises were on Grafton Street, opposite the Provost's House in a building known as 'The Navigation House' and next door to the headquarters of the Dublin Society. After sixty years the academy had outgrown the accommodation here, and in 1851 with the help of the Viceroy, the Earl of Clarendon, it purchased Northland House beside the Mansion House in Dawson Street, where it has remained ever since. This building suited the academy as, unlike most Dublin houses, it was free-standing and therefore less susceptible to fire. This was a growing concern as the collections of rare documents and antiquities were expanding.

Northland House previously belonged to the Reform Club; it had been within an ace of having the windows facing the Mansion House blocked up, as some irreverent members had been observed making faces at the lord mayor. As Craig has written: 'Evidently the Club in its dying days had drifted into unseemly conviviality. No such misconduct has been reported of the members of the Academy, and the windows remain unblocked.'

No. 19 was probably built for Sir John Denny Vesey, Lord Knapton, whose son-in-law, Thomas Knox, bought the house in 1769 from Vesey's own son. Thomas Knox later became Viscount Northland and the house is still known as Northland House. The brick front was originally plain, as the pediments, window surrounds, cornice and string courses are made of plaster and presumably date from the tenure of the academy. The rooms are large and some have good, if not exciting, transitional ceilings; the ceiling over the staircase is compartmented; both the passage and landing have groin-vaulting and there is rich freehand wall decoration here by an unknown stuccodore. Because of the additions, the Venetian window on the staircase has been blocked up and unfortunately the elegant pilasters and entablature have been stripped of paint, revealing the inferior wood, knots and all. A new window was cut through the plasterwork on the north wall.

A large meeting room and a smaller reading room were added at the back. Completed in 1854, these were designed by a young architect at the Board of Works called Frederick Villiers Clarendon, who in 1857 went on to design the Natural History Museum on Leinster Lawn. Considering that the christian names of the Viceroy, Lord Clarendon, were George William Frederick and that his family name was Villiers, the architect's name is a remarkable coincidence.

The Meeting Room, lit from windows high up in the walls, is lined in leather volumes with a row of busts above. Some of these were modelled by Simon Vierpyl in the 1750s for the Rev. Edward Murphy, who gave them to Lord Charlemont in 1774; in 1868 his grandson presented them to the academy as well as the Charlemont manuscripts.

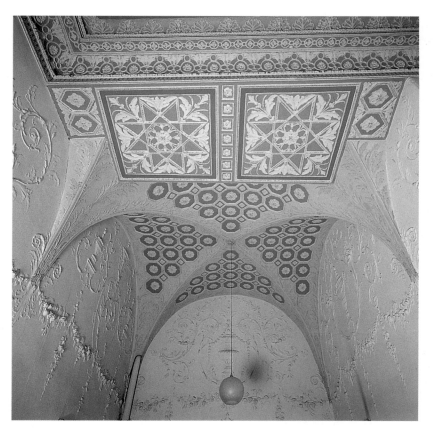

The president's chair was originally in the old House of Lords where it was used by the Lord Chancellor; the bust of Minerva above it was carved by John Hogan. Some of the benches came from the old House of Commons and the three chandeliers are reputed to have hung in the Court of Requests, the ante-room to the Commons Chamber.

The National Museum now houses the remarkable collection of Irish antiquities amassed by the Academy, which were handed over in 1890 so that these priceless treasures could be put on display to the public. Among them are the Ardagh Chalice and the Tara Brooch as well as a major collection of pre-Christian gold ornaments. The library remains in the academy and concentrates on preserving its formidable collection of Irish manuscripts and on acquiring manuscript or printed material relating to the history, antiquities and topography of Ireland. It receives, on an exchange basis, learned journals from similar institutions in other countries. The academy is also the largest scholarly publisher in Ireland; volume v of *A New History of Ireland* has recently been published as part of a ten-volume series. The academy is at present engaged on the first ever monolingual dictionary in the Irish language, and it is a delight to hear this ancient tongue spoken naturally by the young scholars engaged on this work.

The earliest Irish manuscript in existence, known as the Cathach or psalter of St Columba, is believed to date from the latter half of the sixth century and is the library's most prized possession. This priceless collection also includes the Stowe Missal, which contains excerpts from the Gospel of St John and was possibly compiled at St Mael

ABOVE The upstairs landing, with intricately patterned plaster vaulting, is part of the early house still known as Northland House because it was purchased in 1769 by Thomas Knox, later Viscount Northland.

ABOVE LEFT The staircase, with its delicate chinoiserie plasterwork on the walls and compartment ceiling, was originally lit by a Venetian window, which was blocked up when new rooms were built over the garden.

RIGHT The Reading Room. The academy owns a unique collection of early Irish manuscripts accumulated over 200 years. It collects books and other printed material relating to the history, antiquities and topography of Ireland. It is also the largest scholarly publisher in the country, at present engaged on the first monolingual dictionary in the Irish language.

Ruain's monastery at Tallaght in about 800; the manuscript of the Domhnach Airgid of about 750; the Vulgate version of the Gospels; and the Annals of the Four Masters. Many bequests have been added to the library, including the Haliday collection of pamphlets and tracts totalling 25,000 items, mostly relating to Ireland. The widow of the poet Thomas Moore presented his personal library to the academy, where it occupies the shelves of the council room, presided over by a bust of Moore by Thomas Kirk.

The preservation for Ireland of this unique collection of artefacts, manuscripts and printed material owes its existence to the inspired and patriotic vision of the intellectual leaders of the academy over the last 200 years.

BANKING HOUSES

The choice of bank architecture was eclectic during the reign of Queen Victoria, but as a group of buildings the banks of this period had one unifying factor – the wish to impress and at the same time instil a feeling of trust. As the *Dublin Builder* commented in 1863, just as 'a man is generally regarded as a gentleman because he has a good suit of clothes on his back, so too does a respectable show by a commercial establishment inspire confidence in the healthiness of its constitution.' From 1850 a wide variety of banks began to puncture the Georgian streetscape in Westmoreland Street, Dame Street and O'Connell Street. These were built in Lombardo-Romanesque, Ruskinian Gothic and other hybrid styles, the facades ornamented with elaborate carving or moulded terracotta details. Granite was difficult to handle, so limestone and sandstone were the favourite materials.

The Allied Irish Bank, 3 Foster Place, known familiarly as Shaw's Bank, is thought to be the oldest continuously operating bank in Dublin, if not in the whole of Ireland. The origins of the bank go back to 1797 when Sir Thomas Lighton founded it in partnership with Thomas Needham and Robert Shaw. In 1856 George Papworth gave it the present facade with a granite portico, balustrade and urns, and the magnificent cash office was designed by Charles Geoghegan two years later. He created a light and airy space, 80 feet in length; the central span of the large lantern roof is supported by twelve highly ornamental

ABOVE The National Irish Bank, 27 College Green, is one of the finest of Dublin's great Victorian banks on account of the exceptional quality of the carved stonework by C.W. Harrison. The architect was William G. Murray and the bank opened in February 1867.

LEFT The banking hall of the National Irish Bank at 27 College Green, like the lower part of the facade, is in the Venetian style and includes Byzantine columns and an elaborate coved ceiling with coffered plasterwork. The original banking counter, panelled in mahogany, is still *in situ*.

RIGHT The Allied Irish Bank, 3 Foster Place, has a light and airy interior designed by Charles Geoghegan in 1858. Eighty feet in length and with highly decorated iron columns, it is a remarkable survival.

cast-iron columns with decorated capitals. The elaborate ironwork was supplied by Courtney and Stephens. The mahogany banking counter is well carved and shaped like a horseshoe; the original clock, high up in the end wall, used to be wound once a week by climbing onto the roof.

The National Irish Bank, 27 College Green, has an ornate polychrome facade of limestone, Caen and Portland stone as well as polished red Aberdeen granite. The heads that link the windows, carved in limestone, carry on around the building – Victorian successors of the riverine heads on the Custom House. The stonework was carved by C.W. Harrison from Yorkshire, who established a

RIGHT The banking hall of the Allied Irish Bank at 5 College Street is 72 feet long and highly ornamental but exudes a warm welcome.

LEFT Another great city-centre bank by William G. Murray, the Allied Irish Bank, 5 College Street, has a Portland stone facade, and the pediment, carved by Samuel F. Lynn, contains figures representing Manufacture, Commerce and Labour.

leading Dublin firm of monumental masons that survives to the present day. Harrison exhibited 'a technical knowledge, and ... an artistic taste of the very highest order'. The building was designed by William G. Murray for the Union Bank and was completed in February 1867, but by October of that year the company had already collapsed. The banking hall, like some of the lower part of the facade, is in the Venetian style with Byzantine columns and an elaborate coved ceiling.

The present Allied Irish Bank at 5 College Street started life as the head office of the Provincial Bank of Ireland. It was designed in 1862, also by William G. Murray, and opened for business in 1869. The Portland stone facade is busy with carved ornament and decorative features. Immense Corinthian columns support a pediment containing an elaborate composition by the Irish sculptor, Samuel F. Lynn, depicting the genius of banking. The female figure of agriculture is attended by farm workers, a merchant represents commerce and manufacture, a sturdy servant epitomizes the labour force and raw produce is personified by a black man. The vast banking hall measures 72 by 45 feet and is highly ornamented with panelled recesses enclosed by Corinthian pilasters. There are four fireplaces carved in Caen stone; their polished, red Cork marble jambs must have added cheer to the room when the fires were lit.

THE NATIONAL GALLERY
Merrion Square West

The National Gallery of Ireland, which looks across the street at the Rutland Fountain and the great green expanse of Merrion Square beyond, contains a collection of paintings and sculpture of international renown in an ideal setting. It grew out of the International Exhibition of 1853 held on Leinster Lawn, which had been inspired by the Crystal Palace Exhibition of 1851 in London. Whereas the Crystal Palace had enjoyed royal patronage, the Dublin exhibition had only one backer, the philanthropist William Dargan, and it cost him personally the huge sum of £20,000. The son of a Co. Carlow farmer, he had made his fortune from the railways, and by 1853 he had built 600 miles of track in Ireland. The exhibition building, conceived by the Cork-based architect Sir John Benson, was mostly made of timber; the great hall was 425 feet long, 100 feet wide and 105 feet high, with a barrel-vaulted glass roof. Besides displaying the latest industrial exhibits from all over the world, there was a loan exhibition of Old Masters, something which had not been part of the exhibits at the Crystal Palace. Queen Victoria visited the exhibition and offered Dargan a baronetcy which he declined.

RIGHT Sculpture by John Hogan (1852) of Lord Cloncurry embraced by Hibernia with an Irish wolfhound at her feet. The painting behind by Daniel Maclise, 1854, depicts *The Marriage of Aoife and Strongbow on the Battlefield at Waterford.*

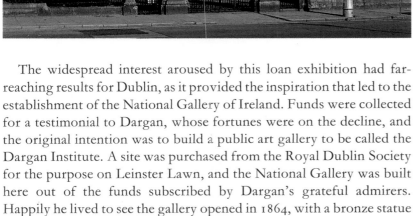

LEFT The National Gallery opened in 1864. It has since built up a magnificent collection of European masterpieces and is especially strong in the Irish School of the eighteenth and nineteenth centuries. The left-hand three bays were designed by Francis Fowke and the gallery has been enlarged twice since.

The widespread interest aroused by this loan exhibition had far-reaching results for Dublin, as it provided the inspiration that led to the establishment of the National Gallery of Ireland. Funds were collected for a testimonial to Dargan, whose fortunes were on the decline, and the original intention was to build a public art gallery to be called the Dargan Institute. A site was purchased from the Royal Dublin Society for the purpose on Leinster Lawn, and the National Gallery was built here out of the funds subscribed by Dargan's grateful admirers. Happily he lived to see the gallery opened in 1864, with a bronze statue of himself by Sir Thomas Farrell in the forecourt.

The National Gallery was designed by Francis Fowke; born in Co. Tyrone, he was a captain in the Royal Engineers and played an important part in the development of 'Albertopolis', the cluster of cultural buildings in South Kensington that were built under the patronage of Prince Albert. The foundation stone of the gallery was laid by the Viceroy, the Earl of Eglinton, on 29 January 1859. The elevations matched those of the Museum of Natural History, which

had been built across the lawn three years previously. The original building occupied the three left-hand bays of the present structure. The portico was added in 1903 to the design of Sir Thomas Manly Deane, and the building was further extended in 1969 by Frank Duberry of the Office of Public Works.

Significant donations, both in funds and works of art, have helped to embellish the collection here which has grown continually since its establishment. Among the most generous patrons have been the last Countess of Milltown, Sir Hugh Lane, Sir Alfred Chester Beatty, George Bernard Shaw and Sir Alfred Beit. Lane gave twenty-one pictures to the gallery during his directorship, 1914–15, and bequeathed his house and property to it; he also designed a uniform consisting of a green tail coat, to be worn by the director of the gallery. Shaw bequeathed it one-third of his royalties, which has enabled significant purchases to be made at a time of spiralling prices for works of art. Pictures purchased with the Shaw Fund include works by Goya, David, Gérard, Fragonard and de La Tour as well as paintings by the

ABOVE A corner of the French gallery with paintings by Yverni (left) and Poussin (right).

BELOW LEFT The main staircase, showing the bold lines of the Victorian interior with its handsome detailing.

leading Irish artists of the eighteenth and nineteenth centuries.

An early director, Henry Doyle, bought many seventeenth-century Dutch masters at a time when they were underrated; he also bought a Fra Angelico and the magical *Rest on the Flight* by Rembrandt as well as two other paintings from the School of Rembrandt. In 1993 an important discovery was made by Sergio Benedetti of the Gallery's restoration studio with the identification of Caravaggio's *The Taking of Christ*. Benedetti had seen the painting on a visit to the Jesuit House in Leeson Street where it had hung unrecognized for many years; the gallery asked the Jesuits for permission to clean and examine it and it was from here that the authenticity of the wonderful painting was established. This masterpiece is now on indefinite loan to the gallery.

The stained-glass artist, Evie Hone, bequeathed a number of Irish and European works of art. The 1986 MacNeill Sweeney bequest included the Picasso painting *Still Life with a Mandolin* (*c.* 1924) and the beautiful composition *The Singing Horseman* (1949) by Jack B. Yeats, the only artist privileged to have a room entirely devoted to his works.

THE ROYAL COLLEGE OF PHYSICIANS
6 Kildare Street

The Royal College of Physicians grew out of the Fraternity of Physicians established in 1654, which included among its members John Stearne, William Petty, Patrick Dun, Richard Steevens and Thomas Molyneux. Stearne was the founder; he was a graduate of Trinity College and left Ireland in 1641 to study at both Oxford and Cambridge. He returned in 1652 to a Dublin ridden with plague and without a hospital to treat the victims of sickness, famine and war – a role which had been undertaken by the monasteries until their dissolution over one hundred years before. Two years later his fraternity was holding regular meetings in Trinity Hall; in return for the use of the hall he agreed to take care of the health of the provost and senior fellows of Trinity without payment. In 1667 Stearne petitioned successfully for a royal charter establishing the Royal College of

RIGHT Graves Hall, named after Robert James Graves whose statue is on the left. On the right is a statue of William Stokes MD, and the portrait in the centre is of John Stearne MD, founder of the Royal College of Physicians in Ireland.

LEFT The Royal College of Physicians, Kildare Street, was designed in 1862 by the great bank architect, William George Murray, on the site of the original Kildare Street Club.

Physicians, of which he was the first president. In the early nineteenth century the college held its deliberations at Sir Patrick Dun's Hospital, before it became established in Kildare Street.

Dr Dominic Corrigan was one of the first of the talented Irish Catholics to achieve prominence in the field of medicine. As an MP he was instrumental in reforming the conditions under which medical practitioners carried out their duties; a quarter of them died from diseases transmitted from their patients. As a politician he was also responsible for education reform and the improvement of Dublin's water supply; the existing system was believed to have caused cholera after the famine. In 1860, under the presidency of Corrigan, the college purchased two houses on Kildare Street as its permanent headquarters. These had belonged to the Kildare Street Club, which had reserved the right to occupy them for some months after the sale while awaiting the completion of their new clubhouse, designed by Deane and Woodward at the junction of Kildare and Nassau Streets. While the club was still in

occupation, the two houses were destroyed by fire with the exception of a billiard room and a racquet court at the back, leaving the Royal College of Physicians with an empty shell. An architectural competition was held for a new building 'in any style other than Gothic' and six designs were entered; these were put on display to the public in Sir Patrick Dun's Hospital. Although John McCurdy was awarded the prize of £50, his design was rejected on the grounds of cost.

William G. Murray, whose father had enlarged the Royal College of Surgeons in 1825, designed the present building. The interior boasts a magnificent double staircase, with Gothic trellis-work in the coving, and an imposing hall, now known as Graves Hall, which contains full-length statues of Dominic Corrigan, Henry Marsh and William Stokes; these are among the finest work of the Irish sculptor, John Henry Foley. A fourth statue of Robert Graves, one of Ireland's greatest physicians, is by Albert Bruce-Joy, a pupil of Foley. In 1863 the billiard room of the old Kildare Street Club was converted into a meeting

ABOVE The magnificent double staircase with cast-iron scrollwork balusters and Gothic trelliswork in the coving.

room but the structure of the roof lights formerly over the billiard table is still in place. The college owns a valuable antiquarian library which was set up in 1713 and has books going back to the sixteenth century as well as an extensive collection of paintings and mezzotints.

By 1963 the stone of the facade was beginning to deteriorate and Desmond FitzGerald, Professor of Architecture at University College, Dublin, was called in to reface the building. The original stonework of the upper floor was taken down and re-erected as a garden ornament at Woodbrook, Bray, the seat of Sir Desmond Cochrane. In the new frontage minor pieces of ornamentation, like dentils, were omitted for reasons of economy, giving it a sterner aspect; iron railings took the place of the original stone balustrade.

The main concern of the college today is postgraduate education; it is governed by some 700 fellows worldwide. The founders set out to raise the standards in the practice of medicine and these are continually being advanced both in Ireland and abroad.

FREEMASONS' HALL

17 Molesworth Street

The Grand Lodge of Freemasons of Ireland was formed in 1725 when on 26 June a hundred gentlemen met at the Yellow Lion in Werburgh Street. Donning their regalia, they proceeded over Essex Bridge and on to the King's Inns, which then stood on the present site of the Four Courts, 'the Grand Master in a Fine Chariot it being a rainey day'. In 1806 the Freemasons were renting Tailors Hall and in 1811 they met in the Assembly Rooms in South William Street.

In 1822 they leased 19 Dawson Street, now the Royal Irish Academy, and in 1829 they took a large room from Mr Inglis, a tavern-keeper in D'Olier Street.

In 1866 a permanent headquarters was at last provided in Molesworth Street on the site of the town house of the first Grand Master, Richard, Earl of Rosse. An architectural competition was held, and was won by Edward Holmes of Birmingham, with Deane and Woodward the runners-up. Holmes employed three architectural orders on the facade, Doric on the ground floor, then Ionic and Corinthian at the top of the building, with the all-seeing eye, symbolic of God, and the Masonic square and compass enshrined in the pediment. The interiors are elaborate, designed to transport the mind to other climes and other

periods of history. The cost of them was met by a voluntary tax which was levied by the Dublin Masons on themselves.

The Grand Lodge Room is in the Classical style with murals by Edward Gibson and life-sized portraits of Grand Masters in elaborate gilt frames, each with their coats of arms above. Edward, Prince of Wales, visited Freemasons' Hall in 1871 and was made a Grand Patron of Irish Freemasonry. His portrait, painted to commemorate this visit, hangs here. The ceremonial chair, carved in Edinburgh, has a coronet and lions' heads on the arms, and the chequered carpet incorporates the Masonic square and compass in the border. The organ is also of note.

The Royal Arch Chapter Room is in the Egyptian style and has Jewish candelabra sitting on Egyptian heads, a combination that no-one has ever been able to explain. It may have derived from the Victorian craze for Egyptology in the 1860s or from an erroneous theory that Freemasonry had evolved from the Egyptian mysteries of

ancient times. The ceremonial chair beneath its multi-coloured Egyptian canopy is flanked by life-sized sphinxes giving the room a slightly Hollywood flavour.

The Prince Mason's Chapter Room, hung with flags, is a cross between Gothic and Tudor; the knightly stalls, with banners incorporating family coats of arms hanging above them, are thought to be based on the choir stalls at St Patrick's Cathedral. The Portland stone mantel is elaborately carved with Masonic symbols.

The Knights Templar Room was built in the form of a medieval chapel, with dim light filtering through the Gothic stained-glass windows on to stone walls. The design was inspired by the twelfth- and thirteenth-century Knights Templar of the Crusades, which is a branch

ABOVE FAR LEFT The Freemasons' Hall, Molesworth Street, was designed by Edward Holmes of Birmingham. Dublin has had a Grand Lodge of the Freemasons since 1725 although this permanent headquarters was not built till 1866.

ABOVE LEFT The Royal Arch Chapter Room – in the Egyptian style but lit with Jewish candelabra.

ABOVE The Grand Lodge Room in the Classical style has murals by Edward Gibson in the lunettes and life-sized portraits of former Grand Masters surmounted by their coronets.

of the order that reflects the chivalric and christian aspects of the medieval orders of knighthood. There is a monochrome portrait of HRH the Duke of Connaught, the son of Queen Victoria, who was Commander-in-Chief of the Irish army and Most Excellent and Supreme Grand Master of the Knights Templar.

Freemasons' Hall contains one of the most fascinating and best-displayed small museums in the city of Dublin that is open to the public. There are portraits, engravings, jugs, bowls, engraved glass, jewels, ceremonial chains, trowels, medals and buckles, all adorned with the mysterious symbolism of the Masons. The apron, a reminder of the stonemason's traditional leather protective garment, is found in every colour, shape and size. Among the myriad symbols are the

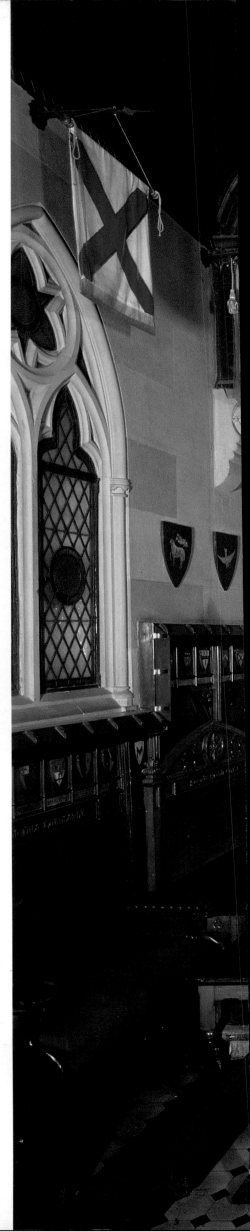

cockerel for the resurrection, the skull and cross bones for mortality and the ark for hope.

Freemasonry flourished in Ireland despite a ban issued by Pope Clement XII in 1738. In 1783 the first Volunteer Lodge was formed as Lodge 620, and it still meets regularly to this day. Augustus Frederick, third Duke of Leinster, was Grand Master for sixty-one years (1813–74). The Duke of Abercorn, the Earl of Donoughmore and the Earl of Charleville were all Grand Masters. Archibald Hamilton Rowan, President of the Society of United Irishmen of Dublin, was a Freemason and even Daniel O'Connell joined the order for a time. In 1814 he defended it declaring that it was based on 'philanthrophy unconfined by sect, nation, colour or religion'.

ABOVE The Prince Mason's Chapter Room contains knightly stalls with banners incorporating family coats of arms, based on the choir stalls of the Knights of St Patrick in St Patrick's Cathedral

RIGHT The Knights Templar Room resembles a medieval chapel with dim light filtering through stained glass.

THE NATIONAL MUSEUM
Kildare Street

The National Museum of Ireland was set up in 1877 with the passing of the Dublin Science and Art Museum Act. The nucleus of the present Decorative Arts and Natural History collections had been assembled by the Royal Dublin Society, which until 1924 had its headquarters next door in Leinster House. The core of the Museum's valuable collection of archaeological and folk items was accumulated by the Royal Irish Academy. This august body began purchasing early Irish treasures in 1785 and it is thanks to it that Dublin has one of the finest displays of antiquities in Europe. The Royal Irish Academy collection was handed over to the museum in October 1890 for public display.

An architectural competition for the museum was advertised in 1881 and sixty-seven architects submitted plans. Of the five chosen, the authorities were embarrassed to discover that not only were they all English but also practically unknown. After much political lobbying and angry letters to the press, a new competition was advertised inviting plans for a National Library, to be built as an entity with the museum. This time Thomas Newenham Deane, Superintendent of Monuments, was chosen; he had entered the competition under the pseudonym 'Crom-a-Boo', the battle-cry of the FitzGeralds. Although the firm of T.N. Deane & Son were determined Gothicists, they produced an essay in Victorian Classicism in deference to Leinster House. The museum and the library were opened on 29 August 1890 by the viceroy, who conferred a knighthood on Deane.

The National Museum which faces the National Library across the front of Leinster House has a vast rotunda inspired by Schinkel's Altes Museum in Berlin, built sixty years before; this serves as the entrance hall and has an attractive mosaic floor. It is said that the marbles from the International Exhibition of 1853 in Dublin were incorporated in the centre court. There is excellent carving in wood by Carlo Cambi whose work can also be seen in the library. The ceramic door surrounds in vivid blue, white and mustard yellow are the most extraordinary feature of the interior and until recently they were covered in magnolia paint; they were made in porcelain by Bermantoft of Leeds. The great entrance hall leads to the museum where the collection of Bronze Age gold is displayed, one of the largest and most important collections in the world. There are gold ornaments dating from 2,000 BC onwards, sun discs and crescent-shaped collars or lunulae, and jewelry of superb craftsmanship. Gold objects from 800 to 600 BC were discovered during the construction of the West Clare railway. Before they could be catalogued by Sir William Wilde, many had been stolen and melted down, but even so the weight of the surviving gold was 174 oz, which made it the greatest find of prehistoric gold ornaments ever discovered in Western Europe. Also on display is the Broighter Hoard, which includes an exquisite model gold boat as well as a collar of the type featured on the 'Dying Gaul' in the third-century BC statue in Rome.

The most famous pieces from the Early Christian Treasury, with their exquisite gold filigree and enamel work, are the Tara Brooch, the Ardagh Chalice, the Cross of Cong and the Derrynaflan Hoard, which was discovered in 1980 beside the ruins of a church on a small green island in a peat bog in Co. Tipperary. This collection is without parallel in Europe.

LEFT Brightly coloured ceramic door surround, with an elaborately carved wooden door by Carlo Cambi of Siena.

RIGHT The domed ceiling has narrow arched windows separated by pilasters that appear to lean inwards, as do those in the Reading Room of the National Library.

BELOW The entrance hall, with the signs of the zodiac in the mosaic floor, surrounded by columns made of Irish marble. The design is modelled on the rotunda of Schinkel's Altes Museum in Berlin.

Excavation work on Viking settlements carried out in Dublin by the National Museum in the twenty years from 1961 to 1981 have brought to light a varied collection of domestic Viking artefacts, which can also be seen here; this includes some wonderful examples of Viking silver. Dr Patrick Wallace, Director of the Museum, is an international expert on the Viking period and led the Wood Quay excavations from 1974 to 1981.

The museum contains extensive collections of Irish silver from the seventeenth century to the Victorian period and there are many fine pieces of early Irish glass. The porcelain collection contains examples from many parts of the world as well as delft made in Ireland. There is a large amount of furniture, mostly Georgian and Victorian, with grandfather clocks, dolls' houses and mantelpieces as well as superb examples of Irish tables and chairs of various dates.

In the extensive textile collection there is a quantity of Irish lace, ball gowns and examples of the Volunteer Fabric, a printed linen depicting the Earl of Charlemont taking a parade of the volunteers in the Phoenix Park in 1783. In another room there is a large variety of Volunteer memorabilia, including flags, uniforms, weapons, medals, drums and printed material. Memorabilia of the 1916 Easter Rising are also on display. Among the sculpture a religious figure in painted wood from Fethard, Co. Tipperary, makes a haunting impression. The great Dublin musical-instrument makers of the eighteenth century, among whom Weber was supreme, are well represented here. A magnificent and unique example of Dublin tapestry-weaving forms part of the collection and was presented by Beatrice, Lady Granard. There is a large collection of folk material, which includes Irish country furniture, examples of traditional basket-weaving and textile-making and implements that were in common use in the Irish countryside.

No. 29 Lower Fitzwilliam Street, a Regency town house just off

Merrion Square, has been restored by the Electricity Supply Board and furnished by the museum. Here can be seen period Irish furniture, glass, silver and other artefacts in an appropriate setting – even the kitchens have been restored to show life below stairs.

The National Museum is fortunate to have been given ethnographical material relating to Captain Cook's third voyage to the South Sea Islands and New Zealand, brought back by the ship's doctor, Dr Patten of Dublin. A collection of Red Indian artefacts comes from Canada, equally far afield. Although the Museum is short of funds and space, the excellence of the collections ensures that visitors will come away enriched by what they have seen and learnt.

The main exhibition area where the superb early Irish gold is displayed. In other departments rich collections of furniture, silver, glass, musical instruments and historical objects of every kind and date will be found.

THE NATIONAL LIBRARY
Kildare Street

The National Library of Ireland developed out of the library of the Royal Dublin Society, which had been established in Leinster House since 1815. The society's objects were 'improving husbandry, manufactures and other useful arts and sciences' and from its inception it accumulated an extensive library. This collection was considerably enlarged when in 1863 Dr Jasper Joly bequeathed his library to the society with the proviso that, in the event of a public library being established, the collection should be given into its care. Since his boyhood he had collected rare books, pamphlets, maps, manuscripts and topographical engravings. The society's library was only accessible to the members and their friends, and it was felt that a library for the general public should be provided.

In 1877 the National Library of Ireland was established by an Act of Parliament and the government bought the society's collection of books, with the exception of certain scientific material, for £10,000. For thirteen years the new National Library remained in Leinster House until a building had been provided for it. William Archer, a Fellow of the Royal Society, was the first librarian and gave valuable

great rotunda surrounded by a Classical colonnade with columns to match those to either side of Leinster House. The walls are of Ballyknocken granite with dressings in soft creamy Mountcharles sandstone which have weathered badly, necessitating replacement. There were formerly groups of statuary on the parapet representing Poetry and Literature and carved by Sir Thomas Farrell, but these have disappeared long since. Deane received a knighthood from the viceroy at the opening ceremony in 1890.

The entrance hall is circular and a perfect Victorian period piece in its decoration. The sun streams onto the mosaic floor through stained-glass windows depicting great literary figures, including Chaucer, Goethe, Shakespeare, Plato and Voltaire; they are the work of Jones and Wallis of Birmingham and the mosaics are by Oppenheimer of Manchester. Between the pillars, up the carved-stone staircase, some ornate woodcarving becomes apparent, executed by Carlo Cambi of Siena. Irish marble from every province was used for the columns throughout the building and the woodcarving of the doors and mantels, also by Cambi, is of the highest quality. The great D-shaped

The design of the National Library reflects that of the National Museum opposite. Both were built by Thomas Newenham Deane, who was knighted at the opening ceremony in 1890. They carry on the line of the string course above the ground floor windows of Leinster House. Deane's firm had entered the competition for the two buildings under the pseudonym 'Crom-a-Boo', the war cry of the FitzGeralds for whom Leinster House was built 150 years before.

advice to the architect on the layout of the new building. For the new library Archer adopted the Dewey Decimal Classification System, which had then only just been invented, but today is in universal use. In 1977 Ireland was one of the few European countries to be awarded a plaque to commemorate the 'early adoption and continuous use' of the system. Archer also designed a special library chair, with a rack under the seat to hold the reader's hat for safety's sake.

Thomas Newenham Deane was awarded the prize in the competition held in 1883 for the design of the library and museum on either side of Leinster House. His plan brought the three buildings into a unified composition; for the library, as for the museum, he designed a

reading room has space for a hundred readers who sit at partitioned tables, each part with its own light, beneath a vast dome with a cherubic frieze by Harrison.

The library possesses a comprehensive record of Ireland and its people, insofar as it has been documented in book, manuscript, map or illustration form. Dr Noel Kissane in his fascinating Heritage Booklet has described the valuable collection of early Irish manuscripts, including the thirteenth-century copy of *Topographia Hibernica* by Giraldus Cambrensis, a scholar and priest who travelled to Ireland twice during the decade following the Norman invasion. On his second visit he accompanied Prince John and stayed for a year; he gives

LEFT Detail of a fireplace carved with grotesque masks by Cambi.

detailed descriptions of the state of the country and its people, depending on travellers he met for his tales of the more distant places.

There are some excellent examples of eighteenth-century Irish bindings, architectural drawings and a vast collection of estate papers including those of Ormonde in Co. Kilkenny, Lismore in Co. Waterford, Fingal in Co. Meath and Inchiquin in Co. Clare. Irish topographical and portrait engravings form part of the collection, in which, as Kissane points out, some historical figures fare better than others – for example, there are over two hundred portraits of Wellington, ninety of O'Connell but only seven of Wolfe Tone. The collection of Irish photographs is extensive and the 40,000 glass negatives forming the Lawrence collection, 1870–1914, are an invaluable record of the period. These photographs came from the firm owned by William Mervin Lawrence which made postcards and sold prints; they chronicle the dress, transportation, architecture, streetscapes and views of the period. The one-armed photographer, Robert French, who worked for Lawrence, was a master of the art. Among the papers of W.B. Yeats in the library there are five drafts of the poem 'The Wild Swans at Coole', which illustrate how the poet strove for perfection in his writing.

The Genealogical Office, headed by the Chief Herald of Ireland, has records going back to the sixteenth century and is now at 2 Kildare Street, close to the library of which it is an important part. It originated as the Office of Arms, which was established in 1552, and it holds the records detailing the grants of coats of arms made over the centuries. People of Irish descent can attempt to trace their ancestry, and the office designs and grants new coats of arms to companies as well as individuals.

There are seven miles of shelves in the library and the material thereon is available to any adult; in addition, exhibitions are mounted both here and round the country for school children. The collection on microfilm of Irish manuscripts held in foreign libraries is much used by researchers as are the old newspapers and parish registers. As technological advances are made, the screen is beginning to take the place of the printed page. Since 1927 publishers in the Republic are obliged to deposit with the library, free of charge, a copy of every publication including all issues of newspapers and periodicals. The library's magnificent collection has also been added to over the years by the generous gifts of many benefactors.

ABOVE The carved woodwork throughout is by Carlo Cambi of Siena whose work is highly individual.

RIGHT The great D-shaped reading room. The library owns a comprehensive record of the history of Ireland and its people in so far as it exists in book, manuscript, map or illustration form.

GOVERNMENT BUILDINGS
Upper Merrion Street

The last great edifice to be erected by the British administration in Ireland was the Royal College of Science. It was also, together with the University College building at Earlsfort Terrace, the last major structure in the city to be built in the Classical idiom. The recent face-lift, removing the grime of nearly a hundred years, has revealed a distinguished example of 'Edwardian Baroque' and has come as a revelation to the Dubliner, for so long oblivious to its beauty.

King Edward VII laid the foundation stone of the Royal College of Science in 1904, an institution originally founded in 1867 under the auspices of the Royal Dublin Society. The building was designed by the English architect, Sir Aston Webb, with the assistance of Sir Thomas Manly Deane of Dublin, the last member of the noted architectural dynasty. The facade of Buckingham Palace and the main front of the Victoria and Albert Museum in London are Webb's best-known works.

The great Portland stone centrepiece of the Dublin building, with its Ionic columns and pediment, is surmounted by a lead dome. An inscription commemorates both the king who laid the foundation stone and his son, George V who declared the building open in 1911.

The two statues at ground level are of Sir William Rowan Hamilton and Robert Boyle. Hamilton was a brilliant mathematician and astronomer, born in Dublin in 1805; he became a professor at Trinity College at the age of twenty while still a student. Boyle (1626–91), the famous scientists, was the fifth son of the Great Earl of Cork. The seated statue in the pediment, designed by Oliver Sheppard and carved by Albert Power, was reputedly inspired by Rodin's 'The Thinker'. Limestone setts from the streets of Dublin have been used to cobble the courtyard, spectacular floodlighting has recently been installed and the central fountain is lit up at night. At the centre of the street frontage there is an attractive colonnaded screen; the design of the two massive blocks to either side, with their pairs of inset Doric columns, owes a debt to the Custom House. On the skyline are enormous sculptured groups of allegorical figures by Albert Power.

The Royal College of Science only remained here until the early

ABOVE LEFT The last great Classical building in Dublin, Government Buildings was also the last to be erected by the British administration in Ireland. It was designed for the Royal College of Science by the English architect Sir Aston Webb, assisted by Sir Thomas Manly Deane. The foundation stone was laid in 1904 by King Edward VII but the entire complex was not completed until 1922.

ABOVE The entrance on Upper Merrion Street. The influence of Gandon's Custom House is evident in the disposition of the columns in the facade. Sir Aston Webb was the great Edwardian architect who gave Buckingham Palace its present facade.

1920s when its students were absorbed into University College, Dublin. In 1926 the laboratories and lecture theatres were taken over by the Engineering and Science Faculties of UCD, which remained here until 1989 when they moved out to Belfield, the new campus on the outskirts of the city.

The north wing of Government Buildings, which now houses the Taoiseach's office, was not completed until 1922 and it was immediately occupied by the Executive Council and government departments of the newly independent country. In those dangerous times armed men had to guard every entrance, not only here at Leinster House and government offices in general.

With the departure of the students the time had come for a major refurbishment programme, completed in 1991, which left the Portland stone facades white where they had been grey and black. This was carried out by K. Unger, D.L. Byers, and A. Rolfe of the Office of

Public Works at a cost of £16 million. The building houses the Departments of the Taoiseach, the Tánaiste (Deputy Prime Minister) and the Attorney-General, together with the Department of Finance, and also provides accommodation for other government ministers. A modern interior has been created using native Irish materials such as oak, sycamore, yew and ash, with linens and wools to furnish it. The Council Chamber is hung with historical Irish portraits; the contemporary Irish paintings which are on display in the corridors come from the loan collections of the Arts Council and the Office of Public Works. In the rotunda outside the Taoiseach's office is a small version of Oisin Kelly's sculpture *The Children of Lir*. A stained-glass window by Evie Hone, originally commissioned for the Irish Pavilion designed by Michael Scott for the New York World Fair in 1939, ornaments the landing of the main staircase; it represents the four provinces of Ireland and is entitled *My Four Green Fields*.

TWO EIGHTEENTH-CENTURY MAPS

Of all the Dublin maps that chart the progress of the city, '*A MAP of the CITY and SUBURBS of DUBLIN . . .*', 1728, by Charles Brooking ranks as one of the most fascinating. The cartographer was a shadowy figure; even the city authorities who gave him a grant of £10 called him Thomas Brooking. The need for an up-to-date map of Dublin was underlined by the publication of a new map of Cork in 1726. Brooking's map is very large, measuring 22½ by 56 inches, and was issued on three sheets, with the twenty-four arms of the Dublin guilds illustrated, as well as twenty vignettes of the principal buildings. It is these that are so revealing to the student of architecture, although Brooking appears to have been a trifle short of edifices, as he included 'A Prospect of the City Bason' amongst them. Dublin's golden age was yet to come – 1728 was the year before the great Parliament House was begun, ushering in Palladian 'correctness' to Dublin, and Ireland for that matter, for the first time. The map was up to date, as it included the new Linen Hall which was only opened in 1728, but it was not entirely accurate – it anticipated the facade of St Ann's Church, Dawson Street, which was never completed as planned, and Maurice Craig says that the house-building on Sir John Rogerson's Quay is depicted more accurately for 1768 than 1728.

There is a plan of the city and above it a panorama showing the principle spires and towers; in later editions a key was added to identify these and the vignettes of buildings were named. The arrangement is unusual in that both the plan and the panorama have the north side at the bottom, because most of the more interesting landmark buildings were on the south side and the Dublin mountains form a picturesque backdrop.

Brooking's venture must have done well as his map was revised subsequently and brought out in further editions with slight variations. For example, the address of Bowles, the printsellers, changed from Cheapside to Cornhill. In 1740 it was reissued on a single sheet without the arms of the guilds and with only two vignettes. The map was plagiarized and re-engraved by the London publishers Overton and Hoole, 'a mean pyratical practice', and published without even Brooking's name. The marginal views were also omitted with the exception of the Poor House – a choice of questionable taste which compounded the offence.

Although Brooking's plan is valuable it does not compare with that of John Rocque, whose four-sheet survey of Dublin was first published in 1756. Entitled the *Exact survey of the city and suburbs of Dublin* it is astonishing for the fine detail with which it marks not only streets and buildings but trees, hedgerows and even the garden layout of each individual Dublin town house. In addition he published the *Plan of the city of Dublin and the Environs*, illustrated here, in 1756, followed by another four-sheet *Survey of the city, harbour, bay and Environs of Dublin* in 1757, in which the *Plan of the city* was reissued as one of the sheets.

The *Plan of the city* shows that the city had expanded east; it illustrates the plan of Phoenix Lodge, the residence of Nathaniel Clements in the Phoenix Park, now Áras an Uachtaráin, as well as Sackville Street as laid out by Luke Gardiner and given the family name of the Viceroy,

Plan of the city of Dublin and the environs, published by John Rocque in 1756.

240

the Duke of Dorset. It is now part of O'Connell Street. Kildare, later Leinster House, whose Burlingtonian forecourt approached through a triumphal arch survived well into the nineteenth century, is illustrated in a bird's eye view as a vignette on Rocque's 1757 survey.

These maps were an amazing feat but Rocque, who was a Frenchman of Huguenot origin, had already published plans of London,

Paris and Rome with great success. In an index to the maps he writes:

After having executed the Plan of London and its Suburbs, I wanted only to do the same by Dublin in order to have the Honour of having traced out two of the largest and most celebrated Cities of Europe.... But we see in this map, that Dublin is one of the finest and largest Cities of Europe, as well on Account of its Quays, which reach with Order and regularity from one End of the Town to the other, as on Account of many grand Buildings in different Parts on either Side . . . and also on Account of several spacious and magnificent Streets, the Gardens, Walks, &c . . . But what contributes yet more than either Nature or Art, to the Embellishment of Dublin, is the Temper of the Inhabitants, obliging, gentle, and courteous.

A map of the city and suburbs of Dublin, published by Charles Brooking in 1728.

ARCHITECTS, ARTISTS
AND CRAFTSMEN

AHERON, JOHN (d. *c.* 1761). Probably born in Limerick, Aheron worked at Dromoland for the O'Briens, building the rotunda and gazebo as well as the house, later demolished to make way for the castle. His other works include the eighteenth-century Stradbally House, Co. Laois, and Rockforest, Co. Cork, both now demolished. He wrote the first Irish architectural book, *A General Treatise on Architecture,* Dublin, 1754.

ASHLIN, GEORGE (1837–1921). Ashlin was born in Co. Cork and educated in England. He was a prolific architect of churches in Ireland. He trained under, and then worked in partnership with, Edward Welby Pugin from 1860 to 1868, running the Irish branch of the practice. In 1867 he married Pugin's sister, Mary. Among the best works of the partnership are the church of St Augustine and St John in Dublin (1862–78) and Cobh Cathedral, Co. Cork, which was begun in 1867 but not finished for half a century. About 1868 Ashlin split with Pugin, later going into partnership with Thomas A. Coleman. Ashlin succeeded James F. Fuller in rebuilding Ashford Castle, Co. Mayo, where he designed the north entrance gateway. His most important country house was Tulira Castle, Co. Galway. With Coleman and Robert Atkinson in 1917 he designed Clery's Department Store in O'Connell Street, Dublin, in a Classical style influenced by Selfridge's department store in London. Ashlin was President of the RIAI from 1902 to 1904.

BAILLIE ROBERT (*fl.* 1716–30?). In 1716 he was appointed Upholsterer to the Government by the Earl of Sunderland and in 1728/29 he entered into a contract to provide tapestries for the House of Lords. Of the six pieces originally commissioned only two, *The Defence and Relief of Derry* and *The Battle of the Boyne,* were ordered and Baillie was paid £200 compensation for the loss of the remainder of the order. He employed Johann van der Hagen to take 'prospects' of the places to be used in the designs of the tapestries and Jan van Beaver to weave them.

BAKER, HENRY AARON (1753–1836). Apprenticed to Thomas Ivory, he became Gandon's collaborator after Ivory's death. Baker succeeded Ivory as Master of the Dublin Society's School of Architectural Drawing from 1786 and retained that position for half a century. He continued work on the King's Inns after Gandon's resignation. His most important commission was the laying out of Westmoreland and D'Olier Streets for the Wide Streets Commissioners in a co-ordinated plan of shops and houses. He restored the old tower of St Audoen's Church (Church of Ireland).

BANKS, THOMAS (1735–1805). An English sculptor. A cenotaph to the memory of Banks in Westminster Abbey refers to him as one 'whose superior abilities in his profession added a lustre to the arts of his country'. His father was William Banks, steward to the Duke of Beaufort, and surveyor of works during the building of Badminton. Thomas Banks was apprenticed to William Barlow and worked for the architect William Kent as well as spending time in the studio of Peter Scheemakers. He received premiums from the Society of Arts and a gold medal and travelling scholarship from the Royal Academy. He married a lady of means and was able to stay in Rome for seven years; he had a year in St Petersburg in 1781, where he executed several commissions for the Empress. From 1776 to 1778 he worked for Sir William Chambers making statuary at Somerset House in London; in 1783 he executed the stone figures of Europe, Asia, Africa and America on the north front of the Custom House in Dublin. He received numerous commissions for busts, memorials and chimneypieces.

BENSON, SIR JOHN (1811–1862). Born in Co. Sligo and appointed surveyor to Cork City and County in 1851, he spent the rest of his career in Cork. In 1852 he won a competition for the design of the buildings for the Irish Industrial Exhibition held in Dublin in the following year. His building combined timber and glass and was widely praised; Benson was knighted at the opening ceremony. Among his architectural works in Cork were the Athenaeum, the Magistrate's Court in Cornmarket Street and several churches. He was surveyor of the Catholic cathedral in Cork and prepared an elaborate plan for its rebuilding, but only the design for the west front with its central tower was executed. Among his engineering works was the Cork Waterworks, which provided a constant supply to nearly every house in the city through 52 miles of pipes. During his time as surveyor he built hundreds of miles of roads and forty-eight bridges in the county, including St Patrick's and North Gate bridges in Cork City.

BOLGER, JAMES (*fl.* 1820–40). A nephew of Bryan Bolger (d.1834), who was a 'measurer of buildings' for the Board of Works in the late eighteenth and early nineteenth centuries, and whose detailed records of building jobs and the craftsmen employed are an important and rare source of information on this period. Bryan Bolger was closely associated professionally with Richard Morrison and it is possible that James received his training from Morrison. James worked with his uncle as measurer and architect, and in 1825 they designed a house for Abraham Bradley King in Fermanagh. James was appointed architect to Trinity College after Morrison in

1832, a position he held for only six months. A church for St Andrew's parish designed by James Leeson was half completed when Bryan Bolger condemned the construction and recommended a new church be built on a new site. The parish priest died; his replacement and Daniel O'Connell approved the suggestion of a new church so, in 1832 with James Bolger as the architect, the foundation stone of St Andrew's in Westland Row was laid.

BOSSI, PIETRO (*fl.* 1785–1798). 'Inlayer in marble and stucco-worker', he was thought to have come from Venice and is noted for the chimneypieces which he made for many Dublin houses. He inlaid white marble with designs of coloured stone, composition and earthen pastes in simple Adam-styled patterns of flowers and leaves, urns or medallions. The method he used was said to be jealously guarded. He worked in Dublin from *c.* 1785 to 1798, and fine examples are to be found in Charlemont House and Belvedere House.

BOWDEN, JOHN (d. *c.* 1822). Bowden studied at the Dublin Society Schools and served his apprenticeship with Richard Morrison. He was architect to the Board of First Fruits of the Church of Ireland from 1813 to 1821, and also architect to the Board of Education by 1818. He designed churches and courthouses throughout the country, and in Dublin designed St Stephen's Church which was completed by his pupil, Joseph Welland, after his death.

BRUCE-JOY, ALBERT (1842–1924). A sculptor from Belfast who studied at the Royal Academy Schools in London. He was a pupil of Foley and executed the statue of Robert Graves in the Royal College of Physicians. His other works include the statue of Lord Kelvin (1912) in the Botanic Gardens, Belfast, and that of Bishop Berkeley in Cloyne Cathedral.

BURGH, THOMAS (1670–1730). The first great Irish architect and engineer, he was the son of the Bishop of Ardagh, educated at Delany's school in Dublin and at Trinity College. He joined King William's army and after the war in Ireland served on the Continent spending part of his time in the army as an engineer. He returned to Ireland in 1697 and in 1700 succeeded Sir William Robinson as Surveyor-General. He was responsible for extending military establishments all over Ireland; his first recorded building was the Dublin or Royal Barracks (now Collins Barracks), begun in 1701. This was followed by the old Custom House on Essex Quay in 1707, which has not survived. His crowning achievement was the magnificent library at Trinity College, begun in 1712 but not completed until 1733. From 1716 he signed payments for the building of St Werburgh's Church, which is attributed to him although the design may have come from Alessandro Galilei. He also designed Dr Steevens' Hospital (begun in 1718), which was a scaled-down version of the Royal Hospital at Kilmainham. His architecture was sober and restrained and depended on great massing; he made use of arcades on the ground floor, as at Trinity College Library, Collins Barracks and Dr Steevens' Hospital, and frequently a centre block of five bays with a heavy pediment. It must have been a severe blow to him when he was passed over for the commission to design the new Parliament House, which was awarded to Pearce in 1728. Burgh owned an estate, Oldtown, near Naas, where his descendants still live.

BURLINGTON, EARL OF (1694–1753). Richard Boyle, third Earl of Burlington and Fourth Earl of Cork, succeeded his father at the age of ten; he was the heir to vast estates in England and Ireland and was appointed Lord Treasurer of Ireland by George I in 1715. He made the tour to Italy in 1715–16 and again in 1719. He became interested in Palladian architecture, which he endeavoured to restore to the place it had held with Inigo Jones. In 1717 he designed a garden pavilion at Chiswick House, and during the next thirteen years redesigned the entire structure. In the 1720s his first public work was to plan the Dormitory of Westminster School, and in 1730 he designed the Assembly Rooms at York, his most revolutionary structure and his last great building. It was due to his influence that the style of Palladio was accepted for public buildings and country house alike. Burlington worked with his protégé William Kent as architect and influenced Kent's designs for the Horse Guards, the Treasury buildings and the Royal Mews. Burlington commissioned Edward Lovett Pearce to carry out a survey of Jigginstown, Co. Kildare, the unfinished brick palace begun in 1637 by the ill-fated Earl of Strafford. Burlington had a great influence on Pearce and Castle, which was reflected in the introduction of Palladian architectural ideas to Ireland.

BURTON, DECIMUS (1800–1881). The son of a builder, he had a successful practice in London partly due to the family friendship with John Nash. He built the arch on Constitution Hill and the Colosseum in Regent's Park as well as many other public buildings. In his domestic architecture, he favoured a Classical Regency style. He was much involved with the redesign and landscaping of the Phoenix Park, where he also provided plans for several gate lodges. Burton was consulted by the Board of Trinity College, who were considering plans drawn up by Darley for a Museum Building. He

advised against the site, and the Museum Building designed by Deane and Woodward was built later in a different location.

BUTLER, RUDOLPH MAXIMILIAN (1872–1943). He became editor of *The Irish Builder* in 1899 and was the principal commentator on contemporary architecture for the next twenty-five years. He was a leading architect of Catholic churches, particularly in Ulster and Connaught, though not a Catholic himself. He won the competition for and constructed the University College Dublin building in Earlsfort Terrace, and was later appointed Professor of Architecture in the College, a post he held from 1924 to 1943. He built the Hiberno-Romanesque church of St Patrick at Newport, Co. Mayo, with stained-glass windows by Harry Clarke.

BUTLER, WILLIAM DEANE (d. 1857). Architect and civil engineer. He studied under Henry Aaron Baker at the Dublin Society Schools, where he was awarded a premium in 1811. From 1847 to 1849 he was architect to the Commercial Buildings Co. of Dublin, and was then made Architect in Ordinary to the Lord Lieutenant. He was a founding member of the RIAI and also the Society of Irish Artists, serving as their President 1845–47. Amiens Street Station (1844) was his most important work in Dublin. He also built the Sligo Asylum (1848), the Catholic cathedral of Kilkenny and St Kieran's College, Kilkenny. He favoured Gothic churches but his courthouses were built in a Classical style. Among his pupils were William Caldbeck and John Skipton Mulvany.

BYRNE, HUGH (d. 1866). Byrne was city architect to Dublin Corporation until his death in 1866 and made alterations to the Mansion House in 1851. In 1858 he was responsible for alterations to Santry Court, Co. Dublin, an early eighteenth-century house built by Lord Barry of Santry.

BYRNE, PATRICK (1783–1864). A leading designer of churches during the first half of the nineteenth century, Byrne studied under Henry Aaron Baker at the Dublin Society Schools, winning a first class premium in 1798. From 1820 until 1848 he worked first as a measurer then as an architect for the Wide Streets Commissioners, and from 1848 to 1851 he was architect to the Royal Exchange. He designed many churches after Catholic Emancipation; he worked in a Neoclassical mode and gave his churches fine interiors. Among his churches in Dublin are the Franciscan Church at Merchants Quay (1830), St Paul's, Arran Quay (1835–37), St Audoen's, High Street. (1841) and the Church of Our Lady of Refuge, Rathmines (1850). He also designed the Turf Gas Company's building in Great Brunswick St, now Pearse St, as well as many suburban and country churches. He was a Vice-President of the RIAI 1854–64.

CALDBECK, WILLIAM FRANCIS (*c.* 1825–72). He built the Bridewell Gaol in Newry, Co. Down, the courthouse in Newtownards (1849) and bank buildings all over the country, mainly for the National Bank (later absorbed by the Bank of Ireland). He was also employed on ecclesiastical works around Drogheda and built several rows of houses in Dublin. Caldbeck had few commissions from wealthy clients, but is credited with the service wing at Emo Court, Co. Laois. He also designed the Brown Thomas Department store in Dublin. His account book from 1844–60 has survived.

CAMBI, CARLO (*fl.* 1880s). A talented woodcarver from Siena, he was responsible for the carved doors and panelling in the National Museum and National Library. His carving may also be seen in the prayer desk of St Stephen's Church, and on a chimneypiece in the former council chamber of the Rathmines Town Hall. He is also believed to have worked at Heywood House, Co. Laois (now demolished).

CARLINI, AGOSTINO (d. 1790). From Genoa, he settled in London as a young man and was one of the foundation members of the Royal Academy, exhibiting there between 1769 and 1787. He became Keeper in 1782. An early commission was a statue of his friend 'Dr' Ward, the inventor, with the sculptor's assistance, of Friar's Balsam. This statue is now in the Royal Society of Arts. In 1783 Carlini made two statues for the south front of the Dublin Custom House and designed the pediment.

CARPENTER, RICHARD CROMWELL (1812–1855). An able Gothic architect, he practised in London and was one of the most successful English church architects of his day. He was a close friend of A.W.N. Pugin and brought Pugin's concepts into the Anglican church. Carpenter designed St Paul's, Brighton, and St Mary Magdelene, Munster Square, London; Pugin designed the painted glass for both. Inverness Cathedral and Lancing College, Sussex, were designed by Carpenter but completed after his death. He worked on the restoration of St Patrick's Cathedral and completed the renovation of the Lady Chapel there but retired as he found that he could not work with Sir Benjamin Lee Guinness. Anthony Symondson says of him: 'His work is distinguished by exquisite colours, harmony, scholarship, and control.'

CARROLL, JAMES RAWSON (1830–1911). Articled to George Fowler Jones of York, he was a successful Dublin architect and was one of those responsible for the reorganization of the RIAI in 1863. He built the Assize Courts at Sligo in 1874–9 and added a tower to the stable court at Tullynally, Co. Westmeath. He designed Classiebawn, Co. Sligo (1874–5), for Lord Palmerston and built Christ Church School, Leeson Park, Dublin, in 1882, as well as remodelling the Richmond Institute for the Blind (1875) in Upper O'Connell Street. Towards the end of his life he worked in partnership with Frederick Batchelor, with whom he built the Richmond Hospital and the Royal Victoria Eye and Ear Hospital, both in Dublin.

CASTLE, RICHARD (c. 1690–1751). Born in Hesse-Cassel of a Huguenot family, he came to England in 1725, after a career as an army engineer travelling in France, Germany and Holland studying fortifications and canals. He designed his first country house in Ireland in 1728, Castle Hume, Co. Fermanagh, for Sir Gustavus Hume and became one of the country's most important architects. He was employed by Sir Edward Lovett Pearce on the Parliament House in Dublin and worked on the Newry Canal. Inheriting Pearce's practice, he designed 85 St Stephen's Green, Tyrone House, Leinster House and the Rotunda Hospital. He also built many of Ireland's most important country houses including Powerscourt, Co. Wicklow; Westport House, Co. Mayo; Carton, Co. Kildare; Russborough, Co. Wicklow and Bellinter, Co. Meath. Nicholas Sheaff says of Castle: 'His Palladian style is distinctively robust and masculine and influenced particularly – apart from Pearce – by James Gibbs.'

CHAMBERS, SIR WILLIAM (1723–1796). He was the son of a Scottish merchant living in Sweden. Although educated in England he returned to Sweden and worked with the Swedish East India Company from 1738 to 1749. He became interested in architecture during his travels and studied in Paris, coming under the influence of the leading French Neoclassicists such as J. F. Blondel; he also studied in Rome. Back in London he became tutor to the future George III in 1755 and later remodelled Buckingham House for the Royal family; he also designed the State Coach. The first edition of his influential book *A Treatise on Civil Architecture* was published in 1759 and became the standard work. Somerset House, a collection of public offices under one roof, was the pinnacle of his achievement. He became Comptroller of Works in 1769 and combined this with the position of Surveyor-General. Although he never came to Ireland, Chambers had a powerful Irish patron in the first Earl of Charlemont, for whom he designed Charlemont House in Dublin, today the Hugh Lane Municipal Gallery of Modern Art, and the Casino at Marino. Chambers designed the Theatre, or Examination Hall, and the College Chapel at Trinity College, and his pupil, James Gandon, gave Dublin some of its finest public buildings. In 1768 Chambers was one of the founders of the Royal Academy of Arts and two years later he was given the Knighthood of the Polar Star by the King of Sweden; George III allowed him to assume the rank and title of an English knight. He was a Fellow of the Royal Society and a member of the French Academy of Architecture. He is buried in Westminster Abbey.

CLARENDON, FREDERICK VILLIERS (1820–1904). A graduate of Trinity College Dublin, in 1839 he acted as assistant in the erection of the Kenmare Suspension Bridge. He was engaged as architectural assistant to the Board of Works in 1841 and supervised the erection of additions to the Clonmel Lunatic Asylum. In 1844 Clarendon was resident engineer in the construction of the Galway docks and the Tralee ship canals. He was made Surveyor to the Board of Works in 1854. Clarendon designed the Meeting Room and the Reading Room for the Royal Irish Academy (1852), and also in 1856 the Natural History Museum. Although he was christened Frederick Villiers Clarendon by ambitious parents, it was a coincidence that the Viceroy in Dublin at the time of the RIA commission was George William Frederick Villiers, Earl of Clarendon.

CLARKE, HARRY (1889–1931). A designer of stained glass and talented illustrator, he was part of the Celtic Revival movement in Ireland. His father was English and came to Dublin, where he set up a business in church decoration and his mother was Irish. He was born in Dublin, educated at Belvedere College and encouraged by his father to be a stained-glass artist. He worked in the Clarke studios under William Nagle, a gold medallist from the RHA schools and skilled stained-glass artist, while studying at the Dublin Metropolitan School of Art. Scholarships enabled him to study full time and travel to France. He achieved success with his book illustrations in England. In Ireland he designed and made eleven windows for the Honan Hostel at University College, Cork (1915); another great work, the *Geneva* window, with dramatic scenes from Irish literature was commissioned by the Irish Government for the Office of the International Labour Organization in Geneva but never installed. Clarke's *Eve of St Agnes* window, displaying fourteen scenes from Keats's poem, showed his brilliant use of colour, his originality and technical skill.

CLEMENTS, NATHANIEL (1705–1777). By the age of twenty-two he was a Member of Parliament, becoming Deputy Vice-Treasurer, then Deputy Paymaster-General of Ireland. In association with Luke Gardiner, he organized the building of Henrietta Street. Clements leased land and built houses in Sackville Street and was closely associated with Richard Castle. Castle and Clements became respectively Gardiner's architect and contractor after Pearce's death. On being appointed Ranger of the Phoenix Park in 1751 Clements built himself a Palladian villa which, much enlarged, is now Áras an Uachtaráin. The Knight of Glin attributes to him a number of houses in Leinster, including Beau Parc, Co. Meath, in 1755 and Lodge Park, Co. Kildare which was built for Hugh Henry in 1775.

COLBOURNE, THOMAS (fl. 1805–08). Architect and engineer employed by the Grand Canal Company. In 1805 it was decided to terminate their passage boats at the harbour at Portobello Lock instead of St James's Street Harbour. Colbourne drew up plans for a hotel on the banks of the canal, which was completed in 1807. The stone used for the building was brought forty-five miles from the company's quarries at Tullamore.

COOLEY, THOMAS (c. 1740–1784). Little is known of Cooley's early years except that he served his apprenticeship in London with Mr Reynolds, a carpenter, and that he was a pupil of Robert Mylne, who built Blackfriars Bridge. He settled in Dublin having won the competition for the Royal Exchange, now the City Hall. In 1775 he was appointed Clerk and Inspector of Civil Buildings, i.e. chief architect to the Board of Works. He designed Newgate Gaol and worked in Armagh for Primate Robinson building the Archbishop's Palace, the Royal School and the public library there. He designed Caledon, Co. Tyrone, for the Earl of Caledon in 1779, and built Mount Kennedy, Co. Wicklow, for Lt-Gen. Cunningham, later Lord Rossmore. The house was completed in 1784 to a modified version of a design of James Wyatt. Cooley designed a Public Records Office which after his death was incorporated into Gandon's Four Courts.

CRAMILLION, BARTHOLOMEW (fl. 1755–72). A plasterworker of unknown origins who came to Dublin in 1755 to work on the decoration of the chapel of the Rotunda Hospital for Dr Mosse. For this he was paid 500 guineas, and on 29 December 1757 he agreed to do the altarpiece in the chapel for 200 guineas. Recent research has attributed to him the ceilings at Mespil House, now demolished, which were divided between Dublin Castle and Áras an Uachtaráin. He may also therefore have been responsible for the ceilings at Belvedere, Co. Westmeath. Joseph McDonnell suggests that the strong German influence in Cramillion's stuccowork comes from the Wessobrun School.

CRANFIELD, RICHARD (1731–1809). Born in Dublin, he also lived there. He exhibited sculptures carved in wood at the Society of Artists in George's Lane, 1765–69. He was responsible for the carving in the Dublin Society's old premises in Grafton Street including the President's chair. In 1771 he worked at carving and gilding in the Provost's House and also in the Blue Coat School, where he carved the reredos in the chapel – now removed. His daughter Emily married William, son of the architect Thomas Cooley. His son and partner John Smith Cranfield was also a woodcarver and an example of his work can be seen in the Mansion House, where he carved the frame on the portrait of the Marquess of Buckingham, painted by William Williams in 1769.

CUMING, WILLIAM (1769–1852). He attended the Dublin Society's Schools from 1785, winning a silver medal in 1790 for figure drawing. He then set up as a portrait painter in Crow Street. He was a successful artist, particularly with his female portraits, and in 1811 he was President of the Society of Artists. Cuming was one of the original founding members of the Royal Hibernian Academy and its president from 1829 to 1832. His output was limited, perhaps because he had independent means.

CUVILLIÉ, JOHN BAPTISTE (d. 1728). According to Dr Barra Boydell he was the leading organ builder in the early part of the eighteenth century. Thought to be of French origin, he came to Dublin c. 1697 and worked as assistant to Renatus Harris, who was building the organs for both cathedrals in the city. Cuvillié built or enlarged organs for Trinity College (1700), St Finbarre's Church, Cork (1710), and St Mary's Church, Dublin (1713) as well as others. He built the organ for St Michan's in 1725, although little more than the case now survives. A keyboard, which Dr Boydell believes may be part of the original organ of 1725, is displayed in the porch of the church.

CUVILLIÉ, JOHN BAPTISTE (d. 1788). Thought to have been a son of John Baptiste Cuvillié, organ builder. He was a house painter, gilder and decorator in Dublin who was admitted to the Corporation of Painter-Steyners in 1763. He was Warden of the Corporation in 1750 and Master in 1777. He invented a composition for tables and chimneypieces which imitated marble.

DARLEY, FREDERICK (1798–c. 1873). He was an architect, son of Alderman Frederick Darley of the well known quarry-owning family. He built the Merchant's Hall (1821) in Dublin and designed the King's Inns Library (1826). In the 1840s he redesigned the main staircase of the King's Inns and possibly, according to Frederick O'Dwyer, designed the north wing of the building. The balancing south wing is by Jacob Owen. Darley was also responsible for the Magnetic Observatory, Trinity College (given to UCD, Belfield, in 1974) and the Royal Irish Institution, College Street (demolished). He lived at 25 Lower Fitzwilliam St between 1830 and 1850, one of the houses demolished by the ESB in 1965. He was architect to Trinity College from 1834 and designer of New Square. He was a founding member and secretary of the RIAI.

DARLEY, GEORGE (b. 1731). A member of the quarry-owning family. The Dining Hall chimneypiece at Trinity College was carved in 1765 in the workshop of George Darley and cost £55 15s 8d. Dr McParland says that this included £7 10s for the 'Large Festoon and 2 Flower potts', and £8 for 'a Carlow marble tombstone laid as a hearth Stone'. He employed 100 men to prepare stone for the College. He also designed the Tholsel in Drogheda (1765–70).

DARLEY, HENRY (b. 1717). His family owned the Ardbraccan (limestone) and Golden Hill (granite) quarries. He worked on the Parliament House and also on the Rotunda where, by 1756 his stonecutting bill, including the capitals of the 'cupiloe', amounted to £3,395 7s 3d with other later substantial payments. Henry Darley supplied fireplaces to the Rotunda and also to Dr Mosse for his house at No. 9 Cavendish Row, where he was paid £35 for those on the first floor and £100 for those 'in the middle floor'.

DARLEY, HUGH (1701–1771). An architect and member of the quarry-owning family in Co. Meath who were associated with the consruction of buildings in the eighteenth century, including Dr Steevens' Hospital and the Library at Trinity College. Darley built the Protestant church of St Peter's in Drogheda (1749), supervised the building of the west front of Trinity College for Theodore Jacobsen, and was apparently the effective architect of the present Dining Hall in the College.

DARLEY, MOSES (d. 1754). Together with his father Henry, he was employed on the stonework of the Library at Trinity College,

designed by Thomas Burgh and begun in 1712. The Darley family are thought to have come from the north of England and settled in the north of Ireland towards the end of the seventeenth century.

DAVIS, WHITMORE (fl. 1782–96). He designed the Green Street Court House, scene of many of Dublin's famous trials, and was surveyor of the Paving Board. He was employed on minor works at the St Mary's Abbey premises of the Bank of Ireland. Dr McParland says he was a busy second-rate architect, protégé of the La Touche family to which he surely owed his appointment with the Bank. He was sacked by the bank in 1791 for not paying attention to his responsibilities.

DEANE, SIR THOMAS (1792–1871). He belonged to one of the most prominent Irish architectural dynasties and was based in Cork, where he was responsible for building Queen's College, now University College; he also built the Killarney Lunatic Asylum. He was the foremost architect/builder in Cork for many years. In 1853 the firm, by then joined by Benjamin Woodward and Thomas Newenham Deane, moved to Dublin. The partnership of Sir Thomas Deane, Son and Woodward designed the Museum building in Trinity College, Dublin (1853–7), and the Kildare Street Club, Dublin (1858–61), as well as the Oxford Museum. Deane was Vice-President of the RIAI 1851–54 and President 1868–9.

DEANE, SIR THOMAS MANLY (1851–1933). Born at Ferney, Co. Cork, eldest son of Sir Thomas Newenham Deane. He was a pupil of William Burges A.R.A. and studied at the Slade School, London, and later in France and Italy joining his father's Dublin practice in 1878. The firm, T.N.Deane & Son, won the competition for the building of the National Library and the Museum which were completed in 1890. Deane made alterations to the National Gallery and with Sir Aston Webb was joint architect for the Royal College of Science in Dublin, now Government Buildings. McArthur Hall, Belfast and St Bartholomew's Church in Dublin were among his works.

DEANE, SIR THOMAS NEWENHAM (1828–1899). Born in Cork and educated at Trinity College, he joined his father's practice in 1850. In 1851 he was made a partner together with Benjamin Woodward. The firm of Deane and Woodward developed a Gothic style founded on the naturalistic principles of John Ruskin and played an important role in the nineteenth-century Gothic revival in England. Their most famous buildings were the Museum Building at Trinity College and the Oxford Museum (1854–60). They designed the Crown Life Assurance Company Office, London (now demolished), and the Kildare Street Club, Dublin (1858–61). The partnership ended with the death of Woodward in 1861, but Deane continued to practice in Dublin and Oxford and in 1878 he formed a partnership with his son Thomas Manly Deane as T.N. Deane & Son. The firm won the competition for the building of the National Library and Museum, which was opened in 1890 when T.N. Deane was knighted by the viceroy.

DOBBS, ARTHUR (1689–1765). Appointed Surveyor-General after Pearce in 1734. He was MP for Carrickfergus 1727–30. A gentleman and political economist rather than an architect, he wrote many papers including *The Trade and Improvement of Ireland*. He devoted his time to local politics and the improvement of his estate at Castle Dobbs; his advice on agricultural matters was sought by progressive landowners. He was appointed Governor of North Carolina (1754–65) and he induced the Admiralty to send an expedition 'in search of the North West passage'.

DREW, SIR THOMAS (1838–1910). One of the most distinguished architects of the nineteenth century. He was the son of a Belfast clergyman and was articled to Sir Charles Lanyon. Aged twenty-four, Drew joined the Dublin office of William G. Murray and married Murray's sister, Adelaide. Among his Dublin works were the Ulster Bank, Dame Street, the Trinity College Graduates' Memorial Building, alterations to the Reading Room and Library at Trinity, the spiral staircase to the organ chamber at St Patrick's Cathedral, work at Christ Church Cathedral, the law library at the Four Courts (since destroyed), the Rathmines Town Hall and the Romanesque-styled Belfast cathedral. He built a triumphal arch for Queen Victoria's visit to Dublin in 1900. Drew was President of the Royal Hibernian Academy, President of the Royal Society of Antiquaries, President of the RIAI and Fellow of the Royal Institute of British Architects, and held the Chair of Architecture at the new National University of Ireland. Each St Stephen's Day he gave a lecture at Strongbow's tomb in Christ Church Cathedral.

DUCART, DAVIS (d. c. 1784/85). A Savoyard architect and canal engineer, he worked mostly in the south-west of Ireland. He built the Limerick Custom House (1760–69), Kilshannig (1765) and Castletown Cox (from 1767), using Patrick Osborne for the plasterwork as he did at the Mayorality House in Cork and possibly at Neptune, now St Patrick's Infant Hospital, Blackrock, Co. Dublin. His style is described by the Knight of Glin as 'Baroque-Palladian', and he was the most important Palladian country house builder in Ireland after the death of Richard Castle.

ENSOR, JOHN (d. 1787) AND GEORGE (d. 1803). John Ensor came to Dublin from Coventry in the 1730s. He became assistant to Richard Castle and on Castle's death inherited some of his practice. He completed the Rotunda Hospital, and laid out the east side of Rutland (now Parnell) Square for Dr Mosse. He built speculatively in Rutland Square, St Stephen's Green, and Hume Street, and laid out Merrion Square North for Lord Fitzwilliam from 1762. He also laid out Gardiner's Row for Luke Gardiner three years later. He designed and built the circular assembly room beside the hospital which later came to be known as the Rotunda, the exterior of which was later altered by Gandon. George Ensor was appointed Clerk of Works to the Surveyor-General at Dublin Castle in 1744. His most accomplished building was the church of St John the Evangelist (demolished) in Fishamble Street – the Classical façade may be seen in engravings. In Armagh he built the County Infirmary and houses for Primate Robinson. He married the heiress to Ardress House, Co.

Armagh, a seventeenth-century building which he enlarged and modernized. It is now owned by the National Trust.

EYRE, COLONEL THOMAS (d. 1772). He was Surveyor-General from 1753 to 1763, and MP for Fore and Thomastown. Joseph Jarratt was his deputy, and substantial building was carried out at Dublin Castle during this period.

FARRELL, TERENCE (1798–1876). A native of Co. Longford where his grandfather owned stone quarries, he was placed in the modelling school of the Dublin Society. He received instruction from Edward Smyth. He worked with Thomas Kirk for seven years and in 1828 he set up his own practice. He exhibited from 1826 onwards and excelled at miniature busts. He executed three memorials in St Patrick's Cathedral, two to the memory of those who fell in the wars with Burma and China, and one to the Rev. Charles Wolfe. His third son was Sir Thomas Farrell.

FARRELL, SIR THOMAS (1827–1900). The son of Terence Farrell, he studied at the Royal Dublin Society's Schools under Constantine Panormo. His practice increased after 1852 when he won the competition for a memorial to Archbishop Murray in the Pro-Cathedral, defeating, among others, John Hogan. He also executed the statues of Cardinal Cullen and Henry Baldwin in the Pro-Cathedral, the statue of Capt. John McNeill Boyd in St Patrick's Cathedral, the bust of Cardinal Newman in the University Church, the memorial to Canon Doyle in St Andrew's, Westland Row, and the bronze statue of Lord Ardilaun in St Stephen's Green. In 1850 he was invited to execute one of the bronze panels for the Wellington Testimonial in the Phoenix Park. Farrell was made President of the Royal Hibernian Academy in 1893 and knighted the following year. Homan Potterton says of him: 'Unfortunately Farrell was by no means a sculptor of genius or even of any great imaginative powers . . .' but in the absence abroad of John Hogan and Patrick MacDowell he received most of the top commissions.

FOLEY, JOHN HENRY (1818–74). One of the most successful sculptors in Britain in his day, Foley was born in Dublin and trained at the Royal Dublin Society's Schools under John Smyth, winning many prizes. He moved to London and studied at the Royal Academy. Success came rapidly and he was elected a member of the Academy in 1858. He executed the statue of the Prince Consort and the group *Asia* for the Albert Memorial in Kensington, besides many statues for Dublin including Edmund Burke and Oliver Goldsmith for Trinity College. In 1866 he was given the commission for the O'Connell monument and had the sketches and clay models completed when he died. His studio was in Osnaburgh Street in London. Strickland says his work had a vitality, a knowledge and sense of structure and movement, and a decorative feeling which were absent in the cold and lifeless works of his contemporaries. He is buried in the crypt of St Paul's Cathedral, London.

FOWKE, CAPT. FRANCIS (1823–65). An architect based mainly in London, he was born in Ulster. He received his commission in the Royal Engineers, distinguished himself in Bermuda, and was given the task of designing the Raglan Barrack at Devonport which became the model of its class. In 1853 he was appointed Inspector of the Department of Science and Art. He built the Royal Scottish Museum in Edinburgh, and designed the building for the London Exhibition of 1862. He played a major part in the development of 'Albertopolis', the cultural centre built in South Kensington under the patronage of Prince Albert, which followed after the Great Exhibition of 1851. He designed the National Gallery in Dublin to match the Natural History Museum on the south side of Leinster House. Fowke produced designs for the Royal Albert Hall and won the competition for the Natural History Museum in South Kensington. After his untimely death the architects who executed these buildings drew heavily on his designs.

FREEMAN, D. J. (d. 1902). Appointed City Architect in 1879, he designed the first Corporation housing scheme at Benburb Street (1887) followed by another, Bride's Alley (1895). He designed the iron and glass porch for the Mansion House in 1896.

FULLER, JAMES FRANKLIN (1835–1924). A native of Kerry, he was articled in England to F.W. Porter. He later worked in the offices of Alfred Waterhouse and others. In 1862 he was appointed architect to the Representative Church Body in Ireland. He was a sound and competent architect, and built a number of small churches. He was architect to the National Bank, designing many branches, and built the Great Southern and Western Hotels at Kenmare and Parknasilla. With Samuel Ussher Roberts he designed Kylemore Castle, now Kylemore Abbey, for Mitchell Henry in the 1860s and was responsible for additions to Ashford Castle. He built Lord Ardilaun's mansion at St Anne's, Dublin, and made extensive alterations to Iveagh House. Fuller was a first-rate genealogist and wrote extensively on this subject.

GALILEI, ALESSANDRO (1691–1737). The first Viscount Molesworth brought Galilei from Florence to England in 1714 and to Ireland in 1718, and probably introduced him to Speaker William Conolly, for whom he produced designs for Castletown. Galilei returned to Italy in 1719, so he could not have been concerned with the construction of Castletown which began in 1722. He later designed the façade of San Giovanni in Laterano, Rome.

GANDON, JAMES (1742–1823) Born in New Bond St, London, to a Huguenot family, he was a pupil of Sir William Chambers from c. 1757 to 1763. In 1768 he entered a design in the competition for the Royal Exchange in Dublin, being awarded second place after Thomas Cooley. He received the Royal Academy's first gold medal in architecture in 1769. With John Woolfe he produced Vols IV and V of *Vitruvius Britannicus*, and in c. 1769 he obtained his only major commission in England, the Nottingham Courthouse. He was offered employment in St Petersburg by Princess Dashkova but he accepted the invitation of John Beresford to come to Ireland in 1781 to build the Dublin Custom House. He remained in Ireland for the rest of his life. Gandon's other great works in Dublin include the

Four Courts, the King's Inns, the eastern extensions to the Parliament House, and Carlisle Bridge (later widened and reconstructed as O'Connell Bridge). His houses include Abbeville and Emsworth, Co. Dublin, Emo Court, Co. Laois, and the farmyard and stable complex at Carrigglas, Co. Longford. He was the foremost Neoclassical architect in Ireland and his contribution to Dublin must be greater than that of any other architect. In 1808 he retired to his home in Lucan.

GEOGHEGAN, CHARLES (1820–1908). Initially trained as an engineer, Geoghegan left Dublin where he was born and educated, and took up architecture in the offices of George Godwin in London. After studying on the Continent he practised in London for a time before returning to Dublin, where he established a successful practice designing in both Classical and Gothic styles. Among his works in Dublin were alterations to the Royal Bank at Foster Place (now the Allied Irish Bank)1858, the Cabra Deaf and Dumb Institute, St Mary's Blind Asylum, the Whiskey Distillery at Fairview and the Jervis Street Hospital (1884). He was the first member of a family of architects which continued to practise for a hundred years.

GIBBONS, GRINLING (1648–1721). Born in the Netherlands of an English father, he was a sculptor and woodcarver. He came to England c. 1667. John Evelyn, the diarist, showed his work to Charles II; he was appointed Master Carver in Wood to the Crown (1693) and also employed by Sir Christopher Wren. He worked at Windsor Castle, St Paul's Cathedral, Blenheim Palace and Hampton Court. He made statues of Charles II, Edward VI, Queen Mary, James I and James II for the Royal Exchange. In 1714 he was made Master Carver to George I. He worked in wood, marble, stone and brass employing skilled assistants, but wood was his favourite material; in his day he was unsurpassed. He executed the statue of King William III (1701) in College Green (demolished) and the monument to Archbishop Narcissus Marsh (d. 1713) in St Patrick's Cathedral.

GIBBS, JAMES (1682–1754). The pupil of Carlo Fontana, the leading Baroque architect in Rome. His church of St Martin-in-the-Fields (1720), London, set the standard for eighteenth century church architecture in England. In 1728 he published *A Book of Architecture* which was widely used as an architectural pattern book in England, Ireland and \merica. He favoured window surrounds with heavy blocking, known as 'Gibbsian surrounds'. He worked for the Barrymores of Fota Island at their English seat, Marbury Hall, Cheshire, but never had an Irish commission.

GIBSON, EDWARD (fl. 1870–90). The son of James Gibson of Mary Street, Dublin, he was based in Great Russell Street, London. His design for the decoration of the Masonic Hall was selected from a competition judged by 'Mr' T. Jones, President of the RHA, and 'Brother' Drew, RHA (Sir Thomas Drew). For the five semi-circular arches on the walls each side of the Grand Lodge Room he painted ten cartoons depicting the building of Solomon's Temple. In 1877 the Rev. Benjamin Gibson, his brother, presented these cartoons to the lodge. Edward Gibson also painted the decorations on the series of door panels in the drawing room of the Writers' Museum, which are signed 'Gibson'.

GRACE, OLIVER (fl. 1750s). The Graces were an ascendancy family listed in Burke's Landed Gentry of Ireland, and a member of the family may have been the Oliver Grace who published an engraving *View of Sackville Street* in the 1750s, dedicated 'To his grace Lionel Duke of Dorset Lord Lieutenant General and Governor Gen of Ireland'. An Oliver Grace was responsible for the original house at Lyons, Co. Dublin, which was built in 1797 for Lord Cloncurry.

DE GREE, PETER (d. 1789). Born in Antwerp, he was a pupil of Martin Joseph Geeraerts, a master of *grisaille* painting. David La Touche brought him to Ireland to decorate No. 52 St. Stephen's Green, where his painted panels are in green and white to match the marble mantelpiece. Other examples of his work are found at Lucan House in the Wedgwood Room and at Luttrellstown Castle, Co. Dublin. The latter were formerly at the Oriel Temple, Co. Louth, the residence of Speaker Foster.

GROSE, FRANCIS (1731–91). Described as a topographical draughtsman, he was born in Middlesex, the son of a Swiss jeweller. After studying drawing at Shipley's School he exhibited architectural views. He was Adjutant and Paymaster of the Hampshire and Surrey Militia. Independent means enabled him to indulge his taste for antiquarian pursuits and he published a number of books on the antiquities of England, Wales and Scotland. He came to Ireland to prepare a similar work but died suddenly while at dinner with James Gandon at the house of Horace Hone the miniature painter. The book was completed after Grose's death with engravings taken from works of other artists and published as *Antiquities of Ireland*. His eldest son Francis Grose later acted as Governor of New South Wales, 1792–94. His nephew Lieutenant Daniel Grose compiled an account of Irish monuments, including eighty-nine watercolours which he painted. This volume has recently been published by the Irish Architectural Archive as a supplement to his uncle's book.

HAGUE, WILLIAM (1840–c. 1900). Born in Cavan where his father was a builder, he moved to Great Brunswick Street, Dublin. He designed a number of Catholic churches in Co. Cavan, Ballyboy (1859), Butlersbridge (1861), Kingscourt (1869), and Swanlinbar (1869). The chancel of St Augustine and St John's Church, designed by Pugin and Ashlin, was finished by Hague in 1895.

HARRIS, RENATUS (c. 1652–1724). The son and grandson of English organ builders who worked in France when organ building was suppressed during the period of the Commonwealth in England. The family returned to England in 1660 and Harris went on to become a famous organ builder. He built thirty-nine organs for churches including King's College Chapel, Cambridge, and cathedrals including Chichester, Winchester, Ely, Bristol, and Salisbury. He built the organ at St Patrick's Cathedral in 1697 and later that at Christ Church Cathedral.

HARRISON, CHARLES W. (1837–1905). Born and trained as a stonecarver in Yorkshire, he came to Dublin during the 1850s. *The Building News*, 29 May 1905, describes Harrison as a sculptor of considerable eminence whose works may be seen in churches and public buildings throughout Ireland and in many parts of England. He was the senior member of the well known firm of architectural sculptors, Messrs Harrison & Sons, Monumental Works, Great Brunswick Street. He worked with Deane and Woodward from 1858 to 1861 and succeeded the O'Sheas as 'master carver' in Dublin when they remained in England after 1861. The naturalistic carving on the exterior of the Kildare Street Club, which was designed by Deane and Woodward, is his work.

HARWOOD, FRANCIS, (fl. 1748–1769). Rupert Gunnis in his *Dictionary of British Sculptors, 1660–1851* states that all Harwood's statues and busts known to him are either copies of, or based on, Greek and Roman originals, but holds that they are, none the less, fine works. He executed statues of Marcus Aurelius for Gordon Castle in 1762 and a bust of 'A Vestal' in 1765. A letter quoted in Whitley's *Art in England, 1821–37* from Nollekens to Thomas Banks in 1769 states: 'there is F.H. at Florence who is knocking the marbil about like feway & belive he as got more work to do than any One Sculptor in England'. Harwood worked in Ireland at the Marino Casino for Lord Charlemont.

HEITON, ANDREW (1823–94). Son of an architect, he was a pupil of David Bryce, then joined his father's practice in Perth, succeeding his father as the city architect. He specialized in designing Scottish baronial country houses. He restored the old church of St John's, Perth, and he built three churches in Dublin, the Rathgar Presbyterian Church, the Presbyterian Mission Church in Jervis Street, and the Abbey Presbyterian (or Findlater's) Church in the neo-Gothic rather than the traditional Classical style more commonly used for the Nonconformist churches. In Scotland Heiton built Castle Roy, Broughty Ferry.

HEWETSON, CHRISTOPHER (1739–98). The best Irish sculptor of the eighteenth century, he was born in Thomastown, Co. Kilkenny. He assisted John Van Nost the younger at the Rotunda Gardens and he was in Rome from 1765, where he worked successfully for the rest of his life. His outstanding work in Ireland is the monument to Provost Baldwin in Trinity College which the sculptor himself describes: 'The piramid is of the Red Oriental Granite and makes a much better ground for the white figures than any other hitherto used for the purpose. N.B. – I was the first who applied Granite to this use.' Hewetson received £1,000 for the monument which cost £416 to transport to Dublin where it arrived in 1784 and was erected by Edward Smyth. In the Provost's House there is a bust by Hewetson of Richard Rigby.

HICKS, FREDERICK (1870–1965). He was born in Oxfordshire, and served his apprenticeship with J.W. Stephens. He left London to become assistant to J. Rawson Carroll, whose chief assistant at the time was Francis Batchelor. Hicks and Batchelor became partners until 1922, and during the 1930s Hicks was joined by Alan Hope. He was President of the RIAI from 1929 to 1931, and was the first architect to be awarded the RIAI Gold medal for his design of the Lombardo Romanesque Church of St Thomas, Cathal Brugha St, Dublin. In 1907 he designed the Iveagh Markets to house the street traders selling old clothes, vegetables and fish.

HOBAN, JAMES (c. 1762–1831). Born in Ireland, he worked as an 'artisan' in Dublin before emigrating to America. His entry in the competition for the President's house in Washington, DC, won the first prize of $500 and a gold medal. His original plan was based on Leinster House, Dublin (1745), but this was reduced to a two-storey design at the request of George Washington for reasons of economy.

HOGAN, JOHN (1800–58). The son of a master builder and carpenter, he was born in Co. Cork where he worked in the office of Sir Thomas Deane. Turning to sculpture, he carved twenty-eight wooden statues of apostles and saints for St Mary's Pro-Cathedral in Cork, known locally as the North Chapel. Assisted by a group of patrons including the RDS, he went to Rome where he set up a studio and where he remained for 24 years. During this time he carved some altarpieces and statues for Irish churches. He spent his last ten years in Ireland but received few commissions. Among Hogan's best works are the bust of *Lord Cloncurry Embraced by Hibernia* (1852) in the National Gallery; the *Dead Christ* in the St Teresa's Church, Clarendon St (1829) and the memorial to Bishop Brinkley, Professor of Astronomy, in Trinity College, Dublin (1835), which portrays him with a globe and telescope.

HOLMES, EDWARD (1832–1909). He practised as an architect in Birmingham and London in the 1860s. He designed a number of churches near Birmingham and in Burton-on-Trent, and also designed the Exchange Buildings and the Birmingham and Midland Bank in Birmingham. The Freemasons' Hall is his only Dublin building. The RIBA has in its collection seven of his drawings of the New Palace of Westminster, 1862.

HONE, EVIE (1894–1955). Painter and stained-glass artist, she was a member of an artistic Dublin family. She studied at the Byam Shaw School of Art, London and in addition received some training from Walter Sickert and Bernard Meninsky. She and Mainie Jellett spent some time in Paris with André Lhote and Albert Gleizes. Deeply religious, she converted to Catholicism and much of her work has a religious content. From painting she turned her vivid sense of colour to stained glass and her works are to be seen in many Irish churches, the National Gallery of Ireland, the Hugh Lane Municipal Gallery, Government Buildings in Merrion Street and the Ulster Museum, Belfast. Her most famous commission was the large *Crucifixion and Last Supper* window in Eton College Chapel.

HOUGHTON, JOHN (fl. 1741–75). A sculptor who worked principally as a woodcarver, he won premiums from the Dublin Society in 1741 and 1742. He carved the frame on Bindon's portait of Swift in St Patrick's Deanery and collaborated with David Sheehan on church monuments, carving the two angels on the monument to James,

Earl of Barrymore in the mausoleum at Castle Lyons, Co. Cork. He also worked at Carton for the Earl of Kildare in collaboration with John Kelly.

HUDSON, THOMAS (1709–79). One of the most fashionable English portrait painters in London from the mid-1740s to the mid-1750s. He was a pupil of Jonathan Richardson, whose daughter he married. Joshua Reynolds was his pupil.

IVORY, THOMAS (c. 1732–1786) Born in Cork, where he started life as a carpenter. He moved to Dublin and was employed by a gunsmith making stocks. He studied in Dublin and was the best of the Irish architects eclipsed by the arrival of Gandon. In c.1760 Ivory became the first master of the Dublin Society's School of Architectural Drawing and held this post until he died in 1786. His principal works are the Blue Coat School, the Newcomen Bank and the bridge at Lismore, Co. Waterford. Ivory was a superb draughtsman and his elevation of the Blue Coat School in the British Museum shows the tower as he intended it to be. He was also Surveyor to the Revenue Commissioners.

JACOBSEN, THEODORE (d. 1772). Of German origin, Jacobsen was actively engaged in running the family commercial business in London, but found time to practise as an amateur architect. He designed the building for the East India Company in Leadenhall St and also designed both the London Foundling Hospital (1742–52) and the Royal Naval Hospital for Sick Sailors (1745), near Portsmouth, with James Horne in charge. Main charged fees. Dr McParland has established that the main quadrangle at Trinity College, known as Parliament Square, was built to Jacobsen's designs (1752–9). Hugh Darley, the architect in charge, wrote to John (sic) Keene to say that the north range and north-west pavilion were ready for their cornice, and alternative suggestions had been put forward about the elimination of a dome over the central pediment and of cupolas on the pavilions. Henry Keene and John Sanderson were paid £74 11s 8d for their detailed plans.

JARRATT, JOSEPH (fl. 1745–74). Maurice Craig in Dublin 1660–1860 identified the shadowy figure of Jarratt, architect for the Irish Public Works between the periods of Ensor and Cooley, but little was known of him until an album of his designs was discovered and purchased for the Irish Architectural Archive in 1984. Nicholas Sheaff, former Director of the Archive, has written that Jarratt 'was clearly one of the most gifted young architects in Palladian circles in Dublin' and suggests similarity in draughtsmanship style to Richard Castle, which may mean that he trained in Castle's office in the late 1750s. Jarratt designed the Weavers' Hall (demolished) in the mid-1740s. The drawings suggest that Jarratt worked on the garden front of the State Apartments at Dublin Castle formerly attributed to Pearce, on the north side of the Upper Castle Yard during the period 1753–63 when he acted as deputy to the Surveyor-General. He also rebuilt the La Touche Bank nearby, which had collapsed. In 1763 on the abolition of the post of Surveyor-General this office closed down and Jarratt's job was redefined as 'clerk and inspector of the civil buildings'. He appears to have been a kinsman of Thomas Jarratt who submitted three designs for the Royal Exchange competition.

JOHNSTON, FRANCIS (1760–1829). One of Ireland's greatest native-born architects, from Armagh, he was sent to Dublin by Richard Robinson, Primate of Armagh, to study with Thomas Cooley and Samuel Sproule. He was appointed architect to the Board of Works in 1805. He built many public buildings including the GPO and St George's Church; he converted the Parliament House for the Bank of Ireland. Townley Hall, Co. Louth, begun 1794, is a fine example of a Neoclassical country house and his castellated houses include Charleville Forest, Co. Offaly and Gothic alterations to Tullynally Castle (Pakenham Hall), Co. Westmeath. The Chapel Royal of Dublin Castle (1807–14) is another example of his Gothic work. He was one of the founders of the Royal Hibernian Academy, Lower Abbey St, and its President from 1824 to 1829, designing and building its premises out of his own pocket; only the façade now remains.

JOHNSTON, RICHARD (1759–1806). Son of a prosperous builder from Armagh and elder brother of the better-known Francis Johnston, he was the architect of the Rotunda Assembly Rooms (now the Gate Theatre) with Frederick Trench. He drew the original plans for Castle Coole, which were modified by James Wyatt. He also designed Daly's Club House in College Green.

JONES, ALFRED GRESHAM (1822–1915). He died in Melbourne, Australia, at the age of 93, having left a substantial practice in Ireland to start again in Australia. His chief work in Dublin was the construction of the Dublin Exhibition Palace and Winter Garden in Earlsfort Terrace, which was built to hold an International Exhibition of Arts and Manufactures in 1865 and intended to be a permanent centre in Dublin for exhibitions, public meetings, flower shows and concerts – the largest room was to hold 3,000 people. These buildings were handed over to University College, Dublin, in 1908. He was the architect for the enlargement of Trinity Church, Rathmines, and designed some private houses on Morehampton Road. In 1862 Jones designed Merrion Hall, Dublin, an Evangelical Hall recently rebuilt and renamed the Davenport Hotel, and in 1877–9 he designed Wesley College, a Gothic building off St Stephen's Green (demolished in the 1970s).

JOSEPH, N. SOLOMON (1834–1909) AND SMITHEM, CHARLES JAMES (d. 1937). English architects who specialized in designing synagogues and industrial dwellings. They were commissioned to build the Iveagh Buildings for the Iveagh Trust from 1894. The terracotta and brick buildings with Dutch gables provided flats, a men's hostel with 508 cubicles and public baths in an Art Nouveau building with segmental arches over the doorways. The English architects were assisted by the Dublin firm of Messrs Kaye, Parry and Ross. A new park was also created on the north side of St Patrick's Cathedral.

KAUFFMAN, ANGELICA (1741–1807). A native of Switzerland and daughter of the painter Joseph Johann Kauffman, she was an accomplished decorative painter and also a musician. She went to Rome in 1763, and a portrait of Winckelmann painted there greatly helped her reputation. She was a founder member of the Royal Academy in 1768. She was a close friend of Reynolds, Goethe, and Winckelmann, and did decorative work for Robert Adam among others. She visited Dublin in 1771 for six months, staying with Bishop Clayton's widow, and during this visit painted the portrait of the Ely family now in the National Gallery. While in Dublin she decorated No. 52 St Stephen's Green but could not possibly have carried out all the painting commonly attributed to her. She returned to Rome and concentrated mainly on historical and mythological themes.

KEANE, JOHN B. (d. 1859). He was probably the John Kane of Brookeborough, Co. Fermanagh, who applied to be Richard Morrison's drawing clerk in 1809 (Bolger papers). He worked for Morrison at Killruddery, Co. Wicklow, in 1820 and Ballyfin, Co. Laois, in 1822 and first appears in the directories in 1823 at 33 Mabbot St. He competed against William Vitruvius Morrison for courthouses at Tralee, Carlow and Tullamore – he was successful at Tullamore and built courthouses also at Waterford, Ennis and Nenagh. He designed the fine Church of St Francis Xavier, Gardiner St (1829–32), and completed the Pro-Cathedral; in 1846–50 he designed Queen's College, Galway for the Board of Works but he failed to supervise the project and it was taken over by the Board's own architects. He designed Longford Cathedral (begun 1840) and the Church of St Lawrence O'Toole (1850) in Dublin, besides some country houses. He was a founding member of the RIAI but his name was removed from the list of members in 1850 after he was imprisoned for debt. His whereabouts between 1850 and his death in 1859 are not known.

KEENE, HENRY (1726–1776). The son of a Middlesex builder, in 1746 he became Surveyor of Westminster Abbey. He worked for Sir Roger Newdigate at Arbury Hall (c. 1750–76), a house in the Gothic style contemporary with Strawberry Hill. He was one of the first to initiate the Gothic revival, using details from Westminster Abbey in his designs. In the Classical style he designed the Guildhall in High Wycombe for the first Earl of Shelburne in 1757, and he worked on a number of Oxford colleges. In 1761 Lord Halifax, the Lord Lieutenant, brought him to Ireland as 'Architect to the Barrack Board' in Dublin. In the 1750s he made the working drawings for the west front of Trinity College, which was designed by the amateur architect Theodore Jacobsen. The collaboration between Jacobsen, Keene and an English architect called Sanderson remains something of a mystery. Dr McParland believes that Keene may have been responsible for the interior of the Provost's House.

KEYSER, WILLIAM DE (1603–after 1685). The son of Dutch architect and sculptor Hendrik de Keyser, William worked with his father in Amsterdam. He was also an architect and sculptor, living in England from 1621 to 1640, and was probably employed by Nicholas Stone, Hendrik's brother-in-law and former pupil. William went back to Amsterdam in 1640, where he stayed until his return to England in 1658. Rolf Loeber considers it likely that de Keyser set up a workshop in Dublin and that in 1683 he carved the statues of Charles I and II for the Dublin Tholsel; he was paid for this work in 1685. The statues are now in the crypt of Christ Church Cathedral. De Keyser is also mentioned in connection with a fountain executed for the Duke of Ormonde at Kilkenny Castle in 1681.

KIRK, JOSEPH ROBINSON (1821–94). Irish sculptor and eldest son of Thomas Kirk, he studied under his father and became master of the Dublin Society's Modelling School. He was one of three sculptors invited to design a panel cast in bronze for the Wellington Testimonial in the Phoenix Park– the others were Farrell and Hogan. He also executed the extraordinary Crampton Memorial, 1862, which stood at the junction of College Green and Hawkins St until it collapsed in 1959, and a bust of Sir Philip Crampton for the Royal College of Surgeons. He was a member of the RHA and exhibited regularly.

KIRK, THOMAS (1781–1845). The son of William Kirk from Edinburgh, who settled in Newry near to Cork. Thomas Kirk studied at the Dublin Society Schools then worked with Henry Darley, the stone cutter. An early commission was the 13-foot-high statue of Nelson (now blown up) for the pillar in O'Connell St. He carved the military trophies above the Ionic archway of Johnston's armoury in Foster Place. In Dublin, memorials carved by him may be found in St Ann's Church, Dawson St, St Patrick's Cathedral, Christ Church and the Pro-Cathedral; they are also in many churches throughout the country. He frequently used a relief portraying the Good Samaritan, as in the memorial to Thomas Dillon in the Pro-Cathedral. He was considered one of the best Irish sculptors in the first half of the nineteenth century and was a founding member of the RHA in 1823.

LAFRANCHINI, PAOLO (1695–1770) AND FILIPPO (1702–1779). Born in Ticino, Switzerland, Paolo appears to have worked in northern Germany in 1721–22 and in England in 1731, where he was associated with James Gibbs. The brothers came to Ireland to decorate the saloon at Carton in 1739 and worked at fifteen houses during their forty years of activity in Ireland. They have been credited with the introduction of the human figure into plaster decoration in Ireland, and they had a profound influence on native Irish stuccodores. Examples of their work may be seen in Dublin at 85 St Stephen's Green and at the St Stephen's Green Club; also in country houses such as Riverstown House and Kilshannig, Co. Cork, Russborough, Co. Wicklow, and Castletown, Co. Kildare.

LANYON, SIR CHARLES (1813–1889). A native of Eastbourne, Sussex, he was articled to Jacob Owen, the engineer and architect of the Irish Board of Works in Dublin in 1832, later marrying his daughter. He became County Surveyor of Antrim and remained in Ulster, where he supervised the construction of bridges, railways and roads as well as designing some of the finest country houses there, such as Drenagh, Co. Derry, Dunderave, Co. Antrim, and the flamboyantly Italianate Ballywalter, Co. Down. He designed Queen's College, Belfast, in the 1840s and the splendid Custom House in Belfast in 1857. Lanyon was head of the flourishing Belfast firm of Lanyon and Lynn and a prominent public figure, President of the RIAI from 1863 to 1868, a Conservative MP and Mayor of Belfast. In the words of C.E.B. Brett, 'His is certainly the greatest name in the development of Belfast.'

LANYON, JOHN (c. 1840–1900). The eldest son of Sir Charles Lanyon of Belfast, he joined his father's firm in 1860. He ran the Dublin office from 1860 returning to Belfast in 1867 where he was architect to the Northern Counties Railway Co. In 1879 he constructed additional buildings at the Northern Railway terminus at Amiens St, Dublin, and in 1883 he added new offices for the company. He built many public buildings in Belfast and in 1873 he restored Belfast Castle, the seat of the Marquess of Donegall.

LE BAS, LOUIS HIPPOLYTE (1782–1867). Professor at the École des Beaux-Arts in Paris (1819–1867) and architect of civil works there, he designed the Church of Notre-Dame de Lorette and the prison at Petite Roquette. He also remodelled the Academy of Medicine, Paris. Frederick O'Dwyer believes he could be the architect of St Mary's Pro-Cathedral in Dublin.

LEESON, JOHN (fl. 1820s–30s) studied in the Dublin Society's School of Architectural Drawing where he was awarded a premium in 1813. He appears as Clerk of Works in the records of the Building Committee of the Pro-Cathedral, 1819–21. He designed the church of St Nicholas of Myra, Francis St, Dublin, which opened in 1834. The portico, bell tower and cupola were added later by Patrick Byrne. He also designed and commenced the building of St Andrew's Church in Townsend Street, which was abandoned and left unfinished in favour of Bolger's plans for the new site in Westland Row.

LUTYENS, SIR EDWIN (1869–1944). One of the most important English domestic architects in the first half of the twentieth century, he worked closely with Gertrude Jekyll, the landscape and garden designer. Their work over a period of twenty years was marked by the integration of house and garden. In Ireland, Lutyens worked at Heywood, Co Laois, and Lambay Castle, Co. Dublin, as well as carrying out extensive alterations and additions at Howth Castle, Co. Dublin. He planned the Garden of Remembrance at Islandbridge, recently restored, and designed an art gallery in the form of a bridge over the Liffey which was never built.

LYNN, SAMUEL F. (1836–1876). Born in Co. Wexford, he worked with his talented elder brother the architect William Henry Lynn in Belfast, where he attended the School of Design. He decided to train as a sculptor and went to London, enrolling at the Royal Academy Schools where he won silver and gold medals. He assisted John Foley in the execution of the statue of Prince Albert for the Albert Memorial in Kensington. He exhibited in the Academy regularly, and before his untimely death at forty had produced sculpture for many public buildings including the tympanum of the present AIB Bank in College St. He was made an associate of the RHA in 1872 when he left London to live in Belfast. His only church monument in Ireland is in Waterford Cathedral. He executed statues of Dr Henry Cooke for Belfast, and Lord Farnham in marble for Cavan.

LYNN, WILLIAM H. (1829–1915). The son of a naval lieutenant, he grew up in Co. Wexford; at eighteen he was apprenticed to the architect Charles Lanyon in Belfast. Lynn was Clerk of Works on Lanyon's Queen's College, Belfast (1846–7) and became his partner. Lynn was influenced by Ruskin, as exemplified by the use of polychromatic stone and brick for Queen's University Library (1865–8), and was also at home with the Classical style which he used in the design of Belfast Central Library (1883). In Dublin he restored the medieval church of St Doulagh's, and as a result became interested in the Hiberno-Romanesque style. He has been described as 'an eclectic of the eclectics'. Innovative, he won many competitions and had considerable success outside Ireland. Lynn was a skilled draughtsman and a very competent watercolour artist; his elaborate perspective drawing for Carlisle (now O'Connell) Bridge took the prize for design but it was not executed. He won a gold medal at the Universal Exhibition in Paris for his complex Gothic design for the New South Wales Houses of Parliament in Sydney (1867), and also designed the Canadian viceregal residence in Quebec. Before leaving Lanyon in 1872 he had designed seventeen churches, including the Church of St Andrew's, Suffolk Street (1860), some twenty-five public buildings and many country houses. He designed the Unitarian Church on St Stephen's Green, Dublin and was President of the RIAI from 1886 to 1888.

McCARTHY, JAMES JOSEPH (1817–1882). Born in Dublin, he studied at the Royal Dublin Society Schools. Known as the 'Irish Pugin', he chose a career as an ecclesiastical architect. He was a Catholic, had strong nationalistic leanings and greatly admired Irish medieval architecture. His domestic practice was small; he designed Cahirmoyle, Co. Limerick, for Edward O'Brien in the Celtic-Romanesque style. His churches include the Catholic cathedrals in Monaghan and Thurles, and the completion of the Catholic Cathedral in Armagh, begun by Thomas Duff. In Dublin he designed the chapel (now rebuilt) and collegiate buildings of All Hallows Missionary College, Drumcondra, as well as St Saviour's in Lower Dominick Street. He also designed the Romanesque Church of St Paul of the Cross, Mount Argus.

McCULLAGH, JAMES (d. 1795). Variously called McCullogh and McCulloh, he was admitted to the Plasterers' and Bricklayers' Guild in 1761 and worked in Dublin as a plasterer and stuccodore. He became Master of the Guild in 1778, and a member of the City Council in 1781. His best known work is at Powerscourt House, South William Street, built between 1771 and 1774, where he was responsible for the walls and ceiling of the staircase. He worked here with Michael Stapleton, whose stuccowork in the dining room and drawing room appears by contrast less heavy and more elegant. A description of this work and costings are given in The Georgian Society Records, Vol. I. In 1774 he executed plasterwork in the Rotunda for John Ensor.

McCURDY, JOHN (1823–1885). A pupil of Frederick Darley, he became architect to the Board of Trinity College. His plans, modified by the Board, were the starting point for Deane and Woodward's Museum Building at Trinity. He worked mainly in the Dublin area and in 1857 won a prize for the enlargement of Kilmainham Gaol which was completed in 1863. He designed the Shelbourne Hotel (1867) and the Royal Marine Hotel in Dun Laoghaire (1863). From 1873 he was in partnership with William Mansfield Mitchell. He was President of the RIAI from 1875 to 1885.

McDONAGH, IGNATIUS (fl. 1771). Woodcarver, Powerscourt House, South William Street.

McGRATH, RAYMOND (1903–77). Described by Bruce Arnold as a man of prodigious and diverse talents, whose direct influence has been felt in at least three countries, Australia, Britain and Ireland. After winning two scholarships from Sydney University he studied architecture at Clare College, Cambridge. He practised in London as an architect and interior designer from 1930 to 1939, using new techniques and materials; his writings during this period were influential. He worked for the property developer J.A. Philips in London, decorated the RIBA and was design consultant for the BBC and the Aspro factory at Slough. St Anne's Hall, Chertsey has been described as his most notable architectural achievement. In 1940 he moved to Ireland, taking up a position with the Board of Works. He became its principal architect from 1948 to 1968 carrying out improvements to Áras an Uachtaráin in the late 1940s and also to Dublin Castle; he worked on Irish embassies abroad. He designed the RHA (begun in 1973) and was the Professor of Architecture as well as President in 1977. He also exhibited paintings. One of his major works in Ireland was the designing of the unexecuted John Kennedy Memorial Concert Hall.

MACK, ROBERT (fl. 1753–80). Mack was a mason-builder who built the Essex Bridge over the River Liffey to the designs of George Semple in 1753–55. He designed and built Powerscourt House, South William Street, commencing in 1771. The day book of the builder states that Lord Powerscourt approved of Mack's plan and elevation for his house and agreed to pay him 'five pr.Cent for Conducting the whole of sd.works, as also that sd. Mack is [to] Execute all the Stone cutting parts of sd. house'. Mack entered the competition for the Royal Exchange; he designed the dairy at Newbridge House, Donabate, a house designed by George Semple in 1749. Gandon, critical of local architects, consulted Mack during the financial struggles attendant on the building of the Four Courts, begun in 1786, and seemed to accept him along with Ivory and Cooley as his professional equal.

MACLISE, DANIEL (1806–70). Born in Cork, the son of a Scottish soldier who left the army and became a shoemaker, he studied art at the Cork Institute and opened a studio there, making enough money from small pencil sketches to go to London. His portrait of Walter Scott made during Scott's visit to Cork in 1825 helped his success. He studied at the Royal Academy, where he won a silver medal and a gold medal for his painting *The Choice of Hercules* . He exhibited for many years in the Academy and won fame for his historical, biblical and literary paintings. In 1830 he began to create character portraits of literary personalities of the day for *Fraser's Magazine*; the series was published as a book. He illustrated books such as *Moore's Melodies*, he painted frescoes for the Prince Consort and was one of six artists chosen to decorate the Houses of Parliament where his two great historical paintings, *The Death of Nelson* and *Wellington and Blücher on the Field of Waterloo* still hang. He was an excellent draughtsman and in his historical paintings, such as *The Marriage of Strongbow and Aoife* (1854) in the National Gallery of Ireland, he went to great lengths to get the details of costumes correct. The symbolism of Aoife sacrificed to the Normans shows his sensitivity to his Celtic nationality and he retained contact with Ireland throughout his career. His popularity began to decline before his death, as his paintings were thought to be wooden and exaggerated.

MAGUIRE, MICHAEL (fl. 1750s–89). During the rebuilding of St Werburgh's in the 1750s Michael Maguire and Thomas Tierney are known to have carried out the plasterwork. Maguire's work in the chancel may be seen in a pair of panels, the lower pair with swags of natural foliage, and the upper with palmiers coming from a head. Bryan Bolger's papers mention that Maguire also worked in Dawson Street for Francis Sandys in 1789.

MALLET, ROBERT (1810–1881). His father came from Devonshire and established a brass and copper foundry in Dublin. Educated at Trinity, Mallet was an exceptionally talented engineer, inventor and scientist. He travelled on the Continent, returning to expand the business to cater for most of the engineering requirements of Ireland. He raised and supported the roof of St George's Church, Hardwicke Place, which had become dangerous, using an iron truss framing. He devised ventilating and heating systems for Dublin buildings including Dublin Castle, the Chapel Royal, the Records Office, the Law Courts and numerous public buildings throughout the country. He worked at Trinity and designed the railing which bounds the College along Nassau Street. He built a locomotive to haul the mails between Dublin and Kingstown (Dun Laoghaire); he constructed a 40-ton crane. He established a permanent water supply for Guinness's brewery, and made steam presses for Messsrs. Grierson, printers of *The Irish Times* and the Dublin *Freeman's Journal*. He built five swivel bridges for the Shannon in 1845–46, and the passenger sheds at Amiens Street and Kingsbridge Stations. He built the Fastnet Rock lighthouse. Buckled plate, patented in 1852, was one of his most successful inventions and was used in the construction of London Bridge and Westminster Bridge. From 1861 he acted as a consultant engineer in London. He was an expert on earthquakes and volcanoes and wrote seventy-four papers in the Royal Society's catalogues.

MALTON, JAMES (c. 1764–1803). Thomas Malton (1726–1801), the father of James, was a talented architectural draughtsman and writer on perspective in London. Faced with financial difficulties, he moved to Dublin in 1785. His elder son Thomas (1748–1804)

studied at the Royal Academy Schools and is known for his beautiful series of watercolours of Bath, London and Oxford. He also taught perspective drawing, and Turner was among his pupils. There is confusion between the father and two brothers. James Malton, the younger son, became a skilled topographical artist. He worked for three years as a draughtsman in the office of James Gandon during the building of the Custom House but was dismissed for 'irregularities'. The set of twenty-nine drawings of Dublin buildings, from which engravings were made, was completed in 1791 when Malton moved to London. He reproduced them himself as aquatints, selling them first in sets and later in a handsome bound volume with a 'brief authentic history'. The engravings were not finished until 1797 and he wrote that he had updated the drawings where necessary. He included a dedication to the Lord Mayor, Sheriffs, Common Council, Freemen and Citizens of Dublin. These views are a valuable record of late eighteenth-century Dublin.

MANNIN, JAMES (d. 1779). A French artist who came to Dublin in 1746, he was appointed teacher of ornamental and landscape drawing at the Dublin Society Schools. He excelled at painting flowers, exhibiting flower and landscape paintings at the first exhibition of the Society of Artists in 1765; he also won premiums from the Dublin Society. He held the position at the Dublin Society Schools until 1779, teaching well known artists such as J.J. Barralet, Thomas Roberts and George Barret.

MILLS, JOHN (fl. c. 1638–c. 1673). Loeber states that as a foreigner or non-resident Mills was admitted as Freeman of the City of Dublin in 1638. From 1655 to 1656 he was employed on works in and around Dublin, including alterations to the old Custom House, additions to Phoenix House for Henry Cromwell, and repairs to one of the towers in Dublin Castle. In 1661 he received the patent as Master Carpenter in Ireland; the Lord Chancellor of Ireland, Sir Maurice Eustace wrote that Dr John Westley, [John] 'Mylls' and Capt. John Paine [the Surveyor-General] were the only experts on building in Ireland. In 1663 he appears to have supervised the rebuilding of the Vicars' Choral Hall in St Patrick's Cathedral.

MILLS, RICHARD (fl. 1671–1719). Mills was a native of Gloucestershire and admitted a Freeman of Dublin in 1671. He started work as a bricklayer and mason working on the buildings at Trinity College. According to Rolf Loeber he is mentioned in documents as the Overseer of Structures. He was appointed assistant to the Masters of City Works in 1702, which involved overseeing the public buildings and the craftsmen working on them and keeping account of materials used. It is not known if he designed buildings but, according to Loeber, he was overseer of the Tailors Hall (1703–7), Molyneux House (1706), St Werburgh's Church (c. 1716) and the Marshalsea (1717). In the year he died he is reported as being one of the benefactors of the Blue Coat School.

MITCHELL, MICHAEL (fl. 1711–1750). The son of Sir Michael Mitchell, MP, Sheriff of Dublin and Lord Mayor from 1691 to 1693, he was a portrait painter but little is known of his work. A receipt for £20 for the picture and £5 for the frame shows that he painted 'Dean Drelincourt' for the Blue Coat School; he repaired and restored paintings in the Tholsel and the Mayor's Hall and in 1738 painted portraits of King George II and Queen Caroline. In 1741 he was paid £11 16s 6d for the painting of Grizel Steevens which hung in Dr Steevens' Hospital.

MORRISON, SIR RICHARD (1767–1849). Born in Co. Cork, he was the son of John Morrison, an architect and builder from Midleton. On completion of his studies at the Dublin Society's Schools, he set up a practice in Clonmel. Archbishop Agar of Cashel commissioned him to construct a tower and spire for the cathedral there; this Gibbsian design was not executed but he did build the tower and a changed spire in 1807. In 1793 he published *Useful and Ornamental Designs in Architecture*; this was one of the few pattern books produced by architects in Ireland at the time. Around 1800 he moved to Dublin and established a thriving country-house practice, building in addition courthouses and gaols. He also built a number of highly sophisticated villas such as Castlegar, Co. Galway, and Cangort Park, Co. Offaly. Morrison was architect to Trinity College, building the Anatomy House and encasing the upper storeys of Burgh's Library in granite. His plans for a dome over the West Front were not executed. He designed Sir Patrick Dun's Hospital, 1803–16. In collaboration with his son William Vitruvius, who joined his practice in 1809 he worked at Killruddery, Co. Wicklow, Fota Island, Co. Cork, and Baron's Court, Co. Tyrone. He was one of the founders of the RIAI in 1839 and was its first Vice-President; he was knighted in 1841.

MORRISON, WILLIAM VITRUVIUS (1794–1838). The second son of Richard Morrison, he was born in Clonmel. He was said to have produced a plan for Ballyheigue Castle when only fifteen. William travelled abroad, spending time in Rome and Paris. In England he learned to admire the Tudor style, which he subsequently favoured. He worked on the Anatomy House in Trinity with his father and he was responsible for the designs of Mount Stewart, Co. Down, and Baron's Court, Co. Tyrone. He built the court houses at Tralee and Carlow and was a pioneer in the development of cottage-style houses with steep gables. He died when only forty-four; his brother John described him as being of delicate health, suffering from a nervous illness and having a highly sensitive nature, in contrast to his father who was both ambitious and energetic and may have resented his son's ability.

MULVANY, JOHN SKIPTON (1813–1870). The son of Thomas J. Mulvany, who was an artist and the close friend and biographer of James Gandon. T. J. Mulvany had four sons: William Thomas, an engineer and Commissioner of the Board of Works; George Francis, a painter like his father, and the first director of the National Gallery of Ireland; Richard Field, who owned a newspaper; and John Skipton, a successful architect. John Skipton was articled to William Deane Butler and appointed architect to the Dublin and Kingstown Railway, designing stations along the route; and to the

Midland Great Western Railway, designing the terminus hotel at Galway, and stations at Athlone and Galway. His outstanding work was the Broadstone Station, terminus of the Midland Great Western Railway. He also designed two yacht clubs at Kingstown (now Dun Laoghaire), the Royal Irish and the Royal St George. Professor A.E. Richardson in his work *The Monumental Architecture of Great Britain and Ireland* writes: 'Ireland has produced many architects of renown, but few with the genius of J. S. Mulvany. He was nurtured in the traditions of Gandon and emanated from a family of artists.' R.M. Butler, in an appreciation of the architect in the *Tuam Herald* of 1924, says his work was simple, massive and dignified and that his virile and original manner was marked by scholarship.

MURRAY, WILLIAM (d. 1849). A cousin of Francis Johnston, he became his assistant at the Board of Works in 1822. He was appointed architect to the Board of Works in 1827 and took over Johnston's practice when he died in 1829. He built gaols and asylums, mostly in the Classical style, throughout the country; he designed houses in an Italianate style. He was responsible for the present front of the College of Surgeons, enlarging Edward Parke's original façade in 1825.

MURRAY, WILLIAM GEORGE (1822/23–1871). Son of the architect William Murray, he had a successful practice in Dublin building for the public, private and ecclesiastical sectors. He worked for the Provincial Bank and built the main branch in Dublin at 5 College Street; he also designed the South Mall branch in Cork. Murray built the Union Bank, College Green, which is now the National Irish Bank, and the Royal College of Physicians in Kildare Street. He was the father of the architect Albert Edward Murray (1849–1924).

MYERS, CHRISTOPHER (d. 1789). He was appointed to succeed Acheson Johnston as Director of the Works of the Newry Canal in 1762, and in 1767 argued the case for the canal before a Committee of the House of Commons. The same year he succeeded Henry Keane as architect to the Commissioners and Overseer of the Barracks. In the 1771 *Journal of House of Lords* there are architects' estimates for barracks in Cork, Waterford and Limerick signed by Christopher Myers. Appointed architect to Trinity College in 1775, he carried out the building of the Theatre, or Examination Hall, on the southern side of Parliament Square to a design by Chambers; a letter from Chambers says that he is too busy to do the work and suggests that 'the operator, Mr Myers' do it. Myers completed this work in the mid-1780s and work on the Chapel was begun in 1788.

MYERS, GRAHAM (1777–1800). He succeeded his father, Christopher Myers, as executive architect of Trinity College Dublin in 1789, the year after the start of work on the Chapel. Father and son between them were responsible for erecting the Theatre and Chapel at Trinity from 1777 to 1800 to the designs of Sir William Chambers, who never came to Ireland. In 1776 Myers subscribed to George Richardson's book of ceilings and he unsuccessfully submitted designs for the King's Inns in 1800. He gave Pakenham Hall, Co. Westmeath (now renamed Tullynally Castle), a five-bay Classical facade in the 1770s .

NASH, JOHN (1752–1835). An English architect best known for his planning of Regent's Park and Regent Street in London in his later years, he established a vast country-house practice, working in the Picturesque style. When James Wyatt died in 1813 the office of Surveyor-General was reorganized and shared by John Soane, Robert Smirke and Nash. Nash was the personal architect of the Prince Regent (later George IV) and remodelled the Brighton Pavilion for him (1815–21). He also rebuilt Clarence House and laid out Carlton House Terrace. In Ireland his work includes the Swiss Cottage, Co. Tipperary, Rockingham, Co. Roscommon, Shanbally Castle, Co. Tipperary, Lough Cutra Castle, Co. Galway, and Killymoon Castle, Co. Tyrone.

O'CONNOR, ANDREW (1874–1941). A sculptor born of Scottish parents in Massachusetts. His first assignment was to help assemble the Chicago World Exhibition, 1891–2. He worked with Sargent in London and executed the bronze doors of St Bartholomew's in New York. After the Great War he lived in Paris executing American commissions. In the 1930s he divided his time between Paris and Dublin; he left several pieces of sculpture to the Hugh Lane Gallery. Homan Potterton describes his style as derived from nineteenth-century French sculpture, especially Rodin, but that it is 'rougher in handling'.

O'CONNOR, MICHAEL (c. 1801–1867). Born in Dublin, he went to London to be apprenticed to Thomas Willement as a heraldic artist and became a successful designer of stained glass. He returned to Dublin for a time but settled in London in 1845 where, with his son, he ran a successful firm, providing stained glass for many English churches. He exhibited in Ireland and undertook Irish commissions. In 1859 he supplied the east windows for the church of St James, James Street, and in the International Exhibition of 1862 in London his studio won the gold medal in the stained-glass section. He provided the heraldic stained glass for the windows of the chapel of the Royal Hospital, Kilmainham.

OLDHAM, THOMAS (fl. 1748–77). Dublin woodcarver. A Thomas Oldham is listed in the Directories as living at No. 35 Moore Street, Dublin, in 1777. An entry in the Commons Journal showed that the chimneypiece in the House of Lords was finished by him in 1748/49 but not necessarily carved by him. He executed carving in 1749 in the House of Commons and repairs to the capitals of the pillars and pilasters of the House of Lords. In 1764 he carried out some carving in the Rotunda Chapel. Although little information is available about him he was one of the more distinguished Dublin carvers of the time.

OMER, ROWLAND (fl. 1755–1767). Strickland describes him as an architectural draughtsman, and he is remembered for his five drawings of the Parliament House in Dublin, engraved by Bernard Scalé and published in 1767. He was probably the son of the Englishman Thomas Omer, who was employed by the Inland

Navigation Board to construct the Grand Canal from Dublin to the Shannon and to improve the Boyne and Lagan rivers. Rowland Omer was also an engineer with the Navigation Board.

O'SHEA, JAMES AND JOHN (*fl.* 1850s–1860s). The brothers are believed to have been natives of Ballyhooly in Co. Cork; they came to Dublin about the same time as Deane and Woodward who employed them on the Museum Building (1853–7) in Trinity College and the Oxford Museum (1854–60). Little is known of them after the death of Benjamin Woodward in 1861 although there is evidence that they were working in Oxford on the Corn Exchange, and the carving in Exeter College Chapel. They worked on Waterhouse's Manchester Assize Courts and in 1862 they executed carving at Cowley House, Oxford, their last known job for the firm of Deane. In 1863 they carved statues for the Catholic church in Rhyll, Wales, designed by John Hungerford Pollen. The O'Sheas had a remarkable and original talent for naturalistic carving, especially for rendering plants, leaves and animal forms; they were ideally suited to Woodward's expression of Ruskin's principles.

OWEN, JACOB (1778–1870). Born in North Wales, he served under William Underhill, an engineer engaged in canal works in South Staffordshire. In 1832 he transferred to the Irish Board of Works, an appointment he held until his retirement in 1856. He designed the lunatic asylum at Dundrum and was executant architect for Mountjoy Prison, additions to the Four Courts, and Queen's Inns, now King's Inns. His son James succeeded him as architect to the Board of Works, and his fourth daughter married Charles Lanyon.

PAINE, JOHN, (*fl.* 1642–*c.* 1670). He was Director-General and Overseer of the King's Fortifications from 1644 and again from 1660. He was MP for Clogher, Co. Tyrone, in 1661. He made extensive alterations to Dublin Castle for the Duke of Ormonde from 1662 to 1667 and also worked at Chapelizod House, Co. Dublin, and at Chichester House, Dublin, the home of the parliament at the time.

PAPWORTH, GEORGE (1781–1855). A member of a distinguished family of architects and craftsmen in London, Papworth came to Dublin in 1806 after training with his brother John. He was inventive and original in his methods of construction and had great skill as a draughtsman. In 1818 he designed the Dublin Library in D'Olier Street. He worked at Portumna Castle for the Marquess of Clanricarde (1824–26) and in 1827 he built the King's Bridge (1849) over the Liffey, a novelty in bridge building for its precautions taken against expansion. It was cast by the Phoenix Iron Works nearby. Papworth acted as architect for the Dublin and Drogheda Railway. Among numerous commissions were the Whitefriars or Carmelite Friary Chapel, the Museum of Irish Industry, St Stephen's Green and the Royal Bank, Foster Place, in 1856. Papworth's private houses included Brennanstown for Joseph Pim (1842), and in the same year the grand remodelling of Kenure Park, Co. Dublin, of which only the portico now survives. He designed an extensive warehouse for the British and Irish Steam Packet Co. which was built in the marsh by the side of the Liffey below the Custom House. The building sank 18 inches without needing repair beyond screwing up ironwork already in place. He was Vice-President of the RIAI, 1854–55.

PARKE, EDWARD (*fl.* 1794–1816). He was a protégé of the last Speaker, John Foster of Oriel Temple, Co. Louth. In 1806 Parke designed the Royal College of Surgeons, which was later enlarged by William Murray. He designed the Commercial Buildings in Dame Street (1794–8), and in 1816 an infirmary and dwelling for the Hibernian Marine School. He also designed the Greek Revival courthouse at Dundalk (1813–19).

PARKE, ROBERT (*fl.* 1787–1800). Architect with a large practice in Dublin. From 1787 to 1794 he worked on the Parliament House; he designed the Ionic portico in Foster Place and the western colonnade which connected Pearce's front of the Parliament House to the portico.

PEARCE, SIR EDWARD LOVETT (*c.* 1699–1733). His father, who died in 1715, was a major-general and a first cousin of Sir John Vanbrugh. His mother's grandfather had been Lord Mayor of Dublin. Pearce joined the dragoons then travelled in Italy and France in 1723–4, studying the architecture. His annotated copy of Palladio's *I Quattro Libri* is in the RIBA in London. He is thought to have been a pupil of his cousin Vanbrugh, the architect of Blenheim Palace, and he was associated with the Burlingtonian circle in London. He returned to Dublin in 1724 and succeeded Thomas Burgh as Surveyor of Works and Fortifications in Ireland in 1730. He was knighted by the Viceroy in 1732. His works include Bellamont Forest, Co. Cavan, the Cashel Palace, Co. Tipperary, the Parliament House, Dublin, and some of the interior of Castletown, Co. Kildare. He also designed Nos 9, 10, 11 and 12 Henrietta St. Pearce was Ireland's greatest Palladian architect and his untimely death was a great loss to the country.

PEARSE, JAMES (1839–1900). An artisan from Bloomsbury who came to Dublin in his teens looking for work. He found a job with C.W. Harrison and set himself up as a monumental mason in the 1870s. His firm, O'Neill and Pearse (later James Pearse & Son), executed the statues on the Church of St Augustine and St John. The family, including Patrick Pearse who was one of the leaders of the 1916 rebellion, was received into the Catholic church at St Paul of the Cross, Mt Argus.

PETIT, PAUL (*fl.* 1731–33). Gilder and frame maker. In 1731 he is known to have made frames for Frederick, Prince of Wales. In 1731–2 he received £252, then another £7 10s for altering, mending and gilding the oars of the Royal Barge. In 1733 he was carving in the 'Best Parlour' of Newcastle House, London.

POLLEN, JOHN HUNGERFORD (1820–1902). He was the nephew of Charles Robert Cockerell who built the Ashmolean Museum in Oxford and who worked in Ireland designing Loughcrew in Co. Meath. Pollen was educated at Eton and Oxford, was a Fellow of Merton College from 1842 to 1852 and took Holy Orders in the

Anglican faith. Interested in art and architecture, and encouraged by his uncle, he became a decorative artist and undertook the decoration of Merton College Chapel in 1850. By 1852 his extreme views had led him into conflict with the church authorities and he was received into the Catholic church that year, visiting Rome over the next few years. In 1854 Dr Newman invited him to Dublin to become Professor of Fine Arts at his new Catholic University and to build and decorate the University Church. While in Dublin Pollen became friendly with Benjamin Woodward and decorated some of his buildings. In 1857 he collaborated with Rossetti, Burne-Jones and others in decorating the Oxford Union. In 1862 he completed the decoration of Kilkenny Castle for the Marquess of Ormonde. He received many ecclesiastical commissions in England and he was appointed keeper of the South Kensington Museum (now the Victoria and Albert). In 1876 he resigned his Kensington post and became private secretary to Lord Ripon, with whom he journeyed to India in 1884.

POOL, ROBERT AND CASH, JOHN (*fl.* 1770s–1790s). Pupils in the Dublin Society's Architectural School, taught by Thomas Ivory, they published *Views of the most remarkable Public buildings, Monuments and other edifices in the City of Dublin* in 1780. In 1777 they had placed the drawings, which later became plates, before the Dublin Society which gave the required support and received the dedication. Apart from Brooking's map, the publication was the first to illustrate the architecture of Dublin, and it appeared the year before Gandon arrived to begin the Custom House. Maurice Craig in his introduction to the reprint of 1970 says it is possible that Cash was related to a Cash who worked under Vanbrugh at Blenheim, and that Pool was related to a John Pool who practised in London between 1802 and 1817. Pool designed the Pigeon House Hotel, erected 1793–98, on the South Wall to cater for passengers crossing to and from England.

POWER, ALBERT (1883–1945). A sculptor and member of the RHA, he worked on the Munster and Leinster Bank in O'Connell St. For University College Dublin, on Earlsfort Terrace, his work included a series of heads depicting philosophers and sages of Greece, Rome and the Renaissance period as well as early Irish figures. He also carved a series of figures of Irish saints for the reredos of the church at Balla, Co. Mayo. His enormous sculpted figures may be seen on the skyline of Government Buildings, and also by him is the seated statue which resembles Rodin's *The Thinker*, in the pediment designed by Oliver Sheppard.

PRESTON, JOHN (*fl.* 1793–1825). A 'Cabinet Maker, Upholsterer and Auctioneer' whose premises were in Henry St from 1793 to *c.* 1825. He was joined by his son in 1806 and was Dublin's leading upholsterer. He refurnished Castle Coole in the Regency style between 1807 and 1825 on the instructions of the second Earl of Belmore, supplying sumptuous curtains with ornate fringes and tassels, elegant gilded tie-backs and gilded furniture in the Grecian manner; four lamp stands alone cost £944. The house is as important for its interior decoration as it is for its Neoclassical architecture.

PUGIN, AUGUSTUS WELBY NORTHMORE (1812–1852). His father, a refugee from France after the execution of Louis XVI, became a draughtsman under John Nash. A.W.N. Pugin was a celebrated English Gothic Revival architect and writer who converted to Catholicism in 1835. He believed the quality and character of the people was reflected in their architecture and that Classicism was allied to paganism. He passionately believed that Gothic architecture was the true expression of the Catholic faith. He held that the form of a building should echo its function and that it should be constructed of local materials. Through his writings and his buildings he was extremely influential, and his talents extended to the decorative arts such as furniture, stained glass, vestments, metalwork and embroidery. He established a significant Irish practice from 1838, and in Dublin built the Rathfarnham Loreto Convent Chapel (1839). His work in the provinces includes St Mary's Cathedral, Killarney (begun 1842), Enniscorthy Cathedral and works at Maynooth College. Pugin was involved in the design of the interiors both at Adare Manor, Co. Limerick, and Lismore Castle, Co. Waterford. In England his work included St Chad's Cathedral, Birmingham, St George's Cathedral, Southwark, and the Church of St Oswald, Liverpool (now demolished), which is supposed to have been the model for many Gothic Revival parish churches in England and abroad. He also designed the interiors, furniture and other works for the Houses of Parliament, 1844–52.

PUGIN, EDWARD WELBY (1834–75). Educated by his father A.W.N. Pugin, he began to practise at the age of eighteen after his father's death. Like his father's, his buildings were in the Gothic Revival style and more than one hundred Catholic churches and schools as well as private houses were listed in his obituary in *The Builder*. He practised with James Murray of London; in 1860 George Coppinger Ashlin opened a joint office with him in Dublin, and in Ghent J. Bethune was his partner. Among the best works of Pugin's Irish partnership are the church of St Augustine and St John (1862–78) and the Sacred Heart Church, Donnybrook (1866), both in Dublin, and Cobh Cathedral, Co. Cork, which was begun in 1867 but not finished for half a century. He was made a Knight of St Sylvester by Pope Pius IX in 1859 for his church of Notre Dame in Dadizele, Belgium.

ROBINSON, ANDREW (1858–1929). A native of Antrim, he was articled to L.L. Macassey, the waterworks engineer of Belfast. In 1884 he was appointed assistant surveyor to the Commissioners of Public Works in Ireland. In 1888 he successfully underpinned the structure of the GPO, Dublin, which had shown signs of imminent collapse. He attended on the Prince and Princess of Wales during their visit to lay the foundation stone of the National Library and Museum in 1885, on Queen Victoria, and later, on King Edward and Queen Alexandra when the foundation stone of the College of Science was laid. He was involved in a further royal visit from King George V and Queen Mary when the College was opened in 1911. On this occasion he was given membership of the Royal Victorian Order for 'personal services to the Sovereign', and for his services

during the war he received the CBE. He became Principal Architect in 1920 and Commissioner of the Board of Works in 1921. During his seven years as Inspector of Ancient and National Monuments important works were carried out at the Rock of Cashel, Roscrea Castle, and Carlingford Castle.

ROBINSON, SIR WILLIAM (*c.* 1643–1712). Born in England of a Yorkshire family. Little is known of his life before he was made Surveyor-General of Ireland in 1671. At the instigation of the Duke of Ormonde he designed and built the Royal Hospital at Kilmainham in Dublin. He also built Essex Bridge (1677–78), and Marsh's Library in Dublin, redesigned Dublin Castle after a fire in 1684, and designed Charles Fort, Kinsale. By 1691 he had built himself a residence at Islandbridge. In 1700 he resigned as Surveyor-General on the grounds of ill health. He was knighted in 1701 or 1702 but in 1703, because of a financial scandal, he was dismissed as Deputy Receiver-General and briefly imprisoned in Dublin. He was an MP for various periods between 1692 and 1712. He spent much time in England from 1703 to 1709, leaving Ireland for good in 1709; he died in London. In his will he assigned £100 for a monument to be erected at his Royal Hospital with an inscription stating that he had been 'Contriver and Builder'.

RYAN, FRANCIS (*fl.* 1780s). Stuccodore and builder; No. 35 North Great George's Street, built in 1783, is attributed to him.

SANDBY, THOMAS (1721–98). He grew up in Nottingham where he was apprenticed, and took up a situation in the military drawing office in the Tower of London. He was attached to William Augustus, Duke of Cumberland, and stayed with him during military campaigns sketching battle scenes. He was appointed Draughtsman to the Duke and later Deputy Ranger of Windsor Great Park. With his brother he formed Virginia Water, the largest artificial lake in the kingdom with grottoes, bridges and waterfalls. Sandby was also favoured by Henry Frederick, Duke of Cumberland, and George III, who took over Windsor Great Park when the duke died in 1790. Sandby was made Architect of the King's Works. He exhibited at the Royal Academy where he was the first Professor of Architecture; in his buildings he favoured a Neoclassical style. He gave a series of influential lectures each year until he died. He entered the competition for the Royal Exchange in Dublin in 1769 and received the third premium; the drawings are in the RIBA. Few of Sandby's architectural works have survived, but his accomplished watercolour drawings may be seen in museum collections.

SANDYS, FRANCIS (d. 1795). There were two Francis Sandys and it is difficult to disentangle information about them. The elder was a late eighteenth-century Dublin architect and it was probably he who entered the Royal Exchange competition of 1768 and designed some street fountains (such as Rutland Fountain in Merrion Square). Sandys also worked at Bellevue, Co. Wicklow, for the La Touches, and probably designed Luggala there. His son, also Francis, was patronized by the Earl-Bishop of Derry, for whom he supervised the building of Ickworth in Suffolk. Dr McParland believes that the younger Sandys' career was largely, or wholly, in England.

SAVAGE, JAMES (1779–1852). In 1798 he studied at the Royal Academy and exhibited there until 1832. He won a competition for rebuilding Ormonde Bridge in Dublin in 1805, but this was not undertaken. In 1808 his plans for Richmond Bridge were accepted and the bridge was built to his design between 1813 and 1816. He was able to handle difficult problems of construction, and in 1823 his plan for rebuilding London Bridge was only defeated by the casting vote of the chairman of a House of Commons Committee. He designed the Classical church of St James, Bermondsey, and St Luke's Church, Chelsea, the first Gothic Revival church to have a loadbearing stone vault. As architect to the Society of the Middle Temple he completed the Plowden Buildings.

SCHEEMAKERS, PETER (1691–1781). The son of a sculptor from Antwerp, he was determined to study sculpture in Rome and walked there from Copenhagen. He left for a short stay in London but returned to Rome with his friend Laurent Delvaux and worked there for several years. Returning to London with some models in clay and several marble statues copied from antiques, he established his reputation with a statue of Shakespeare for Westminster Abbey which, as George Vertue writes, 'tossd this sculptor above on the summit of the wheel and so [he] became the admiration of the publick …' Scheemakers executed many statues, monuments, busts, and chimneypieces. In 1743 Trinity College commissioned fourteen busts from Scheemakers to fulfill a bequest of Dr Gilbert, who left £500 'for the purchase of busts of men of eminent learning to adorn the library'. Scheemakers returned to Antwerp in 1771, dying there ten years later.

SEMPLE, GEORGE (*fl.* 1748–d. 1782). His family was extensively involved in building in Dublin during the second half of the eighteenth century. He was an engineer and architect, building St. Patrick's Hospital in 1749 and adding a spire to St. Patrick's Cathedral, Dublin, the same year. He designed Headfort, Co. Meath (1760), although the interior is by Robert Adam. He wrote a treatise *The Art of Building in Water,* with reference to Essex Bridge which he designed and rebuilt 1753–5 (demolished 1874); he was a skilful canal engineer. He also built the bridge at Graiguenamanagh in Co. Kilkenny.

SEMPLE, JOHN (*fl.* 1820s). One of the Semple family who were connected with the building trade during the eighteenth and nineteenth centuries as architects, engineers, bricklayers, plasterers, and painters. Maurice Craig says John Semple built and probably designed the Round Room of the Mansion House in 1821. He was in business with his son as John Semple and Son, Architects and Engineers, at No.13 College Green; father and son were sheriff's peers.

SEMPLE, JOHN (*c.* 1801–*c.* 1873), son of John Semple. Frederick O'Dwyer has established that he was almost certainly the grand-nephew of George Semple. He was city architect from 1829 to 1842 and architect for the city prisons, the piped water works and roads. He was Dublin architect to the Board of First Fruits which provided funds for Protestant church building. In the years immediately preceding the abolition of this board in 1834, Semple designed fourteen or fifteen churches in the Dublin and Kildare dioceses. Among his Dublin churches were St Mary's Chapel of Ease, known as the Black Church, Donnybrook Church in Anglesea Road, and Rathmines Church. Maurice Craig notes that the typical Semple church has narrow lancet windows between closely spaced buttresses finishing in gablets, also sometimes pinnacles, a slender tower and needle spire if money permitted, and a plain west door without a frame. In the Black Church Semple used a parabolic arch springing from the floor, and masonry vaults rather than wood and plaster.

SHEEHAN, DAVID (d. 1756). A member of the stone-cutting family with premises in Marlborough Street. He was a sculptor and his monuments are found in churches throughout the country – his most impressive sculpture being the monument to James, Earl of Barrymore in the mausoleum at Castle Lyons. Two angels on the entablature were carved by John Houghton. He worked in Dublin Castle and, according to Strickland, was involved in the stonecarving on the front of Trinity College, *c.* 1751.

SHEPPARD, OLIVER (1864–1941). A native of Co. Tyrone and son of a sculptor, he was trained in Dublin at the Metropolitan School of Art. He studied also at the Central Art Training School, South Kensington, under Edouard Lanteri whose assistant he became. He was appointed Instructor in Modelling at the Dublin Metropolitan School of Art and designed figures for the Government Buildings which were executed by Albert Power. His work *Cúchulainn* was executed in 1911–12 and chosen to be placed in the GPO as a memorial to the 1916 Rising. He also designed the 1798 memorial in Wexford.

SMYTH, EDWARD (1749–1812). A noted sculptor, he was born in Co. Meath and apprenticed to, and subsequently employed by, Simon Vierpyl. In 1771 he won a competition for a memorial to Dr Charles Lucas, beating the famous John Van Nost the younger. Smyth was then employed by the builder Henry Darley, for whom he did stonecarving and plasterwork. Darley recommended him to James Gandon, who, having seen Smyth's design model for the Royal Arms, which was to be placed over the eastern and western wings of the north and south fronts of the Custom House, cancelled further commissions of sculpture from Agostino Carlini and Thomas Banks in London. Smyth carved the figures of *Plenty* and *Industry* above the south portico of the Custom House and *Commerce* above the dome together with the allegorical group in the tympanum of the river-front portico to Carlini's design. The fourteen riverine heads are among his finest work. He executed all the carving for the Four Courts and the King's Inns for Gandon; he carved the three additional statues of *Fidelity*, *Hibernia* and *Commerce* for the roofline of the old Parliament House when it was converted for the Bank of Ireland by Francis Johnston. In 1811 he became the first head of the Dublin Society School of Modelling. Smyth died suddenly while working on the plaster heads for the Chapel Royal in 1812. Edward's son John carried on the practice, and his great-grandson George Smyth repaired some of his statues in the 1940s.

SMYTH, JOHN (*c.* 1773–1840). Son of Edward Smyth; he attended the Dublin Society Schools and worked with his father in Montgomery Street. With his father he carved the statuary for the Chapel Royal in Dublin Castle. In 1827 he was commissioned by the members of the bar to execute the monument in St Patrick's Cathedral to John Ball, Sergeant-at-Law. Although he did not have the ability of his father he was responsible for many statues on public buildings, including the statues on the GPO and the Royal College of Surgeons; he carved the arms over Johnston's gateway to the King's Inns at the top of Henrietta Street. In 1836 he gave a new head, left arm and leg to the equestrian statue of King William III in College Green after it had been blown up. He succeeded his father as Master of the Dublin Society Modelling School and was one of the original associates of the RHA.

SMYTH, or SMITH, JOHN (*fl.* 1758–1775). He designed the Church of St Thomas, Marlborough St, 1758–62 (now demolished) and the Poolbeg Lighthouse, South Wall, 1761–68. There is a memorial to Archbishop Smyth in St Patrick's Cathedral designed by Smith and executed by John Van Nost the younger, who may bear no relation. Smith seems to have been involved in the execution of the Provost's House; until recently the design of St Catherine's Church and alterations to St Werburgh's were attributed to him.

SPROULE, SAMUEL (*fl.* 1785–1803). A prominent but artistically undistinguished architect involved in the development of Merrion Square, he provided plans for the Wide Streets Commissioners and designed the Newry White Linen Hall. Francis Johnston seems to have worked in his office. He entered the Royal Exchange competition and received a consolation prize. Sproule carried out repairs and alterations for the Bank of Ireland's first premises at St Mary's Abbey. His engravings of unexecuted designs for a new bank there survive. By 1786 he seems to have been succeeded by Whitmore Davis.

STAPLETON, MICHAEL (*fl.* 1770–1801). A native of Dublin, he built and lived in No. 1 Mountjoy Place until his death in 1801. He was the major Irish Neoclassical stuccodore as well as an accomplished architect. His most important Dublin interiors are at Belvedere House, of which he was also the architect, the chapel of Trinity College and Powerscourt (town) House, which has a room almost identical to the Wedgwood Room at Lucan House, Co. Dublin.

STEWART, RICHARD (*fl.* 1807–19). He carved the pulpit for the Chapel Royal which is now in St. Werburgh's Church. He did extensive work for Francis Johnston, and among the Bryan Bolger papers is a detailed bill for his work at Carton in 1819. He executed carving at St George's Church and was responsible for the coat of arms of the Duke of Richmond, designed by Francis Johnston, which may be seen at St Brendan's Hospital, Grangegorman, the former Richmond Asylum. Frederick O'Dwyer located an official document concerning the castle chapel in which Stewart is described as the 'mad carver'.

STIRLING, ROBERT (1841–1915). Born in Dublin, he graduated in engineering from the University of Dublin; he worked for the Board of Works for many years before starting in private practice as an architect and civil engineer. He was later architect and surveyor to Trinity College, where he built gables to the top floor of the Rubrics facing west and also designed the Pathology Building. He was the architect for the rebuilding of the Queen's Theatre in 1909.

STREET, GEORGE EDMUND (1824–81). He trained under George Gilbert Scott in London and practised in Oxfordshire before returning to London in 1856. He adapted the Gothic style of purists such as Pugin to the vigorous High Victorian Gothic style. Most of his buildings were for ecclesiastical use, but one of the most important was the Royal Courts of Justice in London for which he won a competition in 1866. Among his best known churches is St James the Less, Westminster (1859–61). In Dublin he restored Christ Church Cathedral for Henry Roe and designed the adjoining Synod Hall as well as the bridge connecting the two buildings. In London, Street employed or trained three of the leading designers of the late nineteenth century, William Morris, Philip Webb, and R. Norman Shaw. Street was a member of the Royal Academy in 1871 and Professor of Architecture there in 1881. He was awarded the gold medal of the RIBA in 1874 and was President of the RIBA in 1881.

TABARY, JAMES (*fl.* 1655–87). A Huguenot carver and designer, and a member of the Academy of St Luke in Paris. He fled to London from Paris to escape persecution and soon afterwards came to Dublin, where he became a freeman of the city in 1682. Joined by his brothers John and Louis he worked on the chapel at the Royal Hospital, Kilmainham from 1682 to 1687. In 1687 James Tabary petitioned the Governors of the hospital for the full value of his work on the altarpiece and was granted £250. Rolf Loeber suggests that Tabary may have been responsible for the Baroque characteristics and detail of the fine Kilmainham chapel woodwork rather than the architect William Robinson, as the interior seems to derive from a French source.

TAYLOR, JOHN (d. *c.* 1841). Taylor attended the Dublin Society's Schools and was awarded premiums in 1791 and 1792. He practised in Dublin, designing the Church of St Michael and St John, an early Gothic revival Catholic church with almost identical front and rear elevations. Another stylistically similar church is the St Michan's Catholic Church in Halston Street, beside the Green Street Court House. Maurice Craig attributes to Taylor the Church of St Michael and All the Angels, which was demolished and the tower incorporated into the Synod Hall of Christ Church. He supervised the erection of St Mary's Pro-Cathedral and in 1820 became Chief Clerk to J. E. Davis, the Surveyor of Revenue Buildings in Ireland, subsequently taking over that post. Taylor designed the Custom House in Waterford. In 1830 he was made Surveyor of Buildings to HM Customs, and designed the Custom Houses at Glasgow and Dundee.

THORP, CHARLES (d. 1817/18). Builder and stuccodore, he built in Hume Street, Ely Place, and in the area of Mountjoy Square; he was elected a Commissioner of the Square in 1808. He was a member of the Fine Arts Committee of the Dublin Society, an alderman for many years, and Lord Mayor in 1800–1. He decorated the Grafton Street premises of the Royal Irish Academy in 1793. His best known plasterwork is in the Blue Coat School, particularly the Board Room ceiling which was damaged by fire in the 1930s and was repaired by John Sibthorpe. Thorp built Nos 38 and 41 North Great George's Street and worked with Francis Johnston on the Bank of Ireland in 1804. His ceiling in the Council Chamber of the City Hall was destroyed by fire and replaced, but unfortunately his work in the round hall above the entablature and between the *oeil de boeuf* windows was removed; the staircase ceilings are by him. His son Charles, stucco plasterer and painter, was master of his guild and a member of the City Council.

TINGHAM, EDMUND (*fl.* 1630s). He carved the Boyle monument in St Patrick's Cathedral for Richard, First Earl of Cork in 1630, for which he was paid £300. He was commissioned by the Earl to make the monument to the design of Alban Leverett, Athlone Pursuivant-at-Arms. Tingham was a sculptor and also acted as architect, builder and contractor. He came from Chapelizod, Co. Dublin, where Lord Valencia had a house and may have employed him. He worked on Lord Caulfeild's Dublin house in 1631 on Cork Hill, which was later bought by the First Earl of Cork. Lord Cork was guardian of George, Sixteenth Earl of Kildare, and in this capacity engaged Tingham to restore and rebuild Maynooth Castle, Co. Kildare. Tingham's wife seems to have managed the finances, as she is frequently mentioned in the accounts of the Earl of Cork. In 1632 she received from the Earl a grey hackney and two cows 'to help to encourage them in forwarding the buildings' at Maynooth.

TRAILL, SIR JOHN (*fl.* 1757–95). He lived at Islandbridge, Dublin, where he built Kilmainham Gaol on a site acquired from Sir Nicholas Lawless, later first Lord Cloncurry. The gaol, almost completed in 1795, was to hold 800 men and was to be 'superior to any Prison in Europe'. Traill was an engineer and in 1768 was employed to work on the Grand Canal; the dam he had constructed near the River Morrell collapsed owing to bad masonry work on locks, bridges and the aqueduct. In a submission Traill says he has during twenty years 'built Locks entirely of Wood, others of brick ty'd with Wood, and Bricks ty'd with Stone, and some entirely of Stone, but thank God never experienced the failure of any part of my Work' and that the fault was due to bad execution when he was ill; he was replaced by Capt. Tarrant as engineer for the Grand Canal. Traill designed the lighthouse at Wicklow Head and acted as architect for the Royal Hospital, Kilmainham. He was knighted later for his work for the County Grand Jury; juries preceded the county councils.

TRENCH, FREDERICK (*c.* 1747–1836). An amateur architect, he designed a parish church at Swords and his own house, Heywood, Co. Laois. He was one of the powerful Wide Streets Commissioners

and took ten lots when North Frederick St was being developed; he was given the right to arrange floor height and fenestration. At the Rotunda Richard Johnston and Trench collaborated in the 1780s, building the new Assembly Rooms. The building committee included Lord Charlemont, Luke Gardiner, David La Touche and Frederick Trench, all Wide Streets Commissioners. Gandon looked over Trench's plans and made some minor alterations. The foundation stone was laid by the Duke of Rutland. The façade was designed by Richard Johnston. Trench was about to carry out improvements to Belvoir Castle when the Duke of Rutland died in 1787.

TROTTER, JOHN (d. 1792). He was a portrait painter who studied in the Dublin Society Schools and in Italy, where he spent sixteen years. His portrait of Thomas Ivory and the building committee of the Blue Coat School now hangs in their new premises in Palmerstown.

TURNER, RICHARD (*c.* 1798–1881). The Turner family was long associated with the iron trade, Timothy Turner having supplied the ironwork for the stairs in the Provost's house while Richard's uncle, also called Richard, operated an ironmonger's business from 1813 in St Stephen's Green. The family opened the Hammersmith Iron Works in Dublin in 1834, specializing in conservatories. Richard Turner constructed the Palm House in the Belfast Botanic Gardens. In 1845–8 he was responsible for the two largest iron and steel structures of the day: the Winter Garden in Regent's Park and the Palm House at Kew Gardens. In both these buildings Turner was involved with Decimus Burton in the design as well as the construction. He erected the iron and glass building for the Great Exhibition of 1853 in Dublin and constructed railway sheds, including the original roof of the Broadstone Station in 1847. He was involved in the construction of the first iron roof to cover a terminus in a single span at Lime Street Station (1849–50) in Liverpool. With his son Thomas, an architect, he submitted a design for the Crystal Palace but it was rejected as being too costly. Another son, William, took over the Hammersmith foundry on Turner's retirement in 1863.

TURNERELLI, PETER (1774–1839). His father, of Italian origin, worked as a statuary in Belfast and Dublin. Peter studied for the priesthood but moved to London in 1793 and became a pupil of Peter Francis Chenu. He attended the Royal Academy, where he distinguished himself winning a silver medal in 1799. His bust of Francis Drake for Lord Heathfield attracted much attention and he was appointed teacher of modelling to the Royal Family. He executed busts of all its members, including the Jubilee bust of George III in 1810, and started a fashionable and successful practice in London. In 1812 he came to Ireland and among his many commissions were busts of Henry Grattan; Dr Elrington, Provost of Trinity College; and later John Philpot Curran. He was appointed sculptor to the Queen in 1814. He returned again to Ireland several times, creating a bust of Daniel O'Connell of which ten thousand plaster copies were supposed to have been sold. He exhibited at the RHA during the 1820s and 1830s and carved the high altar for the Pro-Cathedral in Dublin.

VAN DER HAGEN, JOHANN (*fl.* 1720–45). A native of The Hague, he came to Dublin via London in the early part of the eighteenth century. He is believed to have painted on copper a small portrait of Carolan, the famous Irish harpist. Van der Hagen was employed by Robert Baillie to take 'prospects' of the places to be featured in the tapestries commissioned for the House of Lords in Dublin. He painted in various parts of the country and Strickland says that his seascapes were particularly esteemed. Several paintings by him are at Curraghmore including *The Landing of King William at Carrickfergus*. His view of the Powerscourt waterfall was engraved by John Brooks in 1745; an advertisement describes it as being by 'the late ingenious Mr Vander Egan'. He also worked for the theatre, painting scenery for Smock Alley in 1733.

VAN NOST, JOHN, THE YOUNGER (*fl.* 1750–87). Son of the sculptor J. Van Nost who worked in London and in 1722 executed the statue of George I for Dublin, which was set up on Essex Bridge, Van Nost the younger came to Dublin around 1750, and for the next thirty years monopolized sculptural work in Ireland. Among his first commissions was a statue of George II for the Guild of Weavers which, according to *Faulkner's Journal*, was received with 'acclamations and demonstrations of joy'. In 1753 his statues of *Justice* and *Fortitude* were finished for Dublin Castle. Dublin Corporation described him as 'the most knowing and skilful statuary in this Kingdom' and in 1753 commissioned the equestrian statue of King George II for the centre of St Stephen's Green, which cost £1,000. The Friendly Brothers of St Patrick commissioned a brass statue of General Blakeney from Van Nost for the centre of Gardiner's Mall, richly gilded on a white marble plinth. It was damaged and had disappeared by 1783. Among his countless commissions were monuments in Christ Church and St Patrick's Cathedrals and a statue of George III, presented to the merchants of Dublin by the Lord Lieutenant, the Duke of Northumberland. He was also commissioned by Dr Mosse to execute metal statues for the Rotunda Gardens and marble busts for the Assembly Rooms – six of the garden statues were delivered but not paid for and the sculptor took them back. The Rotunda entrance hall contains busts by him of the Bishop of Clogher, Lord Shannon and Lord Arran.

VANBRUGH, SIR JOHN (1664–1726). He was of Flemish origin and born in London where his father was a merchant; he was the fourth of nineteen children. He joined the army and in 1688 was arrested in France as a spy and thrown into prison for four years, passing the last part of his sentence in the Bastille. In England again he became a successful playwright. His friend Nicholas Hawksmoor, Christopher Wren's assistant, helped him draw up a plan for Castle Howard for the Earl of Carlisle. Swift wrote:

Van's genius without thought or lecture
Is hugely turn'd to architecture.

Vanbrugh and Hawksmoor drew up a design for Blenheim Palace, which was a present from Queen Anne to the Duke of Marlborough. The Duke fell out of favour and eventually Vanbrugh resigned. His other outstanding works were his own residence, Vanbrugh Castle, Greenwich (1718–21), Eastbury, Dorset (1718), and Grimsthorpe, Lincolnshire (1723–5). He was Comptroller of Works from 1702 to 1713 and again from 1715, and was knighted in 1714. He was the uncle by marriage of Edward Lovett Pearce and it is thought that Pearce was his pupil.

VIERPYL, SIMON (c. 1725–1810). Born in London, he studied under the sculptor Peter Scheemakers. Lord Charlemont employed him in Rome about 1750 to make terracotta copies of antiquities in the Capitoline Museum for the Rev. Edward Murphy, who was Lord Charlemont's tutor and companion on the trip. Twenty-two statues and seventy-eight busts of Roman emperors were completed and sent to Ireland five years later – the busts are now the property of the Royal Irish Academy. Vierpyl came to Ireland to work on the Marino Casino for Lord Charlemont; Sir William Chambers wrote that the Casino at Marino 'was built by Mr Verpyle with great neatness and taste'. Vierpyl's work survives on many public buildings in Dublin including the Royal Exchange (1769), now the City Hall, and the Blue Coat School (1773), presently the headquarters of the Incorporated Law Society. He also carved the busts of Dr Claudius Gilbert and Dr Baldwin which are in the Trinity College library. Edward Smyth was his pupil.

WALDRÉ, VINCENT (c. 1742–1814). Born in Faenza, Italy, he worked as an artist in Rome and went to London in 1774. Employed by the Marquess of Buckingham at Stowe to paint the ceiling of the Music Room, he accompanied his patron to Ireland when Buckingham was appointed viceroy for the second time. Waldré painted the ceiling of St Patrick's Hall at Dublin Castle. He was appointed architect to the Board of Works on the death of Thomas Penrose. He rebuilt the House of Commons after the fire of 1792; his plans included a dome which was not executed. He supervised the decoration of the Crow Street Theatre, and painted the ceiling of the Fishamble Street Music Hall when it became a private theatre. Little else is known of his work as an architect. Strickland relates the story of Waldré's marriage: being invited to a wedding, and the bridegroom failing to appear, Waldré gallantly offered himself to the disappointed bride as a substitute, and was promptly accepted. Strickland also relates that while living near Leixlip, Waldré and his wife were robbed and severely beaten; the perpetrator later being convicted and hanged.

WALL, WILLIAM, JOHN, PATRICK AND JOSEPH (fl. 1715–58). The Walls were a family of Dublin plasterers in the early eighteenth century. William was a Dublin Freeman in 1715, and John his son was a Freeman in 1751. Patrick was the father of Joseph Wall who was a Freeman in 1758. Patrick was on a list of plasterers who were not on the Freeman's Roll.

WARE, ISAAC (c. 1707–1766). English architect. After an apprenticeship with Thomas Ripley he was appointed Clerk Itinerant and later Purveyor of the Royal Works; he held a senior official's job there for over thirty years. He seems to have been patronized by Lord Burlington, who may have sent him to Italy. He translated Palladio's *I Quattro Libri* in 1738 and even today it is said to be the most reliable translation; he dedicated this work to the Earl. Among other books he published *A Complete Body of Architecture*, a valuable treatise on architectural theory and practice of the time. He worked on Lord Chesterfield's house in London, 1748–9 (demolished 1934) and, according to Frederick O'Dwyer, may have been engaged by Chesterfield on the rebuilding of Dublin Castle. After the death of Castle, Ware worked on the completion of the interior of Leinster House, Dublin, from c. 1759 onwards. On the ground floor he worked on the dining room and the garden hall, and designed the present library, the main staircase and the first floor suite of rooms on the garden front. His designs for the picture gallery, now the Senate Chamber, were not carried out. He probably designed the interiors of the Green and Red Drawing Rooms at Castletown and also the Dining Room. He designed the bridge at Carton for the Earl of Kildare, and during the 1760s produced designs for rebuilding the main block of Carton – these plans were not executed.

WEBB, SIR ASTON (1849–1930). Edward Webb, the father of Aston, was a watercolour artist and engraver. His son was articled to Banks & Berry and began practising in 1873, winning the RIBA Pugin prize that year. With his partner, E. Ingress Bell (1837–1914), he won the competition for the Victoria Law Courts in Birmingham and by early years of the twentieth century had built up the largest practice in public buildings in England. His work included the Victoria and Albert Museum, Kensington (1891–1909), the Royal Naval College, Dartmouth (1899–1903), Birmingham University (1900–09), the Imperial College of Science and Technology, Kensington (1900–06), and the new façade of Buckingham Palace and the layout of the Mall and the Admiralty Arch (1901–13). In

Dublin he designed the Royal College of Science (with Thomas Manly Deane) in the Classical style. He was knighted in 1904; in 1905 he received the Royal Gold Medal for Architecture, and in 1907 the American Gold Medal.

WEBER, FERDINAND (d. 1784). He came to Dublin c. 1749; Dr Barra Boydell describes him as the outstanding organ and harpsichord builder in Dublin in the mid-eighteenth century, maintaining and tuning the organs in the most important Dublin churches as well as throughout the country. On Weber's death his wife Rachel continued to run the business.

WELLAND, JOSEPH (1798–1860). Born in Midleton, Co. Cork, he served his apprenticeship with John Bowden in Dublin. He completed the Church of St Stephen when Bowden died. For seven years he was architect to the Board of First Fruits and when this was abolished in 1838 he was appointed by the Ecclesiastical Commissioners as one of the architects for the four provinces. In 1843 the Commissioners decided to centralize the architects' department and he was sole architect for the Established Church. He built more than 100 churches as well as planning enlargements, restorations and alterations, always constrained by limited funds. Important churches he designed were St Nicholas, Cork, and St John's, Limerick. In Dublin in the 1850s he designed the Church of Ireland churches Zion Church at Zion Road and St John's, Monkstown. Among his other works were the Monaghan Gaol and Courthouse.

WEST, ROBERT (d. 1770). The son of an alderman from Waterford, Robert West studied art in Paris under François Boucher and Charles-André Van Loo before setting up a school of drawing in George's Lane. The Dublin Society engaged him to teach twelve boys in his own academy. In 1757 the Society set up its own premises in Shaw's Court, off Dame Street, and West was appointed master of the Drawing School established there. He was a most successful teacher, and many artists owed their later achievements to him, including George Barret.

WEST, ROBERT (d. 1790). The West family of Dublin was long associated with bricklaying and plastering. Robert West continued the tradition as well as being an architect and builder. He was the first of the Irish stuccodores to imitate the Lafranchini brothers, and was made Freeman of the City of Dublin in 1752. He was responsible for the plasterwork at 20 Lower Dominick Street, a house he built for himself, and at 86 St Stephen's Green, now part of Newman House. He also executed the plasterwork on the staircase leading to the Rotunda Chapel, besides the ceilings in Dr Mosse's house at No. 9 Cavendish Row.

WILKINSON, GEORGE (1814–1890). In 1838 the English Poor Law was extended to Ireland, which was divided into 130 unions each of which was to have a workhouse; a million pounds was allocated to build them. George Wilkinson, a twenty-five-year-old architect, was employed by the Poor Law Commissioners and built 160 workhouses in five years. The son of a builder from Oxfordshire, he had already built workhouses in his native county. He designed Harcourt St Station in 1859 and the colonnaded shelter for jarveys at Broadstone Station two years later; in 1860 he added to the courthouse at Castlebar, Co. Mayo. He wrote *Practical Geology and Ancient Architecture of Ireland* (1845).

WILLS, ISAAC (fl. 1720s). The design of St Ann's Church in Dawson St is attributed to him, and Maurice Craig presumes he is the same as the Isaac Wills who worked as master carpenter under Burgh at Dr Steevens' Hospital. In Brooking's map of 1728 the west front of the church is shown as a naïve example of Queen Anne baroque, but this was not executed. A Michael Wills (fl. 1721–52) served as clerk of works during the building of Dr Steevens' Hospital and he submitted a design for St Patrick's Hospital in 1749 which, however, was not accepted.

WILSON, HUGH (fl. 1730–60). A master carpenter who worked on Dr Steevens' Hospital, designed by Thomas Burgh and completed by Sir Edward Lovett Pearce after Burgh's death. Wilson executed the panelled library which held the Worth collection. He was probably the Hugh Wilson, carpenter, who signed a report supporting Colonel Eyre when he was in difficulties with the Dublin Barracks Board in 1760.

WILTON, JOSEPH (1722–1803). His father was an ornamental plasterer with a factory near Charing Cross. Joseph decided to study sculpture and, after eight years in Paris at the Academy, he went to Rome in 1752 where he received the 'Jubilee' gold medal from Pope Benedict XIV. Three years later he returned to England in the company of Sir William Chambers, the architect, and Giovanni Battista Cipriani, the decorative painter. Wilton became coach carver to the King, and in 1764 Sculptor to His Majesty. He produced richly carved chimneypieces for many commissions, including Blenheim Palace, and carvings for Somerset House, as

well as many important memorials and statues. He executed William Chambers' designs for patrons including Lord Charlemont. Wilton carved many objects for Lord Charlemont's houses; the lions, or Egyptian leopards, at the Marino Casino are attributed to him.

WOOD, JOHN, THE ELDER (1704–1754). Born in Bath and son of a builder, he went to London during the period 1723–30, and was employed as a builder on the Earl of Oxford's Cavendish-Harley estates; he saw how speculative builders were made to work to a unified plan. Bath was a city becoming prosperous with acts passed to improve the roads, to pave, clean and light the streets, and to make the Avon navigable. Wood formed designs for a grand place of Assembly, a Grand Circus for Sports and a Gymnasium for the city. The Duke of Chandos enabled him to enter into agreements to build 'a court of houses'. He assembled carpenters, joiners and plasterers and, in addition, took on the execution of the Avon scheme, employing labourers who had worked on the Chelsea waterworks. After the death of George I and lack of enthusiasm from the corporation he became sole contractor for Queen Square, a great residential square where individual houses were grouped to form a single palace. In a volume containing drawings in the Bath Reference library is a design for Ranger's Lodge, later the Viceregal Lodge in the Phoenix Park. His son, also called John, continued his work in Bath.

WOOD, SANCTON (1815–86). He was articled to Robert and Sydney Smirke and worked in London where he was architect for the districts of St Luke's Chelsea, Putney and Roehampton. He worked chiefly with railway companies and designed many railway buildings, including stations at Rugby, Cambridge, Blackburn and Peterborough between 1840 and 1860. He entered a competition in 1845 for Kingsbridge Station, Dublin, which he won with John Skipton Mulvany in second place. He also built Neo-Gothic stations on the Great Southern and Western Railway line. In London in 1852 he built the Queen's Assurance and Commerical Chambers in Cheapside, and in 1864 Hackney Town Hall.

WOODGATE, ROBERT (d. c. 1805). A carpenter by trade, he was apprenticed to Sir John Soane from 1788–91 and brought to Ireland by him to act as his Clerk of Works at Baron's Court, Co. Tyrone. Woodgate set up as an architect, working mostly in Ulster where he designed the County Infirmary at Londonderry. He settled in Dublin and succeeded Vincent Waldré at the Board of Works. He added the wings to the Viceregal Lodge from 1803, which were still under construction when he died after only three years in office.

WOODWARD, BENJAMIN (1816–1861). Born in Tullamore, Co. Offaly, he was the son of a captain in the Royal Meath Militia. Trained as a civil engineer, Benjamin developed an interest in medieval architecture. He made measured drawings of Holy Cross Abbey in Co. Tipperary which were exhibited at the RIBA in London in 1846, the year he joined the office of Thomas Deane in Cork. He became a partner in the firm together with Thomas Newenham Deane in 1851. His work was influenced by John Ruskin. Deane looked after the the financial matters in the firm, leaving the design and site supervision to Woodward. Among his best loved creations are the Museum Building at Trinity College (1853–7) and the Kildare Street Club (1858–61), both in Dublin. The firm also designed and built the Oxford Museum (1854–1860).

WYATT, JAMES (1746–1813). Wyatt's family were well-known builders in Weeford, Staffordshire, in the eighteenth century. Wyatt studied architecture in Venice and Rome and favoured the Neoclassical style, which he was influential in introducing and disseminating though he was equally adept later at Gothic. In 1796 he succeeded Sir William Chambers as Surveyor-General and Comptroller of the Office of Works. He had a vast practice in England and among his important commissions in Ireland were Abbey Leix, Co. Laois (1785), and Castle Coole, Co. Fermanagh (1790–97). He remodelled the picture gallery of Leinster House, now the Senate Chamber, for William Robert FitzGerald, second Duke of Leinster.

YOUNG, WILLIAM (1843–1900). A Scottish architect who worked in London in the office of the Surrey County Surveyor. Asked by Lord Elcho (later Lord Wemyss) to provide a wooden marquee at Wimbledon Common for the National Rifle Brigade with seating for 1,000, he succeeded so well that he received commissions from the nobility including a Chelsea house for Lord Cadogan; he built Gosford Park, Haddington, East Lothian, with its grand staircase, for Lord Wemyss. In Dublin he designed a ballroom for Lord Iveagh's house on St Stephen's Green. Young won a competition for the Glasgow Municipal chambers, having visited Rome and Florence to get ideas for his design. He was also given the commission to build the new War Office in Whitehall, but died at the age of 57 when it had only just begun. It was completed by his young son Clyde, jointly with Sir John Taylor who had been the chief architect to the Office of Works.

SELECT BIBLIOGRAPHY

AALEN, F.H.A. and WHELAN, KEVIN (eds), *Dublin City and County: From Prehistory To Present*, Dublin, 1992.

AALEN, F.H.A., *The Iveagh Trust, The First Hundred Years, 1890–1990*, Dublin, 1990.

ARCHITECTURAL ASSOCIATION OF IRELAND, *Public Works, The Architecture of the Office of Public Works, 1831–1987*.

BENCE-JONES, MARK, *Burke's Guide to Irish Country Houses*, London, 1988.

BENNETT, DOUGLAS, *Encyclopaedia of Dublin*, Dublin, 1991.

BERNELLE, AGNES, *Decantations – A Tribute to Maurice Craig*, Dublin, 1992.

CLARKE, AUSTIN, *Twice Round the Black Church*, London, 1962.

CLARKE, HOWARD (ed.), *Medieval Dublin – The Living City*, Vols I and II, Dublin, 1990.

CLARKE, HOWARD (ed.), *Medieval Dublin – The Making of a Metropolis*, Dublin, 1990.

COLVIN, HOWARD, *A Biographical Dictionary of English Architects, 1660–1840*, London, 1954; republished 1978.

COLVIN, HOWARD, and CRAIG, MAURICE (eds), *Architectural Drawings, Sir John Vanbrugh and Sir Edward Lovett Pearce*, Oxford, 1964.

COSGROVE, ART (ed.), *Dublin Through the Ages*, Dublin, 1988.

COSTELLO, PETER, *Dublin Churches*, Dublin, 1989.

COWELL, JOHN, *Where they lived in Dublin*, Dublin, 1980.

CRAIG, MAURICE, *The Volunteer Earl*, London, 1948.

CRAIG, MAURICE, and GLIN, KNIGHT of, *Ireland Observed – a Guide to the Buildings and Antiquities of Ireland*, Cork, 1970.

CRAIG, MAURICE, *Architecture of Ireland*, London, 1982.

CRAIG, MAURICE, *Dublin, 1660–1860*, Dublin, 1980.

CROOKSHANK, ANNE and GLIN, KNIGHT of, *The Painters of Ireland, c. 1660–1920*. London, 1978.

CROOKSHANK, ANNE and WEBB, DAVID, *Paintings and Sculpture in Trinity College Dublin*, Dublin, 1990.

CROWL, PHILIP, *The Intelligent Traveller's Guide to Historic Ireland*, Dublin, 1990.

CRUICKSHANK, DAN, *A Guide to the Georgian Buildings of Britain and Ireland*, London, 1985.

CRUISE O'BRIEN, MARIE and CONOR, *A Concise History of Ireland*, London, 1985.

CURRAN, C.P., *Dublin Decorative Plasterwork of the Seventeenth and Eighteenth Centuries*, London, 1967.

CURRICULUM DEVELOPMENT UNIT, *Viking and Medieval Dublin*, Dublin, 1988.

D'ALTON, JOHN, *The History of the County of Dublin*, Dublin, 1838.

DALY, MARY E., *Dublin, The Deposed Capital*, Cork, 1985.

DAY, A. (ed.), *Letters from Georgian Ireland – the Correspondence of Mary Delany, 1731–68*, Belfast, 1991.

DE BREFFNY, BRIAN (ed.), *Ireland: A Cultural Encyclopedia*, London, 1983.

DE BREFFNY, BRIAN (ed.), *The Irish World – The History and Cultural Achievements of the Irish People*, London, 1977.

DELANEY, FRANK, *The Celts*, London, 1986.

DEVLIN, POLLY, *Dublin* (American Express Travel Guide), London, 1993.

DICKSON, DAVID (ed.), *The Gorgeous Mask – Dublin, 1700–1850*, Dublin, 1987.

DIXON, R. and MUTHESIUS, S., *Victorian Architecture*, London, 1978.

FAGAN, PATRICK, *The Second City, Portrait of Dublin, 1700–1760*, Dublin, 1986.

FLANAGAN, LAURENCE, *A Dictionary of Irish Archaeology*, Dublin, 1992.

FOSTER, R.F. (ed.), *The Oxford Illustrated History of Ireland*, Oxford, 1989.

FOSTER, R.F., *Modern Ireland, 1600–1972*, London, 1988.

FOX, PETER (ed.), *Trinity College Dublin: Treasures of the Library*. Dublin, 1986.

GANDON, JAMES and MULVANY, THOS, *The Life of James Gandon, Esq.*, reprint, London, 1969

GARNHAM, TREVOR, *Oxford Museum, Deane and Woodward*, London, 1992.

GEORGIAN SOCIETY RECORDS, 1909–13, Vols I–V.

GILBERT, J.T., *History of the City of Dublin*, Vols 1–3, Dublin, 1854.

GILLIGAN, H.A., *A History of the Port of Dublin*, Dublin, 1989.

GORDAN BOWE, N., *The Life and Work of Harry Clarke*, Dublin, 1989.

GPA *Irish Arts Review Year Books*.

GRABY, JOHN and O'CONNOR, DEIRDRE, *Phaidon Architecture Guide*, Dublin, London, 1993.

GRAY, A.S., *Edwardian Architecture, A Biographical Dictionary*, London, 1985.

GUINNESS, D. and RYAN, W., *Irish Houses and Castles*, London, 1971.

GUINNESS, D., *Georgian Dublin*, London, 1979.

GUNNIS, RUPERT, *Dictionary of British Sculptors, 1660–1851*, London, 1951.

HAIGH, CHRISTOPHER (ed.), *The Cambridge Historical Encyclopedia of Great Britain and Ireland*, New York, 1985.

HALL, F.G., *The Bank of Ireland*, Dublin, 1949.

HARBISON, PETER, *Guide to the National Monuments in the Republic of Ireland*, Dublin, 1970.

HARBISON, PETER, POTTERTON, HOMAN and SHEEHY, JEANNE, *Irish Art and Architecture*, London, 1978.

HARVEY, JOHN, *Dublin – A Study in Environment*, London, 1949.

HOLLAND, C.H. (ed), *Trinity College Dublin and the Idea of a University*, Dublin, 1991.

IRISH ARCHITECTURAL ARCHIVE, *The Architecture of Richard Morrison and William Vitruvius Morrison*, Dublin, 1989.

IRISH BUILDER, THE, 1867–1961. (From 1859 to 1866 it was known as *The Dublin Builder*.)

IRISH GEORGIAN SOCIETY *Bulletins*, 1958 onwards.

IRISH HERITAGE BOOKLETS, Easons Series, Dublin, from 1974.

JACKSON, VICTOR, *The Monuments in St Patrick's Cathedral, Dublin*, Dublin, 1987.

JONES, A., *Biographical Index*, Irish Architectural Archive (unpublished manuscript).

KEARNS, KEVIN, *Georgian Dublin, Ireland's Imperilled Architectural Heritage*, Devon, 1983.

KEE, ROBERT, *Ireland, A History*, London, 1980.

LALOR, BRIAN, *Ultimate Dublin Guide*, Dublin, 1991.

LEASK, HAROLD G., *Irish Churches and Monastic Buildings* (Vols I–III), Dundalk, 1987.

LEWIS, SAMUEL, *A History and Topography of Dublin City and County (1837)*, Dublin, 1980

LINCOLN, COLM, *Dublin as a Work of Art*, Dublin, 1992.

LOEBER, ROLF, *A Biographical Dictionary of Architects in Ireland, 1600–1720*, London, 1981.

LUCE, J.V., *Trinity College Dublin – The First 400 Years*, Dublin, 1992.

McCREADY, C.T., *Dublin Street Names*, Dublin, 1987.

McCULLOUGH, NIALL, *Dublin: An Urban History*, Dublin, 1989.

McDERMOTT, MATTHEW J., *Ireland's Architectural Heritage*, Dublin, 1975.

McDONALD, FRANK, *The Destruction of Dublin*, Dublin, 1985.

McDONNELL, JOSEPH, *Irish Eighteenth-century Stuccowork and its European Sources*, Dublin, 1991.

MacLOUGHLIN, ADRIAN, *A Guide to Historic Dublin*, Dublin, 1979.

McPARLAND, EDWARD, *A Bibliography of Irish Architectural History*, Dublin, 1988.

McPARLAND, EDWARD, *James Gandon – Vitruvius Hibernicus*, London, 1985.

MALCOLM, ELIZABETH, *Swift's Hospital – A History of St Patrick's Hospital, Dublin, 1746–1989*, Dublin, 1989.

MALTON, JAMES, *A Picturesque and Descriptive View of the City of Dublin*, London, 1799; reprinted Dublin, 1978.

MAXWELL, CONSTANTIA, *Dublin under the Georges, 1714–1830*, Dublin, 1946.

MITCHELL, G. FRANK, HARBISON, PETER, de PAOR, LIAM, de PAOR, MAIRE and STALLEY, ROGER A., *Treasures of Irish Art, 1500 BC–1500 AD*, New York, 1977.

MOODY, T.W. and MARTIN, F.X. (eds), *The Course of Irish History*, Cork, 1967.

NATIONAL GALLERY OF IRELAND, *Illustrated Summary Catalogue of Paintings*, Dublin, 1981.

NEILL, KENNETH, *An Illustrated History of the Irish People*, Dublin, 1979.

NOKES, DAVID, *Jonathan Swift*, Oxford, 1987.

O'BRIEN, JACQUELINE and GUINNESS, DESMOND, *Great Irish Houses and Castles*, London, 1992.

O'DONNELL, E.E., *The Annals of Dublin – Fair City*, Dublin, 1987.

O'DWYER, FREDERICK, *Lost Dublin*, Dublin, 1988.

O'REILLY, SEAN and ROBINSON, NICHOLAS K., *New Lease of Life – The Law Society's Building at Blackhall Place*, Dublin, 1990.

PAKENHAM, THOMAS and VALERIE, *Dublin – A Travellers' Companion*, London, 1988.

PLACZEK, ADOLF (ed.) *Macmillan Encyclopedia of Architects*, Vols I–IV, London, 1982.

POOL, ROBERT and CASH, JOHN, *Views of the most remarkable Public Buildings Monuments and other Edifices in the City of Dublin, 1780*, reprinted Shannon, 1970.

POTTERTON, HOMAN, *Irish Church Monuments, 1570–1880*, Belfast, 1974.

POYNTZ, S.C., *St Ann's, the Church in the Heart of the City*, Dublin, 1976.

ROBERTSON, IAN, *The Blue Guide to Ireland*, London, 1992.

ROBINS, JOSEPH, *Custom House People*, Dublin, 1993.

ROTHERY, SEAN, *Ireland and the New Architecture*, Dublin, 1991.

ROYAL INSTITUTE OF THE ARCHITECTS OF IRELAND, *1839–1989, 150 Years of Architecture in Ireland* (ed. John Graby), Dublin, 1989.

ROYAL INSTITUTE OF BRITISH ARCHITECTS, *The Directory of British Architects, 1834–1900* (compiled A. Felstead, J. Franklin and L. Pinfield), London, 1993.

ROYAL IRISH ACADEMY, *Giraldus Cambrensis, Expugnatio Hibernica – The Conquest of Ireland* (eds A.B. Scott and F.X. Martin), 1978.

ROYAL IRISH ACADEMY, *A New History of Ireland*, Vol. II (ed. Art Cosgrove), Vols III and VIII (eds T.W. Moody, F.X. Martin and F.J. Byrne), Oxford, 1982–1993.

ROYAL IRISH ACADEMY, *Treasures of Ireland: Irish Art 3000 BC–1500 AD*, Dublin, 1983.

SHAW, HENRY, *The Dublin Pictorial Guide and Directory, 1850*, Dublin, 1988.

SHEAFF, NICHOLAS, *Iveagh House – An Historical Description*, Dublin, 1978.

SHEEHY, JEANNE, *J.J. McCarthy and the Gothic Revival in Ireland*, Belfast, 1977.

SHEEHY, JEANNE, *The Rediscovery of Ireland's Past – The Celtic Revival, 1830–1930*, London, 1980.

SMITH, CORNELIUS F. and SHARE, BERNARD (ed.), *Whigs on the Green*, Dublin, 1990.

SOMERVILLE-LARGE, PETER, *Dublin*, London, 1979.

STRICKLAND, WALTER GEORGE, *A Dictionary of Irish Artists*, Vols I and II, Dublin, 1989.

SWEENEY, CLAIR, *The Rivers of Dublin*, Dublin, 1991

TRINITY COLLEGE DUBLIN, *Treasures of the Library*, Dublin, 1986.

TURPIN, JOHN, *John Hogan – Irish Neoclassical Sculptor in Rome*, Dublin, 1982.

WALLACE, PATRICK F., *The Viking Age Buildings of Dublin*, Dublin, 1992.

WARBURTON J., WHITELAW, Rev. J. and WALSH, ROBERT, *The History of Dublin*, 2 vols, London, 1880.

WILMONT, HARRISON, *Memorable Dublin Houses*, Dublin, 1971.

INDEX